PERSPECTIVES

ON CANADA'S

POPULATION

PERSPECTIVES ON CANADA'S POPULATION

An Introduction to Concepts and Issues

Edited by
FRANK TROVATO
AND
CARL F. GRINDSTAFF

Toronto   **OXFORD UNIVERSITY PRESS**   1994

Oxford University Press
70 Wynford Drive, Don Mills, Ontario M3C 1J9

Toronto   Oxford   New York
Delhi   Bombay   Calcutta   Madras   Karachi
Kuala Lumpur   Singapore   Hong Kong   Tokyo
Nairobi   Dar es Salaam   Cape Town
Melbourne   Auckland   Madrid

and associated companies in
Berlin   Ibadan

Oxford is a trademark of Oxford University Press

Canadian Cataloguing in Publication Data

Main entry under title:

Perspectives on Canada's population : an introduction
   to concepts and issues

Includes bibliographical references and index.
ISBN 0–19–540960–4

1. Canada – Population.   I. Trovato, Frank, 1951–   .
II. Grandstaff, Carl F., 1937–   .

HB 3529.P47 1994   304.6'0971   C94–930965–6

Design by Heather Delfino

1 2 3 4 — 97 96 95 94

This book is printed on permanent (acid-free) paper ∞.

Printed in Canada

CONTENTS

ACKNOWLEDGEMENTS

T.R. BALAKRISHNAN, KAROL KRÓTKI, and EVELYNE LAPIERRE-ADAMCYK. Reproduced with the permission of The Alan Guttmacher Institute from T.R. Balakrishnan, Karol Krótki, and Evelyne Lapierre-Adamcyk, 'Contraceptive Use in Canada, 1984', *Family Planning Perspectives*, Volume 17, Nunber 5, September/October 1985.

T.R. BALAKRISHNAN and GEORGE JARVIS. 'Is the Burgess Concentric Zonal Theory of Spatial Differentiation Still Applicable to Urban Canada?', *Canadian Review of Sociology and Anthropology*, Volume 28:4, 1991. Reprinted by permission.

RODERIC BEAUJOT. 'The Family and Demographic Change in Canada: Economic and Cultural Interpretations and Solutions', *Journal of Comparative Family Studies*, Volume XXI, Number 1, Spring 1990. Reprinted by permission.

RODERIC BEAUJOT and KEVIN MCQUILLAN. 'The Social Effects of Demographic Change: Canada 1851-1981', *Journal of Canadian Studies*, Volume 21, Number 1, 1986. Reprinted with the permission of the *Journal of Canadian Studies*.

ELLEN BOBET. 'Indian Mortality' from *Canadian Social Trends*, Statistics Canada, Winter 1989, pages 11-14. Reproduced with the permission of the Minister of Industry, Science and Technology, 1993.

MONICA BOYD and EDWARD PRYOR. 'The Cluttered Nest: The Living Arrangements of Young Canadians', *Canadian Journal of Sociology* 14(4): 461-77, 1989. Reprinted by permission.

THOMAS BURCH. 'Age-Sex Roles and Demographic Change: An Overview', *Canadian Studies in Population*, Volume 14 (2), 1987. Reprinted by permission.

MARY ANNE BURKE. 'Interregional Migration of the Canadian Population' from *Canadian Social Trends*, Statistics Canada, Autumn 1987, 17-25. Reproduced with the permission of the Minister of Industry, Science and Technology, 1993.

A. GORDON DARROCH and WILFRED G. MARSTON. 'Patterns of Urban Ethnicity: Toward a Revised Ecological Model', from *Urbanism and Urbanization: Views, Aspects, and Dimensions*, Iverson, Noel (ed.), 1984. Reprinted by permission of E.J. Brill.

DAVID K. FOOT and ROSEMARY A. VENNE. 'Population, Pyramids and Promotional Prospects', *Canadian Public Policy—Analyse de Politiques*, XVI:4, 1990. Reprinted by permission.

ELLEN GEE. 'The Life Course of Canadian Women: An Historical and Demographic Analysis', *Social Indicators Research*, 18, 1986, © 1986 by D. Reidel Publishing Company. Reprinted by permission of Kluwer Academic Publishers.

CARL GRINDSTAFF. 'The Baby Bust Revisited: Canada's Continuing Pattern of Low Fertility', *Canadian Studies in Population*, Volume 12 (1), 1985. Reprinted by permission.

JACQUES HENRIPIN. 'From Acceptance of Nature to Control: The Demography of the French Canadians Since the Seventeenth Century', *Canadian Journal of Economics and Political Science*, 23:1, June 1957. Reprinted by permission of the author and The Canadian Political Science Association.

WARREN KALBACH. 'Growth and Distribution of Canada's Ethnic Populations, 1871-1981' from *Ethnic Canada's Identities and Inequalities*, Leo Driedger (ed.), Copp Clark Pitman, 1987. Reprinted with permission of the publisher.

MARGARET KING, JOHN GARTRELL, and FRANK TROVATO. 'Early Childhood Mortality: 1926-1986' from *Canadian Social Trends*, Statistics Canada, Summer 1991, pages 6-10. Reproduced with the permission of the Minister of Industry, Science and Technology, 1993.

SUSAN McDANIEL. 'Reconceptualizing the Nuptiality/Fertility Relationship in Canada in a New Age', *Canadian Studies in Population*, Volume 16 (2), 1989. Reprinted by permission.

DHRUVA NAGNUR and MICHAEL NAGRODSKI. 'Epidemiologic Transition in the Context of Demographic Change: The Evolution of Canadian Mortality Patterns', *Canadian Studies in Population*, Volume 17 (1), 1990. Reprinted by permission.

CONSTANCE NATHANSON and ALAN LOPEZ. 'The Future of Sex Mortality Differentials in Industrialized Countries: A Structural Hypothesis', *Population Research and Policy Review*, 6, 1987. © Martinus Nijhoff Publishers (Kluwer), Dordrecht. Reprinted by permission of Kluwer Academic Publishers.

BALI RAM. 'Family Formation' from *Current Demographic Analysis: New Trends in the Family*, Statistics Canada, 1990. Reproduced with the permission of the Minister of Industry, Science and Technology, 1993.

BALI RAM, MARY JANE NORRIS, and KARL SKOF. *The Inner City in Transition*, Statistics Canada, 1989. Reproduced with the permission of the Minister of Industry, Science and Technology, 1993.

ANATOLE ROMANIUC. 'Fertility in Canada: Retrospective and Prospective', from *Forum*, Statistics Canada, 1991. Reproduced with the permission of the Minister of Industry, Science and Technology, 1993.

JAMES STAFFORD. 'Welcome but Why? Recent Changes in Canadian Immigration Policy'. *American Review of Canadian Studies* 22:2 (Summer 1992): 235-58. Reprinted by permission.

LEROY O. STONE. *Urban Development in Canada*, Dominion Bureau of Statistics, 1967. Reproduced with the permission of the Minister of Industry, Science and Technology, 1993.

LEROY STONE and SUSAN FLETCHER. *The Seniors Boom: Dramatic Increases in Longevity and Prospects for Better Health*, Statistics Canada, 1986. Reproduced with the permission of the Minister of Industry, Science and Technology, 1993.

JEAN VEEVERS. 'The "Real" Marriage Squeeze: Mate Selection, Mortality, and the Mating Gradient', from *Sociological Perspectives*, Volume 31, Number 2, April 1988. Reprinted by permission of JAI Press Inc.

SURINDER WADHERA and JOHN SILINS. Reproduced with the permission of The Alan Guttmacher Institute from Surinder Wadhera and John Silins, 'Teenage Pregnancy in Canada', *Family Planning Perspectives*, Volume 22, Number 1, January/February 1990.

ROBERT WRIGHT and PAUL MAXIM. 'Canadian Fertility Trends: A Further Test of the Easterlin Hypothesis', *Canadian Review of Sociology and Anthropology*, Volume 24:3, 1987. Reprinted by permission.

PREFACE

Intended primarily for students in undergraduate courses in population studies, this collection presents 28 papers on demographic issues in Canadian society. It is designed to be used either alone or as a supplement to a standard population textbook.

A brief introduction to each section highlights the dominant themes contained in the readings that follow. In addition, each introduction includes a set of technical notes outlining some of the more relevant basic measures of population analysis.

At the end of each introduction is a list of references to which students can turn for further study. These include some of the standard references in the field as well as Canadian works that could not be included as chapters in a book of this size.

We examined a multitude of papers for possible inclusion in this reader, but space restrictions demanded that we limit ourselves to a small proportion of them. Ultimately, we decided to publish those papers that (a) covered important demographic issues for Canada, (b) were written at a level appropriate for undergraduate students in university or college, and (c) were representative of research in Canadian demography. We believe that all the readings included in this book satisfy these three criteria. Those items excluded are by no means inferior; their exclusion was based on their fit and adequacy in relation to our objectives.

The book is divided into seven sections. The first focuses on population growth and social demographic change in Canadian society, with emphasis on the interrelationships of population components with social structure. The two factors are so highly intertwined that it is not always readily apparent which is the prime cause of change; for example, while a rise in fertility may be a function of economic change, fertility can also be a determinant of economic change. Part II focuses on issues involving the age and sex composition of Canadian society; a dominant theme in this section is the aging of the population and its sociological implications for both individuals and the society. Part III examines the first component of population change, mortality, providing an overview of epidemiological change over time and mortality discrepancies in contemporary Canada. Part IV addresses historical and contemporary changes in fertility, the second component of population change. Family formation and dissolution is the subject of Part V. The third component of population change, migration and population movement, is examined in Part VI. Finally, the selections in Part VII examine issues of urbanization and the inner city.

PART ONE

CANADA'S POPULATION

Social and Demographic Change

WORLD POPULATION IN HISTORY

The history of humanity can be divided into two distinct stages: the first is characterized by a very long period of slow growth of the population; the second, and most recent, by a relatively short period of explosive growth. From about 5000 BC to approximately AD 1750, the average rate of population growth rarely exceeded .05 per cent per year; from 1750 to 1800 the average annual rate of growth was .44 per cent, bringing the world's population at the end of this 50-year interval to about one billion. The second billion of human population was reached around 1930. The three-billion mark was attained in 1963. In 1975 the world's population grew to four billion; and in 1987 it reached five billion. By the end of this century, the population of our planet is projected to reach more than six billion.

Sooner or later this exponential growth pattern of the human population will stabilize: the major questions are when, how, and under what conditions. On a world scale, there are only two ways in which reduction in the growth of human numbers can be attained: either (1) the fertility rate must come down significantly, or (2) mortality must go up. Clearly, the former mechanism is the most desirable.

In the first chapter of this section Grindstaff and Trovato provide a general overview of the history of population growth and of the issues and arguments surrounding it, both globally and from the point of view of Canada. All industrialized countries have gone through three stages of demographic transition, from a period of high vital rates (births and deaths) to an intermediate interval of high fertility and declining mortality, to a final stage of low vital rates. The developing nations have completed Stage I and are currently in Stage II—a phase of explosive rates of natural increase. While these countries will eventually complete their demographic transitions, what is uncertain is how long this process will take. Countries in Western Europe took roughly 200 years to complete their transitions. But the less developed regions of the world cannot wait so long if social upheaval and environmental disaster on a global scale are to be avoided.

CANADA'S POPULATION

As one of the most advanced nations in the world, Canada enjoys favourable demographic dimensions. It is currently in the final stage of demographic evolution, with low rates of fertility and mortality, and its population is growing at the slow pace of less than one per cent per year. The 27 million people now residing in Canada are concentrated in a small geographic area, raising concerns of overpopulation in the largest cities. The sustained low rates of fertility since the mid-1970s have contributed to an increase in the median age of the population. This fact, plus the low rates of natural increase, means that population growth can be maintained only by an increase in immigration, which by its very nature engenders its own set of social, economic, and demographic implications. The demographic components of Canada have changed drastically over the last one hundred years, and the society has been transformed from a pioneer social organization to an advanced urban industrial multicultural nation.

In a paper first published in 1957, Henripin describes this transformation for the province of Quebec. Tracing the demographic patterns of French Canada from the seventeenth century to the mid-1950s, he finds that they reflect a cultural shift from 'acceptance of nature' in the formative stages of New France, when French-Canadian couples had an average of 8.5 to 9 children, to 'control of nature' with the advent of the industrial era and the possibility of limiting family size. Nevertheless, French-Canadian fertility remained relatively high, above the national average, until the early 1960s, when the modernization process in Quebec intensified, the Roman Catholic church's hold on the populace was loosened, and the ideology of the 'revenge of the cradle' succumbed to a new ethos of individualism in a context of new economic opportunities.

Beaujot and McQuillan provide an extensive overview of the social effects of demographic change in Canada from 1851 to 1981. They argue that while much emphasis has been placed on short-term phenomena such as the 'baby-boom', little attention has been paid to the long-term changes in Canada's mortality and fertility rates and consequences of these changes. For example, life expectancy has increased from just over 40 years in 1851 to 72 years for males and 79 years for females in 1981, while the total fertility rate (the number of children a women would have during her lifetime if she were to experience the fertility rates of the period at each age) has declined from 7.02 to 1.70 over the same period. Among the consequences of these changes are significant shifts in attitudes and behaviour. The fall in mortality has made it possible for our society to avoid facing the reality of death on a day-to-day basis. At the same time, the fall in infant mortality has led to the development of a culture of parental love towards children. Now that parents can expect their two offspring (on average) to reach adult-hood, they can afford to invest emotionally and materially in their well-being. Given the high probabilities of infant survival, parents have opted for quality over quantity of children.

Gee continues on the general theme of social effects in her examination of the life course of Canadian women over the last 100 to 150 years. As a result of massive reductions in mortality, life-course events that were 'expected' in the early society — such as the loss of a husband in one's thirties, or the death of a child — have become relatively rare: life has become more 'predictable' in this sense.

While non-marriage was relatively common during the formative stages of this coun-try, the exchange of marriage vows has in recent decades become an increasingly universal and predictable component of the life course of Canadian women. The per-centage of ever-married women who remain childless has also followed a long-term downward trend, from approximately 13 per cent in 1941 to just over 7.2 per cent in 1981. In fact, the levels of childlessness experienced by the cohorts of women who produced the baby boom are exceptionally low. Thus while the number of children women bear has been declining, the numbers of childless couples have also been following a declining trend overall.

The contemporary woman in Canada, according to Gee, is likely to experience a higher chance of divorce, but the majority of women who marry stay married; they tend to space their children close together and to have the last child fairly early in life in comparison to previous generations of women. These tendencies have generated a high degree of homogeneity in the occurrence and timing of family life-cycle events in contemporary women's lives.

TECHNICAL NOTES

1. Population growth between two points in time (t_1 and t_2) can be computed with the following formula:

   Population growth between t_1 and t_2 = (births$_{t_1-t_2}$ – deaths$_{t_1-t_2}$) + (immigration$_{t_1-t_2}$ – out-migration$_{t_1-t_2}$ = (natural increase + net migration).

   As demonstrated by this balancing equation, population growth is a function of the interplay between births, deaths, and migration. The difference between births and deaths is called *natural increase*. The difference between in-migration and out-migration is *net migration*.

2. There is a non-linear (inverse) relationship between a population's rate of natural increase (RNI) and the number of years it would take for the population to double its size. Generally, the lower the RNI, the longer the doubling time. For example, an RNI of 1.0 per cent per year would result in

a doubling time of approximately 70 years. If the RNI is 2.0 per cent, the doubling time would be close to 35 years, while an RNI of 3.0 per cent would result in a doubling time of 23 years; and if RNI is 4.0 per cent, the doubling of the population would take only 18 years, approximately.

If RNI remains constant, the doubling time would also be a constant. For example, at a 1.7 per cent rate of natural increase in 1992, the world's population would double in 41 years; if this rate remained constant, the population would quadruple in 82 years, would grow eightfold in 123 years, and so on. Thus the population would continue to double every 41 years, assuming that the rate of growth remained unchanged at 1.7 per cent per year.

The doubling time of population can be approximated with a simple formula:

$$Doubling\ time\ =\ 70\ /\ RNI$$

Thus if RNI = 1.7 per cent, the doubling time is approximately 70/1.7 = 41.17 years.

SUGGESTED READING

Beaujot, Roderic, and Kevin McQuillan (1982). 'The population of Canada before confederation'. Pp. 1–26 in Beaujot and McQuillan, *Growth and Dualism: The Demographic Development of Canadian Society*. Toronto: Gage.

Caldwell, Gary, and Daniel Fournier (1987). 'The Quebec question: A matter of population'. *Canadian Journal of Sociology* 12, 1–2: 16–41.

Coale, Ansley J. (1974). 'The history of the human population'. Pp. 15–28 in Scientific American, *The Human Population*. San Francisco: W.H. Freeman.

Henripin, Jacques, and Yves Peron (1972). 'The demographic transition of the province of Quebec'. Pp. 213–31 in D.V. Glass and Roger Revelle, eds, *Population and Social Change*. London: Edward Arnold.

Kalbach, Warren E., and Wayne W. McVey (1979). 'The demographic transition and population growth in Canada'. Pp. 15–38 in Kalbach and McVey, *The Demographic Bases of Canadian Society*. Toronto: McGraw-Hill.

Keyfitz, Nathan (1987). 'Canada's population in comparative perspective'. Pp. 95–110 in P. Krishnan, F. Trovato, and G. Fearn, eds, *Contributions to Demography: Methodological and Substantive. Essays in Honour of Dr Karol J. Krótki*. Vol. I. Department of Sociology, University of Alberta. Edmonton, Alberta, Canada, T6G 2H4.

CHAPTER 1

CANADA'S POPULATION IN THE WORLD CONTEXT

Carl F. Grindstaff and Frank Trovato

A BRIEF HISTORY OF THE HUMAN POPULATION

During the last 200 years the world has seen unprecedented population growth. While human beings have been around for many hundreds of thousands of years, it took all of that history until the nineteenth century to populate the planet with a billion people. From the time of Christ until 1840 (when the world's people reached one billion), the doubling time of population growth was on average about 1,250 years, with an average growth rate of about .056 per cent per year, compared to the 1.6 per cent currently experienced by the world's population (Population Reference Bureau, 1993).

The historical growth curve of the human population is indicated graphically in Figure 1 and numerically in Table 1. It was not until the 1970s that the rate of growth of the world's population reached 2 per cent per year—a rate that would result in a doubling of the population in just thirty-five years. In the past two

Figure 1: World population growth, 8000 BC–AD 2000

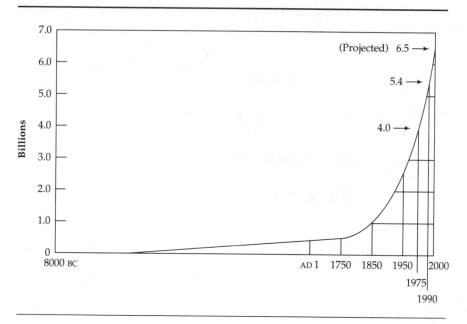

decades, this growth rate has slowed, but at 1.6 per cent it is still one of the highest rates of population increase in the history of humanity. At this rate, the world's population would double in a period of approximately 42 years.

The planet attained its first billion of population shortly after 1800. It had taken all of human history—perhaps a million years or more—to reach this point. The two-billion population figure was reached at the beginning of the Great Depression in North America, around 1930. Thus a billion more people had been added to the world's total in approximately one century. The three-billion figure was achieved in 1963, some 33 years later, and at current rates of growth nearly one billion people are being added to the population every 11 years.

In the 1990s, approximately 140 million people are born each year (more than the total population of Japan) and about 50 million die, for a net natural increase of some 90 million. This number works out to approximately seven million people born per month; about 230,000 a day; nearly 10,000 per hour; 170 per minute. As we enter the next millennium, close to three people are being added to the population of the world every second. With numbers projected to exceed six billion by the end of the twentieth century, the population of our planet is currently increasing by nearly a billion a decade.

The United Nations designated 11 July 1987 as the day on which the world would reach the population total of five billion people. It was indicated at that time that the birth of the five billionth person alive on the earth would be a cause for celebration of the human ingenuity and adaptability that have made it possi-

Table 1: History of world population growth

| | World population growth | | |
	Population (millions)	Annual rate of growth from the preceding period	Years to double
10,000 BC	.1–1	—	—
5,000 BC	5	—	—
AD 0	200	—	—
1000	350	—	—
1650	545	.10	700
1700	600	.20	350
1750	728	.34	206
1800	900	.46	152
1850	1,171	.53	133
1900	1,608	.63	111
1950	2,454	1.00	70
1960	2,800	1.70	41
1970	3,632	2.00	35
1980	4,414	1.70	41
1993	5,506	1.60	42

SOURCES: C.F. Grindstaff (1981), *Population and Society: A Sociological Perspective* (West Hanover, MA: The Christopher Publishing House), p. 23; Population Reference Bureau World Population Data Sheet for 1993.

ble for the world to support such a large number of people. By many yardsticks, especially demographic ones, life for most of the people on earth is now better than ever before in the history of humanity—higher life expectancies, lower rates of infant mortality, freer movements of people. However, the UN also indicated that 11 July 1987 would be a day for contemplation of the necessity to control the growth of the world's population and come to terms with population-related issues of environmental pollution, resource depletion, hunger, poverty, and political justice. It is conservatively estimated (allowing for major decreases in the current annual growth rate of 1.6 per cent) that the population of the world will reach nearly 15 billion in the next 100 years. We need to explore carefully the implications of that growth.

The cultural, economic, and social consequences of such population numbers are tremendous. At current rates of increase, the population of the planet at the end of the next century would be approaching not 15 billion but 30 billion! This type of growth cannot continue indefinitely. Sooner or later the growth must be curtailed and a condition of stability obtained. In the long run, only an agenda of low fertility is compatible with the world goal of minimum human suffering and premature mortality (Coale, 1987).

The major questions are when, how, and under what conditions the population will stabilize. Since on a global scale growth is a function of the interplay of fertility

Figure 2: World population growth by region, 1975–2000

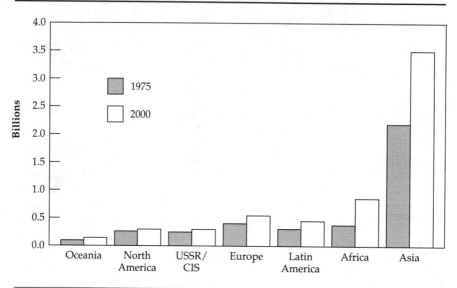

SOURCE: C.F. Grindstaff (1981), *Population and Society: A Sociological Perspective* (West Hanover, MA: The Christopher Publishing House), p. 25.

and mortality, it is clear that for a reduction of growth, only two alternatives are possible: either (1) the fertility rate must come down, or (2) the mortality rate must go up. There are no other possibilities in a finite world. The most important question facing the world today may be how to deal with population growth.

Figure 2 illustrates estimated population change in the world by region between 1975 and the year 2000. There can be no doubt that the regions of the world that will see the greatest increases in the next generation are those that already have large populations and are economically underdeveloped. Almost all experts in all countries agree that this growth needs to be curtailed (but for a contradictory assessment, see Simon, 1987). The question is how—and here there is a great deal of controversy. Obviously it is unacceptable that the problem be solved by raising death rates. Thus the only alternative is reduction and control of fertility. There are three basic schools of thought relating to fertility reduction, and ultimately the conflicts between them have to do with timing and cause.

The first school argues for the importance of social and cultural networks that spread the norms and values of a society with respect to any behaviour. In this view, the basic orientation to reduce fertility is promoted through the dissemination of information from the developed to the developing world, through various agencies, communications media, and contact. The basic mechanisms of change may relate to economic rationality and the concept of the nuclear family (Caldwell, 1976). Crucial in this orientation is the readiness of the society for *family planning* (Coale, 1973). Once the basic normative system is in place, the effective use of contraception becomes possible (Tsui and Bogue, 1978). It is argued that once a society recognizes the value and necessity of family planning in the context of other social goals (economic development, educational advancement, women's rights), people will in fact reduce their fertility (Brackett et al., 1978). In the order of things, this reduction in fertility will in turn allow for investment in economic development; in fact, economic development cannot come about until a relatively low fertility norm is established and a fertility control program is under way. This argument relies on the operation of social and cultural norms that support low fertility within the context of effective birth-control technology and dissemination.

A second view, which might be labelled the *developmentalist* strategy, is endorsed by many developing countries. Perhaps most clearly enunciated at the major population conference held in Bucharest in 1974, it argues that fertility is a pattern of behaviour that is closely tied to the total institutional and organizational structure of society, and that if people recognize that economic and social developments are taking place, they will be motivated to control their family size in order to take part in the developmental process. The key is to ensure that economic development takes place, with the aid of other parts of the world. Central to this approach is the idea that the Western world must share its wealth in every way, and not exploit the resources of the rest of the world to benefit only itself. It is incumbent upon the West to provide large-scale economic assistance and opportunities to the developing world. Once this process is under way, then fertility, along with other types of behaviour associated with economic self-sufficiency (desire for education, changing roles for women, change in family organization) will automatically follow.

A third option is what one author has called the *societalist* approach (Demerath, 1976). This method of change depends on 'deliberate alteration of selected institutions to produce desired changes in the demographic behavior of a particular society' (Demerath, 1976: 22). A more wide-ranging approach, and certainly more costly, it involves changes in natural-resource development, social structure (i.e., economic and stratification systems), culture and religion, marriage patterns, and age at marriage, and may even require political coercion. Such radical change would undoubtedly take a very long time. However, this approach might work well in societies that have the dedication and the ability to exercise relatively total control over institutions. China has been used as an example of a society controlling population through the societalist approach.

Most likely, elements of all three positions are necessary, but the key is time. Many areas of the world are already stretching their economic, political, and social resources to the maximum just to keep pace with population growth. It would appear that in the short run, the family planning/normative approach through effective leadership within countries might alleviate the present crisis, while the long-run solutions would involve economic development and societal change. Tsui and Bogue (1978) indicate that the essential features are in place for family planning to be successful and that this allows for an optimistic stance. Others argue that the problem of overpopulation is so great that only total economic and social transformation can have any impact (Davis et al., 1986; Ehrlich and Ehrlich, 1990). The control of population growth—that is, fertility—is indeed one of the most important issues of our time, and the resolution to the problem of 'exploding populations' will dramatically affect the conditions of life on this planet.

THEORIES OF POPULATION CHANGE

A theory can be defined as a scientific attempt to state an order, system, and/or relationship among facts and variables to explain and predict phenomena. The key components of a theory are definition, specification, and measurement of both dependent (outcome) and independent (predictor) variables. This section will outline some of the general theories as to how and under what conditions populations change.

The Demographic Transition

In the history of the world, three revolutions have enabled humans to begin to control their environment: (1) the acquisition of tools, (2) the agricultural revolution, and (3) the industrial revolution. The last of these has dominated world development, particularly in the West, for the past 300 years. This era has brought about massive changes both in the structure of human society and in population size, composition, and distribution. A central feature of this change was the transformation of the working world. Before the eighteenth century, 95 per cent of all productive labour was performed by physical human and animal power (Brown, 1954); today, 95 per cent of all such work is performed by non-animal power (e.g., machines and other forms of technology). The use of natural resources to control the human environment continues unabated. For the first time, people have attained the ability to control natural phenomena to a significant degree. Accompanying the industrial revolution have been corresponding changes in society that result in dramatic differences in the way people live together. For example, 100 years ago Canadian society was 75 per cent rural, with very few cities over 50,000 people; today more than 75 per cent of the population live in urban areas, and more than half reside in one of the 22 major metropolitan areas with more than 100,000 inhabitants. From a demographic perspective, the major change associated with the industrial revolution is what is known as the vital revolution, or the demographic transition.

Until the seventeenth and eighteenth centuries, the societies making up all of the world's population were essentially agrarian and lacking in any major form of technological development. Various types of evidence have indicated that these societies were characterized by high fertility and high mortality, resulting in relatively low or no population growth. This pattern of the relationship of fertility to mortality is often called the 'old balance'. Populations were stable in terms of numbers. Frank Notestein (1945), reworking a model developed by Warren Thompson (1929), called this Stage I of the demographic transition, or a phase of high growth potential. Generally, the life of the average person was, as Hobbes put it, nasty, brutish, and short. Food was often scarce and unwholesome, water supplies were unstable, sanitation was primitive, communication and transportation facilities were minimal, and life expectancy was most likely around 30 years. Examining the population variables specifically, birth and death rates hovered around 35 to 40 per 1,000 people.

Stage II of the demographic transition is what Notestein called the period of transitional growth. While there were many changes in Western societies in the fifteenth and sixteenth centuries that set the stage for the industrial transformation (the voyages of discovery, the invention of the printing press, the increasing use of salt for food preservation and soap for cleanliness), it was primarily the two centuries from 1750 to 1950 that witnessed the major improvements in life chances. Throughout this period, according to the formulators of the demographic-transition theory, the effects of improvements in agriculture, transportation, communication, sanitation, public health, and medicine were evident first in the area of death control. Over the decades, death rates came down as the overall standard of living improved, first in the upper classes and then throughout the society (Cowgill, 1963). Fertility rates, however, remained high. The resulting period of growth represented the beginnings of Stage II, the transition phase. The fact that advances in technology were not immediately applied to the control of fertility reflected the cultural norms and values of the earlier high-mortality regime, in which fertility had to be high to ensure survival. Fertility levels remained high, at or above mortality levels, primarily as a result of pressures and motivations from the whole range of social institutions—religious, economic, and political—all of which continued to stress the biblical injunction to 'be fruitful and multiply'. In the early stages of the industrial revolution many agrarian values persisted, among them the desire among most people for large numbers of children. In addition, of course, contraception was simply not available to the average family; children were the inevitable result of unprotected sexual intercourse.

Into the nineteenth century in the West, the emerging demographic picture is one of traditional values supporting high fertility (crude birth rates between 30 and 40 per 1,000 population, in some cases even reaching as high as 50) coupled with emerging technologies that enabled populations to implement their values emphasizing the preservation of life. Overall, the nineteenth and early twentieth centuries saw approximately twice as many births as deaths, and a rapidly expanding population. For example, England's population in 1800 was about 10 million; by 1900, it was over 30 million, despite the emigration of vast numbers of people to North America and other parts of the world. Roughly 60 million European immigrants settled in the New World in the century ending in the 1920s; they represented a significant portion of the population growth of the New World. The availability of the New World as an outlet for Europe's swelling population enabled high fertility rates to continue. In time, however, as industrialization spread and its tempo increased, high fertility came to be seen as incompatible with improved living standards and the more individualized value systems that developed out of the changing economic, political, and social circumstances of Europe and North America. Changes in religious and family values, the roles of men and women, economic needs, etc., were reflected in changes with respect to the value placed on having children.

Of course, these dramatic changes in societal structure took place gradually, over centuries. The transition to low fertility did not really go into high gear until well into the twentieth century. The decline in fertility has been relatively linear (a temporary fluctuation in North America was the 'baby-boom' of the 1950s and early 1960s) until by the 1990s, the levels of fertility and mortality are once more in balance—except that this time the balance is achieved through low fertility and low mortality (10–15 per 1,000). This is the new balance, Stage III of demographic transition, which Notestein called the period of incipient decline.

This general description of demographic change in history, in which the large family declines in response to the necessities of the industrial and urban life (Teitelbaum, 1987) is primarily based on an economic model of development: first the industrial revolution transforms the mortality experience, and then, later, the patterns of fertility (a dependent variable) follow the dictates of the economic development pattern (independent variable). It was on this model that the Bucharest World Population Conference of 1974 based its opinion that if economic development took place around the world, the population issue would be solved.

But how likely is it that this general transition model can be repeated in the less developed areas of the world, where industrialization is still in its earlier stages? In Europe, the transition took place over a period of 200 years: there was time to adopt various strategies to reduce fertility, such as prolonged education and late marriage (Davis, 1963). Mortality declined gradually, and emigration, particularly to North America, siphoned off much of the accumulating surplus population. The developing countries currently going through the modernization process have no such outlet to release population pressure.

Moreover, the nations that are striving for development today face other disadvantages. The technology capable of reducing mortality is already invented, available, and being applied, having been imported from industrialized nations. In the developing world, mortality reduction can take place within a few years rather than the centuries that were necessary in the Western societies. Thus the population in some of these areas is growing very quickly, at rates of 2 and 3 per cent per year; around the world, the average birth rate is 27 per 1,000, with Africa, parts of Latin America, and Western Asia closer to 40 per 1,000. There has been no time for a corresponding reduction in fertility to match the pace of mortality reduction. It has been argued that in the Western world, fertility was reduced only after widespread industrial development—and where the changes in the norms and values associated with high fertility occurred slowly, in conjunction with other 'modernization' changes in society. In the non-industrialized world, such time is a luxury that cannot be afforded.

However, some experts (including Coale, 1973; van de Walle and Knodel, 1980; Caldwell, 1976) have argued that it is more likely that economic development will *follow* rather than precede fertility decline in the developing world. For example, Caldwell (1976) argues that the industrialized world has exported not only technology to the developing countries but also the concepts of the nuclear family and alternatives to the maternal role for women. He predicts that fertility will decline in the developing world as these cultures accept the changing role of women and focus on the 'quality' rather than the 'quantity' of children, independent of economic modernization:

> From the demographic viewpoint, the most important social exports have been the concept of the predominance of the nuclear family with its strong conjugal tie and the concept of concentrating concern and expenditure to one's children. The latter does not automatically follow from the former, although it is likely to follow continuing Westernization; but the latter must be preceded by the former. *There probably is no close relationship in timing between economic modernization and fertility — and, if true, this may be the most important generalization of our time*. . . . The major implication of this analysis is that fertility decline in the Third World is not dependent on the spread of industrialization or even on the rate of economic development. It will of course be affected by such development in that modernization produces more money for schools, for newspapers and so on; indeed the whole question of family nucleation cannot arise in the nonmonetized economy. But fertility decline is more likely to precede industrialization and to help bring it about than to follow it (Caldwell, 1976: 356; emphasis added).

Generally, according to this view, the change from high to low fertility is a consequence of changing norms and values relating to children and women, and the economic development patterns that come out of these social variables. The next generation in the developing world will provide the evidence to test this hypothesis.

Malthusian Theory

Thomas Malthus, a professor of history and political economy in England in the late eighteenth and early nineteenth centuries, wrote his famous treatise *An Essay on the Principle of Population* in 1798, and in many respects the issues he raised then are still being debated today. Malthus was writing in reaction to European utopians who believed that nineteenth-century Europe was the best of all possible worlds, and that increases in population numbers were fundamental to the further progress of the human race. Malthus, more of a pessimist, argued that people were victims of passion, and that any progress would suffer by the addition of large numbers of people.

Malthus's basic thesis was that human populations tend to increase at a more rapid rate than does the food supply needed to sustain them. In fact, in the second edition of his essay he wrote that, when unimpeded, populations grow in a geometric (doubling) fashion — 2, 4, 8, 16, 32, 64, 128, etc. — whereas the food supply most likely would increase in an arithmetic (additive) way — 1, 2, 3, 4, 5, 6, 7, etc.

Malthus based his ideas on the relationship of population to the social and economic world on several propositions:

1. Sexual passion is a powerful, virtually uncontrollable characteristic of humans and cannot be modified. The result of this uncontrollable desire is children.

2. People need food in order to exist.
3. The need for food and the need for sexual expression are inescapably in conflict, in that the satisfaction of the latter drive ultimately requires that more food be produced to support the additional population.

From these ideas, Malthus developed several conclusions:

1. Population is necessarily limited by the means of subsistence or growing food.
2. Population invariably increases where the means of subsistence increase, unless prevented by some very powerful and obvious checks.
3. These checks, which keep the effects of population growth on level with the means of subsistence, include moral restraints, vice, and misery.

Moreover, if population always increases to the ultimate point of subsistence, progress can have no long-term, lasting effects. The population will always 'catch up', and literally eat away the higher standards of living. Ultimately, therefore, human beings will always live on the edge of survival.

Those elements in society that produce 'vice' and 'misery' are called *positive checks*: for example, wars, plagues, and famines. In essence, these are checks that limit population by raising the death rate. *Preventive checks*, on the other hand, are those that lower the birth rate. Malthus's prime examples were abstinence from sex and late marriage. Although he held little hope that human sexual appetites were capable of such restraint, abstinence and late marriage were, in his opinion, the only permanent ways to improve society. It is important to note that Malthus was also an ordained minister who defined 'artificial' birth control, the most widespread preventive check in use today, as sinful and beneath human dignity; he objected to birth control on moral grounds, saying that people would be giving in to their sexual urges rather than taking personal responsibility to overcome and control them. In addition, he wanted some increases in population, for he believed that people were by nature lazy, and that having some children would keep them working for progress; without children as a 'push', no progress, even short-term, could be expected. Thus there is an important duality in Malthus's thinking: people need moral restraint to control population, and at the same time they need population growth to push them to make a contribution to society.

Some of the limitations of the Malthusian theory are fairly obvious. First, Malthus could not have foreseen the full possibilities of the industrial revolution, which was beginning to expand productive capacities to an extent previously unimaginable. In fact, in the industrialized world the standard of living has risen dramatically in the past 200 years; for example, the life expectancy (the number of years any person at birth can expect to live) has more than doubled in such countries. It could be argued that, although the population has not yet caught up with the advances made possible by the industrial revolution, in time people will 'use up' the advancement. The counter-argument is that given the existing political and economic structures, the higher standards of living are here to stay.

Second, although Malthus did not specifically define what he meant by the level of subsistence, generally this term refers to the level of food supply necessary to keep people alive, along with shelter and clothing. However, these basics may no longer be the minimum criteria. We also 'need' cars, TVs, schools, recreation; all of these are perceived as necessities in the industrialized nations. In this sense, many people may be living at a subsistence level, but now that level of subsistence is culturally and not biologically defined.

Third, Malthus could not have foreseen the possibilities of birth-control technology and its widespread application. Almost everywhere in the developed world, birth rates have been declining for the past 100 years. Thus Malthusian arguments are most applicable today in the developing countries of Asia and Africa, where the population growth rates may in fact be detrimental to social and economic advancement. It is in this part of the world that positive checks are most likely to occur. Finally, Malthus blamed the problem of poverty not on the selfishness of capitalist social structure, but on the poor themselves and thus, from a Marxist conflict perspective, never got to the heart of the so-called 'over-population problem'. A better sharing of wealth and resources might help to alleviate some of the problems associated with high numbers and rates of population growth.

In general terms, what Malthus was stating in his formulation of positive and preventive checks was that people will, one way or another, be restrained from their full reproductive capacity, but that the necessary restraint can in large part be the product of human judgement and motives. For his time, this theory represented a significant breakthrough. In the industrialized world in particular, including Canada, such judgements and motives have indeed become central in the curtailment of population growth through control of fertility.

The Theory of Demographic Change and Response

In 1963, Kingsley Davis wrote an article in which he attempted to augment demographic-transition theory by examining the complexities of the changes in demographic patterns in the industrialized countries. Focusing on Japan and, later, Ireland as test cases, he argued that societies make multiphasic responses to bring down fertility (for example, late marriage, contraception, out-migration, abortion) in the face of significant stimuli that cause population increase.

In the case of industrialization in the Western world, a major stimulus was the significant decline in mortality and the sustained increase in fertility during Stage II of demographic transition. A sustained high rate of natural increase was the demographic stimulus for the multiphasic response: that is, society reacted to population pressure. Industrialization provided an additional stimulus for an eventual reduction in fertility. According to Davis, the shift from high to low fertility is brought about not by national or political goals, but rather by *personal, individual goals and initiatives*. The decrease in fertility was not related to poverty or lack of resources, but rather to the desires of individuals for personal advancement. In the stimulus-response theory, a key component is the idea that individuals act not out of collective consciousness, but on the basis of personal choice, in recognition of fundamental issues of economic and social advantage:

> Under a prolonged drop in mortality with industrialization, ... people ... found that their accustomed demographic [fertility] behavior was handicapping them in their effort to take advantage of the opportunities being provided by the emerging economy. ... Thus it was the rising prosperity itself, viewed from the standpoint of the individual's desire to get ahead and appear respectable, that forced a modification of reproductive behaviour (Davis, 1963: 348).

Davis also notes that in the face of high natural increase, households wanted to maximize the increased economic opportunities brought about by the industrial revolution, and controlled fertility through what Bongaarts (1982) calls the 'proximate determinants': such biological and behavioural factors as marriage, marriage disruption, contraception, sterility, abortion, foetal mortality, and post-partum infecundability.

A decade later, Coale (1973) outlined three general preconditions for a sustained decline in fertility, all of which have been met by the industrialized world:

1. 'Fertility must be within the calculus of conscious choice.' That is, family size must be dictated by personal considerations, not tradition and custom.
2. 'Reduced fertility must be advantageous.' Taking the precautions necessary to limit fertility must be seen as having advantages for the couple, usually within the framework of economic circumstances.
3. 'Effective techniques of fertility reduction must be available.' Procedures to limit family size must be available and known, and couples must be comfortable in using them.

Relative Income and the Role of Women: Cycle and Trend

Two of the most important recent theoretical positions relating to fertility patterns, especially in North America, are those proposed by Easterlin (1978) regarding 'cycle' and Ryder (1979) regarding 'trend'. The former is an economic analysis set in a framework of what has been called *relative income*, while the latter is based primarily on what has happened to the role of women in our society in the past century.

Generally, Easterlin argues that in an industrial society fertility follows an autoregulatory cyclic process: current levels of childbearing are partly a function of past fertility levels, and future reproductive rates in turn will be determined in part by the current levels of childbearing, etc. This cyclic process is a consequence of the interplay between economic conditions in society and the age composition arising from past fertility. In other words, when times are good—when relative income is high—fertility will be higher than when times are bad: for example, in the 1930s, when people restricted their family size at least in part in response to the depressed economic conditions that were widespread in North America. The fertility rate in North America during the 1930s was the lowest up to that period in recorded history (the low point in Canada was 1937, when the total fertility rate stood around 2.7 and the crude birth rate at 20 per 1,000).

Throughout the 1940s, especially in the post-war period, the economic situation improved dramatically in North America, and the small cohort that had been born in the 1930s were able to move into an expanding economy. In the 1950s, when this cohort began to form families, they had relatively high incomes compared to the previous generation. According to Easterlin, it was the relative wealth of this period that prompted couples to have more children. The children born in this 'baby boom' period were a part of a large cohort. As the young adults of this generation entered the working world during the 1960s and 1970s, the economic conditions facing them had deteriorated. As a result, into the 1970s marriage was delayed and fertility declined dramatically, until by the middle of the 1970s, the total fertility rate was below replacement (2.1) and the crude birth rate hovered around 15 per 1000 population. Thus a cycle had been completed, from low births during the 1930s to high births in the baby-boom period, to low births in the baby-bust period, all in the context of changing economic and demographic conditions.

In the 1930s, many population experts were predicting low levels of fertility in the foreseeable future. Easterlin says those forecasts were wrong because they 'ignored a major demographic influence tending to turn fertility behaviour around: the growing scarcity of young adults and the resulting rise in their relative affluence.' Predicting that the late 1980s and the 1990s would see a rise in fertility as the small cohort of the 1970s began to come to adulthood and move into an expanded economic situation similar to that of the 1950s, Easterlin emphasizes the idea of cycle: 'Current fertility depends on current age structure. Current age structure depends on past fertility. Hence, deleting the mediating role of age structure, current fertility depends on past fertility' (1978: 418). (For a more recent review of the Easterlin hypothesis, see Chapter 13 in this book.)

In the late 1980s and early 1990s, fertility rates have edged up ever so slightly (total fertility rates in Canada rose from 1.7 to 1.8), but low fertility is certainly a fact in the North American experience of the past generation. Norman Ryder has developed the argument that low fertility is here to stay, and that while cycle may have some influence, trend is the key pattern, and that the overall fertility trend for a century has been following a downward path to replacement and sub-replacement. He bases his thesis primarily on 'change in the family institution, in particular the increased respectability of non-maternal roles for women and the decreased importance of parents and children for each other' (1979: 359). According to Ryder and others (Keyfitz, 1986; Grindstaff, 1993), changes in the roles of men and women, particularly the latter, have precipitated major adjustments within the family, expanding opportunities for women outside the home and reducing dramatically the rate of childbearing.

The decrease in the numbers and rates of children being born in the past generation is closely related to the changing role of women. Keyfitz (1986) has written that low fertility is a certain outcome of increased gender equality. Societies that do not constrain women will contract: women want the alternative life choices available to men, and having fewer children in their lives makes it possible to choose those alternatives. Ryder (1979: 366) provides a concise, clear statement on the changing role of women and the reproductive aspects of the family:

> . . . the principle reason for the recent decline in fertility is the possibility now gradually opening for women to derive legitimate rewards in the pursuit of activities other than motherhood. At considerable risk of oversimplification, I would assert that our past success at population replacement, throughout all of human history, has been conditional on the discriminatory treatment of women. If we are now prepared to consider this as fundamentally inequitable, and we are ready to respect the woman who chooses a non-maternal way of life, we may be pulling out the prop that has all along made possible our survival as a species. Although I am apprehensive about the consequences, I believe we must accept them, because . . . it is right and proper for women as well as men to be self-determining persons. . . . In summary of this account of the present family, I believe that there is less satisfaction from parenthood today, and there are alternative modes of living which appear preferable to a significant portion of young women.

Caldwell (1976) indicates that in societies where children are costly—that is, where the flow of wealth goes from parent to child and not in the other direction—the economically rational behaviour is to have few children. Obviously, the number of children born per woman has decreased substantially over the past 100 years, but it is important to recognize that having children is still one of the most important aspects of most people's lives. Studies have shown that 95 per cent of young people want to have children when they are adults. In our society, having a child is a very powerful norm, and the vast majority of women do want, and indeed do have, children, even in the 1990s. What has changed dramatically is the number of children that couples have and the timing of their births (relatively later in the reproductive life course).

These two theories of cycle and trend, of relative income and the changing role of women, point to the complexity of analysing and predicting fertility in North America as we approach the twenty-first century. Certainly the 55 per cent decline in fertility in the past 30 years and the changing role of women have had a profound impact on the Canadian family and society. At the same time, it can be argued that this dramatic change in reproductive behaviour has taken place within the context of a society in which children are highly valued by men and women, and that value is reflected and supported by the various mass media and the institutions of government and religion. In some sense we hold contradictory values. We want to have adult freedoms and choice with many alternatives available to both women and men in terms of education, employment, and recreation. At the same time, we continue to want children and to care deeply about their well-being, and about the future of the next generation (Bumpass, 1990).

CANADA'S POPULATION

Canada is the second largest country in the world in geographic area (nearly four million square miles) and ranks thirty-first in population size, with a total of 27 million inhabitants in 1991. Given its area, Canada has always been sparsely populated. It is estimated that, at the time of the European colonization of North America in the early 1600s, there were only between 200,000 and 1,000,000 Native people in the land that is now Canada. The European settlement grew slowly (almost exclusively from France and Great Britain) and by the time of the Treaty of Paris in 1763 there were probably only about 100,000 non-Native inhabitants in the country (Beaujot, 1978).

In the nineteenth century, Canada's population grew rapidly, mainly through immigration. At the time of Confederation, the number of people in this country was over 3 million. The average growth rate in the century preceding 1870 was nearly 4 per cent, an increase that is greater than that in any of today's rapidly growing developing countries.

While Canada's projected population at the end of this century (30 million) will be relatively small by the standards of most of the rest of the world's countries, this figure represents an increase of approximately 600 per cent from the figure of 5.3 million in 1901. Through natural increase and international immigration, Canada's growth rate in the past century has been higher than that of the United States, the fourth-largest country in the world.

This growth in the Canadian population has followed the general pattern of other industrialized countries. Since the middle of the twentieth century, Canada's population has grown by about 1.7 per cent per year, two-thirds of which has been accounted for by natural increase and one-third by net immigration. In the 1990s, Canada's crude birth rate is around 15 per 1,000, while the death rate is approximately 9, accounting for a natural increase of just over one-half of one per cent—or about 170,000 people per year. Projected immigration levels for the 1990s will add at least that many people yearly.

It is part of the conventional wisdom of our country that we are a nation of immigrants from lands all over the world. From one perspective this analysis is correct: few of us, except for the Native peoples, would be here were it not for immigration on the part of ourselves or our ancestors. And since the 1960s that immigration has come from more diverse areas of the world. However, it should be noted that historically most of Canada's population growth was due to the fertility of those immigrants and their descendants, and not to immigration *per se*. To illustrate this point, one has only to examine fertility/mortality and immigration/emigration statistics (see Table 2). From 1851 to 1991 there were about 12.5 million immigrants coming to Canada and 7.5 million leaving, for a net gain of roughly 5 million through immigration. Over this same 140-year period, there were more than 33 million births and 14.5 million deaths, for a natural increase of approximately 18.5 million. Thus fertility has been a more important factor in the growth of the Canadian population than has immigration. In general, there were about three births for every one immigrant during this period in our nation's history.

In fact, Table 2 shows that natural increase accounted for at least half of the population change in every decennial period, and in five periods it accounted for all the growth that took place in Canada, since those decades saw a greater flow of emigrants out of the country than immigrants into it. With low levels of fertility

Table 2: Components of population growth in Canada: 1851–1991[1]

Census year	Total population ('000s)	Natural increase[2] ('000s)	Net migration[3] ('000s)	Ratio of natural increase to total growth	Ratio of net migration to total growth	Average annual growth rate (%)
			Change since preceding census			
1851	2,436	—	—	—	—	—
1861	3,230	611	182	77.0	23.0	2.9
1871	3,689	610	−150	132.6	−32.6	1.3
1881	4,325	690	− 54	108.5	− 8.5	1.6
1891	4,833	654	−146	128.7	−28.7	1.1
1901	5,371	668	−130	124.2	−24.2	1.1
1911	7,207	1,025	810	55.9	44.1	3.0
1921	8,788	1,270	311	80.3	19.7	2.0
1931	10,377	1,360	230	85.5	14.5	1.7
1941	11,507	1,222	− 92	108.1	− 8.1	1.0
1951[4]	14,009	1,972	169	92.1	7.9	1.7
1956	16,081	1,473	598	71.1	28.9	2.8
1961	18,238	1,675	482	77.7	22.3	2.5
1966	20,015	1,518	259	85.4	14.6	1.9
1971	21,568	1,090	463	70.2	29.8	1.5
1976	22,993	934	350	75.5	24.5	1.3
1981	24,343	978	310	75.9	24.1	1.1
1986	25,354	901	110	89.1	10.9	.9
1991	27,297	1,000	850	54.1	45.9	1.5

[1] Figures for 1851–1976 are from Beaujot (1978).
[2] Births minus deaths.
[3] Immigrants minus emigrants.
[4] Newfoundland included as from this year.
SOURCES: M.V. George (1976), *Population Growth in Canada, 1971 Census of Canada Profile Studies* (Ottawa: Statistics Canada, Cat. 99–701) pp. 5 and 7; Statistics Canada (1977), *Estimates of Population for Canada and the Provinces*, Cat. 91–201; Beaujot (1978); Statistics Canada, *Quarterly Demographic Statistics*, vol. 6, no. 4, 1992; *Vital Statistics, Births and Death 1990* (Statistics Canada, 1992).

prevalent in Canada for the past generation, and with plans for increasing immigration, it is probable that for the 1990s natural increase will account for a smaller proportion of Canada's growth, and net immigration a greater one (Dumas, 1990). As the 1986–91 data show, there were nearly as many people added to the Canadian population through net migration as through natural increase, with the smallest ratio of natural increase to total growth in the history of the country.

As one of the most developed societies in the world, Canada's population enjoys favourable demographic dimensions. As Beaujot (1991: 49) points out, 'Only 2.3 per cent of the world population lives in countries with higher life expectancy than Canada's, and only 7.5 per cent in countries with lower fertility.' As a result of these demographic patterns, an increasing proportion of Canada's people is over 65 years of age (more than 10 per cent as we move into the twenty-first century, compared to about 3 per cent 100 years ago) and a substantially smaller youthful population (from nearly 40 per cent of the population 15 years of age and under in 1901 to just over 20 per cent in the 1990s). One of the major challenges facing Canada in the next century will be to develop policies that take into account the major changes in age structure that are currently taking place.

Perhaps the most important feature of Canada's population is the distribution of people across the country. While we are relatively small in numbers, we are heavily concentrated in a small part of the country. First, the population remains heavily concentrated along the border with the US. About 55 per cent of Canadians live in a 250 km-wide corridor, from Windsor to Quebec City. Second, more than 70 per cent of the population west of Ontario lives in the metropolitan areas of Winnipeg, Regina, Saskatoon, Edmonton, Calgary, and Vancouver. Overall, about 70 per cent of our population resides on something less than one per cent of the land area of Canada. Thus, although the population of the country is not large, especially in relation to geographic size, it is heavily concentrated and urban in character—a characteristic that Canada shares with an ever-increasing part of the world. Such population concentration has important political and economic consequences relating to nationalism, housing, and resource development and distribution.

While not critical in the Canadian context, perhaps the most important question facing people in the world today is how to deal on a global level with population growth. Certainly population growth is implicated in many other pressing problems, such as pollution and resource depletion. In order to understand the policies and programs that are being developed to combat high levels of population increase, an understanding of some of the theoretical aspects of demographic change is essential.

SUMMARY

On a world scale, population growth and overpopulation are controversial and important issues, the solutions to which will shape world events in the foreseeable future. Some authorities argue that the impact of the birth-control policies of the 1970s and 1980s is about to be felt in the high-fertility countries, and that the social, economic, and political mechanisms necessary to bring about population stabilization are in place (Tsui and Bogue, 1978); it is just a matter of time, they believe, until fertility decreases to a point where the growth rate is manageable. Other experts, however, maintain that the population-development equation has been overwhelmed by the population variable, and that only drastic action to control fertility can reduce the growth rate sufficiently to allow any significant improvement.

There is some evidence, based on world fertility surveys, that in the past decade natural increase around the world has declined by approximately 15 per cent, and that much of this decline has occurred in the developing world. As calculated by the Population Reference Bureau (1977, 1993), between 1977 and

1993 the world's crude birth rate has gone down from 30 to 26. However, in 1993 the natural increase is still 1.6 per cent per year—which means the addition of just under 90 million people annually. In effect, then, the world is caught in a race between economic development, broadly defined, and population growth that can literally eat away any possible economic improvement. Ultimately, as has been stressed in this chapter, birth and death rates must come into balance: the only questions are how, when, and under what conditions. The only really acceptable long-run alternative is for fertility rates to continue to fall to match the lowered mortality levels, but the potential always exists that death rates will rise to match the higher levels of fertility. This is the Malthusian dilemma of positive and preventive checks, and the reality is that one of these checks must eventually occur. It will take a great deal of planning, foresight, organization, and co-operation to achieve a population balance where birth and death rates are both at low levels.

In Canada and the rest of the industrialized world the demographic transition is completed: mortality is under control, birth rates are low (at or below replacement), and immigration policies reflect government estimates of population needs (Beaujot, 1991). But demographic issues are still vitally important for Canadians. Population variables interact with social and economic factors in complex ways, as both causes and effects, and changes in one area of society have a ripple effect throughout the social structure. For example, it is obvious that declining fertility has important implications for the educational system, housing and recreational needs, support for the aged, etc. In turn, economic conditions, attitudes towards marriage and family, and the changing role of women all have important implications for childbearing.

If Canadians from the 1890s were suddenly transported to the Canada of the 1990s they would be hard pressed to recognize their country. The demographic realities of the past have been transformed, and the social structure has changed radically, largely in response to demographic forces. The next century will undoubtedly bring as many—or more—technological, social, and economic changes, and it is certain that the population size, distribution, composition and change will have important roles to play in the future of Canadian society.

REFERENCES

Beaujot, R. (1978). 'Canada's population: Growth and dualism'. *Population Bulletin*, vol. 33. Washington, DC: Population Reference Bureau.

——— (1991). *Population Change in Canada*. Toronto: McClelland and Stewart.

——— and K. McQuillan (1982). *Growth and Dualism*. Toronto: Gage.

Bongaarts, J. (1982). 'Fertility determinants: 1. Proximate determinants'. Pp. 275–9 in J. Ross, ed. *International Encyclopedia of Population*, vol. 1. New York: Free Press.

Brackett, J., R. Ravenholt, and J. Chao (1978). 'The role of family planning in recent rapid fertility declines in developing countries'. *Studies in Family Planning* 9, 12: 314–23.

Brown, Harrison (1954). *The Challenge of Man's Future*. New York: Viking Press.

Bumpass, L. (1990). 'What's happening to the family? Interactions between demographic and institutional change'. *Demography* 27, 4: 483–98.

Caldwell, J. (1976). 'Toward a restatement of demographic transition theory'. *Population and Development Review* 2, 3–4: 321–66.

Coale, A. (1973). 'The demographic transition'. Procedings, Symposium on Population and Development, Cairo: 347–55.

——— (1987). 'How a population ages or grows younger'. Pp. 365–9 in Menard and Moen (1987).

Cowgill, D. (1963). 'Transition theory as general population theory'. *Social Forces*, 41: 270–4.

Davis, K. (1963). 'The theory of change and responses in modern demographic history'. *Population Index* 29, 4: 345–62.

———, M. Bernstam, and R. Ricardo-Campbell (1986). *Below-Replacement Fertility in Industrialized Societies*. New York: Population Council, Supplement to *Population and Development Review*, 12.

Demerath, N. (1976). *Birth Control and Foreign Policy*. New York: Harper and Row.

Dumas, J. (1990). *Report on the Demographic Situation in Canada: 1988*. Ottawa: Statistics Canada, Cat. 91–209–E.

Easterlin, R. (1978). 'What will 1984 be like? Socioeconomic implications of recent twists in age structure'. *Demography* 15, 4: 397–421.

Ehrlich, P., and A. Ehrlich (1990). *The Population Explosion*. New York: Simon and Schuster.

Grindstaff, C. (1993). 'A vanishing breed: Women with large families, Canada in the 1980s'. *Canadian Studies in Population* 19, 2: 145–62.

Keyfitz, N. (1986). 'The family that does not reproduce itself'. Pp. 139–54 in K. Davis et al. (1986).

Menard, S., and E. Moen (1987). *Perspectives on Population: An Introduction to Concepts and Issues*. New York: Oxford University Press.

Notestein, F. (1945). 'Population: The long view'. In Theodore Schultz, ed. *Food for the World*, Chicago: Chicago University Press.

Population Reference Bureau Inc. (1977 and 1993). *World Population Data Sheets for 1977 and 1993*. Washington, DC: Population Reference Bureau Inc.

Ryder, N. (1979). 'The future of American fertility'. *Social Problems* 26, 3: 359–69.

Simon, J. (1987). 'World population: An anti-doomsday view'. Pp. 123–8 in Menard and Moen (1987).

Teitelbaum, M. (1987). 'Relevance of demographic transition theory for developing countries', in Menard and Moen (1987).

Thompson, Warren (1929). 'Population'. *American Journal of Sociology* 34, 6: 959–75.

Tsui, A., and D. Bogue (1978). 'Declining world fertility: Trends, causes, implications'. *Population Bulletin* 38, 4. Washington, DC: Population Reference Bureau.

van de Walle, E., and J. Knodel (1980). 'Europe's fertility transition: New evidence and lessons for today's developing world'. *Population Bulletin* 34. Washington, DC: Population Reference Bureau.

CHAPTER 2

FROM ACCEPTANCE OF NATURE TO CONTROL

The Demography of the French Canadians Since the Seventeenth Century

Jacques Henripin

Toward the end of Louis Hémon's novel *Maria Chapdelaine*, which is perhaps the work most representative of traditional French Canadianism, one finds this lyrical passage: '. . . in the country of Quebec, nothing has changed. Nothing will change, because we are a testimony.' This was written in 1916, but evidently many things have changed since that time. Economic evolution, urbanization, spread of knowledge, technical progress have greatly modified individual and family life as well as social environment. And these transformations have affected the very core of both French-Canadian society and French-Canadian individuals. As a matter of fact, they have burst the old framework of self-sufficient social life and they have transformed the most fundamental motivations of the individual and of conjugal behaviour. Even in the observance of formal moral rules their impact has been felt. It is not surprising that such changes have affected the demographic pattern to a large extent. Most French-Canadian scholars, social philosophers, and political leaders, who are specially interested in the French-Canadian ethnic group, are relatively unaware of the extent of this demographic change and some would not readily admit it. In this paper, I would like to try to throw some light on the main demographic facts and problems of this evolution or, as one might be tempted to name it, revolution.

THE OLD DEMOGRAPHIC PATTERN: ACCEPTANCE OF NATURE

There is generally not much statistical material that would enable one to formulate an answer to the question 'What is the demographic behaviour that corresponds to acceptance of nature?' for the reason that when a population has a natural, spontaneous, or non-controlled behaviour, it lives in social and cultural conditions that are almost incompatible with a system that allows the statistics to be gathered that are necessary for analysing population phenomena. Even today, in what I would call 'natural' populations, there is no adequate statistical material available. However, the common practice of keeping parish registers in the French Catholic parochial institutions, that was enforced from the very beginning of the French colony, has made possible an analysis of the whole historical demographic pattern of the French-Canadian population. It is possible to give sufficient proof that, from a statistical point of view, these certificates of baptism, marriage, and burial are satisfactorily complete. When these documents are classified on a family basis, they provide even more complete information on demographic phenomena than any modern vital statistics.

The gathering and classification of statistically useful information on a family basis has been done by Mgr Tanguay, a priest who spent twenty-five years of his life, around 1870, visiting all the French parishes in the North American continent which, at that time, spread along the Mississippi as far as New Orleans. One million, two hundred thousand certificates were gathered and 120,000 families were reconstituted. The data were finally presented in 4,200 pages containing the genealogy of Canadian families from 1621 until approximately the British Conquest. Moreover—and this is comforting enough—the analysis permits cross-checking, which gives the results an appreciable degree of validity.[1] I will group the findings of the analysis around three main phenomena.

Mortality

Here, I will just recall that in Canada the mortality rate—the annual number of deaths per 1,000 persons—seems to have been lower than the rate observed in Europe. Between 1720 and 1750, the mean rate in Canada was about 26 per thousand, whereas for approximately the same period, that is, around the middle of the eighteenth century, the rate of 33 per thousand is accepted for France.[2] It is possible that plague and other epidemic diseases worked less havoc in Canada than in France.

The data also permitted the measurement of infant mortality: 25 per cent of the children died before reaching their first anniversary. We may also assume—

on the basis of less reliable information—that almost 45 per cent died before the age of ten years, and 50 per cent before the age of twenty. Only 44 per cent survived at the age of thirty, and 30 per cent reached the age of fifty. According to the present Canadian life table, 86 per cent of female children survive till the age of fifty. This infant mortality rate does not support the testimony of the observers and writers of that time, who apparently had a tendency to brighten the picture. The Venerable Mère Marie de l'Incarnation wrote in 1664: 'Owing to the very healthy air of the country, few children die in their cradle.' The rate obtained from our data suggests that infant mortality in Canada was nearly equal to that in France.[3]

Nuptiality

The mercantilism that dominated policy during this period was *populationist*. But this populationism favoured more the mother country than her colony, so that emigration from France to Canada amounted only to 10,000 persons for the total period of the French Régime which lasted for 150 years: an average of 66 persons a year. As a result of the lack of an effective emigration policy, there were, in 1760, only 65,000 people in New France against 1½ million in New England. Of course this situation was related to the military and political issues of 1760.

Nevertheless, France tried to counterbalance the deficiency of immigration into Canada by encouraging the development of the established population. This could only be done by instituting means of favouring early marriages, because the population was non-malthusian. But this policy did not succeed in bringing the mean age to a sufficiently low level to permit us to believe that very early marriage was a universal or general practice. For the marriages celebrated in Canada during the period 1700–30, the mean age was 22.4 for spinsters and 26.9 for bachelors. In 1951 it was 23.8 and 26.6 respectively.

Fertility

The possibility of analysing in great detail the fertility of this non-malthusian population is probably Mgr Tanguay's most important and least expected contribution to demographic science. I will not dwell, here, on overly technical aspects of this question. However, some results can be put forward. The fertility of married couples can be expressed simply by saying that until the age of thirty-five, married women had one child every two years (see Figure 2). This estimate is far from another belief that, on an average, non-malthusian couples could have a child every year, a belief which even Intendant Talon stated in one of his letters. Of course, some couples did, but they were not representative of the total married population.

Another way of expressing the rate of fertility will show that it was nevertheless sizeable. A woman who married at the age of fifteen, who remained married until the end of the child-bearing period, and who represented the mean fertility of all married women, would have had 13 children. This figure, at the mortality rates of that time, represents a doubling of the population every twenty-two years; at the rate of mortality now prevailing, a doubling every nine or ten years. But minimum mortality is in practice incompatible with maximum fertility. Moreover, most women did not marry until they were considerably older than fifteen. Actually, eighteenth-century French-Canadian couples who survived until the mother reached the age of fifty had 8.5 to 9 children [on average] during their life. This, at the mortality rates that probably prevailed, corresponds to a doubling of the population in each generation, that is, every thirty years. With the present mortality, it would mean a doubling every sixteen years.

This rate of increase is verified by the numerous censuses which took place during the French Régime. Georges Sabagh,[4] on the basis of other data, has been able to estimate the total fertility at the end of the seventeenth century, that is, the number of children born to a woman who married at the age of fifteen and who lived through the entire child-bearing period. This total fertility was found to be 12 children. With Mgr Tanguay's data and a more direct method, I found the total fertility for the first half of the eighteenth century to be 13 children. It is probable that a high fertility was not only a governmental policy but also a socially prevalent and a generally and individually internalized value, as is pointed out by Mr Sabagh: 'It was still the time when children were economic assets; in New France, they were also potential defenders against the Indians and the English colonists who were growing in strength and threatened to absorb New France.'

Is the fertility of the French Canadians of the eighteenth century exceptional? Besides Mr Sabagh's study, there has been another attempt to measure the fertility of a non-malthusian population. A survey[5] conducted in 173 villages of an agricultural region of Iran in 1950 indicated a rate of fertility much lower than that of the French Canadians. But the scholars who conducted that survey think that the rate represents an underestimate, owing to the often faulty memory of the women interrogated. It seems that Canadian marital fertility, during the eighteenth century, was exceptionally high; it was much higher than that in Iran in 1950, and higher than that in Norway, in 1875, when contraception was not yet practised on a large scale.[6] But I would endorse Mr Sabagh's conclusion that 'there is nothing mystically amazing about this.'

THE NINETEENTH CENTURY

During the French Régime, except for some exceptional periods, the rate of increase of the Canadian population does not support Malthus's hypothesis that, if unrestricted, population would double every twenty-five years. Malthus's statement is based on Franklin's observations of the American population. Surprisingly enough, during the English domination, from 1760 to 1850, French-Canadian population effectively doubled every 25 years, and probably without any substantial *net* immigration.

The marriage rate was maintained at the high level of nine per thousand of population, until 1830. Then it decreased rather regularly to approximately six per thousand for the decade 1890–1900; this last decline—whose beginning coincides with the interruption of the tremendous rate of increase of the period 1760–1850—is the result of a serious problem that faced the French-Canadian population toward the beginning of the nineteenth century: the scarcity of land. Around 1820, all seigneurial lands had been occupied. Outside these domains, three million acres of land fell into the hands of 200 speculators or friends of the political régime in power. This land policy resulted in the emigration of the *habitants*, which started on a large scale around 1830 and lasted until 1930. Other factors—the most important of which was the industrialization in the United States—contributed, of course, to sustain this large emigration.

As shown on logarithmic scale in Figure 1, where the slope of the curves is representative of the *rate* of increase of population, the French-Canadian population never resumed the rate of increase of the period preceding 1850. A great proportion of young adults were leaving the country and this explains the decline in both marriages and births. This decline has been observed from 1830 to the middle of the economic depression of the thirties.

It is generally accepted that the limitation of families by birth control did not occur on a large scale in Europe, except in France, before the last quarter of the nineteenth century. It would be surprising if Canadian couples and especially French-Canadian couples started to practise voluntary contraception earlier. It is difficult to ascertain when voluntary limitation did start in French-Canadian society. Some facts tend to lead to the conclusion that it started relatively late: the fertility of women living on Quebec farms, in 1951, was apparently as high as fertility in the eighteenth century. As to urban population, Mrs Enid Charles, studying the fertility of married women from 1941 census data, concluded that, even in Montreal, the effect of urbanization is noticeable only for young women.[7] Broadly speaking, this would mean that family limitation hardly started in Montreal before 1925, among French-Canadian families.

During the last two centuries, world population has been multiplied by three, European population by four, and French-Canadian population by eighty, in spite of net emigration which can be estimated roughly at 800,000. Without this constant drain of its population, the number of French Canadians would be nearly twice the present number. This leads us to the present situation.

THE PRESENT SITUATION

Maria Chapdelaine's nephews and nieces have modified the main facts of their life. Of course, not only the material facts of birth, health, and death have changed, but also their psychological and cultural attitude toward life. 'Nature' is controlled, to the extent that the very core of family life is thereby affected.

The measurement of fertility, in itself, may be interpreted as quite a superficial and external aspect of the life of a society. But a change in behaviour concerning procreation implies fundamental modifications in the psychological, cultural, or spiritual approach to existence. These last modifications are necessary conditions for family limitation and perhaps the correlation between demographic and cultural factors is one of the main results of studies on the population problems of

Figure 1: French-Canadian population, 1680–1951

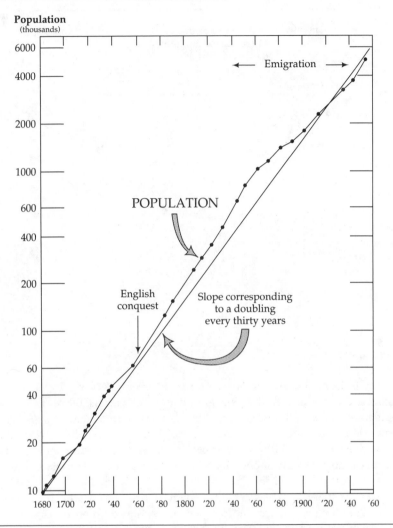

SOURCES: Censuses of Canada, 1871 to 1951; Georges Langlois, *Histoire de la population canadienne-française* (Montreal, 1934).

underdeveloped countries. So we may say that if marital fertility has changed, something else also has changed that is related to what is commonly referred to as the philosophy of life.

Now, how can we measure the evolution of marital fertility? We may limit the technical aspect of this question to Figure 2, which represents fertility rates of married women by age. The upper curve represents eighteenth-century fertility which we may assume to have been maintained till the First World War. This

Figure 2: Fertility rate of married women by age of mother (annual number of children born to 1,000 married women of specific age)

I. French-Canadian couples, eighteenth century. II. French-Canadian couples, 1951.
III. British-Canadian couples, 1951.

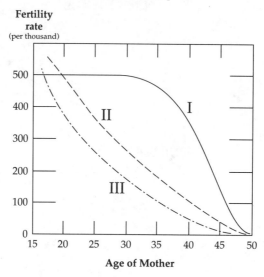

SOURCES: Census of Canada, 1951; J. Henripin, *La Population canadienne au début du XVIIIe siècle* (Paris, 1954), 59–60, 124.

curve results from the analysis of a sample of over 1,000 of Mgr Tanguay's families. We see that the fertility rate kept up at its high level (500 per thousand) until the mother reached the age of thirty. It is easy to understand that this rate corresponds to one child born every two years. The rate has not declined much at the age of thirty-five. But after thirty-five it decreases sharply. The rate is 320 per 1,000 at the age of forty and about 100 per 1,000 (that is, one child every ten years) at the age of forty-five.

Curve II corresponds to the same phenomenon, in 1951, for French-Canadian married women. At a glance one can see clearly the difference between the acceptance of nature and the control which now prevails. We may sum up the difference in the following manner: whereas, before family limitation, a woman who married at the age of fifteen had 13 children during her life, she now has only 8.7 if she is submitted to the present rate of French-Canadian marital fertility. That means that, inside marriage, fertility has decreased by 35 per cent.

But there is another aspect which is worth noting: the difference between the two curves is not equal for every age. Practically no difference exists at twenty years old, which means that voluntary limitation is not yet effective at the very beginning of marital life. When the wife is twenty-five, the difference is 30 per cent; at thirty, it is 50 per cent; and at forty, about 65 per cent. These figures suggest that birth control is getting more effective as the wife grows older. Parents control their fertility more effectively *after* they have had a few children. This is a classical phenomenon not peculiar to French Canadians. The pattern is the same for English Canadians, as shown by curve III.

Incidentally, English-Canadian fertility is appreciably lower. The difference is about 25 per cent. It is interesting to note that this difference tends to lessen as time goes on: the difference was 38 per cent in 1941. It is possible that part of the difference in 1941 is due to accidental factors. Nevertheless, the trend toward a decrease in the difference between present English- and French-Canadian fertility is also confirmed by other methods of computation.

Among French Canadians, family limitation is far from being evenly distributed. Mrs Enid Charles, using 1941 census data, showed that such factors as education and rural or urban residence had a very important effect on fertility. It is possible to get a rough idea of the present situation from this point of view. We have seen before that fertility is still as high as it was during the eighteenth century for farm families of the province of Quebec. But at present, in Montreal, French-Canadian marital fertility is only half the fertility of the French-Canadian couples who live on farms.

The relatively high fertility of French Canadians is partly compensated for by their relatively low nuptiality. Canadians of British origin marry earlier than Canadians of French origin. Doubtless, reluctance to use birth control, on the part of many candidates for marriage, places an added burden on family budgets. If the impossibility of divorce and the less favourable economic conditions are added, one understands easily that French-Canadian young men and girls face marriage a little less merrily!

As compared to fertility in other so-called developed modern countries, French-Canadian fertility seems unique. This is partly due to the fact that the other citizens of Canada also have a relatively high level of fertility. It is also due to the fact that a relatively high proportion of the French Canadians belong to the socio-economic classes that normally have larger families. But the main reason probably lies in religious and cultural characteristics.

TWO PROBLEMS

Two main problems are related to the high fertility of French Canadians. First, does quantity work against quality? Second, how is it possible to justify the French-Canadian reluctance to use birth control, without referring to Roman Catholic authority?

The number of other Canadians has increased at the same rate as the number of French Canadians. But part of that increase comes from net immigration, which is a less painful way of increasing, since the population receiving immigrants does not have to support the cost of rearing and educating them. Is the high rate of *natural* increase of French Canadians an obstacle to their quality? I do not claim to have a solution for this problem. The present state of demographic science does not permit a complete answer. But a few observations can be made.

There seems to be an opposition between large families and both a high degree of schooling and the possibility of having access to a higher social class. This is quite a serious problem for French Canadians, since a relatively great proportion of their labour force is engaged in lower occupations. Health, too, is probably affected by high fertility, especially in the case of children during their first year.

But small families carry certain disadvantages; a low fertility corresponds to an aging population, that is, a population with a great proportion of elderly persons, for whom society must foot the bill. The economic consequences of such a phenomenon can be measured in some degree. England and France are at present facing very difficult economic problems resulting from the aging of their population. But the aging of a population has psychological and political consequences that can hardly be measured. French demographers, for example, do not consider the low fertility that has prevailed in their country for a long time to be an advantage. Many of them think that it is responsible for the social sclerosis many traces of which can easily be pointed out. But other problems are related to this question: problems of civilization and culture.

This leads us to the last point of this paper: How can the position of French Canadians—and especially their leaders—regarding birth control, be explained? The explanation does not rest only on Roman Catholic obedience. Reluctance to limit their families is sometimes interpreted by French Canadians as a defence reaction against the threat of disappearing as an ethnic group. Of course, the immediate level of explanation for the resistance of the French Canadians to birth control is largely a question of obedience to moral law as taught by the Roman Catholic Church. But these rules of the church do not rest only on an interpretation of the so-called 'natural law' about sexual intercourse in marriage. They rest also on something which is probably vaguer but, on the other hand, more easily accessible for non-Catholics: a certain philosophy of life which extends priority of the creative forces over material comfort even to the realm of procreation. Not only Roman Catholics rally to this position. Mr Alfred Sauvy, for example, is an acknowledged anti-malthusian demographer. Communists too, at least for the moment, share the same tendency.

Malthusianism has been caricatured in the following way: when there are not enough hats for everybody, one solution consists in cutting off a certain number of heads (this is the malthusian solution). The other one is: to produce more, and look after a better distribution. The problem is not whether births should be controlled or not controlled. Everybody would admit the necessity of some control, at least in some cases. Even the Roman Catholic church admits it, when there are serious reasons, but to the exclusion of the use of technical or mechanical methods. Periodical continence is permitted, and it is said to be at the same time a means of birth control and of self-control. So what is the difference? It seems to me that the anti-malthusian position can be summarized in these two points:

First, the same material phenomenon has a different meaning when, on the one hand, it refers to particular instances, and when, on the other hand, it is promoted to a legal and socially sanctioned status. The difference can be illustrated by the case of France. In that country, the practice of birth control has developed more precociously and perhaps more effectively than anywhere else. But one finds there more objection than elsewhere to neo-malthusianism, for example to the preaching of birth control. In France, birth control has never been a doctrine. Father de Lestapis writes that what is to be feared is that contraception be raised to the rank of a core value of a civilization.

Second, nobody can predict the effect of technical birth control. From a purely demographic point of view it is not naïve to fear that populations may reach a stage when they would not have what one might call the courage to reproduce themselves. Many urban populations do not reproduce themselves. The population of Vienna, for example, has been reproducing only a quarter of its generations. With the expansion of urbanization, a great proportion of humanity may be in the same case.

But there are other *possible* effects of contraception. They are more obscure, less tangible than the purely demographic ones. An analogy may clarify the outlines of this problem. Father de Lestapis compares this question to the generalization of the automobile. 'Is there any sociologist,' he says, 'so well informed that he could have predicted, in 1910, which consequences would result from the generalized use of the automobile on family life, its stability, its cohesion, its intimacy? Even today, does automobile civilization reveal all the sociological effects that it entails?'[8] The automobile is still quite an external reality for man. What are the modifications that will result from birth-control civilization?

It is not impossible, after all, that the anti-malthusian doctrine carried some wisdom, some part of a social perspicacity, some warning that birth control might be used excessively if officially sponsored. Evidently, this position is partly outside the scope of science. Nevertheless, I submit that social scientists cannot ignore the sociological content of this doctrine.

One might find that this wisdom is austere. I think it is not easy to answer this objection. One finds in St Matthew a sentence inviting all to take the narrow and difficult path. Obviously French Canadians are also straying from the narrow path.

NOTES

[1] See, for more complete information and analysis, J. Henripin, *La Population canadienne au début du XVIIIe siècle* (Paris 1954).

[2] See Michel Huber, 'Le Mouvement naturel de la population: la mortalité', chap. IV in A. Landry et al., *Traité de démographie* (Paris, 1945).

[3] See Jean Bourgeois-Pichat, 'Evolution générale de la population française depuis le XVIIIe siècle', *Population* 4 (1951): 647–51.

[4] Georges Sabagh, 'The fertility of the French Canadian woman during the seventeenth century', *American Journal of Sociology* XLVII, 5 (March 1942): 680–9.

[5] Mohammed B. Mashayekhi, P.A. Mead, and G.S. Hayes, 'Some demographic aspects of a rural area in Iran', *Milbank Memorial Fund Quarterly* XXXV, 2 (April 1953): 149–65.

[6] See Louis Henry, 'Aspects démographiques d'une région rurale de l'Iran', *Population* 3 (1953): 590–2.

[7] Enid Charles, *The Changing Size of the Family in Canada* (Ottawa, 1948).

[8] Translated from S. de Lestapis, 'Politique de contraception et sociologie', *Revue de l'action populaire* (février 1956), 169.

CHAPTER 3

THE SOCIAL EFFECTS OF DEMOGRAPHIC CHANGE
Canada 1851–1981

Roderic P. Beaujot and Kevin McQuillan

Few people realize how much the framework of their lives has been shaped by demographic changes. The post-war baby boom and its attendant consequences have served to focus attention on the wide-ranging impact of demographic factors on social life. Yet these effects are even more dramatic when we extend the time horizon for comparison and examine the role of demography in helping to shape social patterns in Canada since the mid-nineteenth century. In this paper, we will compare three different periods in Canadian history, looking first at differences in demographic patterns and then commenting on the implications for society of the shifts which have occurred.

CANADA'S DEMOGRAPHIC TRANSITION

Demographers claim that Canada, like all industrialized countries, has passed through a three-stage transition in demographic patterns. Up until the early nineteenth century, Canada experienced high birth and death rates. After this point, both birth and death rates began to fall but the drop in death rates was sharper than the decline in the birth rate. In recent times, the two rates have come back towards a rough equilibrium and the prospects for the near future are for a slow rate of population growth.

To examine the consequences of these changes, we have selected three points in time which illustrate markedly different demographic patterns: 1851, 1921, and 1981. While the selection of particular points in time is arbitrary and determined in part by the availability of data, these years provide good vantage points for examining changes in population patterns. Birth rates were high and relatively stable in the mid-nineteenth century[1] and though the death rate had declined somewhat by this point, the rate of decrease accelerated in the following decades.[2] The year 1921 marks a good mid-way point for our analysis. Increases in life expectancy have been much slower since that date while declines in fertility have been much sharper.[3] Moreover, 1921 marks the beginning of Canada's national system of vital registration. In looking at these three points, we will consider the nature of the demographic changes themselves as well as the social, economic, and psychological consequences which flow from these changes in population.

Since we wish to focus on the demographic transition, we will consider the effects of changes in fertility and mortality. In so doing, we will ignore the third component of demographic change: migration. That is not to say that migration has not itself had important consequences on Canadian society. This importance can be highlighted by the very facts that since Confederation about 17 per cent of population growth was due to net immigration and that in 1971 more than one-third of the population were either foreign-born or had at least one foreign-born parent.[4] As important as immigration and emigration have been for Canadian society, we have chosen to focus here on the factors of natural increase, fertility and mortality.

CHILDBEARING

A major problem with many demographic measures is that they do not communicate to non-specialists the real nature of demographic change. Thus to note that the crude birth rate declined from 46 per 1,000 in 1851 to 15 per 1,000 in 1981 gives us only a vague sense of the dimensions of this change for society and for individuals. More useful is the total fertility rate which measures the number of children a woman would have if she experienced the age-specific rates for a given year. This measure suggests that in 1851 a woman would have slightly over seven children by the end of her childbearing years. This figure declined by roughly 50 per cent by 1921 and was cut in half again between 1921 and the present, to the level of 1.7 births per woman on average.

A different way to look at this issue involves comparing the number of small children to the number of women of childbearing age. As the figures in Table 1 indicate, there were more children in Canada under the age of 5 in 1851 than women aged 20–44. By contrast, in 1981 there were only about 4 small children

Table 1: Measures of fertility and mortality, Canada, 1851, 1921, 1981

	1851	1921	1981
Fertility			
Births per 1,000 population	46.2	29.3	15.3
Births per woman (TFR)	7.02	3.54	1.70
Children 0–4 per 100 women aged 20–44	120.3	68.7	37.5
Mortality			
Deaths per 1,000 population	22.2	11.6	7.0
Infant mortality rate	184.1	102.1	9.6
Life expectancy at birth			
Male	40.0	55.0	71.9
Female	42.1	58.4	79.0
Life expectancy at age 20			
Male	39.6	45.1	53.4
Female	41.4	47.5	60.1
Life expectancy at age 65			
Male	10.6	11.7	14.6
Female	11.4	12.8	18.9

SOURCES: Jacques Henripin, *Trends and Factors of Fertility in Canada* (Ottawa: Statistics Canada, 1972), pp. 30 and 366; M.C. Urquhart and K.A.H. Buckley, eds., *Historical Statistics of Canada* (Toronto: Macmillan, 1965), p. 16; Statistics Canada, *Vital Statistics, Vol. 1, Births and Deaths, 1981* (Ottawa: Statistics Canada Cat. 84–204), pp. 2, 9; *1921 Census of Canada,* Volume III, p. 7; *1981 Census of Canada,* 92–901, Table 1; Robert Bourbeau and Jacques Légaré, *Evolution de la mortalité au Canada et au Québec, 1831–1931* (Montréal: Presses de l'Université de Montréal, 1982), pp. 79, 86; Statistics Canada, *Life Tables, Canada and Provinces, 1980–1982* (Ottawa: Statistics Canada, Cat. 84–532, 1984), pp. 16–19.

for every 10 women in this age group. One direct result of this decline in fertility has been a shortening of the period in a woman's life devoted to childbearing and childrearing. The century since 1851 has seen the virtual elimination of childbearing among women over 35. And, while there has been some move toward an older pattern of childbearing among some groups of women in recent years, their childbearing experiences are limited to a short part of the life cycle. Indeed, one of the most remarkable changes in recent years has been the steady increase in the proportion of first births occurring to women over 30 years of age. This suggests that women who begin their childbearing early finish early as well; those who begin later also restrict the period of childbearing to a small number of years.

Along with the decline in the birth rate has come a marked change in the distribution of Canadian families by size. The change, however, is not precisely what one might have expected. Obviously, there has been a large decline in the number of families with four or more children. But in the years from 1921 to the 1970s, there has also been a large decline in the proportion of women who are childless or who have only one child. Put differently, there has been increasing adherence to the norm of the two-child family. Whether this will continue to be the case in the future is debatable. There are some indications that rates of childlessness may again be on the increase. Nevertheless, the data for the recent past demonstrate that the relationship between declining fertility and family size is not as simple as we might have predicted.

DEATH

The decline in death rates has been as dramatic as the decline in fertility. The crude death rate has declined from 22 per 1,000 in 1851 to 12 per 1,000 in 1921 and to 7 per 1,000 in 1981. However, because it is affected by the age composition of the population, the crude death rate is not a particularly good indicator of changes in mortality. Several other figures are more illuminating. Expectation of life at birth, for example, has increased from approximately 40 years for males living in 1851 to 72 years for males living in 1981. For females, the gains have been even larger, with life expectancy rising from 42 years in 1851 to 79 years in 1981.

It is particularly important, when examining changes in mortality, to identify the groups in the population which have benefited the most from changes in the overall patterns. Doing this, we note that the most significant change concerns the drop in infant mortality. The infant mortality rate, which measures the proportion of children who do not survive the first year of life, declined from 184 per 1,000 in 1851 to 102 per 1,000 in 1921. Thus while considerable progress was made during this period, the rate remained very high. In the more recent period, however, infant mortality has fallen precipitously. In 1981, only about 10 of every 1,000 live born children failed to celebrate their first birthday. Stated differently, almost 1 in 5 children did not survive their first year in 1851, compared to 1 in 100 in 1981. It is this decline which has helped to boost life expectancy so dramatically. As the figures in Table 1 indicate, the gains in life expectancy for those who reach their sixty-fifth birthday have been relatively small. What these data show is that the most important consequence of falling mortality rates has been to allow the vast majority of the population to reach retirement ages. The proportion of persons living to age 65 has increased from 32 per cent in 1851 to 80 per cent in 1981.

As another way of demonstrating the salience of these figures, let us assume that at each year we could look at a 'representative village' of 1,000 people whose age structure and mortality pattern by age reflected that of the entire country. In 1851, the village of 1,000 people would experience a death of a child under one year of age every month and a half, while in 1981 one would occur every seven years. Similarly, at ages 1 to 4, a death occurs every 2.5 months under 1851 conditions but every 33 years under the 1981 conditions. One can say that deaths of children aged 1 to 4 are now virtually non-existent. Let us take the point of view of a doctor who is the general practitioner for this village. If we assume a professional life of 35 years, the doctor would experience 465 deaths of children before their fifth birthday in 1851 conditions, but only 6 such deaths under 1981 conditions. At later stages of life, deaths of older people are now more frequent. In a village of 1,000 people there would be 1 death of a person over age 80 every 15 months in 1851 but every 6 months in 1981. The greater frequency of deaths of older people is not because their death rates have increased—in fact the rates have decreased—but because there is a higher proportion of older people in the population.

Life expectancy at age 20 gives a picture of the proportion of adult life that might be spent in retirement. In 1851, having reached age 20, an average person could expect to live another 40 years. If we consider retirement to be after age 65, this means that on average people could not expect to retire. In fact, retirement as we know it now was non-existent. In 1921, people could expect at age 20 to spend 3 per cent of their adult life in retirement while in 1981 it would be 21 per cent. Stated differently, in 1921 having reached age 20 one could expect to work an average of 34.6 years for each year of retirement, but by 1981 it would be 3.8 years of work for each year of retirement.

These changes in demography have had far-reaching effects on the Canadian community and no doubt on the attitudes of Canadians toward a number of important issues. The family, perhaps more than any other institution, has been transformed by the decline in mortality. The orphan was a significant figure in much nineteenth-century literature and the regular appearance of such characters reflected the frequency of the status in society. Under conditions of life expectancy similar to those experienced in Canada in 1851, 11 per cent of children would have been maternal orphans by the age of 10 while under 1981 conditions such would be the case for only 1 per cent of children.[5] More generally, under high mortality conditions, a large amount of chance and variability are injected into human affairs.[6] For instance, it is estimated that in seventeenth-century New France, half of couples would have lost a child before their sixth wedding anniversary, while now in only 10 per cent of cases would a child die or leave the family by the fifteenth wedding anniversary.[7] It can be argued that the greater role played in the past by relatives outside the nuclear unit was a response to the greater likelihood of family disruption due to mortality. As death rates have fallen, the need for this form of insurance has declined as well.

Other social and psychological consequences of falling mortality rates, though no less important, are harder to measure. It seems almost certain, for example, that our increasing ability to relegate death to the older ages of life has profoundly affected attitudes towards and customs surrounding death. Philippe Ariès has traced the evolution of customs associated with death in Western societies and has argued that modern societies attempt to banish death from sight in order not to be constantly reminded of the inevitability of dying.[8] The dead and dying are increasingly removed from public eye in order to limit contact between the living and the dead. There can be little doubt that the decline in death rates and the increasing concentration of deaths among a restricted group of the population, a group whose participation in society is limited generally, has facilitated the development of these practices. The increasing predictability of death has allowed us to handle it in a more business-like and orderly fashion. Blauner has argued that 'the disengagement of the aged in modern societies enhances the continuous functioning of social institutions.'[9] That is, companies, bureaucracies, and other institutions can suffer from the sudden disappearance of a given person in the structure. By setting old people aside, institutions are less subject to this disruption. The problem of course is that while the disengagement of the aged may be beneficial to the social structure, older people themselves bear the social costs of this isolation.

The fall in mortality has also revolutionized relationships between parents and children. A number of authors have pointed to the poor quality of care accorded to small children in pre-modern societies.[10] Much of this can be traced to the generally low standard of living in such societies, but it can be argued that the high infant mortality rates also discouraged the development of strong emotional bonds between parents and children. Parents resisted making large emotional investments in their children until they demonstrated their ability to survive. The delay in naming infants and the practice of giving the name of a child who had died to a subsequent child are cited as practices which demonstrate this relative lack of attachment.[11] Thus, a situation of high infant mortality is in a sense a vicious circle, with children valued less because they are less likely to survive, and with the lower emotional investment in children reducing their survival chances.

Children's views of parents must also have been transformed by changing mortality experiences. Not only can most children expect that their parents will live until they achieve adult status, but a large proportion can expect to interact with their parents as adults for as long or longer than they did as children. Indeed, for many, at least one parent may be dependent on them for as long as they themselves were dependent on their parents during childhood. These changing roles of parents and children are likely to affect both family relationships and the decisions of young couples to have children.

Another consequence of the increased length of life is that the various parts of the life cycle have become more differentiated and more strictly tied to age. For instance, the boundaries between middle age and old age have been sharpened. In addition, as we will see in the next section, new stages of life have emerged, especially the empty-nest period, retirement, and a long period of widowhood.

MARRIAGE AND THE FAMILY

Marital patterns have changed radically in some ways in the period since 1851, though not always in the manner one might have expected. For example, as Table 2 indicates, average age at first marriage has fluctuated somewhat, but the overall trend has been downward since 1851.[12] Contrary to what is sometimes thought, marriage did not occur at a particularly young age in the nineteenth century. But while age at marriage has changed very little, the potential length of marital life has been altered considerably. If all marriages are assumed to end in the death of one partner, the average duration of marriage will have increased from 28 years in 1851 to 47 years in 1981. In the mid-nineteenth century, only 6 per cent of couples would have celebrated their fiftieth wedding anniversary compared to 39 per cent under 1981 conditions. When romantic love was introduced into Western civilization as the basis for marriage, the promise to 'love each other for life' had a vastly different time horizon. When young lovers make a lifetime promise, they proba-

Table 2: Measures of the marital life cycle, Canada, 1851, 1931, 1981

	1851	1931	1981
Singulate mean age at first marriage:			
Wife	23.8	24.6	23.1
Husband	26.8	27.7	25.2
Mean age of mother at:			
All births	30.7	29.9	26.6
Birth of first child	25.4[1]	26.6[1]	24.8
Birth of last child	35.9[1]	34.9[1]	31.1[1]
Marriage of last child	63.0	58.3	55.3
Mean age at death of one spouse:			
Wife	51.7	62.8	69.7
Husband	54.7	65.9	71.8
Mean years between marriage and first birth	1.6	2.0	1.7
Mean years of childbearing	10.5	8.3	6.3
Mean years of empty nest (marriage of last child to death of one spouse)	NIL	4.5	14.4
Mean years of marriage	27.9	38.2	46.6
Percentage reaching 50th wedding anniversary	6.1	16.6	39.4
Percentage never married at age 50:			
Females	7.7	10.4	5.9
Males	8.0	13.6	7.7
Percentage of 15+ married	54.8	56.0	63.3

[1] Very approximate estimates were derived using United States data on average intervals between marriage and birth of first and last child from Paul Glick, 'Updating the life cycle of the family', *Journal of Marriage and the Family* 39 (1977): 6.

NOTE: For procedure used in calculation of mean age at death of one spouse, see Henry S. Shryock and Jacob S. Siegel, *The Methods and Materials of Demography* (Washington: US Government Printing Office, 1973), p. 311. In calculating mean age at marriage of last child, we used singulate mean age at first marriage for 1881, 1956 and 1981 respectively.

SOURCES: R.G. Basavarajappa, *Marital Status and Nuptiality in Canada* (Ottawa: Statistics Canada Cat. 99–704, 1978), p. 62; Bourbeau and Légaré, *Essai sur la mortalité par génération au Canada et au Québec, 1831–1931*, Université de Montréal, Département de Démographie, document de Travail, No. 11; Dominion Bureau of Statistics, *Life Expectancy Trends: 1930–32 to 1960–62* (Ottawa: DBS Cat. 84–518, 1967), p. 16; Statistics Canada, *Life Tables, Canada and the Provinces, 1980–82* (Ottawa: Statistics Canada Cat. 84–532, 1984); Statistics Canada, *Vital Statistics, Volume I, Births and Deaths, 1981* (Ottawa: Statistics Canada Cat. 84–204, 1983), pp. 6, 17; *1981 Census*, Cat. 92–901; Table 5; *1931 Census*, Vol. III: Table 12; *1851–52 Census*, Vol. I: Nos. 5 and 6; Henripin, *Trends and Factors of Fertility in Canada*, p. 378.

bly do not realize that it is for almost 50 years. This change in the average length of marriage has changed the meaning of the phrase 'till death do us part'. An unhappy marriage is probably more likely to be broken when one has the horizon of a long life to 'endure'. The longer life provides the opportunity for a 'new' life, including the possibility of a new spouse. In fact, it can be argued that the longer married life and the sharpening of boundaries between the various stages of life are an additional strain on marriage, as not all couples can successfully adapt to the successive sets of new roles that are implied.[13]

Thus the instability in family life caused by death is gradually being replaced by instability caused by voluntary dissolution. Whereas 98 per cent of marital dissolutions in 1921 were caused by the death of one partner, death was responsible for only 55 per cent of dissolutions in 1981.[14] And, of course, in the younger age groups the importance of divorce as the source of family break-up is even greater.

It is significant to note that the difference between typical ages of men and women at marriage has also decreased, by one year or one-third of the earlier difference. While this decrease is not particularly large, we would argue that it has considerable social significance. The younger person in a marriage is likely to have less education, to be less experienced at taking responsibility and leadership, and generally to have a lower status. The decrease in the typical age difference at marriage is thus probably associated with an increase in the relative status of wives in marriages and of women in society.

One other consequence of changing demographic patterns for marriage and the family deserves attention. The combination of declining fertility and mortality has served to create new stages in the marital life cycle which did not previously exist for most couples. The emergence of the empty-nest stage between the marriage of the last child and the death of one of the spouses has become an important feature of comtemporary marriages. This stage did not exist for the typical couple living in the mid-nineteenth century, but by 1981 the average couple could expect to live together for 14 years beyond the marriage of their last child. And interestingly, research on marital satisfaction suggests that many couples view this stage as among the happiest in their marital life.[15]

In general, compared to the mid-nineteenth century, couples now have 5 less children, they end childbearing 5 years earlier, and they have 14 more years of married life after the last child marries. In other words, there is a longer family lifetime. The family life cycle is longer even if divorce is included in the calculations. Under 1976 conditions, it was estimated that the average duration of marriage was 31.5 years.[16] Women spent an average of 9.5 years as widows and 3.5 years as divorced; for men the figures were 2.0 years as widowers and 1.7 years as divorced.

AGE STRUCTURE

Much attention has been focused recently on the aging of the Canadian population. The reasons for this phenomenon are not well understood, however, nor have many of the consequences been fully explored. Again, it is a problem better analysed by looking at long-term changes rather than by restricting our view to the post-World War II period as is often the case.

The age structure of the population is a function of the level of fertility and mortality and migration. But contrary to popular beliefs, it is the fertility rate which is by far the most important determinant. The population aging that Canada is now experiencing is the result of the continuing decline in fertility since the end of the baby boom and is only marginally a product of increases in expectation of life. Immigration has tended to moderate slightly the aging of the Canadian population, but over the more recent period its impact on the age distribution has been 'almost imperceptible'.[17] The aging of the population is thus

Table 3: Measures of age structure, Canada, 1851, 1921, 1981

	1851	1921	1981
Percentage aged 0–19	56.3	43.6	32.0
20–64	41.0	51.5	58.3
65+	2.7	4.9	9.7
Persons 65+ per 100 persons aged 20–64	6.6	9.5	16.6
Median age	17.2	24.0	29.6

SOURCES: Urquhart and Buckley, *Historical Statistics of Canada*, p. 16; Joseph A. Norland, *The Age–Sex Structure of Canada's Population* (Ottawa: Statistics Canada Cat. 99–703, 1976), p. 22; *1981 Census of Canada*, Cat. 92–901: Table 1.

a long-term process which parallels the decline of fertility since the mid-nineteenth century. Although it was common during the 1960s to emphasize the youthful nature of the population, in fact nineteenth-century Canadian society was far younger. As Table 3 shows, the median age of the population has risen from 17.2 in 1851 to 29.6 in 1981. And this figure is projected to increase to 41.0 by the year 2026![18] The changes can be highlighted by comparing the relative predominance of older and younger persons in the population. In 1851 there were 5 persons aged 65 and over for every 100 persons aged 0–19, while in 1981 there were 30, and in 2026 there would be 82 older persons for every 100 younger persons. In 1921 there were 10 persons of retirement age (65 and over) for every 100 persons at working ages (20–64). In 1981 there were 17 retirement-age persons for every 100 working-age persons but this figure will double to 32 by 2026.

The aging of the population is a complex phenomenon. Most of the attention given this question has centred on the increase of the aged population and the potential difficulties facing governments charged with providing social services to this group. And indeed, difficult problems are likely to emerge in the near future in this regard. Retirement funds such as the Canada Pension Plan, which are funded by the contributions of current workers, are destined to encounter severe problems in the future.[19] Health costs are also likely to rise given the disproportionate use of medical facilities by the elderly population.[20] These trends suggest the need for a rearrangement of procedures for the organization and funding of many forms of social services. Patterns with respect to retirement itself may also need to change. An increase in employment rates among senior citizens would counter part of the transfer-payment burden that will be associated with population aging after the turn of the century.

It is worth noting that the funding of retirement through year by year transfers from the working to the retired population is an attractive scheme when each generation is larger than the one before, but is considerably less attractive when the relative size of working-age cohorts is decreasing. Stated differently, cohorts that give birth to many children will be more easily taken care of in their old age than those with few children. Thus, after the turn of the century, the baby-boom cohorts will be at a disadvantage because the smaller baby-bust cohorts that follow will be hard pressed to make contributions necessary to support their elders. One frequently hears the argument that pre-transition fertility was high partly because parents needed their children as a source of support in old age. While providing for the elderly no longer occurs through family relationships, the argument that large families are useful for support in old age may still be true at the level of a total society.

Important as these issues are, however, they have deflected attention from other consequences of shifts in age structure, some of which are of benefit to Canadian society. As Richard Easterlin has pointed out in his analysis of American society, a decline in the proportion of the population in the young age groups can yield major benefits for the members of those groups and for society as a whole.[21] The rapid growth of the Canadian labour force during the last half of the 1960s and throughout the 1970s exacerbated the problem of unemployment. While increases in female participation rates contributed to this phenomenon, the major factor was the entrance into the labour force of the baby-boom cohorts.[22] The recent slowdown in fertility will contribute to a slower rate of growth in the labour force and may well ease the problem of providing jobs for new entrants.

Shifts in age structure can have other beneficial effects as well. Since certain age groups are primarily responsible for certain forms of behaviour, changes in the relative weight of age groups within the population can produce important changes in the prevalence of certain types of activity. Crime is a particularly good example. Young males are responsible for a disproportionate share of most major crimes, particularly violent crimes. Thus the aging of the population will bring about a decline in the population of these high-risk groups in the population and, other things being equal, lead to a decline in rates of crime.[23] Similar kinds of arguments can be extended to other issues such as traffic fatalities.[24]

One final consequence of shifts in age structures should be noted. While being a member of a relatively large cohort can have disadvantages, it can also yield a number of advantages to the members of such a group. Thus a society such as Canada in 1851, in which the median age of the population was quite young, may accord to the young more power and privileges than would be the case in older societies. In this regard, it is interesting to note how young many Canadian political leaders were when they began their careers. Both Sir John A. Macdonald and Sir Wilfrid Laurier were first elected to public office by the age of thirty.[25] Indeed young people generally assumed positions of importance at an earlier age in nineteenth-century societies.

One might then expect that the current aging of the Canadian population will have analogous effects. While the elderly may well suffer certain disadvantages, they may also find that their power and influence as a group is increasing. The potential for such change can be seen clearly if we look at the proportion of the voting population 65 years of age and over. In 1981, 13.5 per cent of voters belonged to this age category, and by 2026 the proportion will rise to approximately 23.3 per cent.[26] Combined with the fact that elderly people are more likely to turn out to the polls, these trends suggest that senior citizens will be able to wield increasing political power in the future.

IMPLICATIONS FOR THE FUTURE

The effects of demographic change have received considerable attention recently in both popular and professional journals. The effect of a declining birth rate on school enrolment and the continuing growth of the elderly population are now widely known and efforts are being made to come to terms with some of the problems created by these developments. However, in focusing on these particular issues, attention has been directed away from long-term trends which have had profound and far-reaching effects on Canadian society. From this perspective, the post-war baby boom is best seen as a deviation from the trend of declining fertility which stretches back to the mid-nineteenth century. Understanding the impact of demographic forces on social behaviour will require that more attention be paid to these less obvious but no less important long-term changes.

Projections of future demographic developments envision further small improvements in mortality rates and continued low fertility. If true, Canada will experience further changes in the age composition of the population; we may expect that, in the early decades of the next century, close to 1 in 5 Canadians will be over the age of 65. However, while assuming a continuation of present trends is the easiest strategy to follow when making projections, there is no guarantee that it is the most accurate. Preparing for the future demands that we examine the possible consequences of at least two other plausible paths of development. The first would entail a cyclical pattern of growth based on alternating periods of relatively high and relatively low fertility. Such a pattern would exacerbate problems of social planning, particularly in sectors such as education which are directly affected by population changes. The second alternative would see further declines in fertility and the prospect of population decline. This route would also necessitate major rearrangements in the structure of Canadian society.[27] Given the profound effects past demographic changes have had, it is essential that demographers and social planners pay more attention to the potential effects of future changes in population patterns.

NOTES

[1] Ellen M. Thomas Gee. 'Early Canadian fertility transition: A components analysis of census data.' *Canadian Studies in Population* 6 (1981): 23–32; R. Marvin McInnis, 'Childbearing and land availability: Some evidence from individual household data', in Ronald Demos Lee. ed., *Population Patterns in the Past* (New York: Academic Press, 1977), pp. 201–28.

[2] Jacques Légaré and Bertrand Desjardins. 'La situation des personnes âgées au Canada', *Canadian Review of Sociology and Anthropology* 13, 3 (1976): 321–36.

[3] Roderic Beaujot and Kevin McQuillan, *Growth and Dualism: The Demographic Development of Canadian Society* (Toronto: Gage, 1982).

[4] *Ibid.*, Chapter 4.

[5] Thomas K. Burch, 'Some social implications of varying mortality', United Nations World Population Conference, Belgrade, 1965.

[6] Norman B. Ryder, 'Reproductive behaviour and the family life cycle', in United Nations, *The Population Debate: Dimensions and Perspectives*, Vol. III (New York: United Nations, 1975), pp. 278–88.

[7] Evelyne Lapierre-Adamcyk et al., 'Le cycle de la vie familiale au Québec vues comparatives, XVIIe-XXe siècles', *Cahiers Québécois de Demographie* 13, 1 (1984): 59–77. See also Yves Peron and Evelyne Lapierre-Adamcyk, 'Les répercussions des nouveaux comportements sur la vie familiale: la situation canadienne', paper presented to the Conference on the Family and Population, Hanasaari, Expoo, Finland, May 1984.

[8] Philippe Ariès, *Western Attitudes Towards Death* (Baltimore: Johns Hopkins University Press, 1974).

[9] Robert Blauner, 'Death and social structure', *Psychiatry* 29, 4 (1966): 378–94.

[10] Edward Shorter, *The Making of the Modern Family* (New York: Basic Books, 1975); Lawrence Stone, *The Family, Sex and Marriage in England 1500–1800* (New York: Harper and Row, 1977).

[11] Shorter, *Modern Family*.

[12] See also Roy H. Rodgers and Gail Witney. 'The family cycle in twentieth century Canada', *Journal of Marriage and the Family* 43 (1981): 727–40.

[13] Holger R. Stub, *The Social Consequences of Long Life* (Springfield: Charles C. Thomas Publisher, 1982).

[14] K.G. Basavarajappa, 'Incidence of divorce and the relative importance of death and divorce in the dissolution of marriage in Canada, 1921–1976', paper presented at the meetings of the Canadian Population Society, Saskatoon, June 1979; Statistics Canada Cat. 84–204 (1981), p. 48 and 84–205 (1981), p. 14.

[15] Boyd C. Rollins and Harold Feldman, 'Marital satisfaction over the family life cycle', *Journal of Marriage and the Family* 32 (1970): 20–28; Eugen Lupri and James Frideres, 'The quality of marriage and the passage of time: Marital satisfaction over the life cycle', *Canadian Journal of Sociology* 6 (1981): 283–305.

[16] Owen B. Adams and D.N. Nagnur, *Marriage, Divorce and Mortality: A New Life Table Analysis for Canada 1975–1977* (Ottawa: Statistics Canada Cat. 84–536, 1981).

[17] David K. Foot, 'Immigration and future population', paper prepared for Policy and Program Analysis Branch, Employment and Immigration Canada, 1984, p. 13.

[18] Statistics Canada, *Population Projections for Canada and the Provinces* (Ottawa: Statistics Canada Cat. 91–520, 1979), p. 468.

[19] A. Asimakopulos, 'Financing Canada's public pensions — Who pays?', *Canadian Public Policy* 10 (1984): 156–66.

[20] David K. Foot, *Canada's Population Outlook: Demographic Factors and Economic Challenges* (Toronto: James Lorimer, 1982): L.A. Lefebvre, Z. Zigmund, and M.S. Devereaux, *A Prognosis for Hospitals* (Ottawa: Statistics Canada Cat. 83–250, 1979): Leroy O. Stone and Michael J. Maclean, *Future Income Prospects for Canada's Senior Citizens* (Montreal: Institute for Research on Public Policy, 1979).

[21] Richard Easterlin, 'What will 1984 be like? Some socioeconomic implications of recent twists in age structure', *Demography* 15, 4 (1978): 397–432.

[22] Foot, *Canada's Population Outlook*, pp. 191–4.

[23] Easterlin, 'What will 1984 be like?' C.F. Wellford, 'Age composition and the increase in recorded crime', *Criminology* (May 1973): 61–71.

[24] A.C. Irwin, 'A new look at accidental deaths', *Canadian Journal of Public Health* 66 (1975): 457–60; I. Waldron and J. Eyer, 'Socioeconomic causes for the recent rise in death rates for 15–24 year olds', *Social Science and Medicine* 9 (1975): 383–96.

[25] *The Macmillan Dictionary of Canadian Biography* (Toronto: Macmillan, 1978), pp. 444, 495.

[26] Statistics Canada, *Population Projections*.

[27] For an extensive discussion of the long-term effects of low fertility see André Lux. 'Un Québec qui vieillit: Perspectives pour le XXIe siècle'. *Recherches Sociographiques* 24 (1983): 326–77.

CHAPTER 4

THE LIFE COURSE

OF CANADIAN WOMEN

An Historical and

Demographic Analysis

Ellen M. Gee

INTRODUCTION

Empirical research on the life course is just beginning in Canada. While one would wish for a comprehensive, integrated understanding of this subject, such is not possible at the present time.... The life-course perspective holds the promise of theoretical integration of micro- and macro-sociological concerns, or in different words, the linking of the individual and society, that long-standing thorn in the side of the sociological enterprise. However, this paper does not make an attempt at such integration. Rather, the concerns here are more narrow: to focus on *objective* changes in the life course of Canadian women that have occurred over the last 100–150 years. The work is clearly, and unashamedly, macro-sociological with an historical and demographic focus.

The underlying theoretical premise is that the life course has become a core social institution, in the sense of 'a pattern of rules ordering a key dimension of life' (Kohli, 1986). These rules will be examined by looking at changes in the *occurrence* and *timing* of age-related life-course transitions related to the family. As these changes are examined, three themes emerge: the increased *predictability, standardization,* and *compression* in age-related family life-course transitions.

The data sources are, for the most part, aggregate data provided in Canadian censuses and vital statistics publications. Due to the nature of the data bases, two types of analysis are performed: *cohort* analysis, in which the differential life-course experiences of real cohorts of women, as traced through successive censuses, are compared; and *synthetic cohort* analysis, in which the differential life-course experiences of hypothetical cohorts are constructed from cross-sectional, age-specific data. In the tables that are presented, the term 'birth cohort' signifies that cohort analysis was used while the terms 'approximate birth cohort' or 'synthetic birth cohort' indicate that a synthetic technique was employed. . . .

MORTALITY REDUCTION

As a backdrop to an understanding of the changing life course of Canadian women, it is necessary to appreciate the implications for the life course resulting from mortality reduction. We are well aware that life expectancy has increased dramatically in the past 100–150 years. These improvements mean that increasingly larger percentages of birth cohorts can expect to live long enough to experience the full range of life-course events. Simply put, one of the most significant changes that has occurred in the life course over time is the increased probability of surviving to ages at which one is at least 'eligible' to take on, or exit from, age-related roles.

Let us assume that age 20, age 45, and age 65 are 'marker' ages: age 20 is the minimum age for life-course changes relating to marriage and family formation; age 45 represents middle age and a reduction in childrearing responsibilities; and age 65 marks the commencement of old age and retirement. We can then ask the question: What changes have occurred in the likelihood that numbers of a birth cohort will survive to these three 'marker' ages?

Table 1 presents data relevant to this question for synthetic cohorts born from 1831 to 1981. Of 1,000 females born in 1831, approximately two-thirds would survive to age 20, less than one-half to age 45, and substantially less than one-third to age 65. In other words, high mortality levels meant that large numbers of women simply did not live long enough to experience many life-course events. The situation today is radically different. The vast majority of women survive to ages 20 and 45, and a large percentage (approximately 86 per cent) are alive at age 65.

A related dimension is that early widowhood and death of children have become increasingly rare events. Recent literature indicating that it is 'unexpected' life-course events such as the loss of one's husband in one's 30s or death of a child that create severe psychological trauma and stress are further evidence of the degree to which *predictability* has become an entrenched feature of the contemporary life course.

Table 1: Female survivorship at ages 20, 45, and 65, Canada, 1831–1981

	N	20 years	45 years	65 years
1831	1000	650	480	302
1841	1000	661	506	328
1851	1000	668	520	342
1861	1000	669	529	354
1871	1000	661	543	361
1881	1000	716	576	391
1891	1000	718	584	401
1901	1000	762	636	448
1911	1000	807	693	504
1921	1000	857	751	557
1930–32	1000	885	794	617
1940–42	1000	920	854	682
1950–52	1000	950	910	755
1960–62	1000	967	940	809
1970–72	1000	976	949	831
1980–82	1000	985	965	861

SOURCES: For 1831–1921, Bourbeau et Légaré (1982); for 1930–32 to 1980–82, Canadian Life Tables.

THE OCCURRENCE OF FAMILY LIFE EVENTS

We will first examine historical changes in the occurrence of family life events. Here, the relevant questions are: What proportion of a cohort experiences a given family-related event, and how have the proportions changed over time?

Marriage

Let us begin with the variable of marriage, examining the extent of historical change in the proportion of female cohorts who experience this life-course event (at least once) and, conversely, the proportion who never marry. Demographers typically measure extent of marriage by examining census data on the percentage of the population that is ever-married, and never-married, at ages 45–49. As it is rare for first marriages to occur after these ages, this measure provides a reasonably accurate estimate of the extent to which persons in a cohort experience the role transition into marriage.

As can be seen in Table 2, the majority of women in all cohorts marry. The overall trend over time is for marriage to become an increasingly universal life event. For cohorts born between 1862 and 1906, a rather high incidence of non-marriage occurred, with approximately 11 per cent of women never marrying. From a global perspective, this percentage is very high but it is in line with the

Table 2: Percentage of women ever-married and never-married at ages 45–49

Census year[1]	Birth cohort	Ever-married[2]	Never-married
		%	%
1881	1832–1836	88.7	11.3
1891	1842–1846	90.6	9.4
1911	1862–1866	88.0	12.0
1921	1872–1876	88.9	11.1
1931	1882–1886	89.7	10.3
1941	1892–1896	88.8	11.2
1951	1902–1906	88.3	11.7
1961	1912–1916	90.5	9.5
1971	1922–1926	93.0	7.0
1981	1932–1936	94.2	5.8

[1] No data available for 1901.

[2] Consists of married, divorced, separated, and widowed at census year.

SOURCES: Computed from data presented in Censuses of Canada: 1881 (v. 4, Table G); 1891 (v. 4, Table H); 1921 (v. 2, Table 29); 1931 (v. 3, Table 12); 1941 (v. 3, Table 7); 1951 (v. 2, Table 1); 1971 (Cat. 92–730, Table 1); 1981 (Cat. 29–901, Table 5).

experience of European and European-origin populations. As first pointed out by Hajnal (1965), European populations, particularly Western European populations, were characterized by a substantial proportion of persons never marrying (often exceeding 15 per cent), a pattern which is believed to have commenced in the seventeenth century and which lasted until the 1940s. In contrast, in societies of non-Western European origin, less than 5 per cent of the population never marries.

The trend away from high rates of non-marriage becomes evident in the 1961 data, i.e., the data relating to cohorts born between 1912–16. These women would have come to prime marriage age around 1940; thus, the Canadian experience is in keeping with that of other populations originating in Western Europe. Further rather marked declines in never-marriage occur among the cohorts born in 1922–26 and 1932–36. These cohorts reached young adulthood in the prosperous post-World War II years, a time when marriage would be 'easy' from a financial point of view. This is particularly so for the cohort 1932–36 (the Depression cohort) whose financial prospects in adulthood were particularly favourable given the competitive advantage in the labour market provided by its small size.

While comparable information on more recently-born cohorts cannot be provided until they have reached ages 45–49, some speculations can be offered, at least for the 'baby-boom cohorts' of 1946–1961. These cohorts have experienced the twin economic disadvantages of a declining economy and a high degree of job competition due to their large size. Therefore, it can be expected that their level of non-marriage will increase due to these economic factors, coupled with a, perhaps related, increased social acceptance of 'living together'. But, will it increase to the level experienced by earlier cohorts of Canadian women? In 1981, 10.4 per

Table 3: Percentage of childless ever-married women

Census year	Birth cohorts	Percentage childless
1941	1861–1876	12.8
1941	1877–1886	13.2
1941	1887–1896	12.3
1961	1897–1901	14.6
1961	1902–1906	15.5
1961	1907–1911	15.3
1961	1912–1916	13.1
1971	1917–1921	11.8
1971	1922–1926	9.6
1981	1927–1931	8.4
1981	1932–1936	7.2

SOURCES: Computed from data presented in Canadian Censuses: 1941 (v. 2, Table 51); 1961 (Cat. 98–507, Table G1); 1971 (Cat. 92–718, Table 24); 1981 (Cat. 92–906, Table 7).

cent of women aged 30–34 (the cohort of 1947–51, the leading edge of the 'baby boom') had never married. Given that these never-marrieds have another 15 years in which to marry, it would appear that their eventual levels of never-marriage will not be as high as those of the cohorts born before 1912–16.

In summary, then, taking on the status of 'married' has become an increasingly universal and predictable component of the life course of Canadian women.

Childbearing

Now, let us turn to the question: What changes have occurred in the proportion of cohorts of Canadian women who have made the transition into parenthood? This question can be answered by examining trends in the incidence of childlessness among ever-married women in the post-reproductive ages.

Although there is some variation, generally for cohorts born before 1916 the percentage of ever-married women who remain childless is in the range of 13–15 per cent. The percentage is particularly high (over 15 per cent) for women born between 1902 and 1911, women whose childbearing was undoubtedly affected by their historical location in time, i.e., these cohorts reached prime childbearing ages during the Depression. [See Table 3.]

The incidence of childlessness steadily declines among the cohorts born after 1922 to the degree that the percentage of childless ever-married women among the cohort of 1932–1936 is approximately one-half that of earlier cohorts of women. These more recently born cohorts (i.e., the cohorts born between 1922 and 1936) are the mothers of the 'baby boom'. Hence, one aspect of the 'baby boom' was a pronounced trend away from historically established levels of childlessness.

Accounting for trends in childlessness is a complex task, given that the causes of childlessness are twofold, both voluntary and involuntary. It has been estimated that the incidence of involuntary childlessness (i.e., sterility) among Canadian women aged 30–44 in 1961 was approximately 5 per cent and that some decreases have occurred over time, due largely to improvements in medical treatment (Veevers, 1972). The levels of childlessness observed for Canadian women, particularly for cohorts born before 1921, are significantly higher than this figure of 5 per cent. Even allowing for increases in sterility as one moves back in time, it seems that childlessness was deliberately chosen by some portion of Canadian women throughout the century. It appears that Canadian society, although evaluating childlessness negatively, provided avenues such that some percentage of ever-married women could exercise the option of remaining childless. This finding has been reported for the American population as well (Tolnay and Guest, 1982).

The levels of childlessness experienced by the cohorts of women who produced the 'baby boom' are exceptionally low. Keeping in mind that some women are married to sterile men, and assuming that sterile women and sterile men do not deliberately seek out one another as marriage partners, virtually every ever-married woman in a union that was not sterile produced at least one child. For reasons that remain unclear, voluntary childlessness among these cohorts was virtually non-existent.

Canadian women currently under the age of 35 exhibit relatively high rates of childlessness (Grindstaff, 1984). These data may indicate trends toward increased childlessness, later childbearing, or both. Experts in the field generally agree that permanent childlessness among today's young women will be in the range of 15 to 20 per cent (Veevers, 1985). If the figure is around 15 per cent, the level of childlessness will return to the 'traditional' level in Canada; if the figure exceeds 20 per cent, childlessness will be higher than experienced by earlier cohorts of women.

Another important dimension of the life course concerns the *number* of children that are born. It is well known that Canadian fertility has declined substantially. Indeed, this fertility decline is the major cause of population aging.

In assessing the magnitude of Canadian fertility decline, both a synthetic cohort measure (the total fertility rate, which gives the number of children that 1,000 women [all marital statuses combined] would bear by the end of their reproductive years if they bore children throughout their lives at the rates observed in a given year) and a cohort measure (the number of children ever-born to 1,000 ever-married women by the end of their reproductive years) are available. . . .

Although the two measures are not strictly comparable, they both indicate the major decreases that have occurred in the number of children that cohorts of women have borne. See Table 4. The total fertility rates cover a greater time period and, therefore, illustrate more dramatically declines in family size. The cohorts of 1817–1831 bore about 6.6 children per woman whereas the cohorts of 1947–1961 are expected to bear approximately 1.7 children per woman—a decrease of approximately 75 per cent. The cohort measure captures only part of the picture of fertility decline, in that data for the high-fertility early cohorts are not available and the substantial fertility decline of cohorts born after 1936 is not indicated.

Parallel with the declines in the number of children ever-born has been an

Table 4: Canadian fertility trends

		(A) total fertility rates (per 1000 women)			
Census year	Approximate birth cohorts	Rate	Census year	Approximate birth cohorts	Rate
1851	1817–1831	6562	1921	1887–1901	3536
1861	1827–1841	5858	1931	1897–1911	3200
1871	1837–1851	5513	1941	1907–1921	2832
1881	1847–1861	4975	1951	1917–1931	3503
1891	1857–1871	4575	1961	1927–1941	3840
1901	1867–1881	4644	1971	1937–1951	2187
1911	1877–1891	4396	1981	1947–1961	1704

		(B) number of children ever-born per 1000 ever-married women			
Census year	Birth cohorts	Number of children	Census year	Birth cohorts	Number of children
1941	1861–1876	4818	1961	1912–1916	3110
1941	1877–1886	4398	1971	1917–1921	3189
1941	1887–1896	4167	1971	1922–1926	3315
1941	1897–1901	3650	1981	1927–1931	3407
1961	1902–1906	3385	1981	1932–1936	3260
1961	1907–1911	3154			

SOURCES: For children ever-born: Canadian Censuses, 1941 (v. 2, Table 51); 1961 (Cat. 98–507, Table G1); 1971 (Cat. 92–718, Table 24); 1981 (Cat. 92–906, Table 7).

interesting convergence in family size. . . . As would be expected, the percentages of women bearing large numbers of children have decreased rather steadily over time. The interesting data relate to the percentages of women bearing only one child. As family size has decreased, we would expect an increase in the production of only children. However, the data indicate the reverse. While the women whose chief childbearing ages spanned the Depression years display some increase in the production of 'onlies', the overall trend over time is one of decrease. It appears that a 'norm' of sorts has emerged among couples—a small family is seen as desirable, but one child is too small. Of course, our data end with the cohorts of 1932–36, and younger couples may be more desirous of only children. The jury is still out on this issue, but my speculation is that the majority of young women today are opting for either no *or* two children.

Another dimension of convergence in family size concerns the trend away from traditional differentials in number of children born. While data are not provided here, it is well-established that former differentials in family size, related to variables such as rural/urban residence and ethnicity, have virtually disappeared (Veevers, 1983).

Table 5: Percentage distribution of ever-married women, by number of children ever-born

Census year	Birth cohort	Percentage of ever-married women by number of children ever-born					
		1	2	3	4	5	6+
1941	1861–1876	10.6	12.7	12.5	11.5	9.9	42.3
1941	1877–1886	12.9	15.5	14.2	12.0	9.4	35.7
1941	1887–1896	14.1	17.6	15.2	12.0	9.1	31.7
1961	1897–1901	16.1	20.5	16.7	12.0	8.8	26.0
1961	1902–1906	17.7	22.5	17.0	11.7	8.1	22.9
1961	1907–1911	18.5	25.2	17.6	11.5	7.7	19.4
1961	1912–1916	17.4	25.9	19.4	12.5	7.8	17.1
1971	1917–1921	14.9	25.4	20.4	13.9	8.7	16.8
1971	1922–1926	12.5	24.3	21.7	15.4	9.3	16.7
1981	1927–1931	10.3	23.2	22.7	16.8	10.3	16.6
1981	1932–1936	9.7	24.7	24.7	17.8	10.0	13.2

SOURCES: Canadian Census, 1941 (vol. 2, Table 51); 1961 (Cat. 98–507, Table G1); 1971 (Cat. 92–718, Table 24); 1981 (Cat. 92–906, Table 7).

Divorce

The rate of divorce in Canada has increased markedly since the liberalization of legal access to divorce in 1968. We have little hard data on the extent of marital breakdown prior to this, because: (1) inaccurate data have been provided in vital statistics publications and censuses (Nagnur, 1985); and (2) the difficulty in obtaining a divorce prior to 1968 masked the number of marriages that had broken down in fact if not in law.

Given severe data problems, it is not possible to perform either cohort or synthetic cohort analysis on the life-course event of divorce. However, preliminary findings from the Canadian Family History Survey can shed some light on the changing incidence of divorce (Burch, 1985). Approximately 10 per cent of ever-married women aged 50–64 in 1984 (cohorts of 1920–1934) and approximately 16 per cent of ever-married women aged 30–49 (cohorts of 1935–1954) have ever been divorced. These figures reflect an increase in the incidence of divorce among younger cohorts. Yet even among the younger cohorts, the vast majority of women who get married stay married.

THE TIMING OF FAMILY LIFE EVENTS

One of the major dimensions of the life course is social timetables. Here the concern is with changes that have occurred in the *ages* at which women experience major life-course events or role transitions. In turning to this issue, it is

Table 6: Median ages at family life-course events

Median age at:	Approximate birth cohorts					
	1831–1840	1841–1850	1851–1860	1861–1870	1881–1890	1891–1900
First marriage	25.1	26.0	24.9	24.3	25.1	23.4
First birth	27.1	28.0	26.9	26.3	27.1	25.4
Last birth	41.0	40.0	38.2	36.2	36.2	33.9
Empty nest[1]	61.0	60.1	58.2	56.2	56.2	53.9
Widowhood	58.2	59.5	58.9	58.3	60.1	59.4

Median age at:	Approximate birth cohorts					
	1901–1910	1911–1920	1921–1930	1931–1940	1941–1950	1951–1960
First marriage	23.3	23.0	22.0	21.1	21.3	22.5
First birth	25.0	25.4	23.5	22.9	23.3	24.5
Last birth	29.1	28.8	29.5	29.1	26.7	26.3
Empty nest[1]	49.1	48.8	49.5	49.1	46.7	46.3
Widowhood	61.3	63.0	67.0	67.2	68.8	69.9

[1] Age at which last child is 20 years old.

important to keep in mind that a sizeable (and variable) minority of cohort members do not ever experience the role transitions we will be discussing here.

Table 6 provides an overview of changes that have occurred in the average ages at which cohorts of Canadian women experience the following: age at first marriage; age at birth of first and last child; age at which mothers experience the departure of their last child ('empty nest'); and age at widowhood. . . .

Significant declines have occurred in age at first marriage. The relatively old age at marriage experienced by cohorts born in the nineteenth century is in keeping with the high percentage of persons never-married (see Table 2); both are charac-teristic of the European marriage pattern (Gee, 1982; Hajnal, 1965). This marriage pattern, termed 'restrictive' (van de Walle, 1968), was abandoned when economic and social change made it possible. As argued by Gee (1980: 462), an important change occurring in this century affecting lowered age at marriage is increased female labour-force participation. Greater proportions of women in the paid labour force have affected the desirability and the feasibility of marriage. The desirability of marriage is a function of the availability of socially rewarding alternatives to marriage (Dixon, 1971). Presumably, increased female labour-force participation provides more options for women outside of the traditional sphere of the home. However, given that women working outside the home are concen-trated in low-wage clerical and service jobs, their labour-force participation has *not* led to a situation in which the worker role is a viable (i.e., socially rewarding)

Table 7: Percentage distribution of ages at first marriage

| | Percentage of women marrying at ages: | | | | |
	−19	20–24	25–29	30–34	35+
1931[1]	23.0	43.7	18.5	6.2	8.6
1941[1]	19.3	42.9	22.2	7.9	7.7
1951	27.0	46.4	16.3	5.4	4.9
1961	34.7	46.0	11.3	4.0	4.0
1971	30.2	54.0	10.4	2.6	2.8
1981	16.4	55.3	20.5	5.1	2.7

[1] Data refer to age at all marriages, not first marriages only. In 1931 and 1941, the percentages of marriages that were first marriages were 87.3 per cent and 88.5 per cent, respectively.
SOURCES: Vital Statistics, Cat. 84–202 and 84–205.

alternative to the wife role for many women. Rather, the occupational role has become supplemental to the familial role—this incorporation of roles implies a loss of alternatives to marriage. The fusion of the worker and familial roles for women has resulted in an opportunity structure that makes marriage *more* desirable by removing, or at least obscuring, alternatives to it.

While the increased labour-force participation of women has indirectly, and perhaps paradoxically, operated to increase marriage desirability, it has also functioned to affect the feasibility of marriage. It is more economically feasible to marry, and to marry at younger ages, when two incomes contribute to the setting up of the new household.

There is a slight trend toward older age at first marriage for recent cohorts. Increased incidence of 'living together', economic recession, and normative change are likely contributing factors. However, it must be kept in mind that age at first marriage remains young when viewed historically.

Coupled with the overall trend towards younger age at first marriage is a trend of increased *homogeneity* in the ages at which women marry. As shown in Table 7, there has been a pronounced move away from marrying at older ages and a steady trend towards first marriage in the early 20s.

Age at first birth has declined over time, generally paralleling the declines in age at first marriage. Among cohorts of the nineteenth century, median age at birth of first child for women was about 27. Median age at first birth reached an all-time low (22.9) among the cohorts of 1931–40, the mothers of the 'baby boom'; a combination of young age at marriage and a short interval between marriage and first birth. Indeed, decreased age at marriage and accelerated childbearing have been identified as the major factors accounting for the 'baby boom' (Gee, 1978, 1980; Henripin and Légaré, 1971).

As with age at first marriage, there is a slight increase in average age at first birth among recent cohorts. While much has been made in recent years of delayed parenthood, most women continue to have their first child at relatively young ages, given that the median age of first birth is 24.5 years for the most recent cohort. Only a two-year interval exists between age at marriage and age at birth of the first child for the most recent cohort. The majority of women who have children continue to have them early in marriage. It seems likely that a class phenomenon is involved: the people who are delaying childbearing are the well-educated, successful middle class — a highly visible and publicized minority.

Age at last birth has decreased dramatically over time. For cohorts born in the middle of the nineteenth century, the last child was born to women when they were approximately 40. A virtually steady decline over cohorts can be observed, so that, for the most recent cohort, the average age for women is 26.3. While decreasing age at marriage is partially responsible for this trend, the major factor involved is declines in the number of children women have, in conjunction with a childbearing pattern in which children are born early in marriage and spaced closely.

The data concerning age at 'empty nest', calculated by simply adding 20 years to the age at which the last child is born (and assuming that all last-born children survive to age 20), illustrate the same substantial declines as do the data on age at birth of last child. Whereas women born in the middle of the last century were approximately 60 when the last child left home, this experience is now expected to occur to women in their mid- to late 40s. This represents a fundamental change in the life course of Canadian women. I have estimated that for female cohorts born between 1831 and 1840, 90 per cent of the years lived after marriage were spent rearing dependent children; the comparable figure for the cohorts of 1951–60 is 40 per cent. Canadian women have, in other words, *compressed* their child-rearing into a much smaller part of their adult lives.

The average age at which women become widows has increased quite substantially over time. Whereas women born in the nineteenth century would become widows in their late 50s, their present-day counterparts can expect to be nearly 70 before this life-course event occurs. While a narrowing in the male/female gap in age at marriage is partially responsible for this trend, the major factor involved is increased longevity.

CONCLUSIONS

This paper has attempted to provide an overview of the changes in family-related life events among Canadian women. Major *changes* include the following:

1. Major reductions in mortality have made it increasingly possible for members of birth cohorts to experience age-related family life-course events. The predictability of the life course has been enhanced considerably.
2. An increased propensity to marry and to marry at younger ages is evident. While there has been a recent trend towards later marriage, the median age at marriage for women remains young when viewed with an historical lens. Also, a trend towards convergence in age at first marriage is evident.

3. A trend away from childlessness occurs among ever-married women, particularly for cohorts born between 1922 and 1936. It is speculated that the incidence of childlessness will return to, and perhaps exceed, earlier levels.
4. Substantial declines in fertility can be observed. A significantly smaller proportion of adult life is devoted to childrearing responsibilities. The median age at birth of the last child decreases dramatically over cohorts, as does the median age at 'empty nest'. Hence, a compression effect is observed.
5. A large increase occurs in the median age at which women become widows, largely the result of improvements in longevity.

However, it is important to keep continuities in mind as well. The major *continuities* include:

1. The majority of Canadian women marry. There is no trend away from the institution of marriage.
2. There is a continuing trend for married women who have children to do so early in marriage and to space their children closely. The recent trend towards delayed childrearing appears to be characteristic of a highly visible minority.
3. There is no discernible trend towards one-child families. Such families continue to be avoided.
4. While divorce has increased since the legal changes instituted in 1968, the vast majority of Canadian women who marry do not divorce.
5. The majority of women can expect to become widows. Indeed, increasing sex differentials in life expectancy favouring women suggest an intensification of this phenomenon.

IMPLICATIONS

1. This analysis points to the atypical life-course experience of the women who produced the 'baby boom'. From an historical perspective, they display a young age at first marriage, a low incidence of never-marrying, an extremely low incidence of childlessness, and a short interval between marriage and birth of the first child. It is easy, even tempting, to look at today's trends in family life-course behaviour in light of the experience of these atypical cohorts (who are, for many of us, our mothers) and thereby *exaggerate* trends away from marriage, childlessness, and early childbearing within marriage. If we cast our net further back, however, the resulting overview of the family life course of Canadians allows for a more accurate, historically-based assessment of change.
2. The general trend of standardization—observed in data relating to age at marriage, proportions marrying, and number of children born—is intriguing. One would expect the opposite, given the wider societal process of individualization. A plausible explanation has been provided by Kohli

(1986). He argues that mechanisms of social control have changed with the development of modern society. In the past, social control operated through family membership and ties to the local community. [With modernization] individualized social control mechanisms [emerged]. One such mechanism is the institutionalization of the life course. In other words, 'rules of membership have been replaced by rules of temporal order.' How this happened is yet to be worked out, and is a fruitful area for further investigation.

REFERENCES

Barclay, G.W. (1958). *The Techniques of Population Analysis*. New York: John Wiley.

Bloom, D.E., and A.R. Pebley (1982). 'Voluntary childlessness: A review of the evidence and implications'. *Population Research and Policy Review* 1: 203–24.

Bogue, D.J. (1969). *Principles of Demography*. New York: John Wiley.

Bourbeau, R. et J. Légaré (1982). *Evolution de la mortalité au Canada et au Québec, 1831–1931*. Montréal: Les Presses de l'Université de Montréal.

Burch, T.K. (1985). *Family History Survey: Preliminary Findings*. Ottawa: Statistics Canada, Cat. 99–955.

Dixon, R.B. (1971). 'Explaining cross-cultural variations in age at marriage and proportions never marrying', *Population Studies*. 25: 215–33.

Elder, G.H., Jr. (1978). 'Approaches to social change and the family', *American Journal of Sociology*. 84: S1–S38.

——— and R.C. Rockwell (1976). 'Marital timing in women's life patterns'. *Journal of Family History*. 1: 34–53.

Gee, E.M. (1978). Fertility and Marriage Patterns in Canada: 1851–1971. University of British Columbia, doctoral dissertation.

——— (1980). 'Female marriage patterns in Canada: Changes and differentials', *Journal of Comparative Family Studies* 11: 457–73.

——— (1982). 'Marriage in nineteenth-century Canada', *Canadian Review of Sociology and Anthropology* 19: 311–25.

Glick, P.C. (1977). 'Updating the family life cycle', *Journal of Marriage and the Family* 39: 5–13.

Grindstaff, Carl (1984). 'Catching up: The fertility of women over 30 years of age, Canada in the 1970s and early 1980s', *Canadian Studies in Population* 11: 95–109.

Hagestad, G.O. and B.L. Neugarten (1985). 'Age and the life course', in *Handbook of Aging and the Social Sciences* (second ed.), ed. R.H. Binstock, E. Shanas and Associates. New York: Van Nostrand Reinhold, pp. 35–61.

Hajnal, J. (1953). 'Age at first marriage and proportions marrying', *Population Studies* 7: 111–36.

——— (1965). 'European marriage patterns in historical perspective', in *Population in History: Essays in Historical Demography*, ed. D.V. Glass and D.E.C. Eversley. London: Edward Arnold, pp 101–43.

Henripin, J. and J. Légaré (1971). 'Recent trends in Canadian fertility', *Canadian Review of Sociology and Anthropology* 8: 106–18.

Hogan, D.P. (1985). 'The demography of life-span transition: Temporal and gender comparisons', in *Gender and the Life Course*, ed. A.S. Rossi. New York: Aldine. pp. 65–78.

Kohli, M. (1986). 'The world we forgot: A historical review of the life course', in *Later Life: The Social Psychology of Aging*, ed. V.W. Marshall. Beverly Hills: Sage.

Nagnur, D. (1985). Personal communication.

Potter, R.G. Jr. (1963), 'Birth intervals: Structure and change', *Population Studies* 17: 155–166.

Rodgers, R.H. and G. Witney (1981). 'The family cycle in twentieth century Canada', *Journal of Marriage and the Family* 43: 727–740.

Shryock, H.S., J.S. Siegel and Associates, (1973). *The Methods and Materials of Demography*. Washington: U.S. Printing Office.

Tolnay, S.E. and A.M. Guest (1982). 'Childlessness in a transitional population: The United States at the turn of the century', *Journal of Family History* 7: 200–19.

van de Walle, E. (1968). 'Marriage and marital fertility', *Daedalus* 97: 486–501.

Veevers, J.E. (1972). 'Factors in the incidence of childlessness in Canada: An analysis of census data', *Social Biology* 19: 266–74.

Veevers, J.E. (1983). *Demographic Aspects of Vital Statistics: Fertility*. Ottawa: Statistics Canada.

——— (1985). Personal communication.

PART TWO

AGE AND SEX COMPOSITION

FERTILITY'S ROLE IN AGE COMPOSITION

The age composition of society is primarily determined by changes in fertility and, to a lesser degree, mortality. The high fertility rates that prevailed around the turn of the century ensured Canada of a young age structure well into the early 1930s and 1940s. The low fertility of the 1930s and the war years, on the other hand, was partly responsible for the dramatic and unpredicted rise in childbearing after the Second World War. During the prosperous 1950s and 1960s, people born during the Depression and war were entering adulthood and establishing themselves in the labour market. The economy was booming, and the age structure was such that there was a relative shortage of young workers — conditions that favoured not only relative prosperity but early age at marriage and more childbearing. Thus the fertility declines of the 1930s and early 1940s produced an undersupply of young workers twenty years later, with the result that structural conditions were favourable for this relatively small generation as it entered adulthood.

Such has not been the case for the baby-boom generation. The high fertility rates of the post-war years meant that in the 1980s and 1990s large numbers of young adults would be seeking to make their fortunes in the labour market at a time when a series of recessions has weakened public confidence in the economy. The relative size of this large cohort, combined with uncertain economic conditions and rising material aspirations, has produced the current 'baby bust' era in Canadian demography. Here again we note the importance of age structure in determining life chances and the effect of past fertility trends on age composition. Any significant change in fertility will work through its economic effects after a lag of 20 to 25 years. Thus a small generation of babies will enjoy certain advantages throughout its life cycle that cannot be shared by a large cohort.

This is the theme of the chapter by Foot and Venne, who argue that upward career movement may be out of reach for many Canadian baby boomers. They demonstrate that if one considers the career prospects of this generation in the market economy, the closest match between the age structure of the labour force and a typical hierarchical organizational pyramid occurred in the late 1970s, and that over the 1980s a substantial mismatch has emerged. The baby boomers are overflowing the middle ranks of the organization hierarchy during their prime working years. This means that there are few opportunities for upward movement beyond the middle ranks of the organizational ladder. At the same time, organizations face a shortage of entry-level workers coming from the much smaller baby-bust. According to Foot and Venne, a flattening of organization hierarchies and the adoption of rewarding spiral career paths are among the responses that may help the Canadian labour force to cope with the effects of changing demographic structures.

DEMOGRAPHIC AGING

Another demographic reality facing Canada and much of the industrialized world is the aging of the population. The continuation of this process into the future will have significant implications for both society and the individual. Burch outlines a series of propositions that derive from the mutual interrelationships of demographic change (including aging) and change in sex roles. For example, declining mortality rates at older ages (beyond the reproductive ages) have yielded a higher proportion of elderly in the population (although declining fertility is a more important causal factor), and the same underlying forces that have lowered mortality have meant that the elderly population is generally healthier and more active than in the past. The growing number of 'elderly' people will likely change society's expectations of what it means to be 'old'; and the weakening of the associations between old age and infirmity will also change elderly people's conception of themselves. Burch predicts that older persons will have more power by reason of their voting strength and even their accumulated wealth.

Another dimension of an aging population is the large sex differential in mortality favouring women. This means that many women will spend their old age without a spouse, and society will witness a growing tendency towards the 'feminization of old age'. The lower remarriage prospects of widowed and divorced women, together with their numerical preponderance in old age, will tend to define the role of the older woman as 'spouseless'. The prospect of being alone in old age may even diminish the centrality of marriage in women's conception of their lives.

As Canada enters the twenty-first century, the population aged 65 and older will number nearly 4 million. In the second decade of the next century, the baby-boom generation (born between 1946 and 1966) will enter the ranks of the senior population. This is the demographic scenario for the near future as outlined by Stone and Fletcher. By the year 2031, seniors will account for 7.5 million people in Canada. An important contributor to these projected changes is the unprecedented decline in mortality at the older ages that began in the 1970s. Stone and Fletcher place this phenomenon in the same class as the baby boom in that both were unexpected.

TECHNICAL NOTES

1. The relative importance of fertility and mortality in determining age composition can be ascertained with the following simulation provided by the United Nations. The table (p. 66) shows six panels, each reflecting a certain level of mortality (expectation of life at birth) and fertility (gross reproduction rate, or GRR). (The GRR is computed by multiplying the total fertility rate by the proportion of female births. This measure can be interpreted as the average number of daughters that would be born to a women during her lifetime if she were to experience the fertility rates of the period at each age.) The percentage of the population within three broad age classes is shown in each panel. If one varies mortality while keeping fertility constant, the effect on age distribution is minimal. For example, in panel I life expectancy is 20, and in panel VI it is 70 — a difference of 50 years. Yet the proportion aged 0–14 changes by only about 4 per cent (from 14.8 per cent in panel I to 19.5 per cent in panel VI) when fertility is kept constant at GRR = 1.00. By contrast, when we vary fertility within each mortality level (i.e., within each panel), from a GRR of 1.00 to a GRR of 4.00 the proportions within each age class change dramatically (e.g., from 14.8 per cent to 45.2 per cent). This exercise shows that fertility is the key determinant of change in the age composition, and that mortality plays a relatively minor role.

2. The sex ratio in the population is computed by dividing the number of males by the number of females and then multiplying by 100. Sex ratios can be computed for any age class, such as for the prime marriageable ages (15–34), to better ascertain imbalances in the relative numbers of men and women. Sex ratios in infancy typically reflect a relative numerical advantage for males (about 105 for every 100 females), but this advantage gradually erodes, until by age 45 the ratio reverses, primarily because of sex differences in mortality (higher death rates for males). Immigration, if it is sex-selective, can also have a distorting effect on the relative balance of the sexes.

3. Dependency ratios are often calculated as rough proxies for the degree of economic burden on the working population. For example, the youth dependency ratio is the number of children aged 0–14 divided by the number of people in the working ages 15–64 and then multiplied by 100. Similarly, the old-age dependency ratio can be computed by taking the number of people aged 65 and older and dividing it by the number of people in the working ages 15–64. The total dependency ratio is the sum of the two ratios. In general, industrial nations have a lower youth dependency ratio than developing countries, because of their much lower fertility, but a larger old-age dependency burden — another consequence of sustained low fertility, together with the effects (small but growing in significance) of increased survival in old age.

Gross reproduction rate (GRR)	Percentage of population			Gross reproduction rate (GRR)	Percentage of population		
	0–14 years	15–59 years	60 years and over		0–14 years	15–59 years	60 years and over
(I) Expectation of life at birth: 20 years				(IV) Expectation of life at birth: 50 years			
1.0	14.8	68.3	16.9	1.0	17.8	60.7	21.5
2.0	28.9	64.0	7.1	2.0	34.2	57.2	8.6
3.0	38.5	57.6	3.9	3.0	44.6	50.9	4.5
4.0	45.2	52.4	2.4	4.0	51.5	45.8	2.7
(II) Expectation of life at birth: 30 years				(V) Expectation of life at birth: 60.4 years			
1.0	16.3	65.0	18.7	1.0	18.7	59.4	21.9
2.0	31.4	60.9	7.7	2.0	35.6	55.8	8.6
3.0	41.3	54.5	4.1	3.0	46.0	49.6	4.4
4.0	48.2	49.2	2.6	4.0	52.9	44.4	2.7
(III) Expectation of life at birth: 40 years				(VI) Expectation of life at birth: 70.2 years			
1.0	17.0	62.6	20.4	1.0	19.5	58.6	21.9
2.0	32.9	58.8	8.3	2.0	36.8	54.7	8.5
3.0	43.1	52.5	4.4	3.0	47.3	48.4	4.3
4.0	50.0	47.3	2.7	4.0	54.1	43.3	2.6

SOURCE: United Nations (1973) *The Determinants and Consequences of Populations Trends* (New York: United Nations Publications), p. 274.

SUGGESTED READING

Coale, Ansley J. (1964). 'How a population ages or grows younger'. Pp. 47–69 in Ronald Freedman, ed., *Population: The Vital Revolution*. Garden City, NJ: Doubleday.

——— and Paul A. Demeny (1983). *Regional Model Life Tables and Stable Populations*. Second Ed. New York: Academic Press.

Day, Lincoln (1978). 'What will a ZPG society look like?'. *Population Bulletin* 33, 3.

Denton, T. Frank, Christine H. Feaver, and Byron G. Spencer (1986). 'Prospective aging of the population and its implications for the labour force and government expenditure'. *Canadian Journal of Aging* 5, 2: 75–98.

Easterlin, Richard E. (1987). *Birth and Fortune*. Chicago: University of Chicago Press.

Guttentag, Marcia, and Paul F. Secord (1983). *The Sex Ratio Question: Too Many Women?* Beverly Hills, CA: Sage.

Kettle, John (1980). *The Big Generation*. Toronto: McClelland and Stewart.

McDaniel, Susan (1986). *Canada's Aging Population*. Toronto: Butterworths.

Norland, A. Joseph (1976). *The Age-Sex Structure of Canada's Population*. Ottawa: Statistics Canada. Cat. 99-703.

Preston, Samuel H. (1984). 'Children and the elderly: divergent paths for America's dependents'. *Demography* 21, 4: 435–58.

United Nations (1973). *The Determinants and Consequences of Populations Trends*. Vol. 1, Chap. 8. New York: United Nations Publications.

Wigdor, T. Blossom, and David K. Foot (1988). *The Over Forty Society*. Toronto: Lorimer.

CHAPTER 5

POPULATION, PYRAMIDS AND PROMOTIONAL PROSPECTS

David K. Foot and Rosemary A. Venne

INTRODUCTION

The baby-boom generation has been the subject of considerable attention. Because of its sheer size in North America, it is easy to document historically the enormous impact the baby boom has had on society and its institutions, which have often been stretched to their limits to accommodate its requirements. Some would say the baby-boom generation has changed the shape of these institutions. Jones (1980) views this generation as a tidal wave effecting massive changes in society's institutions as it ages, causing disruption, for example, in schools and the labour force. Similarly, Russell (1987) documents the myriad of institutions that will be affected by the baby boom over the next half century.

The baby-boom generation in Canada is defined as those born during the high fertility period from post-World War II to the mid-1960s (1947–1966). Following this period, fertility rates declined to below replacement levels, resulting in a subsequent 'baby bust' generation (1967–1980). During the 1960s and 1970s labour-force growth in Canada reached unprecedented levels (over 3 per cent per annum) due in large part to the baby boom entering the labour force (see Foot, 1987). No other country in the Western world approached these rates of labour-force growth. Over the 1980s, with the baby-bust generation entering the Canadian labour force, average annual growth has slowed considerably, despite an economic boom that has characterized much of this period. These new trends can be expected to continue as the much smaller baby-bust generation continues to enter the labour force over the 1990s.

Corporate hierarchical structures with a broad base of entry-level positions were well designed to accommodate wave after wave of new labour-market entrants over the post-war period, and especially over the 1960s and 1970s. However, over the 1980s they are gradually becoming less appropriate as shortages of entry-level workers gradually become more widespread in the economy. Over the 1990s it is likely that, unless modified, these structures will prove to be inadequate for the new labour-force environment. This emerging 'mismatching' between organization structures and the labour force is the foundation for recent concern over the promotional prospects for the large baby-boom generation.

The labour-force experiences of the baby-boom cohort, and more specifically their likely decreased promotional prospects in the years ahead, are the focus of this paper. This is a relatively new concern. Recently, both demographers and human-resource planners have expressed interest and concern over possible blocked career paths and 'plateauing' for this large generation (see, for example, Keyfitz, 1973; Malkiel, 1983; Walsh and Lloyd, 1984; and Bardwick, 1986). This paper relates the baby-boom generation in the labour force to a typical organization hierarchy and develops an empirical measure of the 'mismatch' between the two. The discrepancy between labour-force age structure and the typical organization hierarchy is then examined, both historically and in the future. The implications for human-resource planning for individuals, organizations and the society are then outlined, with particular attention to the baby-boom generation in the 1990s.

. . .

THEORY

Individuals work within organizations. Consequently, individual career paths and promotional possibilities are largely determined by organization structures and behaviour. Organizations in turn are influenced by the 'external environment'. This especially includes demographic developments, over which both individual and organizational decisions effectively have no control. The monitoring of this external environment as an input into these decisions has become an important focus of the literature in human-resource planning (see, for example, Kochan and Barocci, 1985; or Dolan and Schuler, 1987).

At the individual level, a number of researchers (for example, Keyfitz, 1973; Cantrell and Clark, 1982; and Denton and Spencer, 1982; 1987) have explored the relationship between the rate of population growth and the promotional prospects for individual employees. Using US life tables with various steady-state rates of population growth, Keyfitz (1973) concluded that a 2 percentage point decrease in the growth rate resulted in an average delayed promotion of 4 1/2 years for employees in the middle levels of organization hierarchies. Cantrell and Clark (1982) extended this idea to include the impacts of labour-force participation rates on promotional prospects. More recently Denton and Spencer (1987), in an update of their earlier (1982) work, examined the impact of both population and labour-force changes on promotional prospects. Using population projections for Canada under a variety of 'realistic' assumptions with regard to fertility, mortality, immigration, labour-force entry, participation rates, and retirement, they conclude that, 'to the extent that age matters in promotion prospects, the baby boom generation suffers some disadvantages as a result of its size'. This conclusion is rather robust: other demographic or participation-rate assumptions make little difference to the age of promotion over the next 25 years — for that period they note that 'the die is already cast'.

The relationship between individual promotional opportunities and organization structures has only recently received attention in the literature. Jones (1980) notes that 'the baby boom will find that just as there once was not enough room for all of them to climb onto the occupational ladder, there later will not be enough room at the top. As each person tries to climb up the business and professional hierarchies, he or she will find other baby boom competitors blocking the way . . . crowded on the first steps of management [they] will be forced to stay right there'. He then goes on to explore some of the implications: for example, longer climbs to the top will become commonplace, frustration will become acute, the mid-career job switch could become a way of life, and emphasis will be increasingly placed on job rotations, and the 'psychic benefits' of work.

Morgan's (1981; 1985) case study actually documents the problem of blocked career paths for the decision-making group of the Canadian federal public service. For approximately a decade (1965–75) this organization experienced rapid expansion during which time there was considerable career advancement, with promotions according to seniority being the norm. This rapid expansion was followed by a period of slow growth. Having been recruited at entry levels over the previous decade, the bulge of baby boomers advanced to middle management positions and subsequently found that there was, in Morgan's terminology, 'nowhere to go'.

Bardwick (1986) refers to this phenomenon as the 'plateauing trap'. She notes that the fundamental factors determining overall rates of promotion are impersonal; they have nothing to do with individual competence and they cannot be changed by any individual. While plateauing is inevitable for most employees, it is occurring sooner for the baby boomers due to the large size of their cohort group. As a result of these promotional blockages, employee frustration and a serious problem with morale emerge. Possible solutions to this problem are outlined, including psychological counselling for employees and changes in organization culture, such as retraining and lateral transfers.

Implicit in these analyses are the dual assumptions of linear individual career paths and pyramidal organization hierarchies. Driver (1979; 1985) argues that

Table 1: Career paths and associated characteristics

Career path	Direction of job movement	Number of occupations	Organizational structure	Reward systems
Steady state	None	One	Rectangular	Tenure, fringe benefits
Linear	Upward	Two	Tall pyramid	Promotion, power
Spiral	Lateral/upward	Five (?)	Flat pyramid	Re-education, retraining
Transitory	Lateral	Many	Temporary teams	Variety, time off

SOURCE: Adapted by the authors from Driver (1985).

these two concepts are linked. He points out that there are alternative career paths and associated organizational structures and cultures. He presents a classification of four individual career concepts linked uniquely with four organizational structures (and, ultimately, cultures). (See Table 1.)

The first two career paths are the most familiar. Briefly, the steady-state career represents a lifelong career path where an employee is committed to an occupation for life (for example, a minister of religion or a professor). Since there are many employees at the same level, the associated organization structure is almost flat with an accompanying culture that emphasizes tenure, seniority and fringe benefits. The linear career path is perhaps most pervasive in North America today. Here the employee seeks upward movement towards the top of a tall, increasingly narrow pyramid structure with numerous salary levels. Changes in occupation are infrequent, with promotions and accompanying salary increases and bonuses the main measures of career success.

The next two career paths may be less familiar. The spiral career, which combines mainly lateral moves with a few vertical moves, is associated with a moderate number of changes in occupation over a lifetime. The supporting organization structure is a flat pyramid with a few, broad levels. Here the emphasis is on occupational flexibility with liberal opportunities for lifelong re-education and retraining. Last, the transitory career is characterized by a 'consistent pattern of inconsistency', with frequent occupational change and lateral mobility. The associated organization structure consists of temporary teams and the organization culture revolves around variety and possible breaks between assignments.

Driver (1985) touches on the relevance of these concepts for the baby boom. After noting that demographic boom and bust conditions strongly affect work mobility—a proposition that was established by earlier writers—he concludes (for the US) that 'the bust generations born in the 1920s and 1930s carry an image of high mobility and demand [but] the 1940s and 1950s generation [that is, the baby boom] have faced a world of fierce competition, low demand and mobility'. The former group entered management during a period of economic expansion when a disproportionate increase in white-collar and middle management jobs occurred (see Bardwick, 1986). This small birth cohort experienced rapid promotions up the increasingly tall hierarchies. According to Bardwick (1986) these economic conditions held sway long enough that they came to be viewed as the

Table 2: A 'representative' pyramidal organization hierarchy (percentage distribution of employees)

Level	Total
6 (top)	2.8
5	8.3
4	13.9
3	19.4
2	25.0
1 (bottom)	30.6
Total	100.0

norm and formed the basis for the expectations of today's baby boomers. Thus it is not surprising that these linear expectations are supported by MBA and similar programs that have a strong linear career focus.

However, given the current demographic situation and recent organizational restructuring (for example, the shrinking of middle management positions; see Naisbitt and Aburdene, 1985) the linear focus of these programs is increasingly at odds with reality. Recent graduates who now face the 'career blocking' or 'plateauing' phenomenon identified by Morgan (1985) and Bardwick (1986) are becoming increasingly frustrated as their linear expectations clash with reality. They are on a collision course and in Driver's (1985) evaluation 'organizations are [currently] geared to reinforce precisely the wrong career concept from a societal point of view'. With the peak of the baby boom recently graduating from these programs, this linear career 'crisis' (as termed by Driver, 1985) can only become worse over the 1990s.

The following sections document this assertion quantitatively by developing an index of the 'mismatch' between the labour force and organizational structures based on the linear career concept. A subsequent section then reviews possible policy implications for the 1990s and beyond.

MEASURING THE 'MISMATCH'

. . .

To derive an empirical measure of the extent of mismatching, it is first necessary to develop a representation of a typical organization hierarchy. Following in the spirit of Keyfitz (1973) and Denton and Spencer (1987), six career levels are considered. A pyramidal hierarchical structure then identifies the percentage of employees at each level (see Table 2). The numbers show that under these conditions the 'representative' pyramidal organization hierarchy contains 30.6 per cent of employees at the bottom level, 25 per cent at the next level and so on to the top of the hierarchy where 2.8 per cent of the employees are located.

To develop a measure of how closely the labour force distribution matches this hierarchy, it is then necessary to relate the hierarchical levels in Table 2 to age groups in the labour force. Six ten-year age groups were chosen, the lowest being the youth aged 15 to 24 years and the highest being aged 65 years and over. These age groups are obviously mutually exclusive and exhaustive. By encompassing the entire labour force, a measure of the hierarchical mismatch for the entire society can be developed.

The statistical literature is replete with aggregate deviation measures. The most popular is the sum of squared deviations (on which 'standard deviations' and 'least squares' regression are based). This measure can be used to derive a squared deviation index (*SDI*) of the mismatch between the observed labour-force distribution in each year and the representative hierarchical distribution summarized in Table 2 as follows:

$$SDI_t = S \sum_i (H_i - L_{it})^2$$

where i indexes the age groups, H_i are the 'representative' hierarchical distribution percentages (Table 2), L_{it} are the observed labour-force distribution percentages in each time period t and the scaling factor S is chosen so that the index takes on the value 1.0 at its minimum value. A relatively high value for this index indicates a substantial mismatch, while a relatively low value (near 1) indicates closer coincidence of the observed labour-force and hierarchical distribution.

RESULTS

The *SDI* index was calculated for the Canadian labour force for the historical period from 1961 to 1986 and was projected a further 25 years to the year 2011 using one of Statistics Canada's recent population projections. The calculations follow the suggestions of Cantrell and Clark (1982) and the procedures of Denton and Spencer (1987) by incorporating labour-force participation rates. For the projection period, these age-specific rates were set at their 1986 values, which was the most recent census year and the starting year for the population projection.

The results are presented in Figure 1. The years when there was the closest coincidence between the labour-force distribution and the representative organization hierarchy occurred over the late 1970s. The general u-shape of the index indicates that over the 1960s and the 1970s, a gradually improved match between the labour force and organization hierarchy emerged as wave after wave of baby boomers entered the labour force, thus filling out the lower levels of organization hierarchies and reducing the index of mismatching. By 1976 the peak of the baby boom born in 1960 reached the minimum labour-force age of 16 years and by 1982 the last of the baby boomers born in 1966 reached this age.

Over the 1980s the trend has been dramatically reversed as the aging early baby boomers experienced mismatching in the middle career levels and the smaller baby-bust generation began entering the lower levels of the organization hierarchies. Therefore, over the 1980s mismatching takes two dominant forms. First, there is a scarcity of younger employees at the bottom career levels. The

Figure 1: Squared deviation index (SDI) of mismatching, Canada, 1961–2011

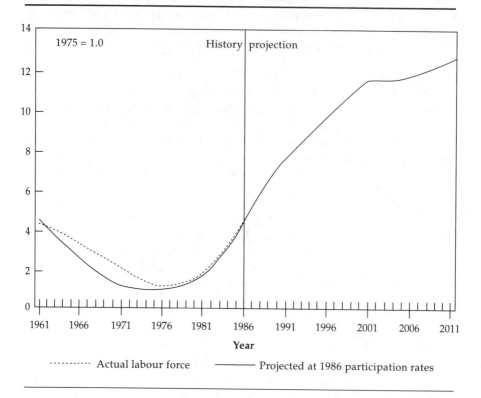

emergence of 'Help Wanted' signs in retail establishments where younger work-ers often start their careers (often in part-time positions) is evidence of this form. Second, there is a surplus of middle-aged employees in the middle career levels, which explains the recent concerns with career blocking and plateauing. By 1986 these calculations suggest that the mismatching is already worse than it has been throughout much of this historical period. Moreover, this trend is projected to continue through the 1990s and into the next century, when the degree of mismatching will be at unprecedented levels.[1] In essence, the mismat-ching problem that is emerging over the 1980s represents a reversal of the trend of the previous two decades, and can be expected to intensify over the 1990s and into the next century. It is important to remember that the baby-boom cohort in Canada encompasses a 20-year span. Since most people work for approxi-mately 40 to 45 years, the baby-boom generation from beginning to end impacts on the labour force for a span of at least 60 years. Hence the mismatch and associated career blockage problems are likely to persist for a long time unless corrective action is taken.

IMPLICATIONS

These conclusions, based on the *SDI* measure of the mismatch between the labour force and organization structures, verify not only the theoretical results of Keyfitz (1973), Cantrell and Clark (1982) and Denton and Spencer (1982; 1987), but also the more case-based works of Jones (1980), Morgan (1981; 1985) and Bardwick (1986). By the early 1980s, the entire baby-boom generation had become of labour-force age. The more slowly growing labour force over the 1980s, due in large part to the labour-force entry of the following smaller baby-bust generation, began intensifying the problems of slower promotional opportunities and increasing ages of promotion at each level in organization hierarchies. This led to blocked career paths, or the plateauing of the baby-boom generation. And the situation is not going to improve. In fact, over the 1990s with continuing slower labour-force growth, the problem can be expected to intensify as baby boomers continue to accumulate in the middle career levels with 'nowhere to go'.

These findings also provide dramatic verification of Driver's (1985) contention that currently 'organizations are geared to reinforce precisely the wrong career concept—the linear concept—from a societal point of view'. While it is likely that some organizations will continue to maintain structures and cultures that foster the linear career path, many linear-oriented organizations will adapt to this new reality by flattening their tall pyramidal organizational structures. A motivation may be to reduce the importance of promotions by reducing the number of hierarchical levels (Bardwick, 1986). When there are fewer levels, less upward movement is possible and much of the employee's attention is directed laterally rather than vertically; in other words, employees are encouraged to move from the linear career path towards the spiral career path.

The likely resurgence of the spiral career path in North America, where the pressures from the baby-boom generation are the most intense, will intensify education as a lifelong process and likely see the emergence of the 'generalist'. The employee with a solid training in basic skills and a variety of experiences who can be flexible and move laterally into new positions, is likely to be the most challenged and productive to his or her employer. Lateral swaps or exchanges are likely to become much more common. For example, employees plateaued as Directors of Marketing, Communications and Human Resources may well be rotated to provide new challenges for each employee. In this way, lateral moves are both a solution to an individual employee's plateauing problem, as well as to the entire cohort of employees at that particular organizational level.

And, of course, the 'sensible' employer will recognize these employee contributions and reward the employee appropriately even though no promotion to the next hierarchical level has taken place. In other words, employers who wish to keep their potentially plateaued employees challenged and productive will make sure that lateral as well as vertical moves are reflected in the financial rewards of the employees. With fewer levels in the hierarchy, each level will carry a much broader compensation range. Consequently, the broader pay level as a result of hierarchical flattening will provide the opportunity for monetary rewards to be provided even though there has been no elevation of the employee in the corporate structure.

Other changes for both employers and employees will also be necessary. Employers will likely have to provide more information and support services to assist employees in establishing career 'paths' (as distinct from career 'ladders') as they adapt to the new work environment. In addition, it will be increasingly necessary for employers to provide and purchase more training and education services to facilitate preparation for occupation changes associated with lateral moves. Employees for their part will find it advantageous to encourage and use these services rather than to resist their introduction.

On the human-resource planning side, far more attention will need to be paid to programs designed to encourage lateral movement. Information bases will need to be expanded to include data on employees' 'other' skills and interests; policies to encourage the use of educational and training opportunities outside of the employee's current responsibilities will need to be developed; exchange programs must be designed so that employees are encouraged to seek out other employees and positions that may be of interest for lateral moves; and salary structures that position employees in the organization hierarchy may have to be abandoned because an employee who has been rewarded for three lateral moves may well have a higher salary than the 'boss' who may be in the higher level position as a result of one vertical (or promotional) move.

Other changes within organizations are likely to be more subtle. Success in the workplace is likely to be redefined to include the variety of positions held as well as their level in the organization hierarchy. Reducing hierarchical levels may reduce formality, make leaders more accessible, improve communication and information flows, and lead to a more participatory style of management. See Naisbitt (1982); Naisbitt and Aburdene (1985); and Walton and Lawrence (1985) for an elaboration of these arguments. Increased concern for team work and 'followership' rather than leadership is likely to emerge. Emphasis will need to be on the opportunities for increasingly independent and challenging work— embracing challenge and mastering it will have to be rewarded. Extended study leaves or sabbaticals may become necessary to achieve these goals, as may employee access to improved health and recreation facilities.

This is only a representative and by no means exhaustive list of the changes that can be expected. The key ingredient, however, is the likely transformation of the corporate hierarchy and the workplace in North America over the 1990s and beyond from tall pyramids and linear career paths to flatter pyramids and spiral career paths. This transformation is likely to be accompanied by a much greater emphasis within organizations on human-resource management issues than in the past.

Changes are also likely outside of individual organizations. Several public policy issues dealing with the baby boom in the labour force will need to be addressed. To facilitate the spiral career path it will be increasingly necessary for educational institutions, especially post-secondary institutions, to offer timely and relevant courses. Naisbitt and Aburdene (1985) predict a boom in adult education as the new information society transforms people into 'lifelong learners'. This boom will be fuelled to a large extent by the baby boomers as would-be career changers, by people upgrading in fast-changing fields and as a preparation for lateral career moves. Courses will need to be scheduled at times that do not conflict with work (for example, on evenings and weekends) and redesigned into compact, modular courses that can be completed during a short-term leave (for example, three weeks). Teaching methods will also have to change, as the older student often has different 'expectations' than the younger student. Not only do they have more life and work experiences to draw on, they also are more likely to face and recognize a higher opportunity cost on their time (especially if the workload continues to pile up back at the office). In addition, since employers are likely to be willing to pay the fees for these students, educational institutions will be provided with an opportunity to broaden (and increase) their funding bases. The myriad of possible effects on educational policies deserve careful consideration and cannot be adequately explored here.

In the case study of the federal public sector, Morgan (1981; 1985) recommends early retirement as one measure to ease the career blockage problem. Early retirement incentives and flexible retirement policies, such as easing the employee into retirement by allowing employees to become part-time mentors or consultants, are becoming more common. Bardwick (1986) refers to the latter as 'transitional retirement' policies and recommends that these part-time employees should receive a proportionate fraction of their salary and benefits. Of course, the removal of mandatory retirement provisions and the introduction of various flexible retirement policies, such as has been recently introduced into the Canada/Quebec Pension Plan, could work in the opposite direction by allowing employees to remain longer in the senior levels of the organizational hierarchies.

Another public policy that can potentially impact on the promotional prospects of the baby boomers is immigration. Immigration policy in Canada has often been influenced by labour-market considerations, and, more recently, has been presented as a solution to population aging and low fertility. However, Foot (1986) has pointed out that because people are most geographically mobile in their early working lives, currently more than half of the immigrants are approximately the same age as the baby boomers. The similar age distribution of these two groups is potentially intensifying the career blockage problems for the baby boom generation. As a way of ameliorating this situation, Foot (1986) recommends an 'age-directed' component be added to Canada's immigration program that would be directed at younger age groups, corresponding to the age range of the baby-bust generation. Moreover, bringing in a larger share of younger immigrants would have the benefit of alleviating the shortage of entry-level workers and, consequently, would contribute to a lessening of the mismatch at the lower end of the hierarchy.

CONCLUSIONS

The baby-boom generation in Canada (1947–66), by its sheer size, has had an enormous impact on society and its institutions. This paper focused on the workplace experiences of the baby-boom generation; in particular, their promotional prospects. The widely held concept of a linear career (meaning upward career movement in a tall organization hierarchy) is likely to be out of reach for many baby boomers.

A measure of the extent to which the Canadian labour force deviates from typical organization hierarchies indicates that over the 1960s and 1970s the mismatch between the labour force and the hierarchical pyramid was lessening as a result of wave after wave of baby boomers entering the lower levels of corporate hierarchies. These calculations suggest that the closest match between the two structures occurred in the late 1970s and that over the 1980s a substantial mismatch has been emerging. The baby-boom generation is saturating and overflowing the middle ranks of the organization pyramid during their prime working years.

These results concur with other research findings from studies that have examined population aging and promotion prospects in slower-growing populations and from studies concerning career blockage and employee plateauing. In addition, the reduction in youth unemployment and the appearance of 'help wanted' signs in retail establishments indicate that human resource flexibility in organizations is being further hampered by the emerging shortage of entry-level workers who come from the much smaller baby-bust generation.

Moreover, these new trends are not likely to be transitory. The inevitable aging of the Canadian population into the 1990s and beyond is likely to intensify further the mismatch that has emerged over the 1980s. As a result, changes in policies for the individual, the organization and, ultimately, society are likely to be both desirable and necessary.

The major changes involve flattening the pyramidal structure of organization hierarchies and changing employee career paths from the linear to the spiral concept. In addition, specific human-resource planning policies to deal with the promotion squeeze that the baby-boom generation will continue to experience are necessary. A strong emphasis on human-resource planning is needed by all organizations to accommodate the inevitably changing structure of the future Canadian labour force. Finally, these changes also impact on a variety of public policies such as education, retirement and immigration. It is important that decisions taken in these areas be consistent with the changes taking place in the population, organizational pyramids and promotional prospects of the nation.

NOTE

[1] The 'flattening' of the index in the first decade of the 21st century reflects the entry of the children of the baby boomers — the so-called baby-boom 'echo' generation — which provides some relief at the entry levels of the 'representative' hierarchy at that time. Beyond the end of this projection period, the baby-boom generation will begin reaching retirement age (that is, those born in 1947 reach age 65 in 2012), which will also contribute to some flattening of the index.

REFERENCES

Bardwick, J. (1986). *The Plateauing Trap*. New York: Amacom.

Bean, C.R., P.R.G. Layard, and S.J. Nickell (1986). 'The rise in unemployment: A multi-country study'. *Economica* 53, 210: S1–22.

Bourgeois, R.P. and T. Wils (1987). 'Career concepts, personality and values of some Canadian workers'. *Relations Industrielles* 42, 2: 528–43.

Cantrell, R.S. and R.L. Clark (1982). 'Individual mobility, population growth and labour force participation'. *Demography* 19, 2: 147–59.

Crocker, O.C., C. Charney, and J. Chiu (1984). *Quality Circles: A Guide to Participation and Productivity*. Toronto: Methuen.

Denton, F., and B. Spencer (1982). *Population Aging, Labour Force Change and Promotion Prospects*, QSEP Research Report No. 30. Hamilton: Faculty of Social Sciences, McMaster University.

—— (1987). *Age Structure and Rate of Promotion in the Canadian Working Population*, QSEP Research Report No. 210. Hamilton: Faculty of Social Sciences, McMaster University.

Dolan, S.L., and R.S. Schuler (1987). *Personnel and Human Resource Management in Canada*. New York: West Publishing Company.

Driver, M.J. (1979). 'Career concepts and career management in organizations'. Pp. 79–139 in C.L. Cooper, ed., *Behavioral Problems in Organizations*. Englewood Cliffs: Prentice-Hall.

—— (1985). 'Demographic and societal factors affecting the linear career crisis,' *Canadian Journal of Administrative Studies*, 2, 2: 245–63.

Foot, D.K. (1986). *Population Aging and Immigration Policy in Canada: Implications and Prescriptions*, Population Working Paper No. 1. Ottawa: Employment and Immigration Canada.

—— (1987). *Population Aging and the Canadian Labour Force*, IRPP Discussion Paper No. 87.A.5. Ottawa: Institute for Research on Public Policy.

—— and R.A. Venne (1988). 'The baby boom generation in the labour force: New human resource challenges'. Pp. 428–41 in J. Boivin (ed.), *Some Aspects of International Industrial Relations: Proceedings of the 25th Meeting of The Canadian Industrial Relations Association*. Quebec: Laval University.

Freeman, R.B., and J.L. Medoff (1984). *What do Unions do?*. New York: Basic Books Inc.

Jones, L.Y. (1980). *Great Expectations: America and the Baby Boom Generation*. New York: Ballantine Books.

Keyfitz, N. (1973). 'Individual mobility in a stationary population', *Population Studies*, 27, 2: 335–52.

Kochan, T.A., and T.A. Barocci (1985). *Human Resource Management and Industrial Relations*. Boston: Little Brown.

Malkiel, B.G. (1983). 'The long run economic and demographic outlook: Implications for government policy and human resource planning', *Human Resource Planning*, 6, 3: 143–52.

Morgan, N. (1981). *Nowhere to Go? Possible Consequences of the Demographic Imbalance in Decision Making Groups of the Federal Public Services*. Montreal: Institute for Research on Public Policy.

—— (1985). *Implosion: An Analysis of the Growth of the Federal Public Service in Canada (1945–1985)*. Montreal: Institute for Research on Public Policy.

Naisbitt, J. (1982). *Megatrends: Ten New Directions Transforming our Lives*. New York: Warner Books.

—— and P. Aburdene (1985). *Re-Inventing the Corporation*. New York: Warner Books.

Russell, C. (1987). *One Hundred Predictions for the Baby Boom: The Next 50 Years*. New York: Plenum Press.

Statistics Canada (1988). 'Population projections for Canada, provinces and territories, 1986–2011', unpublished.

Walsh, D. and A.D. Lloyd (1984). 'Personnel planning's new agenda', *American Demographics* 6, 9: 34–8.

Walton, R. and P. Lawrence, eds (1985). *Human Resource Management: Trends and Challenges.* Boston: Harvard Business School Review Press.

CHAPTER 6

AGE-SEX ROLES AND DEMOGRAPHIC CHANGE

An Overview

Thomas K. Burch

INTRODUCTION

This report deals with the interrelationships among modern demographic changes in developed nations, including Canada, and changes in age and sex (gender) roles. More specifically, it discusses ways in which demographic trends may have affected and been affected by the role definitions and behaviour of men and women, married and non-married persons, the young and the old. Demographic variables considered include fertility (level and timing); mortality; migration; age–sex composition; union formation (marriage, divorce, remarriage, cohabitation); and household formation (extension, home leaving, living alone). Roles are considered primarily in terms of education, labour-force participation, leisure, and family responsibilities.

This system of interrelationships is so large and complex that a detailed discussion of the whole system is not possible [here]. . . . The propositions set forth below, although stated without qualification, should be viewed not as fact or verified theory but as plausible hypotheses.

DEFINITIONS

The term *role* as used in everyday speech and in social science has at least three different meanings: behavioural, normative, and attitudinal. The behavioural meaning refers to what people occupying a certain status actually do. The normative meaning refers to what society thinks they should do — to widely accepted social definitions of appropriate or acceptable behaviour for persons in that status. The attitudinal meaning refers to what individuals or specific sub-groups of society consider appropriate behaviour. This report discusses roles in all three senses, but the emphasis is on actual behaviour, which is easiest to document.

In a discussion of the relationships among demographic changes and role changes, it is sometimes difficult to distinguish the two, since they are so close conceptually. For example, the decline in fertility, a demographic change, is so immediately and directly bound up with a change in the extent of child-care for parents — what they do in the parental role — that it is not clear one should speak about a causal relationship; the level of fertility is almost a dimension of the role.

In a related vein, the system of interrelationships involves so many elements of mutual causation that there is no obvious starting point for discussion. Apart from temporal leads and lags that might emerge from a detailed historical treatment, it may be better to think of a functional system of relationships. The discussion then can begin anywhere in the system, but repetition becomes inevitable, as one discusses a relationship first with demographic change as cause, and then with role change as cause.

This report will begin with a review of demographic change and then move to age and sex-role changes. Along the way, key propositions, stated in summary form, will be underlined and numbered for easy reference. 'D' propositions emphasize the causal role of demographic change, 'R' propositions the causal role of role change.

MODERN DEMOGRAPHIC CHANGE IN CANADA

Mortality

Modern mortality trends are well known and need not be described here in any detail. Two aspects of these trends are relevant for present purposes: (a) the rise in average life expectancy, with associated declines in infant and child mortality; and (b) the large and increasing excess of female over male life expectancy.

Around 1931, male life expectancy at birth in Canada was 60 years, that of females 62 years. By 1981, these had climbed to 72 and 79 respectively, with the differential thus increasing from two to seven years. Around the turn of the century, a forty-year-old male or female both had a life expectancy of 33 additional years. By 1981, 40-year-old males had a life expectancy of 35 years, but the figure for females at that age had risen to 41 years, a six-year differential.

These changing patterns of mortality have had the following effects relevant to age–sex role change:

D1. *Declining infant and child mortality has increased the number of surviving children from a given number of live births. It has made it easier to 'have a family', in the sense of raising two or more children to adulthood and beyond.* Since a couple can have a family with as few as two births, and can even count on an only child surviving, there is less felt need for a larger number of live births, and the 'required' reproduction can be accomplished over a relatively short period. For both sexes, but for women in particular, given past sex roles, this means a much shorter portion of adult life involved with childrearing.

D2. *Declining mortality rates at older ages, beyond the reproductive ages, have yielded a higher proportion of elderly in the population (although declining fertility is a more important causal factor), and the same underlying forces that have lowered mortality have led to generally healthier and more active elderly.* It is taken as axiomatic that the relative number of persons in an age–sex category can help shape the social role associated with that category, although this relationship is not well understood. In the present case, it seems likely that a weakening of the empirical association of old age with infirmity (at least for persons in the lower ranges of old age — say 65 to 75) would change society's expectations of the elderly, and their expectations of themselves. At the same time, older persons have less 'scarcity value' when they constitute 25 per cent of the population than when they constitute a much smaller fraction, say 5 or 10 per cent. On the other hand, they will tend to have more power in a democratic society by reason of their votes, and in any society will tend to have whatever power is associated with accumulated wealth.

D3. *Declining mortality has tended to increase the social worth or importance of the individual; the lower the probability that any given individual will die in the near future, the more likely one is to invest in him/her emotionally and economically.* This relationship has been discussed most often in the context of infancy and childhood, but it applies at other stages of life as well.

D4. *The higher life expectancy at every age — the prospect of a longer life — has changed the time horizon for individual decision-making; one has more time for one's life, indeed one has time for 'many lives', in terms of residence, career, marriage, and so forth.* One consequence is that conventional 'lifetime' commitments — permanent marriage, job tenure — become more serious, but often more unrealistic, especially in view of the scope and rapidity of social and individual change. Another is that new commitments may be undertaken late in life that previously would not have been. Persons in their thirties or forties attend professional school with some confidence of being able to pursue the profession for a reasonable period. Spouses facing the 'empty nest' and 25 or more years of life remaining are often motivated to try a new marriage as part of a new life. Younger people may see no need to rush in order to make conventional commitments to adult roles.

D5. *The less frequent first-hand experience of the event of death — to a relative, neighbour, or close friend — the more apt the individual is to invest in his or her personal life, and the less apt she or he is to seek continuity through commitment to the group (notably the family) and to future generations.* Since the frequency of deaths is a function of age composition as well as of age-specific mortality risks, this may be expected to rise as the population ages—indeed a crude death rate of 14 or 15 per 1,000 is likely early in the next century, barring substantial further declines in mortality rates at older ages. It is possible that the personal consciousness of death as a human reality will increase over the next decades.

A summary statement of these last three propositions would be that modern low mortality has helped reinforce a Western cultural emphasis on the value of the individual over the group.

D6. *The large sex differential in mortality has led to an excess of women over men at older ages, and to a high probability that such women will be unmarried (single, widowed or divorced).* The situation has been complicated by high divorce rates, since divorced males tend to marry younger women. The remarriage prospects for the divorced or widowed woman are uncertain. A realistic expectation for the middle-aged woman is that she will spend her old age without a spouse. Differential mortality (along with the age difference between spouses, and the differential remarriage rates) has promoted what might be called the 'feminization of old age'.

Fertility

There has been a long-term secular decline in the level of fertility, the number of children born per woman or per married woman, whether viewed on a period or cohort basis. Around 1900, the Canadian period total fertility rate was approximately 4.8; by 1985 it had dropped to 1.7. The post-World War II baby boom constitutes only a partial exception, since much of the rise in period rates was due to changes in timing of childbearing, and most of the rise in cohort completed fertility was due to an increase in the proportion of women having at least two children, rather than an increase in the mean number of children among women having at least two (see Ryder, 1982).

Associated with this decline in the number of children per woman have been changes in the tempo of childbearing—the average age of childbearing, the average age at first birth, the average age at last birth, etc. These dimensions of fertility have been volatile over time. But with some exceptions (for example, the Depression), there has been a secular trend toward earlier cessation of childbearing, typically around 30 years or younger for the woman.

The combination of low mortality and low fertility allows for considerable flexibility in family formation, as childbearing and rearing occupy a smaller fraction of adult life. In the typical case, to have two children would only require about five years out of a woman's total reproductive span of 35 years. To raise them to the beginning of full-time school attendance would require an additional five or so years, so that full-time mothering might require only 10 years of a woman's 50 or more years of adult life remaining after age 20. Even to raise her children to age 18 would require less than half of her adult life (see Davis and van der Oever, 1982). Similar patterns affect males, with qualifications to take account of higher male mortality.

Couples are able to take advantage of this flexibility due to the availability of modern contraceptives, including surgical sterilization and abortion. It is feasible to avoid accidental pregnancies or unwanted births over long periods of married life to a much greater extent than was the case prior to 1960.

The rise of this modern fertility pattern has had several direct consequences for age and sex roles:

D7. *Low fertility, concentrated within a brief period of the life span, has made child-bearing and childrearing a temporarily less important part of the adult role. Since in the past women tended to specialize in child-related activities, their role change has necessarily been the greater.* This fertility effect has combined with the extension of the average life to create what Davis and van der Oever (1981) describe as a new phenomenon — 'prolonged parental survival beyond the last child's coming-of-age'. In high fertility/high mortality societies of the past, they point out, the period of such survival was virtually zero; in a low fertility/low mortality society like Canada today, by contrast, this so-called 'empty nest' period can exceed 30 years.

D8. *Low fertility has been the major demographic determinant of the increase in the proportion of elderly in the population.* Thus, whatever effects on age and sex roles flow from the rise in the proportion of elderly are due indirectly to declining fertility.

D9. *Low fertility tends to reduce the average number of kin of any given individual, which in turn tends to reduce the centrality of familial roles for that individual, regardless of his/her age or sex.* The generic effect is to reduce the salience of kin in everyday life, even though in some sense kin may be greatly valued because of their scarcity. A specific effect reinforcing the trend toward low fertility is the decline in kin support with the overall task of childrearing. The importance of kin in everyday life has been further eroded by migration and by residential independence of the elderly.

D10. *Low fertility and delayed childbearing have contributed to the continuing high divorce rate, which in turn probably yields a net decline in fertility.* The popular view is that couples 'stay together for the sake of the children'. Becker et al. (1977) have formalized this in the argument that children constitute 'marriage-specific capital', which the couple is loathe to risk through divorce. The rise in divorce, as discussed in more detail below, has been particularly influential in the breakdown of the traditional familial division of labour between males and females.

D11. *The diminution of the temporal importance of childbearing for adults reinforces the tendency toward low fertility, and tends to increase the proportion of adults who will have no children or only one child.* This will be true whether childbearing begins early or late. In the former case, there will be motivation to 'get it over with', and get on with the main business of life, typically a job or career. Since many of the logistical problems associated with children tend to increase exponentially with number (at least for the first few parities — before economies of scale set in), such a pattern favours at most two children, and there are signs that the only child is rapidly becoming culturally acceptable. If childbearing begins late, couples will tend to have fewer children, other things equal, even though two remains the culturally stereotypical ideal. Some will simply never get around to it until it is too late in some sense, including the onset of infecundity. Some will be reluctant to have a child given higher age-associated risks to the mother and the child. Others will find that the disruptive effects of one child are sufficient to discourage having a second or third. Overall, it seems doubtful that women now having their first child in their early and mid-thirties will ever have as many children as earlier cohorts, who started childbearing in their twenties. Indeed feminist analyses of the consequence of early childbearing have noted that it tends to 'lock women into' the mother/housewife role.

Age–Sex Structure

A demographic consequence of the changes in mortality and fertility described above has been a major shift in age structure: a declining proportion of children; a rising proportion of elderly, especially elderly females. The sheer relative number of persons in a particular age–sex category may be expected to shape the associated age–sex role, although the relationship is not direct and deterministic— other factors are at work and may well be more important. The effects in general are not well understood, although the following seem likely:

D12. *The decline in the relative number of children may make them more highly valued in some senses, due to scarcity, but in general they will come to occupy a smaller part of the social consciousness, and command a smaller proportion of societal investment.* Children are largely passive recipients of whatever society and their parents care to give them of the overall social good. As their centrality in the life of active adults diminishes, their share may be threatened. Preston (1984) has argued at length that this has already happened in the US; and Hunsley (1987) has recently applied the same general argument to Canada.

D13. *The rise in the proportion of elderly in the population will tend to enhance their visibility and power, perhaps at the expense of other age groups.* The elderly not only vote, but given their low labour-force participation rates, they have more time than other adults to engage in political or quasi-political activity. By contrast with the young, they have experience and a certain credibility that conventionally has been associated with old age. All in all, the elderly are a powerful political force in the competition for social and economic advantage. In the past, as Davis and van der Oever (1981) have argued, competition between the generations was muted by family ties of co-residence and mutual dependency. Increasingly, the competition is impersonal and political.

Marriage, Remarriage and Divorce

The single most important trend in this demographic area has been the sharp rise in the divorce rates, especially since 1970. In some marriage cohorts, the proportion divorced or separated thus far (at medium durations, of 10 to 15 years) is well over 0.20. The proportion eventually divorcing for recent marriage cohorts almost certainly will exceed 0.30 and may reach 0.40 or more.

Other important trends are the rise in premarital cohabitation among the young (as many as 25 per cent of young people report having cohabited at least once), generally as a prelude to marriage, and the rise in post-marital cohabitation among the middle-aged, as a postlude to divorce or prelude to remarriage.

A third important pattern is the lower (than men) remarriage rates among widowed or divorced women, a factor that increases the proportion and number of nonmarried women at older ages.

D14. *The rise in divorce rates has been one of the most powerful demographic determinants of the changing roles of women. It has undermined the woman's ability to fulfil her conventional role as mother, and the viability of that role as conventionally defined, in the sense that a woman who commits herself to that role at the expense of a career and financial independence is at high risk of eventual poverty or a least downward economic mobility.* Davis and van der Oever (1982) argue that what they term the 'breadwinner' system contained the seeds of its own destruction. As the husband moved out of the home to work, leaving the wife behind with the children, he encountered other females, typically young, with involvements often leading to divorce. To hedge against the risk of divorce the married woman had to leave the home to have a career and financial independence. Having achieved these, she too could then entertain the notion of initiating divorce, driving rates up still further.

D15. *The high probability of divorce may well have led to a postponement or even a devaluation of the conventional roles of marriage and parenthood.* If divorce is likely, then marriage should be delayed in favour of cohabitation, and children should be avoided, whether in marriage of cohabitation, until the union seems likely to last. But the absence of commitment to marriage and children in itself increases the likelihood of union dissolution, in a circular fashion. In general, young people may ask why they should commit themselves to a role that has such a high failure rate.

D16. *The lower remarriage rate for divorced or widowed women together with their numerical preponderance in old age will tend to define the role of the older woman as 'spouseless'.* The prospect of being 'alone' in old age may diminish the centrality of marriage in women's conceptions of their lives.

Household Formation

The period since World War II has seen substantial increase in the proportions of persons living alone in a separate house or apartment. In absolute numbers, the rise has been especially pronounced among young adults and among older never-married or previously-married women, but the proportion has increased among virtually all adult age–sex categories. The causes of this trend include rising real income and (for elderly women) the decline in the number of living children, and probably cultural changes (not well documented or easy to measure) relating to privacy and independence of the individual and to the very definitions of age–sex roles, which are becoming more homogeneous (Burch, 1985).

A concomitant set of changes has seen the decline of extended households, containing persons other than related members of a nuclear family of husband, wife and children. The proportions of households with in-laws, other relatives, servants, boarders and lodgers has declined to near-zero.

These changes are due in part to changes in cultural definitions of age–sex roles, but in turn may be expected to affect age–sex roles in a variety of ways:

D17. *The increase in separate living may be expected to reinforce the breakdown of a family division of labour based on age and sex.* Separate living promotes the homogenization of social roles, as the individual has no one with whom to share various domestic tasks. A male living alone is thus more apt to cook and clean house, a female to fix plumbing or shovel snow—more or less by necessity. At the same time, changing ideology makes such departures from conventional roles acceptable. Separate living, and the privacy it affords, also is related to the introduction of 'universality' in regard to regular sexual relations among adults, in particular the trend toward regular sexual relations on the part of young, unmarried adults, and on the part of the elderly.

D18. *Separate living and the decline of the extended family have tended to focus child-care responsibility even more closely on the parents and particularly the mother.* There probably never was a time when the majority of households were extended, but the proportion was appreciably greater in the past (plus there was greater residential propinquity, even if not co-residence), and the extra persons in the household typically played a non-trivial role in assistance with child-care (in some modern societies they still do, for example, Eastern Europe, Japan). This development, along with the increasing labour-force participation of married women and mothers, has led to increased demand for governmental or commercial child-care services, entailing yet another major departure from the conventional definitions of the parental role: the parent is the one responsible for the purchase of third-party child-care services for infants and young children.

Geographic Mobility

The last decades have seen a continuation of high rates of residential mobility, including inter-community and inter-provincial migration. Given the increasing urbanization of the population, a larger fraction of this migration is from urban to urban places, much of it inter-metropolitan. This plus Canadian geography means that much migration in Canada involves long distances.

There has been relatively little research on how migration affects age–sex roles, but a few important relationships seem clear:

D19. *Increasing dispersal of kin has diminished their salience, and therefore the importance of family-related roles, and has weakened family solidarity based on co-operation in day-to-day living.*

D20. *Continuing mobility, often job-related, has increased the costs of family relationships.* Migration is more costly in dollars, time and effort if it is a family rather than an individual move. Similarly, one's ability to move at all is restricted by family ties; the most common example relates to dual-career couples, who will only move if both find suitable employment in another place. Mobility also increases the probability of divorce, with consequences for age, sex and family role definitions as described above.

MAJOR CHANGES IN AGE ROLES

Education

The primary role of the young in any society is the learning of their eventual adult roles—the standard sociological jargon is 'primary socialization'. In highly industrialized societies like Canada, this process is handled to a large extent by specialized institutions (schools) and involves nearly all young people up to age 18 or so—the age at which they are considered more or less ready to undertake the full range of adult roles. Among persons between the ages of six and 13, for example, virtually 100 per cent are enrolled in elementary school; and, at ages 14–17, 90 per cent or so are enrolled full-time in secondary school, even though the law allows the termination of formal education after age 16.

The near-universal attendance of elementary school has characterized Canada at least since the end of World War II. But the high rates of secondary school enrolment represent the result of a sharp upward trend (see Leacy, 1983, Series W10–20). The ratio of full-time enrolments to persons age 14–17 doubled between 1951 and 1975. Some of the increase represents the tendency of older persons to return to high school, but much of it represents a decline in the tendency of 17- and 18-year-olds to drop out for employment or marriage.

A substantial minority of Canadians prolong their education past the age of 18, and that number has increased markedly since the 1950s. The ratio of full-time post-secondary enrolments to persons 18–24 has risen more than threefold during that period, reaching about 20 per cent in 1975 (Leacy, 1983, Series W10–20).

Perhaps the most striking trend in school enrolments is that for persons in what used to be known as the 'pre-school' ages—under six years, the traditional age for beginning grade one. The full-time enrolment of persons under age six as a ratio to the population of five-year-olds rose from 0.28 per cent in 1951 to well over 1.00 in 1975, partly due to the rise in the proportion of five-year-olds attending kindergarten, but partly because of the extension of schooling (or combination schooling and day-care) to four- and even three-year-olds (Leacy, 1983, Series W10–20). By now this ratio would be even higher, given the growth of day-care in the intervening decade.

In summary, the student role has become more nearly universal among age groups traditionally associated with schooling—6 to 18—but has also been extended outside that age range in three important ways: (a) more young adults (18–24) are enrolled in some form of post-secondary education; (b) more older adults are returning to school for further education; and (c) children are beginning full-time enrolment at earlier ages, often as early as three.

Some demographic consequences of these changes in age-related educational roles include the following:

R1. *For parents, the extension of education to the secondary and post-secondary level means greater costs of childrearing over a longer period of dependency.* There are direct economic costs, but also indirect costs associated with the young person's post-ponement of entry into productive work. There also are psychological costs, as parent–child struggles associated with adolescence are prolonged to higher ages, with legal and chronological adults wishing to be independent while *de facto* dependent on their parents. In general, modern attempts to raise 'quality' chil-dren, of which prolonged education is symptomatic, have made children very expensive, and contributed to the decline of fertility and to the delay of child-bearing.

R2. *The increasing resort to pre-schools or day-care for very young children should ease the time costs of childrearing, especially for women, but the money costs remain high, and in any case the pattern reduces the centrality of childrearing in a woman's life.* Day-care both symbolizes and reinforces the secondary position occupied by motherhood for the contemporary woman. Note that fatherhood has long tended to be sec-ondary for males.

Labour-Force Participation

At the turn of the century, Canada had what Davis and van der Oever (1982) have called the 'breadwinner' system: virtually all able-bodied males worked for pay (all except the very young, the very old, and the infirm); women's participation in the labour force was marginal, at least by comparison to the present. Their main tasks were the rearing of children and housekeeping—although on farms and in other family enterprises, clearly their labour was financially productive.

Two important age-related trends in labour-force participation can be noted since that time. The first is the steady decline in the participation rates of males ages 14–19 (Leacy, 1983, Series D107–122). From 1921 (the earliest date for which the relevant data are available) until 1961, the rate for this age–sex group declined from 68 per cent to 41 per cent. Since then the rate may have risen somewhat, but there are problems with the comparability of data for more recent dates. The decline presumably is related to the rise noted above in the proportion of young males attending secondary school. But some part of it also may be related to the rising unemployment rates among males in this age group, which discourage labour-force participation. Unemployment rates for this group, which ranged between 4 and 7 per cent between 1946 and 1953, had climbed to 16 per cent by 1975. Among males 15–24 in the labour force, 13 per cent were unemployed in 1983.

The other important trend is the decline in the labour-force participation rates of older males, that is, those 65 and over. In 1921, 60 per cent of these men were reported as in the labour force. By 1961, this proportion has been cut in half, and stood at 31 per cent. It was more than halved between 1961 and 1981, reaching 14 per cent in the latter year. Part of this trend is due to the decline of the quantitative importance of agriculture as an occupation; part is due to the growth of the notion of mandatory retirement, and of private and government pension schemes to support it.

Whatever the causes, this trend, together with that noted for young males, signals a withdrawal of males under 20 and over 65 from 'productive' labour, and a focusing of productive effort in those between 20 and 65, among whom labour-force participation rates have remained virtually constant over the last several decades, at rates above 90 per cent. As will be seen below, some of this effort increasingly has been shared by women.

Stated most generally, the trend in the youth role has been toward education, consumption and leisure, and in the elderly role toward consumption and leisure.

Some demographic implications are as follows:

R3. *Declining labour-force participation rates and high unemployment rates among the young, especially young males, increase the costs of children to parents, and diminish the readiness of young adults to assume the responsibilities of marriage and childbearing at any early age.*

R4. *The declining labour-force participation rates among older males and the continuing low rates among older females do not seem to have helped make jobs available to young adults, since their unemployment rates remain high. Nor has the new-found leisure of the elderly been employed in any effective way to assist in the raising of the younger genera-tion.* In fact, as Davis and van der Oever argue, the slack caused by the retreat of males from the labour force has largely been taken up by middle-aged women (see below). They also suggest that the elderly have become a greater financial burden on those in the prime working ages (through taxation), with delayed marriage and lower fertility a result.

MAJOR CHANGES IN SEX ROLES

Education

The main sex-related trend in education has been the increasing participation of women in higher education, specifically university education.

The proportion of university undergraduates who were female rose sharply from 1920 to 1925–30, and then remained at about the same level (actually there was a slight decline in the period 1945–55) until it began a sustained rise from 1955 on. The trends in the percentage of graduate students who were female were similar, although there was a more pronounced decline from relatively high levels in the 1920s to a trough in 1955. Not until 1975 did the proportion exceed the levels achieved in the years 1920–35 (Leacy, 1983, Series 340–438). Full-time undergrad-uate enrolments of females as a proportion of women ages 20–24 show a roughly similar trend, with a plateau in the 1930s, and a sharp upward trend beginning after 1955.

Not only have women increased their overall participation rates in university education; they also have shown a greater tendency to take advanced degrees, and to take programs related to professions or specializations traditionally reserved to males, although pronounced sex differences remain in these regards. An increasing proportion of women clearly view university education as preparation for a career.

R5. *The increasing pursuit of higher education by women tends to delay their entry into marriage and childbearing.* This effect is all the more pronounced since men are increasingly neither willing or able to support women in such a way that they could undertake both education and family formation at an early age.

R6. *Both the content and the experience of higher education are apt to broaden women's horizons and to give them a sense of role options other than the conventional roles of marriage, motherhood, and housekeeping.*

Labour-Force Participation

While the overall labour-force participation rates of males 15 and over have remained virtually unchanged since the turn of the century (at around 80 per cent), those of women have climbed steadily from 14 per cent in 1901 to 29 per cent in 1961, roughly doubling, and then nearly doubling again to 52 per cent by 1981 (Leacy, 1983, D107–122). A similar trend can be observed in the proportion of the total labour force accounted for by women, which rose from 13 per cent in 1901 to 27 per cent in 1961 and 40 per cent by 1981 (Leacy, 1981, D86–106). The bulk of this increase has been among women between the ages of 20 and 65. Among women 20–24, the rise between 1921 and 1981 has been from 40 to 73 per cent. Among those 25–34, the rate rose from 20 per cent in 1921 to 68 in 1983.

Even more striking, in terms of the gradual breakdown of the 'breadwinner' system, has been the rise in labour-force participation by married women and by women with young children. Among women with a husband at home and pre-school-age children, for instance, the percentage in the labour force rose from 34 in 1975 to 52 in 1983 (Statistics Canada, 1985).

These changing patterns of female labour-force participation probably constitute the single most important change in sex roles, in general and specifically in respect to demographic change. Their effects may be summarized as follows:

R7. *The expectation on the part of young women that they will work full-time for most of their adult life, possibly in a career, has led to a postponement of marriage and childbearing.*

R8. *These same expectations have led to a curtailment of family size.* One or two children may be managed on the basis of part-time parenting, but with three or four, the logistics become difficult if not impossible. The problem is exacerbated by the facts (a) that the redefinition of the male parental role has not yet reached the point of equal sharing of the responsibilities for childcare or housekeeping; and (b) that adequate and reasonably inexpensive day-care is not generally available. As is well known, the additional responsibilities borne by women as full-time workers have not been fully compensated for by release from residual responsibilities for domestic tasks. Lower fertility is the inevitable result.

Increasing Role Homogeneity

A strong cultural emphasis on the value and rights of the individual seems to have had two effects on the definitions of age–sex roles: (a) the individual is seen as 'transcending' any particular social role in the sense that he/she is not expected to subordinate her/himself to a role, except by personal choice; and (b) individuals of different ages and sexes are increasingly seen as having the same rights, prerogatives, privileges, and responsibilities. The two trends are closely related, since equality of rights may be seen as a logical consequence of the overarching value of the individual.

R9. *The increasing homogeneity of age–sex roles has diminished family/household solidarity based on a division of labour, and has increased intra-family/household competition for scarce goods; this in turn has fostered the formation of smaller and less complex households, as is manifested in demographic trends such as declining fertility, the rising divorce rate, and increased proportions living alone (Burch, 1985).*

CONCLUSIONS AND SUGGESTED RESEARCH

The above overview of age–sex roles and demographic change suggests the following general conclusions:

1. Demographic change has played an important causal role in the shaping of modern conceptions of age–sex roles, but modern roles and role definitions have in turn affected demographic trends. Many of the key relationships tend to be mutually reinforcing.
2. The relationships thus constitute a system, such that any one factor is unlikely to change in isolation. From a policy point of view, this implies both options and constraints—options, since the system provides many potential points for intervention; constraints, since superficial or narrow policy interventions may be ineffectual.
3. The changes in age–sex roles and in demographic patterns are deeply rooted in the very nature of Canadian society—a modern, urban-industrial society, in which the vast majority of adults work as individual employees of large organizations. Many of the changes described above result ultimately from the virtual disappearance of family-owned productive enterprises, a major source of traditional family solidarity. Many also derive from a central cultural emphasis—in the Western cultural tradition of which Canada is a part —on the pre-eminent importance of the individual. This suggests that demographic policy will be able at best to introduce marginal corrections in levels and trends (where this is seen as desirable). Demographic policy cannot change the nature of Canadian society.
4. From the standpoint of demographic impact, the single most important change in age–sex roles described above is the entry of women into the labour force on a full-time, permanent basis.

5. The increasing centrality of work as opposed to childbearing and rearing in women's lives suggests that minor changes in the costs of children to parents are not apt to encourage higher fertility. The savings are more apt to be devoted to career enhancement, leisure and to investments in 'child quality', notably for female children.

6. The above review is consistent with the view that the burdens of productive work and of childcare have been increasingly focused on middle-aged adults, with less help than previously from the young and the old. If true, then the trend has to be critically examined from the viewpoint of demographic implications (divorce, fertility, morbidity) as well as from the viewpoint of social equality.

The research agenda associated with the broad area of this report is potentially endless. A few specific topics seem to stand out as especially timely and important:

1. There is need for a more detailed description of Canadian age–sex roles. Behavioural indicators of certain aspects of roles are readily available in *Historical Statistics of Canada*, in some cases valuable time series back to the early part of the century. But most of the time series end around the mid-1970s or before, and updating them with comparable data is not always a routine matter. In any case, they deal only with behaviour (school attendance, employment, etc.) and tell us nothing directly about attitudes or cultural definitions. Some digging is necessary to see if sample surveys, including public opinion polls, can yield some direct measures of role attitudes and their changes. Further analysis of such surveys and polls (as well as other micro-data) might also yield some insights into variations in role definitions across subgroups, and into causes of attitude change. But for a demographic review, the mere detailed documentation of changes is important.

2. The Preston–Davis thesis, namely, that a disproportionate share of the societal goods has begun to flow to the elderly, at the expense of children and perhaps of middle-aged adults, needs to be evaluated for Canada (see conclusion 6 above). It is political dynamite, but is potentially too important in terms of social and demographic implications not to be tested and answered one way or the other. Clearly it is not entirely a scientific question, since values and notions of justice and equity are central. But a clarification of the relevant facts would be a major contribution.

3. The likely demographic effects of extended child-care services, whether commercial or governmental, need to be assessed. Such an extension currently seems to be the most popular proposal to mitigate the conflicts between labour-force participation and child-rearing. But such a result is hardly certain (see 5 above). A related investigation would look into other approaches, including remuneration (through tax breaks, guaranteed income, 'parent's allowances') for those—whether men or women—who forego labour-force participation in favour of the 'household management' role.

4. Further research is needed on the forces leading to the increase in separate living noted above, with particular attention to role homogenization (Burch, 1985) and the supply of housing (size, type, etc.). Detailed analysis of census public–use tapes and of available surveys, notably the Quality of Life survey, could provide new empirical information on these matters.

REFERENCES

Becker, G.S., E.M. Landes, and R.T. Michael (1977). 'An economic analysis of marital instability'. *Journal of Political Economy* 85: 1141–87.

Burch, T.K. (1985). 'Changing age-sex roles and household crowding: A theoretical note'. Proceedings, International Population Conference, Florence. Liege: International Union for the Scientific Study of Population. 3: 253–261.

Davis, K. (1984). 'Wives and work: The sex role revolution and its consequences'. *Population and Development Review* 10: 397–418.

Davis, K., and P. van der Oever (1981). 'Age relations and public policy in advanced industrial societies'. *Population and Development Review* 7: 1–18.

—— (1982). 'Demographic foundations of new sex roles'. *Population and Development Review* 8: 495–512.

Hunsley, T. (1987). 'A blueprint for providing tax reform for children'. *Globe and Mail,* 10 August, p. A7.

Leacy, F.H. (1983). *Historical Statistics of Canada,* 2nd ed. Ottawa: Statistics Canada.

Preston, S.H. (1984). 'Children and the elderly divergent paths for America's dependents'. *Demography* 21: 435–458.

Ryder, N.B. (1982). 'Fertility trends'. In J.A. Ross, ed., *International Encyclopedia of Population,* Vol. 1.

Statistics Canada, Social and Economic Studies Divison (1985). *Women in Canada: A Statistical Report*. Ottawa, Ontario: Minister of Supply and Services.

CHAPTER 7

THE SENIORS BOOM

Dramatic Increases in

Longevity and Prospects

for Better Health

Leroy O. Stone and Susan Fletcher

RAPID GROWTH OF THE SENIOR POPULATION

[In 1986] some 2.7 million Canadians are 65 years of age or more. This is three times more than just 55 years ago and represents a much faster rate of growth than for the total population, which slightly more than doubled over the same period.

As Canada enters the 21st century, the population aged 65 years of age or more will number nearly 4 million people. In the second decade of the next century, the baby-boom generation (those born between 1946 and 1966) will enter the ranks of the senior population. It will then escalate in size, reaching 6 million by 2021 and 7.5 million by 2031. Thus, in the next 45 years the older population is expected to triple in size. (See Figure 1.)

Within the older population itself, the next 45 years will see rapid growth in the group with advanced age. The population aged 75 and over is expected to triple in size from approximately 1 million, while the group aged 85 plus will increase from 224,000 to nearly 750,000.

Figure 1: Population in selected age groups, Canada, 1931–2031[1]

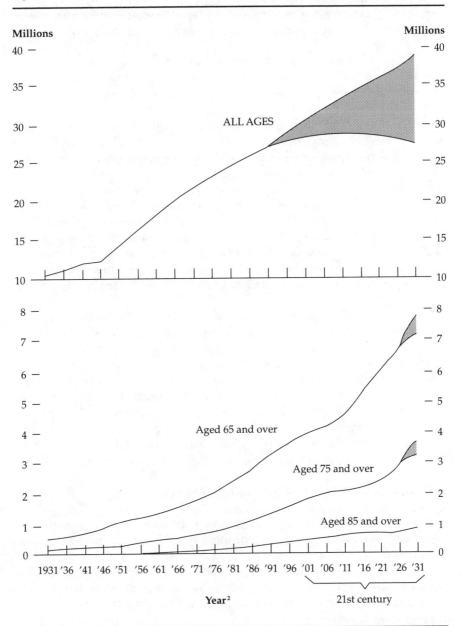

[1] Projections start in 1986. Shaded areas represent ranges of possible numbers of people.
[2] The numbers shown above refer to years starting with 1931 and ending with 2031. The values '01', '06', etc., refer to 2001, 2006, etc.

SOURCES: Dominion Bureau of Statistics, 1953: Table 14; 1958: Table 16; 1968a: Table 19; 1968b: pp. 13, 23, 33; Statistics Canada, 1973a: Table 14; 1982a: Table 1; 1985a: pp. 110–51, 294–335, sec. D3, D4.

These population projections represent a substantial revision of earlier projections by Statistics Canada. For example, in [the 1979] projections, a 58 per cent growth rate was forecasted for the population aged 80 years or more from 1986 to 2001. In the 1985 projections this growth rate was revised upwards to 77 per cent.

DRAMATIC GROWTH AT THE TOP

Over the next 15 years, the growth rate for Canada's older population will be dramatically higher than that for the rest of the nation. For instance, between 1981 and 1991, the population aged 65 years or more will show an average annual increase in size of 3 per cent, while the entire population will be expanding at a rate barely above 1 per cent per year. A slowdown in growth rate to 2 per cent per year will take place for the population aged 65 and over in the last decade of this century and in the first decade of the next century. Beginning in the second decade of the next century there will be another period of explosive growth for this population as the baby boomers invade the ranks of senior population.

Over the 1980s Canadians aged 75 years or more will show the greatest growth rate, within the senior population, by increasing in size at an average annual rate of at least 3.5 per cent. They will be contributing to a huge growth rate of 4 per cent or more per annum for those aged 85 and over in the last decade of this century. (See Figure 2.)

From 1926 to 1961, there was little appreciable difference between the growth rates of men aged 80 years or more and those of women the same age (Figure 3). Since 1961 the number of women in this age group has grown much more quickly than that of similarly-aged men. For instance, while the growth rate for women aged 80 and over remained very high (near 4 per cent per year) throughout the 1960s and 1970s, that for similarly-aged men declined steadily from 4.5 per cent per year over the 1956–61 period to about 1 per cent per year during the 1971–76 period.

According to the latest Statistics Canada projections, both men and women aged 80 and over will join in showing very high growth rates over the next 15 years.

FUTURE POPULATION AGING

The older population will itself be aging over the next 25 years (Figure 4). A particularly sharp rise will occur among those aged 85 and over, relative to those 65 and more, over the period from 1991 to 2011. After 2011, the percentage of seniors aged 85 years or more will begin to decline as the baby-boom generation will move strongly into the youngest ranks of the older population. The population aged 85 and over will remain at much less than 5 per cent of the total population up to 2031.

As a result of the aging of the baby-boom cohorts, the proportion of Canadians aged 65 and over will sweep strongly upwards after 2011; and by 2021, nearly one in every five Canadians will be aged 65 years or more.

Figure 2: Average annual growth rates for selected age groups, Canada, 1971–81 to 2011–21[1]

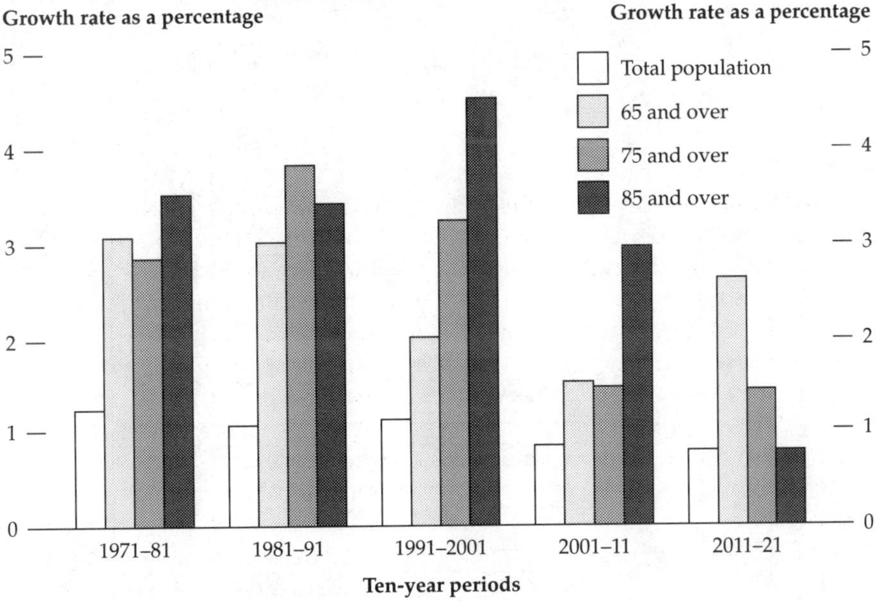

Growth rate as a percentage

Growth rate as a percentage

☐ Total population
▨ 65 and over
▨ 75 and over
■ 85 and over

Ten-year periods

1971–81   1981–91   1991–2001   2001–11   2011–21

[1] Data for 1986 and beyond are averages of the latest Statistics Canada highest and lowest projections.
SOURCES: See Figure 1 sources.

MAIN SOURCE OF POPULATION AGING

The principal immediate cause of the population aging that has been highlighted to this point has been the major fall in the birth rate since the early 1960s. A declining fertility rate means relatively fewer children are being born than in previous years. Figure 5 shows that in 1946 the total fertility rate (a measure of the potential number of children per women born in the year in question) was 3.5. Rates of this level or higher prevailed during the baby-boom period. Since 1961 Canadian fertility rates have declined significantly. For instance in 1971, the total fertility rate was 2.2, and has decreased still further to 1.6 in 1986.

The shaded area that represents 1986 and beyond in Figure 5 shows a degree of uncertainty in predicting future fertility rates for Canadian women. It is important to note, however, that Statistics Canada projections do not anticipate any rates like those experienced during the baby-boom years for Canada in the near future.

Figure 3: Average annual growth rates for the population aged 80 and over, by sex, Canada, 1926–31 to 2021–26

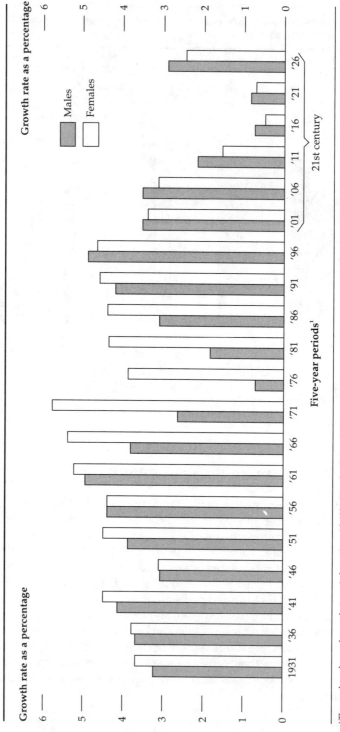

[1] The numbers shown above refer to periods starting with 1926–31 and ending with 2021–26. The values '01,' '06,' etc., refer to 1996–2001, 2001–2006, etc.
SOURCE: See Figure 1 sources.

Figure 4: Percentage of the total population in three selected age groups and the percentage aged 85 and over among those aged 65 and over, Canada, 1931–2031[1]

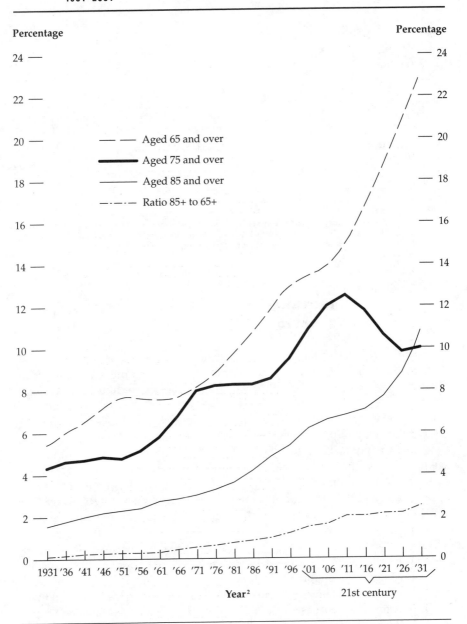

[1] Data for 1986 and beyond are averages of the latest Statistics Canada highest and lowest projections.
[2] See Note (2) of Figure 1.
SOURCES: See Figure 1 sources.

Figure 5: Total fertility rate, Canada, 1921–1998

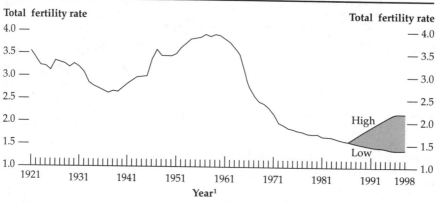

[1] The data for 1984 and beyond are 'High' and 'Low' assumptions used in the latest Statistics Canada population projections.

SOURCES: Statistics Canada, 1973b: Table 10; 1974a: Table 7; 1974b: Table 10; 1975: Table 10; 1976: Table 7; 1978a: Table 6; 1979: Table 6; 1980: Table 4; 1981: Table 5; 1982a: Table 5; 1982b: Table 5; 1983: Table 5; 1984: Table 5; 1985b: Table 5 and unpublished data from Demography Division.

STRUCTURAL CHANGES IN THE SENIOR POPULATION

There will be dramatic changes in the age structure of the senior population over the next three decades. A comparison of the two sides of the age pyramids in Figure 6 indicates that women will account for most of these shifts in age composition.

The changing areas covered by the age pyramids in Figure 6 reflect the growing sizes of the age groups comprising the senior population. The maturing of the baby-boom cohorts will be the major factor in the shape of the senior population age structure, as they will increase the proportion in the lower part of the structure (ages 55 to 65) up to 2021. By 2031 these cohorts will form the middle and upper sections of the senior population age structure. As a result, between 2021 and 2031 the age structure of the senior population will look more like an oval than a pyramid.

This development could bring new pressures to bear on social-service delivery systems in so far as those aged 75 and over will be reliant upon a relatively smaller and younger population for social supports of various kinds.

By 2001, those who fought or were building families during the First World War will be practically all deceased. By 2021, the cohorts that raised families around World War II will be almost all gone. The replacement of dying cohorts with new ones is a demographic process of great consequence because cultural values and social norms unique to the dying cohorts could be lost to the remaining popula-

Figure 6: Age pyramids for the population aged 55 and over, Canada, 1981–2031 (population in thousands)

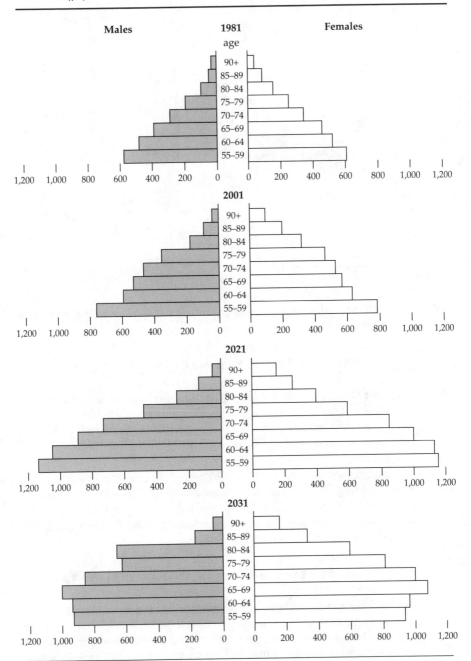

SOURCES: Statistics Canada, 1982a: Table 1; 1985a: sec. D.3, D.4.

Figure 7: Ratio of females to males in selected age groups, Canada, 1986

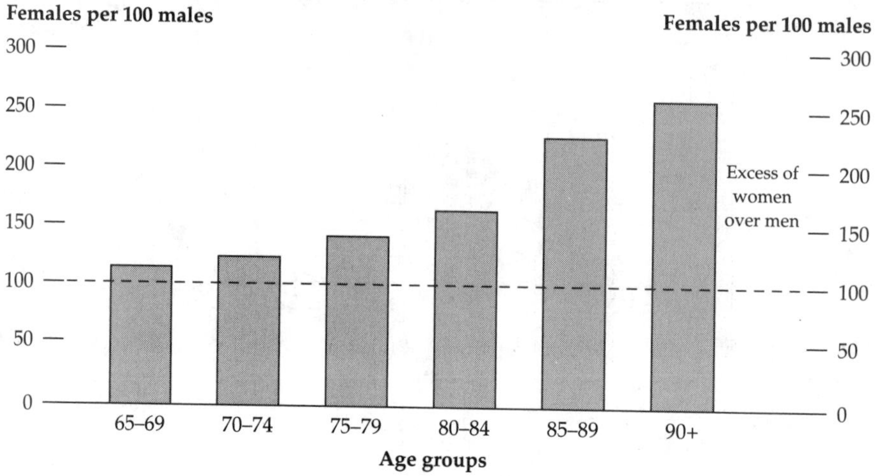

Females per 100 males

SOURCE: Statistics Canada (1985a): pp. 110–51, 294–335.

tion. As a result, the older population of the future may well be very different in character from the one we presently know.

IMBALANCE OF THE SEXES

Women account for a rising proportion of the older population as age increases (see Figure 7). For instance, in 1986 for every 100 men aged 65 to 69 years of age there were 125 women, while for every 100 men aged 80–84 years there were 175 women the same age, and for every 100 men aged 90 years or more there were 267 women the same age.

Since the mid–1950s, the ratio of women to men in all the older age categories has risen enormously (see Figure 9). For example, in the 75 and over age group the ratio of women to men was 125 to 100 in 1956; however, the ratio had increased to 195 to 100 women to men by 1981. The rise in the ratio of women to men among older Canadians seems to have practically stopped.

IMPRESSIVE DECLINES IN MORTALITY RATES

It has been said that the second most consequential development (after the baby boom) in the recent demographic history of developed countries has been the marked decline in mortality rates at the oldest ages. The upsurge of life expectancy among seniors is similar to the baby boom in that both phenomena surprised most of the demographic forecasters. . . .

Figure 8: Population in selected age groups, by sex, Canada, 1986

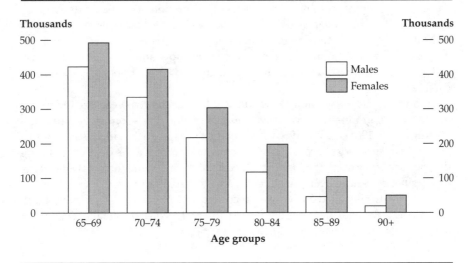

SOURCES: See Figure 1 sources.

Figure 9: Ratio of females to males in selected age groups, Canada, 1931–2031[1]

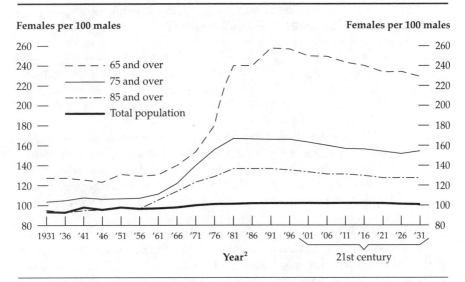

[1] Data for 1986 and beyond are averages of the latest Statistics Canada highest and lowest projections.

[2] The numbers shown above refer to years starting with 1931 and ending with 2031. The values '01', '06', etc., refer to 2001, 2006, etc.

SOURCES: See Figure 1 sources.

The story begins with older women back in the 1950s, since for some 30 years now they have shown a remarkable series of substantial falls in mortality rates. For example, among women aged 70 years of age or more, the death rate declined by 6 per cent or more over each of the six five-year periods between 1951 and 1981 (see Figure 10). Much more recently, in the late 1970s, older men had a similar fall in mortality rates. Prior to that time, as the jagged appearance of the lower graph in Figure 10 shows, older men have had only poor and sporadic death-rate declines.

Among the oldest women shown in the figure, the five-year decline in the mortality rate gradually grew larger and larger after 1951–56, but was not outstanding until 1966–71. The 1966 to 1971 period was a benchmark of sorts for this group because a very sharp fall of 11.8 per cent occurred in the death rate during that period. Since then, the highest or nearly highest declines of female mortality at the older ages have been registered by those aged 80 and over.

For 1976–81, men aged 50–54 years recorded a 14 per cent fall in death rate. In fact, all the older age categories of men in this chart recorded mortality declines of 6 per cent or more during that time.

COHORT PATTERNS OF IMPROVING SURVIVAL RATES

The sustained strong declines in mortality rates among older women since the 1950s, along with much less impressive showings for men, imply that the female population has a much better chance of surviving over a portion of the later years of life. Each curve in Figure 11 plots an aspect of the life course of a birth cohort. Each one of these curves refers to a group who were in the 45–49 age range on 1 June of a specific year. For example, the top curve of the graph for females refers to the group of women who were aged 45–49 years old on 1 June 1946, and who would then potentially be 85–89 years of age in 1986. The decline in this curve reflects the decreased likelihood that all those women aged 45–49 years in 1946 would attain ages of 85–89 years in 1986.

A comparison of the birth-cohort curves for women indicates that survival chances have improved most notably in the 80 and over age range. For instance, the earliest cohort (45–49 years in 1921) had a 50 per cent chance of surviving from the age group 80–84 to that of 85–89; but the later cohort of women aged 45–49 years in 1946 had a 70 per cent chance of survival between these two age groups. Now if one measures the improvement in chances of surviving from age group 70–74 to 75–79 one will see that they are distinctly less.

The improvements in survival chances for men are far less notable. These curves decline more sharply with age, and practically merge into a single curve, indicating little change over time, except for the age group 80–84. The male cohort aged 45 to 49 years in 1921 had slightly less than a 50 per cent chance of surviving from age group 80–84 to that aged 85–89; whereas the male cohort aged 45 to 49 years in 1946 had about a 55 per cent chance of surviving between these two age groups.

Figure 10: Percentage change in death rates over five-year periods for selected
age groups, by sex, Canada, 1951–56 to 1976–81

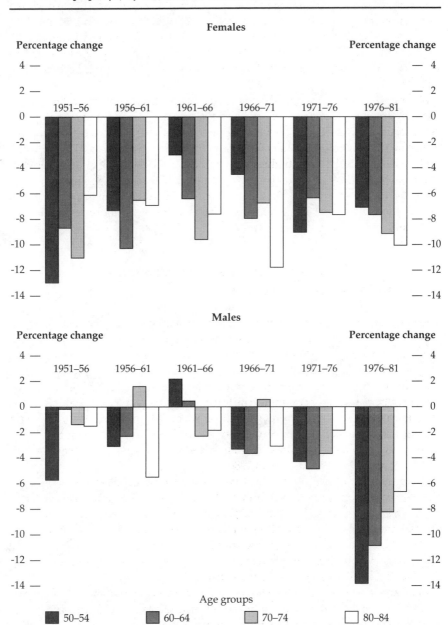

SOURCES: Dominion Bureau of Statistics, 1954: Table 20; 1957: Table 23; 1963: Table D6; 1968c: Table D5;
Statistics Canada, 1974a: Table 14; 1978b: Table 9; 1980a: Table 13; 1980: Table 20; 1981: Table 19; 1982b: Table 19;
1983: Table 19.

Figure 11: Life-table survival rates[1] for selected cohorts at nine time points, by sex, Canada

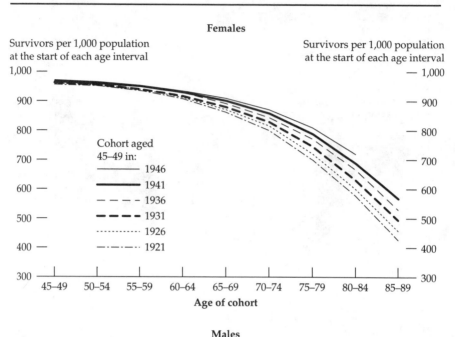

Females

Survivors per 1,000 population
at the start of each age interval

Survivors per 1,000 population
at the start of each age interval

Cohort aged
45–49 in:
——————— 1946
————— 1941
— — — — 1936
━ ━ ━ ━ 1931
················ 1926
—·—·—·· 1921

Age of cohort

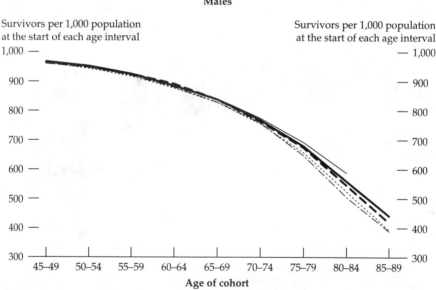

Males

Survivors per 1,000 population
at the start of each age interval

Survivors per 1,000 population
at the start of each age interval

Age of cohort

[1] The estimated probability of surviving to the next age group is multiplied by 1,000.
SOURCE: Nagnur (1985), Appendix Tables.

Figure 12: Census survival rates, by sex, for cohorts aged 55–59 in 1926, 1936, 1961 and 1996, Canada[1]

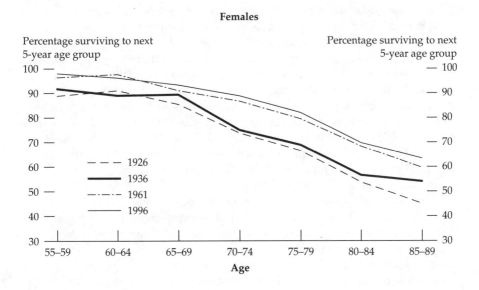

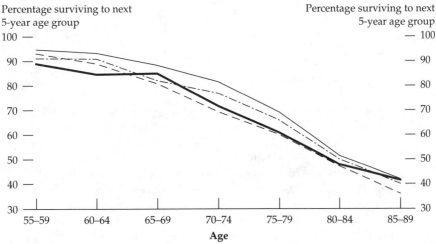

[1] Each curve pertains to one cohort. A point plotted on that curve is 100 times the ratio of the cohort's size at the next age group to its size in the age group shown. For example, the point above 55–59 is the ratio of the cohort's size at age 60–64 to its size at age 55–59, based on census data and population estimates for non-census years.

SOURCE: Dominion Bureau of Statistics, 1962: Table 20; 1968a: Table 19; 1968b: pp. 13, 23, 33; Statistics Canada, 1973a: Table 14; 1982a: Table 1; 1985a: sec. D2, D3, D4.

SLOWER RATES OF DECLINE IN COHORT
SIZES IN THE FUTURE

It is often helpful to place mortality rates against a background of actual population changes. In Figure 12 census data, population estimates, and projections are used to portray the pattern of decline in population size for four selected cohorts.

Each successive point on each curve indicates the percentage of a population cohort who survived (or will survive) to be counted among the next oldest age group five years later. For example, the lowest curve of each graph indicates that nearly 90 per cent of men and women who were in the 55–59 age range in 1926 survived to be in the 60–64 age category in five years' time (1931). Of the female cohort aged 55–59 years in 1926, 66 per cent of those who reached the 75–79 age range in 1946 succeeded in going on to the 80–84 age range in 1951. Of the latter group, 53 per cent then went on to live to 85–89 years of age in 1956.

The two curves for the male and female cohorts aged 55–59 years in 1996 have the highest profiles compared to the other curves. This means that the levels of improvement this birth cohort is expected to experience are unparalleled in Canadian history. Some 70 per cent of the men and above 80 per cent of the women who will be in the 75–79 age range in 2016 will go on to join the ranks of the 80–84 year olds in 2021. Of that group of women surviving to be 80–84 years old, over 70 per cent are projected to live to be 85–89 years of age in 2026. Of the men aged 55–59 years in 1996 who will survive to be in the 80–84 age range in 2021, just over half (51 per cent) will then survive to be 85–89 in 2026, and of these, 42 per cent will live to be 90–94 years old in 2031.

REFERENCES

Canada. Dominion Bureau of Statistics (1948). *Census and Estimated Populations of Canada and the Provinces by Sex and Age Group 1931–1948.* Ottawa: Minister of Trade and Commerce.

——— (1953). *Ninth Census of Canada, 1951. Population, General Characteristics.* Vol. 1. Ottawa: Minister of Trade and Commerce.

——— (1954). *Vital Statistics 1951.* Ottawa: Minister of Trade and Commerce.

——— (1957). *Vital Statistics 1956.* Ottawa: Minister of Trade and Commerce.

——— (1958). *1956 Census of Canada, Population, General Characteristics.* Vol. 1. Ottawa: Minister of Trade and Commerce.

——— (1962). *1961 Census of Canada, Population. General Characteristics.* Vol. 1. Part 2. Ottawa: Minister of Trade and Commerce.

——— (1963). *Vital Statistics 1961.* Cat. 84–202. Ottawa: Minister of Trade and Commerce.

——— (1968a). *1966 Census of Canada, Population, General Characteristics.* Cat. 92–610. Vol. 1. Ottawa: Minister of Trade and Commerce.

——— (1968b). *Population 1921–1966 — Revised Annual Estimates of Population by Sex and Age, Canada and the Provinces.* Cat. 91–511. Ottawa: Minister of Trade and Commerce.

—— (1968c). *Vital Statistics 1966*. Cat. 84–202. Ottawa: Minister of Trade and Commerce.

Canada. Statistics Canada (1973a). *1971 Census of Canada, Population, General Characteristics*. Cat. 92–716. Vol. 1, Part 2. Ottawa: Minister of Industry, Trade and Commerce.

—— (1973b). *1971 Census of Canada. Population, General Characteristics*. Cat. 92–715. Vol. 1, Part 2. Ottawa: Minister of Industry, Trade and Commerce.

—— (1974a). *Vital Statistics: Deaths 1971*. Cat. 84–206. Vol. 3. Ottawa: Minister of Industry, Trade and Commerce.

—— (1974b). *Vital Statistics: Births 1972*. Cat. 84–204. Vol. 1. Ottawa: Minister of Industry, Trade and Commerce.

—— (1975). *Vital Statistics: Births 1973*. Cat. 84–204. Vol. 1. Ottawa: Minister of Industry, Trade and Commerce.

—— (1976). *Vital Statistics: Births 1974*. Cat. 84–204. Vol. 1. Ottawa: Minister of Industry, Trade and Commerce.

—— (1978a). *Vital Statistics: Births 1975 and 1976*. Cat. 84–204. Vol. 1. Ottawa: Minister of Industry, Trade and Commerce.

—— (1978b). *Vital Statistics: Deaths 1976*. Cat. 84–206. Vol. 3. Ottawa: Minister of Industry, Trade and Commerce.

—— (1979). *Vital Statistics: Births 1977*. Cat. 84–204. Vol. 1. Ottawa: Minister of Industry, Trade and Commerce.

—— (1980a). *Vital Statistics: Deaths 1977*. Cat. 84–206. Vol. 3. Ottawa: Minister of Supply and Services.

—— (1980b). *Vital Statistics: Births and Deaths 1978*. Cat. 84–204. Vol. 1. Ottawa: Minister of Supply and Services.

—— (1981). *Vital Statistics: Births and Deaths 1979*. Cat. 84–204. Vol. 1. Ottawa: Minister of Supply and Services.

—— (1982a). *1981 Census of Canada, Population*. Cat. 92–901. Vol. 1. Ottawa: Minister of Supply and Services.

—— (1982b). *Vital Statistics: Births and Deaths 1980*. Cat. 84–204. Vol. 1. Ottawa: Minister of Supply and Services.

—— (1983). *Vital Statistics: Births and Deaths 1981*. Cat. 84–204. Vol. 1. Ottawa: Minister of Supply and Services.

—— (1984). *Vital Statistics: Births and Deaths 1982*. Cat. 84–204. Vol. 1. Ottawa: Minister of Supply and Services.

—— (1985a). *Population Projections for Canada, Provinces and Territories, 1984–2006*. Cat. 91–520. Prepared by M.V. George and J. Perreault. Ottawa: Minister of Supply and Services.

—— (1985b). *Vital Statistics: Births and Deaths 1983*. Cat. 84–204. Vol. 1. Ottawa: Minister of Supply and Services.

Nagnur, Dhruva (1985). *Longevity and Historical Life Tables 1921–1981* (Abridged) Canada and Provinces. Statistics Canada Cat. 89–506. Ottawa: Minister of Supply and Services.

PART THREE

MORTALITY

AND

MORBIDITY

EPIDEMIOLOGIC TRANSITION

Over the last 150 years, Canada's population has moved from an early stage characterized by relatively low life expectancy and a preponderance of deaths attributable to
infectious and parasitic diseases (such as pneumonia, influenza, tuberculosis, and dys-
entery) to one characterized by high life expectancy and a concentration of deaths
caused by chronic and degenerative diseases. As standards of living (nutrition, sanitation, housing, etc.), improved, the infectious and parasitic diseases eventually receded.
Fewer people died from such causes, infant mortality declined, and life expectancy
increased. During the early decades of the twentieth century, modern medicine — in
particular, the development of germ theory — led to the development of antibiotics to
fight viral and bacterial diseases in humans. Other important medical innovations followed, contributing to further gains in human longevity.

In the contemporary society, the major killers are no longer the infectious and parasitic diseases, but ailments associated with aging and life-style. Chronic conditions such

as heart disease and cancer are the inevitable results of our society's having attained a high life expectancy. Because we live longer, on average, we are more susceptible to developing degenerative and chronic conditions associated mainly with aging. In addition, many of our ailments are related to life-style: for example, lung cancer is largely a function of cigarette smoking, while heart disease is partly linked to diet, obesity, and lack of exercise. Another unfortunate characteristic of contemporary society is the increased number of suicides and deaths resulting from accidents (at work and on the road) and violence (murder). Environmental pollution is another growing concern; for example, air quality has been implicated in diseases ranging from chronic asthma to lung cancer. Along with its benefits, therefore, 'progress' has created a number of serious problems for human health.

The chapters in this section focus upon these epidemiological phenomena. Nagnur and Nagrodski provide a detailed analysis of the movement of Canadian mortality from the high levels around the turn of this century to the low levels of recent years. The authors emphasize the trends and levels in the age/sex/cause components of mortality, the increase in life expectancy, and the rectangularization of the survival curve (the tendency for age-specific survival probabilities to increase over time) in the context of epidemiologic transition. An important conclusion suggested by their analysis is that the past improvements in mortality and expectation of life cannot continue indefinitely: the pace of improvement in longevity will be much slower in the future than it has been in recent decades.

King, Gartrell, and Trovato examine early childhood mortality from 1926 to 1986. Canada's success in reducing infant and childhood mortality rates to among the lowest in the world is a great achievement. In 1986, only 7.9 infants died per every 1,000 live births, compared with 101.8 in 1926. In the early 1980s, only 2 per cent of all deaths occurred to children aged less than 5 years, down sharply from the 27 per cent recorded in the 1926–30 period. Whereas in the early 1920s, infection and other environmental causes accounted for most infant deaths, the leading causes of death among infants today are congenital anomalies.

SEX DIFFERENCES IN MORTALITY

While there have been large declines in mortality since the early part of this century, the gains in longevity have not been shared equally by the sexes. In general, the modernization process has been more favourable to women. At the turn of the century, females' advantage over males in life expectancy at birth was around two years. Currently, Canadian women share a seven-year advantage in life expectancy over Canadian men.

Two key factors lie at the root of this phenomenon: biology and life-style. Perhaps females' constitutions are inherently stronger and more resistant to illness and the degeneration of the organism, giving them a 'natural' advantage over males; for example, the death rate *in utero* and in early infancy is substantially higher for males than females. In adulthood, however, a disaggregation of sex differences in death rates by cause of death reveals that about 75 per cent of the discrepancy can be accounted for by differences in rates of death due to lung cancer, cirrhosis of the liver, suicide, homicide, motor vehicle accidents, heart disease, and stroke, all of which have strong life-style components (e.g., stress, diet, substance abuse, etc.). This suggests that life-style differences between the sexes may be at the bottom of the observed sex gap in survivorship. It also implies that sex-role socialization is different for men and women: that is, the higher death rates of men may be a function of their socialization for aggression, risk-taking, and unhealthy behaviours. Thus biology may have an independent effect on the sex–mortality differential, but socialization appears to be a more important factor, particularly in accounting for differences in mortality at ages beyond infancy.

Nathanson and Lopez advance the thesis that the future of sex-mortality differentials in industrialized countries may depend on the future death rates of blue-collar men. Their study reveals that this subgroup in the population plays a significant role in current mortality differentials from ischemic heart disease, which is the leading killer in our society. The authors argue that the sex-social class-mortality differences observed in the Western world correspond to social structural differences in protection against illness and premature death. In Canada, the sex-mortality discrepancy is more than one-and-a half times larger at the lowest than at the highest income level; this difference is due primarily to variation in life expectancy in men rather than in women. Evidence accumulated over the past two decades suggests that, in general, blue-collar men smoke more and consume more alcohol than either upper-class men and women or lower-class women. Moreover, the social environment of the lower classes lacks many of the social support mechanisms available to the upper classes. But women generally have more social ties irrespective of class, and this fact may account for the narrower mortality difference between upper- and lower-class women.

Nathanson and Lopez predict that at the upper class levels, the sex differences in life expectancy will probably converge in the near future, primarily as a function of the presence of supports for healthy behaviour among upper-class males (e.g., emphasis on reduced smoking, better diet, and more exercise). Convergence at lower levels of social status is less likely, since the social supports emphasizing a more balanced and less risky life-style are less accessible to lower-status males.

ABORIGINAL MORTALITY

In the context of epidemiologic transition, Canada's aboriginal subpopulation is anomalous. Although the country's standards of living are among the highest in the world, its aboriginal people show a morbidity pattern that is characteristic of less-developed nations. They share this pattern with disadvantaged racial minorities in other parts of the world as well, such as the Aborigines in Australia, and Black and Native people in the United States. Common to all these peoples has been the experience of conquest and domination by outsiders. This historical process has resulted in their isolation from the mainstream society, extreme poverty, poor living conditions, and high death rates.

According to Bobet, death rates among Indian people in Canada have dropped recently, but continue to exceed those of the general Canadian population. Specifically, Indians are more likely than other Canadians to die from accidents, violence, suicide, and respiratory diseases. The aboriginal population has lower rates of cancer mortality, however, mostly because of its relatively young age structure.

Nevertheless, as Native people enter the final stages of epidemiologic and demographic transition it is expected that chronic and degenerative diseases will begin to claim an increasing number of lives. Since chronic diseases require prolonged care and attention — they cannot be controlled with antibiotics and similar treatments — this development could have severe implications unless health-care facilities become more accessible to Native people. Canadian social policy must face this challenge in the years ahead as the aboriginal population begins to age and, following the demographic trajectory of the larger society, experience a significant rise in chronic and degenerative diseases.

TECHNICAL NOTES

1. The crude death rate (CDR), while insensitive to age composition, is often used as a starting-point in mortality analysis. It is calculated as the number of deaths divided by the mid-year population, multiplied by 1,000.

2. The infant mortality rate (IMR) is a sensitive indicator of the socio-economic conditions prevailing in a society (or subgroup). It is computed by dividing the number of deaths to infants in a given year by the number of live births in the same year, multiplied by 1,000.

3. Life expectancy at age zero is a useful index of mortality for a society (or social category). This index can be calculated only once a life table has been computed. A life table provides a description of mortality for an actual population based on the mortality experience of a hypothetical birth cohort of 100,000 exposed to the prevailing age-specific death rates of the actual population. The objective of this exercise is to arrive at an indication of average life expectancy for each age group in the study population:

   From the life table, life expectancy at age x (E_x) is obtained by dividing T_x by ℓ_x:
   $$E_x = T_x / \ell_x$$
   where: T_x = the number of persons-years left to be lived by the hypothetical cohort given survival to age x,
   ℓ_x = the number of survivors in the hypothetical cohort at age x.

4. In the life table, the rate of natural increase is always zero since it assumes a closed population (no in- or out-migration) of 100,000 hypothetical newborn babies whose numbers are depleted only by the force of mortality, such that eventually all 100,000 will die. Therefore, since the number of births is 100,000, and ultimately the number of deaths is also 100,000, it follows that the difference between births and deaths is zero.

SUGGESTED READING

Adams, Owen (1990). 'Life expectancy in Canada — an overview'. *Health Reports* (Statistics Canada) 2, 4: 361–76.

Bah, Sulaiman M., and Rajulton Fernando (1991). 'Has Canadian mortality entered the fourth stage of epidemiologic transition?'. *Canadian Studies in Population* 18, 2: 18–41.

Barcley, George W. (1958). *Techniques of Population Analysis*. New York: John Wiley .

Gee, Ellen M. (1984). 'Mortality and gender'. *Canadian Women Studies* 5, 3: 10–13.

Kunitz, Stephen J. (1990). 'Public policy and mortality among indigenous populations of Northern America and Australia'. *Population and Development Review* 16, 4: 647–72.

Maxim, Paul S., and Carl Keane (1992). 'Gender, age, and the risk of violent death in Canada, 1950–1986'. *Canadian Review of Sociology and Anthropology* 29, 3: 329–45.

Morrison, H.I., R.M. Semenciw, Y. Mao, and D.T. Wigle (1986). 'Infant mortality on Canadian reserves, 1976–83'. *Canadian Journal of Public Health* 77: 269–73.

Nagnur, Dhruva (1986). 'Rectangularization of the survival curve and entropy: The Canadian experience'. *Canadian Studies in Population* 13, 1: 83–102.

Omran, Abdul R. (1971). 'The epidemiological transition: A theory of epidemiology of population change'. *Milbank Memorial Fund Quarterly/Health and Society* 49: 507–37.

Semenciw, R.M., H.I. Morrison, J. Lindsay, and J. Silins (1986). 'Risk factors for postneonatal mortality: Results from a record linkage study'. *International Journal of Epidemiology* 15, 3: 369–72.

Trovato, Frank (1992). 'Mortality differences by marital status in Canada'. *Canadian Studies in Population* 19, 2: 111–43.

Wilkins, Russell, and Owen Adams (1983). 'Health expectancy in Canada, late 1970s: Demographic, regional and social dimensions.' *American Journal of Public Health* 73, 9: 1073–80.

———, ———, and Anna Brancker (1989). 'Changes in mortality by income in urban Canada from 1971–1986'. *Health Reports* (Statistics Canada) 1, 2: 137–74.

Young, Kue T. (1988). 'Are subarctic Indians undergoing the epidemiologic transition?'. *Social Science and Medicine* 26, 6: 659–71.

CHAPTER 8

EPIDEMIOLOGIC TRANSITION IN THE CONTEXT OF DEMOGRAPHIC CHANGE

The Evolution of Canadian Mortality Patterns

Dhruva Nagnur and Michael Nagrodski

INTRODUCTION

. . .

Epidemiologic transition, according to Omran, focuses on the 'shifting web of health and disease patterns in population groups and their links with several demographic, social, economic, ecologic and biologic changes' (Omran, 1977: 4). He further elaborates the theory of epidemiologic transition by emphasizing the fact that

> Many countries have experienced a significant change or transition from high to low mortality accompanying either social development . . . or a combination of medical development and early social change (. . . when antibiotics, insecticides, sanitation and other medical technology were introduced after World War II) (1977: 4).

In support of these views, Omran (1977) provides some convincing evidence in his paper on the epidemiologic transition in the US.

Figure 1: Demographic–epidemiologic transition: A brief description of the stages

Demographic transition	Epidemiologic transition

Stage I: Age of Pestilence and Famine

High death rate	(a) High & fluctuating mortality
High birth rate	(b) Dominance of infectious and parasitic diseases as causes of mortality
	(c) Low life expectancy
Low growth rate	

Stage II: Age of Receding Pandemics

Low death rate	(a) Accelerated declines in mortality
High birth rate	(b) Shifts from infectious and parasitic disease mortality to degenerative disease mortality
High growth rate	(c) Rising life expectancy

Stage III: Age of Degenerative and Man-made Diseases

Low death rate	(a) Continuation of mortality declines and its eventual approach to stability at low levels
Low birth rate	(b) Dominance of degenerative disease mortality, caused by aging, changing lifestyle, and deteriorating environment
Low growth rate	(c) Further rise in life expectancy

What is more important in Omran's statement, however, is the identification of the commonality of the shifts in the kinds of diseases and causes of mortality that are prevalent at specific time-points in the development of a country or a society. The recurring theme, of course, is that during the final phases of epidemiologic transition, epidemic, infectious and parasitic diseases are progressively replaced by degenerative diseases and diseases of man-made variety, both as leading causes of morbidity and mortality. The infectious and parasitic diseases such as TB, 'diphtheria, plague and the like decline as the leading diseases and causes of death to be replaced by heart diseases, cancer, stroke . . . and the like, together with increased mental illness, accidents . . . and diseases [due to] a deteriorating environment' (Omran, 1977: 4).

Corresponding to the three traditional stages (high mortality and fertility, low mortality and high fertility, and low mortality and fertility) of demographic transition, Omran's identification of the three stages of the epidemiologic transition could be presented as follows: (a) Age of Pestilence and Famine, (b) Age of Receding Pandemics, and (c) Age of Degenerative and Man-made Diseases. Figure 1 presents a comparative perspective of these stages for the classical transition in Western societies. It is clear from this that there is a distinct relationship between demographic changes in mortality and the corresponding epidemiologic shifts.

... To follow through with all the stages of epidemiologic transition requires data for very long periods of time, say 150 to 200 years, which, of course we do not —and perhaps cannot—have with respect to Canadian mortality. Hence, this study is limited to the Canadian experience of the past 50 years.

Fortunately in Canada, as a consequence of federal-provincial agreements dating back to 1918–19, annual mortality data are available for more than six decades, back to 1921. 'Epidemiologic' classifications of mortality data have been available at least since the fourth revision of International Classification of Diseases (ICD). One could reasonably establish a comparative pattern of mortality by leading causes and its transition through time over the past five decades as the Canadian population has progressed to reach one of the lowest overall mortality levels among the developed countries of the world in recent years.

DEMOGRAPHIC CHANGES

Demographic changes in mortality can be assessed by means of several conventional indicators derived annually or quinquennially from the annual series of death data and populations at risk obtained at the time of censuses or revised intercensal estimates. In order to maintain consistency, we have looked at the changes since 1931, though some of the tabulations and mortality indices could be derived and have been available since a decade earlier.

Overall Mortality

The Canadian crude death rate has declined by more than 30 per cent since 1931 (Figure 2). More than half of this improvement occurred during the two decades between 1951 and 1971. Even in the trends of crude rate, a significant differential in the relative improvement has been registered in favour of women. When one examines the age-standardized rates (Table 1), it can be seen that these have consistently and monotonically declined for Canada during the past decades. Between 1931 and 1981, the age-standardized death rate for Canada fell by 54 per cent for the population as a whole. The rate for women improved 50 per cent faster than for men.

Infant Mortality

One of the important links in the chain of improvement of mortality is the significant reduction of infant mortality and its neonatal and post-neonatal components. In 1931, nearly one in 12 live births resulted in infant death; by 1981, infant mortality had declined by nearly 90 per cent, resulting in infant deaths of less than one in 100 live births.

This remarkable achievement has been the consequence of reductions of 85 per cent and 90 per cent in the neonatal and post-neonatal death rates, respectively. The improvements have been uniform for both sexes and, with one or two exceptions, across all provinces. It is of interest to note that in 1931, the neonatal

Figure 2: Death rates and infant mortality rates, Canada, 1931, 1951, 1971, and 1981

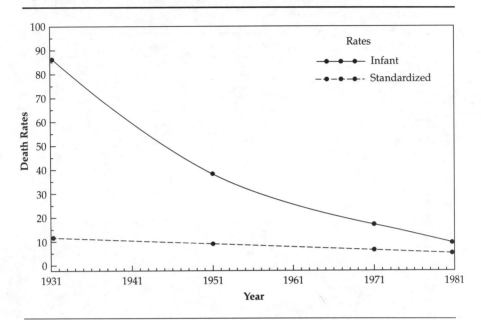

and post-neonatal death rates were practically of the same magnitude, but in 1981, the post-neonatal rate was one-half that of the neonatal rate, as a consequence of the accelerated improvement. As the decomposition of the effects of mortality by age on life expectation shows, these sizeable reductions in the infant, neonatal and post-neonatal rates have contributed significantly to the increases in the expectation of life at birth during the past five to six decades.

Life Expectancy Trends

A comparative profile of life expectancy at birth and at selected ages for the years 1931 and 1981 is presented in Table 2 (see also Figure 3). The trend shows that there has been a considerable increase in life expectancy at birth for both males and females — about 12 years and 17 years, respectively. The average increase during the past 50 years has been about three months per year for males and four months per year for females.

Throughout the evolution of this mortality pattern within the period of study, the life expectancy of females has always been higher than the corresponding life expectancy for males. Moreover, it is generally observed that the difference in life expectancy between males and females tended to increase over time (Table 2). In 1931, the difference in life expectancy at birth was about two years; by 1981, the difference in favour of women was more than seven years. The excess years of

Table 1: Death rates and infant mortality rates, Canada, 1931, 1951, 1971, and 1981

	Rates per 1,000 population		
	Both sexes	**Males**	**Females**
Crude rate			
1931	10.2	10.5	9.6
1951	9.0	10.1	7.8
1971	7.3	8.5	6.1
1981	7.0	8.0	6.0
% Change (1931–81)	−31.4	−23.8	−37.5
Standardized rate			
1931	12.2	12.7	11.7
1951	9.0	10.0	8.0
1971	6.7	8.4	5.2
1981	5.6	7.2	4.3
% Change (1931–81)	−54.1	−43.3	−63.2
Infant rate			
1931	86.0	95.4	74.4
1951	38.5	42.7	34.0
1971	17.6	19.9	15.1
1981	9.6	10.7	8.3
% Change (1931–81)	−88.8	−88.7	−88.9
Neonatal rate			
1931	41.5	46.6	35.4
1951	22.6	25.6	19.4
1971	12.4	14.1	10.6
1981	6.4	7.2	5.4
% Change (1931–81)	−84.6	−84.5	−84.7
Post-neonatal rate			
1931	44.5	47.8	39.0
1951	15.9	17.1	14.6
1971	5.2	5.8	4.5
1981	3.2	3.5	2.9
% Change (1931–81)	−92.8	−92.7	−92.6

Table 2: Life expectancy of selected ages, Canada, 1931 and 1981

Males	Ages	Years of life expected		Percentage change
		1931	1981	
	0	60.00	71.88	19.8
	1	64.57	71.65	11.0
	15	53.41	58.05	8.7
	40	31.99	34.74	8.6
	65	12.98	14.57	12.2
	75	7.57	9.01	19.0

Females	Ages	Years of life expected		Percentage change
		1931	1981	
	0	62.06	79.06	27.4
	1	65.64	78.72	19.9
	15	54.15	65.02	20.1
	40	33.03	40.80	23.5
	65	13.72	18.93	38.0
	75	7.98	11.88	48.9

Ages	Excess years of female life expectancy over male life expectancy	
	1931	1981
0	2.06	7.18
1	1.07	7.07
15	0.74	6.97
40	1.04	6.06
65	0.74	4.36
75	0.41	2.87
85	0.32	1.43

females over males, however, tended to decline with increasing age: in 1981, at age 75, [the difference] was less than three years.

Survival Probabilities to Older Ages

From 1931 to 1981, there were significant increases in the probability of survival and the number of survivors to successively older ages (Figure 4). The values in Table 3 are reproduced from a set of abridged life tables constructed at five-year periods from 1921 to 1981 for Canada and the provinces (Nagnur, 1986a). Generally, the improvements in the numbers of survivors have been greater during the 30 years following 1951, compared to the previous 30 years. Women made greater

Figure 3: Years of life expected at selected ages, males and females, Canada, 1931 and 1981

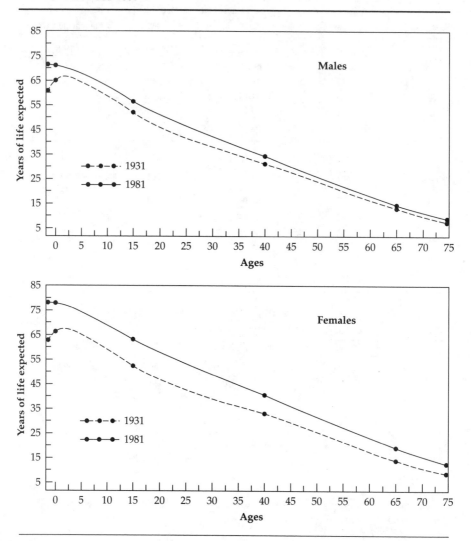

gains than men and remarkable improvements were registered in the probabilities of survival to older ages of 65, 75 and 85.

Among the male birth-cohorts subject to the 1931 life table, nearly three out of
five were expected to survive to the age 65; according to the 1981 life table, the
proportion had risen to three out of four. Slightly more than one out of three
survived to age 75, according to the 1931 life table; while in the 1981 life table, one-
half were expected to make it to that age. Remarkable progress has occurred with

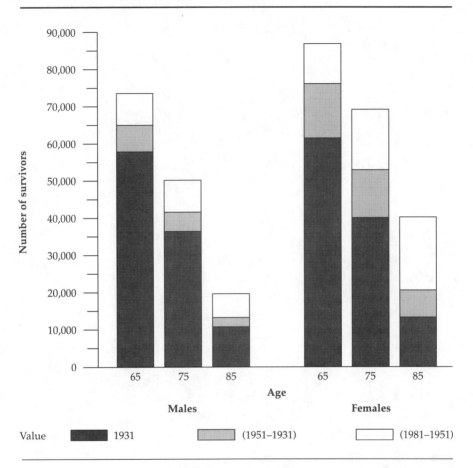

Figure 4: Number of survivors of the synthetic birth cohort of 100,000, to ages 65, 75 and 85, Canada, 1931, 1951, and 1981

respect to the improvements in the chances of survival to the age 85; between 1931 and 1981, the increase in the number expected to reach age 85 was almost three times that between 1931 and 1951—6,500 compared to 2,500 per 100,000.

With regard to women, the improvements in the corresponding survival probabilities have been still more spectacular that those for men (Table 3). According to the 1931 life table, women who were expected to survive to age 65 accounted for more than three out of five; the proportion rose to three out of four by 1951 and was almost seven out of eight in 1981. A similar trend was observed among women expected to survive to age 75: according to 1931 life tables, two out of five were expected to reach that age; the proportion increased to more than one in two by 1951 and was in excess of seven out of 10 in 1981. Similarly, the

Table 3: Survivors of the synthetic birth cohort of 100,000, to ages 65, 75, and 85, Canada, 1931, 1951, and 1981

Number of Survivors

	Males						Females					
	Age: 65		Age: 75		Age: 85		Age: 65		Age: 75		Age: 85	
Years	Number	%	Number	%	Number	%	Number	%	Number	%	Number	%
1931	58,694	58.7	36,626	36.6	11,006	11.0	61,635	61.6	40,716	40.7	13,323	13.3
1951	65,877	65.9	41,931	41.9	13,490	13.5	75,585	75.6	54,046	54.0	20,760	20.8
1981	74,681	74.7	50,367	50.4	19,966	20.0	86,088	86.1	70,503	70.5	40,648	40.6

Increase in Survivors[1]

	Males						Females					
	Age: 65		Age: 75		Age: 85		Age: 65		Age: 75		Age: 85	
Years	Number	%	Number	%	Number	%	Number	%	Number	%	Number	%
1951–1931	7,183	12.2	5,305	14.5	2,484	22.6	13,950	22.6	13,330	32.7	7,437	55.8
1981–1951	8,804	13.4	8,436	20.1	6,476	48.0	10,503	13.9	16,457	30.4	19,888	95.8
1981–1931	15,987	27.2	13,741	37.5	8,960	81.4	24,453	39.7	29,787	73.2	27,325	205.1

[1]Percentage increase was derived with 1931 as the base.

survival to age 85 doubled to more than two out of five by 1981, compared to two out of 10 in 1951.

The increasing rectangularization of the survival curve (the curve on the number of survivors to age x, lx, plotted against age x) illustrates the phenomenon rather dramatically. This aspect has been discussed in considerable detail in Nagnur (1986b).

EPIDEMIOLOGIC CONSIDERATIONS

The foregoing looked at the evolution of some of the changes in mortality and life table parameters which could be considered and grouped as 'demographic'. Now let us examine some of the considerations which could be characterized as epidemiologic shifts that have occurred concurrently with those demographic changes.

Distribution of Deaths by Cause Categories

Table 4 shows the percentage distribution of deaths by selected cause-categories which were leading in 1931 and changes in that distribution over the past five decades. The cause categories are mostly broad chapters in ICD, except in a couple of cases where individual diseases are designated. The total deaths for Canada exclude those for Newfoundland (and for the years 1931 and 1941, exclude those for the Yukon and Northwest Territories, as well). (The percentages in this table do not add up to 100 due to the residual category not being shown.) Table 4 also shows the equivalent ICD codes from the fourth revision to the ninth.

One can clearly see from Table 4 the progressive reduction in the importance of the infectious and parasitic diseases and the increasing importance and impact of the degenerative diseases from 1931 to 1981. For example, TB accounted for more than seven per cent of the deaths in 1931, while it was almost negligible in 1981. Cancer, on the other hand, accounted for less than one in 10 deaths in 1931, while in 1981 it claimed almost one in four deaths. Heart disease claimed two out of five deaths in 1981, while in 1931 it accounted for half that number. Cerebrovascular diseases accounted for three per cent of all deaths in 1931, while that percentage tripled to about 9 per cent in 1981.

The shifts which Omran discusses regarding the epidemiologic transition—the shifts from infectious and parasitic diseases to degenerative diseases—are clearly observed in the evolution of Canadian mortality patterns during the past several decades.

Potential Years of Life Lost (PYLL)

Epidemiologic shifts are also reflected in the examination of the PYLL (potential years of life lost) values by leading causes of death. Table 5 considers 11 categories which were the leading causes of death for men in 1931; these, and the corresponding categories for women, are followed through to 1981. The estimates of the

Table 4: Percentage distribution of deaths by selected cause-categories, Canada, 1931, 1951 and 1981

Selected cause categories	Percentage distribution of deaths			Equivalent ICD cause-categories with respect to different revisions		
	1981 (ICD9)	1951 (ICD6)	1931 (ICD4)	1981 (ICD9)	1951 (ICD6)	1931 (ICD4)
Tuberculosis	0.1	2.8	7.3	010–018, 137	001–019	23–32
Other infectious and parasitic diseases	0.4	1.1	5.0	001–009, 020–139	020–138	1–10, 11e–22, 33–44, 80, 83
Malignant neoplasms	24.1	14.5	9.2	140–208	140–205	45–53
Diabetes mellitus	1.8	1.3	1.2	250	260	59
Cerebrovascular disease	8.9	10.5	3.2	430–438	330–334	82
Other cardiovascular disease	39.3	35.6	19.6	390–429 440–459, 785.4	400–468	56, 90–103
Respiratory disease	6.6	8.0	10.8	460–519	240, 241, 470–527	11a–11d, 104–114
Urinary disease	1.3	3.4	5.5	580–599	590–594 600–609	130–136[1]
Accidental deaths	5.7	6.6	6.6	E800–E949	E800–E962	77, 176 178–194
Total Number of Deaths	104,517	122,819	167,799			

[1] 1931 included some terms that in later revisions were considered circulatory cardiovascular disease.

PYLL were derived by considering the difference between the age at death due to a particular disease and the life expectancy at birth in the corresponding year under consideration.

The total PYLL for Canada as a whole remained in the neighbourhood of about two million years annually for the three decades from 1931 to 1961 in spite of the increases in the population and the number of deaths. It dropped by about 160 thousand years between 1961 and 1971 and remained at about the 1971 level in 1981. However, the epidemiologic distribution by cause-categories changed dramatically during the past five decades.

Consistent with the notion of epidemiologic transition, infectious and parasitic diseases, diseases of the digestive and respiratory systems and certain diseases of early infancy which were leading contributors to the PYLL in the earlier decades under study have gradually declined in significance and importance. Diseases of the circulatory system, neoplasms, and the accidents, poisoning and violence category have been the leading contributors to the total PYLL in recent years.

As the number of deaths due to infant and childhood diseases has decreased and the number of deaths due to degenerative diseases has concurrently

Table 5: Potential years of life lost, by selected cause of death categories, and sex, Canada, 1931 and 1981

	Males			Females		
	1931	1981	Percentage change[1]	1931	1981	Percentage change[1]
Life Expectancy at Birth	60.0	71.9	19.8	62.1	79.0	27.2
Leading Causes of Death	(thousands)			(thousands)		
Certain diseases of early infancy	309.1	61.8	−80.0	235.6	48.5	−79.4
Diseases of the digestive system	232.2	39.6	−82.9	176.1	33.2	−81.1
Diseases of the respiratory system	189.2	34.0	−82.3	161.5	33.2	−79.4
Infective and parasitic diseases	187.1	6.8	−96.4	217.7	7.4	−96.6
Accidents, poisonings and violence	135.7	373.0	174.9	43.1	141.7	228.8
Congenital malformations	47.3	57.2	20.9	38.1	48.3	26.8
Diseases of the circulatory system	42.5	228.9	438.6	45.8	180.1	293.2
Diseases of the nervous system	37.3	20.8	−44.2	32.2	20.8	−35.4
Neoplasms	25.3	170.6	574.3	38.5	239.6	522.3
Diseases of the genito-urinary system	18.9	4.9	−74.1	25.8	6.8	−73.6
All other causes	57.4	53.9	−6.1	89.6	54.9	−38.7
Total	1,282.0	1,051.5	−18.0	1,104.0	814.5	−26.2
Total Both Sexes	2,386.0	1,866.0	−21.8			

[1] Percentage change is derived with 1931 as the base.

increased, the mean number of years lived by those dying has increased. This is consistent with the notion of epidemiologic transition and accounts to a large extent for the total PYLL remaining at the same level or declining somewhat despite an increasing population and more annual deaths.

Causes of Death for Selected Age Groups

Infant Mortality by Cause. As we have observed, the infant mortality dropped by about 90 per cent during the past five decades. Epidemiologically, the leading causes of death for infants in the earlier decades under study were immaturity, infectious and parasitic diseases such as diarrhoea and enteritis, and respiratory diseases such as influenza, bronchitis and pneumonia. Again consistent with the notion of epidemiologic transition, the cause pattern of infant mortality has changed dramatically over the past five decades. Congenital malformations accounted for the highest rate among both male and female babies in 1981. Deaths due to the three leading causes that existed in 1931 were reduced by more than 95 per cent during the past five decades.

Age Group 1–4. The trends in mortality for this age group indicate a precipitous drop in the death rate following the first year of life. The overall death rate for this age group declined by more than 90 per cent between 1931 and 1981. Many of the leading causes of death recorded in 1931 have been either eradicated or reduced to insignificance. The leading causes of death for this age group in 1931 were (a) infectious and parasitic diseases, (b) respiratory diseases, and (c) accidents, poisoning and violence. Of these, the category involving accidents is the only one that remains a predominant cause in 1981.

Age Group 65–74. The leading causes of mortality for this age group were cardiovascular diseases and cancer. Among males, the mortality due to the former increased until 1961 and has been declining since then. In contrast, with the exception of 1951, the mortality rate due to cancer has been increasing steadily from a level of about 700 per 100,000 in 1931 to 1,070 in 1981 — an increase of more than 40 per cent. Among females, the mortality due to cardiovascular disease increased until 1971, but has declined significantly since then. Between 1931 and 1981, the overall mortality declined by about 15 per cent for males and more than 50 per cent for females.

Age Group 75 +. Although cardiovascular disease has been the main cause of mortality for this age group — accounting for more than one-half of the deaths for both males and females — the second cause has been cancer. The cancer mortality rate for males increased by 75 per cent in the past five decades, and in 1981, it accounted for almost 20 per cent of all male deaths. For females in this age group, the cancer mortality rate has changed little since 1931. The overall mortality rate for this age group declined by about 12 per cent for males and about 40 per cent for females during the last five decades.

An interesting point to note is the reappearance of respiratory diseases as a significant cause of mortality for this age group. This may not spell the reversal of the shifts in the epidemiologic transition, but as Osler stated, 'There is truth in the paradoxical statement that persons rarely die of the [chronic] disease with which they suffer. Secondary *terminal* infections carry off many patients with incurable disease' (Gruenberg, 1977: 3).

What is essentially required in this context is a refinement in classifying data and a concerted effort directed towards multiple-cause coding of mortality data; contributory causes take on added importance, especially at older ages. The general practice of classifying deaths only on the basis of an 'underlying cause' might be insufficient to identify important emerging epidemiologic shifts. (For details in the trends of age-cause specific mortality rates, see Nagnur, 1986b.)

Table 6: Years of life expectancy gained at birth if selected causes were deleted, by sex, Canada, 1931 and 1981

	Males		Females	
Cause of Death Categories	1931	1981	1931	1981
No cause deleted	0.00	0.00	0.00	0.00
Respiratory tuberculosis	1.13	0.01	1.45	0.09
Other infectious and parasitic diseases	1.35	0.06	1.36	0.15
Malignant and benign neoplasms	1.48	3.24	2.03	3.53
Cardiovascular disease	4.35	8.69	4.79	13.05
Influenza, pneumonia, bronchitis	2.25	0.37	2.22	0.50
Diarrhoea, gastritis, enteritis	1.60	0.06	1.25	0.19
Certain degenerative diseases	1.12	0.56	1.24	0.66
Complications of pregnancy	0.00	0.00	0.57	0.09
Certain diseases of infancy	2.96	0.33	2.34	0.36
Motor vehicle accidents	0.37	0.78	0.14	0.43
Other accidents and violence	1.68	1.35	0.56	0.73
All other and unknown causes	3.77	1.69	3.44	1.70

Cause-deleted Life Tables

One other important means of looking at the effect of a particular disease on the overall mortality and assessing the impact of epidemiologic shifts is to construct a series of cause-deleted life tables and study the changes over time in the important parameters (such as life expectancy and probability of survival to specified ages) from such life tables. One strong assumption in constructing these tables is that these causes operate independently of each other (which, of course, is not strictly valid).

Preston, Keyfitz and Schoen constructed such tables eliminating 12 leading cause-categories for many national populations (Preston et al., 1972). They included life tables for Canada up to 1964. We have developed similar tables, eliminating the same 12 cause-categories for recent years encompassing the seventh, eighth and ninth revisions of ICD.

For the years 1931 and 1981, Table 6 shows the increases in life expectancy at birth that would result if the deaths due to the cause-category mentioned in the first column were eliminated. One observes the epidemiologic shifts, the decrease in the impact of infectious, parasitic and respiratory diseases, and the increase in the effect of cardiovascular diseases, neoplasms and accidents. For example, according to the 1931 pattern, the elimination of deaths due to TB would have added 1.1 years to the life expectancy at birth for males (Figure 5) and 1.5 years for females (Figure 6); the same elimination in 1981 added a negligible amount of years to life expectancy.

Figure 5: Years of life expectancy gained, at birth, if selected causes were deleted, males, Canada, 1931 and 1981

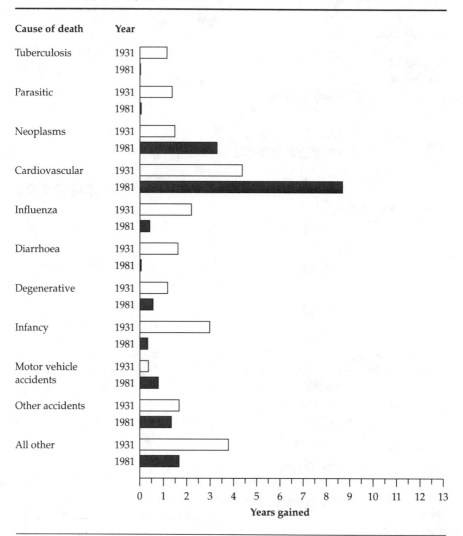

The elimination of cardiovascular diseases would have added 4.4 and 4.8 years for male and female life expectancies, respectively, according to 1931 tables; by 1971, the corresponding years increased to 10.6 and 14.7; by 1981, they declined slightly to 8.7 and 13.1 years, respectively, due to the decrease in cardiovascular disease mortality. The shifts in this cause-category, more than in any other, will have significant impact on the changes in life expectancy in future years.

Eliminating cancer mortality, on the other hand, continues to add increasing

Figure 6: Years of life expectancy gained, at birth, if selected causes were deleted, females, Canada, 1931 and 1981

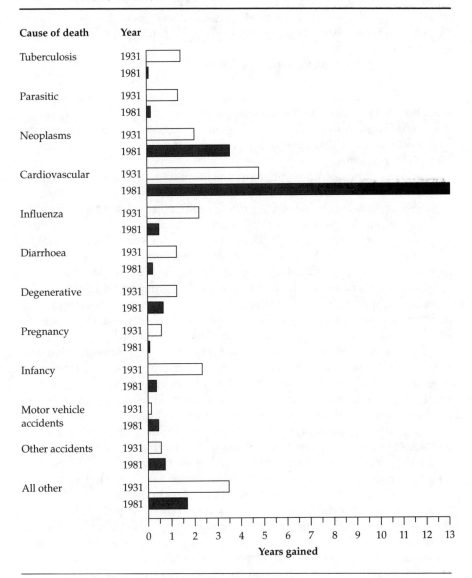

years to the life expectancy of both men and women. In 1931, the years added by eliminating neoplasms were 1.5 years for males and 2.0 years for females; by 1981, the corresponding years were 3.2 and 3.5.

One other category that has shown sustained increase is that involving accidents—motor vehicle as well as other forms of accidents. Elimination of motor vehicle accidents alone would add about half a year to female life expectancy and three quarters of a year to male life expectancy.

Once again, we see the effects of shifts involved in epidemiologic transition on the emerging pattern of life expectancy. A detailed analysis of the cause-deleted life tables and their implications will be dealt with in future publications.

CONCLUDING REMARKS

In the foregoing discussion, we have examined some selected trends in mortality indicators and variations in the life table parameters over the past five decades. We have attempted to provide cause-specific disaggregations and to describe epidemiologic shifts that have taken place concurrent with the demographic changes in mortality.

Now, one might ask how important are the utility and purpose of such a perspective and analysis? There are several important considerations. The first and foremost is its considerable relevancy to health policy. Health, as defined by the World Health Organization (1948), is not just an absence of disease or infirmity, but a state of complete physical, mental and social well-being (see MacMahon and Pugh, 1970). The three important components concerning health — mortality, morbidity and disability — need to be studied in the context of epidemiologic shifts that have already, and are currently, taking place. Epidemiologic transition in morbidity has an equal, if not more important, bearing on the literature related to health-sector accounting and satellite accounting of health and is antecedent to a sizeable portion of health expenditures.

The second most important consideration is in the context of population projections. Most demographers agree that the past improvements in mortality or expectation of life cannot continue indefinitely in the future. Whether there will ever be a cap on the life expectancy or not, the pace of improvement in the future will be much slower than it has been in recent decades. One is certainly on very unsure ground in projecting mortality based only on the trends in age-specific mortality rates or the derived period life tables. In this instance, the past is certainly no prologue to the future; past trends do not offer sufficient clues for the future projections. Thus realistic projections cannot help but take into account the epidemiologic shifts and future plausible changes in them.

Lastly, along with the importance of demographic changes, epidemiologic shifts are important in shaping the future course of population change. There is a need, as Omran implies, to develop models so that epidemiologic shifts and demographic and other relevant changes can be related in such a way that a comprehensive theory of population dynamics could be developed so as to provide a systematic basis for future planning in health, social and economic sectors.

REFERENCES

Gruenberg, E.M. (1977). 'The failures of success'. *Milbank Memorial Fund Quarterly, Health and Society* 55: 3–24.

MacMahon, B. and T.S. Pugh. (1970). *Epidemiology: Principles and Methods.* Boston: Little, Brown.

Manton, K.G. (1982). 'Changing concepts of morbidity and mortality in elderly populations'. *Milbank Memorial Fund Quarterly, Health and Society* 60: 183–244.

Nagnur, D. (1986a). *Longevity and Historical Life Tables, 1921–1981 (abridged): Canada and the Provinces).* Statistics Canada Cat. 89–506. Ottawa: Minister of Supply and Services.

—— (1986b). 'Rectangularization of the survival curve and entropy: The Canadian experience, 1921–1981'. *Canadian Studies in Population* 13: 83–102.

Omran, A.R. (1971). 'The epidemiological transition: A theory of epidemiology of population change'. *Milbank Memorial Fund Quarterly, Health and Society* 49: 507–537.

—— (1977). 'Epidemiological transition in the U.S.' Population Reference Bureau Bulletin 32(2).

Preston, S.H., N. Keyfitz and R. Schoen (1972). *Causes of Death, Life Tables for National Population.* New York: Seminar Press.

Statistics Canada. *Causes of Death.* Annual, 1965 to 1981. Cat. 84–203. Ottawa.

Statistics Canada (formerly Dominion Bureau of Statistics). *Vital Statistics.* Annual, 1931 to 1970. Cat. 84–202. Ottawa.

Statistics Canada. *Vital Statistics, Volume I, Births and Deaths.* Annual, 1971 to 1981. Cat. 84–204. Ottawa.

Statistics Canada. *Vital Statistics, Volume III, Mortality: Summary list of Causes.* Annual 1971 to 1981. Cat. 84–206. Ottawa.

World Health Organization (1948). Text of the Constitution of the World Health Organization. Official Recordings of the World Health Organization 2: 100. Geneva: World Health Organization.

—— (1978). *International Classification of Diseases, 1975 Revision, Vol. 2, Alphabetic Index.* Geneva: World Health Organization.

CHAPTER 9

EARLY CHILDHOOD

MORTALITY

1926-1986

Margaret King, John Gartrell,

and Frank Trovato

Since early in the century, deaths among young children have decreased dramatically as a proportion of all deaths in Canada. This is mainly because of a significant drop in the mortality rate of children under 5 years old. Over the same period, deaths from infectious diseases have been largely brought under control in Canada and non-infectious diseases and conditions have replaced them as the major cause of death in early childhood.

Childhood Deaths Down

Early childhood deaths have declined as a proportion of total deaths since at least the 1920s. From 1981 to 1985, only 2 per cent of deaths occurred among children aged less than 5 years, down sharply from 27 per cent in the 1926–30 period.

Most early childhood deaths occur in the first year of life. During the 1981–85 period, infant deaths (those among children under 1 year) accounted for 83 per cent of all deaths of children under 5 years old. Although down slightly from the

Figure 1: Infant mortality rates, by sex, 1926–1986

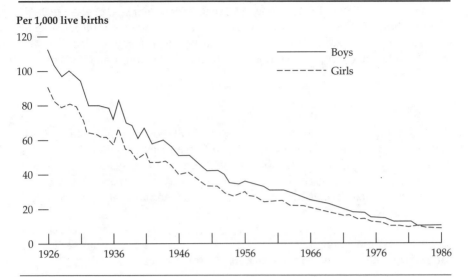

Per 1,000 live births

¹Children under 1 year.
SOURCE: Statistics Canada, Vital Statistics and Causes of Death as published from 1926–1986.

peak of 86 per cent in the 1956–60 period, the proportion was still much higher than in the late 1920s when it was 76 per cent.

Neonatal deaths (those among infants under 4 weeks old) now account for most infant deaths, a change of the pattern that prevailed early in the century. In the 1920s, there was a preponderance of post-neonatal deaths (those among infants 4 weeks and older). During the following two decades, the proportions of post-neonatal and neonatal deaths were generally equal. From 1981 to 1985, however, 65 per cent of infant deaths occurred among children under 4 weeks old, down from a high of more than 70 per cent in the 1966–70 period.

Mortality Rates

A main reason why early childhood deaths now account for a lower proportion of total deaths is that mortality rates among young children, particularly infants, have dropped very quickly.

By 1986, only 7.9 infants died per every 1,000 live births, compared with 101.8 in 1926 (See Figure 1). The decline in the rate was irregular, however, because of periodic infectious disease epidemics in this vulnerable segment of the population.

The magnitude of the decline in mortality rates among post-neonatal and neonatal infants has been similar. Post-neonatal rates, however, dropped some-what faster, to 2.8 deaths per 1,000 live births in 1986 from 54.1 in 1926. Among infants under 4 weeks, the rate was 5.1 in 1986, down from 47.7 in 1926.

Among children aged 1–4 years, mortality rates also have declined throughout the century. However, within this age group, rates consistently have been highest among children 1 year old, declining with each subsequent year of age.

Stillbirths (foetal births occurring after 20 weeks' gestation) are still considered less responsive to medical intervention but also show a steady decline. By 1986, only 6.2 stillbirths occurred per 1,000 live births, down considerably from 30.5 in 1926.

Male Rates Still Higher

Throughout the 60-year period, death rates for both boys and girls plummeted. Male mortality rates remained higher than those of females but the gap has narrowed considerably. For example, in 1986, among infants aged 4 weeks and over, the rate for boys was 2.9 deaths per 1,000 live births, compared with a rate of 2.6 for girls. In 1926, male and female post-neonatal mortality rates were 59.0 and 48.8, respectively.

Similarly, in 1986, 5.8 deaths occurred for every 1,000 live births among males under 4 weeks old, compared with a rate of 4.5 for females. Sixty years earlier, the comparable rates were 53.9 for males and 43.1 for females.

Infectious and Non-infectious Diseases

Mortality rates for the broad categories of both infectious and non-infectious diseases have been declining since early in the century. Death rates from infectious diseases, however, have dropped much more sharply than those for non-infectious diseases (See Figure 2).

Consequently, non-infectious diseases and conditions (including accidents, congenital anomalies, prematurity, cancer, and others) now account for most deaths among children under 5 years old. This reverses the pattern of earlier in the century when infectious diseases caused most early childhood deaths.

From 1981 to 1985, non-infectious diseases caused 90 per cent of both deaths among children aged 1–4 years and post-neonatal deaths. In contrast, in the 1926–30 period, non-infectious diseases caused only 28 per cent of deaths in this age range.

Unlike the pattern among other young children, non-infectious diseases have consistently accounted for most neonatal deaths. In the 1981–85 period, such diseases caused 97 per cent of neonatal deaths, up from 90 per cent in the late 1920s.

Communicable Childhood Diseases

From 1926 to 1985, epidemics of communicable diseases (infections transmissable from person to person) have sometimes caused short-term reversals in the overall decline in mortality rates among young children. Tuberculosis and influenza epidemics influenced mortality rates early in this period. At various times, epidemics of measles, mumps, chicken pox, whooping cough, and scarlet fever also affected rates.

Nonetheless, mortality rates for all communicable diseases have dropped

Figure 2: Early childhood mortality rates, by age and type of disease, 1926–1986

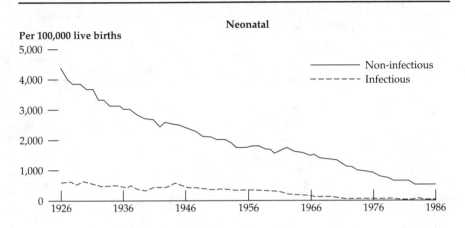

Neonatal

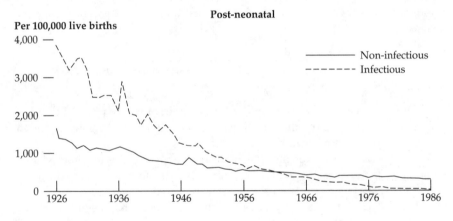

Post-neonatal

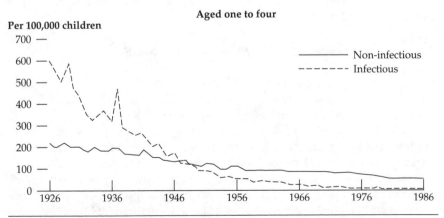

Aged one to four

SOURCE: Statistics Canada, Vital Statistics and Causes of Death as published from 1926–1986.

Table 1: Percentage of deaths among children aged 1-4 due to selected causes, 1926-1985

| | Infectious diseases | Non-infectious | | |
| | | Accidents | Congenital anomalies | Neoplasms |
	%	%	%	%
1926–1930	72.6	8.4	1.3	0.8
1931–1935	66.8	11.1	1.7	1.6
1936–1940	64.8	12.0	2.3	2.0
1941–1945	58.5	17.1	4.0	3.1
1946–1950	49.6	23.2	5.8	5.0
1951–1955	41.2	29.2	7.1	7.3
1956–1960	33.3	32.6	10.4	9.5
1961–1965	26.9	37.3	11.2	10.6
1966–1970	22.0	41.1	13.2	11.1
1971–1975	15.6	44.4	14.7	10.4
1976–1980	12.5	45.0	14.8	10.3
1981–1985	10.2	41.5	16.3	11.0

SOURCE: Statistics Canada, Vital Statistics and Causes of Death as published from 1926 to 1985.

throughout the century. In fact, such diseases now cause very few childhood deaths. However, rates of illness from whooping cough are rising again due to decreased levels of immunization.

Of all infections, those of the gastrointestinal area and the respiratory tract accounted for most deaths in children under 5 year old since 1926. Although major outbreaks of gastrointestinal infections occurred several times up to 1941, the overall decline in mortality rates for such infections has been rapid. For respiratory infections, rates were high and fluctuating for children under 5 until 1945, but dropped off sharply after that.

Leading Non-infectious Causes of Death

Among young children, mortality rates for all non-infectious diseases except cancer have declined sharply over the century. Differences in the magnitude of declines have resulted in shifts in the leading causes of death.

Children aged 1–4 years: Accidents have been the leading cause of death among children aged 1–4 years since the 1960s. For example, in the 1981–85 period, they accounted for 42 per cent of deaths in this age range. In contrast, only 8 per cent of deaths among 1–4-year-olds resulted from accidents in the 1926–30 period, even though there were fewer actual deaths from accidents from 1981 to 1985 (See Table 1).

Table 2: Percentage of infant deaths due to selected causes, 1926–1985

	Infectious diseases		Congenital anomalies		Non-infectious diseases					
					Prematurity		Accidents		Neoplasms[1]	
	N	P-N	N	P-N	N	P-N	N	P-N	N	P-N
	%	%	%	%	%	%	%	%	%	%
1926–1930	10.3	72.0	8.9	4.0	41.1	2.9	0.7	1.2		
1931–1935	9.5	71.1	9.7	5.1	41.0	3.3	0.8	1.5		
1936–1940	8.5	67.9	11.2	6.9	40.6	4.3	0.6	2.1		
1941–1945	11.6	68.5	14.1	9.4	37.9	2.4	0.9	3.1		
1946–1950	10.4	62.7	14.0	11.3	38.1	2.1	1.0	5.1		
1951–1955	9.3	60.8	15.2	14.5	23.1	1.7	1.0	7.0	0.1	0.6
1956–1960	8.7	56.1	15.3	16.7	25.1	1.7	0.8	9.6	0.1	0.7
1961–1965	6.3	48.6	16.1	20.3	26.5	1.1	0.7	13.3	0.1	0.8
1966–1970	4.8	40.0	17.7	23.9	23.0	0.5	0.7	15.4	0.1	1.0
1971–1975	3.9	28.8	21.4	23.4	14.5	0.2	0.6	13.9	0.1	1.1
1976–1980	3.5	16.2	27.9	25.4	12.0	0.2	0.5	9.7	0.2	1.0
1981–1985	3.0	10.4	34.5	23.5	10.5	0.1	0.5	7.5	0.2	1.2

[1] Data not subdivided into neonatal and post-neonatal age groups until 1950.
SOURCE: Statistics Canada, Vital Statistics and Causes of Death as published from 1926 to 1985.
N = Neonatal.   P-N = Post-neonatal.

Congenital anomalies, such as an incompletely formed nervous system or major organ, have accounted for a growing proportion of deaths as the decades advanced, and are now the second leading cause of death among children aged 1–4 years. From 1981 to 1985, 16 per cent of young children died as a result of congenital anomalies, compared with only 1 per cent in the late 1920s.

Cancer accounts for a larger proportion of deaths among children aged 1–4 years now than in the early 1930s. From 1981 to 1985, 11 per cent of deaths among children this age resulted from cancer. Although this proportion has been relatively stable since the late 1950s, it is up considerably from 1 per cent in the 1926–30 period.

Infants: Since the early 1930s, congenital anomalies have accounted for an increasing proportion of infant deaths. Now the leading cause of death, these anomalies made up about one-quarter (24 per cent) of post-neonatal and one-third (35 per cent) of neonatal deaths in the 1981–85 period. These figures were up from 4 per cent and 9 per cent, respectively, in the 1926–30 period (See Table 2).

Among neonatal infants, deaths due to prematurity have dropped sharply in recent decades. In the 1981–85 period, only 11 per cent of neonatal deaths resulted from prematurity; until the 1950s, the proportion was around 40 per cent.

CHAPTER 10

THE FUTURE OF SEX–MORTALITY DIFFERENTIALS IN INDUSTRIALIZED COUNTRIES

A Structural Hypothesis

Constance A. Nathanson and Alan D. Lopez

The relative longevity of the female sex was observed as early as 1662 (by John Graunt, cited in Lopez and Ruzicka, 1983). However, it is only in the twentieth century that sex differences in mortality have commanded sustained scientific, as well as popular, attention. As the expectation of life for persons living in industrialized countries increased overall, the significant and (until recently) widening male mortality disadvantage became increasingly salient, demanding not only explanation but intervention. The objective of this paper is to suggest an approach to predicting the future of sex–mortality differentials based on the hypothesis of social structural variations in men's and women's exposure to protection against mortality and to mortality risk.

Prediction is a hazardous undertaking, and few serious attempts have been made to predict the future of sex–mortality differentials in industrialized countries. Speculation about future trends, by and large, has been based on two premises: first, that the substantially higher male death rates relative to females observed in these countries are caused by social and environmental, not biological, factors, and, second, that they are the consequence of gender role differences in vulnerability and/or exposure to injurious life-styles (House, 1974; Lewis and Lewis, 1977; Garbus and Garbus, 1980; Verbrugge, 1980).[1] This reasoning has led to the hypothesis that changes in gender roles in the direction of increased participation by women in extrafamilial activities associated (presumably) with the adoption of 'male' life-styles will result in higher female death rates and, *ipso facto*, converging sex–mortality differentials.

There is little evidence for this hypothesis and, we would argue, considerable evidence against it (Nathanson, 1984). It has gained credence by repetition and by the lack of an alternative argument that takes equal (or better) account of known relationships among gender, life-style, and mortality. Such an alternative argument is presented in this paper. This argument has both methodological and substantive components. We will first consider some possible approaches to the question of prediction; we will then proceed to illustrate our preferred approach and to examine its implications for the future of sex–mortality differentials. A very brief review of data describing these differentials will serve to introduce this discussion.

In all developed countries, the expectation of life at birth for females exceeds that for males by 4 to 10 years. Based on average mortality levels in 35 countries, the median difference in 1975–78 was 6.4 years (Lopez, 1983). These figures reflect a steady widening of sex–mortality differentials over the course of the twentieth century, owing both to greater improvement in female relative to male death rates and to increases in male death rates relative to those of females for leading causes of death (Shryock and Siegel, 1975; Preston and Weed, 1976; Wunsch, 1980). Change over this century in the number of years' difference between life expectation for males and females in the United States is shown in Figure 1. Data are shown by race and are for the period 1900–2020. (The projected differences to the right of the vertical line are discussed below.) Between 1920 and 1970, the sex difference increased among whites by a factor of 6 and by a factor of 8 among blacks. Subsequent data (actual and projected) indicate a much slower rate of increase in the size of the differential, particularly among whites.

MORTALITY PREDICTION: ALTERNATIVE APPROACHES

One approach to predicting future change in sex–mortality differentials is to extrapolate from past experience. This approach, based on a mortality model proposed by Manton, Patrick, and Stallard (1980), was used by Olshansky (1985) to generate the sex-race-specific projections of life expectancy used in the construction of Figure 1. Olshansky's projections assume that mortality rates for selected causes (major cardiovascular diseases, diabetes, and some cancers) currently experienced by a given age-sex group are simply *delayed* for a specified number of years (5 years in the data we present). Based on these projections, we would expect a continued increase over time in the sex–mortality differential but

Figure 1: Sex difference in expectation of life at birth by race, United States, 1900–2020

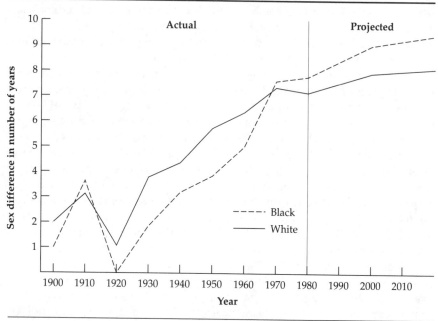

SOURCES: National Center For Health Statistics: *Vital Statistics of the United States, 1983*, Vol. II, Section 6. Life Tables, DHHS Pub. No. (PHS) 86–1104, Public Health Service (Washington, US Government Printing Office, 1986): Table 6–5; S. Jay Olshansky, 'Pursuing longevity: delay versus elimination of degenerative diseases', *American Journal of Public Health* 75 (July 1985): Table 1.

at a substantially lower rate. However, simple (or even, as in this case, sophisticated) projections from past demographic trends have proved inaccurate in the past, in large part because they were based on oversimplified conceptions of the underlying behaviour on which these trends ultimately depend. (For example, neither the 1950s baby boom nor the more recent baby bust were directly predictable from prior trends in fertility.) Ideally, prediction should be based on explanation; indeed, successful prediction is the final test of an explanatory hypothesis. By this standard, in order to predict the future of sex–mortality differentials, we would need to have the answers to at least three questions: First, what variables account for the divergence of sex–mortality rates in the past? Second, how can these explanatory variables be expected to change over time? Third, how will these latter changes differentially affect the mortality rates of males and females?

We will address these questions below. However, first we need to consider the prior and more critical question of what it is precisely that we are attempting to explain. We propose to simplify the explanatory problem on one level and to complicate it on another. First, the simplification: The major contributor to present sex–mortality differentials in industrialized countries (about 50 per cent of the difference) and to the increase in this differential over time (about 80 per cent) is ischemic heart disease (Preston, 1976; Nathanson, 1984). Accounting for sex differences in ischemic heart disease is the central explanatory problem. Second, and herein lies the complication, the *size* of the sex–mortality differential varies widely, not only over time as we have pointed out, but across developed countries: it is very large in Finland and Russia, very small in Japan (Lopez, 1983); among social class and religious groups it is inversely related to social class (see below) and almost nonexistent among Seventh-Day Adventists (Phillips et al., 1980; Berkel and de Waard, 1983); and, finally, among individuals occupying different structural positions it is smaller among married people than unmarried people (Carter and Glick, 1976).

In order to be fully explanatory, proposed causal hypotheses should be able to account for these structural variations in mortality patterns. Furthermore, the very presence of these variations suggests that stating the explanatory problem as one of accounting for sex *differences* in mortality, in so far as it directs attention toward the fact of difference rather than the size of the difference, may be misleading. A too exclusive focus on the *difference* leads to a search for causes intrinsic to the individual; by restating the problem as one of accounting for variation in the *size* of the difference, attention is directed instead to the circumstances under which this difference is greater or less.

GENDER, SOCIAL CLASS, AND MORTALITY

To illustrate the potential for further specification of the explanatory problem offered by these methodological suggestions, we present some data on observed interrelationships among gender, mortality, and social class. Figure 2 is based on data drawn from a paper by W.J. Millar, published in the *Canadian Journal of Public Health* (1983). This figure gives the number of years of life expected at birth by gender and by the income level of the census tract in which the decedent resided. These data were calculated from all deaths in 21 census metropolitan areas of Canada in 1971. It is important to point out that Millar's analysis was based on the assignment of an aggregate income level index to the individual case, not on a comparison of average income with average mortality, mitigating at least to some degree the 'ecological fallacy' problem (cf. United Nations Department of International Economic and Social Affairs, 1982).

The data in Figure 2 demonstrate two important points. First, they show that sex–mortality differences are more than one-and-one-half times larger at the lowest than at the highest income level. Second, they show that this difference is due primarily to variation in life expectation in men rather than in women. Figure 3, drawn from the same paper, shows the gender by income level gradient for mortality rates from ischemic heart disease specifically; the rates are for persons 35 to 64. Again, the size of the difference at the lowest income level is about one and one-half times that at the upper level; the gender-income level interaction effect is caused by the marked influence of income level on male mortality rates.

Measurement of social class for purposes of mortality analysis, particularly when the objective is gender comparisons, presents substantial conceptual and

Figure 2: Expectation of life at birth by income level and gender, Canada, 1971

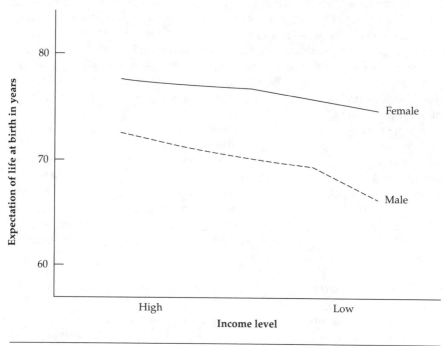

SOURCES: Millar (1983), Table III.

methodological difficulties (United Nations, 1982; Fox and Goldblatt, 1982). Criticism has focused primarily on the use of occupational indices to measure women's social class. (Difficulties are presented both by a wife's occupation and that of her husband.) Aggregate indices of socio-economic status (as employed in the Canada study) or indices where gender-comparability can be assumed more reasonably (e.g., education) are less problematic. Findings from several recently published studies based on the latter indices are consistent with the data presented in Figures 2 and 3 (Yeracaris and Kim, 1978; Valkonen and Sauli, 1981; Wingard et al., 1983). These studies (from the United States and Finland) uniformly show a larger sex difference at lower than at higher social class levels produced by a steeper social class gradient for men than for women. Studies from the United States and Scandinavian countries in which occupation was used as the social class index have had similar results (Passannante, 1983; Lynge, 1981; Koskenvuo et al., 1986).[2]

Consistent observation of the gender–social class–mortality patterns described herein is a fairly recent phenomenon. This pattern is also found in earlier data (e.g., Kitagawa, 1971; Kitagawa and Hauser, 1973; Antonovsky, 1967) but with more frequent exceptions. One reason for this apparent change may be that

Figure 3: Mortality rates for ischemic heart disease by income level and gender, Canada, 1971

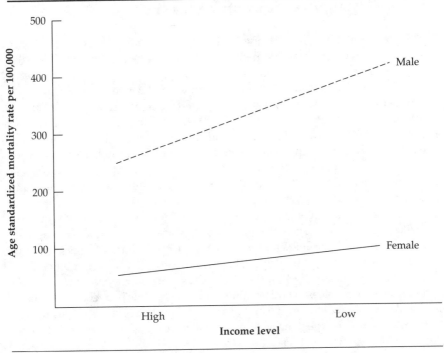

SOURCES: Millar (1983), Table VI.

social-class effects on male mortality have been increasing over time as mortality rates decline (Yeracaris and Kim, 1987; Marmot et al., 1978). A recent analysis of socio-economic status differences in mortality based on data from three cities in the United States concluded that mortality declines (e.g., in ischemic heart disease) were of differential benefit to higher social class groups, that relative increases in mortality (e.g., from cancer) had their greatest impact at the lower end of the social scale, and that both of these social-class effects were more pronounced for men than for women (Yeracaris and Kim, 1978). Parallel trends have been observed in Great Britain. Marmot et al. (1978) reported a reversal of the social-class gradient for heart disease (broadly defined) among men between 1931 and 1971. In the earlier period, upper-class men had the higher rates; by 1961, rates were higher for lower-class men in all age groups. No change was observed in the social-class gradient for women.

Our objective in this presentation of data has been to suggest that a basis exists for narrowing the broad question of sex differences in mortality to the specific question of accounting for increasingly divergent mortality rates from ischemic heart disease of blue-collar men. If we could answer the latter question, we would have gone a long way toward explaining the variance in sex–mortality differentials. With this specification in mind, we will review various hypotheses that have been advanced to account for sex differences in mortality.

EXPLANATORY HYPOTHESES

Explanatory hypotheses may be divided into three categories: biomedical, behavioural, and environmental. Biomedical research has focused primarily on the roles of genetic and hormonal factors in mortality (Waldron, 1983; Sullivan, 1983; Hazzard, 1984). Investigators in this tradition tend to assume constancy of the external environment; for example, in a recent comprehensive review of sex differences in ischemic heart disease, it was stated categorically that 'men and women are similarly exposed to dietary and environmental influences' (Sullivan, 1983: 665). The assumption of environmental constancy may not be necessary for a biological framework. Nevertheless, biological variations alone are insufficient to account for the relatively high mortality rate of blue-collar men, not only compared to women, but to higher-status men as well.

The second category, behavioural (or life-style) hypotheses, attributes the sex-mortality differential to gender-specific differences in risky behaviour (i.e., smoking, drinking, driving, and violence) or to differences in social and/or psychological stress (e.g., the Type A behaviour pattern). (These hypotheses are reviewed in Nathanson, 1984.) If these hypotheses are correct, we should expect to find sharp divergences in critical dimensions of life-style between lower-status men and both higher-status men and women irrespective of social class. Furthermore, we might also expect these differences to have increased over time. Is there any evidence for either of these effects?

The clearest evidence of social class differences in behaviour that correspond to observed gender-social class-mortality relationships is in smoking patterns. Figure 4 is based on national samples of the US population and shows the percentage of current smokers by gender and educational level for three years separated by intervals of approximately 10 years. In all three time periods, men with lower levels of education have been substantially more likely to smoke than either better-educated men or women. The difference between male and female smoking patterns within the two least well-educated categories is particularly sharp in the earliest time period, surely the most relevant for current mortality rates. By contrast, the smoking behaviour of college-educated men and women was quite similar, even in 1964, and has tended to become increasingly similar over time, due primarily to decreases in smoking by better-educated men. Recent US data in which occupation rather than education was used to index socio-economic status provide even starker evidence of the pattern we have described. These data are shown in Table 1. Percentages of current smokers among blue- and white-collar women and white-collar men are virtually identical and markedly lower than the percentage for blue-collar men, among whom 50 per cent are smokers.[3] Thus, inasmuch as life-styles as indexed by smoking behaviour are responsible for sex–mortality differentials, it is the lifestyles of blue-collar men with which we should be concerned primarily.[4]

Figure 4: Percentage current smokers by educational level and gender, United States, 1964, 1975, and 1983

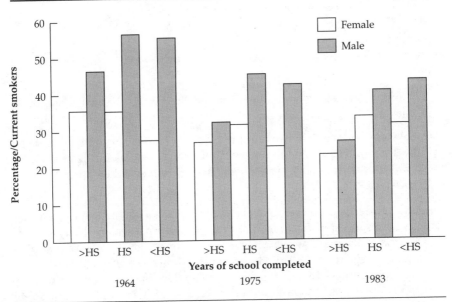

SOURCES: US Department of Health, Education, and Welfare, Washington (1979), Table 6; National Center for Health Statistics, C.A. Schoenborn and B.H. Cohen (1986), Tables 6A and 6B.

Environmental hypotheses, our third and final category of explanatory varia-bles, have focused at the macro level on the differential effects of economic modernization on men and women (Preston, 1976) and at the micro level on sex differences in access to and consequences of social ties (principally, marital sta-tus) (Gove, 1973; Kobrin and Hendershot, 1977; Helsing et al., 1981). Research on the effects of social ties on mortality generally has treated social class as a variable to be controlled rather than examined directly. However, there is enough evi-dence suggesting a social class–gender–social ties interaction effect to make the question worth pursuing.

The relevant data can be very briefly reviewed.

1. The presence of social ties has been shown prospectively to be negatively associated with mortality (Berkman and Syme, 1979; Berkman and Breslow, 1983); these data, from the Alameda County studies, are consistent with a substantial body of social research on the protective effects of social support on health and mortality (reviewed in Berkman and Breslow, 1983).

2. The presence of social ties is positively associated with social class: 'One of the best-established relationships in sociological literature is between socio-economic status and social participation' (Bradburn, 1969:123).

Table 1: Percentage current smokers by occupation and gender, US, 1976

Occupation	Male	Female
White collar	36.6	34.3
Blue collar	50.4	39.0

SOURCE: US Department of Health, Education, and Welfare (1979), Table 7.

3. Women have a greater number of close relationships than men, and these relationships appear to be more central to women's lives (Cancian, 1986).

4. Following from points two and three, it may be that sex differences in the presence (and perhaps the meaning) of social ties, as in the case of sex differences in mortality, are greater at the lower than at the upper end of the social scale.

Empirical evidence on these points is inconsistent. Field studies of blue-collar families have suggested that older blue-collar men are particularly likely to experience social isolation (Townsend, 1963; Komarovsky, 1967). Relative to white-collar men, they are more likely to be widowed, and widowhood is far more consequential for male than for female mortality (Helsing et al., 1981). However, data from other research indicate either no sex-by-social-class difference in social ties (Cancian, 1986) or one that is favourable to men (Berkman and Breslow, 1986). We would argue that this line of inquiry should be pursued actively and with careful attention to both gender and social-class differences, not only in the quantity but also in the quality and meaning of social ties.

DISCUSSION AND CONCLUSIONS

A major weakness of sociologically based environmental hypotheses has been the absence of a clear biological mechanism intervening between social structural or role effects (e.g., social ties), and mortality. Using the example of smoking behaviour, we will advance some tentative suggestions as to how biologically, behaviourally, and sociologically based explanatory models might be integrated in order to account for the relatively high mortality of blue-collar men.

Careful examination of time trends in smoking behaviour reveals a striking pattern of change over time in the *social location* of smoking. In general, cigarette consumption has declined, but these declines are most marked at higher-status levels, particularly among high-status men. Smoking among lower-status women has changed relatively little; among upper-status women, it has declined but not so markedly as among high-status men. (These observations are based on data from the United States, England, and Wales [US Department of Health, Education and Welfare, 1979; National Center for Health Statistics, 1986; Marmot et al., 1978]). Among women, the consequences of these changes reverse what was a slight positive association between social class and smoking; among men, they accentuate an existing negative association. In other words, cigarette smoking has become increasingly concentrated among blue-collar men. The behaviour changes leading to this outcome have taken place during a period of increasing public attention to the deleterious health consequences of smoking.

We present these smoking-related data to make the point that the impact that known risk factors have on behaviour varies both by gender and social class and that initiation, persistence in, and discontinuation of risky behaviours cannot be understood apart from the social context in which they occur. To account for the relatively high mortality of blue-collar men, we must investigate not only their risky life-styles but also the circumstances in which such life-styles are engendered and in which they receive social support (or, conversely, in which 'safe' life-styles fail to be supported). More generally, a complete model to explain variation in the size of the sex–mortality differential by social class would require not only that biological links be established between (to continue the smoking example) cigarette smoking and mortality (as has been done) and that behavioural links be established between gender and cigarette smoking, but also that links based in sociological theory be established between social-class structure and the gender-role dimensions that support or discourage smoking behaviour. Clearly, this general model could accommodate life-style variables other than cigarette smoking as well as social structural variables other than social class.

Finally, we return to the question of predicting the future of sex-mortality differentials. The explanatory model we have proposed would account for some portion of past differentials by reference to social structural variations in the life-styles and (possibly) the social support systems of men. Consequently, in order to establish a basis for predicting future change, we should direct our attention to the probabilities of change in male, not (as popularly believed) in female gender-roles and structural locations. This conclusion is consistent with the results of several recent studies that demonstrate that, in selected social groups with narrow sex–mortality differentials relative to those observed in the general population, reduced male mortality accounts for the difference (Phillips et al., 1980; Berkel and de Waard, 1983; Levitan and Cohen, 1985).

The analysis we have presented suggests that sex–mortality differentials in industrialized societies may converge at upper socio-economic status levels, due primarily to the presence at these levels of structural and cultural supports for relatively healthy male behaviour.[5] Convergence at lower-status levels appears much less likely. How these divergent patterns will affect cross-national variations in sex–mortality differentials is an extremely complex question. If our analysis to this point is correct, the answer would seem to depend on within-country variations in the distribution of the population by social class groups (cf. Myers, 1979) and on what are undoubtedly very large national differences in class-based cultures.

In a recent paper criticizing currently fashionable strategies for health promotion, Becker pointed out that these approaches tend 'to locate the responsibility for the cause and the cure of health problems in the *individual'* and to ignore equally important, but perhaps less readily addressed, social and economic determinants of health and disease (1986: 18, emphasis in original). The analysis we have presented underscores this point. Neither risky life-styles nor behavioural changes that would correct these life-styles are simple matters of individual 'rational' choice. Class- and gender-based differences, both in exposure to health risks and in opportunities for change, are deeply embedded in the social and economic conditions associated with these different locations in the social structure.

NOTES

[1] Biologists are in active pursuit of both genetically and hormonally based hypotheses to account for sex–mortality differentials (recently reviewed by Waldron, 1983 and Hazzard, 1984). However, we believe it is fair to say that the results achieved so far have been inconclusive (and are disputed among biologists themselves) and that biologically based hypotheses cannot account for the marked temporal, geographical, and social variations in the *size* of the differential that are considered in this paper.

[2] Social class mortality studies frequently use mortality ratios rather than rates to examine gradients by social class. This technique makes direct cross-sex comparisons impossible. However, recent studies from the United Kingdom that use this technique have reported steeper social class gradients for men than for women, suggesting that, if rate data were available, gender-social class-mortality patterns would be shown to follow the patterns we have described (Fox and Goldblatt, 1982; Logan, 1982). Similarly, data from the U.S. NHANES follow-up study show a significant effect of residence in a poverty area as compared with a nonpoverty area on survival of 65- to 69-year-old white men but no significant effect for women (Madans et al., 1986).

[3] Apparently similar trends in smoking behaviour were reported for Great Britain by Marmot et al. (1978). They noted that, between 1951 and 1971, smoking remained fairly constant in lower social class groups and decreased in the upper classes. Their data suggest that this latter change was substantially more marked among men than women, but are not presented in such a way as to make a direct comparison with US data possible.

[4] Recent epidemiologic analyses indicate that smoking may have very little impact on women's mortality from ischemic heart disease, lending further weight to the focus of this paper on the behaviour of men rather than women (Kleinman et al., 1979; Patrick et al., 1982).

[5] The precise content of this behaviour is unclear. Access to medical care is greater at upper SES levels (see e.g., Dutton, 1986). In addition, upper-status men may have greater access to improvements in medical technology and/or be more responsive to the influence of health education, and they may receive greater social support for health-promoting activities. Their 'behaviour' may be simply a matter of passive exposure to a healthier, less stressful, more supportive work and/or home environment than that experienced by lower-status men. Research has yet to address these alternative hypotheses directly.

REFERENCES

Antonovsky, A. (1967). 'Social class, life expectancy and overall mortality'. *Milbank Memorial Fund Quarterly* 45: 31–73.

Becker, M.H. (1986). 'The tyranny of health promotion', *Public Health Reviews* 14: 15–25.

Berkel, J. and F. de Waard (1983). 'Mortality pattern and life expectancy of Seventh-day Adventists in the Netherlands', *International Journal of Epidemiology* 12: 455–459.

Berkman, L.F. and S.L. Syme (1979). 'Social networks, host resistance, and mortality: a nine-year follow-up study of Alameda county residents', *American Journal of Epidemiology* 109: 186–204.

―――― and L. Breslow (1983). 'Social networks and mortality risk', *Health and Ways of Living*. New York: Oxford University Press.

Bradburn, N.M. (1969). *The Structure of Psychological Well-Being*. Chicago: Aldine.

Cancian, F. (1986). 'The feminization of love', *Signs: Journal of Women in Culture and Society* 11: 692–709.

Carter, C. and P.C. Glick (1976). *Marriage and Divorce: A Social and Economic Study*. Cambridge, MA: Harvard University Press.

Dutton, D.B. (1986). 'Social class, health, and illness', in L.H. Aiken and D. Mechanic, eds, *Applications of Social Science to Clinical Medicine and Health Policy*. New Brunswick: Rutgers University Press.

Fox, A.J. and P.O. Goldblatt (1982). *Longitudinal Study: Socioeconomic Mortality Differentials*. Office of Population Censuses and Surveys, Series LS, No. 1. London: Her Majesty's Stationery Office.

Garbus, S.B. and S.B. Garbus (1980). 'Will improvement in the socioeconomic status of women increase their cardiovascular morbidity and mortality?'. *Journal of the American Medical Women's Association* 35: 257–261.

Gove, W.R. (1973). 'Sex, marital status, and mortality', *American Journal of Sociology* 79: 45–67.

Hazzard, W.R. (1984). 'The sex differential in longevity', in R. Andres, E.L. Bierman, and W.R. Hazzard, eds., *Principles of Geriatric Medicine*. New York: McGraw-Hill.

Helsing, K.J., M. Szklo, and G.W. Comstock (1981). 'Factors associated with mortality after widowhood', *American Journal of Public Health* 71: 802–809.

House, J.S. (1974). 'Occupational stress and coronary heart disease: a review and theoretical integration', *Journal of Health and Social Behavior* 15: 12–27.

Kitagawa, E.M. (1971). 'Social and economic differentials in mortality in the United States, 1960', in *International Population Conference, London, 1969*. Liege.

―――― and P.M. Hauser (1973). *Differential Mortality in the United States: A Study in Socioeconomic Epidemiology*. Cambridge, Massachusetts: Harvard University Press.

Kleinman, J.C., J.J. Feldman, and M.A. Monk (1979). 'The effects of changes in smoking habits on coronary heart disease mortality', *American Journal of Public Health* 69: 795–802.

Komarovsky, M. (1967). *Blue-Collar Marriage*. New York: Vintage Books.

Kobrin, F.E. and G.E. Hendershot (1977). 'Do family ties reduce mortality? Evidence from the United States, 1966–1968'. *Journal of Marriage and the Family* 39: 737–745.

Koskenvuo, M., J. Kaprio, J. Lonnqvist, and S. Sarna (1986). 'Social factors and the gender difference in mortality', *Social Science and Medicine* 23: 605–609.

Levitan, U. and J. Cohen (1985). 'Gender differences in life expectancy among kibbutz members', *Social Science and Medicine* 21: 545–551.

Lewis, C.E. and R.M. Lewis (1977). 'The potential impact of sexual equality on health', *New England Journal of Medicine* 297: 863–869.

Logan, W.P.D. (1982). *Cancer Mortality by Occupation and Social Class, 1851–1971*. IARC Scientific Publications No. 36/Studies in Medical and Population Subjects No. 44. London: Her Majesty's Stationery Office/ Lyon: International Agency for Research on Cancer. (Joint Publication).

Lopez, A.D. (1983). 'The sex–mortality differential in developed countries', in A.D. Lopez and L. T. Ruzicka, eds., *Sex Differentials in Mortality*. Canberra: Australian National University Press.

Lynge, E. (1981). 'Occupational mortality in Norway, Denmark, and Finland', in *Socioeconomic Differential Mortality in Industrialized Societies*. Vol. 1. United Nations Population Division (New York/World Health Organization (Geneva)/Committee for International Cooperation in National Research in Demography (Paris).

Madans, J.H. et al. (1986). 'Ten years after NHANES I: Mortality experience at initial followup, 1982–84', *Public Health Reports* 101: 474–481.

Manton, K.G., C.H. Patrick, and E. Stallard (1980). 'Mortality model based on delays in progression of chronic diseases: Alternative to cause elimination model', *Public Health Reports* 95: 580–588.

Marmot, M.G., A.M. Adelstein, N. Robinson, and G.A. Rose (1978). 'Changing social class distribution of heart disease', *British Medical Journal* 2: 1109–1112.

Millar, W.H. (1983). 'Sex differences in mortality by income level in urban Canada', *Canadian Journal of Public Health* 74: 329–334.

Myers, G.C. (1979). 'Comments'. Proceedings of the meeting on socioeconomic determinants and consequences of mortality (Mexico City, June 19–24, 1979). Geneva: World Health Organization, 1979.

Nathanson, C.A. (1984). 'Sex Differences in Mortality', *Annual Review of Sociology* 10: 191–213.

National Center for Health Statistics, C.A. Schoenborn and B.H. Cohen (1986). 'Trends in smoking, alcohol consumption and other health practices among U.S. adults, 1977 and 1983'. *Advance Data From Vital and Health Statistics*. No. 118 (Supplement). DHHS Pub. No (PHS) 86–1250. Public Health Service: Hyattsville, Md.

Olshansky, S.J. (1985). 'Pursuing longevity: Delay vs. elimination of degenerative diseases', *American Journal of Public Health* 75: 754–757.

Passannante, M. (1983). *Female Labor Force Participation and Mortality*. Ph.D. Dissertation, Johns Hopkins University, Baltimore, Maryland.

Patrick, C.H., Y.Y. Palesch, M. Feinleib, and J.A. Brody (1982). 'Sex differences in declining cohort death rates from heart disease', *American Journal of Public Health* 72: 161–166.

Phillips, R.L., J.W. Kuzma, W.L. Beeson, and T. Lotz (1980). 'Influence of selection versus lifestyle on risk of fatal cancer and cardiovascular disease among Seventh-day Adventists', *American Journal of Epidemiology* 112: 296–314.

Preston, S.H. (1976). *Mortality Patterns in National Populations with Special Reference to Recorded Causes of Death*. New York: Academic Press.

—— and J.A. Weed (1976). 'Causes of death responsible for international and intertemporal variations in sex–mortality differentials', *World Health Statistics Report* 29: 144–214.

Shryock, H.S. and J.S. Siegel (1975). *The Methods and Materials of Demography*. Vol. 2. Revised Edition. Washington, D.C.: Bureau of the Census, U.S. Department of Commerce.

Sullivan, J.L. (1983). 'The sex difference in ischemic heart disease', *Perspectives in Biology and Medicine* 26: 657–671.

Townsend, P. (1983). *The Family Life of Old People*. Penguin Books.

United Nations Department of International Economic and Social Affairs (1982). *Levels and Trends of Mortality Since 1950*. (ST/ESA/SER/A/7). New York: United Nations.

U.S. Department of Health, Education, and Welfare (1979). *Smoking and Health: A Report of the Surgeon General.* DHEW Publication No. (PHS) 79–50066. Washington, D.C.

Valkonen, T. and H. Sauli (1981). 'Socioeconomic differential mortality in Finland', in *Socioeconomic Differential Mortality in Industrialized Societies.* Vol.1. United Nations Population Division (New York) World Health Organization (Geneva)/Committee for International Cooperation in National Research in Demography (Paris).

Verbrugge, L.M. (1980). 'Recent trends in sex–mortality differentials in the United States', *Women and Health* 5: 17–37.

Waldron, I. (1983). 'The role of genetic and biological factors in sex differences in mortality', in A.D. Lopez and L.T. Ruzicka, eds., *Sex Differentials in Mortality.* Canberra: Australian National University Press.

Wingard, D.L., L. Suarez, and E. Barrett-Conner (1983). 'The sex differential in mortality from all causes and ischemic heart disease', *American Journal of Epidemiology* 117: 165–172.

Wunsch, G. (1980). 'Sex differentials and cause of death in some European countries', in R.W. Hiorns, ed., *Demographic Patterns in Developed Societies.* London: Taylor and Francis.

Yeracaris, C.A. and J.H. Kim (1978). 'Socioeconomic differentials in selected causes of death', *American Journal of Public Health* 68: 342–351.

CHAPTER 11

INDIAN
MORTALITY

Ellen Bobet

In recent years, death rates among North American Indian people in Canada have dropped dramatically. Despite this decline, mortality rates among Indians continue to exceed those of the total population by a wide margin.

Compared with Canadians in general, Indian people are much more likely to die from accidents or violence, including suicide, and from respiratory conditions. They are less likely to die of cancer, while death rates from diseases of the circulatory system are about the same in the Indian and total Canadian populations.

Indian Mortality Data

Data on Indian mortality are provided by regional offices of the Medical Services Branch of Health and Welfare Canada. The information refers only to Status Indians living on reserves. Data collection procedures vary from one region to another.

In the Atlantic provinces, mortality data are provided by Medical Services Branch field personnel, that is, the nurse who serves a particular reserve. Thus, these data pertain only to the on-reserve population. However, in the Atlantic region, Branch personnel visit every reserve, so all reserves are covered.

In Quebec, Indian mortality data include only communities where the Branch has field personnel. In fact, because the Branch does not have employees in a number of settlements, data are lacking for more than half the Indian population of Quebec.

Ontario data collection procedures are the same as in the Atlantic provinces and Quebec. However, figures are not available for 12 communities representing approximately 5 per cent of Ontario's total on-reserve population.

Before 1985, Indian mortality data for British Columbia, covering all Status Indians in the province, were obtained from the provincial government. For human rights reasons, this practice was discontinued in 1985. Consequently, Indian mortality figures for 1985 and 1986 exclude British Columbia.

In the other provinces, information on Indian mortality comes from provincial data systems. Therefore, data pertain to all Status Indians in these jurisdictions.

Death Rate Down

The death rate among Indian people has fallen in recent years, although it remains above the national level. The age-standardized mortality rate among Indians was 9.0 per 1,000 population in 1986, a drop from 11.8 in 1978. Even so, the 1986 figure for Indian people was still about one-and-a-half times the national rate (6.6).

The difference in death rates is particularly pronounced among people under age 35. During the 1983–86 period, for example, Indian death rates were at least three times greater than those for all Canadians in this age range.

By contrast, after age 50, Indian death rates are closer to national levels. For instance, at ages 50–54, the rate among Indians was 956 deaths per 100,000 population, compared with 536 for all Canadians; at ages 70–74, the figures were 3,868 for Indians and 3,282 for the total population.

Infant Mortality Rate Down

Infant mortality rates have declined among both Indians and all Canadians during the past quarter century. But while infant mortality has fallen more rapidly for Indians than for non-Indians, the Indian rate remains substantially above the national level.

In 1986, the Indian infant mortality rate was 17.2 deaths per 1,000 live births, down from 79.0 in 1960 (See Figure 1). The 1986 figure for Indians, though, was still more than twice that for all Canada (7.9).

Much of this difference between Indian and national infant mortality rates is attributable to deaths after the first month of life (post-neonatal). In fact, for the period around birth (neonatal), Indian death rates are fairly close to the national average.

Figure 1: Infant mortality rates for indians and total population, 1960–1986

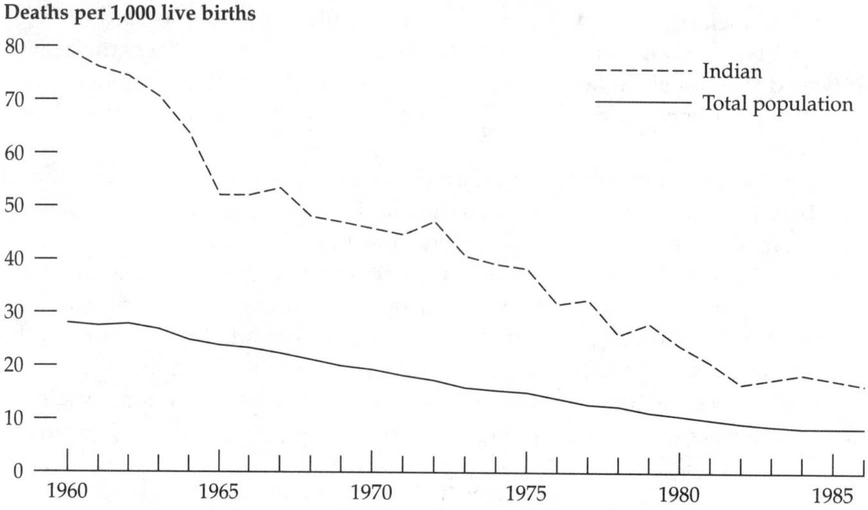

Deaths per 1,000 live births

SOURCES: Statistics Canada, Cat. 84–206, and Health and Welfare Canada, Medical Services Branch.

The Indian neonatal mortality rate averaged 6.9 deaths per 1,000 live births during the 1982–85 period, only 28 per cent higher than the national average (5.4). The post-neonatal death rate among Indians, however, was almost four times the overall Canadian level: 11.0 deaths versus 3.0 deaths per 1,000 live births. During the same period, there were an average of 12.1 stillbirths for every 1,000 live births among Indian women, compared with 4.7 for all Canada.

More Indians Victims of Accidents and Violence

Indian people are far more likely to die as a result of accidents or violence than are Canadians in general (see Figure 2). Accidents and violence accounted for 32 per cent of all Indian deaths reported over the 1978–86 period, compared with just 8 per cent of those in the total population.

Nonetheless, the incidence of accidental deaths among Indian people has declined in recent years. The age-standardized Indian death rate from this cause fell 45 per cent, from 321 per 100,000 population in 1978 to 175 in 1986. Meanwhile, the accidental death rate for the whole population declined 25 per cent, from 69 to 52 per 100,000 people.

About a third of all accidental Indian deaths result from motor vehicle mishaps, while shootings and drownings each account for 10 per cent. The remaining accidental deaths are attributable to a variety of other causes, such as house fires, exposure, and drug overdoses.

Figure 2: Age-standardized death rates for Indians and total population, by cause, 1983-1986 average

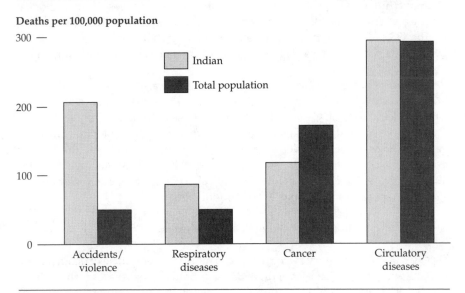

Deaths per 100,000 population

SOURCE: Health and Welfare Canada, Medical Services Branch.

Accidental deaths are highest among Indian men. During the 1983–86 period, there were 378 accidental deaths for every 100,000 Indian men aged 15 and over. This contrasts with a rate of 95 for all Canadian men.

Indian women and children are at a much lower risk of being killed in an accident. The accidental death rate among Indian women aged 15 and older averaged 128 per 100,000 population during the years 1983–86. This level, however, was still over three times the rate for Canadian women in general.

Accidental death rates among Indian children were also relatively low. For example, there were an average of 31 accidental deaths for every 100,000 Indian children aged 5–9 during the 1983–86 period; for those aged 10–14, the figure was 45. Again, these rates were well above those for all Canadian children. In the general population, there were just 12 accidental deaths for every 100,000 5–9-year-olds, and 14 for 10–14-year-olds.

High Suicide Rate

Suicide rates in the Indian population are more than twice the national level. During the 1983–86 period, the suicide rate among Indians averaged 34 per 100,000 population, compared with an average of 14 for all Canada over the years 1983–85.

As is the case for the total population, Indian suicide rates are generally much higher among men than women. Indian men and women differ, however, in the age at which they tend to commit suicide.

Among Indian men, suicide rates are extremely high at ages 15–29, but fall at older ages. The highest Indian suicide rate occurs among men aged 20–24. During the 1983–86 period, the average rate for Indian men in this age group was 171 per 100,000 population, more than five times the rate for all Canadian men the same age.

Suicide rates among Indian men, however, decline at successively older ages, in sharp contrast to the trend for Canadian men overall. In fact, after age 55, suicide rates among all Canadian men exceed those of Indian men.

On the other hand, suicide rates for both Indian and all Canadian women are generally higher among older age groups. For the years 1983–86, the highest average suicide rate for Indian women was 29 per 100,000 population at ages 45–49. The suicide rate for all Canadian women also peaked at ages 45–49, but their 1983–85 average was just 11 per 100,000 population.

Diseases of the Respiratory System

Diseases of the respiratory system are also a more frequent cause of death among Indians than non-Indians. Over the 1983–86 period, these diseases resulted in an average of 88 deaths per 100,000 population among Indians, compared with 51 for Canada overall. Furthermore, unlike many other major causes of death, there is no indication that deaths from respiratory diseases are decreasing in either the Indian or the total Canadian population.

Respiratory ailments are a major cause of death of Indian infants and Native people aged 55 and over. As well, they are generally a more serious problem for men than for women, a pattern similar to that in the total population.

Lower Cancer Death Rate

Indian people are generally less likely than other Canadians to die from cancer. During the 1983–86 period, the age-standardized Indian death rate from cancer averaged 118 per 100,000 population, compared with 172 for all Canada.

The lower cancer mortality rate, however, held only for Indian men, as rates for Indian women age 25–44 were not significantly below the national average for women in this age range.

Diseases of the Circulatory System

Indian people are about as likely as other Canadians to die from diseases of the circulatory system. Over the 1983–86 period, age-standardized death rates for these diseases were 294 per 100,000 population for Indians and 291 for the total Canadian population. Since 1978, death rates from this cause have declined by almost a third for both groups.

Health Problems in Indian Communities

Records of visits to nursing stations operated by the Medical Services Branch of Health and Welfare Canada in seven isolated Indian settlements in Quebec indicate that respiratory conditions, ear/nose/throat diseases, and skin problems were the main reasons residents sought health care. Other frequent health problems for Indians resulted from accidents and digestive diseases.

Relative to their share of the population, infants accounted for a large proportion of all Indian visits to medical facilities. By contrast, those aged 15–24 were less likely than other age groups to visit the nurse.

Data for Saskatchewan present a picture basically consistent with the Quebec findings. In 1987, the most common reasons Indian people required hospital care, aside from childbirth, were respiratory conditions, diseases of the digestive system, and injuries. Hospital separation rates for Indian people were at least double the provincial average at all ages, with Indian children under age 5 four to eight times as likely as non-Indian children to be hospitalized.

Information on chronic diseases among Indian people in the Western provinces suggests that diabetes is a serious problem and that tuberculosis rates continue to exceed the Canadian average by a wide margin.

Data for on-reserve Indians in Saskatchewan, Alberta, and British Columbia show that diabetes was the most frequently reported chronic condition, with rates ranging from 6.2 to 11.9 per 1,000 population.

Although tuberculosis rates among Indian people have been falling, this trend seems to have slowed recently, and there have been outbreaks in some areas. Also, rates of tuberculosis among Indian people remain far higher than among non-Indians. For instance, in 1986, the rate of new active cases among Saskatchewan Indians was 125 per 100,000 population, compared with just 6 for the province as a whole.

Table 1: Summary of health-related conditions in indian communities

---

Location

- 15 per cent of households are on reserves more than 50 km from the nearest large town; 36 per cent are on reserves within 50 km of a major town.
- the other 49 per cent of households are off-reserve, often in large cities.

Water supply

- many communities have several systems.
- about 3/4 of communities have individual or community wells.
- in about half of communities, at least some houses use a piped system.
- in almost 1/4 of communities, some or all residents rely on 'self-haul' methods.

Continued p. 162

Table 1: (continued)

Sewage

– most communities use a septic disposal system or equivalent.
– about 22 per cent of communities have a piped system with treatment.
– a substantial proportion use pit privies or leaching pits.
– 32 per cent of on-reserve households have no indoor bathroom.

Emergency medical evacuation

– in half of communities, patients can be evacuated to hospital in 30 minutes or less; in 5 per cent of communities, medical evacuations can take 3 hours or more.
– most (74 per cent) communities can evacuate patients by road; the rest require some combination of road, water, or air transport.

Community services

– 14 per cent of communities have ambulance service.
– 42 per cent of communities have a childcare worker.

PART FOUR

FERTILITY

AND FAMILY

PLANNING

DETERMINANTS OF HUMAN FERTILITY

Fertility is both an individual issue (involving personal norms, values, and goals) and a collective one (relating to economic conditions and even to societal survival). Trends in fertility affect nearly all of the institutional and organizational systems of society. The fertility level of a society reflects the effects of its economic, educational, social, and political institutions. In particular, the role and status of women in society are closely related to the numbers, timing, and spacing of childbearing. The number of children born to any given group of people, the pattern of that childbearing, and the changes in the pattern can tell us a great deal about the basic organization of the social group.

The complex nature of reproductive behaviour and the large number of factors associated with it have led to numerous attempts to develop a framework that could encompass all the variables necessary to explain fertility. In general, the determinants of fertility can be classified as follows: (1) socio-economic structural variables, (2) demographic and biological factors, (3) psychological factors, and (4) contraceptive factors.

Of major importance for social demographers are the structural factors, including stratification variables such as occupation, income, and education; family structural variables such as divorce and late marriage; non-familial institutions such as religion and the media; and other characteristics pertaining to the social and economic organization of the society. Then there are what have been called the 'intermediate variables' having to do with social organization and norms. These include such factors as age at entry into unions; extent of celibacy and periods of exposure to risk; contraceptive use; extent of fecundity, or, conversely, sterility; and the practice of abortion. Together, these intermediate or proximate variables determine the actual reproductive level of any social group. Sociologists dealing with census and vital statistics data and with sample surveys have concentrated on the relationship between structural and demographic variables and fertility. Characteristics such as religion, ethnicity, residence, educational and income attainment, labour-force participation, age at marriage, age at first birth, divorce, remarriage, and abortion have all been shown to be important variables in the study of fertility patterns in Canada.

At present, Canadian fertility rates are at their lowest levels in history (i.e., below replacement). Yet there is substantial evidence that almost all women want to have children at some point in their lives — usually more than one, but seldom more than two or three. Whereas in the 1950s and 1960s most women began childbearing in their early twenties, over the past generation there has been a definite trend towards delaying the start of childbearing until after the age of 30. While it may seem somewhat at odds with our fertility trends, Canada remains a strongly pro-fertility society if that norm is defined in terms of wanting children in the family: it is only the size of the family that has been reduced. If the appropriate societal supports are in place today (day-care, employment equity, parental leave), it is most likely that even more women who have avoided childbearing in their twenties will begin having children in their thirties. If enough incentive is given, we might even see slight increases at the younger ages. It is also likely that the average number of children for married women will be very close to two, and it is unlikely to be much higher for the near future.

An important proximate determinant of fertility is contraceptive use; sophistication in family planning is one of the major predictors of overall levels of childbearing. In the early 1990s, over 80 per cent of Canadian women in the childbearing ages have used some form of contraception; the figures vary with age, marital status, and sexual activity. We are primarily a bimodal society in terms of contraceptive use: the birth-control pill is widely used by women under the age of 30, while sterilization predominates for older women (although the threat of AIDS has made the condom more appealing in recent years). Overall, about 75 per cent of young women have used the oral contraceptive, while approximately 72 per cent of older women (or their partners) have employed sterilization.

Even though Canadian women are effective users of contraception, many accidental pregnancies still occur, as evidenced by the more than 65,000 therapeutic abortions performed in this country annually in the 1990s. Abortion is a very contentious issue, often drawing pro-choice and pro-life advocates into political and even physical confrontation. But as long as there are failures in the family-planning system, with some women lacking access, knowledge, or interest in effective, reliable, safe, and inexpensive contraception, some may choose an alternative that is not really favoured from any point of view.

The articles in this section bear to some degree on all of the issues raised above. Grindstaff ('The Baby Bust Revisited') documents the continuing low levels of Canadian fertility and suggests that the trend is likely to continue in the future. The widespread use of contraception and the changing role of women in Canadian society receive particular attention in this discussion, which centres around the importance of choice for women in the context of enhanced role opportunities outside of marriage and childbearing. In 'Canadian Fertility Trends: A Further Test of the Easterlin Hypothesis', Wright and Maxim examine the thesis, advanced by Richard Easterlin (see pp. 16–17 above), that the fertility rate of a cohort is inversely related to the relative size of that cohort. That is, small cohorts of women will have relatively large numbers of children (because of economic and social perceptions among members of the cohort) and large cohorts will have relatively few (because of changing economic prospects and social perceptions among members of the cohort). For Canada, however, the authors find that the data do not support the Easterlin hypothesis: in fact, larger cohorts showed higher fertility than did smaller ones. Controlling for age and period effects, the authors argue that in Canada cohort size has no relationship to fertility.

Balakrishnan and colleagues provide a detailed analysis of 'Contraceptive Use in Canada', based on their 1984 Canadian Fertility Survey. Over 80 per cent of all adult women, both married and single, reported having used birth control at some point in their lives. However, the pill is a method employed primarily by younger women: among contraceptive users between the ages of 18 and 24, over 75 per cent were using the pill, while among women aged 30–34, only 17 per cent used it. The contraceptive of choice among women over 30 in Canada is sterilization. A vast majority (72 per cent) of all women between the ages of 35 and 39 practising some form of birth control used sterilization as their means for preventing pregnancy. It is estimated that more than half of Canadian women (or their partners) who have two or more children are sterilized, giving Canada one of the highest sterilization rates in the world—one-third higher than that of the United States, for instance.

One of the age groups in which fertility is most problematic is among Canadian adolescents. When a teenage girl gets pregnant, her life script is written, and most of it is bad: in general, teenage mothers face poor socio-economic prospects throughout their lives. Wadhera and Silins document 'Teenage Pregnancy in Canada, 1975–1987' and find that, overall, both pregnancy and fertility rates among teenage Canadians have shown decreases, corresponding to increases in the average age at marriage and the general decrease in Canadian fertility. Numbers of pregnancies among teenagers declined by over 20,000 in the period under study, and the teenage fertility rate fell by over 60 per cent from its peak in the early 1960s. Much of the decrease is attributable to delays in age at marriage and family formation, along with abortion availability and sexuality/contraception information.

In the concluding article in this section, 'Fertility in Canada: Retrospective and Prospective', Romaniuc traces the broad secular (long-term) pattern of fertility decline in Canada. He indicates that although there are signs of an upward shift in fertility, in the long run the historical developments associated with the secular decline will continue their downward pressures on fertility. This prediction does not seem unreasonable, since in a long-range perspective, only low fertility is compatible with the low mortality conditions of contemporary advanced societies.

TECHNICAL NOTES

Fertility is somewhat more difficult to measure than mortality. Only women can have children (although, with few exceptions, men are generally a necessary ingredient). While death occurs only once, fertility is a renewable process; a woman can have more than one child in her lifetime and she can give birth to multiple children at the same time. Most measures of fertility focus on the women and the frequency of births in a population at some point in time: usually the time is a year, and these measures are called calendar year rates. However, there are a few measures that examine fertility in a longer time frame, usually at the end of an interval or even at the end of the reproductive years. These are called cohort rates.

1. The crude birth rate (CBR) is the simplest measure of fertility; it is defined as a ratio of any particular year's total registered births to the total mid-year population within the same geographical area. It is called 'crude' because it does not take age or gender into account: thus the denominator includes many people — children, women over 55, men — who cannot have a child. It is useful as a first impression of a population (it is often the rate cited in the popular press) and it is easy to calculate. In Canada in the nineteenth century, the crude birth rate was close to 50 births per 1,000 people, one of the highest recorded anywhere in the Western world. In the 1990s, the rate is approximately 15, and it has been so for the past generation. Such a low crude birth rate is indicative of an advanced industrial society.

2. The age-specific birth rate (ASBR) is defined as the number of births to women of a particular age, say twenty-one, or, more likely, an age range (e.g., 20 to 24), divided by all of the women of that age (sometimes restricted to the married women, since about 80 per cent of the children born in Canada are born to married women). This measure allows for an examination of the different magnitudes of childbearing by the various age groups capable of having babies. During the baby-boom period of Canadian history, the age group 20–24 had the highest rates, but into the 1990s women aged 25–29 were having the most children on average, and rates for those 30–34 were higher than for the 20–24 group. This reflects the different timing pattern of childbearing over the past couple of generations.

3. When all of the age-specific birth rates are added together for a calendar year, we have the total fertility rate (TFR). Representing the number of children a woman would have during her lifetime if she were to experience the fertility rates of the period at each age, the TFR is really a snapshot at a particular time of all the fertility currently taking place. The total fertility rate can vary in fairly wide swings because women often time and space the birth of their children in response to social and economic needs and pressures. In Canada over the past 15 years, the total fertility rate has been below replacement (the term used when the population does not reproduce itself), with rates below 2 — as low as 1.65 in the 1980s. The 1990s has witnessed a slight increase to 1.83, but it is too early to know if this is a significant trend upward or a temporary blip reflecting increased numbers of older women who have delayed childbearing and are now catching up.

4. Cohort completed fertility can be calculated in terms of the number of children women have had up to a particular age and at any age in the reproductive cycle; it is usually determined after the women have completed their childbearing, which in our society is by age 40 or 45. Actually, over 95 per cent of all women in Canada complete their fertility by their late thirties. This is one measure that does not refer to any annual period of time; rather, it refers to the completed family, achieved over the total childbearing years (about 30). It is one of the best measures

because the influence of timing and spacing is removed. A major difficulty is that one must wait a long time before getting the completed picture. For the cohort of women born in 1946–51, whose fertility would have been officially completed in 1990, the cohort completed fertility rate was 2.03, or just about at replacement levels. Overall, with the transitory exception of the 1950s (the baby-boom period), both total fertility and cohort fertility in Canada, as in most of the rest of the developed world, have been declining for more than a century.

SUGGESTED READING

Balakrishnan, T.R., G.E. Ebanks, and C.F. Grindstaff (1979). *Patterns of Fertility in Canada, 1971*. Ottawa: Statistics Canada. Cat. 99–759.

————, J.F. Kantner, and J.D. Allingham (1975). *Fertility and Family Planning in a Canadian Metropolis*. Montreal and London: McGill Queen's University Press.

————, E. Lapierre-Adamcyk, and K.J. Krótki (1993). *Family and Childbearing in Canada*. Toronto: University of Toronto Press.

Bongaarts, John (1982). 'Fertility determinants: 1. Proximate determinants'. Pp. 225–79 in J. Ross, ed., *International Encyclopedia of Population*, vol. 1. New York: Free Press.

———— (1983). 'A framework for analyzing the proximate determinants of fertility'. *Population and Development Review* 4, 1: 105–32.

Caldwell, John C. (1976). 'Toward a restatement of the demographic transition theory'. *Population and Development Review* 2, 3–4: 321–66.

Davis, Kingsley (1984). 'Wives and work: The sex role revolution'. *Population and Development Review* 10, 3: 397–417.

————, M.S. Bernstam and R. Ricardo-Campbell, eds (1986). *Below Replacement Fertility in Industrialized Societies: Causes, Consequences, Policies*. Supplement to *Population and Development Review* 12.

Easterlin, Richard (1978). 'What will 1984 be like? Socioeconomic implications of recent twists in age structure'. *Demography* 15, 4: 397–432.

Grindstaff, Carl F., T.R. Balakrishnan, and David J. Dewit (1992). 'Educational attainment, age at first birth and lifetime fertility: An analysis of Canadian fertility survey data'. *Canadian Review of Sociology and Anthropology* 28, 3: 324–39.

Henripin, Jacques (1972). *Trends and Factors of Fertility in Canada*. Ottawa: Information Canada.

Hyatt, Douglas E., and William J. Milne (1991). 'Can public policy affect fertility?'. *Canadian Public Policy* 27, 1: 77–85.

Keyfitz, Nathan (1986). 'The family that does not reproduce itself'. Pp. 139–154 in Davis, Bernstam, and Ricardo-Campbell (1986).

McDaniel, Susan (1984). 'Explaining Canadian fertility: Some remaining challenges'. *Canadian Studies in Population* 11, 10): 1–16.

Needleman, Lionel (1986). 'Canadian fertility trends in perspective'. *Journal of Biosocial Science* 18: 43–56.

Romaniuc, Anatole (1984). *Fertility in Canada: From baby-boom to baby-bust*. Ottawa: Statistics Canada. Cat. 91–524E.

Ryder, Norman (1979). 'The future of American fertility'. *Social Forces* 26, 3: 359–70.

Trovato, Frank, and David Odynak (1993). 'The seasonality of births in Canada and the provinces, 1881–1986: Theory and analysis'. *Canadian Studies in Population* 21, 1: 1–41.

Weinfield, Morton (1990). 'The politics of the birth rate'. *Policy Options* 11, 3: 24–6.

CHAPTER 12

THE BABY BUST REVISITED

Canada's Continuing Pattern of Low Fertility

Carl F. Grindstaff

INTRODUCTION

In an article published in 1975 in Canadian Studies in Population, I documented the low levels of fertility in Canada and argued that these trends in childbearing would continue through the 1970s and into the 1980s (Grindstaff, 1975). It was shown that the decline in fertility during the 1960s and early 1970s came about even though there had been a substantial increase in the number of women in the childbearing ages. In addition, increasing levels of childlessness were documented and it was estimated that by the census year 2001, about 20 per cent of the ever-married women in Canada age 30–34 would be childless. That figure is more than double the rate observed in 1971. It was indicated that these historically low levels of reproduction were associated with both technology (improvements and innovations in contraception) and social norms and values (changes in role opportunities for women).

Table 1:   Crude birth rates and total fertility rates, Canada, 1921–1982

Year	Crude birth rates	Total fertility rates	Year	Crude birth rates	Total fertility rates
1921	29.3	3.53[1]	1970	17.4	2.33
1926	24.7	3.36	1971	16.8	2.19
1931	23.2	3.20	1972	15.9	2.02
1936	20.3	2.70	1973	15.5	1.93
1941	22.4	2.83	1974	15.6	1.88
1946	27.2	3.37	1975	15.8	1.85
1951	27.2	3.50	1976	15.7	1.83
1956	28.0	3.86	1977	15.5	1.81
1961	26.1	3.84	1978	15.3	1.76
1966	19.4	2.81	1979	15.5	1.76
1967	18.2	2.60	1980	15.5	1.75
1968	17.6	2.45	1981	15.3	1.70
1969	17.6	2.41	1982	15.1	1.69

[1] Excluding Quebec.

SOURCE: Statistics Canada, *Vital Statistics*: 1975 and 1976: Vol. 1, *Births*, Tables 1 and 6; 1978: Vol. 1, *Births and Deaths*, Tables 1 and 4; 1980: Vol. 1, *Births and Deaths*, Tables 1 and 5; 1982: Vol. 1, *Births and Deaths*, Tables 1 and 5.

FINDINGS

The purpose of this research is to update the information presented in the 1975 article in terms of crude birth rate, total fertility rate, live births and childlessness. The data used in that article were based on fertility figures in Canada as of 1971. This present presentation provides the fertility trends and patterns into the early 1980s. Table 1 shows that the crude birth rate has been reasonably stable throughout the 1970s and into the 1980s. While the rate of 15.1 observed in 1982 is the lowest point in Canadian history, the range in the past 10 years has been between 15 and 16 births per 1,000 people in the population.

The total fertility rate, which takes the age structure of the women into account, continued to decline throughout the 1970s to reach points below the levels necessary for replacement fertility. In 1982—the last available vital statistics year—the total fertility rate of 1.69 placed Canadian reproductive behaviour approximately 20 per cent under that rate which is necessary for population replacement over a period of time. Clearly, low fertility has been here to stay, at least for the past decade or more in this country.

Table 2 shows that the number of children born over the decade had stabilized at an average of about 360,000 birth per year, but at the same time, the women in the prime childbearing ages (20 to 30) had increased by more than 30 per cent. Once more, these data are an indication that while the numbers of births have stabilized, the rates of fertility have continued to decline in a small but linear fashion throughout the 1970s and into the 1980s.

Table 2:   Number of live births, children aged 0-4, and women aged 15-34,
Canada, 1961, 1971, and 1981

	1961	1971	Percentage Increase (Decrease) 1961 to 1971	1981	Percentage Increase (Decrease) 1971 to 1981
Live births	475,700	362,187	(−19.5)	371,346	+ 2.5
Children 0–4	2,256,401	1,816,155	(−23.9)	1,783,375	(−1.9)
Women 15–34	2,522,834	3,415,500	+35.4	4,412,695	+29.0
15–19	703,524	1,039,915	+47.8	1,132,875	+ 8.9
20–24	596,507	947,625	+58.9	1,169,520	+23.4
25–29	595,400	783,410	+31.6	1,093,200	+39.6
30–34	627,403	644,550	+ 2.7	1,017,100	+57.9

SOURCES: Dominion Bureau of Statistics (1962), *1961 Census of Canada, Population: Age Groups*, Vol. 1, Bulletin 1.2–3 (Ottawa: Queen's Printer); Statistics Canada (1973), *1971 Census of Canada, Population: Single Years of Age*, Vol. 1, Bulletin 1.2–4. (Ottawa: Information Canada); Statistics Canada (1983), *1981 Census of Canada, Population: Age, Sex and Marital Status*, Vol. 1, Cat. 92–901 (Ottawa: Minister of Supply and Services), p. 1.

There is some indication that the low rates of childbearing by women in the prime reproductive ages will be elevated when these same women reach the age of 30 or older (Digest, 1983). In a sense, it is argued that these women will 'catch up' with fertility that has been postponed. Indeed, women aged 30 and over were more likely to be starting a family in 1981 than they were in 1971. That is, for ever-married women aged 30–34 in Canada in 1981, one baby in four was a first-born child compared to one baby in eight for this age group in 1971 (Grindstaff, 1984). However, the actual age specific *rate* of childbearing for women aged 30–34 decreased from 77.3 per 1,000 in 1971 to 68.0 per 1,000 in 1981 (Statistics Canada, 1983a). Again, contrary to some expectations, the actual fertility of these women has declined over the past 10 years or more. The cohort data show much the same trends. In examining a group that has by and large finished its fertility, the number of children ever born to ever-married women 35–39 years of age decreased from 3.16 in 1971 to 2.33 in 1981 (Statistics Canada, 1983).

Table 3 provides evidence that childlessness continues to increase for ever-married women of all age groups except those 40–44, who were in the prime child-bearing ages toward the end of the baby boom. Overall, childlessness rates went up among all women age 15–44, but the largest increases have taken place in the 25–34 age group. Approximately 30 per cent of all ever-married women 25–29 in 1981 had no children, an increase of 45 per cent from the previous decade. Over 14 per cent of women aged 30–34 were childless in 1981, a 50 per cent increase over 1971. In the 'Baby Bust' article of 1975, it was predicted that by the year 2001, fully 20 per cent of women in this age group would be without children (Grindstaff, 1975). It would appear that this outcome is on schedule. Even adolescent fertility has been decreasing, with the number of babies born to teenagers in Canada down to 29,330 in 1981

Table 3: Percentage childless among women ever married, 15–44 years of age, Canada, 1961, 1971, and 1981

	Percentage childless			Percentage increase (decrease) In childlessness	
	1961	1971	1981	1961 to 1971	1971 to 1981
15–44	13.5	18.1	22.7	34.1	25.4
15–19	42.3	49.7	64.9	17.5	30.6
20–24	26.3	42.0	54.0	59.7	28.6
25–29	13.6	20.7	30.0	52.2	44.9
30–34	9.7	9.4	14.2	(−3.1)	51.1
35–39	9.2	7.4	9.3	(−19.6)	25.7
40–44	10.3	8.2	7.3	(−20.4)	(−11.0)

SOURCES: Dominion Bureau of Statistics (1966), *1961 Census of Canada, Population Sample: Women by Age and Number of Children Born*, Vol. IV, Bulletin 4.1–7 (Ottawa: Queen's Printer); Statistics Canada (1973), *1971 Census of Canada, Population: Women Ever Married by Number of Children Born*, Vol. 1, Bulletin 1.2–6 (Ottawa: Information Canada); Statistics Canada (1983), *1981 Census of Canada, Population: Nuptiality and Fertility*, Vol. 1, Cat. 92–906 (Ottawa: Minister of Supply and Services).

from 40,480 in 1971. While the issue of adolescent fertility is still an important one, the volume of children born to these young women has fallen dramatically, paralleling the trend in the rest of the society (Grindstaff, 1985).

CONCLUSIONS

Some writers have argued that the low fertility rates in the 1970s were simply temporal responses to cyclical and economic factors present in the society (Blake, 1974; Easterlin, 1978). It would appear that the force and importance of choice in childbearing have been underestimated. At the present time, women generally have the ability to choose not to be pregnant, and they also have attained increased opportunities outside of the motherhood role (over 50 per cent of all women 15–44 years of age are in the labour force). While it may be that many women in the labour force in the 1980s are there more out of economic necessity than out of occupational choice and that, in better economic circumstances, the participation rates may in fact decline (Easterlin, 1978), it is also true that the number of children in the family is negatively associated with labour-force participation. For example, over 80 per cent of childless ever-married women aged 20–40 are in the employed labour force, compared to about 50 per cent of ever-married aged 20–40 who have children; and ever-married women at age 30 contribute over 40 per cent of the family income when childless, compared to less than 20 per cent when there are two or more children in the family (Grindstaff, 1985). Clearly, children negatively impact both on the labour-force participation of women and on the level of economic contribution provided by women to their families—and women seem to be aware of this situation. It would appear that continuing low levels of childbearing/childrearing would enable women to be better placed in the economic structure. Given these and other factors (Ryder, 1979), it is apparent that low fertility rates and corresponding high levels of childlessness will continue to be part of the social scenario in Canada for some time to come.

While the number of children being born may increase slightly in the next decade due to the movement of the baby boom generation through the child-bearing years, the rates of fertility will most likely remain below the replacement level into the 1990s. More and more women are recognizing that childbearing and childrearing are detrimental in terms of personal long-range economic outcome, and many are not willing to trade potential economic independence for children (Eichler, 1983; Grindstaff, 1985). Women will continue to take advantage of role opportunities outside of motherhood. Even when choosing to begin child-bearing, the pattern begins later in life and fewer babies are born over a reproductive lifetime. If having more children becomes a social goal, then women will need to obtain some form of economic compensation.

As I stated in 1975, 'We must be prepared as a society to recognize that such fertility control has far-reaching implications for social organization and institutional arrangements. For the next decade or more, we must begin to project for total fertility rates at or below the replacement level and for 20 per cent or more of married couples remaining childless' (Grindstaff, 1975: 21). That type of preparation is just as critical in the 1980s. Women will not be content with an exclusive homemaker role, and as a concerned society, we need to find ways for women to be mothers if they so choose, without sacrificing other important life goals.

REFERENCES

Blake, J. (1974). 'Can we believe recent data on birth expectations in the United States?' *Demography* 11: 25–44.

Digest (1983). 'Women having fewer children before age 25, more after age 30'. *Family Planning Perspectives* 15: 193–4.

Easterlin, R. (1978). 'What will 1984 be like? Socio-economic implications of recent twists in the age structure.' *Demography* 15: 397–432.

Eichler, M. (1983). *Families in Canada Today: Recent Changes and Their Policy Consequences* Toronto: Gage.

Grindstaff, C.F. (1975). 'The baby bust: Changes in fertility patterns in Canada'. *Canadian Studies in Population* 2: 15–22.

—— (1984). 'Catching up: The fertility of women over 30 years of age, Canada in the 1970s'. *Canadian Studies in Population* 11: 95–109.

—— (1985). *Long Term Economic Consequences of Adolescent Marriage and Fertility.* Ottawa: Statistics Canada.

Ryder, N. (1979). 'The future of American fertility.' *Social Problems* 26: 359–70.

Statistics Canada (1983). *1981 Census of Canada, Population: Nuptiality and Fertility.* Ottawa: Ministry of Supply and Services.

CHAPTER 13

CANADIAN FERTILITY TRENDS

A Further Test of the Easterlin Hypothesis

Robert E. Wright and Paul S. Maxim

INTRODUCTION

Fertility has declined considerably in Canada since the peak of the 'baby boom', and is now well below the replacement level.[1] Although the consensus among demographers is that fertility will likely remain low in the future, such a conclusion is probably premature given past trends in fertility rates. Even though the long-run trend has been downwards, there have been major short-run fluctuations. There was a sizeable decline in fertility in the Great Depression which was followed by a sharp increase that resulted in the post-war baby boom. Since about 1960, however, fertility has once again declined and is presently at a historical low. Given what appears to be the 'erratic' nature of past fertility rates, one could easily conclude that forecasting fertility levels is an extremely risky, if not impossible, task.[2]

Nevertheless, having some idea of future fertility levels is of utmost importance. If fertility remains low and there are no drastic increases in immigration, the Canadian population will 'age' dramatically with population proportions concentrating in the older age groups. It is often assumed that such a shift in age composition is undesirable for a variety of reasons. For example, it has been suggested that a heavy financial burden will be placed on society in order to maintain existing social welfare programs aimed at accommodating the elderly population.[3] Since population aging is primarily a function of low fertility (see Coale, 1957), an increase in fertility would, to a certain extent, alleviate some of these projected problems. With this in mind, this paper will speculate on future levels of fertility in Canada by testing the so-called 'Easterlin Hypothesis' using a statistical procedure known as 'age–period–cohort' analysis.

THE EASTERLIN HYPOTHESIS

Richard Easterlin (1961; 1968; 1973; 1978; 1980) has argued that the relative size of one's birth cohort has a major impact on one's overall life chances. Central to Easterlin's thesis is his conclusion that there are two distinctly different demographic groups composed of (1) individuals born in a period when the birth rate is 'low'; and (2) individuals born in a period when the birth rate is 'high'. The first group, which he terms a 'small' generation or cohort, is composed of individuals born in the low fertility years of the 1930s. The second group, which is a 'large' generation or cohort, consists of those individuals born in the high fertility baby boom period.

According to Easterlin, there are definite advantages associated with being born in a relatively small cohort which persist throughout life. For example, there is a direct relationship between the number of births and the number of people reaching working age. Therefore, those individuals born in the 1930s found, on entering the work force in the 1950s, a favourable labour market where young workers were in short supply compared to older workers. This in part resulted in low levels of unemployment and high relative incomes for young workers. However, the situation has reversed for individuals born in the 1950s who started entering the labour force in the 1970s. As they are from a high-fertility generation their numbers were large in relation to their parents' generation. They have found a labour market unfavourable to young workers and this (again in part) has contributed to higher levels of unemployment and lower relative incomes.

What ties Easterlin's overall argument together is his notion of 'relative income' which must not be confused with 'absolute' or 'real' income. For all age groups real income has risen steadily in the post-war period. Relative income, however, is the ratio of 'earnings potential' to 'material aspiration' which Easterlin demonstrates has declined for members of the baby-boom cohort. 'Relative income is critical in determining the behavior of young adults as well as their feelings of well being' (Easterlin, 1980: 23). In short, the baby-boom cohort grew up in a period of relative affluence which led to high aspirations among its members. On entering the labour force, however, they have found themselves in an unreceptive environment which has severely curtailed their initial high expectations.

Easterlin has used this argument to partially explain various social, economic and political conditions that have widely been interpreted as indicators of an increased level of social demoralization. Examples include such trends as rising rates of divorce, suicide, crime and illegitimacy; higher levels of political alienation, and declining rates of college and university participation (Easterlin, 1978; 1980). His proposed relationship concerning fertility behaviour is, however, of particular importance for the purpose of this paper. He writes:

> . . . both the postwar baby boom and the subsequent baby bust were in large part the products of swings in generation size that affected the economic circumstances of young adults. Because of their exceptionally favorable economic situation, those from the small generation of the 1930s tended to marry earlier and have more children; the relatively unfavorable economic situation of the large generation of the 1950s made for later marriage and reduced childbearing (Easterlin, 1980: 38–9).

Therefore, in its simplest interpretation, *the Easterlin Hypothesis implies that, ceteris paribus, relatively large cohorts will exhibit lower fertility rates vis-à-vis small cohorts.* If Easterlin is correct, fertility should fluctuate cyclically depending on the relative economic status of young adults.

PREVIOUS RESEARCH

Easterlin bases his argument on the experience of the United States where his model seems to fit the data very well. Consequently, he has argued that his explanation should be applicable to other industrialized nations that have completed their demographic transitions. One crude way of testing the Easterlin Hypothesis is to construct a measure of 'relative cohort size' which Easterlin considers to be a suitable proxy for relative income. This measure is usually expressed as a simple ratio of the population age 30–64 to the population age 15–29 (i.e., $N\,30\text{–}64/N\,15\text{–}29$). Upward movement in this ratio indicates a *decrease* in the number of 'young' people relative to 'older' people which is assumed to correspond to an *increase* in relative income for the former group. Of course, one problem with this proxy, as Ermisch (1979) has pointed out, is that the stability of the relationship between cohort size and relative income has not been demonstrated rigorously for nations outside the United States. Leaving this problem aside, changes in relative cohort size should exhibit a direct association with changes in fertility.

Easterlin and Condran (1976) have shown that the movements in relative cohort size and the total fertility rate correspond closely in Australia, Canada, England and Wales, and the United States in the 1940 to 1970 period.[4] They note that the timing and amplitude of the changes in these two variables are 'remarkably similar' for the United States and Canada in both the period of fertility increase (1940–60) and the period of fertility decline (1960–70). For Canada they find that the amplitude of the fertility trend is greater than for Australia and the United States, and the post-1960 fertility decline is more pronounced. With respect to England and Wales, the amplitude of the fertility trend is smaller, and there is a

Figure 1: Relative cohort size and total fertility rate, 1922–1984

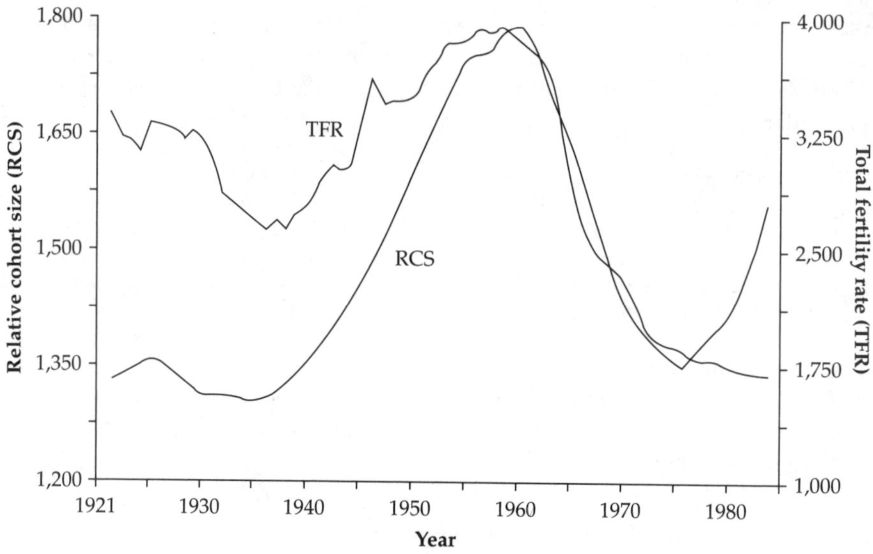

time lag between the decline in fertility and the decline in relative cohort size. Overall, there is a 'rough correspondence between the movement of the age ratio and the fertility rate' (Easterlin and Condran, 1976: 143). Based on this general observation, the authors support the validity of the Easterlin Hypothesis and predict upturns in fertility in these four nations.

Chesnais (1983) tested the Easterlin Hypothesis by considering changes in the net reproduction rate and relative cohort size for eighteen industrialized nations.[5] The time series of observations used covered the 1930–80 period. Overall, he found little support for Easterlin's idea of post-transitional fertility cycles. He concluded that fertility trends in only two nations—the United States and Australia—clearly fit the pattern suggested by Easterlin.

COHORT SIZE AND FERTILITY IN CANADA[6]

Figure 1 displays changes in the total fertility rate (TFR)[7] and relative cohort size (RCS) for the 1922–84 period in Canada. The pronounced increases and decreases in the TFR that have occurred in this period are immediately clear from the graph. In 1922 the TFR was estimated at 3.402 live births per woman; by 1939 it had declined to 2.654. This change represents a decrease of about 22 per cent. Beginning in 1940, the fertility rate began to climb. By 1959 the TFR surpassed the 1922 value, and reached almost 4 births per woman—the peak of the baby boom as measured by this index of fertility. Between 1940 and 1959, the TFR increased by

Table 1: Estimates of total fertility rate (TFR) and relative cohort size (RCS), Canada, 1922-1984

Year	TFR	RCS
1922	3.402	1.33146
1925	3.132	1.35352
1930	3.282	1.32536
1935	2.755	1.30860
1940	2.766	1.34089
1945	3.018	1.43110
1950	3.455	1.56634
1955	3.831	1.72166
1960	3.895	1.78287
1965	3.145	1.65478
1970	2.331	1.44897
1975	1.852	1.35777
1980	1.746	1.40492
1984	1.686	1.55458

SOURCE: See text.

over 40 per cent. As was stated earlier, the fertility rate has been on a steady downward trend since 1960. By 1966 the TFR bypassed its previous low set in 1939, and in recent years (1982–84) has levelled off at a value of about 1.680 live births. The post-1960 decline represents a decrease of approximately 57 per cent.

Of equal interest is the observed trend in relative cohort size. Like the TRF, RCS has fluctuated considerably in the 1922–84 period. Of special importance is the period 1940–75. In this period, changes in the TFR closely shadowed changes in RCS. Between 1940 and 1959, the zero-order correlation (r) between RCS and the TFR is a very high +.958. Between 1960 and 1975, it is even higher at a calculated value of +.990. These simple correlations clearly indicate a very close direct statistical relationship between the two variables in the 1940–75 period. However, since 1975, movements in the TFR and RCS have been in opposite directions ($r = -.881$). Fertility has continued to decline in unison with an increase in RCS. Table 1 presents some selected estimates of RCS and TFR.

The post-1975 trends in RCS and TFR point to two possible conclusions concerning the relevance of the Easterlin Hypothesis . The first is its rejection within the context of the Canadian experience. As RCS is supposed to proxy relative income, according to Easterlin, its steady rise in the past ten years should have corresponded with a rise in fertility. Of course just the opposite has occurred. The second is that there may be a lag time between an upturn in RCS and an upturn in fertility. Given the undoubtedly crude way in which RCS 'measures' the central theoretical concept of relative income, such a hypothesis is indeed reasonable and fertility may still increase. What is required is a more rigorous test before any confident conclusions can be formed.

Figure 2: Age specific fertility rates, 1922–1984

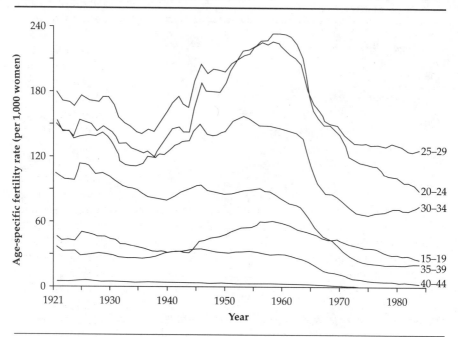

AGE, PERIOD, AND COHORT EFFECTS: THEORETICAL RELEVANCE

In order to further test the Easterlin Hypothesis, a time series of fertility data will be decomposed into age, period, and cohort effects. With respect to fertility behaviour, there is a vast amount of research positing the importance of each of these factors; however, space does not allow for a detailed discussion of this literature.

It is well established that age is one of the most important predictors of fertility. In most societies, almost all childbearing occurs within the age range 15 to 49 years, the approximate biological limits set by the age of puberty and menopause. However, there are considerable differences across societies and through time in how births are distributed in this age range.

This point is well illustrated by considering Figure 2. This graph displays changes in age-specific fertility rates for Canada in the period 1922–84. As Figure 2 indicates, there are considerable differences in the rate of childbearing by age across all points in time. The age specific rates for the younger age groups (15–19, 20–24, 25–29, and 30–34) have followed a pattern of change that roughly parallels the trend in the total fertility rate (see Figure 1). However, the changes for the older age groups (35–39, 40–44, and 45–49) have been primarily downward throughout the 1922–84 period. This trend is especially pronounced for the two oldest age groups. Given the importance of age in the explanation of fertility behaviour, it is essential to control for age in temporal models of fertility determinants.

The concept period effect '. . . refers to all events which have taken place at or between the moments of observation and which have influenced the phenomenon being studied' (Hagenaars and Cobben, 1978: 71). In short, period effects represent events which influence all age groups at a particular point in time.

Important period influences with respect to fertility behaviour in Canada would be variant economic conditions brought about by what economists term 'business cycles'. In fact, it has long been recognized (outside the work of Easterlin) that there is a direct relationship between fertility and fluctuations in economic conditions (Basavarajappa, 1971; Galbraith and Thomas, 1941; Kirk, 1960; Yule, 1906). As Hagenaars and Cobben (1978) point out, however, period effects not only refer to 'clearly demarcated events' but also include longer-term social, cultural and economic processes. Important post-war period influences on fertility behaviour include such important factors as rising female labour-force participation (Chaudhry and Choudhry, 1985), more efficient methods of birth control, and changing role opportunities for women (Grindstaff, 1985).

Of particular importance, within the context of this study, are cohort effects. According to Ryder (1965: 845): 'A cohort may be defined as the aggregate of individuals (within some population definition) who experienced the same event within the same time interval.' In this study we are concerned exclusively with whether or not an individual belongs to a relatively large or small birth cohort. We have already presented our justification for positing the importance of birth cohort in fertility behaviour. Therefore, within this age–period–cohort framework, relative cohort size should be inversely associated with fertility after controlling for age and period effects.

Somewhat surprisingly, very little empirical research has differentiated between age, period and cohort influences on fertility behaviour (Hobcraft et al., 1982). Pullum (1980), using data for the United States (1917–73), found little support for independent cohort effects. His empirical results indicate that age-period models are better predictors of fertility trends than age-cohort models. He also found that adding a cohort effect to an age-period model did not produce a significantly better fit. Likewise, Page (1977), using fertility data for Australia, England/Wales and Sweden, discovered that age and period alone adequately describe changes in fertility rates in these selected nations. On the other hand, Sanderson (1976), also working with US data, found significant cohort effects, especially for lower order births. Lee (1964; 1977; 1980) also found that US fertility rates in the past appear to vary with changes in cohort size. The studies by Sanderson and Lee suggest that fertility does fluctuate in accordance with the Easterlin Hypothesis. However, the above studies differ considerably in terms of the models estimated, the estimating procedure used, and the time periods covered. Therefore, it is still too early to confidently comment on the relative importance of cohort influences.

ESTIMATING AGE, PERIOD, AND COHORT EFFECTS

The technique of age–period–cohort analysis has been used in many areas of sociological research. For example, trends in juvenile delinquency (Maxim, 1985, 1986; Pullum, 1977), political party affiliation (Knoke and Hout, 1974), and labour force participation (Clogg, 1982; Evers and Halli, 1984) have been modelled using age–period–cohort analysis. Detailed reviews of the technique and its applications are to be found in Hagenaars and Cobben (1978) and Hobcraft et al. (1982).

In this paper, we analyse fertility data using what Hobcraft et al. (1982: 6) term the 'conventional linear model approach.' . . . The technique used here is the one adopted by Maxim (1985; 1986), and discussed by Hobcraft et al. (1982: 7). It is a two-step procedure. In the first step, the age and period effects are estimated by regressing the age and period variables on the transformed age–period–cohort-specific rates. In the second step, cohort effects are estimated by regressing the cohort variables on the residuals generated . . . by the age-period model.

DATA

The data used in this study pertain to Canada as a whole, and cover the period 1921–85 inclusive. Age-specific female population totals for the period 1921–49 were available in published form (Statistics Canada, 1973). The totals for the period 1950–85 were obtained from Statistics Canada via their CANSIM data base (Matrix numbers 00698.2.4 to 00698.2.10). Five-year age-specific fertility rates for the 1922–83 period were also available in published form (Statistics Canada, 1979; 1981; 1982; 1983a; 1984). Estimates for 1984 were obtained directly from the Vital Statistics Division of Statistics Canada. Age-specific fertility rates were not available for 1921 and 1985 so the rates were estimated using logarithmic extrapolation. In order to make the period intervals consistent with the five age-specific fertility rates, the single year categories were collapsed into five-year periods.

In total, the seven age intervals and the thirteen period intervals generated nineteen distinct cohorts. The Lexis diagram illustrating the relationships between the various age, period and cohort groups is shown as Table 2.

RESULTS

. . .

Figure 3 shows the distribution of age effects (B_i) by age group. The pattern is for the most part self-explanatory and is consistent with the temporal fertility data displayed in Figure 2. Fertility peaks in the 20–29 age group and then decreases sharply as age increases. This distribution quite strikingly illustrates the major non-linear impact that age has on the reproductive process.

Figure 4 shows the distribution of period effects (B_j) by period interval. Three distinct period effects are well reflected in this distribution. The first is the negative

Table 2: Diagramatic representation of the relationships between age, period and cohort groups

Period

Age	1921–1925 (P₁)	1926–1930 (P₂)	1931–1935 (P₃)	1936–1940 (P₄)	1941–1945 (P₅)	1946–1950 (P₆)	1951–1955 (P₇)	1956–1960 (P₈)	1961–1965 (P₉)	1966–1970 (P₁₀)	1971–1975 (P₁₁)	1976–1980 (P₁₂)	1981–1985 (P₁₃)
15–19 (A_7)	C_7	C_8	C_9	C_{10}	C_{11}	C_{12}	C_{13}	C_{14}	C_{15}	C_{16}	C_{17}	C_{18}	C_{19}
20–24 (A_6)	C_6	C_7	C_8	C_9	C_{10}	C_{11}	C_{12}	C_{13}	C_{14}	C_{15}	C_{16}	C_{17}	C_{18}
25–29 (A_5)	C_5	C_6	C_7	C_8	C_9	C_{10}	C_{11}	C_{12}	C_{13}	C_{14}	C_{15}	C_{16}	C_{17}
30–34 (A_4)	C_4	C_5	C_6	C_7	C_8	C_9	C_{10}	C_{11}	C_{12}	C_{13}	C_{14}	C_{15}	C_{16}
35–39 (A_3)	C_3	C_4	C_5	C_6	C_7	C_8	C_9	C_{10}	C_{11}	C_{12}	C_{13}	C_{14}	C_{15}
40–44 (A_2)	C_2	C_3	C_4	C_5	C_6	C_7	C_8	C_9	C_{10}	C_{11}	C_{12}	C_{13}	C_{14}
45–49 (A_1)	C_1	C_2	C_3	C_4	C_5	C_6	C_7	C_8	C_9	C_{10}	C_{11}	C_{12}	C_{13}

NOTE: A_1, A_2, A_3, …, A_7 represent the 7 age groups
P_1, P_2, P_3, …, P_{13} represent the 13 period groups
C_1, C_2, C_3, …, C_{19} represent the 19 cohorts

Figure 3: Fertility effects by age

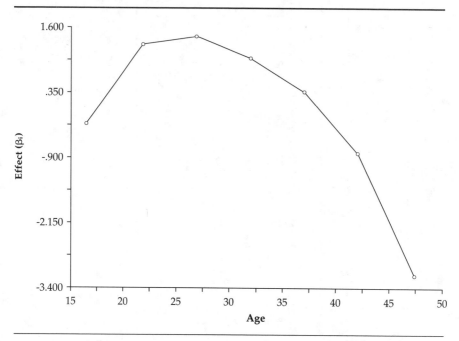

effect that the Depression period of the 1930s exerted on fertility. The second is the positive effect of the immediate post-war period that corresponds with the baby boom. And the third is the precipitous negative effect of the post-1960 period.

It must be remembered that these period effects are controlling for age and thus represent influences that are independent of changes in age structure. It must also be remembered that period effects, at best, only 'proxy' underlying causal factors and hence are not in a strict sense 'explanatory'. The observed distribution is not, however, inconsistent with previous explanations of fertility trends in Canada. In a relative sense, they suggest that the period influences that affected fertility behaviour in the Great Depression and baby boom are 'less significant' than the period influences of the post-1960 fertility decline.

In Figure 5, the estimated cohort fertility effects (B_k) are plotted against their respective cohort groups. The resulting distribution is very surprising. The U-shaped curve indicates that for the 'older' cohorts (i.e., C_1 through C_{13}), the effect of cohort membership on fertility behaviour is increasingly negative. However, for the 'younger' cohorts (i.e., C_{14} through C_{19}) the opposite holds and the effect is increasingly positive.

As the main goal of this paper is to test the Easterlin Hypothesis, Figure 6 shows the distribution of cohort effects by relative cohort size for cohorts 10 through 19.[8] Members of the oldest cohort (C_{10}) were born in the 1921–25 period while members of the youngest cohort (C_{19}) were born in the 1966–70 period. As

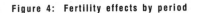

Figure 4: Fertility effects by period

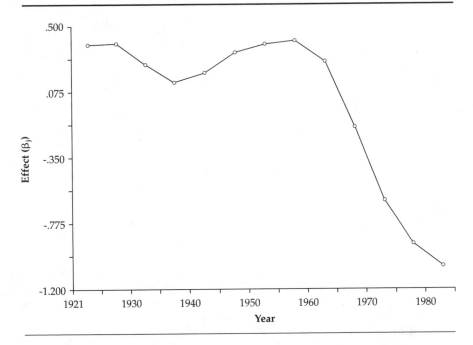

the reader can see, the resulting trend line shows no relationship whatsoever between cohort fertility effects and relative cohort size. Regressing relative cohort size on the cohort fertility effects gives an R^2 = .002, further confirming our visual inspection of the graph.

CONCLUSIONS

Prima facie, our findings concerning relative birth cohort size and fertility suggest no direct association. That is, after controlling for age and period influences, relatively small birth cohorts exhibit no greater fertility rates than do large birth cohorts. There appears to be no well-developed theoretical justification for this observed relationship beyond the conclusion that fertility rates in Canada *do not* fluctuate in accordance with the Easterlin Hypothesis.

At the beginning of this paper, it was suggested that by more rigorously testing the Easterlin Hypothesis, one might be able to comment more confidently on the future levels of fertility in Canada. According to Easterlin, the upturn in relative cohort size which has occurred since 1975 (see Figure 1) should correspond with an upswing in fertility. Ten years have passed and this has not happened. The current findings suggest that the relative birth cohort size–fertility relationship, which is supposed to be adequately proxied by the relative cohort size–fertility relationship, is inconsistent with Easterlin's interpretation. Based on this conclu-

Figure 5: Fertility effects by cohort

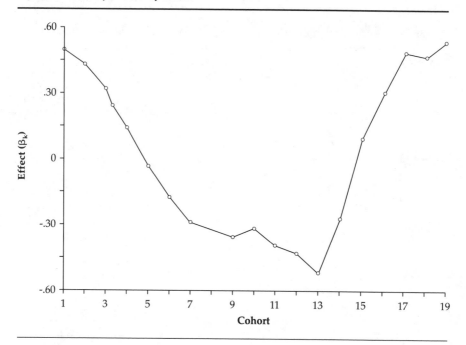

Figure 6: Cohort fertility effect by relative cohort size (C_{10} through C_{19})

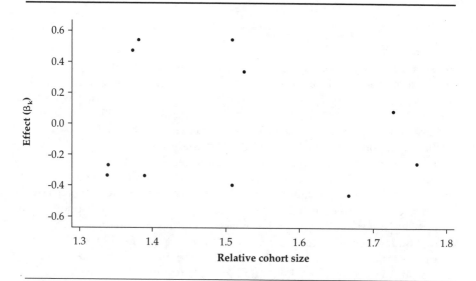

sion, and the strong negative period effects of the post-1960 period, it is unlikely that fertility will increase in the immediate future without the inclusion of some dramatic, unforeseen factor.

These conclusions tend to echo the work of Chesnais (1983) who noted that Easterlin's hypothesis held only for the United States and Australia. Given the apparent cultural similarities and close economic relationship between Canada and the United States, it is interesting to speculate as to why differential fertility trends are observed in these two countries.

Two possible explanations readily come to mind—one sociologically based; the other economic. First, while there are major similarities between these two countries, there are also significant differences. In Canada, for example, the Catholic French-Canadian sector of the population (which composed about 25 per cent of the national population over the period of study) did not experience the general secular downtrend in fertility which occurred in the US and English-speaking Canada until the early 1960s. Concomitant with shorter-term cyclical trends, most of North America's population exhibited a general decrease in fertility from the turn of the century onward. The conservative, and predominantly rural, Catholic culture in Quebec appears to have acted as an insulator to this more widespread pattern for many years.

Second, although it is true that the economies of the United States and Canada are tightly linked, there has been a much stronger 'social net' of economic and social benefits available to Canadians which has insulated them from the full impact of fluctuations in the overall economy. Some benefits, such as family allowance payments and universal medicare, are unavailable in the US, and others, such as unemployment insurance payments, are less well developed.

In its current form, Easterlin's model does not account for cultural variables and assumes a market economy which is largely immune to central planning. As a result, it is not too surprising that Easterlin's model has met with limited success outside the United States.

NOTES

[1] In 1984 the total fertility rate (TFR) was estimated at 1.686 live births per woman. The replacement level of fertility is a TFR of approximately 2.1.

[2] For example, the Scripps Foundation writing in 1948 about probable post-war fertility levels in the United States erroneously concluded: 'No one anticipates the restoration of levels of fertility that could be regarded as high in a world setting. The range of uncertainty is between rates somewhat below permanent replacement and rates slightly above such replacement' (Scripps Foundation, 1948: 190). Such a forecast is strikingly similar to a more recent statement concerning future fertility levels in Canada: '. . . the rates of fertility will most likely remain below the replacement level in the 1990's' (Grindstaff, 1985: 109). Of course, in 1948 the American birth rate jumped signalling the beginning of the baby boom!

[3] Detailed studies of the possible social and economic consequences of the aging Canadian population are Foot (1982), Kettle (1980), and Statistics Canada (1983b). A contrary argument to this mounting conventional wisdom regarding the 'evils' of an aging society is quite eloquently presented in McDaniel (1986).

[4] In this study, the authors used N_{35-64}/N_{15-34} as the relevant measure of relative cohort size. 'The particular age ratio used here was chosen after some experimentation as to the one providing the best fit to the fertility rate, when the experience of all four countries put together is considered' (Easterlin and Condran, 1976: 146).

[5] The eighteen nations considered by Chesnais (1983) were: United States, Canada, Australia, Norway, France, Finland, England and Wales, Netherlands, Denmark, Sweden, Switzerland, West Germany, Austria, Belgium, Italy, Spain, Portugal, and Japan.

[6] The sources of the estimates used in this section are described in the 'Data' section.

[7] Total Fertility Rate is a central concept in demography which refers to 'the sum of the age-specific birth rates of women over their reproductive span, as observed in a given year' (Shryock and Siegel, 1980: 524). While this statistic is generally easy to calculate and quite useful in a variety of circumstances, it does have a number of limitations. Primarily, the TFR does not account for the quantity or timing of births which may take place over the reproductive lifespan of a cohort — the completed fertility rate. In Canada, the completed or cohort total fertility rate generally moves in unison with the TFR although it exhibits less overall variability. By decomposing period and cohort effects the ensuing analysis incorporates both of these effects in a single model.

[8] Average birth cohort size was calculated by taking the arithmetic average of the single year birth cohorts.

REFERENCES

Basavarajappa, K.G. (1971). 'The influence of economic conditions on fertility and marriage rates, Australia, 1920–21 to 1937–8 and 1946–47 to 1966–67.' *Population Studies* 25, 1: 39–53.

Chesnais, J.C. (1983). 'La notion de cycle en démographie. La fécondité post-transitionelle, est-elle cyclique?' *Population* 38, 2: 361–90.

Chaudhry, M.D., and N.K. Choudhry (1985). 'The fertility rate in Canada, 1950–1976: A socio-econometric analysis.' *Canadian Studies in Population* 12, 1: 1–30.

Clogg, C.C. (1982). 'Cohort analysis of recent trends in labor force participation.' *Demography* 19, 4: 459–79.

Coale, A.J. (1957). 'How the age distribution of a human population is determined.' *Cold Spring Harbor Symposia on Quantitative Biology* 22: 83–9.

Easterlin, R.A. (1961). 'The American baby boom in historical perspective.' *American Economic Review* 51, 5: 869–911.

―――― (1968). *Population, Labor Force, and Long Swings in Economic Growth: the American Experience.* New York: National Bureau of Economic Research.

―――― (1973). 'Relative economic status and the American fertility swing.' Pp. 166–233 in E.B. Sheldon, ed., *Family Economic Behavior: Problems and Prospects.* Philadelphia: Lippincott.

―――― (1978). 'What will 1984 be like? Socioeconomic implications of recent twists in age structure.' *Demography* 15, 4: 397–432.

—— (1980). *Birth and Fortune: The Impact of Numbers on Personal Welfare.* New York: Basic Books.

—— and G.A. Condran (1976). 'A note on the recent fertility swing in Australia, Canada, England and Wales and the United States.' Pp. 140–51 in H. Richards, ed., *Population, Factor Movements and Economic Development: Studies Presented to Brinley Thomas.* Cardiff: University of Wales Press.

Ermisch, J. (1979). 'The relevance of the Easterlin hypothesis and the new home economics to fertility movements in Great Britain.' *Population Studies* 33, 1: 39–57.

Evers, F.T., and S.S. Halli (1984). 'Age, period, cohort analysis of Canadian labour force participation: 1950–1982.' Mimeo. Department of Sociology, University of Western Ontario.

Fienberg, S.E., and W.M. Mason (1979). 'Identification and estimation of age-period-cohort models in the analysis of discrete archival data.' Pp. 1–67 in K.F. Schuessler, ed., *Sociological Methodology, 1979.* San Francisco: Jossey-Bass.

Foot, D.K. (1982). *Canada's Population Outlook: Demographic Futures and Economic Challenges.* Toronto: Lorimer.

Galbraith, V.L., and D.S. Thomas (1941). 'Birth rates and interwar business cycles.' *Journal of the American Statistical Association* 216: 465–76.

Glenn, N.D. (1976). 'Cohort analysts' futile quest: Statistical attempts to separate age, period and cohort effects.' *American Sociological Review* 41, 5: 900–4.

Grindstaff, C.F. (1985). 'The baby bust revisited: Canada's continuing pattern of low fertility.' *Canadian Studies in Population* 12, 1: 103–11.

Hagenaars, J.A., and N.P. Cobben (1978). 'Age, cohort and period: A general model for the analysis of social change.' *Netherlands Journal of Sociology* 14: 59–91.

Hobcraft, J., J. Menken, and S. Preston (1982). 'Age, period, and cohort effects in demography: A review.' *Population Index* 48, 1: 4–43.

Kettle, J. (1980). *The Big Generation.* Toronto: McClelland and Stewart.

Kirk, D. (1960). 'The influence of business cycles on marriage and birth rates.' Pp. 241–60 in National Bureau of Economic Research, *Demographic Change in Developed Countries.* Princeton: Princeton University Press.

Knoke, D., and M. Hout (1974). 'Social and demographic factors in American political party affiliations, 1952–72.' *American Sociological Review* 39, 5: 700–13.

—— (1976). 'Reply to Glenn.' *American Sociological Review* 41, 5: 905–8.

—— (1974). 'The formal dynamics of controlled populations and the echo, the boom and the bust.' *Demography* 11, 4: 563–85.

—— (1977). 'Target fertility, contraception and aggregate rates: Towards a formal synthesis.' *Demography* 14, 4: 455–79.

—— (1980). 'Aiming at a moving target: Period fertility and changing reproductive goals.' *Population Studies* 34, 2: 205–26.

Mason, K.O., et al. (1973). 'Some methodological issues in cohort analysis of archival data.' *American Sociological Review* 38, 2: 242–58.

Maxim, P.S. (1985). 'Cohort size and juvenile-delinquency: A test of the Easterlin hypothesis.' *Social Forces* 63, 3: 661–81.

—— (1986). 'Cohort size and juvenile delinquency in England and Wales.' *Journal of Criminal Justice* 14, 6: 491–9.

McDaniel, S.A. (1986). *Canada's Aging Population.* Butterworths: Toronto.

Page, H. (1977). 'Patterns underlying fertility schedules: A decomposition by both age and marriage duration.' *Population Studies* 31, 1: 85–106.

Palmore, E. (1978). 'When can age, period and cohort be separated?' *Social Forces* 57, 1: 282–95.

Pedhauser, E.J. (1982). *Multiple Regression in Behavioral Research.* New York: Holt, Rinehart and Winston.

Pullum, T.W. (1978). 'Parameterizing age, period, and cohort effects: An application to U.S. delinquency rates, 1964–1973.' Pp. 461–84 in K.F. Schuessler, ed., *Sociological Methodology, 1978.* San Francisco: Jossey-Bass.

———— (1980). 'Separating age, period, and cohort effects in white U.S. fertility, 1920–1970.' *Social Science Research* 9, 3: 225–44.

Rodgers, W.L. (1982a). 'Estimable functions of age, period, and cohort effects.' *American Sociological Review* 47, 6: 774–87.

———— (1982b). 'Reply to Smith, Mason and Fienberg.' *American Sociological Review* 47, 6: 793–6.

Ryder, N.B. (1965). 'The cohort as a concept in the study of social change.' *American Sociological Review* 30, 6: 843–61.

Sanderson, W. (1976). 'Towards an economic analysis of the baby boom: A test of the Easterlin hypothesis.' Mimeo: Stanford University.

Scripps Foundation (1948). 'The population forecasts of the Scripps Foundation.' *Population Index* 14, 3: 190–5.

Shryock, H.S., and J.S. Siegel (1980). *The Methods and Materials of Demography* Vol. 2. Washington D.C.: U.S.G.P.O.

Smith, H.L., W.M. Mason, S.E. Fienberg (1982). 'More chimeras of the age-period-cohort accounting framework: Comment on Rodgers.' *American Sociological Review* 47, 6: 787–93.

Statistics Canada (1973) *Population 1921–1971.* Cat. 91–512. Ottawa: Information Canada.

———— (1979). *Vital Statistics* (Volume I) *Births 1977.* Cat. 84–204. Ottawa: Information Canada.

———— (1981). *Vital Statistics* (Volume I) *Births and Deaths 1979.* Cat. 84–204. Ottawa: Information Canada.

———— (1982). *Vital Statistics* (Volume I) *Births and Deaths 1980.* Cat. 84–204. Ottawa: Information Canada.

———— (1983a). *Vital Statistics* (Volume I) *Births and Deaths 1981.* Cat. 84–204. Ottawa: Information Canada.

———— (1983b). *Fact Book on Aging in Canada.* Ottawa: Information Canada.

———— (1984). *Births and Deaths. Vital Statistics* (Volume I) *1982.* Cat. 84–204. Ottawa: Information Canada.

Yule, G.U. (1906). 'On the changes in the marriage and birth rates in England and Wales during the past half century: With an enquiry as to their probable causes.' *Journal of the Royal Statistical Society* 69: 122.

CHAPTER 14

CONTRACEPTIVE USE IN CANADA, 1984

T.R. Balakrishnan, Karol Krótki,
and Evelyne Lapierre-Adamcyk

SUMMARY

Canada's first national fertility survey, carried out by telephone in 1984, found that 68 per cent of all women aged 18–49—73 per cent of currently married women, 69 per cent of the previously married women and 57 per cent of single women—are practising contraception. Overall, the most widely used method of birth control in Canada is sterilization (male and female), which is relied on by almost 60 per cent of all married users and 66 per cent of previously married users. Among single women, the preferred method is the pill, chosen by 7 out of 10 of such users.

Among all women, the major determinant of method choice is age: the pill is overwhelmingly chosen by women under 25, and sterilization, by those 30 and over. While the IUD and the condom are used by roughly 10–14 per cent of women in their 20s who practice contraception, these methods decline in importance with increasing age. Highly educated women are less likely than those with little education to elect sterilization, and more likely to rely on barrier methods. Differences in contraceptive prevalence and patterns of use between Catholics and Protestants have all but disappeared in Canada, but church attendance and country of birth appear to exert a modest influence on method choice. As might be anticipated, women whose family size is complete have considerably higher levels of contraceptive use than those who expect to have more children.

The survey reveals no difference in contraceptive use between Quebec women and those in the rest of Canada, thus confirming both the accuracy of earlier Quebec studies showing extremely high levels of sterilization and the applicability of these findings to all other Canadian women.

Comparisons between the 1984 Canadian data and 1982 US data from the National Survey of Family Growth indicate somewhat higher overall use of a contraceptive method among married women in Canada and greater recourse to sterilization (although Canadian married women tend to be somewhat older, on average, than their US counterparts). Among single women, contraceptive prevalence is also higher among Canadians (58 per cent) than among Americans (43 per cent), and considerably higher proportions of never-married Canadian users than of their US counterparts rely on the pill (72 per cent vs. 52 per cent).

The investigators speculate that as divorce and remarriage continue to increase in Canada, and with improved levels of education among women and better knowledge of various contraceptive methods, Canada's high rates of sterilization may decline in future years.

BACKGROUND

In 1984, the first Canadian survey conducted at the national level and devoted exclusively to an examination of fertility and contraceptive practice among women of childbearing age (including single women) was carried out. Because there had previously been only partial fertility surveys in Canada, limited data on patterns and trends in contraceptive use were available. A national survey carried out in 1976 collected some information on contraceptive practice.[1] However, the findings were narrow in scope, since the study was designed primarily to study the attitudes of Canadian adults toward abortion. More detailed information about family planning practices is available at the local and regional levels.[2] In fact, a great deal more is known about the population of Quebec than about the rest of Canada, as a result of the large number of demographic studies carried out in that province. However, since Quebec society is largely Catholic and French-speaking, with a different historical and cultural background from that of the rest of the country, it is not generally representative of the whole of Canada.

Examination of commercial sales records and of provincial government health plans shows that contraceptive use in Canada has changed dramatically in recent years. The use of oral contraceptives, as estimated on the basis of pharmacy sales, declined from a high of 27 per cent of all women aged 15–44 in 1977 to about 19 per cent in 1981.[3] After analysing data from the Quebec provincial health plan for the years 1971–79, investigators reported an extraordinary increase in reliance on sterilization in that province.[4] By 1979, according to that study, one-half of Quebec women reaching the age of 40 had become surgically sterilized. The researchers surmised that these levels would increase further if current trends continued. One of the important objectives of the 1984 Canadian Fertility Survey (CFS) was to find out whether this projection had, in fact, been correct. The present article is the first published report on the 1984 survey findings.

The CFS was conducted in April–June of 1984; selection of the sample and interviews were carried out by telephone. A two-stage probability process was used. The first stage involved the selection of households through the random generation of telephone numbers. The second stage involved the choice of eligible respondents (women aged 18–49) in each selected household. A total of 22,169 random dialings yielded 13,642 residential telephone numbers, 7,574 households with an eligible respondent and 5,315 subsequent completed interviews. Thus, the overall response rate was 70 per cent, slightly lower than that found in face-to-face surveys dealing with similar subjects, but comparable to that of other telephone surveys.[5]

Because the entire interview was conducted on the telephone, the complexity and length of the questionnaire had to be minimized. Moreover, because the investigators believed that sexual activity was too sensitive a topic to be raised on the telephone, no information on the subject was collected. However, 17 per cent of never-married women, and 27 per cent of the previously married (separated, divorced and widowed women), reported that they were living with a partner in a common-law relationship.

It should be emphasized that since information on current sexual activity was not gathered in the CFS, it is not possible to describe the contraceptive practice of women exposed to the risk of pregnancy. In particular, many previously married women who obtained a tubal ligation while they were married and who count, therefore, as current users of a method, may not have been sexually active at the time of the survey.

Despite the intrinsic limitations of a telephone interview, it was found possible to collect information on most of the standard topics covered in fertility surveys, including contraceptive practice, birth histories, attitudes toward marriage and areas such as the woman's work experience and economic status. The average interview lasted 36 minutes, although there was considerable variation in duration. In a pretest, using the same questionnaire, the investigators found that telephone interviews take a slightly shorter amount of time to complete than face-to-face interviews.

Telephone interviews reduced costs considerably. They also cut down on the time spent in the field, because all operations were centralized. There also appear to have been an improvement in the quality of responses and lower levels of non-response to certain questions, possibly because better supervision of interviews could be maintained, and more direct assistance could be provided at the central offices from where the calls were made. Telephone interviews in households throughout Canada were conducted from five central cities: Edmonton, Montreal, Regina, Toronto and Vancouver. Thus, the 5,315 women who were reached constitute a nationally representative sample of the population of Canadian women aged 18–49.

Current contraceptive status (including male and female sterilization) was measured as of the time of the interview. Information on ever-use, on use of a birth control method in the open birth interval [the period when a woman has not has a child in the last two years and is not breast-feeding] and on sterilization procedures was used to double-check the accuracy of the findings on current contraceptive status. If a woman mentioned using more than one method of birth control, the most effective method was reported as her current method. If both the woman and her husband or partner had been surgically sterilized, only the woman's procedure was counted in the use estimates.

All women other than current users are classified into three groups: those who are currently pregnant, have recently given birth or are seeking pregnancy; women who are sterile for non-contraceptive reasons (including those experiencing difficulty in conceiving, those who have had a hysterectomy or other operation that has made them sterile, and those whose husbands are sterile as a result of an operation other than vasectomy); and women who are presumably fecund, not seeking a pregnancy, but using no method of contraception.

Women who had had a hysterectomy following a tubal ligation were considered to be users of a contraceptive method. However, those who had only had a hysterectomy were classified as non-users of a method, among the non-contraceptively sterile. Almost half of the women who had had a hysterectomy said that if they had not had that operation they would have had a tubal ligation. Women who said that they were not practising contraception because they were postpartum made up a very small proportion of the sample.

Because the CFS data are based on a sample, the findings are subject to sampling variability. All the differences discussed in this article are statistically significant (p < 0.05). Moreover, percentages with a high relative standard error are so designated in the tables.

CONTRACEPTIVE USE PATTERNS

As Table 1 shows, among all Canadian women aged 18–49 in 1948, 68 per cent said they were using a method of birth control at the time of the interview. A further 9 per cent were pregnant, postpartum or seeking pregnancy, and 7 per cent were non-contraceptively sterile. Fifteen per cent were non-users. The table reveals large differences in contraceptive prevalence by the woman's marital status. Currently married women show the highest overall level of use (73 per cent), followed by the previously married (69 per cent) and the never-married (57 per cent). Moreover, only 5 per cent of currently married women are not using a method of birth control. The high level of current contraceptive practice among the previously married can be explained largely by the fact that these women are somewhat older than average and, therefore, are more likely to have been contraceptively sterilized while they were still married. Similarly, the higher average age of the previously married also helps account for the fact that these women

Table 1: Percentage distribution of women aged 18–49, by current reproductive and contraceptive status, according to marital status, Canada, 1984

Status	All women	Currently married	Never-married			Previously married		
			Total	Cohabiting	Not cohabiting	Total	Cohabiting	Not cohabiting
	(N = 5,315)	(N = 3,283)	(N = 1,430)	(N = 289)	(N = 1,141)	(N = 601)	(N = 162)	(N = 439)
Using a method	68.4	73.1	57.4	83.1	50.8	68.8	78.9	65.2
Pregnant, postpartum or seeking pregnancy	9.2	13.0	3.0	11.0	1.0	3.2	8.7	1.1[1]
Non-contraceptively sterile	7.0	8.7	1.5	1.4[1]	1.7	10.6	11.2	10.2
Not using a method	15.4	5.2	38.1	4.5	46.6	17.4	1.2[1]	23.4
Total	100.0	100.0	100.0	100.0	100.0	100.0	100.0	100.0

[1]Relative standard error of 0.30 or more.

report a higher incidence of non-contraceptive sterility (mostly hysterectomy) than do the other groups.

Levels of contraceptive use among single cohabiting women are high in Canada (83 per cent), as Table 1 also indicates, and even somewhat higher than the level reported among the previously married now living with a partner (79 per cent). Moreover, the level of contraceptive use among single women not cohabiting (51 per cent) suggests that at least half of the women in this group are sexually active. This finding indicates that there is no longer any justification for excluding single women from contraceptive prevalence surveys.

Table 2 summarizes patterns of contraceptive use by method. The leading method in Canada—accounting for almost half of all use—is sterilization, both male and female. The pill is the second most widely used method, accounting for 28 per cent of all use, followed by the condom and the IUD (9 per cent and 8 per cent, respectively). Use of other methods is so low as to be of no importance.

As Table 2 illustrates, there are considerable differences in the choice of a method between never-married and married women. Never-married women predominantly rely on the pill (71 per cent of users), while married women overwhelmingly rely on sterilization (59 per cent); the pill, condom and IUD assume considerably less importance among married women as ways of avoiding pregnancy (15, 11 and 8 per cent, respectively). Much of this pattern among currently married women, when compared with that of single women, is, of course, a function of the differing age structure of the two groups. The finding that a large proportion of married women resort to sterilization is consistent with conclusions of an earlier study carried out in Quebec,[6] and reflects the fact that many of these women have already had as many children as they want. The high level of

Table 2: Percentage distribution of women aged 18–49 who are using contraceptives, by current method, according to marital status

Method	All women (N = 3,635)	Currently married (N = 2,400)	Never-married			Previously married		
			Total (N = 821)	Cohabiting (N = 241)	Not cohabiting (N = 580)	Total (N = 414)	Cohabiting (N = 127)	Not cohabiting (N = 287)
Female ster.	35.3	41.8	4.3	4.1	4.3	59.7	53.5	62.4
Male ster.	12.7	17.6	1.7	3.3[1]	1.0[1]	6.3	11.8	4.2
Pill	28.0	15.0	71.2	66.0	73.4	17.4	16.5	17.8
IUD	8.3	8.0	7.9	9.5	7.2	10.6	11.0	10.5
Diaphragm	1.7	1.4	2.8	2.1[1]	3.1	1.2[1]	3.9[1]	0.0
Condom	9.1	10.8	7.9	9.1	7.4	2.2[1]	1.6[1]	2.1[1]
Foam	0.8	0.7	0.4[1]	0.4[1]	0.3[1]	2.2[1]	0.8[1]	2.8[1]
Rhythm	2.3	3.0	1.7	2.1[1]	1.4[1]	0.2[1]	0.0	0.3[1]
Withdrawal	1.2	1.3	1.3[1]	2.9[1]	0.7[1]	0.2[1]	0.8[1]	0.0[1]
Other	0.6	0.6	0.9[1]	0.4[1]	1.0[1]	0.0	0.0	0.0
Total	100.0	100.0	100.0	100.0	100.0	100.0	100.0	100.0

[1] Relative standard error of 0.30 or more.

female sterilization among the previously married reflects this same relationship. Reliance on male methods (vasectomy and the condom) is, as one might expect, lower among separated, divorced and widowed women than among those still living with a husband.

DIFFERENTIALS IN USE

Levels of contraceptive use according to selected background characteristics and method are presented for all women and for currently married women in Table 3. The table adds further evidence to the finding that a woman's age is by far the most important determinant of her method choice. For example, among all women, the proportion of users who became contraceptively sterilized increases sharply after the age of 30. By ages 30–34, 36 per cent of users have obtained a tubal ligation, and by ages 45–49, this proportion has climbed to 68 per cent. If the incidence of vasectomy is also included, 83 per cent of women aged 40–49 rely on sterilization to prevent pregnancy. Even among women 35–39, combined male and female sterilization constitutes more than two-thirds of all use. Correspondingly, reliance on the pill among older women almost disappears, with only 3 per cent of contraceptive users aged 40–44 depending on this method. Even among women aged 30–34, pill use amounts to only 17 per cent of all contraceptive practice. It is clear then, that the pill in Canada is now predominantly used only during the early years of a woman's reproductive life.

Table 3: Percentages of all women and of currently married women who are using contraceptives; and percentage distribution of current users, by method; according to selected characteristics

Characteristic	N	% using	Female ster.	Male ster.	Pill	IUD	Condom	Other[1]	Total
All women	5,315	68.4	35.3	12.7	28.0	8.3	9.1	6.6	100.0
Age group									
18–24	1,323	56.9	2.1	1.6	76.6	6.5	8.1	5.0	100.0
25–29	986	67.7	16.5	7.9	39.2	11.7	14.5	10.2	100.0
30–34	925	74.8	35.7	16.8	17.3	13.4	10.0	6.8	100.0
35–39	846	78.5	54.1	17.8	6.5	8.6	7.4	5.7	100.0
40–44	644	76.2	61.3	21.6	2.9	3.9	4.7	5.7	100.0
45–49	591	63.6	67.6	15.4	0.3	1.6	8.8	6.4	100.0
Birth expectations									
Expect more	1,898	57.0	0.0	0.0	66.0	10.2	14.3	9.5	100.0
Expect no more	3,375	75.4	50.2	18.2	11.9	7.5	6.9	5.3	100.0
Religion									
Catholic	2,548	67.3	34.5	12.2	30.0	8.0	7.9	7.4	100.0
Protestant	1,871	70.7	38.7	14.8	25.7	7.7	8.7	4.4	100.0
Other or none	886	66.3	30.7	10.1	27.6	10.4	14.0	7.3	100.0
Church attendance									
Weekly	1,367	60.9	43.8	14.8	15.2	5.9	9.7	10.6	100.0
Sometimes	2,047	70.2	33.1	12.3	31.8	8.1	9.2	5.4	100.0
Rarely or never	1,893	72.1	32.4	11.9	31.6	9.9	8.7	5.4	100.0
Education (in years)									
≤8	408	62.0	68.8	9.1	10.7	3.2	3.6	4.7	100.0
9–11	1,207	70.4	47.4	16.5	21.1	6.1	5.2	3.8	100.0
12–13	1,977	69.0	30.0	13.7	33.3	8.2	8.4	6.4	100.0
≥14	1,721	67.9	25.5	9.5	30.5	11.0	13.9	9.6	100.0
Nativity									
Native-born	4,576	68.8	34.8	12.8	30.2	8.4	8.0	5.9	100.0
Foreign-born	738	66.5	38.7	11.8	13.8	7.9	16.3	11.4	100.0
Currently married	3,283	73.1	41.7	17.6	15.0	8.0	10.8	7.0	100.0
Age group									
18–24	326	61.3	6.0	4.0	58.5	10.5	14.5	6.5	100.0
25–29	645	68.2	18.4	10.2	33.0	10.9	16.1	11.4	100.0
30–34	679	75.4	36.5	20.1	13.1	12.9	11.3	6.2	100.0
35–39	663	81.4	53.1	20.7	4.1	7.8	8.5	5.7	100.0
40–44	513	78.0	58.5	26.0	2.0	2.8	5.5	5.3	100.0
45–49	457	68.1	65.0	16.4	0.3	1.6	10.6	6.1	100.0
Birth expectations									
Expect more	761	53.2	0.0	0.0	49.0	12.5	23.0	15.5	100.0
Expect no more	2,509	79.4	50.2	21.2	8.1	7.1	8.1	5.3	100.0

[1] Diaphragm, spermicides, rhythm, withdrawal and others.

Continued p. 196

Table 3: (continued)

Characteristic			Method						
	N	% using	Female ster.	Male ster.	Pill	IUD	Condom	Other[1]	Total
Religion									
Catholic	1,544	72.2	42.2	17.4	16.2	7.8	8.8	7.6	100.0
Protestant	1,224	74.4	44.1	19.4	13.6	7.4	10.2	5.4	100.0
Other or none	511	73.6	34.4	13.8	14.8	10.1	18.0	9.0	100.0
Church attendance									
Weekly	1,017	69.4	46.1	17.2	9.9	6.0	10.9	9.9	100.0
Sometimes	1,277	75.2	40.9	16.7	17.6	8.4	10.8	5.6	100.0
Rarely or never	985	74.3	38.6	19.2	16.6	9.4	10.5	5.6	100.0
Education (in years)									
≤8	296	64.9	71.0	11.9	7.3	2.6	4.7	2.5	100.0
9–11	810	73.1	50.3	22.1	11.5	5.2	5.9	5.0	100.0
12–13	1,174	73.8	37.0	19.0	19.0	8.1	10.1	6.8	100.0
≥14	1,003	74.8	32.6	13.8	15.2	11.5	16.8	10.1	100.0
Nativity									
Native-born	2,751	73.3	42.0	18.3	16.3	8.2	9.2	6.0	100.0
Foreign-born	532	72.4	40.5	14.0	8.6	7.0	18.7	11.2	100.0

[1] Diaphragm, spermicides, rhythm, withdrawal and others.

Sixty-three per cent of all women do not expect to have any more children (excluding the current pregnancy), as Table 3 shows. Among these women, overall contraceptive use is very high (75 per cent). Moreover, among users who expect no more children, 68 per cent are protected against pregnancy by female or male sterilization.

The traditional differences observed between Catholics and Protestants have all but disappeared in Canada, Table 3 reveals. Sixty-seven per cent of Catholics and 71 per cent of Protestants were using some form of contraception at the time of the survey, and method choices are remarkably similar. For example, 35 per cent of Catholic users, compared with 39 per cent of Protestant women using a contraceptive method, had been sterilized. No appreciable religious differences can be seen in the use of vasectomy, the pill, the IUD or the condom. Moreover, the rhythm method, which used to be widely relied on by Catholics, accounts for only 3 per cent of current use among Catholics, compared with 1 per cent among Protestants (not shown). In fact, the differences found in the use of the various methods between Catholics and Protestants are less than if either of these two groups were compared with other religious groups.

However, religiosity, as measured by church attendance, does appear to be associated with some differentials in contraceptive use. Women who go to church at least once a week have lower overall levels of use (61 per cent) than do all others (70–72 per cent). In addition, regular church attenders report higher rates of sterilization and lower levels of pill use than do other groups.

Wide differentials in the use of various methods are to be found by educational level. Women with eight or fewer years of schooling report the lowest overall level of contraceptive practice (62 per cent) and appear to depend very heavily on tubal ligation (69 per cent of all users). The proportion sterilized among all users then decreases with rising levels of education, to 47 per cent of those with 9–11 years of schooling, 30 per cent among women who attended school for 12–13 years, and 26 per cent among those with at least some university education. In contrast, use of the IUD and the condom rises with increased educational level and use of the pill reaches its peak level among high school graduates. However, a strong relationship between education and type of method cannot be inferred in the absence of controls for age. A long-term secular trend in developing countries is for younger women to be more educated than their older counterparts. Therefore, the higher level of sterilization seen among less-educated women is due partly to the fact that older women are heavily represented in this group. Future multivariate analysis of the CFS data should further clarify these relationships.

A substantial proportion of the Canadian population is made up of foreign-born residents. In the CFS sample, 14 per cent of all women had been born outside Canada. During the last two decades, the countries of origin of immigrants to Canada have changed dramatically. A larger proportion are now coming from Asia and Third World countries in other continents than from Western Europe, and this factor probably accounts for the somewhat different pattern of method use seen among women born outside Canada when compared with that of native-born women. Although the levels of overall use and the proportions relying on sterilization do not differ greatly, pill use is much lower among the foreign-born (14 per cent of all use vs. 30 per cent), while condom use is much higher (16 per cent vs. 8 per cent).

Since 62 per cent of all women in the CFS sample (and 77 per cent of those over the age of 30) were married, the findings in Table 3 with reference to married women do not differ greatly from those for all women. Among the currently married, as with all women, pill use declines rapidly after age 30. Only 13 per cent of married users aged 30–34 rely on this method, and yet further declines occur with increasing age. Overall contraceptive use among currently married women who do not expect to have any more children is very high (79 per cent); moreover, 71 per cent of these women are protected against pregnancy by male and female sterilization.

Table 4 presents the findings of the CFS on contraceptive use among all unmarried women (never-married and previously married), in terms of their age and religion. Since never-married women tend to be concentrated among the younger age-groups, and previously married women, among the older age-groups, in this table the age-groups have been collapsed into three categories: 18–24, 25–34 and 35–49. Two-thirds of single women are in the age-group 18–24. Of these, 17 per cent said that they were living with a partner (cohabiting). Even if these cohabitants are removed from the denominator and the numerator, contraceptive prevalence among single women is as high as 49 per cent (not shown). Eighty-four per cent of single women aged 18–24 practising contraception use the

Table 4: Percentages of never-married and of previously married women who are using contraceptives; and percentage distribution of current users, by method; according to age and religion

Characteristic			Method						
	N	% using	Female ster.	Male ster.	Pill	IUD	Condom	Other	Total
Never-married	1,430	57.4	4.3	1.7	71.2	7.9	7.9	7.0	100.0
Age group									
18–24	960	55.1	(0.4)	(0.8)	84.1	4.2	5.9	4.6	100.0
25–34	369	65.9	7.4	3.7	51.4	14.0	12.8	10.7	100.0
35–49	101	49.5	32.0	(2.0)	24.0	18.0	(6.0)	18.0	100.0
Religion									
Catholic	752	57.2	5.3	1.6	68.9	7.9	7.9	8.4	100.0
Protestant	428	60.5	2.7	2.3	74.5	8.1	8.1	4.3	100.0
Other or none	246	51.6	3.9	(0.8)	74.0	7.8	7.1	6.4	100.0
Previously married	601	68.8	59.7	6.3	17.4	10.6	2.2	3.8	100.0
Age group									
18–24	37	59.5	9.0	0.0	59.1	27.3	4.5	0.0	100.0
25–34	217	75.1	43.6	7.4	27.0	14.1	3.7	4.2	100.0
35–49	347	66.3	76.1	6.1	6.5	6.5	0.4	4.4	100.0
Religion									
Catholic	252	67.1	58.0	4.7	21.9	10.1	1.8	3.6	100.0
Protestant	219	73.5	64.0	7.5	14.3	8.7	0.6	5.0	100.0
Other or none	129	65.1	53.6	7.1	14.3	15.5	6.0	3.6	100.0

NOTE: Numbers in parentheses denote cases in which there were fewer than ffve women in the category.

pill, while only 6 per cent rely on the condom. Pill use decreases with age, even among single women. However, since most single women are relatively young, pill use dominates their overall contraceptive practice—71 per cent of all use. The analysis reveals virtually no differences by religion in the contraceptive practices of single women.

Except for patterns of use of male methods and somewhat higher recourse to female sterilization among previously married women, the use of birth-control methods among previously married women is very similar to that of currently married women. As might be expected, very small proportions of the previously married rely on vasectomy or the condom. However, in the absence of any information on sexual activity, it is not possible to infer whether this pattern is the result of method preference or whether it stems from the fact that these women are not involved in a sexual relationship.

The rapid decline in fertility in Quebec, where the total fertility rate dropped from 4.0 children per woman, on average, in 1967 to 1.5 in 1983, has received a great deal of attention but no really satisfactory explanation. A once traditionally conservative society, under strong Catholic influence with regard to reproductive

Table 5: Percentage distributions of married women 18–49, by current reproductive and contraceptive status, and of currently married users, by method, Quebec and the rest of Canada

Status and method	Total (N = 3,283)	Quebec (N = 858)	Rest of Canada (N = 2,425)
All married women			
Pregnant, post-partum or seeking pregnancy	13.0	12.7	13.1
Non-contraceptively sterile	8.7	8.9	8.7
Not using a method	5.2	3.5	5.7
Using a method	73.1	74.9	72.5
Users			
Female ster.	41.7	42.1	41.6
Male ster.	17.6	17.7	17.5
Pill	15.0	17.0	14.3
IUD	8.0	7.0	8.4
Diaphragm	1.4	0.5[1]	1.7
Condom	10.8	9.8	11.1
Foam	0.7	0.2[1]	0.9
Rhythm	3.0	3.7	2.7
Withdrawal	1.3	1.0[1]	1.4
Other	0.6	1.1[1]	0.4[1]
Total	100.0	100.0	100.0

[1] Relative standard error of 0.30 or more.

and contraceptive behaviour, has transformed itself into a society in which fertility levels have reached unprecedented lows. A recent study of trends in Quebec between 1971 and 1979 revealed a very rapid increase in the incidence of female sterilization, vasectomy and hysterectomy during that period.[7] The CFS data have made it possible for the first time to compare patterns of contraceptive practice in Quebec with those of the rest of Canada (see Table 5). As the table indicates, the differences are minimal. In Quebec, 4 per cent of married women aged 18–49 are using no contraceptive; for the rest of Canada, the proportion is almost 6 per cent. Among users, 42 per cent of Quebec women and of women in the other provinces had been sterilized, and the incidence of vasectomy is also almost identical. Even rhythm, in the past the traditional method in Quebec, has lost all importance as a method of birth control (4 per cent vs. 3 per cent in the rest of Canada).

Because Quebec women are mainly Catholic, it is of some interest to compare the contraceptive practice of Catholics and Protestants in Quebec with that of the two religious groups living outside the province (see Table 6). Since there are so few Protestant women in Quebec, detailed comparisons by contraceptive method

Table 6: Percentage distributions of married women 18–49, by current reproductive and contraceptive status, and of currently married users, by method; according to religion, Quebec and the rest of Canada

Status and method	Total	Catholics		Protestants	
		Quebec	Rest of Canada	Quebec	Rest of Canada
	(N = 3,283)	(N = 780)	(N = 764)	(N = 37)	(N = 1,187)
All married women					
Pregnant, post-partum or seeking pregnancy	13.0	12.9	13.2	[2]	12.4
Non-contraceptively sterile	8.7	9.1	9.4	[2]	9.2
Not using a method	5.2	2.9	8.4	[2]	3.9
Using a method	73.1	75.1	69.0	73.0	74.5
Users					
Female sterilization	41.7	43.8	40.5	[2]	44.2
Male sterilization	17.6	18.9	15.5	[2]	19.8
Pill	15.0	16.9	15.5	[2]	13.4
IUD	8.0	6.3	9.5	[2]	7.1
Diaphragm	1.4	0.0	0.9[1]	[2]	2.1
Condom	10.8	8.2	9.5	[2]	9.9
Foam	0.7	0.0	0.4[1]	[2]	1.2
Rhythm	3.0	3.7	4.9	[2]	1.2
Withdrawal	1.3	1.0[1]	2.5	[2]	0.6[1]
Other	0.6	1.2[1]	0.8[1]	[2]	0.3[1]
Total	100.0	100.0	100.0	[2]	100.0

[1] Relative standard error of 0.30 or more.
[2] Too few cases for analysis.

were not possible for this group. Nevertheless, the table shows that there are slightly greater differences between Catholics in Quebec and those in the rest of Canada than between Catholics in Quebec and Protestants in the other provinces, especially with respect to non-use (8 per cent among Catholic women outside Quebec province, compared with 3 per cent among those within and 4 per cent among Protestants elsewhere in Canada). The use of permanent methods of contraception is slightly lower among Catholics in the rest of Canada, whereas the use of barrier methods is somewhat higher.

US COMPARISONS

The striking results of the CFS, particularly the finding that such a high proportion of Canadian couples have resorted to sterilization, prompted us to compare the CFS data with those from recent US surveys.[8] Because the age-range of respond-

Table 7: Percentage distribution of women aged 18–44, by current reproductive and contraceptive status, and of currently users, by method; according to marital status; Canada, 1984, and United States, 1982

Status and method	Currently married		Never-married		Previously married	
	Canada	United States	Canada	United States	Canada	United States
All						
Pregnant, post-partum or seeking pregnancy	15.1	13.7	3.1	3.7	3.5	4.4
Non-contraceptively sterile	6.3	13.1	0.9	1.8	6.9	16.4
Not using a method	4.6	5.0	38.0	51.6	17.3	25.6
Using a method	73.9	68.2	58.0	42.6	72.2	53.6
Users						
Female sterilization	38.3	25.6	4.0	3.6	55.6	37.0
Male sterilization	17.8	15.4	1.7	2.0	5.4	3.5[1]
Pill	17.2	19.7	71.6	52.1	20.3	29.5
IUD	9.0	7.1	7.8	5.9	12.4	12.0
Diaphragm	1.6	6.7	2.6	14.6	1.1[1]	6.9
Condom	10.8	14.4	8.0	10.3	2.5	1.6[1]
Foam	0.7	2.9	0.4[1]	1.3	2.0[1]	2.0[1]
Rhythm	2.9	4.7	1.7	2.7	0.3[1]	2.5[1]
Withdrawal	1.2	1.7	1.3	3.4	0.3[1]	0.6[1]
Other	0.5	1.7	0.9	4.3	0.0	4.4
Total	100.0	100.0	100.0	100.0	100.0	100.0

[1] Relative standard error of 0.30 or more.

US DATA SOURCES: See note 8; and special tabulations from the data tapes of the 1982 National Survey of Family Growth, Cycle III.

ents in these US surveys was 15–44, for the sake of comparison women aged 45–49 were excluded from the Canadian sample. Moreover, since the Canadian survey did not interview women aged 15–17, special tabulations were made of the 1982 US data, excluding women in this age-group. Table 7 presents a comparison of the contraceptive practice of US and Canadian women aged 18–44 for various years.

The difference between the proportions of US and Canadian married women classified as non-contraceptively sterile is probably due in part to differences in the wording of the questionnaires.

In the US survey, according to one researcher, 16 per cent of tubal ligations were reported as having been obtained for non-contraceptive purposes.[9] If this were also so in the Canadian survey, the percentage of all Canadian users who had been contraceptively sterilized would drop from 38 per cent to 33 per cent—a level still higher than the 26 per cent reported in the United States in 1982, although representing only half as great a difference. (A second factor may play a minor, although non-negligible, role: Canada has an older age distribution of married women than does the United States. In Canada, 42 per cent of married women are between the ages of 35 and 44, whereas the comparable proportion in the United States is 37 per cent.)

Table 7 also shows that levels of non-use are similar among currently married US and Canadian women (around 5 per cent) and indicates roughly comparable levels of pill use. However, Canadian women tend to rely less on barrier methods than do women in the United States.

Among unmarried women in the two countries, as the table reveals, Canadian women appear to have higher rates of contraceptive prevalence. For example, among the never-married (who are largely women in the 18–24 age group), 58 per cent of Canadian women, compared with 43 per cent of US women, were using a method of birth control at the time of the survey. Furthermore, among single Canadian women using a contraceptive method, 72 per cent were taking the pill, whereas only 52 per cent of the equivalent US group were doing so. Diaphragm use accounts for only 3 per cent of use among never-married Canadian women, compared with 15 per cent in the United States. Condom use is also slightly higher in the United States.

The differences are equally pronounced between US and Canadian women in their late teenage years (not shown). Analysis indicates that whereas 50 per cent of all 18–19-year-olds in Canada (92 per cent of whom are unmarried) practise contraception, the comparable proportion of 18–19-year-olds in the United States (88 per cent of whom are single) is 37 per cent. Moreover, 84 per cent of Canadian users in this age-group rely on the pill, compared with 64 per cent of US teenage users. Concomitantly, 19 per cent of US 18–19-year-old users rely on condoms, in contrast to 9 per cent of their Canadian counterparts.[10]

Comparisons between the contraceptive practices of previously married women in the two countries also show higher levels of use in Canada. However, the problem of the differing definition of sterilization for contraceptive purposes also applies in the case of these women. Adjustment for the difference brings the rates of contraceptive use for the two countries much closer. Apart from higher levels of diaphragm use among previously married US women, patterns of contraceptive practice are similar for formerly married women in both countries.

TRENDS IN CANADA

Because the 1984 CFS is the first genuinely national fertility survey undertaken in Canada, temporal comparisons are hazardous to make. Table 8 presents data on contraceptive use provided by a number of different surveys carried out in Canada since 1968. However, it should be emphasized that the target populations were not the same for all surveys, and geographic coverage differed considerably. The national rates for 1976 come from a survey carried out among adults to find out their attitudes toward abortion, but the survey contained only a small section on contraceptive use, and the number of women in the survey who were of reproductive age was quite small. Bearing these shortcomings in mind, certain

Table 8: Percentage distribution of currently married users, by contraceptive method, surveys of various years and regions, Canada

Method	Toronto[1] 1968 (N = 1,132)	Quebec 1971 (N = 386)	Edmonton[2] 1973 (N = 442)	Quebec[3] 1976 (N = 325)	Canada 1976 (N[4])	Canada 1984 (N = 2,400)
Age range	18–45	≥ 45	18–54	20–40	≥ 15	18–49
Pill	43.2	38.1	46.2	28.8	39.2	15.0
IUD	3.1	3.9	5.7	8.5	6.0	8.0
Diaphragm	9.5	4.2	3.3	u	2.2	1.4
Condom	16.7	6.6	8.4	8.2	6.0	10.8
Rhythm	9.0	32.0	4.3	15.6	6.1	3.0
Withdrawal	8.8	7.9	2.9	4.3	3.4	1.3
Douche	3.5	1.5	u	u	u	u
Foam or jelly	3.4	2.2	u	1.1	2.5	0.7
Other	u	1.1	u	1.8	4.1	0.6
Female ster.	8.7	1.5	u	21.3	30.5	41.8
Male ster.	1.1	1.0	u	10.0	u	17.6
Total	107.0[5]	100.0	100.0	100.0	100.0	100.0

[1] Includes women married only once.

[2] Refers to women of all marital statuses. See Table 4.4 of P. Krishnan and K. Krótki (1976)[note 2].).

[3] Includes women aged 20–40 in March 1976, married for at least five years.

[4] The survey was of adults aged 15 and older. An estimated 1,000 were aged 15–49.

[5] Total exceeds 100 per cent because for women using more than one method, all methods being used are included.

NOTE: u = unavailable.

SOURCE: A. Romaniuc *Fertility in Canada: From Baby-Boom to Baby-Bust,* Current Demographic Analysis, Statistics Canada, Ottawa, 1984, Table 3.1.

clear trends emerge, particularly with regard to the dramatic increase in dependence upon sterilization that has taken place in Canada over the past 17 years or so. In Quebec, for example, male and female sterilization rates increased 13-fold between 1971 and 1976 alone. Since that time, the incidence of sterilization appears to have increased substantially at the national level. Even allowing for the fact that the 1984 CFS includes tubal ligations performed for both non-contraceptive and contraceptive reasons, the increase is nothing less than spectacular. The second major conclusion to be drawn from the examination of trends in contraceptive practice is that use of the pill has declined over time, largely because of increasing recourse to sterilization among women over the age of 30. The IUD and the condom are still important methods, but all other techniques of birth control appear to have lost their relevance for today's Canadian woman.

CONCLUSIONS

Canadian women practice contraception extensively, both in and outside of marriage, and they mainly use the most effective methods. The CFS data substantiate the major findings of an earlier study, carried out in Quebec province, and show very high rates of adoption of sterilization in that province and also throughout the rest of Canada. High levels of contraceptive use, delayed age at marriage and increased rates of marital dissolution have all contributed to the below-replacement level of fertility that has existed in Canada since 1972.

Because Canadian women are opting for sterilization at ever earlier ages, late child-bearing is virtually eliminated for these women, despite many remaining years of reproductive life. Divorce and remarriage are increasing in Canada, and many women who have had a tubal ligation during their first marriage may regret the decision later. About 10 per cent of the women in the CFS sample reported that if they were to make the decision now, they would not elect to become sterilized. Women with more education tend to resort less to sterilization than do other women. It is, therefore, possible that in the future, with growing levels of education among women, with better general knowledge about contraceptive methods and, perhaps, with the availability of improved methods of birth control, the high rate of sterilization that exists in Canada will decline.

NOTES

[1] Justice Canada, *Report of the Committee on the Operation of the Abortion Law*, Ottawa, (Supply and Services Canada, 1977).

[2] T.R. Balakrishnan, J.F. Kantner and J.D. Allingham, *Fertility and Family Planning in a Canadian Metropolis* (Montreal: McGill Queen's University Press, 1975); J. Henripin and E. Lapierre-Adamcyk, *La fin de la revanche des berceaux: qu'en pensent les Québécoises?* (Montreal: University of Montreal Press, 1974); P. Krishnan and K. Krotki, *Report on the Growth of Alberta Families Study*, Population Research Laboratory, University of Alberta, Edmonton, 1976; J. Henripin, *Les enfants qu'on n'a plus au Québec* (Montreal: University of Montreal Press, 1981); and N. Marcil-Gratton and E. Lapierre-Adamcyk, 'Sterilization in Quebec,' *Family Planning Perspectives* 15: 73 (1983).

[3] Population Information Program, 'Oral Contraceptives in the 1980s', *Population Reports*, Series A, No. 6, (1982).

[4] N. Marcil-Gratton and E. Lapierre-Adamcyk (1983), op. cit. (see reference 2).

[5] Centre de Sondage, *Enquête sur la fécondité au Canada: rapport méthodologique* (Montreal: University of Montreal, 1984).

[6] N. Marcil-Gratton and E. Lapierre-Adamcyk (1983), op. cit. (see reference 2); and ———, 'La stérilisation au Québec 1971–1979', research report, University of Montreal, Montreal, 1981, p. 165.

[7] Ibid.

[8] C.A. Bachrach, 'Contraceptive Practice Among American Women, 1973–1982', *Family Planning Perspectives*, 16: 253 (1984).

[9] W.F. Pratt, 'The Motivation for Surgical Sterilization', paper presented at the annual meeting of the American Public Health Association, Anaheim, Calif., 11–15 Nov. 1984.

[10] Special tabulations from the 1984 Canadian Fertility Survey and the 1982 US National Survey of Family Growth.

CHAPTER 15

TEENAGE PREGNANCY

IN CANADA,

1975 – 1987

Surinder Wadhera and John Silins

INTRODUCTION

Culturally, Canada is composed of two nations—the predominantly franco-phone province of Quebec and the anglophone provinces whose culture is similar to that of the United States. In Canada, racial minority groups make up a very small proportion of the total population. (In 1971, American Indians and Eskimos constituted less than 2 per cent of the population, Asians made up only 1.3 per cent and blacks and West Indians, just 0.3 per cent.[1])

The recent fertility history of Canada parallels that of its southern neighbour, the United States. After World War II, the countries experienced a baby boom that peaked at roughly the same time,[2] with fertility reaching its highest post-war level in 1959 in both.[3] In 1986, the total fertility rate (TFR) in Canada was 1.67 children per woman, slightly lower than the US TFR of 1.84.

This [paper] focuses on fertility among Canadian teenagers. We report the numbers of pregnancies and the pregnancy rates per 1,000 15–19-year-old women from 1975 to 1987. Also included is a discussion of trends, age differentials, pregnancy outcomes and regional variations in rates.

SOURCES AND METHODOLOGY

In our calculation of teenage pregnancies, we have included the following: registered live births; therapeutic abortions (induced abortions) performed in accredited and approved hospitals in accordance with the abortion law amended in 1969; and other pregnancy terminations including foetal deaths occurring after 20 weeks' gestation, hospitalized cases of spontaneous abortion, and 'other' and unspecified abortions. (The hospitalized cases include those taking place elsewhere that were admitted for treatment.)

Data on abortions performed in hospitals were available according to the calendar year for 1975–78 and according to the fiscal year for 1979–84. Because data were not available for 1985–87, we assumed that the calendar-year and fiscal-year abortion data are comparable and then extrapolated the number of abortions performed in hospitals for that period by applying the three-year average increase occurring between 1981 and 1984 to the 1984 figures.

We define the teenage pregnancy rate as the number of pregnancies per 1,000 women who were 15–19-years old at the time of the pregnancy's outcome rather than at its conception. The national and regional data used in this paper were extracted from reports published by Statistics Canada on population, births, therapeutic abortions and hospital morbidity.[4] These data are provided to Statistics Canada by the provinces and territories. No data are included from the province of Newfoundland because data on births were not available by mother's age. (In 1987, Newfoundland accounted for 2.3 per cent of Canada's total population of approximately 26 million, for 2.1 per cent of the live births occurring annually, and for 0.7 per cent of the number of therapeutic [induced] abortions performed annually in the country.)

As no data are available at the national level from Statistics Canada on induced abortions performed in clinics or on spontaneous abortions not requiring hospitalization, these are not included in our analysis. Our estimates also exclude data on abortions obtained by Canadians outside the country. Including those abortions obtained in the United States in our calculations would have raised the pregnancy rates somewhat for several provinces.

NATIONAL AND PROVINCIAL DATA

Both the number and the rate of pregnancies among teenagers in Canada declined each year from 1975 through 1987 (Table 1). For example, in 1987 there were 36,694 pregnancies to 15–19-year-old women—26 per cent fewer than the 49,825 pregnancies recorded in 1981 and 37 per cent fewer than the 58,610 pregnancies registered in 1975. Similarly, the pregnancy rate in 1987 among women in that age-group was 11 per cent lower than that for 1981 (41 per 1,000 women aged

Table 1: Number of women aged 15-19, number of pregnancies among women aged 15-19 and age-specific pregnancy rates (per 1,000 women), by year, Canada

Year	Population (in 000s)	Number of pregnancies	Pregnancy rate		
			15-19	15-17	18-19
1975	1,098	58,610	53.4	34.1	83.3
1976	1,119	58,315	52.1	32.8	82.0
1977	1,127	57,594	51.1	32.4	79.8
1978	1,135	56,816	50.1	31.5	77.8
1979	1,134	53,886	47.5	30.1	73.2
1980	1,122	52,895	47.1	28.8	69.4
1981	1,090	49,825	45.7	28.8	69.4
1982	1,065	48,043	45.1	28.3	67.4
1983	1,018	42,626	41.9	26.2	62.0
1984	971	40,108	41.3	25.7	61.6
1985	933	37,693	40.4	24.8	62.0
1986	915	37,529	41.0	25.5	63.7
1987	903	36,694	40.6	24.9	64.3

NOTE: In this and the following table, data for the province of Newfoundland are not included.

15-19, compared with 46 per 1,000), and 24 per cent lower than that for 1975 (53 per 1,000 women 15-19).

During the period 1981-87, the number of pregnancies to teenagers declined by an average of 4.4 per cent annually, almost twice the average annual decline of 2.5 per cent registered during 1975-81. Furthermore, the rate of teenage pregnancy declined annually by an average of 1.9 per cent during the period 1981-87 and by an average of 2.4 per cent during 1975-81. (If we apply the 1987 rate of 41 pregnancies per 1,000 teenage women to the 1975 population, 14,000 fewer teenage pregnancies would have taken place than the actual number recorded in 1975.)

In 1987, approximately 40 per cent of the 903,000 women in the 15-19 age group were 18-19 years old. These older teenagers contributed 63 per cent of the nation's 36,694 pregnancies to teenagers that year, 68 per cent of the 20,981 live births to teenagers and 58 per cent of the 13,501 induced abortions among teenagers. In 1987, the pregnancy rate among 18-19-year-olds (64 per 1,000 women 18-19) was two and one-half times that of 15-17-year-olds (25 per 1,000 women 15-17). During 1975-87, the average decline in the annual pregnancy rate among 18-19-year-olds was slightly less than the average decline among 15-17-year-olds (1.9 per cent compared with 2.2 per cent).

As the data in Table 2 indicate, 57 per cent of pregnancies among teenagers in 1987 resulted in a live birth, 37 per cent ended in an induced abortion and the remaining 6 per cent, in foetal death or some other pregnancy termination. While the number of pregnancies among 15-19-year-olds decreased by 37 per cent

Table 2: Number of pregnancies and age-specific pregnancy rates (per 1,000 women), by age group, according to pregnancy outcome and year

Outcome and year	Number			Rate		
	15–19	15–17	18–19	15–19	15–17	18–19
All pregnancies						
1975	58,610	22,687	35,923	53.4	34.1	83.3
1981	49,825	18,267	31,558	45.7	28.8	69.4
1987	36,694	13,489	23,205	40.6	24.9	64.3
Births						
1975	38,818	13,190	25,628	35.4	19.8	59.4
1981	29,062	9,107	18,955	26.7	14.3	43.9
1987	20,981	6,790	14,191	23.2	12.5	39.3
Abortions						
1975	14,716	7,371	7,345	13.4	11.1	17.0
1981	17,575	7,841	9,734	16.1	12.3	21.4
1987	13,501	5,674	7,827	14.9	10.5	21.7
Other[1]						
1975	5,076	2,126	2,950	4.6	3.1	6.9
1981	3,188	1,319	1,869	2.9	2.0	3.7
1987	2,212	1,025	1,187	2.5	1.9	3.3

[1] Includes foetal deaths of at least 20 weeks' gestation, hospitalized cases of spontaneous abortion and other unspecified abortions.

between 1975 and 1987, the number of live births among women 15–19 decreased by 46 per cent during that period (from 38,818 in 1975 to 20,981 in 1987). Induced abortions followed a different pattern; their annual number increased steadily, from 14,716 in 1975 to a peak of 18,739 in 1979 (not shown). The number of procedures then dropped in each of the following years so that by 1987, 13,501 induced abortions were performed among Canadian teenagers, even fewer than in 1975.

As mentioned earlier, the Canadian baby boom peaked in 1959.[5] The fertility rate among 15–19-year-olds decreased from a high of 60 births per 1,000 women in that year to 35 per 1,000 in 1975, a decline of 41 per cent. During the next 12 years, it declined by another 36 per cent to reach 23 per 1,000 by 1987. The average annual fertility rate for 18–19-year-old women was three times that for 15–17-year-olds during the 1975–87 period. The fertility rate for the older women declined by an average of 2.8 per cent annually and the rate for the younger teenagers, by 3.1 per cent annually over the 12 years.

The rate of induced abortion per 1,000 15–19-year-olds increased by 24 per cent over the five-year period 1975–80 (from 13 abortions per 1,000 teenagers to 17 per 1,000). It then decreased during each of the following five years (to 14 per 1,000 in 1985), before rising again slightly to 15 abortions per 1,000 teenagers in 1987.

During 1980–87, the average annual decline in the rate of induced abortion for 15–17-year-olds was more than three times the decline for 18–19-year-olds (1.8 per cent vs. 0.5 per cent), and by 1987, the induced abortion rate among 18–19-year-old women was twice the rate for 15–17-year-olds.

As previously stated, the category of 'other' pregnancy outcomes includes foetal deaths from 20 weeks' gestation and hospitalized cases of spontaneous abortions and other unspecified abortions. Both the numbers and rates of these other outcomes among pregnant teenagers declined by about half during the study period—the number fell by 56 per cent and the corresponding rate, by 48 per cent.

The teenage pregnancy rates during the period under examination were generally higher in the western provinces than in the eastern provinces (with the exception of Newfoundland, for which no age-specific data were available), and ranged from a low of 26 pregnancies per 1,000 teenage women in Quebec to a high of 60 per 1,000 in Manitoba (Figure 1). Moreover, from 1975 to 1987, teenage pregnancy rates declined by 6 per cent in Manitoba; by 20–35 per cent in Saskatchewan, Alberta, British Columbia, Ontario and Nova Scotia; by 44 per cent in Prince Edward Island; and by 52 per cent in New Brunswick (not shown). In Quebec, however, the pregnancy rate per 1,000 15–19-year-olds increased by 6 per cent.

In 1987, as in prior years, the proportion of teenage pregnancies resulting in births was greater for Prince Edward Island (92 per cent), New Brunswick (82 per cent) and Saskatchewan (78 per cent) than for Alberta (64 per cent), Manitoba (63 per cent), Nova Scotia (63 per cent), Quebec (60 per cent), British Columbia (45 per cent) or Ontario (50 per cent). Conversely, the proportion of pregnancies terminated by induced abortion was less than 1 per cent for Prince Edward Island; less than 10 per cent for New Brunswick; 10–35 per cent for Saskatchewan, Alberta, Manitoba, Nova Scotia and Quebec; and 45–50 per cent for Ontario and British Columbia.

Because there are very few cases recorded for the Atlantic provinces—especially of induced abortions and 'other' pregnancy outcomes—the rates and numbers should be interpreted with caution. The induced abortion rates are, to a great extent, a reflection of the availability and accessibility of abortion services. The abortion rates for provinces east of Ontario are lower than the national rate while rates in the provinces west of Ontario are higher. If it were possible to include those abortions obtained either outside of Canada or in Quebec clinics in calculations of abortion rates for the women's province of residence, the rates for the eastern provinces would be higher than those published by Statistics Canada. The high fertility rates in the Atlantic provinces, Manitoba, Saskatchewan and Alberta may be partially explained by the social and religious composition of the population in those provinces.

Our estimate of a 24 per cent drop in the teenage pregnancy rate in Canada from 1975 to 1987 is supported by other research. Maureen Orton and Ellen Rosenblat, for example, calculated a pregnancy rate of 44 pregnancies per 1,000 teenage women in 1981, which represented a decline of more than 10 per cent from 49 per

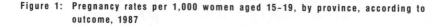

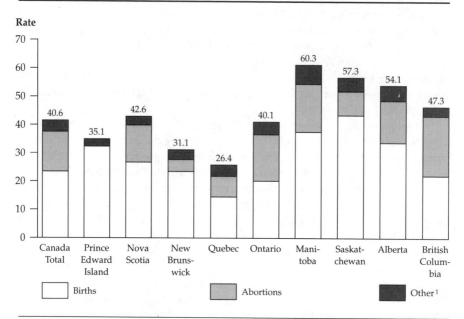

Figure 1: Pregnancy rates per 1,000 women aged 15–19, by province, according to outcome, 1987

1Includes foetal deaths of at least 20 weeks' gestation, hospitalized cases of spontaneous abortion and other unspecified abortions.

1,000 registered in 1976.[6] Furthermore, Elise Jones and colleagues noted a national rate of 44 per 1,000 for 1981 (a decline of 13 per cent from about 51 per 1,000 in 1971).[7] Our data indicate a 1981 teenage pregnancy rate in Canada of 46 per 1,000, a decrease of 14 per cent from 53 per 1,000 in 1975. However, these teenage pregnancy rates were calculated on a slightly different basis: While our calculation took into account stillbirths of at least 20 weeks' gestation and hospitalized cases of spontaneous abortion and other unspecified abortions, the other two studies did not. Moreover, the other studies included induced abortions performed in Quebec clinics and legal abortions obtained by Canadian women visiting the United States, information not included in our investigation.

The addition of these clinic abortions and those performed out of the country would clearly raise the number and rates of teenage pregnancy in Canada. Based on incomplete reports from several US states, most along the Canadian border, an average of 3,000 Canadian women obtained legal abortions in the United States each year from 1975 to 1987.[8] An estimated 22 per cent of these were obtained by teenagers, which would increase the pregnancy rate for Canadian teenagers by 1.3 per cent for the period. If we were to add the number of induced abortions performed in Quebec clinics[9] to our calculation, assuming that the two sets of data have identical age distributions, the average annual number of teenage pregnancies would increase by 10 per cent for the province of Quebec and by 1.4 per cent for Canada as a whole. The inclusion of Quebec clinic data would thus raise the average teenage pregnancy rate for Quebec from 24 pregnancies per 1,000 teenagers to 27 per 1,000.

The available data indicate that teenage fertility is much lower in Canada than in the United States. There were 40 pregnancies for every 1,000 Canadian women aged 15–19 in 1983, compared with 110 pregnancies per 1,000 women aged 15–19 in the United States.[10] In that year, the fertility rate among Canadian teenagers (24 births per 1,000 women aged 15–19) was less than half that of teenage women in the United States (52 per 1,000). The difference between the two countries in the legal abortion rate among teenagers is slightly greater than the difference in fertility rates—in 1985, the abortion rate among Canadian teenagers was 14 per 1,000, one-third of the 44 per 1,000 in the United States.[11]

For further international comparison, we derived teenage pregnancy rates for a group of selected countries (Czechoslovakia, England and Wales, Finland, Hungary, the Netherlands, Norway, Sweden and the United States) by adding the teenage fertility rates to legal abortion rates. We selected countries based on their similarity to Canada in general cultural norms and in level of economic development, as well as on the availability of recent reliable birth and abortion data.[12]

The 1983 teenage pregnancy rate for Canada (39 pregnancies per 1,000 women aged 15–19) was very close to the rate for Norway in the same year (41 per 1,000). Canada's 1983 rate was 12 per cent less than that for England and Wales (45 per 1,000), 39 per cent lower than the 1982 rate for Czechoslovakia (65 per 1,000) and about 60 per cent less than the 1982 rate for the United States (97 per 1,000). However, the Canadian rate was somewhat higher than the 1983 rates for Sweden (30 per 1,000) and Finland (33 per 1,000). In a comparison of fertility rates, Canada's rate of 25 live births per 1,000 15–19-year-old women is very close to the rate for England and Wales (27 births per 1,000), and is roughly one-half the rates for Czechoslovakia (51 per 1,000), the United States (53 per 1,000) and Hungary (54 per 1,000). Only two of the selected countries—Czechoslovakia and the Netherlands—had a lower legal abortion rate for 1983 than Canada (14 abortions per 1,000 teenagers).

DISCUSSION

Rates of fertility and induced abortion are influenced to a great extent by changes in such factors as marital patterns, availability and access to abortion facilities, sexual behaviour, and knowledge and use of contraceptives. For example, marital patterns in Canada have changed considerably over the past few decades: both the annual number and the rate of all marriages have declined, and the marriage rate among teenage women has decreased by 79 per cent in the 15-year period from 1972 to 1987—from 58 marriages per 1,000 unmarried women aged 15–19 to 12 per 1,000. The median age at first marriage for women rose by three years from 21.3 in 1972 to 24.3 in 1987. The significant declines in both the number and rate of marriages in Canada and the increase in the median age at first marriage tend to slow the pace of fertility.

To some extent, the decline in the teenage fertility rate paralleled the decline in the general fertility rate. Both rates increased appreciably during the baby boom of the 1950s and then declined in the following three decades. By 1987, the teenage fertility rate had fallen by 62 per cent from its peak in 1959 and the general fertility rate had fallen by 55 per cent. This drop in the teenage fertility rate may be attributed, in part, to recent trends of delayed marriage and family formation: by 1987, the median age at first birth rose by 3.7 years to 25.8 years from 22.1 years in 1965. As a proportion of all births, births to teenagers decreased to 6 per cent in 1987 from 10 per cent in 1965, while the proportion of births to women aged 20–29 increased to 63 per cent in 1987 from 58 per cent in 1965.

The declines in teenage pregnancy rates could better be explained if there were trend data of both sexual and contraceptive behaviour. However, only limited data are available. According to the 1976 National Population Survey conducted by the Badgely Committee,[13] for example, only 8 per cent of 15–year-old women had had coitus, with an increase to 19 per cent among those 16–17 years of age and to 60 per cent among women 18–23 years of age. Furthermore, data from the 1978–79 Canada Health Survey indicate that 17 per cent of the 1.1 million Canadian teenage women were using oral contraceptives.[14] And results from the 1985 Canadian Fertility Survey show that 50 per cent of 18–19-year-old women use a contraceptive method, with the pill accounting for more than 80 per cent of use in this age-group.[15] Studies conducted in some Ontario counties between 1976 and 1981 have indicated that the provision of sex education and clinic contraceptive services have resulted in considerable declines in adolescent pregnancy.[16] Similar data for future years would be a definite asset to the study of teenage pregnancy in Canada.

In conclusion, there were 36,694 pregnancies in 1987 to Canadian women aged 15–19, a figure that represents a decline of 37 per cent from the 58,610 pregnancies recorded in 1975. During the 12-year period, the rate of teenage pregnancies in Canada declined by 24 per cent, so that 41 out of every 1,000 teenage women in Canada conceived in 1987 compared with 53 of every 1,000 in 1975. Fifty-seven per cent of pregnancies to teenagers in 1987 resulted in a live birth, 37 per cent in an induced abortion and the remaining 6 per cent in some other abortion or in foetal death occurring after 20 weeks' gestation.

The decrease in the overall annual numbers and rates of teenage pregnancies and births may be attributable to delays in age at marriage and family formation; a decline in the proportion of teenagers in the female population over the last three decades; wider availability of contraceptives and the increased prevalence of their use; the impact of negative coverage of high rates of teenage pregnancy in the media; possible infertility resulting from sexually transmitted diseases among teenagers; higher rates and availability of abortion; and a greater emphasis on sex education and the prevention of unwanted pregnancy. However, the association between many of these factors and declines in teenage fertility rates has yet to be thoroughly documented.

NOTES

[1] Statistics Canada, *Census of Canada: Population of Ethnic Groups, 1971*, Volume 1 (Ottawa, Oct. 1973), table 4.19, p. 137.

[2] E.F. Jones et al., *Teenage Pregnancy in Industrialized Countries* (New Haven: Yale University Press, 1986).

[3] Statistics Canada, *Births and Deaths*, Cat. 84–204, Annuals for 1975 through 1987, Ottawa, publication dates 1977–1989; and National Center for Health Statistics, *Vital Statistics of the United States, 1986: Vol. I—Natality* (Washington, D.C., U.S. Government Printing Office, 1988).

[4] Statistics Canada, *Therapeutic Abortions*, Cat. 82–211, Annuals for 1975 through 1987, Ottawa, publication dates 1977–1989; ———, *Population Estimates*, Vol. 4, Cat. 91–210, Annuals for 1975 through 1987, Ottawa, publication dates 1977–1989; and ———, *Hospital Morbidity*, Cat. 82–206, Annuals for 1975 through 1983, Ottawa, publication dates 1977–1985.

[5] Statistics Canada, *Demographic Aspects of Vital Statistics, Report on Summary and Recommendations from Statistics Canada Workshop* (Ottawa, Nov. 1983).

[6] M.J. Orton and E. Rosenblat, 'Adolescent Pregnancy in Ontario, Progress in Prevention', paper submitted to the Ontario Ministry of Health, Feb. 1986.

[7] Jones et al. (1986); (see note 2).

[8] Unpublished data from the Health Departments of the following states: Connecticut, Hawaii, Maine, Minnesota, Montana, New Hampshire, New York, North Dakota, Oregon, Pennsylvania, South Dakota and Washington.

[9] Quarterly and annual Reports on Abortions, 1978–1987, Régie de l'assurance-maladie du Québec, Province of Quebec, Canada.

[10] S.K. Henshaw et al., *Teenage Pregnancy in the United States: The Scope of the Problem and State Responses* (New York: The Alan Guttmacher Institute, 1989).

[11] Ibid.

[12] United Nations, *Demographic Year Book, 1984*, 36th edition (New York, 1986).

[13] Justice Canada, *Report of the Committee on the Operation of the Abortion Law* (Ottawa: Supply and Services Canada, 1977).

[14] Statistics Canada, *The Health of Canadians, Report of the Canada Health Survey, 1978–79*, Cat. 82–538E (Ottawa, June 1981).

[15] T.R. Balakrishnan, K. Krótki and E. Lapierre-Adamcyk, 'Contraceptive Use in Canada,' *Family Planning Perspectives* 17: 209 (1985).

[16] Orton and Rosenblat (1986); (see note 6).

CHAPTER 16

FERTILITY

IN CANADA

Retrospective

and Prospective

Anatole Romaniuc

In recent years, there has been an upsurge of public interest in population issues. Aging and slowdown in population growth; immigration and rising ethnic and cultural diversity; and emergence of new trends in family and living arrangements are increasingly capturing the attention of social scientists and policy-makers alike. At the root of some of these developments is the dramatic decline of the fertility rate since 1960, to a level that is no longer sufficient to ensure the renewal of generations, and in the longer run that of the population as a whole. This paper takes a long view of the fertility evolution in Canada. Structurally it consists of three sections. The first singles out the main stages of secular decline in fertility; the second identifies the significant underlying factors, particularly those more closely associated with the recent baby bust; and the third speculates about the future course of fertility in Canada.

SECULAR DECLINE OF FERTILITY: THE MAIN STAGES

In less than one hundred years, Canada has gone from a regime of traditional high fertility, characterized by the quasi-absence of birth control within marriage, to a regime of low fertility with almost perfect contraception. Prior to the onset of the decline, the crude birth rate was in the range of 45–55 per 1,000; it now stands at 15 per 1,000. From about six births per woman, the total fertility rate has declined to a below-replacement level of 1.7 in recent years. The progression towards ever-lower reproductive targets has not, however, been monotonic. The transition from high to low fertility has followed a trajectory punctuated by phases of fast and slow deceleration, and by upward and downward swings (Figures 1 and 2). Viewed in its historical context, even the post-war baby boom, its magnitude notwithstanding, is not out of character, and the present baby bust is well in keeping with a secular decline that may not yet have run its course. This section attempts to depict the broad configurations of this fertility transition from traditional high to modern low levels.

THE PRE-DECLINE LEVEL OF FERTILITY

Though much of the past remains shrouded in mystery, enough information has been retrieved — all due to the remarkable achievements of historical demography in Quebec — to reconstruct the main reproductive features of the early French Canadian population. Birth rates in the range of 50 to 60 per 1,000 were estimated to have prevailed through the seventeenth and eighteenth centuries (Henripin, 1954: 50). With plenty of land available for settlement by new households, marriage and childbearing were encouraged by kin, and, to some extent, by the state through various material and administrative incentives. Similar reproductive patterns were found in other provinces in the earlier days of settlement. Birth rates of over 55 per 1,000 have been estimated for the provinces of Ontario and Manitoba for one or another period during the nineteenth century (Henripin, 1968: 370). High fertility, typical of frontier settlements, and large-scale immigration of young people with a high propensity to marry and have children, were some of the significant factors.

THE ONSET AND EARLY PERIODS OF THE DECLINE

Eventually, Canada was caught up in what is called the long-term or secular downward movement of fertility among nations undergoing modernization. At first hardly perceptible, the decline picked up momentum in the 1870s and 1880s. After a protracted lull, and even an increase in Quebec's birth rate, the earlier downward tendency resumed its course around 1910. By the mid-1930s, however,

Figure 1: Crude birth rate per 1,000 population, Canada and Quebec,[1] 1801–1989

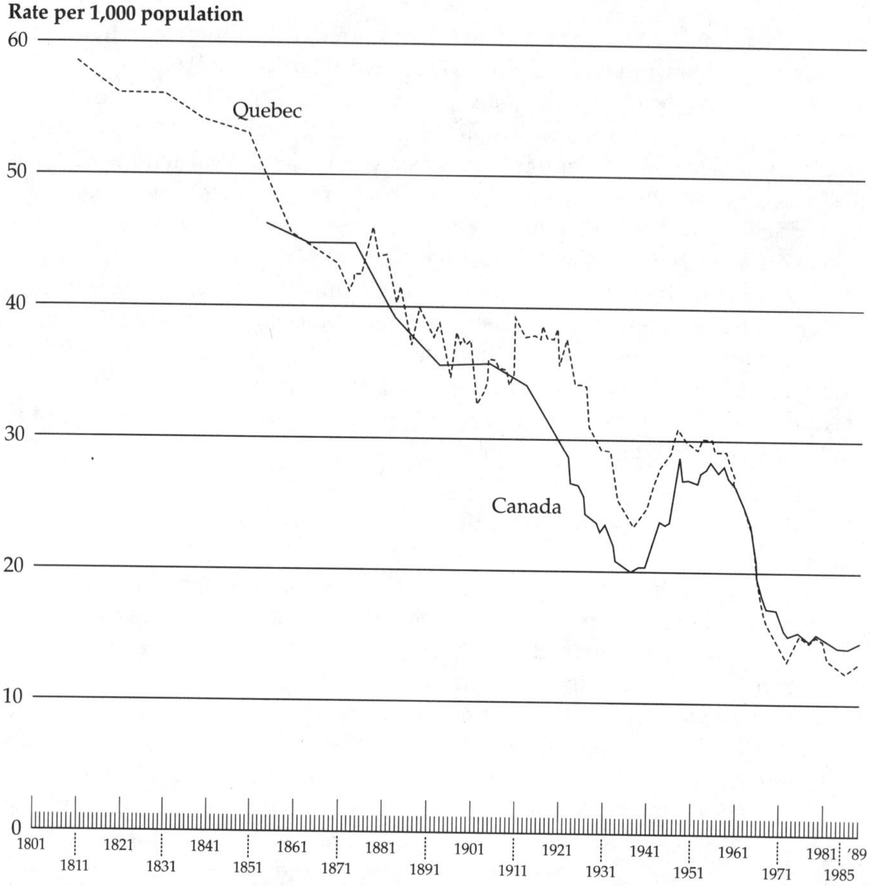

Rate per 1,000 population

[1] Crude birth rates from 1801 through 1867 refer to the Catholic population of Quebec.

SOURCE: Statistics Canada, *Vital Statistics, Births and Deaths*, Cat. 84–204, Annual; J. Henripin, *Trends and Factors of Fertility in Canada* (Statistics Canada, 1972), p. 5, 366; *Historical Statistics of Canada*, M.C. Urquhart and K.A.H. Buckley (eds) (Toronto: Macmillan 1965), p. 43.

it came to an abrupt halt. To the extent that these early estimates of birth rates are valid, they reveal an interesting pattern of alterations between fast and slow phases in the decline. As such, they were harbingers of the more turbulent swings that were to come.

This early period of the decline was characterized by the co-existence of old and emerging models of reproduction. Large and small families co-existed to varying degrees, depending upon social class, ethnicity and region. Even as late as the 1930s, when fertility had reached its historical low, almost 20 per cent of ever-

Figure 2:   Total fertility rate per 1,000 women, Canada[1] and Quebec, 1871–1989

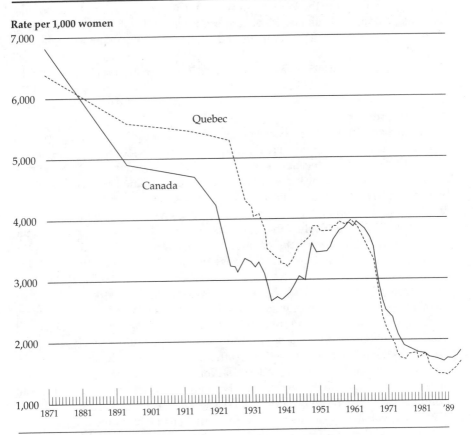

Rate per 1,000 women

[1] Data for Newfoundland excluded.
SOURCE: Statistics Canada, *Vital Statistics, Births and Deaths*, Cat. 84-204, Annual; J. Henripin, *Trends and Factors of Fertility in Canada* (Statistics Canada, 1972), p. 5, 366; *Historical Statistics of Canada*, M.C. Urquhart and K.A.H. Buckley (eds) (Toronto: Macmillan 1965), p. 43.

married women who had fully or nearly completed their childbearing, had six or more children, and this occurred at a time when as many as 16 per cent of couples were permanently childless, many most probably by design. During the 1930s, urban/rural and regional variations were wider than ever before or since. The contrast between Quebec, with 3.3 births per woman, and British Columbia, with 1.9 births per woman, epitomizes the amplitude of the regional variations. What is amazing is that a reduction of childbearing of this scale was possible in an era when most of the methods of contraception used were rudimentary and not very efficient.

THE BABY BOOM

At the very time when the Western world was haunted by the spectre of population stagnation, with its attendant dire economic and political consequences, fertility played havoc with forecasters and produced a baby boom that lasted for more than two decades. The increase in the total fertility rate, from its low of 2.6 in 1937 to a high of 3.9 in 1959, was the outcome of a combination of shifts in both the *timing*—women having children earlier in life and at shorter intervals—and the *level* of childbearing, resulting in larger family sizes. Roughly half of the increase was due to the former.

A remarkable feature of the baby boom is that it was an all-embracing movement involving, in varying degrees of intensity, practically all social strata, irrespective of cultural background, education or income. While spearheaded by the generations in their prime childbearing years, the baby boom was sustained by all but the oldest generations. The rise in nuptiality (with a marked tendency toward earlier marriage and a higher proportion marrying in each age), which significantly broadened the pool of young and relatively stable unions ideally suited for reproduction, was the key factor in the post-war baby boom. And those who married did so with the intention of having children. Childlessness among ever-married women fell dramatically from 16 per cent in the 1930s (cohorts born between 1902 and 1911) to 7 per cent in the 1950s (cohorts born between 1932 and 1936).

While describing the unfolding of the baby boom is a relatively straightforward proposition, unravelling the underlying factors is not. Yet, there is no lack of competing theories. In Easterlin's (1980) well-known interpretation, the baby boom was the product of the long-term effects of growing up during the Depression on people's values—their modest taste for material goods and aspirations for home and family—and the favourable labour market which these relatively small cohorts enjoyed in the environment of post-war economic expansion. For Ryder (1984), what changed was not so much fundamental family values as the material conditions of family formation. Owing to both the high demand for labour—brought about by the post-war economic recovery—and to the short supply of younger workers—the result of the low birth rate of the 1930s—more people at younger ages were in the position, economically speaking, to begin families. Furthermore, and notwithstanding the consumer choice argument, the baby boom took place in an environment of tremendous expansion in the market for durable goods. As Rostow (1965: 80) puts it, 'Americans began to behave as if they preferred the extra baby to the extra unit of consumption.'

All these are probably valid points. However, what is important to recognize in any interpretation of the baby boom is the uniqueness of its historical setting—the Great Depression and World War II that preceded, and the post-war prosperity that accompanied it. As one leading American economist (Feldstein, 1980: 1) states, 'the first two decades of the post-war period were a time of an unsurpassed economic prosperity, stability and optimism.' And all this succession of historical events happened at a time when traditional pro-family values were still strong in the populace.

THE BABY BUST

The baby boom came to a halt as unexpectedly as it began. Who, indeed, in the heyday of the baby boom, would have predicted a collapse in the fertility rate from almost four births per woman in 1959 to about 1.7 in recent years? The drama, curiously enough, unfolded according to a childbearing *quantity/timing* stratagem that was characteristic of the baby boom, but in reverse, and at a significantly swifter pace. It took 22 years for the baby boom to reach its peak, but only eight years for total fertility to revert to its previous low of 2.6, and 12 years to hit replacement level. Couples of all childbearing ages were caught in the down-sizing of the family. Women in the upper age brackets and higher birth orders initiated the decline, but were quickly overtaken by those under age 25.

Today, large families have virtually disappeared, while childlessness is on the rise. According to Canadian census data, the proportion of childless, ever-married women aged 25–29 rose from 14 per cent in 1961 to 30 per cent in 1981. It is difficult to say how many will remain without offspring either by choice or because, after repeated postponements, their 'biological clocks' will have run down. Concomitant with the downward reappraisal of family size, there has been an upward shift in the age pattern and a slower tempo of childbearing. There is now a tendency to have children later in life, and to space them farther apart. The number of first-time parents in their thirties is on the increase of late, possibly signifying the realignment of women's priorities in life.

This drive toward unprecedented low childbearing involves all social strata, ethnolinguistic groups and regions. The province of Quebec, which in earlier times enjoyed the highest fertility in the country, has seen its fertility rate plunge to 1.4 births per woman (1985), the lowest of all the provinces. The sub-replacement fertility is now the national norm. Even Canada's aboriginal people, who maintained a high reproductive profile until about the mid-1960s, have seen their total fertility rate wind down from 7 to 3.5 births per woman (Romaniuc, 1987).

FACTORS IN THE FERTILITY DECLINE

The secular decline of fertility in industrialized countries has received a great deal of attention within the framework of demographic transition theory (Coale and Watkins, 1986). While an earlier version of the theory emphasized declining mortality as the driving force of transition, the more recent version stresses the economics of childbearing. The explanation of modern reproductive behaviour is enunciated in terms such as the opportunity cost of childbearing, cost and benefits of children to parents, socialization of support for the aged, and reversal in flow of wealth from parents to children. More recent attempts aim at the broadening of the explanatory framework. Thus, Kaufman (1990) singles out three key components in the current low fertility: widening of options, primacy of individual choice over normative constraints in marriage and parenthood, and downgrading of socio-economic status of the family — all these due to a combination of factors such as economic development and institutional changes, resulting in greater employment opportunities for females, cultural liberalization, and greater control over procreation.

The explanation attempted here is neither comprehensive nor systematic. It is restricted to the developments that basically took place in the areas of contraceptive technology, female employment, and family and marriage, concomitantly with the most recent stage in the secular decline of fertility, that is, the post-1960 baby bust. Due to lack of space, other potentially promising explanatory avenues, particularly those that could be subsumed under the label of 'ideational' undercurrents of fertility decline, had to be left out, or are touched upon only incidentally.

CONTRACEPTIVE TECHNOLOGY

The advent of highly effective contraceptive technology—the pill and intrauterine devices in the 1960s, and contraceptive sterilization in the 1970s— revolutionized birth-control practices. One immediate consequence has been a much tighter control of the timing of childbearing and the size of the family. If so-called 'unwanted births' have not been completely wiped out, their occurrence has been significantly reduced.

The spread of sterilization is particularly revealing both as a method of contraception and as mental disposition toward procreation. According to the Canadian Fertility Survey (1984), sterilization in the province of Quebec has been carried out on one or the other spouse in 38 per cent of marriages where the wife was 30 to 34 years old. Similarly, as many as 28 per cent of families with one child and 52 per cent with two children, now have at least one medically sterile partner. That so many couples at the earlier stages of family formation have resorted to a method that for all practical purposes is irreversible speaks a great deal about their determination to put an irrevocable end to their reproduction.

There is, however, more to this than meets the eye. Highly reliable, coitus-independent birth control has had far-reaching behavioural implications. Parenthood is no longer a matter of faith and biology, but an act of choice. Preston (1986) has argued that the availability of highly effective contraception has raised the cost of adherence to pro-family values and contributed to the erosion of their legitimacy. Traditional sexual morality and marriage have been weakened by the modern coitus-independent contraceptive technology. As a result, writes Preston (1986: 183) 'the social value of confining sex to marriage was clearly reduced. Sex became less a social act and more a purely private one, and the institutions contrived to govern access to it predictably began to erode. Rates of entry into marriage declined sharply and rates of exit grew, aided by legal changes reflecting an altered value system.'

We shall carry the logic of Preston's argument from contraceptive technology into the reproductive revolution when later discussing the future of marriage and its generative function. In the meantime, in what follows, we shall address another important factor that affected procreative behaviour directly, and indirectly, via changes in marriage and family.

GROWTH OF FEMALE EMPLOYMENT

In the 1920s, only 20 per cent of females over 15 years of age were employed. Over the next 30 years their participation rate rose slowly, inching up to 24 per cent in 1951. During the baby-boom period of the 1950s, the rise was somewhat faster, reaching 30 per cent by 1961. But it was not until the 1960s that women moved *en masse* into the work place, a trend that continued even during the economic slowdown. High male unemployment and the rising cost of living may in fact have reinforced the move towards women joining the labour force in the 1970s. By 1990, almost 60 per cent of women were gainfully employed. Although still heavily concentrated in the low-paid jobs where they predominated historically, it is in occupations carrying higher salaries that their employment expanded the fastest. Between 1971 and 1981, the number of women in the 20 highest-paid professions increased fourfold, as against one-and-a-half times in the traditional lowest-paid jobs.

Contemporaneously, there was a marked trend toward greater work stability. Women's traditional motherhood-related pattern of exit and re-entry into the labour force has given way to a more stable employment picture. Marital and family status differentials in female labour-force participation are disappearing. One novel development has been the dramatic rise in the labour-force participation of married women with pre-school children (from 28 per cent in 1971 to 58 per cent in 1986 for those under age 35). The division of labour by sex within marriage is less clear cut, and this has meant a weakening of traditional sex roles and of 'gains from trade' within marriage (Michael, 1985). Women and men now behave much more similarly when it comes to gainful employment.

Two arguments could be put forward to explain how women's gainful employment can mediate a procreative pattern. One has to do with role incompatibility: working and mothering compete for women's time and energy; career-building takes place over the same years in which families are formed and children raised. Progress in household technology has barely kept pace with the ever-rising standards of living. The bulk of housework still falls on the shoulders of the wife, even when she is employed, according to contemporary time-budget surveys. Its common-sense appeal, notwithstanding the incompatibility argument, is, however, too narrow to account for the complex decision-making process involving the trade-off between employment and childbearing.

The other argument is that increased opportunities for women's employment, along with advances in contraceptive technology, have opened up alternatives to motherhood. By the same token, childbearing has been brought within the ambit of economic calculus. Improved education and skill have increased the earning power of women in the market, and hence the opportunity cost of staying at home.

MARRIAGE AND FAMILY

The early and almost universal marriage pattern that prevailed in the 1950s and 1960s has given way to a different lifestyle. Today fewer people marry, and among those who do, there is a tendency to marry later in life. The rise in the divorce rate since 1970 has been as spectacular as the fall in the nuptiality rate. The rate of remarriage has not kept pace with the rate of divorce, and second marriages have proven to be even more fragile than first—hence the greater marital instability and conjugal mobility. At the same time, the dominance of the two-parent family, based on a formal marriage, is increasingly being challenged by the still small but rising incidence of mono-parental families, headed largely by women, and by the soaring practice of non-marital cohabitation, a less stable, and less procreation-oriented, conjugal arrangement (Burch and Madan, 1986; Ram, 1990). As a result, the pool of people enjoying the optimum conditions for procreation that stable and lasting marriage offers has shrunk in our society.

However, there is more to it. Families are undergoing profound change, not only in structure but in substance as well. McDaniel (1986) speaks of an emerging 'feminist' model as opposed to the traditional family model. Roussel speaks of the deinstitutionalization of marriage, the loss of social control over it, and its transformation into a simple pact of convenience between two individuals concerned. Lasch (1990) deplores the invasion of the family by the market. What is involved here is a significant change in the relationship between family members that ultimately affects, in fact weakens, the very generative function of marriage and family.

The traditional husband-dominated relationship is giving way to a more egalitarian partnership between spouses (Chapman and Balakrishnan, 1986). Marriage is seen more as a joint venture for meeting certain goals, of which procreation may not be the most important. Robbed of its 'institutional content' in favour of personal gratification and individualistic goals, marriage's vulnerability to internal and external strains is more real today than ever before (Roussel, 1984).

At the same time the parent/child relationship is undergoing a major redefinition. According to some observers at least (Shorter, 1975), adolescents seem to be veering away from parents and towards peer groups for companionship and socialization, and are rejecting their parents' values and their own traditional role as guardians of the family line. Proclivity for separate households and common-law unions are some of the outward manifestations of the prevailing spirit of independence among adolescents and young adults. Indifference toward family identity and continuity weakens their own aspirations of becoming parents.

There are basically two kinds of motivation for having children: one is economic—old age security and the economic return which parents expect from their offspring; the other is psychological—the enjoyment parents derive from children, the transmission of family values, and the projection of themselves onto their offspring. Society has long since taken over much of the welfare function, and now family identity and continuity seem to be on their way out as inducements for having children. The instinct of perpetuation and altruistic sentiments can well be evoked as something intrinsic to human species, but they are far too elusive concepts to provide a meaningful basis for the rationalization of procreative behaviour of human populations.

WHAT CAN BE INFERRED?

The above review of selected social and economic indicators, albeit sketchy, is nonetheless revealing of things happening if not in unison then at least in a cluster, more or less contemporaneously. The period during which the baby bust took place was marked by a number of major social events such as the collapse of nuptiality and the rise in divorce rates, along with the growing incidence of common-law unions and single motherhood as options to the traditional two-spouse family. The economic climate was marred by high unemployment, deterioration in the relative income of young adults, rising inflation and spiralling housing costs (Romaniuc, 1984). Yet all these events picked up momentum when the downward drift of the fertility rate was well under way and had almost reached its low ebb. The collapse of nuptiality followed the onset of the baby bust by almost a decade. Inflation and unemployment reached high levels only during the early 1980s, and are basically cyclical occurrences. Their annual rates dropped from their peaks in the early 1980s of 12.4 per cent and 11.8 per cent, respectively, to something in the vicinity of 5 per cent and 7.5 per cent by the end of the decade, only to begin rising once again as Canada was plunged into an economic recession by 1990. The country's changing economic future probably had a compounding effect, but the driving forces in the fertility decline since 1960 must be sought elsewhere.

Of various indicators reviewed in this paper, the rate of female labour-force participation offers the most coherent picture (Figure 3) — an almost perfect negative correlation with the fertility rate since 1960. In a previous section, it has been shown how employment of women can interfere with their family role. Yet the causal relationship between the two eludes precise determination. Rather, the increasing participation of women in the labour force can be viewed as interacting with low childbearing and marital instability in a mutually reinforcing process driven by deep-seated cultural and economic forces.

On the one hand, the quest for equality between spouses, their economic independence and self-actualization, embedded in the very culture of our individualistic society, makes women seek gainful employment. So also does the pressure for higher standards of living. Aggressive advertisement and skilful salesmanship, combined with a highly efficient credit system, render many pleasurable goods not only desirable but also 'affordable'. The ever higher consumption expectations and indebtedness have probably driven more mothers and potential mothers into the work force than the basic necessities of life ever have.

On the other hand, reduction in family size means less domestic commitment, thus releasing energy that can be redirected towards revenue-generating activities outside the home. This makes women's economic independence more real.

Figure 3: Total fertility rate and labour-force participation rate of women aged 20–44, Canada, 1953–1989

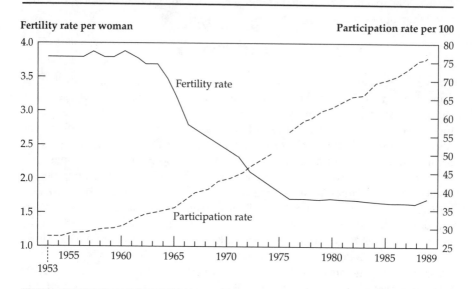

NOTE: The participation rate series breaks in 1975, the year in which major revisions were made to the labour force survey.

SOURCE: Derived from Labour Force Survey, and Statistics Canada, *Vital Statistics, Births and Deaths*, Cat. 84–204, Annual.

While this process may have contributed to marital instability, it also can be argued that the increasing propensity for women to earn income is a rational option to a marriage which no longer provides insurance for the future. And so goes the argument of a circular and self-perpetuating process of low fertility in an individualistic, affluent society.

LOOKING AHEAD

What direction is fertility likely to take? Has the secular decline run its course and reached its nadir in the current baby bust? Is fertility likely to stabilize, break new lows, or rise again adding yet another upward cycle? A short- or medium-term versus a long-term view may be in order when venturing into prognostications about the future course of fertility.

In the Short or Medium Run

The total fertility rate in Canada over the past decade has remained almost stable at around 1.7 births per woman. It would, therefore, be tempting to postulate a stability scenario for the near future. A closer scrutiny reveals, however, that this stability in the total fertility rate is the outcome of two divergent but offsetting tendencies in the age-specific fertility rates. On the one hand, the fertility of young women has continued to decline, while, on the other, the fertility of women in their thirties has increased. What these shifts in the age pattern of childbearing seem to underline is a reordering of life priorities, whereby women's employment is taking precedence over their family aspirations. Women in their thirties seem to 'catch up' with delays in childbearing prompted by work and career commitments in their younger ages. If this interpretation is correct, then the current stabilization of the total fertility rate could be only a lull, albeit a long one. Once the 'catch up' process has run its course and an older age pattern in childbearing has been established, the total fertility rate may well resume its earlier downward trend.

Such a scenario is borne out by the recognition that the forces associated with the baby bust continue to operate in our society. There is still considerable potential for growth in female employment, particularly in occupations that command above-average wages. If such potential is realized, the opportunity cost of childbearing will increase accordingly. Though greatly reduced, unwanted births have not been eliminated. Sex education and greater accessibility to contraception could substantially reduce the still significant incidence of teenage pregnancies. As marriage increasingly gives way to common-law arrangements, downward tendencies in childbearing may well be reinforced. Canada thus will join the growing league of countries and regions in Europe with a fertility rate approaching just one birth per woman.

And yet, after all, history may repeat itself. Another baby boom, at least a mini one, cannot be ruled out. In support of this scenario, one may turn to Easterlin's (1980) autoregulatory process, wherein large cohorts give birth to small cohorts which in turn give birth to large cohorts. Perhaps, indeed, because of their smaller size, when the baby-bust cohorts of the 1960s and 1970s come of age, they will find themselves in a less competitive environment with brighter economic prospects, and will find marriage and larger families more attractive as a lifestyle. It may also be that the scarcity of children will make them more desirable, or that people will swing back to pro-family values. One could cite, in support of a recovery hypothesis, earlier increases in fertility in some Eastern European countries. This turnaround, however, was not spontaneous; rather it was the outcome of pronatalist policies combining material incentives with, in some cases, severe restrictions on abortion. Even so, these policies have not met with unqualified success, for after an initial upturn, the fertility rate resumed its descent.

Yet, there are now renewed signs here and there, that an upward shift in fertility could well be in the offing. The most conspicuous and best-documented case is that of Sweden. In this country, the total fertility rate has risen steadily throughout the 1980s from a low of 1.6 to 2.02 births per woman in 1989. According to Hoem, the rise in the period fertility 'reflects a change in the time pattern of cohort fertility' (1990: 735), but he expects cohort fertility (that is, the number of children born to a generation of women) to rise ultimately as well. He links the change in childbearing behaviour to that country's social policy in support of the family. Sweden's reproductive experience is particularly noteworthy since it has often been in the vanguard of social change and may serve as a harbinger of what may happen elsewhere in the Western world. A rise in fertility, though slower, is already being observed in Norway and Denmark. Other countries, including the USA, seem to be following suit, to the extent one can trust still incomplete data.

On the domestic scene too, the most recent data (1989) seem to reveal a slight upturn in fertility in some provinces, notably in Ontario, and even more so in Quebec. In the latter province, the total (period) fertility rate increased from a low of 1.44 in 1985 to 1.66 in 1989 (Rochon, 1990). Canadian demographers will watch this turn of events closely, if it is one, in view . . . of the Quebec government's policy, implemented in 1988, which provides substantial financial grants to families with two children and even more to those with three.

Occurrences such as those reported above, as infrequent as they are, are important signposts for anyone venturing to predict short-term changes in fertility. If indeed signalling the beginning of a new trend, the emergence of something of a new baby boom, they will cause forecasters to anticipate its likely magnitude. It is tempting in doing so to evoke the historical precedent of the 1950s baby boom. However, what is important to recognize when citing this precedent is, as pointed out earlier, the uniqueness of its historical setting—the Great Depression, World War II and the post-war prosperity, and a social context still largely permeated with familistic values. Though some shifts toward pro-family preferences have been detected among the youngest cohorts (Lesthaeghe and Moors, 1991), they are far too weak to announce a pending break with the ideational trends that have prevailed since 1960. They do not seem to be evolving into an ideational climate capable of triggering and sustaining a major recovery in fertility.

In the Long Run

All the above scenarios—stabilization, resumption of the decline, and upturn—are plausible medium-run assumptions. In the long run, however, this writer's reading of history is that the developments associated with the secular decline will continue their downward pressure on fertility. Once set in motion by the forces of industrialization and by ideologies emphasizing individualistic values, the process of fertility decline is sustained by its own dynamic. A host of mutually-reinforcing factors are at work making low fertility, at below-replacement level, a highly likely long-term prospect for advanced societies. The developments deemed to have brought about the recent baby bust, in particular, are likely to continue holding sway. Four of them call for further elaboration.

First, there is the omnipresent pressure for ever higher standards of living in our affluent, individualistic society. There is something of a paradox here. Common sense (and also marginal utility analysis in the way of the 'New Home Economics') would suggest that as people's basic (and not so basic) needs are satisfied, their interest may turn to other things, such as having children for the sake of their psychic satisfaction. This might well be so to some extent. But as a general proposition, it tends to ignore the inner workings of a society in which, according to Duesenberry (1967), the attainment of an ever-higher standard of living is an end in itself, a major social goal, and, to a large extent, an object of public policy. 'As a society becomes increasingly affluent, wants are increasingly created by the very process by which they are satisfied,' wrote Galbraith (1976: 131). In our consumer-oriented society, there seems to be a never-ending race between the production of goods on the one hand, and the creation of wants by the very process of production and by the power of advertising and salesmanship on the other. 'The more wants that are satisfied, the more new ones are born' (ibid., p. 128).

The implications for procreative behaviours of consumption imperatives in our affluent society, as expounded by Duesenberry, and, in particular, Galbraith, are still awaiting demographers' attention. The argument can be made that the urge for ever-higher standards of living, and the indebtedness that their attainment generates, explains to some extent why so many women are drawn into the labour market and so many men search for extra income. As more income is spent for the acquisition of 'superior' goods, less income is set aside for forming families and having more children.

Second, for the reason just mentioned but also because of the quest for economic independence of spouses and as insurance against the liabilities of marriage breakdown, we should expect the growth momentum of the female work force to continue unabated. However, there is more than just the numbers; there is a shift in quality. More permanent and higher skilled jobs require greater work commitment and thus make the dual role of parenting and working more toilsome.

Third, an argument was made earlier about how modern contraceptive technology has contributed to the erosion of family values and undermined the legitimacy of marriage. The argument could be extended to include the social implications of the reproductive revolution that humanity has embarked upon. Artificial insemination and laboratory-grown embryos (*in vitro* fertilization) and the potential for their intra- and extra-marital transfers through sperm and/or egg donation for both biological and foster (surrogate) mothering, are some of the dimensions of the biomedical reproductive revolution. Yet, these life-giving biomedical advances, no less than the birth-averting ones (coitus-independent contraceptives referred to earlier, and abortive pills being developed), raise serious questions about their long-term social implications, should they, as is likely, become increasingly prevalent. Kass (1985) in particular has made a penetrating, and not too reassuring, analysis of these implications. 'The transfer of procreation to the laboratory and the shuffling of paternity and maternity this shift makes possible, undermines the justification and support that biological parenthood gives to the monogamous marriage.' 'Having babies without sex' may have no less of a weakening effect on the family, kinship and descent than that of 'the possibility of sex without babies'.

The fourth and final point concerns marriage and the family more directly. A great deal has been written about the future of these time-honoured institutions.

This author is inclined to side with those who think that the turbulent times that the family is experiencing are not over. More people are forgoing marriage or opting for alternative, informal, less procreation-oriented conjugal arrangements. Likewise the prospect of a lasting marriage for those who choose it is growing dimmer. The implications for childbearing of these social trends have been outlined earlier. There is, however, one dimension, mentioned sometimes but not stressed enough: the intergenerational transmission of family values. This becomes increasingly more difficult in the prevalent demographic environment of our society. The kinship network and the number of siblings are greatly reduced, as a result of fertility decline. Marriages dissolving and rebuilding entail fragmentation and segmentation of the child socialization process. Even though greater longevity makes it possible for four generations (grandparents, parents, children, and grandchildren) to overlap, the potential for child socialization in acquiring the meaning of family continuity is being defeated by the diminishing physical and social contact among them.

So much for the forces operating in our modern society that may account for the continuing below-replacement fertility in the long run. Is there anything that can be said about countervailing factors; anything that can be learned in the way of meeting the demographic and social challenges in the modern world? A few things are already being done and more could be done to cope with the hardship of being a working parent. Affordable day-care for children, sharing of housework between spouses, and still more efficient labour-saving home appliances are among some of the social and technical innovations one could think of to help alleviate the burden of working parents. In this era of computer technology, work in some occupations could be done at home. Flexible hours, maternity and paternity leave, and many other arrangements could be made to provide a more 'family-friendly workplace', along with various kinds of financial assistance to families.

Yet, although these and similar family-supportive measures have been in operation for quite a while in various degrees in many countries, they have failed to stem the downward tide of the fertility rate. How much more of the same would be needed to reverse the trend? Could anything short of a policy of comprehensive material and institutional family support, on a scale comparable to that applied to public education and health care, avert below-replacement fertility from becoming a lasting feature of advanced societies? Can it be afforded? And if all this is feasible, what will be the long-term implications for the very family, whose 'ills' it intends to cure, of extending the scope of the welfare state in the realm of childbearing and childrearing? These questions alone suffice to reveal the complexity of the issues. It is an open-ended debate which an unprejudiced student of social affairs has to contend with.

There is, however, one message that seems to follow from the retrospective and prospective analysis of fertility undertaken in this paper. Although fertility rates may fluctuate over a relatively short range, their long-term evolution is expected to gravitate toward low ebbs. Advanced societies may well have reached their demographic maturity, a state characterized by low, possibly below-replacement fertility over extended periods, with slow or no growth, and an aging population. The responses to such an emerging demographic environment—be it in the way of social and institutional adjustments or in regard to immigration and fertility— will preoccupy social scientists and policy-makers in the years to come.

REFERENCES

Burch, T.K. and Madan, A.K. (1986). 'Union formation and dissolution in Canada: Results from the 1984 Family History Survey'. Working paper. Ottawa: Statistics Canada.

Calot, G. (1990). 'Fécondité du moment, fécondité des générations: comparaison franco-suédoise'. *Population et société*, Avril, Paris.

Chapman, B.E. and T.R. Balakrishnan (1986). 'Relative sex role deprivation: Equalitarianism and fertility'. Paper presented at the Annual Meeting of the Canadian Population Society, Winnipeg, 5–7 June.

Coale, Ansley J. and S. Cotts Watkins (1986). *The Decline of Fertility in Europe*. Princeton, N.J.: Princeton University Press.

Duesenberry, J.S. (1967). *Income, Saving, and the Theory of Consumer Behaviour*. New York: Oxford University Press.

Easterlin, R.A. (1980). *Birth and Fortune: The Impact of Numbers on Personal Welfare*. New York: Basic Books.

Feldstein, M., ed. (1980). *The American Economy in Transition*. Chicago: University of Chicago Press.

Galbraith, J.K. (1976). *The Affluent Society*. Third ed., rev. Boston: Houghton Mifflin.

Henripin, J. (1954). *La population canadienne au début du XVIII siècle*. Paris: Presses Universitaires de France.

——— (1968). *Tendances et facteurs de la fécondité au Canada*. Ottawa: Bureau Fédéral de la Statisque.

Hoem, J.M. (1990). 'Social policy and recent fertility change in Sweden'. *Population and Development Review* 16, 4: 735–48.

Kass, R.L. (1985). *Toward a More Natural Science: Biology and Human Affairs*. New York: Free Press.

Kaufmann, F.-X. (1990). 'Causes of the fertility decline in the Federal Republic of Germany and possible counteracting measures of the Government. *Zeitschrigt Fur Bevolkerungswissenschaft*, Jg. 16, 3/4–1990, S. 383–96.

Lasch, C. (1990). 'The invasion of the family by the market'. *The World and I*. Washington, D.C., November: 479–89.

Lesthaeghe, R. and Moors, G. (1991). Rationality, Cohorts, and Reproduction. IPD—Working Paper 1990–1, Interuniversity Programme in Demography, Vrije Universiteit, Bruxelles.

McDaniel, S. (1986). 'An alternative to family in crisis model', In J. Légaré, T.R. Balakrishnan and R.P. Beaujot, eds, *The Family in Crisis: A Population Crisis?* Ottawa: Royal Society of Canada.

Michael, R.T. (1985). 'Consequences of the rise in female labour force participation rates: Questions and probes'. *Journal of Labour Economics* 3, 1: S117–S146.

Preston, S.H. (1986). 'Changing values and falling birth rates'. *Population and Development Review* (supplement) 12: 26–47.

Ram, B. (1990). *New Trends in the Family*. Ottawa: Statistics Canada.

Rochon, M. (1990). 'La fécondité des jeunes génerations québécoises'. Colloque Femmes et questions démographiques, 58ᵉ Congrès de l'ACFAS, Québec.

Romaniuc, A. (1984). *Fertility in Canada: From Baby boom to Baby bust*. Ottawa: Statistics Canada.

—— (1987). 'Transition from traditional high to modern low fertility: Canadian aboriginals'. *Canadian Studies in Population* 14, 1: 69–88.

—— (1990). 'Réflexions sur le devenir démographique des sociétés avancées: Un regard sur le Canada'. *Cahiers québecois de démographie*, 19, 2: 179–195.

Rostow, W.W. (1965). *The Stages of Economic Growth*. Cambridge: Cambridge University Press.

Roussel, L. (1984). 'Une nouvelle révolution démographique'. In S. Feld and R. Lesthaeghe, eds, *Population and Societal Outlook*. Bruxelles: Fondation Roi Beaudouin.

—— (1991). 'Les "futuribles" de la famille'. *Futuribles* 153: 3–21.

Ryder, N.B. (1984). 'Some views on the demographic future'. In S. Feld and R. Lesthaeghe, eds, *Population and Societal Outlook*. Bruxelles: Fondation Roi Beaudouin.

Shorter, E. (1975). *The Making of the Modern Family*. New York: Basic Books.

PART FIVE

FAMILY FORMATION AND DISSOLUTION

THE CANADIAN FAMILY IN TRANSITION

In recent years the increasing incidence of divorce, lone-parent families, and fertility outside of marriage has led many observers to claim that the Canadian family is in serious trouble. However, the importance of the family in the overall structure of society is seldom an issue of debate. The family is the central institution in society. While other types of basic social arrangements have been tried, there appears to be no viable alternative that can provide for the ongoing development and socialization of each succeeding generation in the way that the family does. Almost all of us spend most of our lives within some variation of the formal organization that we call the family, and in Canada that family usually takes the 'nuclear' form, as opposed to the 'extended family' arrangements that predominate in other parts of the world. Thus one generation leads to another, and the perpetuation of the species depends on the care that children receive from their parents, whether biological or surrogate.

It is also true, however, that the Canadian family has undergone many fundamental changes in this century, particularly in the recent past (one or two generations). The breadwinning/homemaking family that was typical of earlier decades, where the husband/father went out to earn a living while the wife/mother remained in the household raising the children, is increasingly rare. Today lone-parent families, childless couples, and dual-earning families make up the majority in this country.

The changes in the past thirty years with respect to the position of women within the Canadian family have been remarkable. The proportion of married women in the labour force has increased from 22 per cent in 1961 to nearly 60 per cent in the early 1990s. The age at first marriage has risen from 21.2 for brides in 1965 to 23.7 in 1985. The proportion of women ever marrying has decreased from 95 to 85 per cent in the past generation, and the proportion of marriages dissolved through divorce has increased from 11 per cent in 1965 to 42 per cent at the end of the 1980s. The total fertility rate in Canada has fallen from 3.6 in the early 1960s to about 1.8 in the 1990s. These different patterns imply behavioural changes for individual women, and there are macro-level implications for the society as a whole in terms of gender roles, labour-force activity, educational attainment, familial living patterns, and kinship networks.

THE CHANGING ROLE OF WOMEN

Basic to even a cursory understanding of these alterations in the family is an appreciation of what is one of the most fundamental and important revolutions in human history: the changing role of women. While this revolution has complicated origins, patterns, and developments, the essential components are found in the modernization that is exemplified most clearly in the Western world by the demographic transition. This shift from high birth and death rates to stable low fertility and mortality has been accompanied by a slow but fundamental shift in the position of women in society in general and particularly within the context of the family. Changes in the roles and behaviours of women in Canada are well under way, but the repercussions for economic, social, sexual, and family life are only beginning to be understood. In this context, perhaps the major question to be addressed is the nature of family in the future. A key component of the changing family is the opportunity for women to choose other life-course alternatives: today childbearing and rearing need no longer be the focus of a woman's entire existence. Another important feature may be increased sharing of responsibilities between men and women, both domestically (within the household) and economically (primarily outside the home).

The papers in this section examine the changes that have taken place in the family over the past generation in Canada. Is the family obsolete, an institution that no longer meets the needs of individuals or the society? Or is it still a strong, viable institution in the process of modification? Living arrangements may be more diverse, and individuals may rely less on family for economic and service support, but perhaps the institution is more successful today, in the sense that women have more options within it. Less formal structure in gender roles may bring about more freedom of choice and more emphasis on quality of family life, with less exclusion and dependency on the part of women who choose to have a family.

Ram, in his article on 'Family Formation', follows a family life-cycle perspective in evaluating family formation and dissolution. This process begins at first marriage and ends with the death of a spouse, with childbearing and childrearing taking place in the intervening time. Since the 1950s, the marriage rate has been falling and the divorce rate increasing; however, most divorced people eventually remarry. More children are being reared by lone parents, usually the mother: approximately 15 per cent of all children are in single-parent households. While families are changing dramatically in terms of formation and dissolution, Ram concludes that the family remains an impor-tant aspect of Canadian life.

Beaujot provides both an economic and a cultural interpretation of recent changes in the Canadian family. The economic interpretation of the changes in family structure reflect, on the one hand, the fact that contemporary women are less dependent on marriage (because of increased occupational opportunities) and, on the other, the fact that children are expensive to raise. But economic factors alone are not enough to explain trends in fertility. From the cultural perspective, Beaujot argues that modern secular populations are more 'me'-oriented, more concerned with consumerism and self-gratification; for example, if marriages are not longer 'gratifying', then they are ended, independent of other factors such as children or commitment. He goes on to discuss the solutions suggested by these two perspectives: 'On the economic side, it is time to consider means of decreasing the opportunity costs of children to parents . . . Culturally, one could attempt to build a shared consensus that children are important to the future of the society and that having and caring for children is an important part of normal adult roles, for both men and women.' Clearly, to Beaujot, the family is an institution of continuing importance, and children in the family are essential to social and individual well-being.

Veevers, in 'The "Real" Marriage Squeeze', observes that of the people (about one in five) in midlife who are unmarried, the majority are women. While fertility and mortality factors are relevant here, the major variable accounting for this outcome is the norm that husbands should be older than their wives. She develops several sets of calculations to show that for every 100 women at age 50, there are only 50 eligible men to marry. She then suggests that this unbalanced sex ratio reinforces the male power advantage in a reaffir-mation of the double standard resulting from a surplus of women and a scarcity of men.

McDaniel, in 'Reconceptualizing the Nuptiality/Fertility Relationship in Canada in a New Age', suggests that the traditional link between marriage and childbearing is becoming tenuous. She examines the data associated with fertility outside the tradi-tional patterns, emphasizing changes in sexual behaviour, economic dependencies, the responsibilities for children, social-class factors, desire for children in the context of contraceptive usage, and the general separation of sexual activity from pregnancy. Women's plans most often include both career and children, work and family. McDaniel suggests that marriage is an outcome that must include both of these plans for men and women alike.

The final article in this section, 'The Cluttered Nest', examines the tendency for young people in the 1980s to remain in their parents' homes for longer periods of time than they did in the 1950s through 1970s. Finding that about 30 per cent of single females and 40 per cent of single males aged 25–29 were living with one or both parents in 1981,

Boyd and Pryor find that apart from age, the most common factors associated with living at home are low income and school attendance. They surmise that spending more time in the parental home may make young people more like their parents in terms of norms and values, and could result in more reciprocal relationships later on in life. The authors suggest that such patterns may even result in a resurgence of familism as a central value among the young.

TECHNICAL NOTES

1. The crude marriage rate is computed by taking the number of marriages contracted by couples in a given year, divided by the mid-year population aged 15 years and older in the same year. This rate can be multiplied by a constant, usually 1,000.
2. The crude divorce rate is measured by the number of divorces in a given year divided by the mid-year population aged 15 years and older in the same year. This rate is usually multiplied by 100,000.
3. More precise measurements of marriage and divorce are not so straightforward. With respect to marriage, for example, one may examine either first or subsequent marriages. Also, men and women marry at different ages and in different proportions. A common measure of marriage is the age-specific first-marriage rate by gender. For example, for males this is simply the number of first marriages in a specific age group that occur in any given time frame, usually one year (usually determined at mid-year), divided by the number of males in that age group, multiplied by 1,000:

$$\frac{Number\ of\ males\ marrying\ at\ age\ X}{Number\ of\ males\ at\ age\ X} \times 1,000$$

However, to obtain an overall rate for men, each age category (age 17, 18, 19, 20, etc., up to, say, 50 years of age) must be calculated individually, and then all must be added together. The reason is that age at marriage is not constant across the age range: more marriages take place in the 23–30 age range than among other ages. For example, in 1989, the age-specific marriage rate for males at age 17 was 0.4 per 1,000 (78 marriages out of 195,000 17-year-olds). At age 24 the rate was 63.8 per 1,000 (14,725 marriages out of 230,800 males) and at age 34 it was 12.7 per 1,000 (2,854 marriages out of 224,700 males). If we calculated each single year, say from 17 to 49, and added the rates together, we would obtain the marriage rate for men aged 17 to 49 in 1989. This total was approximately 640 per 1,000.

Obviously, divorce can only take place after a person has married, but it can happen at any time over the life of the marriage—within a few months or after thirty years. One way of examining divorce rates is simply to compare the number of divorces in a year to the number of marriages in that year. In 1989 there were approximately 190,000 marriages and 81,000 divorces, for a rate of 426 divorces for every 1,000 marriages:

$$\frac{Number\ of\ divorces}{Number\ of\ marriages} \times 1,000$$

If marriages and divorces were relatively stable over time, this rate would be an accurate reflection of the patterns. In times of changing rates in marriage and divorce, however, this may not be the best procedure for calculating divorces because the numerator or denominator may vary dramatically from year to year. Another method is based on probability: that is, the likelihood of divorce given current rates of divorce after X years of marriage. Without getting into the technical details (the procedure for this estimation is similar to the one for life-table calculations), at the current rates of divorce about 40 per cent of all marriages would end in divorce, and the average length of first marriage among the divorced would be approximately nine years.

SUGGESTED READING

Balakrishnan, T.R., K.V. Rao, Evelyne Lapierre-Adamcyk, and Karol J. Krótki (1987). 'A hazard model analysis of the covariates of marriage dissolution in Canada'. *Demography* 24: 395–406.

Bumpass, L. 'What's happening to the family? Interactions between demographic and institutional change'. *Demography* 27, 4: 483–98.

Dumas, Jean, and Yves Peron (1992). *Marriage and Conjugal Life in Canada*. Current Demographic Analysis. Ottawa: Minister of Industry, Science and Technology. Cat. 91–534E.

Festy, Patrick (1973). 'Canada, United States, Australia and New Zealand: Nuptiality trends'. *Population Studies* 27, 3: 479–92.

Halli, Shiva S., and Zachary Zimmer (1984). 'Common-law union as a differentiating factor in the failture of marriage in Canada, 1984'. *Social Indicators Research* 24: 329–45.

Hobart, Charles (1991). 'Interest in parenting at the end of the eighties: A study of Canadian students'. *Canadian Studies in Population* 18, 1: 75–100.

Légaré, Jacques, T.R. Balakrishnan, and R.P. Beaujot (1989). *The Family in Crisis: A Population Crisis*. Ottawa: Royal Society of Canada.

Moen, Elizabeth W. (1979). 'What does "control over our bodies" really mean?'. *International Journal of Women's Studies* 2, 2: 129–43.

Moore, Maureen (1987). 'Women parenting alone'. Pp. 121–7 in C. Mackie and K. Thompson, eds, *Canadian Social Trends*. Toronto: Thompson Educational Publishing.

Nett, Emily (1988). *Canadian Families Past and Present*. Toronto: Butterworths.

Rindfuss, Ronald, and A.S. Vandenheuvel (1990). 'Cohabitation: A precursor to marriage or an alternative to being single?'. *Population and Development Review* 16, 4: 703–26.

Trovato, Frank (1988). 'A macrosociological analysis of change in the marriage rate: Canadian women 1921–25 to 1981–85'. *Journal of Marriage and the Family* 50: 507–21.

Veevers, Jean (1991). *Continuity and Change in Marriage and Family*. Toronto: Holt, Rinehart and Winston.

CHAPTER 17

FAMILY

FORMATION

Bali Ram

It is only logical to start an analysis of the family by considering its formation. To capture the process, two approaches are followed—the first via the 'family life cycle', the other via 'factors' that contribute to the formation and dissolution of the family.

THE FAMILY LIFE CYCLE

The succession of stages through which an individual passes is referred to as the family life cycle. Researchers, following the initial work of Paul C. Glick, have identified five general stages, each referenced by a particular event: (1) family formation with first marriage; (2) the beginning of childbearing with the birth of a first child; (3) the end of childbearing at the birth of the last child; (4) the beginning of the 'empty nest' period with the marriage of the last child, and; (5) family dissolution at the death of a spouse.[1] The boundaries between the stages are usually defined by the mean or median age at the time of an event. This broad

Table 1: Median ages of mothers at selected stages of the family life cycle by
period of birth of mother, Canada, 1910–1950

	Generations				
Stages of life cycle	**1910**	**1920**	**1930**	**1940**	**1950**
Median age at:					
First marriage	23.8	23.5	21.7	20.9	21.5
Birth of first child	25.1	24.7	23.8	23.2	23.9
Birth of last child	28.5	28.2	29.2	28.8	26.3
Marriage of last child	51.1	51.0	52.0	51.6	49.1
Difference between age at first marriage and:					
Birth of first child	1.3	1.2	2.1	2.3	2.4
Birth of last child	4.7	4.7	7.5	7.9	4.8
Marriage of last child	27.3	27.5	30.3	30.7	27.6
Difference between age at birth of first and last child	3.4	3.5	5.4	5.6	2.4
Difference between age at birth and marriage of last child	22.6	22.8	22.8	22.8	22.8

SOURCE: Roy H. Rodgers and Gail Witney, 'The Family Cycle in Twentieth Century Canada', *Journal of Marriage and the Family* 43 (August, 1981), Table 1.

typology, however, does not cover all families. Due to the recent rise in premarital births, common–law unions, divorce, separation, remarriage and childless marriage, it no longer accurately depicts all forms of family life and living arrangements. With such limitations in mind, this section describes the changes that have occurred in recent years.

Using the method suggested by Glick, researchers Rodgers and Witney measured the various stages of the family life cycle in Canada.[2] They found a 'long-term stability in the pattern', though there was an appreciable deviation for persons born in the 1930s and 1940s. Most women born in the 1930s, and in particular the 1940s, married during the economic prosperity of the 1950s and 1960s (Table 1). Their family behaviour was rather unusual.

Compared with women born in the 1950s, those born in the 1940s married earlier and had their first child earlier; they also had their last child later and, as a direct consequence, they were older by the time that all their children were married. Their average age at first marriage, and at the birth of their first child, were both lower by about half of a year. Their last child was born 2.5 years later and, in all likelihood, they were 2.5 years older when their last child was married. Though these figures appear small, when they are applied to a mean or median value, they reveal a fairly large discrepancy in the behaviour of individuals between successive birth cohorts of women.

Clearly then, the 1950s cohort has a shorter childbearing period than did the 1940s cohort. Compared to the 1940s cohort, those born in the 1950s married, on average, 0.6 years later at a median age of 21.5, had their first child 0.7 years later at a median age of 23.9, and their last child about 2.5 years earlier at a median age

Table 2: Life expectancy and difference in life expectancy at ages 20 and 65 by sex, Canada, 1920-1922 to 1985-1987

Period	At age 20			At age 65		
	Male	Female	Difference	Male	Female	Difference
1920–1922	48.2	49.1	0.2	13.0	13.6	0.5
1925–1927	49.8	50.3	0.6	13.3	14.0	0.7
1930–1932	49.1	49.8	0.7	13.0	13.7	0.7
1935–1937	49.4	50.5	1.1	13.0	13.9	0.9
1940–1942	49.6	51.8	2.2	12.8	14.1	1.3
1945–1947	50.5	53.1	2.6	13.2	14.6	1.4
1950–1952	50.8	54.5	3.7	13.3	15.0	1.7
1955–1957	51.2	55.8	4.6	13.4	15.6	2.2
1960–1962	51.5	56.7	5.2	13.6	16.1	2.5
1965–1967	51.5	57.4	5.9	13.6	16.8	3.2
1970–1972	51.7	58.3	6.6	13.8	17.6	3.8
1975–1977	52.2	59.1	6.9	14.0	18.2	4.2
1980–1982	53.4	60.2	6.8	14.6	18.9	4.3
1985–1987	54.3	60.7	6.4	14.9	19.1	4.2

SOURCE: Dhruva Nagnur, *Longevity and Historical Life Tables (Abridged), Canada and Provinces, 1921–1981* (Ottawa: Statistics Canada, 1986), Cat. 89–506; *Life Tables, Canada and Provinces 1985–1987* (Ottawa: Statistics Canada, Health Division, Vital Statistics and Disease Registries Section, September 1989).

of 26.3 years. Also, the difference between the median age at first marriage and the median age at the birth of the last child decreased to 4.8 years for the 1950s cohort, from a high of 7.9 years reached by a 1940s cohort. There was a corresponding shrinkage from 5.6 years to 2.4 years in the difference between women's median age at the birth of their first child and that of their last child.[3]

These patterns are not new, however. In some ways, the family life cycle of the 1950s generation resembles that of earlier cohorts, particularly those who were in the family-formation stage immediately prior to the Depression. What sets the 1950s generation apart, though, is the increase in the divorce rate. This phenomenon had no precedent, and among those to whom it occurred, it obviously resulted in a shorter duration of marriage and often in a shorter duration of childbearing.

The family life cycle in the twentieth century has also been heavily influenced by the decline in adult mortality. Both husbands and wives live longer now than ever before. For the 1985–87 period, life expectancy at the age of 20 was 54.3 years for males and 60.7 years for females. In 1920–22, the corresponding figures were 48.9 and 49.1 years, respectively. Among older age groups, the increase in life expectancy, particularly in recent years, is far from insignificant, as shown in Table 2.

Such changes in life expectancy have had an impact on the timing of family cycles. They have reshaped the demographic structure of the contemporary

Table 3: Population and selected ratios for age groups 45–54, 60–64, 65 and over
and 80 and over, Canada, 1921–1986

	Population ('000)				Ratio of number of persons	
Year	45–54	60–64	65 and over	80 and over	65 years and over to number of persons 45–54 years	80 years and over to number of persons 60–64 years
1921	799.2	240.0	420.0	58.4	.526	.243
1931	1,074.4	294.7	576.1	74.5	.536	.253
1941	1,226.8	407.1	768.0	107.2	.626	.263
1951	1,407.3	506.2	1,086.3	149.2	.772	.295
1961	1,898.5	583.7	1,391.2	227.6	.741	.390
1971	2,291.5	777.0	1,744.5	341.6	.761	.440
1976	2,473.0	905.4	2,002.4	385.1	.810	.425
1981	2,498.8	979.3	2,361.0	450.6	.945	.460
1986	2,545.2	1,125.1	2,697.6	537.1	1.060	.477

SOURCES: F.H. Leacy, *Historical Statistics of Canada*, second ed. (Ottawa: Statistics Canada, 1983), Series A78–93; *1981 Census of Canada*, Cat. 92–901, Table 1; *1986 Census of Canada*, Cat. 93–101, Table 3.

family in a number of ways, and have modified the living arrangements of its members. Because of declining mortality, the probability that couples will stay together for a longer time has increased.

These increases in longevity have led to increased overlap between generations: both the number and proportion of aging adults with living parents and grandparents have grown. In 1921, there were 53 persons over age 65 for every 100 persons in the 45–54 year age group; by 1986, the corresponding figure was 106. Over the same period, the ratio of the over–80 age group to the 60–64 age group rose from 24 to 48 (Table 3). It may be inferred from these data that the coexistence of several generations (children, parents, grandparents and great-grandparents) is more common now than in the past.

Lastly, since husbands are, on average, older than their wives, and since life expectancy for women is greater than that for men, the number of widows over age 65 is rising. In 1921, widows over the age of 65 outnumbered widowers by a margin of two-to-one; by 1966, the gap had widened to three-to-one, and in 1986, to approximately five-to-one. . . .

MARRIAGE AND DIVORCE

In most cases family formation begins with marriage. It is therefore logical to begin our analysis with an overview of how nuptiality has evolved in recent years in terms of marriage and remarriage rates, as well as in terms of age at marriage. The marriage rate is falling. As shown in Table 4 and Figure 1, the first marriage rate for all women dropped from 88 per 1,000 in 1971, to 57 per 1,000 in 1986; in the early 1960s it hovered around 80 per 1,000. The recent decline has been

Table 4: First-marriage rate per 1,000 never-married persons by age and sex, Canada, 1951-1986

Age group	1951	1961	1971	1976	1981	1982	1983	1984	1985	1986
Male										
15–19	12.6	12.2	13.0	10.7	5.8	5.2	4.3	3.6	3.2	2.8
20–24	135.6	147.7	157.2	118.1	90.5	83.6	75.0	69.8	65.4	60.2
15–24	65.7	61.2	67.2	51.7	41.4	39.4	36.5	34.8	33.1	30.3
25–29	174.1	167.5	185.2	150.1	138.3	132.7	127.3	126.2	124.9	116.4
30–34	122.6	92.1	102.7	93.3	89.9	88.8	89.3	89.1	88.2	83.7
35–39	69.3	48.5	54.2	52.6	48.5	47.1	47.2	47.9	47.3	48.0
40–44	41.1	27.3	31.3	30.0	25.4	23.6	22.8	25.7	24.5	28.0
45–49	26.3	18.3	19.6	19.5	15.2	14.1	14.3	14.5	14.3	17.7
50+	8.3	6.4	7.6	7.0	5.9	6.0	6.1	6.5	6.6	6.0
Total	74.3	64.9	71.1	58.8	52.4	51.1	49.4	49.1	48.5	46.1
Adjusted[1]	85.1	84.0	91.0	72.3	59.9	56.6	52.9	51.1	49.3	46.1
Female										
15–19	65.6	63.3	54.2	42.5	26.8	24.5	21.8	19.1	17.1	14.9
20–24	204.0	229.9	219.5	168.4	143.6	136.1	125.1	120.4	115.0	106.7
15–24	114.8	106.9	103.8	82.1	69.0	66.8	63.0	61.3	59.0	54.4
25–29	161.4	144.4	146.7	134.7	133.2	132.1	130.5	132.8	133.4	125.8
30–34	86.6	70.7	74.0	71.4	69.1	69.2	70.0	73.7	73.1	69.0
35–39	46.0	36.5	39.1	39.8	33.3	32.5	33.0	33.1	34.5	33.9
40–44	28.0	21.3	23.9	21.7	19.2	18.0	17.4	16.4	18.0	18.6
45–49	18.2	14.4	14.6	13.5	11.3	11.1	10.5	11.9	11.3	10.8
50+	4.9	4.2	4.2	4.0	3.0	3.3	3.3	3.1	3.1	2.3
Total	94.7	84.8	88.4	73.9	65.6	64.3	61.9	61.6	60.6	56.7
Adjusted[1]	108.7	111.4	105.8	85.7	72.3	69.2	65.0	63.2	61.1	56.7

[1] Adjusted using the age distribution of population in 1986 as standard.

SOURCES: Statistics Canada, *Vital Statistics*, Vol. II, Cat. 84-205, various issues.

particularly pronounced in the under-25 age group. Between 1971 and 1986, the first marriage rate among 15–19 year old women decreased by almost two-thirds, from 54 to 15 per 1,000. For those aged 20–24 years, it slipped from 220 to 107 per 1,000.

Remarriages exhibit a similar pattern in time. Although they now form a much larger proportion of all annual marriages than ever—about one-fifth of all marriages in the 1980s—their rates have shown a downward trend (Table 5). The remarriage rate among divorced women, which was 162 per 1,000 in 1961, plunged to 77 per 1,000 in 1986. The same is true for the remarriage rate among widows, which dropped from 10 or 11 per 1,000 during the 1960s and early 1970s, to only 5 per 1,000 in 1986. The remarriage rate remained high among younger women, but showed a steep decline with age. For divorced women between 25

Figure 1: First marriage rate, divorce rate and remarriage rates, women, 15 years and over, Canada, 1961–1986

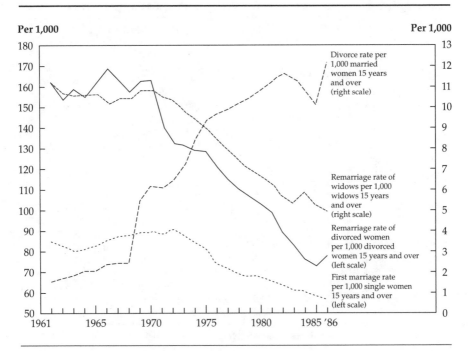

and 39 years of age, the rate shrank by more than 50 per cent, but for those beyond age 40, it dropped by about 45 per cent. The trends in the remarriage rate for widows are similar. Trends in the first marriage and remarriage rates among males have followed a course very similar to that for women. Since the age-adjusted standardized remarriage rates indicate a similar drop over time, the decline in the overall rates (all ages combined) cannot be attributed to a change in the age structure of the population, but rather to altered behaviour.

The age at which people get married is an important factor in the duration of family life. During the last decade, the long-term trend in the mean age at marriage reversed itself. After reaching a record low of 24.4 years for females in 1968, the mean age at marriage rebounded to 27.7 in 1986. Also, the proportion of women marrying at age 25 and over, after a decrease from 33 to 22 per cent between 1950 and 1968, rose to 50 per cent in 1986 (Figure 2). Similar trends are observed for males.

Although delayed marriage is a general phenomenon in Canadian society, in recent years it has become more pronounced among women than among men. Figure 3 shows that the mean age at first marriage for men increased by 2.3 years between 1972 and 1986, while for women it increased by 2.6. Consequently, the

Table 5: Remarriage rates by age and sex, Canada, 1951–1986

Age group	1951	1961	1971	1976	1981	1982	1983	1984	1985	1986
	Remarriage rate of divorced men per 1,000 divorced									
15–24	892.6	600.0	276.0	302.8	211.4	207.0	185.2	171.6	164.5	208.7
25–29	844.5	670.6	408.8	416.8	320.9	321.4	320.2	309.0	275.5	272.4
30–34	716.4	515.7	351.1	362.6	296.7	293.4	286.0	275.6	256.2	220.8
35–39	523.2	359.2	260.7	270.9	222.2	214.3	215.2	204.9	192.2	164.6
40–44	326.4	238.8	213.0	195.3	153.6	150.0	146.0	144.0	135.5	121.1
45–49	257.6	164.3	178.7	155.0	110.3	106.5	109.3	108.1	103.7	93.8
50+	99.0	72.8	98.4	86.4	59.1	54.8	51.4	53.0	51.2	46.9
Total	332.3	229.1	208.6	209.5	159.8	153.5	149.0	143.3	133.1	117.1
Adjusted[1]	346.2	248.1	201.8	195.4	151.1	146.8	144.2	140.7	131.8	117.1
	Remarriage rate of widowed men per 1,000 widowed									
15–24	240.6	112.1	13.0	34.4	27.1	24.3	25.7	25.7	18.6	29.9
25–29	237.9	237.1	83.8	176.3	220.0	185.0	165.0	126.7	123.3	159.7
30–34	231.5	183.4	101.7	185.5	162.5	147.5	151.7	151.7	136.7	129.9
35–39	179.2	151.9	124.2	137.2	131.7	116.3	106.0	117.0	94.8	114.4
40–44	130.1	80.2	97.0	102.8	99.0	92.8	97.0	93.7	95.8	86.3
45–49	97.4	88.6	90.7	80.8	77.7	69.8	64.8	79.8	69.6	70.5
50+	23.9	22.1	29.9	27.3	23.6	22.6	21.4	23.0	21.5	19.9
Total	34.6	29.2	35.9	32.9	28.6	26.8	25.6	27.3	25.4	24.1
Adjusted[1]	31.2	27.6	33.7	32.1	28.4	26.8	25.5	27.3	25.4	24.1
	Remarriage rate of divorced women per 1,000 divorced									
15–24	625.8	631.1	—	325.1	283.1	273.7	259.0	244.8	240.9	290.1
25–29	479.5	456.4	285.1	261.9	246.2	247.7	252.5	240.0	227.9	225.2
30–34	341.8	301.1	203.8	172.0	157.3	155.6	159.8	157.4	151.1	141.9
35–39	203.5	182.0	149.7	118.1	100.9	94.1	96.9	97.0	93.2	86.5
40–44	156.0	116.9	120.1	90.2	72.8	68.6	68.7	66.3	65.3	59.1
45–49	99.7	84.1	104.8	73.5	53.4	52.1	49.8	49.4	48.9	45.3
50+	55.5	35.1	46.1	37.9	24.9	22.3	21.0	19.9	20.2	19.2
Total	216.1	161.8	142.4	121.6	99.3	93.7	91.8	87.0	82.4	11.1
Adjusted[1]	183.0	157.5	121.4	104.3	88.1	85.0	85.5	83.3	80.6	77.1
	Remarriage rate of widows per 1,000 widows									
15–24	210.8	160.9	—	81.3	68.0	60.0	56.3	41.1	35.6	39.5
25–29	171.3	130.3	97.0	111.2	111.0	95.9	86.8	99.0	87.1	86.2
30–34	114.0	98.5	76.1	70.5	65.0	61.6	63.9	73.1	65.8	56.9
35–39	71.9	62.7	50.5	48.5	45.4	37.4	39.2	45.5	39.6	44.0
40–44	48.3	42.2	42.0	33.8	30.3	29.3	27.8	31.4	28.9	27.7
45–49	36.9	31.2	32.5	27.7	21.6	19.0	21.1	22.7	20.6	22.0
50+	6.7	6.0	6.9	5.6	4.2	3.8	3.5	3.9	3.5	3.2
Total	14.1	11.2	10.5	8.3	6.3	5.7	5.4	5.9	5.2	4.9
Adjusted[1]	9.9	8.6	8.9	7.6	6.0	5.4	5.2	5.7	5.2	4.9

[1] Adjusted using the age distribution of population in 1986 as standard.

SOURCE: Statistics Canada, *Vital Statistics*, Vol. II, Cat. 84–205, various issues.

Figure 2: Average age at marriage for women and percentage of brides 25 years and over, Canada, 1950–1986

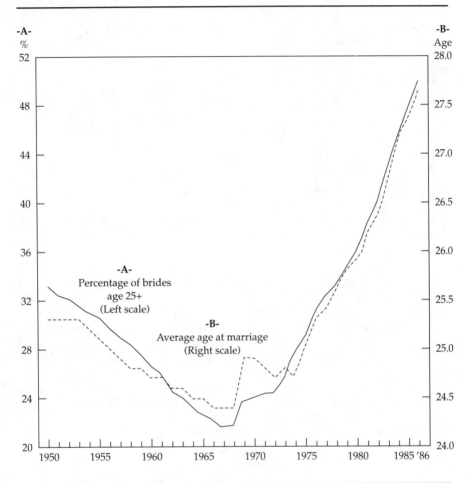

age-gap between first-time brides and grooms has been reduced from 2.5 to 2.2 years — much lower than that observed in the 1950s and 1960s.

The 1986 census results have reinforced the belief that an increasing number of Canadians have recently been delaying getting married. In 1986, 60 per cent of 20 to 24 year-old women had never been married, compared to only 41 per cent in 1961, and 44 per cent in 1971. For the 25 to 29 age group, the proportion of never-married women also increased, from 15 in 1961 to 26 per cent in 1986. Men exhibit similar patterns. While it is likely that many young adults in recent years have been simply postponing their first marriage, considerable increases in the proportion of never-married persons up through the 30–34 age group seem to sug-

Figure 3: Average age at marriage and first marriage of brides and bridegrooms, Canada, 1940-1986

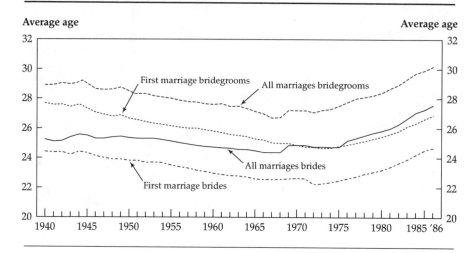

gest that an increasing proportion of men and women may be opting to never marry at all (see Figure 4).

One other factor that has contributed significantly to change in the family in recent years is the rise in the divorce rate, which has been especially dramatic since 1968—the year in which the law was amended to make divorce easier to obtain. Between 1969 and 1986, the annual number of marriages declined from

Figure 4: Percentage of population never married by selected age groups and sex, Canada, 1961-1986

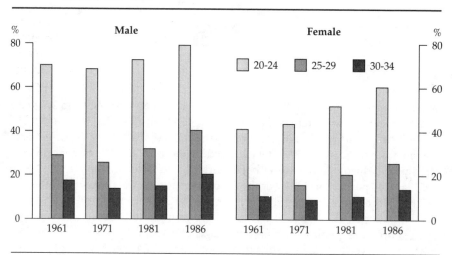

Table 6: Divorce rate per 1,000 married persons by age and sex, Canada, 1971–1986

Age at time of divorce	1971	1976	1981	1982	1983	1984	1985	1986
Male								
Under 25 years	5.5	8.7	9.4	10.6	9.6	9.2	8.8	12.8
25–29	9.4	15.8	19.0	19.1	18.4	16.1	14.9	18.5
30–34	9.4	16.2	19.5	20.3	19.5	17.9	17.1	20.2
35–39	8.0	13.7	16.4	17.3	16.4	16.0	15.0	18.1
40–44	7.1	11.5	13.1	13.9	13.7	13.3	12.8	15.7
45–49	6.0	9.4	10.2	10.6	10.5	10.6	10.1	12.6
50 years and over	3.0	4.3	4.2	2.7	3.8	3.8	3.7	4.7
Total	6.1	9.9	11.4	11.7	11.3	10.6	10.0	12.5
Total adjusted[1]	6.1	9.9	11.4	11.1	11.2	10.6	10.1	12.5
Female								
Under 25 years	7.1	11.1	12.7	13.5	12.8	11.5	11.0	15.1
25–29	9.9	16.7	20.6	20.9	19.8	17.7	16.6	19.9
30–34	8.8	15.1	17.5	18.5	17.7	16.8	15.9	19.1
35–39	7.4	12.4	14.5	15.3	14.8	14.1	13.4	16.1
40–44	6.6	10.1	11.3	12.0	11.7	11.8	11.3	14.2
45–49	5.2	8.0	8.8	8.4	8.2	8.4	8.1	10.4
50 years and over	2.5	3.5	3.3	3.3	3.0	3.0	2.9	3.6
Total	6.1	9.7	11.3	11.6	11.2	10.5	9.9	12.4
Total adjusted[1]	6.1	9.8	11.3	11.6	11.0	10.5	9.9	12.4

[1] Adjusted using the age distribution of population in 1986 as standard.

SOURCE: Statistics Canada, *Vital Statistics* Vol. II, Cat. 84–205, various years.

182,000 to 176,000, but the annual number of divorces boomed, going from 26,000 to 78,000. Alternatively stated, the marriage rate declined from 8.7 to 6.7 per 1,000 population, while the divorce rate more than doubled from 1.2 to 3.1 per 1,000 population. This represents an increase from 5.6 to 12.4 divorces per 1,000 married women aged 15 years and over. Again, the pattern was the same for males and females of all ages (Table 6). It is important to note, however, that the divorce rate declined somewhat between 1983 and 1985, but has since increased slightly. Whether this is a beginning of a trend or a stabilization of the existing pattern is difficult to determine at this stage.

The length of marriages ending in divorce has varied over time. About 40 per cent of the couples who divorced in 1971, when the revised divorce law had already come into effect, had been married less than 10 years. A decade later the proportion has risen to about 50 per cent. During this period, the median duration of marriage among those obtaining a divorce declined from 13 years to 10 years. Even though the catch-up effect immediately following the amendment of the divorce law caused a bulge in the trend, the fact remains that, for whatever reason, divorces did not occur as soon after marriage in the early 1970s as they have done in more recent years. Thus, divorce tables for 1975–77 reveal that

Table 7: Distribution of couples obtaining a divorce by duration of marriage and median duration of marriage, Canada, 1969–1986

Duration of marriage	Year											
	1969	1971	1973	1975	1977	1979	1981	1982	1983	1984	1985	1986
Under 5 years	10.6	14.7	15.8	15.8	17.5	17.9	17.2	17.2	17.0	16.3	15.8	17.2
5–9	21.0	25.2	28.2	29.5	30.3	32.1	32.6	32.1	31.6	30.3	29.5	29.3
10–14	18.6	18.9	17.7	17.7	18.1	19.1	19.7	20.7	21.4	21.7	21.7	20.6
15–19	14.9	14.5	13.4	13.4	12.0	11.0	11.3	11.7	12.2	12.8	13.6	13.5
20 years and over	34.9	26.7	24.9	23.6	22.1	19.9	19.2	18.3	17.8	18.9	19.3	19.4
Total	100.0	100.0	100.0	100.0	100.0	100.0	100.0	100.0	100.0	100.0	100.0	100.0
Median duration	14.9	12.6	11.8	11.4	10.5	10.0	10.0	10.1	10.3	10.7	10.9	10.7

SOURCE: K.G. Basavarajappa, 'Marital Status and Nuptiality in Canada', *Profile Studies*, 1971 Census of Canada, Cat. 99–704, Bull. 5–1–4; Statistics Canada, *Vital Statistics*, Cat. 84–205, various years.

Table 8: Distribution of children under 25 years of age, by type of family, Canada, 1961–1986

Year	Number ('000)			Per cent		
	Total	Husband-wife family	Lone-parent family	Total	Husband-wife family	Lone-parent family
1961	7,777.1	7,281.1	496.0	100.0	93.6	6.4
1966	8,656.2	8,079.0	577.2	100.0	93.3	6.7
1971	8,848.6	8,003.1	845.5	100.0	90.4	9.6
1976	8,520.7	7,621.8	898.9	100.0	89.5	10.5
1981	8,252.4	7,196.9	1,055.6	100.0	87.2	12.8
1986	8,019.5	6,863.8	1,155.7	100.0	85.6	14.4

SOURCE: Sylvia T. Wargon, *Children in Canadian Families* (Ottawa: Statistics Canada, Cat. 98–810, Occasional), Table 20; *Canada's Lone-Parent Families* (Ottawa: Statistics Canada, Cat. 99–933), Table 3; *1986 Census of Canada*, Cat. 93–106, Table 3.

divorce reduced the potential length of the average marriage by almost 10 years.[4] Since 1981–82, however, the trend seems to be moving in the reverse direction. Between 1981 and 1986, the proportion of couples who divorced within 10 years of marriage declined from 50 to 47 per cent, and the median duration of marriage among those who obtained a divorce increased from 10 years to 11 years (Table 7). Again, it is difficult to speculate if this new trend is going to continue into the near future.

A further factor helping to explain the overall change in the forms and functions of the family relates to the growing number of children from 'broken' marriages.

Table 9:   Distribution of children under 25 years in lone-parent families by marital status of parent and age of children, Canada, 1986

Marital status of parent	Number ('000)	% of children by age		
		Under 6 years	6–14 years	15–24 years
Widowed	194.0	3.9	21.4	74.7
Divorced	388.8	10.7	44.2	45.1
Separated	415.8	22.4	41.9	35.7
Never married	156.8	51.7	35.3	13.0
Total	1,155.7	19.3	38.3	42.3

SOURCE: *1986 Census of Canada*, unpublished tabulation.

It is difficult to determine the exact number on the basis of available data because not all children who are affected by broken marriages remain in the household of one of their parents (some are given up for adoption; some go to live with other relatives; etc.), but more children than ever before are now being reared by one parent alone—mostly by the mother. Between 1961 and 1986, the number of children living in lone-parent families climbed from 500,000 to 1.2 million, rising in significance from 6 to 14 per cent of all children (Table 8).

Single-parent families, as such, are not new, but in the past they resulted mainly from the death of one of the spouses. Today, the death of a parent affects children who are, on average, older than those who are affected by parental separation or divorce. In 1986, 25 per cent of children with a widowed parent were 14 year of age or under. In contrast, in the same year, 55 per cent of children whose parents were divorced were under age 14. Table 9 reveals some further features of the age pattern of children according to various parental marital statuses.

NOTES

[1] Paul C. Glick and Robert Parke, Jr., 'New approaches in studying the life cycle of the family', *Demography* 2 (1965): 187–202; Paul C. Glick, 'Updating the life cycle of the family', *Journal of Marriage and the Family* 39 (February 1977): 5–13.

[2] Roy H. Rodgers and Gail Witney, 'The family cycle in twentieth century Canada', *Journal of Marriage and the Family* 43 (August 1981): 727–40.

[3] For convenience without loss of accuracy, the data refer to females only.

[4] D.C. McKie, B. Prentice, and P. Reed, *Divorce: Law and the Family in Canada* (Ottawa, Statistics Canada, Cat. 89-502, 1983), p. 69.

CHAPTER 18

THE FAMILY AND DEMOGRAPHIC CHANGE IN CANADA

Economic and Cultural Interpretations and Solutions

Roderic Beaujot

Certain patterns of family-related behaviour have changed rather extensively in the past 25 years: greater propensities to cohabit, lower marriage rates, older ages at first marriage, higher divorce rates, and lower levels of childbearing. These changes are highly interrelated and they have brought us to a 'demographic turning point' involving markedly lower population growth and significant population aging. . . .

. . . Demographic changes are here placed in the context of the dynamics of marriage, the family and gender roles. An economic perspective is based on structural changes in the economy and its implications for families, women and children. The cultural perspective focuses on changes in norms on matters relating to sex, marriage and childbearing. It is argued that structural changes in the economy have affected the relations between women and men, and that changing cultural norms permit more freedom of choice in family-related matters.

. . .

AN ECONOMIC INTERPRETATION

Fertility trends are frequently attributed to economic trends. One hears that the baby boom was a function of sustained economic growth while the baby bust occurred in a period of greater economic restraint. However, the fertility trends do not relate closely to any simple economic indicator. For instance, why would the sharpest fertility decline have occurred in the period 1961–66? Also, the period 1980–85 has involved the so-called deepest recession since the 1930s, yet the total fertility rate has been basically stable at 1.7 births per woman. On the whole, the periods 1946–64 and 1965–85 do not involve radically different economic climates. While growth was slower in the second period, there was nonetheless sustained economic growth in real terms.

Charles (1936) long ago pointed to the 'paradox' of economic interpretations of childbearing. When real incomes have risen, fertility has declined. At the same time, inadequate means is universally given as the most potent motive for limiting the family. She says it very nicely: 'hence arises the paradox that people limit their families for one of two reasons, because they are prosperous or because they are not' (p. 189).

There is nonetheless a deeper level at which economic factors can be shown to have a bearing. This in turn brings into play the economic side of parent–child and husband–wife relationships.

As McQuillan (1986) notes, our economies have changed in ways that have produced increased demands for workers in areas of the labour force traditionally dominated by women. The consequent change in the integration of women in the paid labour force has altered the relations between women and men and has raised the opportunity costs of children. Women have become less dependent on marriage, making divorce and cohabitation more feasible alternatives. Westoff (1986) also argues that the most important force underlying the weakening of marriage is the growing economic independence of women.

An interesting aspect of this interpretation is that a similar argument can be used in accounting for the earlier demographic transition. In this case, structural transformations in the economic and social system generated by the industrial revolution have decreased the value and increased the costs of children (e.g., Demeny, 1986). Stated differently, the economic role of children changed from that of producer to that of dependent. The movement of economic production out of the household ruptured the link between economic production and demographic reproduction (e.g. Dickinson and Russell, 1986; Boily, 1987). In addition, social security has replaced the family as the basic welfare net in the face of economic hardships and incapacity. Thus the economic rationalities for having children have been seriously undermined.

Ursel (1986) has made an interesting analysis of labour acts in Ontario over the period 1884–1913 showing how these increasingly limited the use of child and female labour in the productive system. The manifest concern was to improve the conditions of children and women, but the laws also entrenched the distinctions between male and female labour. By putting limitations on the hours women could work, the places they could work and the kind of work they could do, it became almost impossible for a female factory worker to make a living wage. As women were in an economically dependent position, their livelihood was contingent on entry into reproductive relations.

The resultant division of labour produced a reciprocal state of dependency between the sexes. Economic and policy structures discouraged women from participation in the labour force, and thus the family was based on a 'breadwinner' model where wives were dependent on their husbands' incomes and the husbands were dependent on wives for the care of home and children.

In recent years, the possibility for women to become more self-sufficient reduced this state of dependency. The greater involvement in work outside the home has obviously cut heavily into the time available for childbearing, a very labour-intensive activity. Davis (1984) has even questioned the extent to which societies based on an egalitarian sex-role system can survive, that is, reproduce themselves. Keyfitz (1986: 152) agrees that low fertility is the ultimate natural outcome of gender equality. He bluntly concludes that societies that do not constrain women will contract.

These broad economic factors are therefore useful for understanding changes in the family, gender roles and childbearing. With the industrial revolution, the family lost much of its function in economic production, and children became economic dependents. Since women became excluded from the economic production that moved outside of the household, they also became more dependent on the extra-familial occupations of their husbands. Only more recently did women regain their roles in the labour force. Fertility went down first when children lost their economic value to parents, and again when childbearing became an opportunity cost to employed women. According to this perspective, we might expect further reductions in childbearing, as labour-force participation of women continues to increase. In 1986, 52.1 per cent of women and 85.2 per cent of men at ages 25–44 were 'employed full-time' (Statistics Canada, 1986: 26, 56). Therefore, there is still room for further labour-force involvement on the part of women.

However, these economic explanations are not definitive. According to economic logic there should be hardly any children, yet the most common family size involves two children. Economic explanations do not suffice in explaining the baby boom. . . . there are no sharp reversals of trends coincident with the beginning or the end of the baby boom. As another example of the difficulty of economic explanations, among women aged 65 and over at the time of the 1961 census, those of English mother tongue indicated 3.2 births on average compared to 6.4 births for those of French mother tongue (Henripin, 1974: 10). Surely economic explanations do not account for this difference, and one needs to consider cultural differences.

A CULTURAL PERSPECTIVE

The cultural explanation proposes that fertility changes spread through societies much [as] new modes of behaviour or innovations are diffused, that is through

channels of communication (van de Walle and Knodel, 1980). Such an explanation holds that 'the things that work inside people's heads' require analysis as
much as the objective conditions that lie outside (Preston, 1986; see also Burch,
1987).

In reflecting on the experience of the world fertility survey, Cleland and Wilson
(1987) argue that ideational rather than structural, economic change lies at the
heart of the earlier demographic transition. The idea of limiting births within
marriage and the use of contraception are innovations whose legitimacy has
spread over time. The deliberate regulation of births within marriage represented
a new model of behaviour that was diffused across societies that were in cultural
contact, first in Europe and eventually around the world. Cultural barriers have
sometimes impeded the spread of the new models of behaviour. In Belgium, for
example, lower fertility gained momentum sooner in the French-speaking population than in the Flemish population. Similarly, French-Canadian fertility for a
long time stayed above that of English Canada. Minorities like the Native peoples
can resist the 'penetration' of different forms of behaviour, including the adoption of changed modes of fertility. The Islamic populations would be another
example of societies that have largely resisted these new fertility norms.

For the more recent trends, this interpretation would point to shift in values and
norms from family or child-centred orientations toward more self-centred pur-
suits (Ariès, 1980; Lesthaeghe, 1983: Roussel, 1987). In particular, there is a
weakening of the normative consensus that marriage and childbearing are integral parts of the adult role. Instead, children are largely viewed as a means
through which adults can receive affective gratification and blossom as individuals (Romaniuc, 1984: 64). Of course, many have concluded that children can
interfere with this affective individualism.

Canada lacks a tradition of social surveys that would make it possible to analyse
these types of trends in social values. For the United States, Preston (1986: 184–8)
shows that 'marriage' and 'children' bring to mind increasingly 'restrictive' con-
notations. American survey data also indicate that behaviour is justified more in
terms of its consequences for personal development, and less on grounds of
adhering to social values.

Based on a survey of people aged 18–30 in France, Roussel (1979) observes a
radical transformation of the concept of marriage. A few see marriage in traditional terms, based on established roles, expectations and mutual obligations,
where the continuation of the relationship is not dependent on the maintenance
of the love that was initially experienced. But the majority feel that a continuation
of strong emotional exchanges and communications is essential to the marriage.
They refuse to abide by the institutionalized prerogatives, they feel that continued personal fulfilment is essential and therefore they do not make definite
commitment to a given partner.

Roussel (1987) suggests that the last two decades have involved a cultural
change wherein people became less interested in living up to external norms and
more interested in living up to what they themselves wanted. In many areas of life
it is not possible to increase the freedom from external norms; for instance

workplaces and bureaucracies have to set limits on the variability of individual behaviour. On questions like child abuse and environmental protection we now accept a higher level of social restrictions on behaviour. However, in family-type behaviour it became possible to live with less social constraints. Here the freedom promised by the Enlightenment, the French Revolution, Existentialism and the Me Generation have become manifest. Legislative changes making divorces easier and equating cohabitation with marriage also signified a greater acceptability of alternate sexual and marital arrangements.

It is, of course, incorrect to say that people's family and fertility behaviour was in the past constrained by strict norms while people are now free to do as they please. In some regards, people may have had more freedom in the past: for instance, to choose celibacy instead of marriage. Cultural norms obviously continue to operate; all societies will constrain individual behaviour in such crucial areas as sex, the family and procreation. Better to argue that the spirit of individualism and self-fulfilment changes, but does not remove, the normative context of these behaviours. For instance, people who remain in a marriage that is not gratifying are going against the norm that 'marriages should be gratifying'. The more importance given to this norm in the culture, the less likely they are to remain married.

By separating sex and procreation, effective methods of contraception also supported a greater freedom in relationships. Partly because of efficient contraception, people could enter into relationships earlier. By becoming accustomed to the idea of relationships or marriages without children, the link between marriage and children was also weakened. Obviously, the relationship between sex, marriage and procreation are shaped not only by contraception but by attitudes, values and norms.

With the rising importance of self-gratification in relationships, people are more likely to be committed to their relationships only to the extent that these remain gratifying. This presents a problem for childbearing since having children involves a long-term commitment. The parent–child relationship, and at least to some extent the relationship to the other parent of one's child, stays with you forever. Thus people may be having fewer children in order to avoid commitments to relationships that may not last a lifetime (see Beaujot, 1986). There is some evidence that less stable relationships involve fewer children. For instance, among women married in the period 1966–81, those with no marital interruptions expect a total of 2.2 children while those with interruptions expect 1.6, a difference of 25 per cent (Lapierre-Adamcyk, 1987). Also, the average expected family size of women aged 18–34 who 'choose only cohabitation' is 1.4 compared to 2.34 those who 'choose only marriage'. Among women who choose cohabitation but not marriage, 30 per cent expect no children.

Clearly, a looseness in relationships does not imply no relationships. For many, long-term relationships and children are a very special form of personal fulfilment. Consequently, most people have children, although it may be counted to the logic of economic rationality, and families of size two are the most popular outcome. Having more than one child allows parents to not only experience children but also relationships among their children.

This interpretation also permits one to envisage variations or 'fads' in the cultural value that gain priority over time. Could that be why marriage and child-bearing were so popular in the post-war period? Skolnick (1978: 6–16) has called the 1950s the 'golden age of the family' where life was family-centred and the roles of women and men revolved around their family roles. There are interesting examples in the popular press of how these roles were promoted:

> What will they [women workers] demand of [post-war] society? Perhaps—and we can only hope—they'll be tired of it all [working outside the home] and yearn in the old womanly way for a home and a baby and a big brave man (*Maclean's*, 15 June 1942: 10; as quoted in Boutilir, 1977: 23).

As the economic climate was favourable and as children did not present an opportunity cost to women who were largely not in the labour force, couples could excel at childbearing, supported by social values that gave strong importance to children. The child's welfare was so important that motherhood was often seen as a full-time vocation. The very fact that people raised the question 'should a mother work?' indicates how much importance was placed on the child's welfare.

It can therefore be argued that questions of culture are useful in interpreting changes in the family, gender roles and childbearing. Persons who have written about the long-term changes in the family speak in such terms as movement from institution to companionship (Burgess et al., 1963), from orderly replacement of generations to permanent availability (Farber, 1964), from instrumental to expressive relationships (Scanzoni and Scanzoni, 1976; Shorter, 1975; Thandani, 1978). When the family was basically a unit of production and survival, relationships were instrumental; as it became a 'private sphere', nurture and affection became the basis for relationships (Hareven, 1977). These perspectives all imply a loosening up of relationships and a greater priority [for] affective gratification. To use Durkheim's terms, the family has changed from a unit of survival where relationships were based on a 'division of labour' to a unit of 'mechanical solidarity' based on commitments to common values. Obviously shared values or sentiment are a weaker basis for relationships and the need for continuous gratification puts heavy, and sometimes contradictory, demands on marriages. Spouses are expected to give the autonomy necessary to develop one's potential, but at the same time to help in this growth. Likewise spouses are to develop to their own potential, but of course to always remain the same person.

There are nonetheless limits to cultural explanations. For one thing, they present difficulties of analysis because the concepts are hard to measure (Burch, 1987). They can be seen as *ex post facto* rationalizations that are difficult to falsify. Also, as Demeny (1986) asks, we can speak of changing cultural aspirations and attitudes, but what determines such aspirations and attitudes? The view proposed here is that the broad economically based structural transformations retain their explanatory priority. These introduce changes in the possibilities of culturally acceptable behaviour. Nonetheless, at any given time, the definition of acceptable alternatives is filtered through not only the economically acceptable possibilities but also the socially acceptable ones.

Going back to the earlier demographic transition, we would say that both Malthus and Marx were poor in anticipating fertility trends. Malthus expected that higher levels of living would produce more children. Marx thought that a socialist revolution was necessary to solve the population problem under capitalism. However, in another sense they were both correct. Following Marx, it was an economic transformation that changed the 'laws of population'. Malthus, a preacher after all, was promoting a new cultural ideal of responsible parenthood. He might say that he was successful in promoting the idea of taking control over one's childbearing. In fact, he might even argue that the new planning attitudes toward childbearing helped the society to take control over other areas of life, including the environment, mortality and the economic sphere. Thus while economic explanations have a more secure base in visible reality, let us not forget the power of attitudes, values and cultural ideals in determining the course of social change.

CONSEQUENCES AND POSSIBLE SOLUTIONS

What about the consequences of these radical changes on the family? Are they sufficiently serious as to justify the term 'crisis' in its negative sense? While some may regret the erosion of 'traditional family values', others can see these changes as liberating. Why should we decry an evolution that allows for more freedom of choice? As Simmons (1986) said, 'living common law is not a problem, except possibly for old-fashioned parents; divorce is often a solution to a poor marriage; and lower fertility is liberating for women in particular'. McDaniel (1986) also says that feminists would not see higher divorce, lower marriage rates and lower childbearing as a crisis. Wargon (1987) prefers to view the changes as a 'challenge' rather than a 'crisis'.

However, there are other dimensions or perspectives which might suggest different conclusions. More divorce means more female lone parents who are worse off economically. Children may be suffering from the new patterns of family behaviour. Marcil-Gratton (1986) notes that smaller family sizes have important consequences on the typical experiences of children. In the average case, children would have parents who are younger and less experienced at child-rearing. Children are less likely to have a brother or sister who is five or more years older and who might give them guidance in life. Using data from Quebec, Duchesne (1986) observes a doubling in the proportion of children living with only one parent, from 6 per cent in 1966 to 13 per cent in 1981.

From the point of view of society, the most important consequence of these family-based changes is a lower population growth and significant population aging (see Henripin, 1986 and Lux, 1983). Population growth remains positive because the baby-boom cohorts are at prime ages for childbearing. However, in the longer term, below-replacement fertility inevitably produces negative natural increase. What is more, there is a 'population momentum' to negative natural increase. Low fertility produces an older population who are even less likely to have children, even if fertility rates increase. Stated differently, there is not a crisis in the family, but there may be a conflict between the interests of adults on the one hand and the reproduction of the society on the other.

In this context, one could certainly argue that it is time for the society to become more supportive of childbearing. In line with the economic arguments on the dynamics of fertility, one could propose that economic inducements, particularly ones that would reduce the opportunity costs of childbearing, could have an impact. These could include more publicly supported quality childcare arrangements, making the workplace more compatible with childrearing (including parental leaves), and generally tax transfers in favour of young families. It could be that the higher fertility in Eastern as contrasted with Western Europe, reversing the previous differences, is not a function of some of the more draconian measures like restricting access to abortion and contraception, but of the basic floor of social welfare in a socialist state which give families a sense of economic security.

This type of economic support for young families is not particularly forthcoming in Canada as we see from the lack of public initiatives in the area of early childcare and for that matter from the constraint on educational budgets. An interesting case in point, as Krótki (1986) observed, involved the 1985 federal budget which had first proposed a slight deterioration both of pension income and of family allowance/child tax-credit type revenues *vis-à-vis* the increase in the cost of living. While the former provoked such an outcry that it was reversed, hardly a word was said about the situation of young families with children. In the short term, we can pay for higher pensions with higher taxes, but in the long term investments in children, and thus in the future labour force, are necessary to pay for the inevitable costs of population aging. As Preston (1984: 451) has argued, the conflict between the young and the old is a serious one. Transfers from the working-age population to the elderly are also transfers away from children since it is people at working ages who have or might have children.

Turning to the cultural argument on the dynamics of fertility, there could be attempts to move the normative consensus in a direction that is more favourable to children. As Gerard (1987) observed, we do not know much about how this can be done. Nonetheless, it seems to have happened in the post-war period, helping to produce the baby boom. Surely part of the dynamic would be to build a shared consensus that children are important to the future of the society and that having children is an important part of normal adult roles. It could be that the higher fertility in France compared to the remainder of Western Europe follows from broadly shared consensus in France that a higher level of childbearing is important for the society. This consensus is supported by policy measures: for instance, giving women who stay home with their third child an allowance equivalent to the average industrial wage for up to three years.

It is important that the promotion of childbearing not be at the expense of the gains that women have made in the last decades. We must take seriously the observations of Davis (1984) and Keyfitz (1986) to the effect that equality implies low fertility. Childlessness is the easiest route to equality; in many marriages it is probably the only route. Children tend to introduce a more traditional division of labour, even to marriages that started out on a relatively equal footing. No doubt . . . childbearing, and even marriage, are more costly to women. That men profit more from marriages is witnessed by the fact that their life expectancy is increased by eight years when they are married, compared to a three-year increase for women (Adams and Nagnur, 1986). As another example, Gold-scheider and Waite (1986: 91) find that in the United States, men are more likely to get married when they have a secure economic status. In contrast, women are more likely to use a higher personal income to 'buy out of marriage'. That is, when women have a choice, which still involves a minority of women given current wage levels, they are more likely to see marriage and childbearing as a cost that might best be avoided.

Another example of the differential costs of marriage comes from the observation that married women are more likely to suffer job interruptions (Robinson, 1986). That does not apply to men since they are less likely to have job interruptions if they are married. As Robinson notes, the differentials are accentuated by the fact that on average marriage involves a wife who is two years younger than the husband. In terms of optimizing family income, if one spouse has to withdraw from the labour force it makes sense to sacrifice the lower salary. In part, wives have lower salaries simply because they are younger. Grindstaff (1986) also documents how childbearing exacts high costs in terms of women's involvement in economic roles, including education, occupation and income.

From this point of view, the 'problem' lies with men's failure to accommodate to women's desire for more role flexibility, and the 'solution' involves men absorbing more of the costs of marriage and childbearing. Presser (1986: 199) observes that a further postponement of childbearing on the part of women would increase their relative power, both because they would become more economically independent, and because a longer child-free context would make them more aware of gender inequalities. Women could then use their greater power to negotiate a more equal deal with their husbands, as well as with the workplace and the broader society, on sharing the costs of childbearing.

In summary, there have been a number of changes in key demographic indicators in the past 25 years, particularly lower fertility, slower population growth and population aging. Many of these trends can be related to patterns of family-related behaviour: later age at marriage, higher proportions not married, higher divorce and more cohabitation. These trends, in turn, can be related to broader economic and cultural questions. Structural changes in the economy have increased opportunities for women in the labour force, increasing the opportunity costs of children and changing the economic aspects of the relations between men and women. Cultural values and norms have promoted a greater concern for self-gratification and a greater freedom of choice in family-related matters.

Inasmuch as these changes pose difficulties in sustaining the reproduction of the society, solutions should also be sought along economic and cultural lines.

On the economic side, it is time to consider means of decreasing the opportunity costs of children to parents, especially through transfers that would benefit young families. Culturally, one could attempt to build a shared consensus that children are important to the future of the society and that having and caring for children is an important part of normal adult roles, for both men and women.

REFERENCES

Adams, O.B. and D.N. Nagnur (1986). 'Marriage, divorce and mortality: A life table analysis for Canada and regions, 1980–82'. Paper presented at the conference of the Federation of Canadian Demographers, November 1986.

Ariès, Philippe (1980). 'Two successive motivations for the declining birth rate in the west', *Population and Development Review* 6, 4: 645–50.

Basavarajappa, K.G. (1978). *Marital Status and Nuptiality in Canada, 1971 Census Profile Studies*. Ottawa: Statistics Canada Cat. 99–704.

Beaujot, Roderic P. (1986). 'Dwindling families'. *Policy Options* 7, 7: 3–7.

Boily, Nicole (1987). 'Dénatalité, immigration et politique familiale: le point de vue des femmes'. Paper presented at the conference of the Association des Démographes du Québec, Ottawa, May 1987.

Boutilier, Marie (1977). 'Transformation of ideology surrounding the sexual division of labour: Canadian women during World War Two'. Paper presented at the Second Conference on Blue-Collar Workers, London, Ontario, May 1977.

Burch, Thomas K. (1985). *Family History Survey: Preliminary Findings*. Ottawa: Statistics Canada, Cat. 99–955.

——— (1987). 'Babel revisited: The role of ideas in explanations of human behaviour.' University of Western Ontario: Centre for Canadian Population Studies Discussion Paper No. 1.

——— and Ashok Madan (1986). *Union Formation and Dissolution: Results from the 1984 Family History Survey*. Ottawa: Statistics Canada, Cat. 99–963.

Burgess, E.W., H. Locke and M. Thomas (1963). *The Family: From Institution to Companionship*. New York: American.

Charles Enid (1936). *The Menace of Under-Population*. London: Watts.

Cleland, John and Christopher Wilson (1987). 'Demand theories of the fertility transition: An iconoclastic view'. *Population Studies* 41, 1: 5–30.

Davis, Kingsley (1984). 'Wives and work: Consequences of the sex role revolution'. *Population and Development Review* 10, 3: 397–417.

Demeny, Paul (1986). 'Pronatalist policies in low-fertility countries: Patterns, performance, and prospects', *Population and Development Review* 12 (Suppl): 335–58.

Dickinson, James and Bob Russell (1986). 'The structure of reproduction in capitalist society'. Pp. 1–20 in James Dickinson and Bob Russell, eds, *Family, Economy & State*. Toronto, Garamond Press.

Duchesne, Louis (1986). 'L'Homogénisation des fratries et l'évolution de la situation domestique et familiale des enfants au Québec de 1951 à 1981'. Paper presented at the conference of the Federation of Canadian Demographers, November 1986.

Dumas, Jean (1985). 'Mariages et remariages au Canada'. *Cahiers Québécois de Démographie* 14, 2: 209–230.

Farber, Bernard (1964). *Family Organization and Interaction.* San Francisco: Chandler.

Gérard, Hubert (1987). 'Les possibilités et les limites d'une politique pro-nataliste'. Paper presented at the conferences of the Association des Démographes du Québec, Ottawa, May 1987.

Goldscheider, Frances Kobrin and Linda J. Waite (1986). 'Sex differences in the entry into marriage'. *American Journal of Sociology* 92, 1: 91–109.

Grindstaff, Carl F. (1986). 'High cost of childbearing: The fertility of women age 30–44, Canada, 1981'. Prepared for the *Review of Demography and its Implications for Economic and Social Policy.*

Hareven, Tamara K. (1977). 'Family time and historical time', *Daedalus* 1977 (Spring): 57–70.

Henripin, Jacques (1974). *Immigration and Language Imbalance.* Ottawa: Manpower and Immigration.

Keyfitz, Nathan (1986). 'The family that does not reproduce itself'. *Population and Development Review* 12 (Suppl): 139–154.

Krótki, Karol (1986). 'The history and methodology of the Canadian Fertility Survey of 1984'. Paper presented at the conference of the Federation of Canadian Demographers, November 1986.

Lapierre-Adamcyk, Evelyne (1987). 'Mariage et politique de la famille'. Paper presented at the conference of the Association des Démographes du Québec, Ottawa, May 1987.

Lesthaeghe, Ron (1983). 'A century of demographic and cultural change in Western Europe'. *Population and Development Review* 9, 3: 411–435.

Lux, André (1983). 'Un Québec qui vieillit: Perspectives pour le XXIe siècle'. *Recherches Sociographiques* 24, 3: 325–379.

Marcil-Gratton, Nicole (1986). 'Les enfants canadiens et l'instabilité conjugale de leurs parents: impact des tendances récentes'. Paper presented at the conference of the Federation of Canadian Demographers, November 1986.

McDaniel, Susan A. (1986). 'An alternative to the Canadian family in crisis model'. Paper presented at the conference of the Federation of Canadian Demographers, November 1986.

McQuillan, Kevin (1986). 'Discussion'. Presented at the conference of the Federation of Canadian Demographers, November 1986.

Needleman, Lionel (1986). 'Canadian fertility trends in perspective'. *Journal of Biosocial Science* 18, 1: 43–56.

Presser, Harriet B. (1986). 'Comment'. *Population and Development Review* 12 (Suppl) : 196–200.

Preston, Samuel (1984). 'Children and the elderly: Divergent paths for America's dependants'. *Demography* 21, 4: 435–457.

―――― (1986). 'Changing values and falling birth rates'. *Population and Development Review* 12 (Suppl): 176–195.

Robinson, Patricia (1986).'Women's work interruptions and the family: An exploration of the Family History Survey'. Paper presented at the conference of the Federation of Canadian Demographers, November 1986.

Romaniuc, Anatole (1984). *Fertility in Canada: From Baby-Boom to Baby-Bust.* Ottawa: Statistics Canada.

Roussel, Louis (1979). 'Générations nouvelles et mariage traditionnel'. *Population* 34, 1: 141–162.

―――― (1987). 'Deux décennies de mutations démographiques (1965–1985) dans les pays industrialisés'. *Population* 42, 3: 429–448.

Scanzoni, Letha and John Scanzoni (1976). *Men, Women and Change: A Sociology of Marriage and the Family.* New York: McGraw-Hill.

Shorter, Edward (1975). *The Making of the Modern Family.* New York: Basic Books.

Simmons, Alan B. (1986). 'Discussion'. Presented at the conference of the Federation of Canadian Demographers, November 1986.

Skolnick, Arlene (1978). *The Intimate Environment.* Boston: Little, Brown.

Statistics Canada (1985). *Population Projections for Canada, the Provinces and Territories, 1984–2006.* Ottawa: Statistics Canada.

—— (1986). *The Labour Force, May 1986.* Ottawa: Statistics Canada Cat. 71–001.

—— (1987). *Postcensal Annual Estimates of Population By Marital Status, Age, Sex and Components of Growth for Canada, Provinces and Territories, June 1, 1986.* Ottawa: Statistics Canada Cat. 91–210.

Thandani, Veena N. (1978). 'The logic of sentiment: The family and social change'. *Population and Development Review* 4, 3: 457–499.

Ursel, Jane (1986). 'The state and the maintenance of patriarchy: A case study of family, labour and welfare legislation in Canada'. Pp. 150–191 in James Dickinson and Bob Russell, eds, *Family, Economy & State.* Toronto: Garamond Press.

Van de Kaa, Dirk J. (1987). 'Europe's second demographic transition'. *Population Bulletin* 42, 1: 1–58.

van de Walle, Etienne and John Knodel (1980). 'Europe's fertility transition: New evidence and lessons for today's developing world'. *Population Bulletin* 34, 6.

Wargon, Sylvia T. (1987). 'Canada's families in the 1980s: Crisis or challenge'. *Transaction* (March): 10–12.

Westoff, Charles F. (1986). 'Perspective on nuptiality and fertility.' *Population and Development Review* 12 (Suppl): 155–170.

CHAPTER 19

THE 'REAL' MARRIAGE SQUEEZE

Mate Selection, Mortality, and the Mating Gradient

Jean E. Veevers

Most people are socialized to expect that they will marry, and that, once married, they will spend most of their lives in the company of a husband or wife. In Canada, about 90 per cent of all men and 92 per cent of all women will marry at least once before the age of 80 (Adams and Nagnur, 1981: 56). The observation that most people marry often leads to the perception that most adults are married, with the unmarried being viewed as a small residual category who are statistically and socially deviant.[1] When considering family life in contemporary North America, however, it is important to distinguish between persons who *have ever been* married, the statistic that is usually given, and persons who are *currently* married. In actuality, the married state is not universal, or even nearly universal. In Canada in 1981 . . . among persons 16 years of age and older, about one-third were not married (Table 1). One adult out of three still constitutes a minority, but it is a substantial one.

Being unmarried is not necessarily problematic for young persons who have not married yet. At the other end of the life span, the approach of senescence may

Table 1: Proportion of population unmarried, by age and sex: Canada, 1981

Age	Males	Females
16–19	92.95	88.31
20–24	79.02	58.25
25–29	39.57	27.42
30–34	21.15	18.20
35–39	16.59	17.47
40–44	14.19	16.71
45–49	12.79	16.23
50–54	13.71	18.88
55–59	14.55	23.52
60–64	15.97	33.29
65–69	16.95	42.74
70–74	22.19	58.48
75–79	28.86	73.86
80+	46.81	91.44
16–29	69.91	56.40
30–64	16.05	19.99
65+	25.22	63.19
All ages 16+	36.28	38.54

NOTE: Total population of Canada (N= 24, 341,700) rounded to the nearest hundred. Unmarried persons includes all persons who are never-married, divorced, or widowed.
SOURCE: Census of Canada (1981).

diminish the centrality of the married state. In midlife, however, marriage continues to be the status preferred by most men and women. Although some persons
elect to remain single, being unmarried is most often viewed as being emotionally, socially, and economically problematic (Adams, 1976; Stein, 1981). Nevertheless, among persons aged 30–64, about 16 per cent of men and about 20 per
cent of women are unmarried.

The study of patterns of nuptiality has tended to focus almost entirely upon
young persons contemplating primary marriages. However, given that more than
one in three marriages now involve remarriages, the systematic study of mate
selection needs to be broadened to include the increasing number of persons who
might marry in midlife or later. The purpose of the present article is to document
some of the demographic and social constraints that affect the mate selection
opportunities for the one in three adults who are currently unmarried, with
special emphasis on the situation of midlife adults aged 30–64.

At least three factors affect the marriage market in midlife. Fluctuations in
fertility . . . may cause a 'marriage squeeze' due to a lack of cross-sex persons of a
suitable age. Alternatively, increasing sex differentials in mortality produce
marked decreases in sex ratios in the later years. A third factor, which to my mind
is the most important, is the operation of age-based mate selection norms that
produce large discrepancies in the *de facto* pool of eligibles for men and for
women. The combined effects of these interacting factors will be illustrated by the

Table 2: Sex distributions by age, marital status, and method of comparison: Canada, 1981

Age	Sex ratios[1] of all persons	Sex ratios of all unmarried[2] persons	Proportionate distribution among unmarried persons % male – % female[3]
16–19	104.13	109.91	52 – 48
20–24	100.41	136.22	58 – 42
25–29	99.19	143.18	59 – 41
30–34	100.43	116.69	54 – 46
35–39	101.77	96.67	49 – 51
40–44	101.72	86.37	46 – 54
45–49	102.27	80.64	45 – 55
50–54	99.97	72.57	42 – 58
55–59	92.95	57.51	37 – 63
60–64	89.46	42.88	30 – 70
65–69	86.07	34.14	25 – 75
70–74	79.86	30.31	26 – 74
75–79	71.59	27.98	22 – 78
80+	54.30	27.80	22 – 78
16–29	101.07	125.28	56 – 44
30–64	102.60	79.40	44 – 56
65+	74.87	29.89	23 – 77
All ages 16+	96.18	88.49	47 – 53

[1] The sex ratio is the number of men divided by the number of women times 100.
[2] Unmarried persons includes all persons who are never-married, divorced, or widowed.
[3] Proportions are rounded to nearest whole percentage point.
SOURCE: Census of Canada (1981).

construction of 'availability indices', which estimate the number of unmarried persons of the opposite sex potentially available for every 100 persons in various age–sex groupings. These 'availability indices' are widely disparate for men and women at different ages, a phenomenon that has major implications for male–female interaction in both familial and non-familial settings.[2]

SEX RATIOS IN THE UNMARRIED POPULATION

In describing mate selection patterns, the first step is to define the pool of eligibles who are considered to be at least minimally suitable as potential partners. In our culture, this ordinarily means persons of the opposite sex who are unmarried.[3] Given the increasing tolerance for remarriage, for most persons eligibles include both the never-married and the divorced or widowed.[4]

The most basic parameter that defines the field of eligibles is simply the relative proportions in a population of males and females of approximately the same ages. Such data are available for Canada for the 1981 census year (Table 2). In adolescence and young adulthood, the sex ratio approximates 100 and remains near unity until the late 50s. If marriage patterns simply involved stable marriages between young persons of the same age, virtually everyone would have the opportunity to marry, and the unmarried population would consist primarily of widows past retirement age. In fact, however, people do not marry others of the same age. A combination of fertility, mortality, and marriage patterns together produce markedly unbalanced sex ratios in the unmarried population. Among persons under 35, such ratios are unusually high; after 35, they decline systematically until, in old age, unmarried women outnumber unmarried men more than four to one. Among the younger populations, the factor of fertility contributes to these outcomes; at the later ages, mortality differentials are more important.

THE FERTILITY FACTOR

During a time of rapid increase in fertility, some young women are 'squeezed' out of the marriage market because there are not enough potential husbands of a suitable age, namely, two to three years older then themselves. The resulting phenomenon is known as the *marriage squeeze*, and has been of concern to demographers for over twenty years (Glick, Heer, and Beresford, 1963: 38).[5] However, this factor does not contribute substantially to the sex ratios of the unmarried at midlife. The only women who are affected by it are those born during the few years of rapid increase in fertility; once high fertility rates have been established, the sex ratios of eligible persons are again stabilized. At the other end of a baby boom, young men who are born during the time of rapid decrease in fertility will also experience a marriage squeeze, in that they will find insufficient numbers of women two to three years younger than themselves. The marriage squeeze seems to account for only a small proportion of persons who never marry, and to have had a substantial impact only on those few select cohorts born during extreme fluctuations in the fertility rate (Veevers, 1988c).

THE MORTALITY FACTOR

In the industrialized Western world, male death rates are consistently and substantially higher than female death rates, a discrepancy that has been increasing (Gee and Veevers, 1983; Veevers and Gee, 1985). Women can now expect to live about seven years longer than men. Although all sex ratios decline with advancing age, it is noteworthy that in the general population the decline does not begin until after age 50, and it is not really pronounced until after age 70. Among unmarrieds, however, the decline begins at age 35 and is much more pronounced. One factor that contributes to this situation is that married persons, especially husbands, have lower mortality rates than the unmarried (Fox, Bulusu, and Kinlen, 1979; Boyd, 1983). Another is the fact that the combination of female longevity plus a preference for marrying older men ensures that the incidence of wives who are widowed will vastly exceed that of husbands who become widowers.[6] At the time of a divorce, the sex ratio of persons involved is obviously balanced. However, once persons become unmarried due to death or divorce, the rates of remarriage are higher for men than for women, and the men's time spent before remarriage is shorter (Adams and Nagnur, 1981: 56; Treas and Van Hilst, 1976).

The effects of differential mortality, differential widowing, and differential remarriage rates combine to produce markedly different sex ratios among the unmarried population compared with the population as a whole, as shown in Table 2. Among persons aged 30–64 in the general population, the sex ratio is 102, which is about equal but slightly in the direction of an excess of males. Among unmarried persons aged 30–64, the sex ratio is only 79.

Before considering other factors that contribute to male-female imbalances, let us consider what sex ratios actually mean. By demographic convention, sex ratios are a convenient means of making between-group comparisons, or of assessing changes within a group over time. In terms of their consequences for a particular population, however, their meaning is less obvious. Another way of expressing the imbalances described by a sex ratio of 79 would be to note that it describes a group composed of about 44 per cent men and about 56 per cent women. Column 4 in Table 2 shows this alternate way of describing sex imbalances. Some imbalances may not seem dramatic for many purposes. However, if the population is to be grouped into cross-sex pairs, as it is in marriage, small distortions may produce significant results.

Let us consider a hypothetical population of 100 persons: 44 men and 56 women. If *all* of the available males were involved in a cross-sex pair, then 44 women could marry 44 men, and 88 per cent of the population could be married. Of necessity, 12 women out of 56, or *21 per cent of all women*, could *not* be married. When talking about marriage markets, this way of looking at sex imbalances may be more relevant than conventional sex ratios.

THE HYPERGAMY FACTOR: AGE-BASED MARRIAGE NORMS

The demographic facts that describe the distribution of the sexes in a population must be considered in light of the social attitudes concerning them. Studies of mate selection provide extensive evidence supporting the generalization that *hypergamy*, the situation where the woman marries up in terms of status, is almost universally more acceptable and more common than the converse, *hypogamy*, in which the woman marries down. These norms structure the patterns of relative ages within marriage. Other things being equal, it is appropriate for a man to marry someone of his own age *or younger*; it is appropriate for a woman to marry someone of her own age *or older*. When women are seeking husbands, they tend to seek men who are considerably older than themselves. In contrast, men seeking wives tend to want relatively young wives. Technically, the word 'nubile' means marriageable, but in common parlance it is synonymous with young.

Casual inspection of marriage patterns suggests that the 'typical' marriage in Canada involves a bride between the ages of 21 and 24 marrying a groom between the ages 23 and 26 who is two or three years her senior. Such an observation would hardly be thought controversial, and yet such a union involves only about one-quarter of all marriages. During the formation of primary marriages, in late adolescence or early adulthood, hypergamy norms are not usually problematic, in that approximately equal numbers of eligible men and women exist, and the age differences of spouses are usually not large. At the later ages, however, the age range of potential mates widens considerably (Bytheway, 1982). In the twenties, most mates are selected from persons within a range of about five years. In later life, potential mates may be 10, 15, or even 20 years younger or older than oneself.

Nearly universal hypergamy norms mean that competition in the marriage market is quite different for men and for women. With advancing age, there are proportionately fewer and fewer unmarried men; those who are available can choose from a large pool of younger women and face few competitors. Conversely, with advancing age, there are proportionately more and more unmarried women; those who are available can choose from only a small pool of older men and face many competitors, including some women who are much younger.

The asymmetrical nature of opportunities for marriage for unmarried men and women in midlife has been discussed from a number of perspectives (Novak, 1983; Guttentag and Secord, 1983; Espenshade, 1985: 231–3). While various authors agree that it exists, and that the disparities involved are 'large', there have been few attempts to assess exactly how large the imbalances are, or how they are affected when a multiplicity of factors are taken into account simultaneously. In addressing this problem, we have developed a method of calculating *availability indexes* in order to quantify the sex-ratio imbalances in the unmarried population.

CALCULATING AVAILABILITY INDEXES

An availability index is defined as the number of eligible persons of the opposite sex available for every 100 unmarried persons. Availability indexes are created by relating two kinds of data: nuptiality data, which allow for a description of probable marriage patterns, and demographic data, which relate those patterns to particular age–sex distributions of unmarried persons. The present illustration will be limited to data on 190,082 registered marriages, with the exact age of brides cross-tabulated by the exact age of grooms. Statistics Canada provided population estimates; men and women classified as never-married, divorced, or widowed were grouped to produce a distribution of unmarried persons by age and sex.

The technique involved in the calculation of availability ratios will be illustrated by examining in detail the steps used to estimate the number of potential brides available for every 100 eligible men who were 40 years of age in Canada in 1981.

Step One: Age range of potential eligibles. Theoretically, it is possible for any single person who is of legal age to marry any cross-sex single person who is also of legal age, and who is outside incest prohibitions. In fact, however, only persons of a 'suitable' age are really viable as potential mates. For some individuals, an age difference of twenty, thirty, or even forty years is acceptable. In most instances, however, persons marry within a few years of their own age.[7] By examining the age distributions of actual brides and grooms in 1981, one can avoid speculation about the choices that individuals might prefer in marriage, or might at least find acceptable, and rely only on what they actually do.

The age range within which persons generally find each other to be acceptable marriage partners was arbitrarily defined as the age range within which 80 per cent of all marriages for persons of a given age occur. The range of ages that are acceptable is relatively restricted among the young, and it increases in midlife. For example, in Canada in 1981, of all brides aged 20, 80 per cent chose grooms between 20 and 25, a six-year span; however, of all brides aged 40, 80 per cent chose grooms between 32 to 52, a 21-year span.

To begin with our specific example: among grooms age 40, 80 per cent chose brides in the age range 26 to 42. As shown in Table 3, Column 4, in 1981, there were a total of 520,200 unmarried women of these ages.

Step Two: The 'fair share' ratio. One way to think about eligible mates would be simply to compare the number of single persons of a given age with the total number of persons in the population who are of the opposite sex, unmarried, and of a suitable age. Thus, in Canada in 1981, there were 18,000 unmarried men age 40 who, theoretically, could choose as brides any unmarried woman age 26–42, of which there was a total of 520,200. Although this superficially seems to constitute very good odds, in reality it overlooks the very important factor of competition.

Although all women aged 26–42 may be suitable as brides for men of 40, they are not all really available, in that 40-year-olds must compete with other unmarried men of all ages. Some of these eigible women will want to marry men who are younger than 40; others will prefer men who are older. Realistically, the best that 40-year-olds can expect is their 'fair share' of all women aged 26–42. How can the competition with men of other ages be taken into account to determine their 'fair share' of the marriage market to 40-year-olds?

To estimate the answer to this question, we need only consider how likely women aged 26–42 are to marry men aged 40 exactly (Table 3). In 1981, of all brides aged 26 (N = 8,712), only 0.459 per cent married men aged 40. Of all unmarried women aged 26 in Canada in 1981 (N = 57,100), we can then assume that 0.459 per cent or 262 are likely to select an unmarried man aged 40 rather than someone of any other age. Similarly, of all brides aged 35 (N = 1,856), 4.149 per cent married men of age 40. Of all unmarried women aged 35 (N = 25,200), we can assume that 4.149 per cent or 1,047 are likely to select an unmarried man aged 40 rather than any other age. This procedure is then repeated for all ages from 26 to 42. The result is that of all unmarried men age 40 in 1981 (N = 18,000), a total of 14,284 unmarried women are theoretically available to them as potential brides. The availability index for men aged 40 is therefore 14,284 per 18,000 or 79 per 100.

Once we know the age range of potential mates, and the 'fair share' that a given group has of that pool, it is easy to calculate the ratio between the number of potential brides of grooms and the number of eligible mates available to them.

Table 3: The calculation of an availability index: An example using unmarried men of 40: Canada, 1981

Age of 'suitable' unmarried women[1]	Number of brides of this age: Canada 1981[2]	Proportion of brides selecting men of 40[3]	Number of unmarried women[4]	'Fair share' of potential brides[5]
26	8,712	.459	57,100	262
27	7,230	.913	49,300	450
28	5,736	1.116	43,300	483
29	4,822	1.224	38,800	475
30	3,994	1.652	35,800	591
31	3,392	2,241	33,200	744
32	2,847	3.410	31,400	1,071
33	2,645	3.251	30,000	975
34	2,340	3.376	29,400	993
35	1,856	4.149	25,200	1,047
36	1,464	4,167	23,200	967
37	1,371	5.616	22,600	1,269
38	1,285	5.370	22,300	1,198
39	1,032	5.717	20,600	1,178
40	983	5.086	19,900	1,012
41	857	3.967	19,200	762
42	819	4.274	18,900	808
Totals:	51,385	2.133	520,200	14,284

[1] Of all men of age 40 who got married in Canada in 1981, at least 80% chose brides between the ages of 26 and 42.

[2] Of all brides who got married in Canada in 1981, there were 51,385 between the ages of 26 and 42.

[3] Of all brides aged 26–42, a total of 2.1% married men aged 40. Of brides aged 37, 5.6% married men aged 40.

[4] In Canada in 1981, there were a total of 520,200 unmarried women aged 26–42.

[5] The 'fair share' for men of 40 is the percentage of unmarried women of a given age who select men of 40 as grooms. There are many young unmarried women aged 26, but only a few (0.5%) select men of 40, so their 'fair share' is estimated to be 0.5% of 57,100 or 262. Conversely, there are fewer unmarried women at age 40, but more (5.1%) selected men of 40, so their 'fair share' is estimated to be 5.1% of 19,900 or 1,012.

These steps were repeated to compute the availability indices of potential brides for selected ages for men aged 20 to 70, as shown in Table 4. The same procedures were applied to compute availability indices of potential grooms for selected ages of women aged 20 to 70, as shown in Table 5.

Step Three: Age–sex differences in availability indices. A comparison of Table 4 and Table 5 shows the differences in circumstances for men and women at different ages in the life cycle. For men, advancing age means a progressive improvement in the availability ratios of unmarried men to potential brides. At age 20, the marriage market is very restricted: their availability ratio is only 46 potential brides for every 100 unmarried men. This ratio improves during the next

Table 4: Availability indexes of potential brides for unmarried men, by age of men: Canada, 1981

Age of unmarried men	Number of unmarried men	Age range of 'suitable' potential brides[1]	'Fair share' of potential brides[2]	Availability indexes[3]
20	217,400	18–21	101,400	46
30	45,100	22–32	33,812	75
40	18,000	26–42	14,284	79
50	16,380	31–52	16,606	101
60	13,440	40–62	19,779	147
70	11,860	54–71	31,003	261

[1] Of all men of a given age getting married in Canada in 1981, at least 80% chose brides within this age range.
[2] 'Fair share' is calculated as shown in Table 3.
[3] An availability index is the number of brides potentially available for 100 unmarried men.

two decades, until it is approximately one to one by age 50. After that time, it increases markedly, until it is better than two to one in old age. Thus men begin with a situation of high competition for a limited number of women, and they end up with a situation of little competition for many women.

Conversely, the availability ratios of women to eligible men begin very high for young girls, who are eligible for many men, and then decline with advancing age, as more and more unmarried women compete for fewer and fewer unmarried men. The availability ratio at age 20 is about one to one; it declines steadily, until at midlife there are only about 50 potential grooms for every 100 unmarried women. The ratio declines sharply from that point on, until in old age there are only about 20 potential grooms for every 100 unmarried women.

Table 5: Availability index of potential grooms for unmarried women, by age of women: Canada, 1981

Age of unmarried women	Number of unmarried women	Age range of 'suitable' potential grooms[1]	'Fair share' of potential grooms[2]	Availability indexes[3]
20	170,600	20–25	176,977	104
30	35,800	26–39	26,176	73
40	19,900	32–52	11,929	60
50	22,820	43–62	11,447	50
60	32,360	53–71	10,652	33
70	38,960	64–75+	7,484	20

[1] Of all Canadian women of a given age getting married in Canada in 1981, at least 80% chose grooms within this age range.
[2] 'Fair share' is calculated as shown in Table 3.
[3] An availability index is the number of grooms potentially available for 100 unmarried women.

An additional complication: Cohabitation.   Although the availability indices as we have presented them provide an estimate of the proportions of men and women available for marriage, they systematically exaggerate the opportunities as they exist in reality. Persons who are not legally married may still be outside the pool of eligibles if they are living in a common-law marriage, an alternative that seems to be increasing (Glick and Spanier, 1980). Strictly speaking, the availability ratios should be based only on unmarried persons who are not cohabiting.

An additional complication: Homosexuality.   For most persons, an important criterion of eligibility for marriage is not only a person of the opposite sex, but one who is exclusively (or at least predominantly) heterosexual. The incidence of homosexuality in the population has been the subject of considerable speculation. Advocates of the Gay Liberation Movement have a tendency to perceive the gay community—both in and out of the closet—as considerably larger than the straight community is likely to believe. The *minimum* estimate of the incidence of persons who are exclusively or predominantly homosexual is 6 per cent of men and 1 per cent of women (Gagnon and Simon, 1973: 131). A *conservative* estimate is at least 15 per cent of men and at least 6 per cent of women (Hyde, 1982: 378). Presumably the rates of homosexuality are generally lower than average among husbands and wives, and substantially higher than average among unmarried persons, especially midlife bachelors and spinsters who have never married. Unfortunately, no data could be found to provide accurate estimates of the prevalence of homosexuality by sex, age, and marital status. Strictly speaking, the availability indices presented should be modified by excluding from the pool of eligibles some percentage of men and women who are homosexual. Since all available studies confirm that homosexuality is much more common among men than among women, the fact of male homosexuality further reduces the sex ratio of the pool of eligibles.

An additional complication: Perennial bachelors.   Many reflections on family life in North America reflect an implicit pronuptialism, in that they assume that almost all unmarried persons would, under beneficent circumstances, want to get married. The present analysis cannot take into account the presence of unmarried persons who are in fact outside the pool of eligibles in that they have no interest or intention of getting married, regardless of their opportunities to do so. This population would include nuns and priests as well as voluntary celibates and other misogamists. Popular wisdom would suggest that men are more likely than women to pronounce themselves 'not the marrying kind', but without additional research this remains speculative.

A singles party. The 'availability index' for unmarried women age 40 is estimated to be 60 men per 100 women (Table 5). A more meaningful conceptualization of these data is possible if we imagine what this distribution of the sexes means in a social setting. Suppose all the unmarried women aged 40 gave a party to which they invited all the unmarried men they considered eligible to become husbands, that is, all unmarried men aged 32 to 52. If their 'fair share' of this group came to a typical party of 100 persons, there would be approximately 38 men and 62 women. Some unknown proportion of those men are not truly eligible, because they are gay, or because they are already living with someone, or because they are uninterested. Nevertheless, if all the men wanted to dance—or all decided to get married—there would only be 38 men to couple with 38 women, leaving 24 women, or 24 per cent of the entire group, without partners. Of all the 62 women who came to the party, *more than one-third* would have no one to dance with.

If a similar singles dance were held by unmarried women of 50, where the 'availability index' is 50, there would be 33 men and 66 women. Half of the women would be without partners. It is this situation that we are referring to as the 'real' marriage squeeze.

IMPLICATIONS: THE DEMOGRAPHIC DOUBLE STANDARD

The double standard of aging is not news. Like other manifestations of the double standard, it has its roots in misogynous attitudes that are a fundamental part of our cultural heritage, and that are accepted, in varying degrees, by both men and women. Like other manifestations, it changes slowly if at all. Contemporary marriage norms do not go to the extreme of the Indian custom of suttee, which dictates that a widow should immolate herself on her husband's funeral pyre. However, contemporary norms do continue to devalue older widows or divorcees and to handicap them in the marriage market.

What is news is the *degree* to which the double standard of aging has become manifest in recent years. Concomitant changes in fertility and mortality have combined to exaggerate greatly the imbalance between the sexes. Moreover, the imbalances, which in the past were a part of life in old age, have now become prevalent in midlife as well.

Dilemmas of mate selection.   To this point, we have considered only the most minimal criteria for defining someone as eligible for marriage, namely, being a cross-sex unmarried heterosexual person within a certain age range. In considering populations in national terms, we overlook regional differences in the distribution of population. Propinquity provides a major constraint, especially for persons outside of major metropolitan areas. Moreover, in addition to important norms of racial and religious homogamy, the mating gradient that dictates that women should marry up and men should marry down applies not only to age, but also to height, weight, socio-economic status, education, and perhaps intelligence (Doudna and Fern, 1980).

When all of the factors constraining mate selection are taken into account, what is amazing is not that some people are unmarried, but that most people do have mates. Saxton (1983: 4) makes this point quite graphically. If one were to assume that a person had six criteria for selecting a mate, and that the chances of each of these standards being met in another person were on the average one in five, then the cumulative odds against finding one person meeting all six of the criteria at once would be five to the sixth power or 15,625. Many individuals will have more than six minimum standards in mind, and for those with idiosyncratic preferences, the odds of finding them in an eligible person may be much more than one in five. A distorted sex ratio such as we have described greatly complicates what was already a very complex problem.

Consequences of male-female imbalances. A full discussion of the implications of the markedly unbalanced sex ratios is beyond the scope of the present article.[8] It is clear, however, that such imbalances will have repercussions, not only for marital relationships, but also for various aspects of all other relationships between the sexes (Heer and Grossbard-Schechtam, 1981). Very low sex ratios will be associated with a cluster of social, sexual, and cultural consequences. Some of these outcomes are suggested by the examination of groups, such as American blacks, who have already experienced very low sex ratios (Guttentag and Secord, 1983: 199–230).

When considering what amounts to demographic determinism, it is important to note that this is one of many factors that may be leading the family in North America toward the same place. The degree of determination by any one factor is difficult to determine, but the sex-ratio factor is clearly one of importance.

In sorting out cause and effect, it is important not to think of the patterns of mate selection as being something 'caused' by the male preference for younger women. It is also 'caused' by the female preference for older men, who are by and large better providers and more established. One response to the 'dilemma' of mate selection might be to accept as husband material persons of one's own age or even younger. However, this alternative does not seem to be happening (Veevers, 1984; Veevers and Gee, 1987).

Among the many sequelae that might result from too many women and too few men, we suggest the following hypotheses for further examination. With declines in sex ratios, one would expect to find:

1. *Single subcultures:* an increase in the proportions of persons who delay marriage or remarriage, or who never marry or remarry.
2. *Antinuptialism:* an increase in supportive ideologies that value a life of *Single Blessedness* (Adams, 1976).
3. *Innovations in mate selection:* a trend to marriage bureaus, classified advertisements, and other unorthodox strategies to increase access to potential mates (Jedlicka, 1978).
4. *Heterogamy:* a broadening in the field of eligibles to include a wider age range of persons, as well as those with dissimilar racial, religious, or marital characteristics (Glick and Spanier, 1980).

5. *Illegitimacy:* an increase in numbers and proportions of out-of-wedlock births (Guttentag and Secord, 1983: 216–20).
6. *Divorce:* an increase in separation and divorce, due to lower marital commitment among husbands and higher marital dissatisfaction among wives (Guttentag and Secord, 1983: 215).
7. *Female independence:* an increase due to a reluctance to depend upon marriage for social and economic status (Guttentag and Secord, 1983: 215).
8. *Female-headed households:* an increase due to illegitimacy and low marriage/remarriage rates.
9. *Man-sharing:* an increase in tolerance for polygamous relationships, both premarital and extramarital (Richardson, 1985).

The principle of least interest. The traditional family system is based upon the ideals of universal and life-long monogamous marriage, which in turn are based upon balanced sex ratios. Assuming that, for most people, getting and staying married are important life goals, the bottom line in marital disputes is the threat of divorce. If a situation is defined as intolerable, walking away from it is an increasingly acceptable solution, as is subsequently entering a new and one hopes more satisfactory union. For young wives, especially attractive young wives, the large pool of men potentially available as mates means that the husband who does not create a satisfactory marital environment is in danger of losing his wife. However, by midlife her pool of eligibles has shrunk while his has expanded considerably. For her, the realistic choice may well be between staying married to her current husband or not being married at all.

In marriage as in other relationships there is a well-known *principle of least interest:* 'that person is able to dictate the conditions of association whose interest in the continuation of the affair is the least ' (Waller, 1938: 275). The demographic reality is that in a marriage at midlife, the onus for maintaining the union is more upon the wife than upon the husband, a situation that, other things being equal, must tip the balance of power in his favour.

If we assume that most adults are heterosexual, and that their first preference is to live out their lives with a husband or wife, in the context of a stable and monogamous marriage, then the imbalance of sex ratios results in a substantial, non-negotiable and pervasive reinforcement of the power advantage that has traditionally been associated with the male role. In essence, what is involved in the 'real' marriage squeeze is a *reaffirmation of the double standard*. The traditional double standard was based upon a philosophy of patriarchy and on vestiges of Victorian morality. These underpinnings have recently been discredited in light of egalitarian norms and increasing permissiveness. In their place, however, there may well emerge a new basis for a double standard. Men and women may continue to be subjected to quite different expectations concerning their sexual and/or conjugal behaviour. The emergent rationale may be based, not upon androcentric ideologies, but upon the demographic reality of a social world in which there is a relative scarcity of men and a relative surplus of women.

NOTES

[1] For example, in a recent textbook, Kelley (1979: 271) writes that 'despite our high degree of interest in alternative lifestyles, it remains true that 95% of American women are married by age 54, and 94% of the men by age 64.'

[2] A comparable situation exists in the white population of the United States (Stein, 1981: 29). In the black population, mortality rates for young males are so high that balanced sex ratios are not found even at the young ages. In 1970, among black women over 20, 30 or more out of 100 did not have a potential partner in the marriage pool (Guttentag and Secord, 1983: 201). The greatly exaggerated marriage squeeze among black populations is discussed separately (Veevers, 1988b).

[3] Farber (1964) has suggested that the family system in North America is moving toward a condition of permanent availability, in which every adult in the society will be considered as potentially eligible as a mate for every other cross-sex adult outside the incest taboo, regardless of their current marital status. While there is evidence of trends towards such a situation, in which divorce and remarriage will be possible and acceptable in a wide variety of circumstances, such expectations are not yet widely shared, and in most circumstances persons who are married and who are living with their spouse are not considered marriageable (Veevers, 1982).

[4] This has not always automatically been assumed to be true. For example, writing in 1961, Petersen notes that 'the sex ratio of that portion able to wed . . . is delimited, first of all, by age (it is usual to include that sector of the population aged 14 and over), and secondly by marital status. . . . Whether to include widowed and divorced persons is a moot point. Legally they are marriageable, but actually in the United States a large proportion of the persons so designated in any census will never marry . . .' (Petersen, 1961: 72). He goes on to discuss sex ratios in terms of marriageable persons, defined as aged 14 years or over and never married. He reports that in 1950, among single persons there were more than five males to every four females.

[5] Alternative strategies for describing and assessing the marriage squeeze are discussed separately (Veevers, 1988c).

[6] In the United States, Nye and Berardo (1973: 600) estimate that if a husband and wife are the same age, there is about a 60 per cent chance that the woman will be widowed. If she is 5 years his junior, the probability increases to 70 per cent, and if she is 10 years younger, it is about 80 per cent. In 1969, widows in the United States outnumbered widowers by more than 3 to 1; in 1970, the ratio was about 4 to 1; in 1980, it was more than 5 to 1 (US Bureau of the Census, 1981).

[7] In defining the field of eligibles that determine mate selection, it is important to remember that what is involved is not a description of all couples who may go together as dating and/ or sexual partners, but rather only that small proportion of all relationships *that lead to marriage*. For example, of the many romantic and/or erotic liaisons between blacks and whites, only a very small proportion lead to marriage. Racially mixed couples are more likely than others to live together without marriage (Glick and Spanier, 1980). In the same way, although there may be many romantic involvements between older men and much younger women, and even some involvements between older women and much younger men, these relationships are unlikely to be formalized by marriage.

[8] The implications of low sex ratios have been discussed in some detail in *Too Many Women? The Sex Ratio Question* (Guttentag and Secord, 1983). A lay person's view of some implications is presented by Novak (1983) in *The Great American Man Shortage and Other Roadblocks to Romance*. The available evidence concerning these nine hypotheses and other possibilities is discussed separately (Veevers, 1988a).

REFERENCES

Adams, Margaret (1976). *Single Blessedness*. New York: Basic.

Adams, O.B. and D.N. Nagnur (1981). *Marriage, Divorce and Mortality: A Life-Table Analysis for Canada*. Ottawa: Statistics Canada, Cat. 84–536.

Boyd, M. (1983). 'Marriage and Death'. Pp. 89–106 in *Marriage and Divorce in Canada*, ed. K. Ishwaran. Toronto: Methuen.

Bytheway, William R. (1982). 'The Variation with Age of Age Differences in Marriage.' *Journal of Marriage and the Family* 43: 923–7.

Doudna, Christine and Fern McBride (1980). 'Where are the men for the women at the top?' *Savvy* (February): 17–24.

Espenshade, Thomas J. (1985). 'Marriage trends in America: Estimates, implications and underlying causes'. *Population and Development Review* 11: 193–245.

Farber, Bernard (1964). *Family Organization and Interaction*. San Francisco: Chandler.

Fox, J.A., L. Bulusu, and L. Kinlen (1979). 'Mortality and age differences in marriage.' *Journal of Biosocial Science* 11: 117–131.

Gagnon, William and John Simon (1973). *Sexual Conduct: The Social Origins of Human Sexuality*. Chicago: Aldine.

Gee, Ellen M. and Jean E. Veevers (1983). 'Accelerating sex mortality differentials: An analysis of contributing factors.' *Social Biology* 30: 75–85.

Glick, P.C., D. Heer, and J.C. Beresford (1963). 'Family formation and family composition: Trends and prospects.' Pp. 30–40 in *Sourcebook of Marriage and the Family*, ed. M.B. Sussman. New York: Houghton Mifflin.

———— and G.B. Spanier (1980). 'Married and unmarried cohabitation in the United States.' *Journal of Marriage and the Family* 42: 19–30.

Gove, W.R. (1973). 'Sex, marital status and mortality.' *American Journal of Sociology* 79: 45–67.

Guttentag, M. and P.F. Secord (1983). *Too Many Women? The Sex Ratio Question*. Beverly Hills, CA: Sage.

Heer, D.M. and A. Grossbard-Schechtman (1981). 'The impact of the female marriage squeeze and the contraceptive revolution on sex roles and the women's liberation movement in the United States 1960–1975.' *Journal of Marriage and the Family* 43: 49–65.

Hyde, Janet Shibley (1982). *Understanding Human Sexuality*. New York: McGraw-Hill.

Jedlicka, D. (1978). 'Sexual inequality, aging, and innovation in preferential mate selection.' *Family Coordinator* 27: 137–140.

Kelley, R.K. (1979). *Courtship, Marriage and the Family*. New York: Harcourt Brace Jovanovich.

Novak, William (1983). *The Great American Man Shortage and Other Roadblocks to Romance*. New York: Rawson.

Nye, F. and F. Berardo (1973). *The Family: Its Structure and Function*. New York: Macmillan.

Petersen, W. (1961). *Population*. New York: Macmillan.

Presser, H. (1975). 'Age differences between spouses.' *American Behavioral Scientist* 19: 190–205.

Richardson, Laurel. (1985). *The New Other Woman: Contemporary Single Women in Affairs with Married Men*. New York: Free Press.

Saxton, L. (1983). *The Individual, Marriage, and the Family*. Belmont, CA: Wadsworth.

Stein, Peter (ed.) (1981). *Single Life: Unmarried Adults in a Social Context*. New York: St. Martin's.

Treas, J. and A. Van Hilst (1976). 'Marriage and remarriage rates among older Americans.' *Gerontologist* 16: 132–136.

US Bureau of the Census, Current Population Reports (1981). *Marital Status and Living Arrangements: March 1980*. Washington, DC: Government Printing Office.

Veevers, Jean E. (1977). *The Family in Canada: Profile Studies 1971 Census of Canada*. Ottawa: Statistics Canada.

—— (1982). 'Permanent availability for marriage: Considerations of the Canadian case.' Paper presented to the International Sociological Association, Mexico City.

—— (1983). *Demographic Aspects of Vital Statistics: Fertility*. Ottawa: Statistics Canada.

—— (1984). 'Age-discrepant marriages: Cross-national comparisons of Canadian-American trends.' *Social Biology* 30: 75–85.

—— (1987). 'Age-discrepant marriages: Some international comparisons of patterns and trends.' Paper presented to the Canadian Sociology and Anthropology Association at their Annual Meeting, Hamilton, Ontario.

—— (1988a). 'Supply and demand: Family implications of skewed sex ratios.' Unpublished.

—— (1988b). 'The marriage squeeze for Black Americans: Causes, trends and consequences.' Unpublished.

—— (1988c). 'Baby boom, baby bust and the marriage squeeze: A simplified measure.' Unpublished.

—— and Ellen M. Gee (1985). 'Accelerating sex mortality differentials among Black Americans.' *Phylon: A Review of Race and Culture XLVI*: 162–175.

Waller, Willard (1938). *The Family: A Dynamic Interpretation*. New York: Dryden.

CHAPTER 20

RECONCEPTUALIZING THE NUPTIALITY/ FERTILITY RELATIONSHIP IN CANADA IN A NEW AGE

Susan A. McDaniel

One need not be a professional demographer to know that in Canada in the late 1980s, marriage and childbearing are changing. Whether viewed with alarm or welcomed as overdue, changes in patterns of marriage and childbearing are dramatic, continuing and not likely to be short-lived. The birth rate in Canada is as low as it has ever been. Marriage, although continuing to be popular, is now entered into later in life and competes as never before with both cohabitation and remaining single. It is thus not surprising that the long-standing relationship between nuptiality and fertility is weakening.

In this paper, the traditional demographic conceptualization of the nuptiality/ fertility relationship is assessed, followed by a look at contemporary Canadian trends in nuptiality and fertility. In an attempt to work toward a reconceptualization of the relationship, one that may be more reflective of contemporary realities, recent research and theory from family sociology and from feminist sociology are reviewed. The basic parameters of a theoretically reconceptualized nuptiality/fertility relationship are outlined, in the hope that a new model might eventually emerge.

THE TRADITIONAL NUPTIALITY/
FERTILITY LINK

Traditionally, marriage marked the beginning of the procreative family. Even though births have always occurred outside marriage, the vast majority occurred within marriage. Childbearing often began soon after marriage, hence the historical association between age at first marriage and age at first birth (Balakrishnan, 1986). Marriage, in the past, tended to be so closely associated with childbearing that the childless married couple was seen as deviant, even pitiable (Veevers, 1980; Ramu and Tavuchis, 1986).

The vast majority of people married, as they indeed still do, and tended to stay married until one spouse, typically the husband, died (Gee, 1986; Beaujot, 1987). There was far less 'conjugal mobility' (Romaniuc, 1984: 59) through divorce and remarriage. Few alternatives to marriage existed. Only exceptional or determined women could opt out of marriage by remaining single or living in 'unconventional relationships', often termed 'living in sin' (Beaujot, 1987). It was not simply social and moral pressure on women to marry, but economic pressure. Few jobs were available to women and even fewer at which they could expect to earn a living wage. For men, marriage denoted entry into full adult status and sometimes resulted in parental gifts of property or money. For both women and men, becoming parents signalled their stability and acceptance of responsibility as full adults.

One of the best recognized and most firm relationships in demography is the inverse relationship between age at first marriage and completed fertility (as summarized by Balakrishnan, 1986; Bumpass, 1982; Westoff, 1987). Two explanations are traditionally offered. One is that early marriers tend to have more familial orientations and hence higher family-size desires. Another is that early marriers have longer exposure to risk of pregnancy, particularly in their highly fertile years, and thus have larger families (Balakrishnan, 1986). So well recognized is this relationship that in the later American fertility surveys, corrections were made for what became known as the 'age at marriage bias' (Ryder and Westoff, 1973). This was also done in some Canadian fertility studies (McDaniel, 1984a).

In short, nuptiality in demographic research has been a proxy for sexual intercourse or exposure to the possibility of pregnancy, at least in the North American context. In Latin America and tropical Africa, nuptiality has been much less often used in this way. Inadequate though nuptiality was recognized to be as a euphemism for sexual intimacy, it provided denominators for rates of exposure to pregnancy. The question now must be raised as to whether, or to what extent, nuptiality can continue to serve this function. To what extent are changing fertility levels and patterns related to changes in nuptiality? The question has been raised by others (Balakrishnan, 1986, 1987; Bumpass, 1982; Burch, 1988; Davis and others, 1987; Westoff, 1987). This paper falls within that literature in offering an assessment of nuptiality/fertility links in this new age.

Table 1:   Mean age of men and women at first marriage, Canada, 1946 to 1985,
           selected years

Year	Women	Men
1946	24.1	27.1
1950	23.8	26.7
1965	22.6	25.3
1970	22.2	24.7
1975	22.5	24.9
1980	23.3	25.5
1985	24.6	26.7

SOURCE: Statistics Canada, *Vital Statistics*.

CONTEMPORARY CANADIAN TRENDS IN FERTILITY AND NUPTIALITY

Among the most dramatic demographic changes in Canada over the past few decades have been those in nuptiality. The baby bust (the historically low Canadian fertility rate) might be seen as an equally dramatic change, of course. Nuptiality change has occurred along several fronts. One of the more significant changes (Westoff, 1987: 155) has been a reversal in the mid-1960s of the tendency towards early marriage (Beaujot, 1987: 2–3). Postponement of marriage has become increasingly popular, as shown in Table 1. The high mean ages of brides and grooms recorded in the mid-1980s are unprecedented in Canada since 1940 when data on age at marriage began to be collected (Beaujot, 1987: 3). This is also occurring in the United States (Bumpass, 1982; Westoff, 1987).

Paralleling the postponement of marriage is a decline in the proportion of people expecting to marry (Dumas, 1987: 18–19; Burch and Madan, 1986). Although most people still expect to marry, the proportions have declined from 95 per cent in 1965 to 86 per cent in 1984 (Adams and Nagnur, 1986). The probability of marriages ending in divorce has also increased, although it has recently stabilized, if not declined (Dumas, 1987: 25). It is difficult to estimate the probability of divorce since what the risk population should be is not straightforward. However, it is clear that divorce rates are high in Canada, with between 15 and 28 per cent of marriages likely to end in divorce (Adams and Nagnur, 1986). Table 2, however, reveals a recent slight decline in divorce levels, the first decline in the upward trend since 1969. Given the volatility of divorce rates in the past, it is prudent as Dumas (1987: 22) suggests not to conclude yet that Canadians are changing their divorce patterns. The small decline in divorce rates may be a function, in fact, of increased cohabitation and self-selection for marriage.

Among divorced people, remarriage is a rather popular option, although somewhat less so than in the past (Dumas, 1987: 21). As shown in Table 3, by 1985 in Canada, for almost 30 per cent of couples marrying, one or both partners had

Table 2: Total divorce index, Canada, 1969 to 1985, selected years

Year	Total divorce index	Based on marriage cohort
1969	1,370	1943–44
1972	2,007	1946–47
1975	2,932	1949–50
1977	3,063	1951–52
1980	3,277	1954–55
1982	3,655	1956–57
1985	3,121	1959–60

[1] Total divorce index is the sum of age-specific rates during a given period, representing behaviour of a fictitious marriage cohort.
SOURCE: Dumas (1987), Table 9, pp. 26–7.

previously been married. The old understanding that high divorce rates did not disrupt fertility too much because of the tendency, particularly of men, to remarry quickly, may be increasingly called into question in the future as fewer divorced people, particularly women, choose to remarry.

Remaining single and cohabiting both compete with legal marriage in Canada now as never before. Over the period from 1966 to 1986, for example, the proportion aged 20–24 who are married has declined from 55.4 to 32.1 per cent for women and from 30.0 to 14.8 per cent for men (as reported by Beaujot, 1987:3). Similarly, according to 1981 census estimates, around 6 per cent of Canadian couples enumerated live in common-law unions (Dumas, 1987: 25). As shown in Table 4, the percentages living common-law tend to be particularly high among younger people. Since data on cohabitation have only recently been collected and tend to be somewhat unreliable, we can only speculate on trends from the past and for the future. However, it seems likely that cohabitation is increasing both

Table 3: Percentage of marriages in which at least one spouse had been previously married, Canada, 1967 to 1985, selected years

Year	% of marriages with one spouse (at least) previously married
1967	12.3
1970	15.9
1973	18.1
1976	23.1
1979	25.7
1982	28.1
1985	29.7

SOURCE: Statistics Canada (1987), *Vital Statistics*.

Table 4: Ratio of common-law/now married by age and sex, Canada, 1981[1]

Year	Males	Females
15–19	56.83	47.83
20–24	27.14	20.77
25–29	12.87	9.80
30–34	7.63	5.81
35–39	5.55	4.46
40–44	4.27	3.37
45–49	3.29	2.65
50–54	2.53	2.14
55–59	1.91	1.62
60–64	1.50	1.38
65–69	1.21	1.11
70+	0.85	0.99
Total	6.28	6.28

[1] Ratio of numbers of common-law couples in each age group, divided by total now married in each age group, multiplied by 100.

SOURCE: Dumas (1987), Table 10, p. 29.

pre-maritally and post-maritally (Burch and Madan, 1986). Whether or to what extent it may be a substitute for marriage is not known. Even if, however, cohabitation is a prelude to legal marriage, it can have fertility consequences since couples tend to postpone childbearing until legal marriage takes place, or seen another way, to enter into legal marriage in order to begin childbearing (Burch and Madan, 1986).

Childbearing has also changed dramatically recently. From a baby-boom high total fertility rate (TFR) of 3.84 in 1961, as shown in Table 5, the TFR hit a low of 1.67 in 1985. As has been suggested by Keyfitz (1987) and others, replacement of the Canadian population is no longer guaranteed. Accompanying the all-time low Canadian fertility rate has been a precipitous decline in large families. Since the baby-boom era, large families have become virtually extinct (Beaujot, 1986). Needleman (1986) argues that the baby boom in Canada, unlike in the US, resulted largely from an increase, during the post-war period, in the proportion of families with three to five children. Families of this size are unusual today. Data from the Canadian Fertility Survey clearly reveal that the family size intentions of all Canadians have been revised downward (Balakrishnan, 1986).

One of the most impressive changes in childbearing patterns has been the increase in births outside of marriage. As shown in Table 6, the largest increases in non-marital childbearing have occurred not among teenagers, as in the past, but among women aged 30–39. In fact, women from age 25 to 40+ have experienced significant increases in their rates of non-marital fertility since 1977.

Table 5: Fertility change in Canada, 1921 to 1984, selected years

Year	Crude birth rate per 1,000 population	Total fertility rate per 1,000 women	Cohort completed fertility rate per 1,000 women
1921	29.3	3,536	3,714
1931	23.2	3,200	3,138
1941	22.4	2,832	2,867
1951	27.2	3,503	3,260
1961	26.1	3,840	3,152
1971	16.8	2,187	2,285
1975	15.8	1,852	2,123
1981	15.3	1,704	—
1985	14.8	1,670	—

SOURCE: Romaniuc (1984). Appendix Table 1.1; Dumas (1987), pp. 25, 28.

Changes in Canadian nuptiality and fertility of late have not only been dramatic, but they have occurred rather suddenly. Analysts have been challenged to explain and interpret them (Beaujot, 1987; Burch, 1987; Lodh, 1987; Preston, 1986; Retherford, 1985; Romaniuc, 1986; Roussel, 1986; Scrimshaw, 1981; Wargon, 1987; Westoff, 1983). Whatever the explanations, it is clear that the traditional link, both temporal and substantive, between nuptiality and fertility is weakening and transforming.

FROM FAMILY AND FEMINIST SOCIOLOGY: HINTS OF CHANGE?

Demography, of course, is not the only discipline which focuses on childbearing and marriage. In different ways, so do family sociology and feminist sociology. Here, a brief overview is provided of some recent research and theory in these two fields in the hope that hints may be gleaned about directions of change in the nuptiality/fertility link, and possible avenues of future exploration as new models are developed.

It seems surprising that family sociology and demography actually rely so little on each other's research, since the areas of overlap are large indeed (DeVos et al., 1987; McDaniel, 1984a). From family sociology, much has been learned about marriage as a social process and social experience (Bernard, 1982), about changing patterns of marriage (Eichler, 1983), about gender aspects of marital and family relations (Burch, 1987; Gerson, 1985; Grindstaff and Trovato, 1987; Pogrebin, 1983), and very importantly, about attitudes toward marriage as a social institution (Greenglass, 1985; Goldscheider and Waite, 1986; among others). Yet, with significant exceptions (Davis, 1985; Burch, 1987; among others),

Table 6: Fertility rates among unmarried women by age in Canada: 1977–1984

Year	< 15	15–19	20–24	25–29	30–34
1977	1.3	15.8	22.9	23.4	16.8
1978	1.3	15.6	23.7	23.9	17.5
1979	1.3	15.5	25.5	27.3	19.3
1980	1.3	16.0	27.5	29.2	21.2
1981	1.4	16.3	29.6	32.6	24.0
1982	1.4	17.2	31.8	36.4	27.2
1983	1.2	16.4	32.0	40.6	31.3
1984	1.3	16.5	31.7	43.1	34.5
Increase 1977–84	0.0	0.7	8.8	19.7	17.7
Increase in %	0.0	4.4	38.4	84.2	105.4

	35–39	40 +	Total
1977	7.8	1.7	17.9
1978	8.5	2.0	18.2
1979	8.4	1.8	18.9
1980	8.6	2.1	20.0
1981	10.4	2.3	21.1
1982	12.4	2.2	22.7
1983	13.6	2.7	24.1
1984	15.1	3.2	25.3
Increase 1977–84	7.3	1.5	7.4
Increase in %	93.6	88.2	41.3

SOURCE: Dumas (1987), Appendix B, Table 1, p. 105.

demography has not benefited fully from these findings and insights. Nor has demography incorporated them into its conceptual schemes of the nuptiality/ fertility link. What follows is a brief overview of some of the more interesting insights from family sociology which may be relevant to an enhanced under-standing of the nuptiality/fertility link.

Bernard, in the 1973 first edition of her book on marriage, was the first to report that marriage for men had a different meaning than for women (Bernard, 1982). The popular belief, of course, is that men are dragged into marriage unwillingly, necessitating a bachelor 'farewell to freedom' party just before the wedding, while women look forward to marriage as the pinnacle of their lives. Bernard, much to the surprise of everyone including probably many sociologists, dis-covered that married men were, on average, healthier and happier than their so-called free bachelor friends. She continued to report that on the basis of the best evidence available, married men are generally happier with marriage than are married women. The happiest, healthiest women are those who are not married. Other subsequent studies, as well as data on life expectancy by marital status, have found support for Bernard's findings (as reported in McDaniel, 1988a).

Greenglass (1985) finds that women tend to regard marriage as security, but paradoxically view the legal commitment as more of a drawback than do men. Women, according to Greenglass, see marriage as something of a 'risky venture'. A 1986 study by Goldscheider and Waite finds that women with more income tend to opt out of marriage, whereas men with more income opt in. This suggests confirmation of Bernard's findings that marriage has very different meanings for men and for women. A study comparing groups of women in therapy in the 1950s and in the 1970s (Moulton, 1977) reports that in the former group, the central concerns were sexuality, marriage and childrearing, whereas in the 1970s, the central issue was anxiety about role proliferation, with women often regarding marriage as a trap. A popular account of the aspirations of teenage girls in Canada (Kostash, 1987) finds that female teenagers are looking forward to having children someday, but are less convinced that marriage is a necessary accompaniment to having children.

Family sociology research is also instructive in attitudes towards balancing work and family roles. For example, Porter et al. (1979) report, on the basis of a survey of female grade 12 students, that having a rewarding relationship with a man was of primary importance (although not necessarily involving marriage) and raising children ranked second, with working outside the home ranked third. Significantly, even in the early 1970s when these data were collected, high school girls wanted their lives to encompass both family and careers. A 1978 study by Gibbins et al. reports that although most Canadians think that mothers of young children should be home with the children full-time, few have any misgivings about mothers working when the children are older. Only a minority felt that a married woman's priority should be to help advance her husband's career. Working-class women are more likely to expect to work throughout their married lives and accept the necessity for day-care for their children (Lindell, 1982). By contrast, professional women more often report that they see childbearing and sometimes marriage too as a trade-off with career expectations (Grindstaff and Trovato, 1987; Swanson-Kauffman, 1987). Dennis (1983) reports ethnic differences in attitudes toward combining work/family, although most Canadian students she interviewed expressed responsibility to both family and work roles. Quebec students were less in favour of mothers working.

Like family sociology, and overlapping with it, feminist sociology also focuses on marriage, family, childbearing and gender structure. In many ways, feminism, as one of the fundamental social movements of our time, has transformed the way social life is seen, analysed and conceptualized (Eichler, 1985). One of the basic insights of feminist sociology is that inequality between men and women in society not only exists, but is one of the cornerstones of the social system (Folbre, 1983; Jaggar and McBride, 1985; Smith 1981). Under the assumption that the personal is political, interconnections between the private and the public worlds have become apparent (Hartsock, 1983).

Among the areas in which the contributions of feminist theory have been most clear are the conceptualization and critique of the nuclear family (Pogrebin, 1983; Smith, 1977). The theoretical perspective through which the nuclear family was largely viewed prior to the advent of feminism was the still popular functionalist perspective, in which the propriety of a gender division of labour was unquestioned. Feminists offered an alternative conceptualization of the nuclear family as a place where the gender inequalities and injustices prevalent in the larger society create particular problems for women, but also for children and for men (McDaniel, 1988a; Pogrebin, 1983; Smith, 1977). Women were thought to be the only ones who might experience role conflict if they also worked outside the home. Not surprisingly, a biased picture of work, status and politics was developed based on incorrect assumptions about women's and men's realms, values and behaviours.

Feminist insights into the nuclear family and women's positions have crucial implications for understanding marriage and childcaring (Folbre, 1983; O'Brien, 1981). Most importantly, feminist theory has revealed the absence from conventional explanations of fertility change, including demographic explanations, any explicit consideration of the inequalities between men and women (Folbre, 1983; Jaggar and McBride, 1985; Maroney, 1985; McDaniel, 1988a, 1988b). Such inequalities, now well documented, provide the means by which society asks women to bear many of the social costs of childbearing through reduced opportunity in the workplace and lowered economic status. This is a factor overlooked by most traditional demographic analyses of childbearing, with a few exceptions (Mincer, 1963; Grindstaff, 1988; Schultz, 1975; Turchi, 1975). Similarly, changes in the costs and benefits of children are related to differential economic power of men and women both within and outside the home.

Feminist theory has powerfully shown (Folbre, 1983; Nolte, 1987; O'Brien, 1981; Petchesky, 1980) that reproduction is not as private as it was thought to be, because it took place in the family and involved biology, but a social and political process imbued with public meaning (Jaggar and McBride, 1985; Greer, 1984; McDaniel, 1988a, 1988b, 1988c; McLaren and McLaren, 1986). This insight allows for a number of fruitful avenues of analysis and further insights. If childbearing is a political process whereby women's reproduction is, to some extent, harnessed for the good of society, then childbearing resulting from violence, economic incentives or denial of reproductive choice to women becomes easier to explain (Love, 1982; McLaren and McLaren, 1986; McDaniel, 1984a). Marriage and childbearing, in light of the limited economic opportunities and negative social sanctions faced by single women who work, may be women's best economic and social option (McDaniel, 1988b; LeBourdais and Desrosiers, 1987). It may be, for example, the division of labour by gender under capitalism which motivates childbearing, rather than women's childbearing which creates the division of labour by gender (LeBourdais and Desrosiers, 1987).

Biases and potential biases in the analysis of marriage and fertility have become apparent by means of a feminist perspective. The distinction, for example, between reproduction and production may be artificial and male-biased. The concept of reproduction as primarily biological (and therefore female) may distort the social reality which involves women's social and economic labour in childbearing and childrearing (Hartsock, 1983; Jaggar and McBride, 1985). It excludes men from significant involvement in the childbearing/rearing process and tends to define reproduction as more biological than social. Further, and importantly, this distinction may ghettoize reproduction in such a way that it is not seen as a purposive and meaningful social activity, like production, changes in which can give rise to societal changes (Jaggar and McBride, 1985). Reproduction, in the means by which it is conceptualized, is thought to be unchanging and biological — and thus becomes both ahistorical and acultural.

TOWARDS A RECONCEPTUALIZATION OF THE FERTILITY/NUPTIALITY LINK

Given the clear weakening of the traditional link between nuptiality and fertility as a consequence of contemporary changes in the patterns of both marriage and childbearing, a new model of the link may be required. Such a new model might build in some greater complexities, as well as give increased attention to the factors and forces addressed in family and feminist sociology. What follows are six tenets on which a reconceptualized model might build:

1. The development of clearer theoretical links between sexuality and nuptiality seems necessary. It may be misleading to continue to assume that nuptiality is a euphemism for sexuality or that in [a] contracepting society sexual activity exposes women to risk of pregnancy (Birdsall and Chester, 1987). Issues of gender inequality and the changing meaning of marriage may be important in elucidating the degree to which nuptiality is a proxy for risk of pregnancy.

2. Hints gleaned from the above overview of research in family and feminist sociology suggest the usefulness of examining links between nuptiality and production. The assumption implicit in demographic approaches traditionally has been that nuptiality is a precondition for reproduction, but that neither has productive value in the same sense, for example, as work. The exception to this is the micro-economic approach to reproduction (Becker, 1981; Schultz, 1975; Turchi, 1975). Given women's attitudes toward and perceptions of marriage, however, as reported above, and persisting gender inequalities which mean that women, except for professionals, find it difficult to live and raise children alone, marriage might indeed have economic rewards and incentives. If this is so, then both marriage and childbearing might be to some extent economically motivated in ways previously unaddressed (Dickinson and Russell, 1986). Women who opt for marriage, then, in these days of alternatives, may be different in terms of their own prospects than those who do not.

3. A need seems to exist for the integration of micro and macro models of nuptiality and fertility. All too often, demographers who specialize in aggre-

gate phenomena seem to jump too quickly to the level of individual decision-making. What exists between these two levels of abstraction may be vitally important. For example, indviduals exist in context—class and gender contexts may matter as much as historical, cultural and political contexts. Attention to these crucial social contexts has been better done by family and feminist sociologists than by demographers. Yet, linking micro-level decisions about marriage and having children to macro-level phenomena such as nuptiality and fertility can only be attempted with reference to the social contexts which impinge on people, often in ways they neither see nor understand.

4. What may be suggested by contemporary socio-demographic trends and existing knowledge is that a tension exists between choice and non-choice with respect to marriage and childbearing. This tension has perhaps been given insufficient attention. The idea of choice in childbearing has become a popular one, yet it is acknowledged that unwanted pregnancy continues to occur, that contraceptives fail, that coerced sexuality and reproduction occur, and that women in situations of gender inequality may use their sexuality and fertility to economic advantage. That fertility might be used explicitly for economic gain in the future is likely if surrogate motherhood becomes institutionalized. The choice rubric, with respect to both marriage and childbearing, once in place, may blind analysts to the elements of non-choice which persist.

5. Another tension may exist between cultural beliefs about marriage and childbearing and the material or real conditions under which these activities are pursued. For example, both men and women might believe in having children once married, but for women the price paid might be discouraging in terms of lost career time, inadequate day-care options, and diminished status at work, among other concerns.

It seems clear, based on the above brief review of research from family and feminist sociology, that the competition between beliefs and material conditions may take different forms for men and for women. This is revealed in Figure 1, where some aspects of the differences are suggested. Although both men and women may *believe* in having children (a positive value relating belief system to desire for children), women's actual circumstances or material conditions—such as lack of maternity leave or inadequate day-care, or the possibility of forfeiting a raise or promotion—are such that her desire for children takes on a negative as well as positive aspect. Similarly, both men and women may have positive predispositions to the use of contraception, while material conditions faced by women mean that they, more often than men, 'pay the price' for contraceptive failure or non-use in terms of life disruption or workplace or mobility losses. Further, and in contradiction to women's strong positive attraction to contraceptive use, are the health risks associated with contraception.

Belief systems may encourage both men and women to commit to marriage, yet each has material conditions which are worrisome. For men, it

Figure 1: Micro-model of childbearing decisions in gender context

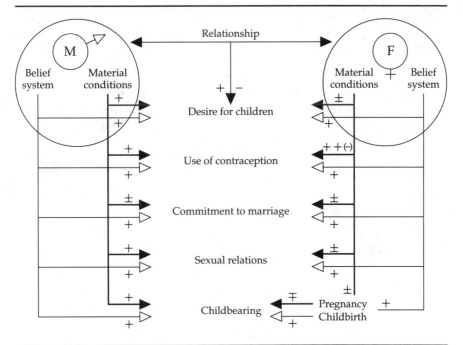

may be that marriage is costly in economic terms. For women, marriage can penalize them in the workplace in terms of their promotion prospects and the seriousness with which they are taken. Sexual relations similarly may have a positive attraction for both men and women, but pregnancy risks and potentially detrimental social labels (the old double standard) may be a negative for women. Risks . . . of pregnancy and childbirth, including the limited alternatives to hospital births, may be an inhibitant to women having children.

6. Lastly, more is assumed in the traditional nuptiality/fertility linkage than that nuptiality is a euphemism for sexuality and a precondition for child-bearing. Fertility is further assumed, implicitly, to have little to do with sexual politics or gender inequality. A demographer once remarked that if a martian were to visit a room where demographers were discussing fertility trends and research, the martian would have the distinct impression that fertility had nothing to do with sexual acts! Most demographers, however reluctantly, would see at least a grain of truth in this. This is nothing short of astounding in this most gender-specific of all human endeavours. It also tends to be assumed, implicitly, that pronatalism exists, that people want to have children and value children, and that society in general values child-ren. Yet it is recognized that single mothers with dependent children are

Figure 2: Macro-model of childbearing in gender context: Men

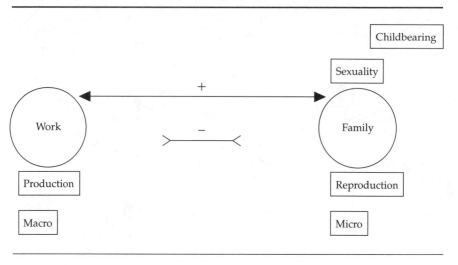

among the poorest in our society, that mothers of young children are less often seen as dependable workers, and that children are not welcome in many apartment buildings, restaurants and social events. The contradictions between presumed pronatalism and antinatalist structures and attitudes could be usefully explored.

It might be instructive to distinguish between a male model of nuptiality/ fertility and a female model. To a large extent, what we have now is a male model, as shown in Figure 2. A sharp separation of work and family is presumed, yet there is an assumed positive functional connection. Work, in the male model, is seen as a production of goods or services for pay. It occurs at the macro, public level. It is valued, as evidenced by the fact that it is paid. It is planned and trained for. Work provides an important source of male identity. It is perceived as rational and instrumental and is evaluated on objective criteria.

By contrast to work, family in the male model is private, a retreat from pressures and technology of the workplace. A man's home is his castle—he is in charge there even if he is not (or cannot be) in charge at work. Sexuality may be increasingly confined to marriage now (possibly due to fear of AIDS), although in the past it was not so much, and still is less confined for men than for women. Childbearing, similarly, is seen as private, although children are costly and thus provide incentives to men to work harder. A family man is perceived as stable and reliable. The male model sees infant- and childcare as largely women's domain, although some men today may increasingly recognize the work and commitment involved in shared childcare.

A female model, which may be emerging largely from family and feminist sociology, is portrayed in Figure 3. The significant difference between this and the

Figure 3: Macro-model of childbearing in gender context: Women

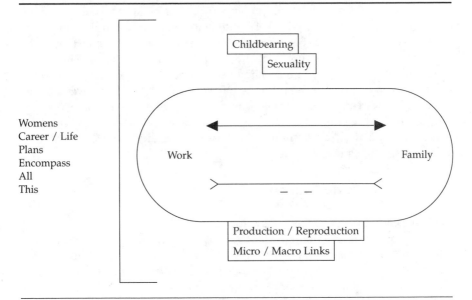

male model is that for females, work and family are linked together in multiple ways (LeBourdais and Desrosiers, 1987). For women, family *is* work, including housework, childcare, caring for the old and sick, emotional labour and intervention. Despite its rewards, childbearing and rearing *is* hard work too, with low pay, limited status, no holidays and no pensions. Home and family are thus not necessarily a retreat for women from work and pressure. For women, reproduction and production are linked, in that reproduction (and childbearing) may be their life's work, no matter what else they also do. It may be work for which they expect rewards, economic and otherwise—a nice house, clothes, labour-saving devices and appreciation. Reproduction itself can be a basis of status for women, a badge of adulthood, of successful femininity. Women's fertility in some places in Africa must be tested pre-nuptially to ensure their marriageability. The new princesses in the royal family in England had their fertility tested before engagements were announced. Reproduction, and marriage too, at the same time, can be a distinct liability for women in that their work commitments might be questioned, their promotion prospects and their mobility constrained.

Sexuality, too, for women may have a productive aspect. The most attractive and sexually 'pure' women may get the 'best' husbands in terms of both attractiveness and earning power. The notion that women's time spent on making themselves attractive is frivolous may be untrue. It may be that women work hard at being attractive as a kind of career planning. Certainly, women's sexual attractiveness within marriage is touted by everyone from marriage counsellors to Ann

Landers as a good way for women to keep their husbands faithful and good breadwinners.

The female model of childbearing and marriage, unlike the male model, reveals that women's career plans may involve *both* work and family and their interconnections. Women may thus be different than men in the ways in which they make career plans, and perhaps should not be evaluated on a male model. The female model reveals ways in which both family and work structures may be inflexible and inadaptable to the necessary trade-offs women must make between them. For example, career paths are male-based and assume that linear paths and promotions are the only way to progress. Work interruptions do not necessarily indicate women's lack of commitment to work or to careers, but only the need to balance responsibilities in two realms.

CONCLUSION

Contemporary trends in Canadian nuptiality and fertility reveal significant changes in patterns and timing. As well, a distinct weakening of the traditional nuptiality/fertility link is apparent. These changes pose challenges to analysts who seek to find meaning in current patterns using existing approaches. A need seems to be emerging for a reconceptualization of the nuptiality/fertility link.

In this paper, contemporary trends in Canada together with some recent findings from family and feminist sociology have been reviewed in an attempt to move close to a reconceptualization of nuptiality/fertility. While this is a small step, it seems an important one to make, however tentatively, toward rethinking this fundamental demographic relationship. . . .

REFERENCES

Adams, O.B. and D.N. Nagnur (1986). 'Marriage, divorce and mortality: A life table analysis for Canada and regions, 1980–82.' Paper presented at Canadian Federation of Demographers, Ottawa, November.

Balakrishnan, T.R. (1986). 'Changing nuptiality patterns and fertility implications in Canada'. Paper presented at The Family in Crisis Conference, Canadian Federation of Demographers and Royal Society of Canada, Ottawa, November.

—— (1987). 'Status of women, development and demographic change'. *Canadian Studies in Population* 14: 9–25.

Beaujot, R. (1986). 'Dwindling families'. *Policy Options* 7, 7: 3–7.

—— (1987). 'The family and demographic change: Economic and cultural interpretations. In *Contributions to Demography, Methodological and Substantive: Essays in Honour of Dr. Karol J. Krótki*. Edmonton: University of Alberta, Department of Sociology.

Becker, G.S. (1981). *A Treatise on the Family*. Cambridge, MA.: Harvard University Press.

Bernard, J. (1982). *The Future of Marriage* (2nd ed.). New Haven: Yale University Press.

Birdsall, N. and L.A. Chester (1987). 'Contraception and the status of women: What is the link?' *Family Planning Perspectives* 19, 1: 14–18.

Bumpass, Larry (1982). 'The changing linkage of nuptiality and fertility in the United States'. In L.T. Ruzicka ed., *Nuptiality and Fertility: Proceedings of a Seminar Held in Bruges (Belgium)*. Liege: Ordina Editions.

Burch, T.K. (1987). 'Age-sex roles and demographic change'. *Canadian Studies in Population* 14: 129–146.

—— (1988). 'Sex role homogeneity, female status and demographic change'. Conference on Women's Position and Demographic Change, Asker (Oslo), Norway.

Burch, T. and A.K. Madan (1986). *Union Formation and Dissolution in Canada*. Results from the 1984 Family History Survey, Cat. 99–963. Ottawa: Statistics Canada.

—— and B.J. Matthews (1987). 'Household formation in developed societies'. *Population and Development Review* 13, 3: 495–511.

Davis, K. with A. Grossbard-Schechtman, eds. (1985). *Contemporary Marriages: Comparative Perspectives on a Changing Institution*. New York: Russell Sage.

Dennis, A.B. (1983). 'Wife and/or worker'. In E. Lupri ed., *The Changing Position of Women in Family and Society*. Leiden: Brill.

Dickinson, J. and B. Russell (1986). 'The structure of reproduction in capitalist society'. In J. Dickinson and B. Russell, eds., *Family, Economy and the State*. Toronto: Garamond.

DeVos, S., A.W. Clark and K.R. Murty (1987). 'Family and fertility in context: Comments on some Caldwellian themes'. *Journal of Comparative Family Studies* 18, 1: 127–136.

Dumas, J. 1987. *Report on the Demographic Situation in Canada* (1986). Current Demographic Analysis, Cat. 91–209E. Ottawa: Statistics Canada.

Eichler, M. (1983). *Families in Canada Today: Recent Changes and Their Policy Consequences*. Toronto: Gage.

—— (1985). 'And the work never ends: Feminist contributions'. *Canadian Review of Sociology and Anthropology* (special issue on the state of the art and new directions) 22: 619–644.

Folbre, N. (1983). 'Of patriarchy born: The political economy of fertility decisions'. *Feminist Studies* 9, 2: 261–284.

Gee, E.M. (1986). 'The life course of Canadian women: An historical and demographic analysis'. *Social Indicators Research* 18: 263–283.

Gerson, K. (1985). *Hard Choices: How Women Decide About Work, Career and Motherhood*. Berkeley, California: University of California Press.

Gibbins, R., J.R. Ponting and G. Symons (1978). 'Attitudes and ideology correlates of liberal attitudes towards the role of women'. *Journal of Comparative Family Studies* 9, 1: 19–40.

Goldscheider, F.K. and L.J. Waite (1986). 'Sex differences in the entry into marriage'. *American Journal of Sociology* 92: 91–109.

Greenglass, E.R. (1985). 'A social-psychological view of marriage for women'. *International Journal of Women's Studies* 8, 1: 24–31.

Greer, G. (1984). *Sex and Destiny: The Politics of Human Fertility*. New York: Harper and Row.

Grindstaff, C. (1988). 'Adolescent marriage and childbearing: The long term economic outcome in Canada in the 1980's'. *Adolescence* 23, 89: 45–58.

—— and F. Trovato (1987). *Junior Partners: Women's Contributions to Total Husband/Wife Family Income, Canada 1981*. Population Studies Centre Discussion Papers no. 87–4. London, Ontario: University of Western Ontario.

Hartsock, N.C.M. (1983). *Money, Sex and Power: Toward a Feminist Historical Materialism*. New York: Longman.

Jaggar, A.M. and W.L. McBride (1985). 'Reproduction as male ideology'. *Women's Studies International Forum* 8, 3: 185–196.

Keyfitz, N. (1987). 'The family that does not reproduce itself'. In K. Davis, M.S. Bernstom and R. Ricardo-Campbell, eds., *Below Replacement Fertility in Industrial Societies: Causes, Consequences, Policies*. New York: Population and Development Review.

Kostash, M. (1987). *No Kidding: Inside the World of Teenage Girls*. Toronto: McClelland and Stewart.

LeBourdais, C. et H. Desrosiers (1987). 'Modifications de la situation socio-économique des femmes: l'interaction entre l'évolution démographique et les changements dans le marché du travail'. *Canadian Studies in Population* 14: 147–169.

Levine, H. (1983). 'The power politics of motherhood'. In J. Turner and L. Emergy, eds., *Perspectives on Women in the 1980's*. Winnipeg: University of Manitoba Press.

Lindell, S.H. (1982). 'Role expectations of adolescent women'. *Canadian Woman Studies* 4, 1: 67–70.

Lodh, F. (1987). *Explaining Fertility Decline in the West (with special Reference to Canada): A Critique of Research Results from Social Sciences*. Ottawa: Vanier Institute of the Family.

Love, C. (1982). 'The regulation of fertility: Some historical and social questions'. *Resources for Feminist Research* 11, 4: 421.

Maroney, H.J. (1985). 'Embracing motherhood: New feminist theory'. *Canadian Journal of Political and Social Theory* 9, 1–2: 40–64.

McDaniel, S.A. (1984a). 'Family size expectations among a sample of Edmonton, Alberta women: A comparison of three explanatory models'. *Canadian Review of Sociology and Anthropology* 21, 1: 75–91.

—— (1984b). 'Explaining Canadian fertility: Some remaining challenges'. *Canadian Studies in Population* 11: 1–16.

—— (1988a). 'The changing Canadian family: Women's roles and the impact of feminism'. In S. Burt, L. Dorney and L. Code, eds., *Changing Patterns: Women in Canada*. Toronto: McClelland and Stewart.

—— (1988b). 'Women's roles and reproduction: The changing picture in Canada in the 1980's'. *Atlantis: A Women's Studies Journal* 14, 1: 1–12.

—— (1988c) 'Women's roles, reproduction and the new reproductive technologies: A new stork rising'. In A. Duffy and N. Mandell, eds., *Restructuring the Canadian Family: Feminist Perspectives*. Toronto: Butterworths.

McLaren, A. and A.T. McLaren (1986). *The Bedroom and the State: The Changing Practices and Politics of Contraception and Abortion in Canada, 1880–1980*. Toronto: McClelland and Stewart.

Mincer, J. (1963). 'Market prices, opportunity cost and income effects'. In *Measurement in Economic Studies in Mathematical Economics and Econometrics*. Stanford: Stanford University Press.

Moulton, R. (1977). 'Some effects of the new feminism'. *American Journal of Psychiatry* 134: 1–6.

Needleman, L. (1986). 'Canadian fertility trends in perspective'. *Journal of Biosocial Science* 18: 43–56.

Nolte, J. (1987). 'Sexuality, fertility and choice: On becoming a woman in the Eighties'. In G.H. Nemiroff, ed., *Women and Men: Interdisciplinary Readings on Gender*. Toronto: Fitzhenry and Whiteside.

O'Brien, Mary (1981). *The Politics of Reproduction*. London: Routledge and Kegan Paul.

Petchesky, R.P. (1980). 'Reproductive freedom: Beyond a woman's right to choose'. *Signs: Journal of Women in Culture and Society* 5, 4: 661–685.

Pogrebin, L.C. (1983). *Family Politics: Love and Power on an Intimate Frontier*. New York: McGraw-Hill.

Porter, M.R., J. Porter and B.R. Blishen (1979). *Does Money Matter?* Toronto: Macmillan.

Preston, S.H. (1986). 'Changing values and falling birth rates'. In K. Davis, M.S. Berstom, and R. Ricardo-Campbell eds., *Below Replacement Fertility in Industrial Societies: Causes, Consequences, Policies*. New York: Population and Development Review.

Ramu, G.N. and N. Tavuchis (1986). 'The valuation of children and parenthood among the voluntarily childless and parental couples in Canada'. *Journal of Comparative Family Studies* 17: 99–116.

Retherford, R.D. (1985). 'A theory of marital fertility transition'. *Population Studies* 39: 249–268.

Romaniuc, A. (1984). *Fertility in Canada: From Baby Boom to Baby Bust*. Cat. 91–524E. Ottawa: Statistics Canada.

——— (1986). *Fertility in Canada: A Long View—A Contribution to the Debates on Population*. Paper presented at the Colloquium, The Family in Crisis; A Population Crisis? Canadian Federation of Demographers and Royal Society of Canada, Ottawa, November.

Roussel, L. (1986). 'Les Changements démographiques des vingt dernières années: Quelques hypothèses sociologiques'. Paper presented at the conference of the Federation of Canadian Demographers, Ottawa, November.

Ryder, N.B. and C.F. Westoff (1973). 'Wanted and unwanted fertility in the United States: 1965 and 1970'. In C.F. Westoff and R. Parke Jr., eds., *Demographic and Social Aspects of Population Growth*, Vol. I of Population Growth and the American Future Research Reports.

Scrimshaw, S.C.M. (1981). 'Women and the pill: From panacea to catalyst'. *Family Planning Perspectives* 13, 6: 254–262.

Schultz, T.W. ed. (1975). *The Economics of the Family: Marriage, Children and Human Capital*. Chicago: Chicago University Press.

Smith, D.E. (1977). 'Women, the family and corporate capitalism'. In M. Stephenson, ed., *Women in Canada* (Rev. edition). Don Mills, Ont.: General.

——— (1981). 'Women's inequality and the family'. In A. Moscovitch and G. Drover, eds., *Inequality: Essays on the Political Economy of Social Welfare*. Toronto: University of Toronto Press.

Swanson-Kauffman, K.M., ed. (1987). *Women's Work, Families and Health: The Balancing Act*. New York: Hemisphere.

Turchi, B.A. (1975). *The Demand for Children*. Cambridge, MA: Ballinger.

Veevers, J.E. (1980). *Childless by Choice*. Toronto: Butterworth's.

Wargon, S.T. (1987). 'Canada's families in the 1980's crisis: Crisis or challenge'. *Transaction* (March): 10–12.

Westoff, C.F. (1983). 'Fertility decline in the west: Causes and prospects'. *Population and Development Review* 9, 1: 99–104.

——— (1987). 'Perspective on nuptiality and fertility'. In K. Davis, M.S. Bernstom and R. Ricardo-Campbell, eds., *Below Replacement Fertility in Industrial Societies: Causes, Consequences, Policies*. Cambridge: Cambridge University Press.

Yaukey, D. (1969). 'On theorizing about fertility'. *American Sociologist* 100–104.

CHAPTER 21

THE CLUTTERED NEST

The Living Arrangements

of Young Canadian Adults

Monica Boyd and Edward T. Pryor

HI, I'M HOME

Assessing changes to the family and pondering the viability and future of the family is a favourite preoccupation of many social scientists. One area of interest is the living arrangements over the family life cycle, with emphasis on the young adult population as well as the living patterns of the elderly (Bianchi, 1987; Goldthorpe, 1987; Grigsby and McGowan, 1986; Glick and Lin, 1986; Heer, Hodge and Felson, 1985; *American Demographics*, 1987; Boyd, 1990; *Future Letter*, 1987; Priest, 1988; Wall, 1988). Recent years have brought unanticipated turns in family composition and living arrangements among both the young and old. While more elderly Canadians have been living alone, the young have been leaving the parental home at earlier ages than in the past. The emptying of the parental nest is one consequence of the increasing trend for young adults to establish their own household (Miron and Schiff, 1982).

However, there is good evidence documenting a reversal of the emptying nest phenomenon. Between 1971 and 1981, the percentage living with parents declined for single adults between 15 and 34 years old (Table 1, panel 1). Between 1981 and 1986, the percentage living with parents rose for these young adults. The shift is particularly noteworthy for the age group 20–29. As of 1986, six out of ten single women and seven out of ten males age 20–24 were living with parents. Even by their late twenties, over three out of ten single women and over four out of ten single males were living at home.

The aging of the young adult population is one consequence of the maturing baby-boom generation. This demographic shift in turn means that the young adult population living at home is older than in previous decades[1] (Table 1, panel 2). From the perspective of the parental household, not only are young adults more likely to be living at home, but they are more likely to be in their twenties, rather than in their teens. As of the mid-1980s, the nest is becoming cluttered with more mature fledglings, whose age would have suggested departure in earlier times.

These trends regarding young adults continuing to live with parents fascinate Canadians at large as well as researchers. The *Montreal Gazette* (Carson, 31 August 1987) picked up the theme with headlines of 'The children are home again' and 'Some kids aren't back—they never left.' Later that year (Zarzour, 19 December 1987), the *Toronto Star* labelled it 'Back to the Nest'. Along similar lines was the *New York Times* report on 'Parenthood II: When a Nest Won't Stay Empty' (Cowan, 12 March 1989) and the article in *The Number News* on 'Focus . . . on the Boomerang Adults' (*American Demographics*, 6 July 1989).

Three interrelated explanations exist for this interest in adult children living with parents:

1. the fact that recent trends in the living arrangements of young adults 'go against the grain' of the previous long-term momentum of the young departing the family of procreation;
2. the implications of young adults living at home for families and for sociological studies of families; and
3. the fact that these trends appear to be part of larger societal changes in the transition from youth to adulthood.

Media accounts leave little doubt about the fact that the young adults living at home evoke changed family dynamics. Social roles and social relationships of parents and their children are challenged and altered, with varying degrees of success, and/or change. Adult children living at home also reshape thinking on the viability/decline of 'the family' as a social unit. In recent years, academic and popular discussions have focused on the changing roles and functions of the family. Reduced fertility, increased labour-force participation of wives, earlier departures of children all are viewed as indicators of the lessening utility of the family. Popenoe (1988: 8–9) identifies five key dimensions of the reduced importance of the family in advanced societies: less family cohesion as a group; weakened traditional social functions including care of its members; reduced institutional power; smaller and

Table 1: Living with parent(s), percentage and age distribution by sex and age group, single population aged 15-34, Canada, 1971 to 1986

Age groups	Females					Males				
	1971 (1)	1976 (2)	1981 (3)	1986 (4)	Difference 1986–1981 (5)	1971 (6)	1976 (7)	1981 (8)	1986 (9)	Difference 1986–1981 (10)
Percentage living with parent(s)										
Total 15–34	76.1	74.0	70.8	68.5	–2.3	77.0	74.9	71.4	70.1	–1.3
15–19	89.5	89.4	89.1	90.3	1.2	90.9	90.0	89.5	91.1	1.6
20–24	61.4	60.1	60.4	63.8	3.4	69.1	67.8	66.2	69.2	3.0
25–29	39.5	34.9	32.3	35.8	3.5	46.8	43.3	41.0	44.9	3.9
30–34	33.4	30.4	25.9	24.7	–1.2	38.3	36.9	32.4	31.9	–0.5
Age profile of single population living at home										
Total 15–34	100.0	100.0	100.0	100.0	—	100.0	100.0	100.0	100.0	—
15–19	72.9	71.9	67.2	58.5	–8.7	62.8	62.0	58.1	49.8	–8.3
20–29	21.4	22.1	25.8	31.1	5.3	28.7	28.8	31.2	34.8	3.6
25–29	4.0	4.3	5.0	7.8	2.8	6.3	6.9	7.9	11.6	3.7
30–34	1.7	1.7	2.0	2.6	0.6	2.2	2.3	2.8	3.8	1.0

SOURCE: Unpublished tabulations, Census of Canada.

more unstable families with a shorter life span; and the decline of familism *vis-à-vis* self-fulfilment. But what is not clear is how to interpret the living arrangements of children at home within a model of family decline.

Adult children living at home also may represent a departure from a traditional model. In this model, the transition from youth to adulthood takes place in sequential stages and with departure from the home occurring early on. Researchers and media writers both concur that the tempo, timing, and sequence of social roles which make up the transition from youth to adulthood are highly dynamic and depart from a linear model of incremental change (see *American Demographics*, 1989; Hogan and Astone, 1986). Terms like 'boomerang' adults depict the fluidity of various transition states in which young adults leave the parental home, return to it, marry, divorce, leave school, hold employment, and return to school. The transition from youth to adulthood in fact is a dynamic process involving a number of dimensions (Hogan and Astone, 1986).

In sum, living arrangements are one dimension of changing patterns in the transitions to adulthood. Leaving home—living alone or with others along with marriage/co-habiting—is extensively studied (see Goldscheider and DaVanzo, 1985; Goldscheider and Goldscheider, 1987; Leppel, 1987; Tanfer, 1987; Wall, 1988; Waite and Goldscheider, 1986; White, 1987). But staying with parents—and not living alone/with others/marriage/co-habiting—also is another option. When this occurs, changes in family dynamics and changes in the role of the family unit in advanced societies also emerge as issues of interest and of research.

WHO IS IN THE BIRDHOUSE?

What factors account for growing numbers of young Canadian adults deciding to live with their parents? The literature on transitions points to three types of factors. First, social-historical conditions affect transitions (Hogan and Astone, 1986). Second, the multidimensionality of transition to adulthood means that change in one dimension often influences another. Third, variables such as sex, race/ethnicity, education, work history, and income underlie subgroup differentials in the transition process.

The first two factors illuminate changes over time. In Canada, the increase between 1981 and 1986 in the percentages of young adults living with parents accompanied changes in economic indicators and in marriage patterns of young adults. Changing socio-economic conditions appear to underlie the increasing percentages of young adults living at home, at least as popularly reported in the press. Between 1981 and 1986, Canadians experienced the worst economic recession since the 1930s (Myles, Picot, and Wannell, 1988). In addition to these economic conditions, or perhaps because of them, young adults are delaying marriage. The percentage ever married by a given age declines between 1976 and 1986 for young adults until they are in their mid-thirties, indicating a delay in the timing of marriages.

The third factor indicates what type of young adult is likely to be living with parents. Such variation shows that living at home is not a uniform experience for all youngsters in their transition to adulthood. From the perspective of the family unit, such variation also implies considerable heterogeneity in the 'functioning' of the family as a social institution. And, it cautions against a ready interpretation of the demise of the family as a social or economic support system.

Who among Canadian youth lives at home with parents? Newspaper articles provide some descriptive vignettes. However, we lack a more comprehensive profile of young Canadian adults who are or who are not living at home. Recent research in the United States shows that the living arrangements of young adults are influenced by a number of factors, including the marital status of parents/children (Bianchi, 1987; Kobrin, 1985; Glick and Lin, 1986; Grigsby and McGowan, 1986; Riche, 1987), sex of children (Bianchi, 1987; Kobrin, 1985; Riche, 1987; Wall, 1987), ethnicity/race (Waite and Kobrin, 1987), education (Bianchi, 1987; Grigsby and McGowan, 1986; Kobrin, 1985; Waite and Kobrin, 1987), labour-force participation (Bianchi, 1987; Grisby and McGowan, 1986; Waite and Kobrin, 1987), and individual income (Grisby and McGowan, 1986).

This body of research indicates who is more likely to be living with parents and why. Since marriage usually results in a new household, living at home is considered more likely if offspring are not currently married. Women are less likely to live with parents than are men, partly because they marry at younger ages than men and form their own husband–wife households. However, even single women are less likely to live with parents than are single men. (Table 1, panel 1). Such differences by gender in the propensity to live with parents may partly reflect gender differences in other characteristics, such as education or place of residence, which are also associated with living arrangements.[2]

Research in the United States also finds that young Blacks and Hispanic adults are more likely to be living with parents than white young adults (Bianchi, 1987). Ethnicity/race is presumed to capture cultural preferences among young adults and their parents for various living arrangements. Differences by ethnicity/race also reflect socio-economic differences among ethnic/racial groups with respect to educational and economic statuses.

Generally, the higher the educational level, the less likely a child is to live with parents, presumably because such education translates into labour-force participation and into higher earnings and purchasing power for alternative living arrangements. However, if young adults are still attending school, monetary considerations may exert strong pressures to reduce costs by living with parents. Similarly, low income and/or unemployment status may increase the propensity to live at home. However, to the extent that availability of apartments affects living arrangements, young adult residents of large cities should be less likely to live with parents than residents of smaller cities or towns.

. . .

PAPA, MAMA AND BABY BIRD

Table 2 provides a basic socio-demographic profile of the single young adult population which is living either at home, alone, or with non-relatives in private households (the small numbers who were living with relatives other than parents have been excluded from the analysis). The variation in living arrangements which are shown for two-year age groups parallel those observed in Table 1. For both females and males, the percentages living with one or more parents is highest for the age group 20–22, tapering off throughout the twenties. Overall, for both men and women, increasing age means rising percentages living as unattached individuals—that is, as individuals who are either living alone or in households with non-relatives. Still, by their late twenties over a third of single females (excluding those living with relatives) and over 40 per cent of the males are still living with parents (Table 2, panel 1).

The age groups which form the single population 20–29 vary from one another with respect to characteristics other than living with parents (Table 2). The percentages with English mother tongue decline slightly with increasing age. The importance of this variable arises out of its relationship not just to age but also to the tendency to live with parents. Mother tongue is used in this analysis as a way of approximating cultural differences in the norms, expectations, and actual living arrangements. Birthplace is a less than perfect variable to tap such cultural variations, since the Canadian-born children of foreign-born parents are allocated to the Canadian-born category.

Residence in a large census metropolitan area (CMA) increases with age as does educational attainment. Younger age groups, especially those under age 20, will not yet have completed university. Thus, the percentages with some or completed university education are higher for the older age groups. Younger men and women are more likely to be attending school full-time.

Labour-force participation rates and income increase with age. Data for labour-force experience as of June 1981 show that the younger ages have the highest percentages of never worked, and last worked in 1980 or 1981 (but not currently in the labour force). Younger adults have much higher rates of unemployment than do older age groups, a phenomenon which could reflect both youth unemployment generally and the higher recent school attendance of the young who by June would be seeking summer employment.

Young adults also have lower incomes than older age groups. Table 2 shows that nearly one third of the women and nearly 20 per cent of the men age 20–21 had 1980 incomes of less than $2,500 compared to 10 per cent in the age group 28–29. Conversely, the percentage with incomes of $11,500 or more increases steadily with age.

Why consider these age variations in CMA residence, mother tongue, highest level of education, school attendance, labour-force experience, and income? The most compelling reason is that all these variables are associated with living arrangements. Differences between various age groups in the percentages of young adults living with parents in part reflect socio-economic differences between the age groups.

. . .

Table 2: Select socio-economic characteristics of single (never married) females and Canada, 1981.

	Females					
	Total (1)	20–21 (2)	22–23 (3)	24–25 (4)	26–27 (5)	28–29 (6)
N[1]	13,885	5,437	3,593	2,289	1,458	1,108
Living arrangements	100.0	100.0	100.0	100.0	100.0	100.0
With parents	60.3	77.1	61.3	46.0	36.8	34.3
Unattached	39.7	22.9	38.7	54.0	63.2	65.7
Living in CMA[2]	100.0	100.0	100.0	100.0	100.0	100.0
Yes	59.9	55.1	59.6	65.0	65.5	66.6
No	40.1	44.9	40.4	35.0	34.5	33.4
Mother tongue	100.0	100.0	100.0	100.0	100.0	100.0
English	63.8	65.0	63.7	63.8	62.4	59.9
French	27.3	27.1	26.9	26.6	28.5	30.1
Chinese	1.1	0.8	1.3	1.2	1.0	1.4
German	1.2	1.0	1.3	1.2	1.3	1.2
Greek, Portuguese	0.6	0.7	0.5	0.4	0.7	0.5
Italian	2.3	2.6	2.6	2.0	1.6	1.1
Ukrainian	0.7	0.6	0.4	0.9	1.1	1.3
Other	3.1	2.2	3.3	3.9	3.4	4.4
Highest education level	100.0	100.0	100.0	100.0	100.0	100.0
Grade 9	3.2	2.5	3.0	3.4	4.3	6.4
9–13	35.2	40.4	34.1	31.4	29.6	28.8
Non-university	29.6	31.7	28.5	27.7	29.6	26.1
University	32.0	25.4	34.5	37.5	36.6	39.5
Attending school	100.0	100.0	100.0	100.0	100.0	100.0
No	64.4	57.2	64.0	71.8	72.8	75.2
Yes, full time	23.1	35.0	23.7	11.8	7.9	6.3
Yes, part time	12.4	7.8	12.3	16.4	19.3	18.5
Labour-force participation	100.0	100.0	100.0	100.0	100.0	100.0
Employed	79.8	75.6	79.4	84.6	84.2	85.2
Unemployed	8.1	10.3	8.7	6.0	5.1	4.2
Last worked in 1981	2.5	3.0	2.0	2.4	2.4	1.9
Last worked in 1980	3.8	4.7	4.7	2.2	1.9	2.2
Last worked before 1980	2.4	2.2	2.4	2.1	3.0	3.4
Never worked	3.3	4.1	2.8	2.5	3.4	3.1
Income ($)	100.0	100.0	100.0	100.0	100.0	100.0
<2,500	21.5	30.5	20.3	14.8	10.4	10.0
2,500–4,499	14.7	19.9	14.9	9.2	8.2	8.4
4,500–6,999	14.9	16.4	15.0	12.8	8.5	8.4
7,000–11,499	24.5	23.9	27.3	25.4	21.8	20.0
11,500 plus	25.3	9.3	22.5	37.8	51.1	53.2

[1] These are the number of cases on the Public Use Sample Database. The numbers are not population counts.
[2] The Public Use Sample provides data for the following Census Metropolitan Areas: Halifax, Quebec, Edmonton, and Vancouver.
SOURCE: Statistics Canada, *1981 Census of Population*, Public Use Sample Tape of Individuals, full count.

males, age 20–29, who are living at home with parents or as unattached individuals,

	Males				
Total (7)	20–21 (8)	22–23 (9)	24–25 (10)	26–27 (11)	28–29 (12)
21,190	7,481	5,501	3,807	2,603	1,798
100.0	100.0	100.0	100.0	100.0	100.0
66.6	81.9	69.6	58.0	46.4	41.1
33.4	18.1	30.4	42.0	53.6	58.9
100.0	100.0	100.0	100.0	100.0	100.0
54.9	51.7	54.6	57.1	58.6	59.1
45.1	48.3	45.4	42.9	41.4	40.9
100.0	100.0	100.0	100.0	100.0	100.0
62.9	63.3	62.1	63.8	64.3	59.3
27.8	28.3	28.6	27.1	25.5	27.7
1.2	0.8	1.0	1.2	1.7	2.4
1.1	0.9	1.3	1.2	1.5	1.3
0.7	0.9	0.8	0.6	0.5	0.6
2.2	2.5	2.2	2.0	1.7	2.3
0.6	0.5	0.4	0.7	0.9	1.2
3.5	2.8	3.6	3.4	3.9	5.2
100.0	100.0	100.0	100.0	100.0	100.0
4.8	4.3	4.5	4.7	5.9	6.8
43.0	50.6	42.2	39.6	35.1	32.4
25.0	24.7	26.6	25.0	24.0	23.5
27.1	20.3	26.7	30.7	35.0	37.3
100.0	100.0	100.0	100.0	100.0	100.0
69.6	62.1	67.0	75.6	78.8	82.2
21.0	30.7	23.8	12.8	9.4	6.7
9.4	7.2	9.2	11.7	11.8	11.1
100.0	100.0	100.0	100.0	100.0	100.0
78.8	75.4	78.7	80.8	82.4	83.4
10.9	12.7	10.9	10.2	8.7	8.4
2.6	2.6	2.7	2.8	2.1	2.1
3.5	4.5	3.8	2.5	2.5	2.1
2.1	1.8	2.1	2.4	2.3	2.0
2.2	3.0	1.8	1.4	2.0	2.1
100.0	100.0	100.0	100.0	100.0	100.0
17.0	23.2	16.3	12.9	11.2	10.7
11.6	15.1	12.0	9.2	7.5	6.8
12.8	15.7	14.4	9.6	9.1	8.1
21.8	23.4	23.3	21.6	17.8	16.1
36.8	22.6	33.9	46.7	54.4	58.2

Montreal, Ottawa-Hull, Toronto, Hamilton, St. Catharines-Niagara, Kitchener, London, Winnipeg, Calgary.

CONCLUSION

Our analysis of trends in living arrangements of young adults between 1971 and 1986 provides empirical evidence for the impressionist reports of increased tendencies among never-married young Canadian adults to live with parents. This increase occurred largely between 1981 and 1986. By 1986, over 60 per cent of all single females and nearly 70 per cent of all single males aged 20–24 were living with parents. The tendency diminished with age, but even so, over 30 per cent of single females and 40 per cent of single males aged 25–29 were living with parents in 1986.

Analysis of 1981 data indicates that for single young adults aged 20–29, the percentage living with parents as opposed to living alone or with non-relatives is above average for persons living in census metropolitan areas; having Greek, Portuguese, Italian, or French as their mother tongue; having a grade 13 education or less; attending school full-time; unemployed or not in the labour force, and having a 1980 income of less than $7,000 if female and less than $11,500 if male. Aside from age, school attendance and income are the most important factors accounting for living with parents.

What are the consequences of young adults living at home for these individuals? The above analysis begs this question, since little research exists to provide the answers. Our findings do raise the possibility that Canadian young adults, unlike their predecessors in the 1970s, will spend more time in a parental setting. This may elicit two kinds of behavioural outcomes. First, greater involvement in reciprocal intergenerational relationships of monitoring may occur in which parents monitor adult children and children monitor middle-aged and elderly parents (see Goldscheider and Goldscheider, 1989). Second, young adults living at home may adopt their parents' behaviour more thoroughly. American research found that marriage for young women was more likely to be delayed if individuals did not live at home in early adulthood but instead lived in separate quarters. Compared to those who continued to live at home, young women who lived away were more likely to plan for employment. These women also departed from a traditional family orientation by lowering family size expectations, showing greater acceptance of non-traditional female roles and holding less traditional expectations regarding gender roles in the family (Goldscheider and Waite, 1987; Waite, Goldscheider, and Witsberger, 1986). These findings appear to reflect two factors: (1) the weaker control which parents have over their children, especially regarding family life values, when the children are not within the same household, and (2) the added skills and confidence acquired by young adults when living on their own.

Young adults living at home also raise important research issues for the future regarding the impact of this trend on families. For instance, what is the effect on family life from young adults at home? What are the implications of living at home not only for the extension of childhood (see Ariès, 1960) but also for prolonged parenting even if reluctantly done (Mancini and Blieszner, 1989)? Furthermore, what does living at home suggest for sociological studies of Canadian families? Two research areas stand out as requiring further investigation. The first focuses on the intersection between youth to adulthood transitions and the parental family. This focus emphasizes the interpretation and study of transitions from a life-course perspective in which individual transitions are mediated by the family. The second area is that of family and social change. In the first section of this paper we observed that the alleged demise of the family commanded considerable attention. Here, family life span, length and degree of economic independence, and care of young members are indicators of familism (or the lack thereof). How are young adults living at home to be interpreted within this perspective? Our findings show considerable socio-economic variability in the propensity of young adults to live at home. This variability raises several possibilities regarding the future roles of the family. Is it possible that family decline is not irreversible, or that — at least temporarily or for select socio-economic groups — there can be a resurgence of certain dimensions of familism? Theories centred on explaining the relevance of the family unit in terms of functions, socialization, and economic dependence look for empirical referents in residence configurations and their longevity. Young adults living with parents are at present an under-interpreted referent within a large literature on family forms and family functions.

NOTES

[1] Direct standardization of the data in Table 1 reveals that change between 1971 and 1986 in the age composition of the total young adult population is responsible for most of the shifts in the age composition of young adults living at home. If the young adult population in 1986 had the age distribution of the 1971 population, but the 1986 rates of living with parents, the living at home population would have the following percentages in the respective 15–19, 20–24, 25–29, 30–34 age groups: 66.3, 26.5, 5.4, 1.8 for females; 57.3, 31.6, 8.4, 2.6 for males.

[2] Parental supervision may also play a role although the socio-demographic data collected by censuses and many surveys do not permit the study of this possibility. The social lives of women may be more closely monitored and they may find themselves under more restrictive 'house rules' than their brothers. Such circumstances in which co-residency elicits supervision for women and less so for men may partly explain the greater tendency of young women to live in non-parental households.

REFERENCES

American Demographics, Inc. (1989). 'Focus . . . on the boomerang adults'. *The Number News* 6 July: 6.

Ariès, Philippe (1960). *L'enfant et la vie familiale sous l'Ancien Régime.* Paris: Plan (English: *Centuries of Childhood.*)

Bianchi, Suzanne M. (1987). 'Living at home: Young adults' living arrangements in the 1980s'. Paper presented at the annual meeting of the American Sociological Association, Chicago.

Boyd, Monica (1990). 'Immigration and living arrangements: Elderly immigrant women in Canada'. *International Migration Review*.

Carson, Susan (1987a). 'Some kids aren't back—they never left'. *The Montreal Gazette* 31 August: B9.

—— (1987b) 'The children are home again'. *The Montreal Gazette* 31 August: Living section.

Cowan, Alison Leigh (1989). 'Parenthood II: When a nest won't stay empty'. *The New York Times* 12 March.

Glick, Paul C. and Sung-Ling Lin (1986). 'More young adults living with parents: Who are they?' *Journal of Marriage and the Family* 48 (February): 107–112.

Goldscheider, Calvin and Frances K. Goldscheider (1987). 'Moving out and marriage: What do young adults expect?' *American Sociological Review* 52: 278–285.

Goldscheider, Frances K. and Calvin Goldscheider (1989). 'Family structure and conflict: Nest-leaving expectations of young adults and their parents'. *Journal of Marriage and the Family* 51 (February): 87–97.

Goldscheider, Frances and Julie Da Vanzo (1985). 'Living arrangements and the transition to adulthood'. *Demography* 22 (November): 545–563.

Goldscheider, Frances Kobrin and Celine Le Bourdais (1986). 'The decline in age at leaving home, 1920–1979'. *Sociology and Social Research* 70: 143–145.

Goldscheider, Frances Kobrin and Linda J. Waite (1987). 'Nest-leaving patterns and the transition to marriage for young men and women'. *Journal of Marriage and the Family* 49: 507–516.

Goldthorpe, J.E. (1987). *Family Life in Western Societies*. Cambridge: Cambridge University Press.

Grigsby, Jill and Jill B. McGowan (1986). 'Still in the nest: Adult children are living with their parents'. *Sociology and Social Research* 70 (January): 146–148.

Heer, David M., Robert W. Hodge, and Marcus Felson (1985). 'The cluttered nest: Evidence that young adults are more likely to live at home now than in the recent past'. *Sociology and Social Research* 69, 3: 436–441.

Hogan, Dennis P. and Nan Marie Astone (1986). 'The transition to adulthood'. In Ralph H. Turner and James F. Short Jr., eds., *Annual Review of Sociology*, Vol. 12, pp. 109–157. Palo Alto, California: Annual Review, Inc.

Leppel, Karen (1987). 'Household formation and unrelated housemates'. *The American Economist* 31: 38–47.

Mancini, Jay A. and Rosemary Blieszner (1989). 'Aging parents and adult children: Research themes in intergenerational relations'. *Journal of Marriage and the Family* 51 (May): 275–290.

Miron, John and Myra Schiff (1982). 'A profile of the emerging empty nester household'. Research Paper No. 130, Centre for Urban and Community Studies, University of Toronto.

Myles, John, Garnett Picot, and Ted Wannell (1988). 'The changing wage distribution of jobs, 1981–1986'. *The Labour Force* (Statistics Canada Cat. 71–001), October.

Priest, Gordon (1988). 'The older old in Canada: How do they live?' Paper presented at the annual meeting of the Canadian Population Society, Windsor.

Riche, Martha Farnsworth (1987). 'Mysterious young adults'. *American Demographics* (February): 38–43.

Statistics Canada (1985). 'Observation: Youth living at home'. *The Labour Force*. Cat. 71–001 (July).

Tanfer, Koray (1987). 'Patterns of premarital cohabitation among never-married women in the United States'. *Journal of Marriage and the Family* 49: 483–497.

Waite, Linda, Frances Kobrin Goldscheider, and Christina Witsberger (1986). 'Nonfamily living and the erosion of traditional family orientations among young adults'. *American Sociological Review* 51: 541–554.

Wall, Richard (1988). 'Leaving home and living alone: An historical perspective'. Unpublished paper. Cambridge University: Cambridge Group for History of Population and Social Structure.

―――― (1989). 'The living arrangements of the elderly in Europe in the 1980s'. In W. Bytheway, ed., *Becoming and Being Old*. Newbury Park, California: Sage Publications, Inc.

White, James M. (1987) 'Premarital cohabitation and marital stability in Canada'. *Journal of Marriage and the Family* 49: 641–647.

Zarzour, Kim (1987). 'Back to the nest'. *Toronto Star* 12 December: H1.

PART SIX

POPULATION

MOVEMENT

Internal and

International

HUMAN MIGRATION

In the absence of catastrophic increases in mortality, migration is the one demographic process by which a population can change quickly. It is also the only area in which policy-makers can respond immediately to social and economic change.

Human migration may be defined simply as the movement of people across signifi-cant boundaries for the purpose of permanent settlement. The key words in this defini-tion are 'boundaries' and 'permanent'; in modern societies, the boundaries are usually political in nature, and 'permanency' refers to settlement for a significant period of time.

While there are several theories about the factors associated with migration, the basic causes may be classified as 'push' and 'pull' factors. 'Push' refers to conditions of undesirability in the place of origin, while 'pull' refers to attractions in the place of destination. The implication of this approach is that people do not move unless induced to do so by some outside force that operates in the context of rational decision-making.

However, human migration does not always occur in such a straightforward way. The decision to move is rarely completely rational, and in some cases the non-rational component may be of even greater importance. Subjective evaluations (e.g., the grass is always greener . . .), transient emotions (e.g., fights with loved ones), accidental occurrences, and personal idiosyncrasies (e.g., a preference for a certain kind of housing) are among the non-rational factors that may complicate a rational decision-making model of migration. A different approach focuses not on individuals and their motivations but rather on those life-cycle events that occur in the lives of most people on a fairly regular basis. The beginning or end of education, marriage or divorce, changes in employment, death in the immediate family, the birth of a child, children leaving home, retirement — all of these stages in the life cycle may well be associated with movement, regardless of the particular motivations or evaluations of positives and negatives at origins and destinations. In other words, there are particular junctions in most people's lives when migration is likely to occur.

INTERNAL AND INTERNATIONAL MIGRATION

Migration can be divided into two basic types: internal and international. Internal migration (e.g., within Canada) is defined as a change in residence across municipal boundaries. Unlike fertility and mortality data, internal migration statistics are not collected in any systematic way by the Canadian government. Most of the data we have comes from Canadian censuses, which contain information concerning residence at the time of the census and five years earlier. Individuals whose current place of residence differs from that of five years earlier are identified as movers. On the basis of these data, the Canadian population appears to be extremely mobile. For example, about half the population, some 12 million people, changed residence in Canada between 1981 and 1986 — a number nearly as large as the total number of people who have immigrated to Canada since 1851! Thus internal movement is clearly an important source of population redistribution. However, of those 12 million people who changed residence in that five-year period, about half were in fact migrants: that is, they changed their residence by moving across a municipal boundary. For the past generation, Canadians have been among the most mobile people in the world.

There are migration differentials between categories of people. Migration tends to be concentrated among young adults aged 20–34, people with higher levels of education or occupational skills, and those in the middle-income group. A composite picture of the very mobile person in Canadian society would be one of either gender, recently married, between the ages of 25 and 29, with some university training, working as a professional, in the middle-income category.

Burke, in 'Interregional Migration of the Canadian Population', describes the migration flows between the various regions and provinces of Canada. Generally, Ontario, Alberta, and British Columbia have gained population from the other regions of Canada. While this theme is not formally developed in the article, it is no accident that the three provinces that attract the most in-migration are the wealthiest in the country.

Although internal migration is the major population movement within Canada, international migration is most often the subject of discussion in both social and political circles. It is part of the conventional wisdom of our country that we are a nation of immigrants from various lands all over the world. From one perspective this analysis is accurate— few of us would be here (except for the Native peoples) were it not for immigration on the part of ourselves or our ancestors. However, it should also be noted that most of Canada's population growth is the result of the fertility of these immigrants and their descendants, and not of immigration *per se*.

In the 140 years since 1851, nearly 13 million immigrants have entered Canada, most of them from Western Europe, particularly Great Britain, although the sources have diversified in recent decades. The latest data indicate that nearly 20 per cent of the Canadian adult population aged 20–50 is foreign-born (16 per cent of the total Canadian population). This is one of the highest proportions of foreign-born people living in any country in the world (double the proportion in the United States).

The ethnic composition of the immigration to Canada has changed dramatically over the years, largely in response to changes in Canada's immigration policy, especially since the 1960s. Historically and through the Second World War, the concentration of people coming from Western Europe was a direct result of an immigration policy that favoured people from England, France, and other areas of Western Europe, and discriminated against populations from the rest of the world, especially Asia and Africa. In the past thirty years, Canada's immigration policies have been amended in a more liberal direction, and immigrant applications have come to be judged more on the basis of skills, economic qualification, and family reunification, and less on country of origin. In the 1960s, about 80 per cent of immigration to Canada was European in origin. For example, in 1966, the British Isles and Italy alone accounted for nearly half of the total number. In the late 1980s, about one-third of the immigration came from Europe and the United States, about one-third from Asia, and the remaining third from the rest of the world.

In 1976 Canada adopted a new immigration act (the first total change since 1952) requiring that potential immigrants be judged on the basis of their acquired characteristics, such as education and skills, and not on the basis of gender, race, ethnicity, religion, colour or national background. This act provided for substantial consultation with the provinces in order to determine the level and distribution of immigration that would be most advantageous both to the country and to immigrants themselves. The most recent immigration act emphasizes the numbers of immigrants that Canada can accommodate and a new management system that divides potential immigrants into three streams: immediate family members (stream 1), other relatives, refugees, self-employed and people who have arranged employment (stream 2), and independent applicants who would be selected on the basis of excellence (stream 3). The new procedure is designed to protect against abuses and to streamline information centres. The number of immigrants is set at approximately 250,000 per year, or about 1 per cent of Canada's population.

Generally, immigration will continue to be an important component of Canadian population growth and economic development. Canadian population policy has been liberalized over the years to accommodate applicants from many diverse areas around the globe. We are becoming more and more a multicultural and multiracial nation, and while this development may result in some problems concerning the different sets of norms, values, customs, attitudes and behaviours of various peoples, in the long run this diversity can add to the strength and character of the Canadian people.

According to Stafford, during certain periods, the Canadian government's immigration policy has been expansionist, while at other times it has been restrictionist in orientation. For example, in 1986 the immigration target was set at between 115,000 and 125,000; four years earlier it has been recommended that the number of new immigrants be reduced from previous levels (about 100,000 per year). Stafford's analysis of immigration policy and objectives since Confederation reveals that, except in wartime periods, prevailing economic conditions have been sufficient to explain Canada's official stance on immigration levels. The humanitarian aspect of immigration, while usually lauded as a key objective of government policy, has really been a secondary concern, after economic exigencies.

In recent years, demographic considerations such as the aging of the population and the possibility of an eventual population decline have also surfaced as essential criteria for setting immigration levels. Increased immigration is seen as a means to counteract the decline, since the early 1970s, in fertility levels and its consequences for Canada's population (i.e., aging and eventual decline in numbers). Stafford argues that, given current fertility levels in Canada, it would be necessary to admit about 250,000 newcomers per year if the objective is to eventually attain a stable population of 35 million inhabitants.

In this connection, he raises the important question of whether Canada is capable of absorbing that many immigrants, from both social and economic points of view. He also challenges many of the rationales behind the new official immigration targets, such as counteracting the aging of the population, and stimulating economic growth. His conclusion suggests that we cannot look to immigrants to solve our unemployment, economic, and demographic problems. Immigrants should be allowed into the country, but not as a means to solve such national concerns. Canada has the means and resources to tackle such problems and issues independently of immigration.

Kalbach's essay on the 'Growth and Distribution of Canada's Ethnic Populations 1871–1981' provides a systematic overview of the changes in the character of the Canadian population that are related to both immigration and the fertility of immigrants. While immigration has a relatively minor impact on the ethnic composition of the total population, it can affect the character of the total foreign-born population rather substantially. In general, differences in fertility among ethnic groups may have more of an impact on the ethnic composition of the Canadian population.

TECHNICAL NOTES

1. The immigration rate is the number of immigrants to a given country (or geographic area) in a given year divided by the mid-year population of the receiving country (or geographic area) during the same year. This rate is usually multiplied by 1,000.

2. The emigration rate for a given country (or geographic area) is the number of persons leaving the country (or geographic area) divided by the mid-year population of the country (or geographic area). This rate is usually calculated for a calendar year and is also multiplied by 1,000.

3. The net migration rate is the number of immigrants to a given country (or geographic area) in a given year minus the number of emigrants from the same country (or geographic area), divided by the mid-year population of the country (or geographic area), multiplied by 1,000.

4. Other, more elaborate procedures for estimating migration have been developed. One such method is based on the application of the components formula. If the population at Time 1 is known (say, 1981), and the population at Time 2 is known (say, 1991), and if the numbers of births and deaths for that specific area are known, then the residual of the differences is net migration. This can be calculated as follows:

(Population [Time 2] — Population [Time 1]) — (Births during the interval minus deaths during the interval) = net migration

For example, if the population of Alberta was two million in 1981 and three million in 1991, and if there were one million births and 400,00 deaths over this ten-year period, then the net migration for Alberta between 1981 and 1991 must have been 400,000:

(3,000,000 — 2,000,000) — (1,000,000 — 400,000) = 1,000,000 — 600,000 = 400,000 migrants

A similar procedure has been developed for estimating the international migration contribution to national population growth. Beginning and ending populations must be known over an interval of time, and the residual from natural increase is the net migration contribution. In Canada, immigration has positively contributed to population growth in every decade of the twentieth century except during the Depression years of the 1930s, when there was more out-migration than population moving to the country.

SUGGESTED READING

Beaujot, Roderic, and K. McQuillan (1982). *Growth and Dualism*. Toronto: Gage.

Beaman, Jay, and Carl D'Arcy (1980). 'A typology of internal migration'. *Canadian Studies in Population* 7: 9–20.

Boyd, Monica (1990). 'Family and personal network in international migration: Recent developments and new agendas'. *International Migration Review* 23, 3: 638–70.

Corbett, D.C. (1957). *Canada's Immigration Policy: A Critique*. Toronto: University of Toronto Press.

George, M.V. (1970). *Internal Migration in Canada*. Ottawa: Queen's Printer.

Goldscheider, Calvin (1971). *Population, Modernization and Social Structure*, Chap. 3 and 11. Boston: Little, Brown.

Halli, Shiva S., Frank Trovato, and Leo Driedger, eds (1990). *Ethnic Demography: Canadian Immigrant, Racial and Cultural Variations*. Ottawa: Carleton University Press.

Hawkins, Freda (1988). 'Canada and immigration: A new law and a new approach to management'. *International Migration Review* 12: 77–94.

Kalbach, Warren E. (1970). *The Impact of Immigration on Canada's Population*. Ottawa: Queen's Printer.

——— and Wayne W. McVey (1979). *The Demographic Bases of Canadian Society*, Chap. 2, 5, 7, and 8. Toronto: McGraw-Hill.

Lee, Everett S. (1966). 'A theory of migration'. *Demography* 3: 47–57.

McVey, Wayne (1978). 'Migration and the smaller community'. *Canadian Studies in Population* 5: 13–23.

Northcott, Herbert C. (1985). 'The geographic mobility of Canada's elderly'. *Canadian Studies in Population* 12, 2: 183–202.

Shaw, Paul P. (1985). *Intermetropolitan Migration in Canada: Changing Determinants Over Three Decades*. Ottawa: Statistics Canada, NC Press, and Supply and Services Canada.

——— (1975). *Migration Theory and Fact*. Philadelphia: Regional Science Research Institute.

Schulman, Norman, and Robert Drass (1979). 'Motives and modes of internal migration: Relocation in a Canadian city'. *Canadian Review of Sociology and Anthropology* 16, 3: 333–42.

Statistics Canada (1983). *Population: Mobility Status*. Cat. 92–907, Vol. 1. Ottawa: Minister of Supply and Services.

CHAPTER 22

INTERREGIONAL MIGRATION OF THE CANADIAN POPULATION

Mary Anne Burke

Migration between the regions of Canada has been one of the key variables affecting the overall distribution of the Canadian population. In fact, interregional population flows have been far more important in shaping population concentrations in Canada than factors such as immigration and natural increase.

The flow of population across regional boundaries in Canada has tended to follow perceived economic opportunities or hardships. Provinces which historically have had strong economies have consistently attracted a large proportion of total Canadian migrants. Economically disadvantaged provinces, on the other hand, have had difficulty attracting migrants, and in most cases have consistently had a net outflow of population. Regional economic booms or busts have resulted in relatively sudden shifts in the flow of the Canadian population, which in turn often have resulted in pressures on the social fabric of the regions concerned.

Changes in technology, shifts in labour-force requirements, the discovery of new natural resources, and changes in the structure of consumer demand have all had differing impacts on regional economies. When viewed from a national perspec-

Table 1: Percentage distribution of Canada's population, 1871–1986

	1871	1881	1891	1901	1911	1921	1931	1941	1951	1961	1971	1981	1986
							Percentage						
Newfoundland	—	—	—	—	—	—	—	—	2.6	2.5	2.4	2.3	2.3
Prince Edward Island	2.6	2.5	2.3	1.9	1.3	1.0	0.8	0.8	0.7	0.6	0.5	0.5	0.5
Nova Scotia	10.7	10.2	9.3	8.6	6.8	6.0	4.9	5.0	4.6	4.0	3.7	3.5	3.5
New Brunswick	7.7	7.4	6.6	6.2	4.9	4.4	3.9	4.0	3.7	3.3	2.9	2.9	2.8
Quebec	32.3	31.4	30.8	30.7	27.9	26.9	27.7	29.0	29.0	28.8	28.0	26.5	25.9
Ontario	43.9	44.6	43.7	40.6	35.1	33.4	33.1	32.9	32.8	34.2	35.7	35.4	35.9
Manitoba	0.7	1.4	3.1	4.7	6.4	6.9	6.8	6.3	5.5	5.1	4.6	4.2	4.2
Saskatchewan	—	—	—	1.7	6.8	8.6	8.9	7.8	5.9	5.1	4.3	4.0	4.0
Alberta	—	—	—	1.4	5.2	6.7	7.1	6.9	6.7	7.3	7.6	9.2	9.3
British Columbia	1.0	1.1	2.1	3.3	5.5	6.0	6.7	7.1	8.3	8.9	10.1	11.3	11.4
Northwest and Yukon Territories	1.4	1.4	2.1	0.9	0.2	0.1	0.1	0.2	0.2	0.2	0.2	0.3	0.3
Total population (millions)	3.7	4.3	4.8	5.4	7.2	8.8	10.4	11.5	14.0	18.2	21.6	24.3	25.4

SOURCE: Statistics Canada, Census of Canada.

tive, the movement of people has facilitated changing uses of Canada's resources. At the same time, imbalances in the movement of people may also have contributed to patterns of economic disparity between the regions of Canada.

Since the 1930s, net interprovincial migration in Canada generally has been from the Atlantic provinces, Quebec, and Manitoba and Saskatchewan to Ontario, British Columbia, and more recently to Alberta. As a result, these three provinces have claimed an increasing share of the Canadian population at the expense of the other regions.

ATLANTIC CANADA

The lack of a strong, diversified economy in the Atlantic region has contributed to the net outflow of its population since 1931. The period 1971–76 was an exception. During this period, there was a net inflow of 6,000 migrants to the Atlantic region. This was attributed mainly to a net inflow of 27,000 migrants from Ontario.

In the last decade, however, Atlantic Canada again lost population through internal migration. There was a particularly large net outflow of migrants from this region between 1976 and 1981. In this period, 37,000 more people left the Atlantic provinces for other parts of Canada than moved to this region. Most of this loss was attributed to migration to Alberta.

The net outflow of population from the Atlantic provinces moderated between 1981 and 1986. Still, in this period, this region had a net loss of 8,000 internal migrants. Included in this figure were a net outflow of 13,000 migrants to Ontario and a net inflow of 1,900 people from Alberta.

QUEBEC

Since 1966, and especially since 1976, Quebec has had large net outflows of its population. During the period 1976–81, Quebec had a net loss of 156,000 internal migrants. Between 1981 and 1986, almost 80,000 more people left than came to Quebec. Most of these losses were accounted for by movement between Quebec and Ontario.

To a large extent, the net outflow from Quebec has been the result of a decrease in the flow of persons moving to Quebec. In-migration to Quebec dropped from 219,000 during the period 1961–66, to around 120,000 during the years 1976–81 and remained at that level during the period 1981–86.

Although Quebec has lost population through net internal migration to all regions in the last decade, the largest losses have been to Ontario. In the period 1976–81, more than 100,000 persons moved from Quebec to Ontario than went in the opposite direction. Quebec also had significant net losses to Alberta (27,000) and British Columbia (16,000) during these years. During the period 1981–86, Quebec had a net loss of 68,000 migrants to Ontario.

Ontario has been the most favoured destination of people leaving Quebec. Over two-thirds (68 per cent) of the 200,000 people leaving Quebec between 1981 and 1986, for example, went to Ontario. Historically, the next largest streams from Quebec have gone to Atlantic Canada and British Columbia. However, between 1976 and 1981, more Quebec migrants went to Alberta than to either of these two areas. Even though the oil and gas boom slowed dramatically in the 1980s, the number of migrants leaving Quebec for Alberta during the period 1981–86 still equalled the number going to Atlantic Canada and exceeded the number moving to British Columbia.

Migrants to Quebec have come mainly from Ontario. That province supplied 56 per cent of all migrants to Quebec between 1981 and 1986. The second largest stream of migrants to Quebec has been from Atlantic Canada, although since 1981, the stream from Alberta has been slightly larger than that from the Atlantic region.

ONTARIO

With its diversified economy and strong industrial sector, Ontario has attracted a large proportion of the total number of Canadian migrants. In fact, the only time Ontario has ever experienced a net outflow of population was during the 1970s when 66,000 more people left than came to Ontario. In the 1980s, however, the flow of migrants reverted to pre-1971 trends. Between 1981 and 1986, Ontario had a net gain of 122,000 internal migrants.

The largest proportion of migrants to Ontario generally has come from Quebec. However, in the period 1981–86, the proportion from Alberta (24 per cent) nearly equalled that from Quebec (30 per cent).

Historically, the largest migration stream from Ontario has been to Quebec. In the 1971–76 period, however, more Ontario migrants went to the Atlantic provinces than to any other region. Since 1976, Alberta has attracted the largest migration stream from Ontario.

MANITOBA AND SASKATCHEWAN

Manitoba and Saskatchewan have had a net loss of migrants since the 1930s. The outflow of people has resulted in a depopulation of the countryside and the disappearance of many small rural communities. Many factors have contributed to the outflow: the Depression and drought of the 1930s; the revolution in farm technology; the expansion of large corporate farms; and an economy heavily dependent on the farm industry and subject to the vagaries of weather and distant markets.

From 1931 to 1961, there were large net outflows of people from these two provinces, especially from Saskatchewan. In fact, during this period, the outflow from Saskatchewan accounted for the largest proportion of the total outflow from all parts of Canada, and led to an absolute decline in the population of Saskatchewan.

Net outflows from Manitoba and Saskatchewan moderated in the 1961–76 period. However, there was a further major net loss of almost 52,000 internal migrants from these two provinces between 1976 and 1981. In the 1981–86 period, the net outflow from these two provinces was just 6,000, a historic low.

Until 1951, nearly all migrants from Manitoba and Saskatchewan went to either British Columbia or Ontario. Since 1951, however, Alberta has been the prime destination of persons leaving Manitoba and Saskatchewan. In the late 1970s, for example, 45 per cent of all those leaving these two provinces went to Alberta. Those moving to Manitoba and Saskatchewan have tended to come mainly from these same three provinces.

ALBERTA

Fluctuations in population movement to and from Alberta have tended to reflect the volatile nature of this province's economy. The drought in the 1930s played havoc with its farm economy, and resulted in a net population outflow during that time. Economic diversification, primarily as a result of the expansion of the oil and gas industry, contributed to the net inflow of population during the 1941–76 period.

The subsequent boom and bust of the oil and gas industry resulted in a massive influx of people from all over Canada during the 1976–81 period, and a population outflow in the 1980s. Alberta had a net gain of 186,000 internal migrants between 1976 and 1981. In the 1981–86 period, however, Alberta experienced a net loss of 29,000 internal migrants. Preliminary data for 1986–87 indicate a continuation of this trend, with Alberta experiencing a net loss of 28,000 migrants in that year alone.

The sudden population inflow to Alberta in the late 1970s placed severe strains on social services and institutions in the province. The housing industry, for example, had difficulty meeting demand, while schools were filled beyond capacity and teachers were in short supply. As well, social service agencies and welfare offices were overburdened with the demand for their services.

Migrants to Alberta have come mainly from British Columbia, Saskatchewan and Manitoba. However, during the period 1976–81, more came from Ontario than from these three provinces. Although the number of persons moving from Ontario to Alberta remained high in the 1980s, British Columbia again became the primary source of Alberta in-migrants in this period.

Those leaving Alberta have gone mainly to these same provinces. Since 1981, however, there have been larger flows than normal from Alberta to all regions, particularly to Ontario.

BRITISH COLUMBIA

British Columbia historically has received net inflows of population from the rest of the country. Its favourable climate, spectacular topography and relatively buoyant economy have all contributed to its attractiveness. Unprecedented low levels of net migration since 1980, however, are a reflection of the recent severe economic recession in British Columbia. Net migration to British Columbia fell from 122,000 during 1976–81, to just 4,100 in the 1981–86 period. During three individual years of the latter period, British Columbia experienced net outflows for the first time.

Alberta has been both the main source of in-migrants to British Columbia and the main destination of those leaving British Columbia. In the period 1981–86, 44 per cent of internal migrants arriving in British Columbia came from Alberta, while 42 per cent of those leaving British Columbia went to Alberta. In fact, the flow of population between British Columbia and Alberta since the mid-1970s has rivalled the stream between Quebec and Ontario as the single largest interregional migration stream in Canada.

PROVINCIAL DISTRIBUTION

The flow of Canadians across regional borders over the years has contributed to shifts in the provincial distribution of the population in a generally westward direction. In the post-war period, the proportion of the Canadian population in Ontario, British Columbia and Alberta has grown, while the remaining regions have seen their shares of the national population decline.

The percentage of the Canadian population in Ontario increased from just under 33 per cent in 1951 to almost 36 per cent in 1986. In the 1981–86 period, Ontario was the only region in Canada to increase its share of the population. During this time, the proportion of the population living in Ontario increased 0.6 percentage points.

British Columbia and Alberta also experienced large post-war increases in their

Table 2: Total interregional migration by origin and destination of migrants, 1981–1986

Origin	Destination						
	Atlantic provinces	Quebec	Ontario	Manitoba and Saskat- chewan	Alberta	British Columbia	Total[1]
Atlantic provinces	—	18,060	82,807	10,396	34,381	16,612	165,164
Quebec	21,693	—	137,267	6,879	21,567	14,043	202,808
Ontario	69,579	69,495	—	42,842	84,780	62,070	333,730
Manitoba and Saskatchewan	10,173	5,541	47,964	—	68,127	37,125	171,941
Alberta	36,309	18,183	110,986	68,054	—	108,260	348,361
British Columbia	16,599	10,845	71,871	33,925	102,044	—	242,453
Total[1]	157,009	123,488	455,791	165,550	319,042	246,679	1,493,539
Net migration	−8,155	−79,320	122,061	−6,391	−29,319	4,226	—

[1] Includes the Northwest and Yukon Territories.
SOURCE: Statistics Canada, Demography Division, unpublished estimates.

shares of the Canadian population. Between 1951 and 1986, the percentage of the population living in British Columbia increased from 8 per cent to 11 percent, while in Alberta the increase was from 7 per cent to 9 per cent. Neither province,

Figure 1: Total in- and out-migration as a percentage of 1981 population, by region, 1981–1986

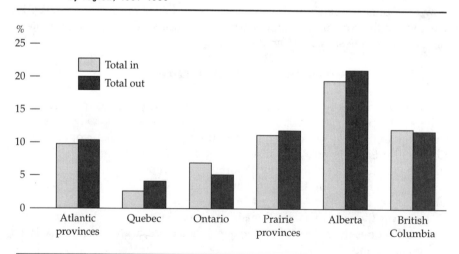

SOURCE: Statistics Canada, Demography Division, unpublished estimates.

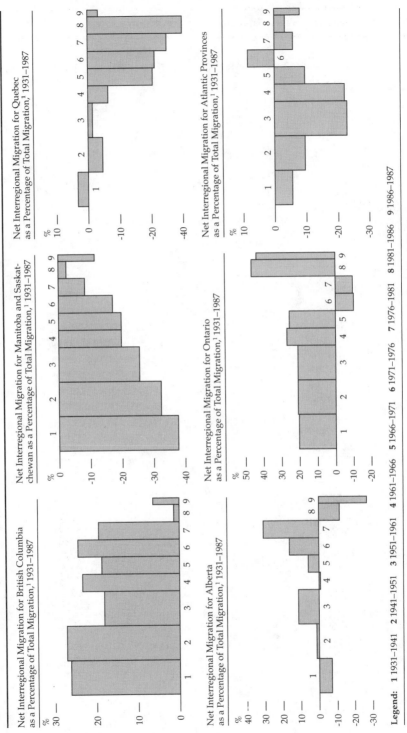

Figure 2: Net interregional migration as a percentage of total migration,¹ by region 1931–1987

Net Interregional Migration for British Columbia as a Percentage of Total Migration,¹ 1931–1987

Net Interregional Migration for Manitoba and Saskatchewan as a Percentage of Total Migration,¹ 1931–1987

Net Interregional Migration for Quebec as a Percentage of Total Migration,¹ 1931–1987

Net Interregional Migration for Alberta as a Percentage of Total Migration,¹ 1931–1987

Net Interregional Migration for Ontario as a Percentage of Total Migration,¹ 1931–1987

Net Interregional Migration for Atlantic Provinces as a Percentage of Total Migration,¹ 1931–1987

Legend: 1 1931–1941 2 1941–1951 3 1951–1961 4 1961–1966 5 1966–1971 6 1971–1976 7 1976–1981 8 1981–1986 9 1986–1987

¹ Figures calculated by dividing net migration (in-migration minus out-migration) by the total volume of net interprovincial migration in Canada.
SOURCE: Statistics Canada, Cat. 91–208, *International and Interprovincial Migration in Canada, 1977 and 1978*, and Demography Division, unpublished estimates.

Table 3: Net region-to-region migration flows, 1961–1986

	Annual net flows [1]				
	1961–66	1966–71	1971–76	1976–81	1981–86
Between Atlantic and					
Quebec	−1,105	672	2,236	8,052	3,633
Ontario	−11,239	−9,514	5,393	−1,298	−13,288
Prairies [2]	−362	−220	139	−3,940	−223
Alberta	−526	−966	−727	−30,088	1,928
British Columbia	−1,001	−1,548	−911	−9,225	−13
Total [3]	−14,197	−11,620	6,001	−37,345	−8,155
Between Quebec and					
Atlantic	1,105	−672	−2,236	−8,052	−3,633
Ontario	−4,497	−19,309	−9,388	−101,519	−67,772
Prairies [2]	176	−74	−314	−3,700	−1,338
Alberta	−53	−1,351	−1,511	−27,208	−3,384
British Columbia	−704	−2,953	−2,063	−15,732	−3,198
Total [3]	−3,972	−24,547	−15,522	−156,498	−79,320
Between Ontario					
Atlantic	11,239	9,514	−5,393	1,298	13,228
Quebec	4,497	19,309	9,388	101,519	67,772
Prairies [2]	1,980	4,163	114	−9,847	5,122
Alberta	869	−289	−4,895	−99,581	26,206
British Columbia	−1,864	−2,671	−6,729	−49,493	9,801
Total [3]	17,074	30,142	−7,712	57,826	122,061
Between Prairies [2] and					
Atlantic	362	220	−139	3,946	223
Quebec	−176	74	314	3,700	1,338
Ontario	−1,980	−4,163	−114	9,847	5,122
Alberta	−5,441	−10,227	−8,229	−42,902	+73
British Columbia	−5,976	−9,965	−4,989	−26,423	−3,200
Total [3]	−13,113	−24,418	−13,516	−51,930	−6,391
Between Alberta and					
Atlantic	526	966	727	30,088	−1,928
Quebec	53	1,351	1,511	27,208	3,384
Ontario	−869	289	4,895	99,581	−26,206
Prairies [2]	5,441	10,227	8,229	42,902	−73
British Columbia	−5,668	−6,243	−3,635	−18,193	−6,216
Total [3]	−397	6,401	11,714	186,314	−29,319

Continued p. 321

Table 3: (continued)

	Annual net flows[1]				
	1961–66	1966–71	1971–76	1976–81	1981–86
Between British Columbia and					
Atlantic	1,001	1,548	911	9,225	13
Quebec	704	2,953	2,063	15,732	3,198
Ontario	1,864	2,671	6,729	49,493	−9,801
Prairies[2]	5,976	9,965	4,989	26,423	3,200
Alberta	5,668	6,243	3,635	18,193	6,216
Total[3]	15,549	22,993	18,457	121,595	4,226

[1] This table outlines differences in interregional migration. A positive figure indicates that more people came to the indicated region from the sub-region than went from that region to the sub-region. A negative figure, of course, indicates the opposite. For example, in 1961–66 an average of 1,105 more people moved from the Atlantic region to Quebec than moved eastward from Quebec each year. In 1966–71, however, the flow reversed and 672 more persons moved from Quebec to the Atlantic region than in the opposite direction.

[2] Includes Manitoba and Saskatchewan.

[3] Total migration figures include persons moving to and from the Northwest and Yukon Territories.

SOURCE: Statistics Canada, Cat. 91–208, *International and Interprovincial Migration in Canada, 1977 and 1978,* and Demography Division, unpublished estimates.

however, experienced any growth in their share of the total population during the 1980s.

The Atlantic provinces have seen their share of the Canadian population decrease the most of any region. The proportion of the population in the Atlantic provinces halved in the post-war period, from 18 per cent of all Canadians in 1951 to 9 per cent in 1986.

Quebec, Manitoba and Saskatchewan also experienced declines in their shares of the population. Quebec accounted for 26 per cent of all Canadians in 1986, compared to 29 per cent in 1951. Quebec was the only region in which the share of population declined in the 1981–86 period. During this time, Quebec's share of the population fell 0.6 percentage points. In 1986, Manitoba and Saskatchewan combined, made up 8 per cent of the total Canadian population, down from 11 per cent in 1951.

The Northwest and Yukon Territories together accounted for just 0.3 per cent of the Canadian population in 1986, up slightly from 0.2 per cent in 1951.

CHAPTER 23

WELCOME BUT WHY?

Recent Changes in

Canadian Immigration Policy

James Stafford

Gerry Weiner, minister of state for immigration in Canada, tabled the *Annual Report to Parliament on Future Immigration Levels* in Parliament on 30 October 1986. The report raised the level of immigration for 1987 to 115,000–125,000. The minister stated that the higher levels were a reflection of 'the significant contribution immigrants make to Canada's economic well-being by giving impetus to capital expansion, job creation for Canadians and consumer demand for Canadian goods and services' (Employment and Immigration, 1986a: 1). This rationale provides an interesting contrast to the 1982 *Annual Report* which recommended a reduction in immigration levels to 'protect jobs for Canadians' (Canada Employment and Immigration Commission, 1983: 28).

The purpose of this paper is threefold: to explain the reversal in government policy, to examine critically the validity of the arguments supporting an increase in immigration, and to provide a framework within which to carry out discussion on the advantages and disadvantages of increasing immigration levels in Canada. It begins with a description of immigration policy as it was applied since World

War II, and [goes] on to examine changes in the policy and factors behind these changes.

The focus is on the economic aspects of Canadian immigration policy. There is no doubt that such policy also contains humanitarian and social dimensions. However, the record of immigration procedures and goals since Confederation reveals that, with the exception of wartime periods, the economic conditions of the time were sufficient to explain immigration policy in Canada.

IMMIGRATION POLICY AFTER WORLD WAR II

During the post-war expansion, the influx of American investment capital into Canada generated a need for a skilled labour force. A shortage of training facilities caused the Canadian state to turn to immigration to meet its employment needs. A number of orders-in-council were introduced by the cabinet from 1947 to 1950 to create new immigration categories or to broaden existing ones. In 1950 the Department of Immigration and Citizenship was established to regulate the selection of desirable immigrants.

The federal government set up the Department of Manpower and Immigration in 1966 to meld further immigration to the supply of labour. A year later immigration regulations were introduced which specified that unsponsored immigrants must have specific skills which were needed in the labour force. A point system was established whereby an applicant was more likely to be admitted into the country if he or she had the appropriate education and occupational training, had arranged employment, and had selected a regional destination to suit the demands for labour in Canada.

The 1975 *Green Paper on Immigration* provided the major statement on policy for ensuing years. It emphasized slow, controlled growth in the face of uncertainties about the impacts of high population growth rates on economic conditions. The policies recommended in the Green Paper were made operational in the 1976 Immigration Act. The only significant change in immigration policy up until the most recent reversal was the freeze in 1982 of selected immigrant workers who did not have prearranged employment, which was put in place because of the high levels of unemployment at the time.

The 1976 Immigration Act, and subsequent amendments, allowed persons to land in Canada as refugees, as family members of citizens and landed immigrants, and as economic immigrants. The last group included business immigrants and persons with skills and work experience that were needed in the labour force. Business immigrants included self-employed persons, entrepreneurs with the experience and capital to establish businesses and create jobs, and, as of January 1986, investors with at least $500,000 and a willingness to invest $250,000 or more in approved investment vehicles in Canada.

An additional act of fine-tuning which was first introduced in 1973 was the enactment of employment visa regulations providing for the employment of temporary workers in Canada. This program was written into the 1976 Immigration Act. It allowed the state to control the flow and the characteristics of temporary workers and was designed to assist employers in obtaining labour at low cost for the type of work which native Canadians were often loath to do. This program has gained in popularity. The number of employment authorizations, which include these workers, has increased from 84,000 in 1973 to 131,000 in 1983 to an estimated 279,000 in 1989 (Canada Employment and Immigration Commission, 1983; Employment and Immigration Canada, 1989: 40).

In summary, immigration policy has always had a strong economic dimension. The changes introduced prior to 1984 reflected a primary concern with the connection between the number of immigrants and the supply of labour. When skills were in short supply or when unemployment rates were low, immigration numbers were boosted to counteract these deficiencies. When unemployment increased, the number of immigrants was reduced accordingly.

PRESENT SHIFT IN IMMIGRATION POLICY

In 1984 the federal government embarked on a policy to push up the number of immigrants coming into Canada. This change took place at a time when there was 15 per cent real unemployment and job-creation programs costing up to $2.7 billion annually (Task Force on Program Review, 1985). Yet the government justified boosting immigration levels by claiming that this effort would create jobs for Canadians. Immigration became part of a job-creation strategy.

The important question is why the government adopted this policy at this point in history. It had been exposed to various arguments in support of such policies for a very long time. In 1949, Mabel Timlin wrote a commissioned report for the government entitled *Does Canada Need More People?* in which, after thorough analysis of the question, she answers with a qualified 'yes' (Timlin, 1951).

This was followed by the *Report of the Royal Commission on Canada's Economic Prospects* in 1957 in which a recommendation was put forward that sustained immigration, even in periods of mild depression, would be beneficial to the country's economic growth. The *Report* disparaged the prevailing, on-again-off-again immigration policy geared to short-term employment conditions (Canada, 1957: 120). Yet the Canadian government continued to disregard this line of advice and to pursue cautious policies that tied immigration closely to immediate, short-term labour force needs until 1984.

A possible answer to the question can be derived from an examination of the sources of the new strategy. Recommendations for the reversal of policy came primarily from two sources in the federal government: the political arm of the state and the Department of Employment and Immigration (Taylor, 1986: 10).

A change in government at that time leads us to a probable explanation for the timing of the policy shift. In the autumn of 1984 the Progressive Conservative party came into power. Among the three major political parties, it is the one which provides greatest support for the business community. Indeed the loss of the previous party, the Liberals, is attributed, in some part, to its lack of support from large corporations. Evidence of the increased support for big business provided by the Conservative government is reflected in a number of its actions. It proceeded to dismantle the National Energy Program and the Foreign Investment Review Agency, to adopt new taxation policies to make Canadian corporate taxation competitive with that of the United States, and to sign a free-trade agreement with the United States. It also deregulated transportation and, to a lesser extent, financial institutions, and privatized some government-owned organizations (Carmichael et al., 1989: 19–72).

These and other policies coincided with the approach known as 'supply side economics' wherein the primary goal of the government was to remove obstacles to investment, innovation, and competitiveness. Finance Minister Michael Wilson provided evidence of the government thrust in this direction when he tabled an initial policy statement in the House of Commons shortly after coming to power:

> Government has become too big. It introduces too much into the market place and inhibits or distorts the entrepreneurial process. Some industries are over-regulated. Others are over-protected, not just from imports but also from domestic competition. Some programs designed to facilitate investment have the perverse effect of distorting investment decisions. Other programs carry on long after the need for them has passed, and are only a fiscal drain. In many cases, the federal government has not done the job it should have, in support of private sector initiatives (Wilson, 1984: 23–4).

It goes without saying that a larger labour force working for lower wages would also enable industry to realize greater profits. Concern with the projections of diminishing numbers entering the labour force in the 1990s would have encouraged such a government to look for alternatives to the normal supply of labour, and increased immigration would have been a logical solution.

The new government did not have time to adjust the numbers in the annual immigration levels report that was due shortly after it came to power, but for the first time, that report signalled concerns about the prospects of population decline. It also announced a review of immigration policy and programs. The following June, Flora MacDonald, minister of employment and immigration, tabled a special report to Parliament on the review of the future directions for immigration levels. It was the first instance in which an immigration report other than the annual one had been tabled in Parliament, suggesting that the government was interested in making immigration policy an integral part of its overall strategy (Howith, 1988, 24).

At the same time, another report was tabled by the Parliamentary Standing Committee on Labour, Employment and Immigration, calling for substantial increases in immigration. The reasons cited for the increase included the needs to counter the decline in fertility and to attain a population of thirty million by the year 2000.[1] Furthermore, it recommended that levels of immigration be manipulated in an attempt to 'smooth out the current age imbalance in the Canadian population' (House of Commons, 1985b: 20:3).[2]

The Standing Committee on Labour, Employment and Immigration is a powerful committee consisting of elected members of the House of Commons. Its major functions are to refine government policy, scrutinize the plans of the Department of Employment and Immigration, and examine policy proposals before they reach the stage of legislation (Van Loon and Whittington, 1987: 620). The standing committee can be very influential because of the experience gained by its members in focusing on the area of responsibility and in hearing expert witnesses. Its power is enhanced by the rules of Parliament which require the government to table a reply to committee recommendations within sixty days of receiving a report (Van Loon and Whittington, 1987: 619).

The minutes of the proceedings of the standing committee provide verbatim reports of all proceedings of the committee with a few exceptions when meetings are held in camera. A careful perusal of these minutes reveals that in spite of the argument put forward that immigrants create jobs, no investigation of the effects of immigration on jobs was carried out. Indeed, one of the members of the committee states that the report in question is really the product of the nine members of the Conservative party and that the committee did not consult a single economist regarding the connection between immigration and unemployment (House of Commons, 1985a: 3622, 3799). Yet, members of the committee and members of the governing Conservative party recited the salubrious effects of immigration on the economy on numerous occasions while discussing immigration on the floor of the House of Commons or while the committee was in meeting.[3] They also presented the same arguments and references to scientific evidence of this connection to the public and were widely quoted in various newspapers and magazines.[4]

Perhaps the most significant statement was made by Benoît Bouchard, minister of employment and immigration, on 6 April 1987, while addressing the standing committee. He pointed out that the government began to set its objectives with respect to immigration immediately after the 1984 election when the Conservatives first came into power (House of Commons, 1987b: 30:7). If this statement is factual, and the prompt change in policy suggests that it is, then one can conclude that the strategy was in place before the numerous justifications were established.

The priority of this policy suggests that it was an integral part of the basic strategy of the new government to adopt supply-side economic policies to support capital. The advantage for capital to have a large and varied labour force at its disposal is evident in both economic theory and historical events.

Capital is aware of this, as is apparent in the briefs submitted to the Macdonald Commission on the Economic Union and Development Prospects for Canada in 1982–84. The briefs of Cominco, Honeywell, and Gulf Canada emphasized the importance of a growing population in Canada to maintain demand for company products. Various organizations representing capital, such as the Canadian Chamber of Commerce, the Retail Council of Canada, the Canadian Life and Health Insurance Association, and numerous chambers of commerce made reference to the advantages of a large and growing population.

In summary, the shift in immigration policy appears to rise out of the general strategy of the new political party in power to use immigration as an economic lever. The Conservative government was influenced by pressure from large capital interests and by ideas inherent in supply-side economics. The economic

Table 1: Immigration to Canada by class, 1984-1988

Class	1984	1985	1986	1987	1988
Refugees/humanitarian	24,507	25,589	32,168	44,599	31,652
Family	43,849	38,556	42,165	53,436	51,003
Assisted relatives	8,188	7,417	5,903	12,316	15,493
Economic/independent	3,303	4,341	9,982	28,631	44,583
Business	6,262	6,490	7,528	11,103	14,913
Retirees	2,317	2,100	1,833	2,666	3,124
Total	88,426	84,493	99,579	152,751	160,768
	Percentage distribution				
Refugees/humanitarian	28	30	32	29	20
Family	50	46	42	35	32
Assisted relatives	9	9	6	8	10
Economic/independent	4	5	10	19	28
Business	7	8	8	7	7
Retirees	3	2	2	2	2
Total	100%	100%	100%	100%	100%

SOURCE: Richmond (1989), Table 1.

emphasis is reflected in the increase in the percentage of immigrants who are destined for the labour force since 1984. Table 1 reveals that the proportion of immigrants admitted to Canada because of family ties has diminished from one-half to one-third and that these have been replaced by an equivalent increase in immigrants admitted for economic reasons.

It found a willing accomplice in the Immigration Branch of the Department of Employment and Immigration. Academic papers and reports by officers in the Department of Employment and Immigration that were being published at the time were lauding the beneficial economic impacts of higher immigration levels.

One example of this foray into academic debate was a criticism of the results of a simulation model of the impact of immigration on unemployment that was reported by Rao and Kapsalis (1982) which found that higher immigration levels contributed to higher unemployment in Canada. The critics, Robertson and Roy (1982) of Employment and Immigration Canada, argued that the structure of the model predetermined its negative impact on unemployment and was irrelevant to contemporary immigration because it was based on the period 1954 to 1976.

A paper by Samuel and Conyers (1985) of Employment and Immigration Canada is most blatant in presenting a case for increasing immigration in order to reduce unemployment. The authors summarized the results of simulations of seven macroeconomic models that, among other things, related immigration to unemployment.[5] Five of these models produced results indicating that increased immigration exacerbated unemployment problems while one failed to establish any relationship. Samuel and Conyers then proceeded to laud the remaining simulation model which showed a reduction in unemployment levels when immigration levels were increased.[6]

Samuel and Conyers then proceeded to generate a model of their own which overwhelmingly supported the contention that immigration generates jobs. They began with the 68,000 immigrants in 1983–84 destined for the labour force, 13,000 of whom had prearranged jobs, leaving 55,000 who must seek work. No suggestion is made that any of the 13,000 took jobs that might otherwise have been filled by Canadians. They calculated that the 2,000 immigrants who came as entrepreneurs or self-employed workers created 24,000 jobs. They then argued that the $1.8 million brought in by the 1983–84 cohort 'may' have created 104,000 jobs over a five-year period. The influx of immigrants itself creates jobs, so they calculated that up to 58,000 jobs could have been created by the physical presence of the immigrants.

Chris Taylor, director of immigration policy development, Canada Employment and Immigration Commission, attempted to identify the sources of the ideas that precipitated the change in immigration policy, but his omissions are as insightful as his inclusions. His position in the immigration department makes him one of the key actors in the development of immigration policy.

Taylor (1986: 11) suggested that 'there has been a gradual reawakening of concern about the immigration-demographic linkage, primarily fostered by federal reports and some discussion among academics and pollsters . . .' The first such report that he mentions was released in December 1984 by Statistics Canada. It estimates varying combinations of levels of immigration and fertility necessary to attain a 1 per cent growth rate in population. Taylor (1986: 11) goes on to suggest that the Statistics Canada publication brought out concerns of the minister of employment and immigration, Flora MacDonald, about links between immigration and population.

What is surprising about the Taylor selection of significant first documents is that he overlooks one produced by his own division that was published eighteen months earlier and which addresses the same issue. Entitled 'The Role of Immigration in Determining Canada's Eventual Population Size' (Employment and Immigration, 1983), it states that under existing fertility rates, Canada must boost immigration in order to maintain its present population size.

Three years earlier a paper was presented in a workshop by immigration division officials. They calculated that annual immigration would have to increase to 263,000 by the year 2001 in order to realize an annual population growth rate of 1 per cent, assuming constant fertility rates (Basavarajappa and George, 1981). Thus the original publications pointing out the need to bolster immigration to counter impending population decline were produced by the Division of Immigration itself.

One would expect the immigration branch of the state to favour long-term programs supporting immigration, given that it is the *raison d'être* of that bureaucratic unit. Bureaucratic politics dictate that a department must compete with other departments for scarce monies, personnel, influence, and prestige. High-ranking officials must adopt a role that is based on the departmental function within the total bureaucratic structure. The role of the immigration branch is to manage immigration. This role is enhanced when immigration becomes a more significant part of government policy. That the branch has played this role is borne out by the record which shows that the immigration branch has a history of promoting immigration for various reasons (Hawkins, 1972: 111).

If the preceding analysis is correct, the explanation for increased immigration lies within the realm of politics more than economics, sociology, or demography. This is so in spite of the arguments put forth by officials that the change was necessary to generate jobs, counter a declining population, or support an aging society. However, these arguments have a validity of their own and deserve analysis in order to evaluate the appropriateness of the policy change.

The arguments that were put forth have considerable merit.[7] The literature provides us with a rich variety of perspectives on these issues, some pro and some con. Space does not allow a complete presentation of all nuances of the arguments, but an attempt will be made to survey the most significant ideas in support of each side. The fact that alternative views exist indicates that the relationship between each factor cited by government and immigration officials is not as simple and clear as was implied.

EVALUATION OF THE RATIONALES FOR HIGHER IMMIGRATION LEVELS

The following sections deal with the three arguments supporting higher immigration levels: the need to maintain a desired population size in the face of declining fertility, the need to counter the effects of an aging population, and the usefulness of immigrants in generating positive economic growth in Canada.

Consequences of a Declining Population

Imminent population decline has threatened ever since fertility rates fell below replacement level in 1972. But the suggestion that higher immigration levels are the appropriate solution to this perceived problem should be questioned. The magnitude of immigration required to balance the decline in fertility is very large.

Employment and Immigration Canada has generated projections of the combinations of fertility rates and immigration levels necessary to maintain Canada's population at various sizes. The results of 1984 projections are presented in Table 2. Rates of total fertility and net migration were approximately 1.7 and 50,000 respectively. If these continued, Canada's population would eventually stabilize at about 10 million. In order to maintain its present population in the long run, given a fertility rate of 1.6, net migration would have to equal about 150,000. If we assume that about 50,000 people leave Canada each year, this requires immigration levels of 200,000.

Table 2: Eventual stable population sizes in Canada with differential combinations of fertility and immigration

Eventual stable population	Total fertility rate	Net immigration
10 million	1.2	100,000
	1.7	50,000
	2.0	20,000
25 million	1.2	250,000
	1.6	150,000
	1.75	100,000
	1.95	50,000
30 million	1.2	300,000
	1.7	150,000
	2.0	50,000
35 million	1.2	350,000
	1.6	200,000
	2.0	60,000
50 million	1.2	500,000
	1.7	250,000
	1.95	100,000

SOURCE: Employment and Immigration Canada (1984), 30.

If higher population levels are desired, a greater influx of immigrants is necessary. For example, if we wish to aim for a stable population of thirty-five million with 1984 fertility rates and emigration levels, we must admit 250,000 immigrants each year.

Such policies are plausible, but the admission of enormous numbers of immigrants year after year will have considerable impact on social and economic institutions in Canada. The projection of net annual immigration of 150,000 to maintain present population levels at present fertility rates would result in one-quarter of the Canadian population being born abroad (Beaujot, 1986: 6).

If we assume that the economy can absorb this quantity of immigrants each year, a question that will be discussed in a later section, we are still faced with the difficulties engendered in the social absorption of such large proportions of the population who have been socialized in a non-Canadian context. In times of economic growth, social diversity is seen as an enriching contribution to the culture, but when unemployment and poverty move into view, such diversity has the potential to spark interracial rancour and conflict.

The most enthusiastic proponent of the utilization of immigration to promote long-term economic growth is Julian Simon. His recent opus, *Theory of Population and Economic Growth* (1986), presents the culmination of his thoughts and research in this area throughout a prolific career. In his model, technological innovation plays a central role in the march toward increasing per capita productivity. He rejects the more common view that technological progress is primarily a function of capital investment and suggests instead that the important factors are education and training, the existence of a large stock of technology, and large industries. The necessary condition for these factors to operate effectively is a large population. Thus he makes a large and increasing population the driving force behind technological development.

Throughout his book, Simon refers to arguments in opposition to his view as he musters support for his own. He acknowledges that the empirical record does not support his model. Numerous studies indicate no association between population size or population growth and rate of technological or economic growth. However, he argues that a longer historical record, something in the order of a century, is needed to assess the ultimate association between the two sets of variables.

He does not eliminate the most important counter-argument which is that capital investment is the most crucial input to technological advancement. Indeed, he acknowledges the importance of this factor, implicitly and explicitly, throughout his text.[8] In this regard, most of his opponents would probably agree with his thesis: that under conditions of continued capital investment and favourable social and economic environments, population growth would probably contribute to economic growth in the long run.

In his exhaustive survey of the literature, Dosi (1988) illustrates the complexity of economic and social forces associated with technological innovation. He discusses the role of scientific knowledge, organizational arrangements within the firm, and the relationships between the innovating firm and its external environment. He points out that various sectors of the economy have different sources of innovation depending on the nature of the sector. Dosi finds that market demand can contribute to innovation in certain sectors, but only within an amenable context of technical and scientific knowledge and organizational structure.

A common justification for increasing population is to attain economies of scale, which gives firms an advantage over other, smaller firms. Such economies are obtained when the size of the market is increased. If the market is the country's population, then it makes sense to increase the latter. However, in an open economy, such as Canada's, the market can be expanded by numerous other means, the most obvious of which is the extension of international trade.

To compete in the domestic or international market, a firm must be able to produce goods that are cheaper and/or of a higher quality than those of other firms. Japanese firms provide us with an exemplary model of how this can be done. Directed by a government that was determined to strengthen certain of its industries and assisted by enormous infusions of capital from government coffers, the Japanese used aggressive marketing techniques and superior production methods to produce and sell higher-quality products than their competitors.

They were assisted by a labour market that was very stable. The knowledge that workers would remain with their firms encouraged them to provide skills training, confident that returns on such human investment would not accrue to a competing corporation. On-the-job training combined with an education system that was superior in imparting scientific and technical knowledge to produce a skilled, competent work force (Prestowitz, 1988; Reich, 1989).

These factors have combined to give Japan enormous advantages in terms of economies of scale. They do not rule out the advantages of a larger domestic population but clearly imply that numerous other avenues are available to attain this end.

In the long run, other things being equal, Simon is probably correct in supporting immigration to assist economic growth. But other things are seldom equal, and in the long run, they are less likely to be equal than in shorter periods.

Consequences of an Aging Population

Many of the arguments supporting continued population growth lie rooted in the mercantile philosophies of the eighteenth century which correlated economic and population growth. Reinforcing this perspective was the French adage that a stationary population consisted of 'old people sitting around in old houses ruminating over old ideas' (Espenshade, 1978: 647).

Teitelbaum and Winter (1985: 109) point out that no empirical evidence is available to provide us with firm conclusions about the association of an aged population and specific societal characteristics. Three countries with the oldest populations are Great Britain, Sweden, and West Germany. While Great Britain has experienced social and economic woes of late, no one blames them on her aged. Sweden and West Germany, on the other hand, are often held up as models of social and economic development.

An important concern with the demographic shift to an older population is based on evidence that public costs per person are two or three times greater for the elderly than for young people. This ratio ignores the significant amount of private costs borne by families in raising their children. Fewer children per family would result in more disposable income per family and would reduce the actual burden of supporting larger numbers of elderly.

Of course, many changes should be made in the redistribution of wealth and the ways by which services are offered in the name of efficiency. For example, health care should be shifted from an emphasis on curative to one on preventive and palliative procedures.

Numerous other variations could be introduced to ease the costs of an elderly population. Age at retirement could be postponed, social security payments could be marginally reduced, and deductions from paychecks going toward private and public pensions could be marginally increased. There is no doubt that a proportionate increase in non-productive elderly would increase the burden of their support for the remainder of the population. But programs could be introduced to provide means by which many of the elderly [would be] able not only to support themselves but to make valuable contributions to society at large.

At the same time, this shift in the age distribution would result in lower expenses for the youth who presently absorb much larger public funds. The increased dependency costs for the elderly would be counterbalanced by diminished public expenditures in the fields of education, family support, day-care, law enforcement, and corrections. The net result need not be an unmanageable increase in the total costs to taxpayers.

On balance, this may be the least convincing argument for increasing immigration. Each immigrant to Canada grows old and becomes a potential source of burden to the public. Thus the problem of dependency is only marginally reduced by the encouragement of immigration.

Another flaw in this argument is the fact that the young and old are the only ones classified as dependents in most standard measures of dependency. Variations in participation and unemployment rates can have a profound impact on actual numbers that are dependent on public support. If immigrants have difficulty finding jobs or if they increase the difficulty for native Canadians to obtain remunerative employment, then their presence defeats this purpose of immigration. This brings us to the last and most important argument put forward.

Immigration and Employment

The most important question to be answered is whether we can be confident that an increase in immigration creates productive jobs. The source of support of this or any other argument can only be empirical evidence or theory.

Turning first to the empirical level, we note a recent study by Borjas (1986) which suggests that immigrants become self-employed to a greater extent than native-born Americans in the United States. When he investigates the types of industries in which self-employed immigrants are engaged, he finds them to be involved significantly more often in retail outlets. Over 27 per cent of self-employed immigrants, compared with 17 per cent of the native-born self-employed, are engaged in retail activities (Borjas, 1986: 488). This suggests that such immigrants establish variety stores, grocery shops, and food establishments which cater to specialized groups of consumers. Although such activity adds to the quality of life in a community, it cannot be construed as a major creator of jobs. Some jobs are created but most often these jobs go to the owner, his spouse, and other members of his immediate family (Borjas, 1986: 494).

Borjas also found that immigrants do not become self-employed until they have worked for five or ten years and have amassed enough capital to invest in a business. Thus, any jobs that are created come into being only after the immigrant has competed with natives in the job market for several years. If we consider a cohort of 100,000 immigrants destined for the labour force, we would see them on state support for an average of eight or ten months before getting a job. This would be followed by about ten years of employment, followed by a shift of about 12,000 of them into self-employment (if we use Borjas's data), wherein many of them would employ members of their own family. This would free up the 12,000 jobs which they had vacated but would leave 88,000 of the immigrants in the labour market. Under conditions of high unemployment rates, this can hardly be construed as a procedure for expanding employment opportunities for native Canadians.

An alternative argument is that immigrants take jobs that are undesirable to natives. There is considerable evidence that this is the case in the United States and that it is becoming so in Canada (Sassen, 1988; US Department of Labor, 1989; Balakrishnan, 1988; Beaujot and Rappak, 1988). Immigrants are accepting many lower-ranking jobs which are opening up as a result of pressure in manufacturing industries to reduce salaries and of the expansion of low-skilled jobs in the service sector.

This process is advantageous to Canadians in that it assists the economy to function efficiently in the short run. However, two long-term effects should be monitored closely. The reliance on low-wage labour in certain manufacturing enterprises may have the opposite effect on technological development to that proposed by Simon (1986) and summarized in preceding paragraphs. Instead of encouraging technological innovation, a large supply of low-wage labour has dampened the need for capital investment and technological innovations in the garment and leather goods industries in the United States (Sassen, 1988; US Department of Labor, 1989).

A second concern has also been manifest in US cities where the structure of the labour market has contributed to a degree of immiseration of visible minorities in larger cities. This in turn has generated ethnic strife and resentment which has created considerable costs both economic and social.

The more usual argument favouring immigration for its job-creating function refers to those jobs created by the demand generated by the purchasing power of immigrants. This argument is based on theory because relevant empirical evidence is not readily obtained. No one can establish empirically that the admission of a number of immigrants in year X is responsible for the sale of more consumer durables in the year X + N than if they had not been admitted.

The major theoretical paradigms that can be applied to immigrant-generated demand are neoclassical economics and political economy. Neoclassical models have been used both to support and to oppose the argument favouring immigration as an engine of growth through demand. In support of it, immigration is seen as a stimulus to the economy because it adds to population size which in turn is transposed into higher expenditures on consumption. Immigrants must purchase clothing, food, housing, cars, and furniture. Their children go to school, attend rock concerts, and buy hockey sticks, all of which increase the level of aggregate demand (Foot, 1984: 6).

In contrast, Star (1975) has argued that immigrants compete with natives for jobs, driving down wages and pushing up unemployment rates. The result of these effects is an increase in government transfer payments to meet the need for larger welfare payments. Canadians are then faced with higher taxes and lower wages that will have the combined effect of reducing rather than augmenting demand.

One of the underlying assumptions in neoclassical economics is the marginality of labour and wages. If additional units are added to the labour force, wages are reduced, but full employment is maintained. The unemployment rates in Canada belie the acceptability of this assumption. The unusually high unemployment rates of young people suggest that an increase in immigrants would lead to displacement of native workers (Ternowetsky, 1985: 3).

The crucial issue on which this debate hinges is the extent to which immigrants displace native workers. If they find gainful employment without displacing workers, they are likely to make a contribution to aggregate supply and demand. But if they are displacing sizeable numbers of the native labour force, the resulting welfare costs will be greater than any economic benefits that are generated.

A second paradigm that can be used in this debate is that of the Canadian political economy of Harold Innis. It may be more appropriate than neoclassical economic models because it is based on historical Canadian development. Canadian political economists treat Canada as a special case of a staple-producing country growing on the periphery of central capitalist powers.

The fundamental principle of the Innis theory is that the economic development of a peripheral society is determined by the nature of the staple product being exported. Canadian staples have been furs, timber, wheat, and minerals. The exports of these staples have created backward linkages such as transportation and energy, rather than forward linkages such as manufacturing, which has locked the entire Canadian economy into a dependency on international markets (Stafford and McMillan, 1986: 14). Monopolistic and centralized political and industrial structures have been put in place to reinforce the economy's dependence on the export of staples. This focus has discouraged industrial diversification and enhanced dependency on external markets for staples and on manufacturing countries for technology and producer's goods.

Innis argued that the location of Canada on the periphery of the international capitalist system has led to structural rigidities in the economic system. Infrastructure is built to meet maximum demand, resulting in capacities which exceed normal requirements. This unused capacity and inelastic supply of the staple, monopolistic controls, and external debts combine to produce rigidities which negate the dynamics of supply and demand that is the engine of growth in neoclassical economics.

Dependency on foreign markets reduces the impact of increases in population brought about by immigration on demand for Canadian-produced goods. The result may be the opposite—an increased demand for foreign-made consumer goods which will adversely affect Canada's balance of payments.

The same negative results may arise when we consider the supply side of the economic picture. An influx of workers in a peripheral society may not reduce wages and costs of production because these do not react in accordance with the maxims of neoclassical economics. Canadian wages are influenced by negotiations between international unions and corporations as much as they are by changes in the supply of labour. The demand for labour is often a function of price fluctuations in foreign markets. It also varies according to decisions made by officers in international corporations to invest in Canadian resource extraction and according to decisions of government officials to invest in large projects designed to improve the infrastructure so as to encourage resource exploitation.

The upshot of the political economic perspective is that immigration cannot be used as a generator of jobs and demand-led growth in a peripheral, staple-producing economy. Growth is primarily dependent on demand and investment from outside the country. Immigration can play an auxiliary role in providing certain skills and bodies for the labour force in response to changes in the economic environment, but it cannot independently create such an environment.

If this approach is valid, then the factor that should have been uppermost in the discussions is the future trajectory of the Canadian economy. Before the government can analyse the effect of immigration on the economy, it must anticipate the evolving structure and dynamics of that economy. This was never considered.

One force which is important in this regard is the evolution of a world industrial system which is dispersing manufacturing activities to countries with economic-factor advantages and which is centralizing management and service industries. Manufacturing activities are being shifted to countries which can provide low wages and docile labour. The likelihood that Canada will be able to attract this sector is fairly small because of the relatively high wages and occupational safety standards that are in place. The types of manufacturing industries that are most likely to be attracted to a country with the characteristics of Canada are capital-intensive ones needing small numbers of skilled workers.

The international centralization of administrative corporate activities and the consequent aggregation of producer services associated with global industrialization are generating a rapid growth of population in some of the major metropolises of the industrialized world. Sassen (1988) identifies Los Angeles and New York as the two major cities adopting these roles in the United States. Toronto, and to a lesser extent, Montreal and Vancouver, are doing so in Canada. Intermediate-sized cities are tending to maintain their economic base by adopting various regional specializations and administrative functions, leading to continued urbanization in Canada. As a consequence, future labour-force growth in Canada will probably continue to be concentrated in southern Ontario and Quebec and in the lower Fraser valley of British Columbia.

Thus, an analysis of immigration effects should focus on specific parts of the country rather than the total area. The 1986 census reveals that out of every six foreign-born residents, two reside in Toronto, two others in Montreal, Vancouver, Edmonton, Calgary, or Winnipeg, and one in other metropolitan areas in southern Ontario. This leaves just one immigrant to live in any other part of the country. Since these geographic areas of attraction are also the location of sectoral areas of economic expansion, the appropriate approach to the problem is to examine the interations of immigrant labour with various service industries in the larger cities of Canada.

These sectors require large numbers of low-wage workers. Recent studies in the United States indicate that significant numbers of immigrant workers are being absorbed in this type of activity, and such may be the case in Canada. If so, they are meeting a need and consequently contributing to the overall growth of the Canadian economy. At the same time, they represent a challenge to the state to provide the necessary social services to assist them in their integration into Canadian society.

This framework for analysis and direction of immigration policy is much more appropriate than the one presently being utilized. Application of this framework may imply that the government is pursuing the correct policies, but if so, these are being carried out for the wrong reasons.

SUMMARY

Canadian immigration policy has always been tied closely to economic needs, although racist aspects in the past and humanitarian concerns in the present have attracted much attention. After World War II, the Canadian state rationalized its procedures for using immigration as an instrument to meet labour-force demands. The two were placed under a single ministerial jurisdiction, the Department of Manpower and Immigration. The Immigration Act was passed which made occupational skills the primary requisite for admission to Canada as an economic landed immigrant.

In 1984 the federal government reversed its policy of reducing immigration. It raised the quotas for immigrants in spite of high unemployment rates that threatened to persist into the next century (Anderson, 1987: B9) and in spite of long-term trends towards the replacement of workers by technology (Leontief, 1983). The rationale that was presented to justify this change in policy was threefold: to counter the long-range projection of a declining population precipitated by below-replacement fertility, to maintain an adequate dependency ratio in the face of an aging population, and to create jobs through the demand for goods generated by the addition of immigrants to the population.

None of these justifications is above question. The action of increasing population to counter future population trends was irresponsible given the existing high unemployment rates. The short-run costs of welfare and social problems far outweighed the anticipated long-term benefits. A more reasonable approach would be to adopt social programs to accommodate changes in our society which will arise from population aging and decline.

The most important justification for increasing immigration, that immigrants will create jobs for natives, is unlikely unless the requisite level of capital investment is maintained. Immigrants will compete with natives for jobs, so that if they are successful, the unemployment of natives will be extended. Even if some immigrants are able to accumulate enough capital to set up businesses, their proportions will be small, and the number of jobs created will be a small portion of those taken by the majority of the immigrants.

Immigrants have made major contributions to Canadian society in the past, and they will continue to do so. But we must not look to immigrants to solve our unemployment and economic problems. These can only be solved by reasonable policies that deal directly with the issues of unemployment and inequality. Immigrants should be admitted into the country for various reasons, but not to counteract low fertility rates and ineffective job-creation policies.

NOTES

[1]They do not address two very obvious questions: why is it necessary to reach that level of population at that point in time, and how would it be possible to bring in so many immigrants in so short a time?

[2]Once again, the report neglects to point out the considerable difficulties in the attainment of this goal which would require immigrants to be children or older workers, nor does it explain why such a goal is worthy of pursuit.

[3]Jim Hawkes, chair of the committee, states on 28 February 1985 that 'we had expert testimony that increased immigration leads to increased GNP. It is a clear-line relationship. According to our expert witnesses, these are no studies which prove, one way or the other, whether or not it costs jobs. There are specific categories where it is clear that you gain jobs' (House of Commons, 1985b: 12:39). In the House of Commons he later announces to all Members of Parliament that 'I think there is unanimous agreement in the Committee that the scientific evidence is clear cut. Increased immigration leads to increased jobs. Increased immigration does not cost Canadian jobs.' (House of Commons, 1985a, 7102). Walter McLean, minister of state for immigration, states in a meeting of the standing committee that 'we will also maintain our commitment to dispelling what remains of the lingering myth that immigrants take jobs away from Canadians' (House of Commons, 1985b: 66:8).

Members of the committee who are not Conservatives also voice support for the policy. Marchi, a Liberal, states that 'Regrettably, immigration has been perceived as contributing to unemployment. It is felt that immigrants place a heavy burden on the social service infrastructures. Yet study after study has painted a very different picture' (House of Commons, 1987a: 4487). He goes on to cite Samuel and Conyers's study (1985) of 'The Employment Effects of Immigration: A Balance Sheet Approach'. This is the only time that a specific study is cited by any of the politicians. He concludes with the statement that 'Immigration can and does increase domestic demand, worker productivity, economic growth and job creation. In addition, there is the value of the skills of immigrants, skills for which Canada does not have to pay.'

Similar arguments are presented by Minister of State for Immigration Gerry Weiner. One significant quote of his is that numbers of immigrants should be increased, 'because of course we have been able to bring forward evidence about the contribution immigrants have been making in job creation and in tax dollars they pay, and the actual benefit in the goods and services they are bringing in[to] the communities across the country' (House of Commons, 1987b: 40:21).

[4]An article in Canada's nationally distributed newspaper, *The Globe and Mail*, reported the announcement of the increase of immigration quotas to the House of Commons by Walter McLean, minister of state for immigration. McLean is quoted as saying that the new quota reflects an attempt to pursue 'the path of the more traditional and widely accepted post-war levels. The Government believes that, contrary to myth, immigrants do not take jobs away from Canadians but instead contribute positively to our economic and social development. . . . We may need to consider in the next two years, significantly higher levels of immigration if we are to sustain our population growth and economic development' (Montgomery, 1985: 1,2). As we shall note, his claim that higher levels of immigration are widely accepted is at variance with evidence collected in public polls.

Two weeks later, the same newspaper ran an article covering a speech by Andrew Witer, a Progressive Conservative member of the Standing Committee on Labour, Employment and Immigration. The opening sentence in the article is erroneous, and is attributed to Witer: 'Canada's population will fall dramatically by the year 2000 unless the immigration process is improved.' Witer is also quoted as saying 'There is a myth that immigrants take jobs away from Canadians and that they are a burden on the Canadian economy. Our research has shown us that immigrants bring good economic times to this country because an influx of immigrants leads to instant consumerism' (*Globe and Mail*, 1986: A5).

A national newsmagazine, *Maclean's*, published an issue a month later which carried the question of immigration as its main feature. Most statements attributed to government officials emphasized the importance of immigration. Gerry Weiner states that 'Immigrants create jobs and expand markets and demand', P.C. member Barbara Turner says, 'Without immigration there will be fewer workers, less revenue to government, less new business', while Jim Hawkes states that the previous government's decision to reduce immigration in 1982 was one of the biggest blunders in Canadian immigration policy (*Maclean's*, 1986: 12–15). Two weeks later, The *Globe and Mail* carried the alarmist front-page headline, 'Population to Decline: Immigration Level Raised to 125,000 for Next Year.' Gerry Weiner is quoted as saying that the increase will help to forestall population decline 'after the turn of the century'. He states that the increase 'will have tremendous potential for Canada's economic growth and help delay any effects of a population decline on Canada's future.' The article also quotes Weiner as labelling the family class of immigrants as the 'cornerstone' of immigration policy in spite of the fact noted in the article that the new policy is having the greatest impact on the economic class of immigrants (*Globe and Mail*, 1986b: 1, 2).

Several months later, the minister of state is quoted as saying, 'What I'm hearing very clearly is that they [Canadians] do understand the contributions immigrants have made. They realize how good they've been for the country.' The article goes on to point out that the minister's statement conflicts with polls showing public resistance to increased immigration and also contradicts earlier statements by the minister that the public opposed higher immigration levels (*Globe and Mail*, 1987: A9).

[5] The models are the TRACE developed by University of Toronto economists, CANDIDE and CANDIDE 2.0 of the Economic Council of Canada, the RDX2 of the Bank of Canada, a model of Informetrica of Ottawa, and the quarterly forecasting model of Data Resources of Canada.

[6] A model based on the Bank of Canada's RDX2.

[7] Except the one which justifies the increase on the grounds that it will 'smooth out' the Canadian population age profile. Shirley Seward (1988) pointed out that the age profile of immigrants contains similar distortions to that of the existing Canadian population, and that the new policy should be delayed if that was its goal.

[8] Explicitly on pages 3, 41, 49, 57, 68, 70, 96, 112, 116 (Simon, 1986).

REFERENCES

Anderson, Ronald (1987). 'Investment growth may result in full employment by 2001'. *Globe and Mail*, 17 February, B9.

Balakrishnan, T.R. (1988). 'Immigration and the changing ethnic mosaic of Canadian cities'. Report prepared for the Review of Demography and Its Implications for Economic and Social Policy. Ottawa: National Health and Welfare.

Basavarajappa, K.G., and M.V. George (1981). 'The future growth and structure of Canada's population: Results and implications of some demographic simulations in demographic trends and their impact on the Canadian labour force'. Ottawa: Department of Employment and Immigration.

Beaujot, Roderic (1986). 'Dwindling families'. *Policy Options Politiques* 7, 7: 3–7.

———— and J. Peter Rappak (1988). 'The role of immigration in changing socio-demographic structures'. Report prepared for the Review of Demography and Its Implications for Economic and Social Policy. Ottawa: National Health and Welfare.

Borjas, George J. (1986). 'The self-employment experience of immigrants'. *Journal of Human Resources* 2, 4: 485–506.

Canada, Royal Commission on Canada's Economic Prospects (1957). *Final Report*. Ottawa: Queen's Printer.

Canada Employment and Immigration Commission (1983). 'Immigration levels, 1984–1986: Federal planning considerations'. Recruitment and Selection Branch. Ottawa.

Carmichael, Edward A., Katie Macmillan, and Robert C. York (1989). *Ottawa's Next Agenda*. C.D. Howe Institute. Scarborough: Prentice-Hall Canada.

Dosi, Giovanni (1988). 'Sources, procedures, and microeconomic effects of innovation'. *Journal of Economic Literature* 26, 3: 1120-71.

Employment and Immigration Canada (1983). 'The role of immigration in determining Canada's eventual population size'. Ottawa: Supply and Services Canada.

———— (1984). 'Background paper on future immigration levels'. Ottawa: Supply and Services Canada.

———— (1986a). 'For release'. Ottawa. 86–36.

———— (1986b). 'Annual report to Parliament on future immigration levels'. Ottawa: Supply and Services Canada.

———— (1989). 'Annual report'. Ottawa: Employment and Immigration Canada.

Espenshade, Thomas J. (1978). 'Zero population growth and the economies of developed nations'. *Population and Development Review* 4, 4: 645–80.

Foot, David K. (1984). 'Macroeconomic-demographic interactions and immigration policy'. Paper presented in the annual meetings of the Canadian Population Society, Guelph.

Globe and Mail (1986a). 'More immigration lauded as beneficial to Canadian growth'. 15 September, A5.

———— (1986b).' Population to decline: Immigration level raised to 125,000 for next year'. 31 October, 1–2.

———— (1987). 'High unemployment spurs fears of immigration'. 7 March, A9.

Hawkins, Freda (1972). *Population and Immigration: Public Policy and Public Concern*. Montreal: McGill-Queen's University Press.

House of Commons (1985a). *Debates*. Ottawa: Supply and Services.

———— (1985b). 'Minutes of proceedings of the Standing Committee on Labour, Employment and Immigration'. Ottawa: Supply and Services.

———— (1987a). *Debates*. Ottawa: Supply and Services.

————(1987b). 'Minutes of proceeding of the Standing Committee on Labour, Employment and Immigration'. Ottawa: Supply and Services.

Howith, H.G. (1988). 'Immigration levels planning: The first decade'. Ottawa: Employment and Immigration Canada.

Leontief, Wassily (1983). 'Technological advance, economic growth, and the distribution of income'. *Population and Development Review* 9, 3: 403–10.

Maclean's (1986). 'Opening the doors'. 13 October, 12–21.

Montgomery, Charlotte (1985). 'Immigration quota raised by 25,000 for 1986'. *Globe and Mail*, 1 November, 1–2.

Prestowitz, Clyde V. (1988). *Trading Places: How We Allowed Japan to Take the Lead*. New York: Basic Books.

Rao, Someshwar, and Constantine Kapsalis (1982). 'Labour shortages and immigration policy'. *Canadian Public Policy* 8, 3: 379–83.

Reich, Robert B. (1989). 'The quiet path to technological preeminence'. *Scientific American* 261, 4: 41–7.

Richmond, Anthony H. (1989). 'Recent developments in Canadian immigration'. Revision of paper presented at Monash University, Melbourne, Australia, 2 August 1989.

Robertson, Matthew, and Arun S. Roy (1982). 'Reply'. *Canadian Public Policy* 8, 3: 383–7.

Samuel T.J., and T. Conyers (1985). 'The employment effects of immigration: A balance sheet approach'. Ottawa: Employment and Immigration Canada.

Sassen, Saskia (1988). *The Mobility of Labor and Capital*. New York: Cambridge University Press.

Seward, Shirley (1988). 'More and younger?' *Policy Options* 7, 1: 16–19.

Simon, Julian L. (1986). *Theory of Population and Economic Growth*. Oxford: Basil Blackwell.

Stafford, James, and Brian McMillan (1986). 'Immigration and the two schools of Canadian political economy'. Report submitted to National Health and Welfare, Ottawa.

Star, S. (1975). 'In search of a rational immigration policy'. *Canadian Public Policy* 1, 3: 328–42.

Task Force on Program Review (1985). 'Job creation, training and employment services' (Neilson report). Ottawa: Supply and Services Canada.

Taylor, Chris (1986). 'Demography and immigration in Canada: Challenge and opportunity'. Paper presented to the Fall Conference of the Association for Canadian Studies in the Netherlands.

Teitelbaum, Michael S., and Jay M. Winter (1985). *The Fear of Population Decline*. Toronto: Academic Press.

Ternowetsky, Gordon (1986). 'The impact of immigration on unemployment, poverty, inequality and state dependency: Counting the costs'. Report submitted to National Health and Welfare, Ottawa.

Timlin, Mabel (1951). *Does Canada Need More People?* Toronto: Oxford University Press.

U.S. Department of Labor (1989). *The Effects of Immigration on the U.S. Economy and Labor Market*. Washington, D.C.

Van Loon, Richard J., and Michael S. Whittington (1987). *The Canadian Political System*. Fourth ed. Toronto: McGraw-Hill Ryerson.

Wilson, Honorable Michael H. (1984). 'A new direction for Canada: An agenda for economic renewal'. Ottawa: Department of Finance.

CHAPTER 24

GROWTH AND DISTRIBUTION OF CANADA'S ETHNIC POPULATIONS, 1871–1981

Warren E. Kalbach

The Canadian government, through its periodic national censuses, has collected data for over a century which have significance for the social, economic, and political development of the country's regional populations and communities. The consistent inclusion of questions in the census dealing with the ethnic and cultural origins, and other characteristics, of individuals permanently residing in Canada has resulted in an impressive accumulation of information concerning the nature of Canadian society. It is possible not only to examine the country's social, economic, and demographic structure, but also to determine the relative contributions made to this structure through migration and the natural increase of Canada's diverse ethnic and cultural groups. The analysis of the growth and distribution of Canada's population presented in this paper focuses on two of these basic data series (country of birth and ethnic origins), which have particular importance for the understanding of the cultural fabric of Canadian society. . . .

POPULATION GROWTH

The Foreign-born Population

The growth and composition of Canada's population varied considerably following Confederation in 1867. In slightly more than a hundred years, Canada's population increased from 3.7 million to 24.3 million. The average annual rate of growth has varied in response to fluctuations in fertility rates and immigration flows. During the 1930s the growth rate was as low as 1.0 per cent compared to almost 3 per cent during the first decade of the twentieth century when heavy immigration coincided with relatively high levels of fertility. The significance of immigration for Canada, in addition to its contribution to population size, is reflected in its effects on the native-born and foreign-born proportions. However, even though Canada was initially settled by immigrants and immigration continues to be one of its major sources of growth, its contribution has never exceeded that of natural increase in the years following Confederation. Since 1871, the proportion foreign-born in Canada has never exceeded the 22 per cent level which was achieved between 1911 and 1941. The size of the foreign-born population continues to reflect the varying significance of Canada's fertility and immigration levels. With the collapse of the 'baby boom' and continuation of fairly high levels of immigration, the foreign-born proportion has increased only slightly. The history of Canada's population growth, immigration, and changes in size of its foreign-born population since 1871 is summarized in Table 1. Note that with the exception of the 1930s, the foreign-born population always increased in numbers during each decade since 1871, but its rate of growth has not always kept pace with that of the native-born.

Children of the Foreign-born

Data on the foreign-born alone do not reveal the full extent of their contribution to the growth of the national population. Children born in Canada to foreign-born residents are generally included with all native-born persons in census publications, so that it is not possible to estimate their direct contribution to total growth. Only twice in recent decades have data been collected on the nativity of the parents that would permit an examination of the generational components and their relative sizes. These data, from the 1931 and 1971 censuses, identifying three generational groupings of the population, are shown in Table 2.

It is apparent that the foreign-born make an additional and rather significant contribution to the population in the form of second-generation Canadians. In 1931, their children made up approximately one-quarter of the population, whereas the two groups combined comprised almost one-half of the total. While the numbers of first- and second-generation Canadians increased from 4.7 million in 1931 to 7.1 in 1971, their combined relative size actually declined to 33 per cent during this period. Nevertheless, in both years the total contribution of the

Table 1: Population increase, immigration, and the foreign-born population: Canada, 1871-81 to 1971-81

Decade	Population			Immigration		Foreign-born	
	Total population[1] ('000)	Percentage decade increase (%)	Annual rate of population increase (%)	Number of Immigrants ('000)	Percentage of average decade population (%)	Total foreign-born ('000)	Percentage foreign-born (%)
1871–1881	3,689	17.2	1.6	353	8.8	602	16.7
1881–1891	4,325	11.8	1.1	903	19.7	603	13.9
1891–1901	4,833	11.1	1.1	326	6.4	644	13.3
1901–1911	5,371	34.2	2.9	1,759	28.0	700	13.0
1911–1921	7,207	21.9	2.0	1,612	20.2	1,587	22.0
1921–1931	8,788	18.1	1.7	1,203	12.6	1,956	22.3
1931–1941	10,377	10.9	1.0	150	1.4	2,308	22.2
1941–1951	11,507	21.7	1.7	548	4.4	2,010	17.5
1951–1961	14,009	30.2	2.6	1,543	9.6	2,060	14.7
1961–1971	18,238	18.3	1.7	1,429	7.2	2,844	15.6
1971–1981	21,569	12.9	1.1	1,447	6.3	3,296	15.3
1981–	24,343	—	—	—	—	3,919	16.1

[1] Population at the beginning of the decade.

SOURCES: Dominion Bureau of Statistics, *Censuses of Canada, 1851 to 1961*; Statistics Canada, *1971 Census of Canada* (Ottawa: Information Canada); *1981 Census of Canada* (Ottawa: Minister of Supply and Services Canada [Cat. 95–941]), Table 1; Employment and Immigration Canada, *Immigration Statistics, 1983* (Ottawa: Minister of Supply and Services Canada, 1985a); W.E. Kalbach, *The Effect of Immigration on Population, The Canadian Immigration and Population Study* (Department of Manpower and Immigration, Ottawa: Information Canada, 1974), Tables 1.1 and 2.6.

Table 2: Population by generations: Canada, 1931, 1971, and 1981

Generation[1]	1931		1971		1981	
	N	%	N	%	N[3]	%
Foreign-born						
1st generation	2,234,600	21.6	3,177,200	14.7	3,919,252	16.1
Native-born	8,125,100	78.4	18,391,100	85.3	20,423,929	83.9
2nd generation	2,509,500	24.2	3,986,700	18.5	—	—
3rd[2] generation	5,615,600	54.2	14,404,400	66.8	—	—
Total	10,359,700	100.0	21,568,300	100.0	24,343,181	100.0

[1] Generations are defined as follows: 1st generation are the foreign-born with foreign-born parents; 2nd generation are the native-born with one or both parents foreign-born; 3rd and subsequent generations are the native-born with native-born parents. The foreign-born also include some who were born outside Canada to native-born parents, of which there were 69,500 in 1931, 118,300 in 1971, and approximately 40,000 in 1981. The question for 'birthplace of parents' was not included in the 1981 Census.

[2] The 1931 total excludes 17,136 persons for whom nativity of parents was not stated.

[3] Estimates of numbers of foreign- and native-born based on the Canada total of 24,431,181 from the 100% enumeration census schedule.

SOURCES: Dominion Bureau of Statistics, *1931 Census of Canada* (Ottawa: Queen's Printer), Vol. III, Table 27, and Vol. IV, Table 15; Statistics Canada, *1971 Census of Canada*, Bulletin 1.3–6 (Ottawa: Information Canada, 1974), Table 46; *1981 Census of Canada*, Cat. 95–941 (Vol. 3—Profile Series B, 1983), Table 1.

foreign-born to the nation's population was actually more than twice as much as it would have been had their children not been taken into consideration. Unfortunately, the question on nativity of parents was dropped from the 1981 census so that no estimate of the change in their proportionate share of the total population can be made for the 1971–81 decade. However, in view of the slight increase in the proportion foreign-born in Canada during this period, it is possible that the proportion second-generation also increased slightly.

Ethnic Populations[1]

The French were the first to establish a foothold in the New World now called Canada. Even after the British secured political control after the Seven Years' War, the majority of the population was still French-speaking. Not until the emigration of British Empire Loyalists from the American colonies after the American Revolution were the British able to achieve numerical superiority in addition to the political control they had won earlier. By the time of Confederation, just under two-thirds, or 60.5 per cent, of the population were of British origins, while almost one-third, or 31.3 per cent, were French. The remaining population was predominantly German, with some Dutch and a scattering of Scandinavians, Russians, and Italians.

The British have managed to maintain their numerical dominance throughout the century; yet, on the other hand, the population of French origin has continued to be the single largest homogeneous cultural group in Canada. On only two occasions have the numbers of French been exceeded by another relatively homogeneous group. In 1921, and again in 1971, the English outnumbered the French. But, in 1981 changed census procedures permitted multiple ethnic responses, making it impossible to develop any reliable estimates that would be comparable with those based on earlier censuses. Of those reporting a single ethnic origin, 6,439,000 were reported to be of French origin, compared to 6,109,000 of English origin. Determining which of the two was actually the largest at the time of the 1981 census, in terms comparable to estimates from earlier censuses, would depend upon the procedures used to allocate those reporting multiple origins. However inconvenient the loss of comparability may be for the analysis of historical trends, the information on multiple origins collected by the 1981 census will provide new insights into the changing nature of Canadian society. In any event, the inherent difficulties in obtaining both valid and reliable data on ethnic origins of individuals from censuses of populations make it advisable to use considerable caution in the interpretation of these data.[2]

The more detailed ethnic composition of the British Isles origin group, shown in Table 3, underscores the greater heterogeneity of the British *vis-à-vis* the French. According to these data, the Irish tended to have numerical superiority over the English until 1901. But, after the heavy influx of immigrants during the early twentieth century, they were exceeded by both the English and the Scottish. Perhaps the other most significant aspect of this particular period of Canadian history was the rising prominence of the 'other' ethnic populations in the Canadian mosaic. In 1871, the British accounted for about two-thirds of the population. Since that time, their proportion has declined rather consistently over the years to about 40 per cent in 1981. The French component of the population was much more stable during this period; nevertheless, it also declined from about 31 per cent in 1871 to approximately 27 per cent in 1981. All of the other ethnic populations combined increased from a negligible 8 per cent to a third of the total population.

The predominance of the Germans and Dutch in this residual group of 'other' ethnic populations prior to the 1900s has already been mentioned. With the opening of the prairies for settlement, and the events in Europe leading up to the First World War and its aftermath, the numbers of Eastern and Southern Europeans in the Canadian population began to increase significantly. However, of the two previously mentioned, only the Germans have consistently maintained their relative numerical position, and are still the largest ethnic origin population in Canada after the British and the French.

In 1911, the Ukrainians, Scandinavians, and Dutch were the next largest ethnic populations after the Germans. After World War II and the resumption of immigration, further changes in their relative sizes occurred. Note in Table 3 that the Dutch surpassed the Scandinavians between 1941 and 1961, while the Italian-origin population exceeded the Ukrainians between 1961 and 1971.

Because changes in procedures for the 1981 census of Canada affected the comparability of its data with earlier censuses, the most recent information on Canada's ethnic populations has been presented separately in Table 4. These data clearly show that a number of Asian and other non-European ethnic populations

Table 3: Population[1] of British Isles, French, and other selected origins: Canada, selected years, 1871–1971

Ethnic group	1871[2]	1881	1901	1921	1941	1961	1971
Total[3]	3,486	4,325	5,371	8,788	11,507	18,238	21,568
British Isles	2,111	2,549	3,063	4,869	5,716	7,997	9,624
English	706	881	1,261	2,545	2,968	4,195	6,246
Irish	846	957	989	1,108	1,268	1,753	1,581
Scottish	550	700	800	1,174	1,404	1,902	1,720
Other	8	10	13	42	76	146	86
French	1,083	1,299	1,649	2,453	3,483	5,540	6,180
Other European	240	299	458	1,247	2,044	4,117	4,960
Austrian, n.o.s.	—	—	11	108	38	107	42
Belgian	—	—	3	20	30	61	51
Czech and Slovak	—	—	—	9	43	73	82
Finnish[4]	—	—	3	21	42	59	59
German	203	254	311	295	465	1,050	1,317
Greek	—	—	—	6	12	56	124
Hungarian[5]	—	—	2	13	55	126	132
Italian	1	2	11	67	113	450	731
Jewish	—	1	16	126	170	173	297
Lithuanian	—	—	—	2	8	28	25
Netherlands	30	30	34	118	213	430	426
Polish	—	—	6	53	167	324	316
Romanian[6]	—	—	—	13	25	44	27
Russian[7]	1	1	20	100	84	119	64
Scandinavian	2	5	31	167	245	387	385
Ukrainian	—	—	6	107	306	473	581
Yugoslav	—	—	—	4	21	69	105
Other	4	6	5	18	10	88	195
Asiatic	—	4	24	66	74	122	286
Chinese	—	4	17	40	35	58	119
Japanese	—	—	5	16	23	29	37
Other	—	—	2	10	16	34	129
Other[8]	52	174	177	153	190	463	519
Native people	—	—	—	114	126	220	313
Blacks	—	—	—	18	22	32	34
Other	—	—	—	21	42	210	172

[1] Numbers rounded to the nearest 1,000.
[2] Four original provinces only.
[3] Excludes Newfoundland prior to 1951.
[4] Includes Estonian prior to 1951.
[5] Includes Lithuanian and Moravian in 1901 and 1911.
[6] Includes Bulgarian in 1901 and 1911.
[7] Includes Finnish and Polish in 1871 and 1881.
[8] Includes 'not stated' prior to 1971. In 1971 'not stated' cases were computer assigned.

SOURCES: Dominion Bureau of Statistics, *1961 Census of Canada*, Bulletin 7:1–6 (Ottawa: The Queen's Printer, 1966), Table 1 and Table I; Statistics Canada, *1971 Census of Canada*, Bulletin 1.3–2 (Ottawa: Information Canada, 1973), Table 1; D. Kubat and D. Thornton, *A Statistical Profile of Canadian Society* (Toronto: McGraw-Hill Ryerson, 1974), Table f–10.

Table 4: Population by selected ethnic origins[1]: Canada, 1981

Ethnic group	Number
British	9,674,245
French	9,439,100
Multiple (British and French)	1,522,075
Other European	
Austrian	40,630
Balkan	129,075
Baltic	50,300
Belgian and Luxembourg	43,000
Czech and Slovak	67,695
Dutch	408,240
Finnish	52,315
German	1,142,365
Greek	154,365
Magyar	116,390
Italian	747,970
Jewish	264,025
Polish	254,485
Portuguese	188,105
Romanian	22,485
Russian	49,435
Scandinavian	282,795
Spanish	53,540
Swiss	29,805
Ukrainian	529,615
Asian/African	
African	45,215
Armenian	21,155
Asian Arab	60,140
Chinese	289,245
Indo-Chinese	43,725
Indo-Pakistani	121,445
Japanese	40,995
North African Arab	10,545
Pacific Island	155,290
West Asian	10,055
Other	
Latin American	117,555
Native People	413,380
Other single origins	176,160
Other multiple origins[2]	316,540
Total population[3]	24,083,500

NOTE: Totals may not equal the sum of components due to rounding.

[1] The 1981 Census is the first to accept more than one ethnic origin for an individual. Therefore, this table includes counts of single and multiple origins.

[2] Includes multiple origins of European, Jewish, and other origins not included elsewhere and multiple origins of Native People and British, French, European, Jewish, or Other Origins.

[3] Excludes inmates.

SOURCE: *1981 Census of Canada.*

surpassed many of the older European ethnic populations. The most notable case is the population of Chinese origin. In addition, and for the first time, the census has provided an estimate of the extent of ethnic mixing that has occurred in Canadian society through intermarriage. The proportion reporting multiple origins at the time of the 1981 census was approximately 8 per cent, with combinations of British and French with each other as well as others comprising the largest portion of this group. This is not unexpected considering that the British and French have been numerically and culturally dominant for so much of Canada's history.

Components of Population Change

Fertility, Immigration, and Population Growth   The actual levels of fertility for the decades following Confederation, and through the first twenty years of the twentieth century, are still subject to considerable debate. Nevertheless, whichever estimates are taken as most correct, it is clear that births have had, and continue to have, greater significance for population growth in Canada than immigration. For the decade of heaviest immigration, i.e., 1901–11, births exceeded immigrants by over 380,000. In fact, for every decade since Confederation, fertility measured in numbers of births has consistently exceeded the reported numbers of immigrants. . . . Between 1901 and 1931, and for the four decades following 1941, additions to the population through natural increase were supplemented by positive net migration. For the first three decades of Confederation, and the Depression decade of 1931–41, the full contribution of natural increase to Canada's growth was inhibited by a negative net migration. The relative contribution made by natural increase and net migration has obviously varied significantly since Confederation. For the two 'peak' growth periods, i.e., 1901–11 and 1951–61, net migration accounted for 44 per cent of the former decade's growth, but only 26 per cent of the latter baby-boom decade's increase. The post-war surge in immigration was clearly overshadowed by the excess of births over deaths during the baby-boom years.

The effective contribution to population growth by births is mitigated by the number of deaths; and, similarly, the direct effects of arriving immigrants are reduced in proportion to the number of emigrants who leave the country. While the later component is extremely difficult to estimate accurately, data from the census, immigration records, and vital statistics show that the net gain from natural increase during the 1901–11 decade exceeded net immigration by at least 220,000. Estimates for other decades consistently show the greater contribution of natural increase over net immigration. For certain single years, the significance of net immigration has occasionally increased dramatically, but for the years following the Second World War, its net effect never reached 50 per cent of the annual population increase. In 1951, an estimated net immigration of 184,000 accounted for 41 per cent of the population increase for that year. The highest net immigration, which occurred in 1956, and amounted to 200,000, contributed somewhat less, or 38 per cent, to that year's growth; and, in 1966, an estimated

131,000 net immigrants contributed 36 per cent of that year's increase. At no time during the post-war period did net immigration ever achieve the distinction of contributing the major share of the country's growth.[3]

Fertility, Immigration, and Ethnic Composition   As fertility and immigration both contribute to numerical changes in the population, they can also affect its ethnic composition. Ethnic differences in fertility can cause the native-born component of some groups to increase more rapidly than others, while shifts in the source countries for immigrants will affect the ethnic composition of the foreign-born whether levels of immigration are rising or falling. Of the two, differences in fertility would most likely produce the greatest effects on the ethnic composition of the native-born population. While changes in the character of the immigrant stream can produce significant shifts in the ethnic composition of the foreign-born in a relatively short period of time, the effects are greatly reduced when the foreign-born are combined with the native-born population, because of their relatively small size compared to the latter population. Similarly, whatever the fertility differentials might be among the foreign-born by ethnic origins, the impact of the annual cohorts of births contributed to the native-born population by the foreign-born would be relatively slight.

It is a well-established fact that the French have maintained their relative position in Canada through high fertility rather than through dependence upon immigration, as has been the case for the British-origins group. Data collected as recently as 1981 show that the fertility of married women is still generally higher for those of French origin than those belonging to most other ethnic groups. The few exceptions are to be found among younger married women under 25 years of age, and women from some Protestant groups (e.g., Hutterites, Mennonites, Mormons, etc.).[4]

Following the post-war baby boom, fertility levels resumed their downward trend for the nation as a whole; rates have been falling faster in Quebec than elsewhere since 1957. By 1968, Quebec had the lowest crude birth rate of any province in Canada. In addition, Quebec was the only province whose gross reproduction rate (GRR) had fallen below 1.0 by 1970, a level somewhat below that required for population replacement.[5] By 1981, the fertility of French-Canadian women still in their childbearing years was close to the lowest levels reported for any ethnic population.[6]

For obvious reasons, these trends have caused alarm among Quebec politicians and others concerned with the province's future. To the extent that Quebec can neither reverse the present trend in fertility nor succeed in attracting French-speaking immigrants, it will have to pursue more drastic measures to preserve the French-Canadian culture and language. Concerns about Quebec's demographic future are now being expressed in the form of legislation aimed at restricting access to English-language schools as well as restricting the use of English throughout the province.[7]

Changes in the source countries of arriving immigrants have been the primary reason for the continuing decline in the proportion of the British-origin popula-

Table 5a: Origins of immigrants arriving in Canada, 1926–66: Immigration by ethnic-origin groups, 1926–45, 1946–55, and 1956–66

Ethnic-origin group	1926–45	1946–55	1955–66
British Isles	47.8	34.1	32.9
Northwestern European	24.4	30.2	20.7
Central and East European	19.1	15.1	7.7
Southeastern and South European	4.5	15.3	29.9
Jewish	3.4	3.5	2.2
Asian and other origins	0.8	1.7	6.5
Totals: %	100.0	100.0	100.0
N	950,944	1,222,318	1,476,444

SOURCES: Department of Manpower and Immigration, *Annual Immigration Reports*; Royal Commission on Bilingualism and Biculturalism, *The Cultural Contribution of the Other Ethnic Groups, Book IV* (Ottawa: Queen's Printer, 1970), Table A-1; and, W.E. Kalbach, *The Effect of Immigration on Population, The Immigration and Population Study* (Department of Manpower and Immigration, Ottawa: Information Canada, 1974), Table 2.1.

tion in Canada following Confederation. The arrival of large numbers of immigrants from other Western and Northern European countries had never been regarded as a problem by those of British origins because of their general cultural similarity. However, the influx of 'new' immigrants from Central, Eastern, and Southern Europe during the early 1900s became the cause of growing concern among the 'old' immigrants, who felt that immigration from non-traditional source areas would have deleterious effects on the established Canadian way of life.

Between 1926 and 1966, the proportion of immigrants of northern and western European origins, including British, declined significantly, as did the proportion of Central and Eastern European origins. In contrast, the relative numbers of immigrants of Southern and Southeastern European origins increased during this period, especially after World War II. While the latter group comprised only 4.5 per cent of all immigrants coming to Canada between 1926 and 1946, their proportion jumped to 15 per cent during the immediate post-war period, and then doubled to 30 per cent for the 1956–66 period. Immigrants of Asian origins, while still relatively small in numbers, also showed significant increases. From less than 1 per cent before the war, they increased to 6.5 per cent during this same period. These data are summarized in Table 5a.

Ethnic-origin data were not collected after 1966, but parallel trends can be seen in data for 'country of last permanent residence' which were also collected during the same post-war years, and are still collected by the Department of Employment and Immigration. These data, presented in Table 5b for the fifteen-year period 1966–80, clearly show the rapidly changing character of Canada's most recent immigrants.

The proportions of arriving immigrants from the British Isles and other Northern and Western European countries have continued to show significant declines.

Table 5b: Origins of immigrants arriving in Canada, 1966–80: Immigration by last country of permanent residence, 1966–70, 1971–75, and 1976–80

Country of last permanent residence	1966–70	1971–75	1976–80
Britain and Republic of Ireland	25.2	16.4	14.1
United States of America	11.4	14.3	9.9
Northern and Western Europe	15.8	6.8	6.8
Central and Eastern Europe	1.8	1.4	2.3
Southern and Southeastern Europe	22.8	15.6	8.8
Israel	0.8	0.6	0.9
Australia and Europe, n.o.s.	2.6	1.7	1.4
Asia			
South, S.E., and East Asia	9.4	20.7	31.7
Middle East and North Africa	2.1	2.3	4.8
All others	8.1	20.2	19.3
Totals: %	100.0	100.0	100.0
N	910,837	834,452	605,869

SOURCES: Canada Manpower and Immigration, *Immigration Statistics*, for years 1966–1976; Employment and Immigration Canada, *Immigration Statistics*, for years 1977–1980 (Ottawa: Minister of Supplies and Services).

While those from Southeastern and Southern Europe had shown spectacular gains up to the 1955–66 period, their proportion of immigrant arrivals declined rapidly since then. Probably the most significant of these recent changes has been the spectacular increase in the proportions of immigrants coming from Asian and other non-European countries. As recently as the 1966–70 period, only 19.6 per cent of arriving immigrants had come from non-European source countries. As the data in Table 5b clearly show, this proportion increased dramatically to 43.2 per cent during the 1971–75 period, and to over half, or 56 per cent, for 1976–80.

A better picture of the changing ethnic mix of arriving immigrants can be obtained by examining the lists of leading source countries presented in Table 6. The shift to non-European source countries is very clear. The effects of these changes on the ethnic composition of the foreign-born population will, of course, be dependent on variations in immigration levels. For the years shown, the small number of arriving immigrants in 1984 would have produced the least effect, while the 1951 immigration of close to 200,000 would have had a considerably greater impact. Of course, a continuation of the shift to non-European source countries, in the long run, will significantly alter the character of both the first and second generations of Canadians.

Much of the shift to non-European source countries in recent decades, apparent in Tables 5 and 6, can be attributed to the elimination of restrictions based on racial and ethnic origins and to the contrasts in economic conditions which had developed between the traditional source countries and many of the Third World countries, *vis-à-vis* the state of the Canadian economy. Faced with a commitment

Table 6: The leading source countries of immigrants: Selected years

1951	1960	1968	1976	1984
Britain	Italy	Britain	Britain	Vietnam
Germany	Britain	United States	United States	Hong Kong
Italy	United States	Italy	Hong Kong	United States
Netherlands	Germany	Germany	Jamaica	India
Poland	Netherlands	Hong Kong	Lebanon	Britain
France	Portugal	France	India	Poland
United States	Greece	Austria	Philippines	Philippines
Belgium	France	Greece	Portugal	El Salvador
Yugoslavia	Poland	Portugal	Italy	Jamaica
Denmark	Austria	Yugoslavia	Guyana	China

SOURCES: Department of Manpower and Immigration, *The Immigration Program, Vol. 2, A Report of the Canadian Immigration and Population Study* (Ottawa: Information Canada, 1974), Table 3.3, p. 84; *1976 Immigration Statistics*, Table 3; and Employment and Immigration Canada, *Annual Report to Parliament on Future Immigration Levels, 1985* (Ottawa: Minister of Supply and Services Canada, 1985b), Statistical Appendix.

to maintain a non-discriminatory policy during a period of rising demand for emigration in many non-European countries, the government was compelled to review and revise its policies and regulations in order to develop a more objective method of regulating immigration in relation to its national requirements.

The government's Green Paper on immigration and population in 1974 provided the arguments and the rationale for the various regulations made by the government under the authority of the old 1952 Immigration Act, including the introduction of the more objective 'point' system in 1967 for determining eligibility for admission of unsponsored or independent workers.[8] The Green Paper also led to the overhauling of the existing immigration laws and regulations and ultimately to the introduction of a new Immigration Act in 1976. The new act explicitly prohibits discrimination on the grounds of race, national or ethnic origin, colour, religion, or sex. It emphasizes the importance of family reunification, fulfilment of international obligations regarding refugees and displaced persons, and the need to tailor the selection of immigrants to the country's economic needs while fulfilling appropriate demographic goals established through consultation with the provinces and other appropriate parties.[9]

The Immigration Act of 1976 established, for the first time in Canada, the basis for a general quota system that would permit better control over the numbers of immigrants admitted to Canada. The new act requires the government to lay before Parliament, prior to each calendar year, its report specifying the numbers of immigrants it 'deems it appropriate to admit' and 'the manner in which demographic considerations have been taken into account in determining that number'.[10] The admission of unsponsored or independent workers was greatly restricted during the period following the enactment of the new Immigration Act as the economy remained depressed and the country continued to be plagued by high levels of unemployment. Continuing annual reviews of immigration by the new Conservative government generally have been consistent with the 'short-term' goals of their predecessors which were primarily concerned with restricting admissions of workers during periods of high unemployment. However, the need to justify their recommended annual intake of immigrants in terms of demographic considerations has succeeded in bringing new problems to the attention of the government that would be a consequence of permitting only minimal immigration while fertility levels in Canada continue at below-replacement levels. The nature of these problems would seem to be sufficiently serious to warrant ameliorative action on the part of government. The fact that the Minister of Immigration recommended increases in immigration levels for 1986 and 1987, albeit modest ones, represents a major change in immigration policy with significant consequences for both the volume and character of future immigration to Canada.

POPULATION DISTRIBUTION

. . .

Ethnic Populations

The population of French descent in Canada has compensated, in part, for its smaller size by maintaining a singularly high degree of regional concentration. Had they been more evenly distributed throughout Canada, they would not have been able to achieve the numerical dominance in any one region that they have in Quebec today. In 1981, slightly more than three-fourths of Canada's population of French origin lived in Quebec, where they comprised 80 per cent of the province's population. Those of British origin, more generally dispersed, numerically dominated the French in every province outside of Quebec. Yet, only in Nova Scotia, Prince Edward Island, and Newfoundland could one find proportions of British nearly as high, or higher, than the concentration of French in Quebec. Of these, only Newfoundland, could be considered to be more British than Quebec is French. In 1821, 92 per cent reported British origins only, while another 2.6 per cent reported multiple British and Other origins. Only 2.7 per cent were of French origin, while the remaining 2.5 per cent were of other origins. The other European origins have tended to be more highly concentrated in the provinces west of Ontario, with the notable exception of the Italians and Jews. The former are highly concentrated in Ontario, while the latter are found in disproportionately greater numbers in Quebec, Ontario, and Manitoba. Asians, whether considering the combined group as a whole, or the Chinese separately, are most concentrated in British Columbia, but are also found in above-average numbers in Alberta and Ontario.

Very little detail was provided on the ethnic composition of the population in 1901. Nevertheless, the data in Table 7 still permit an examination of changes in the relative concentrations of the three major groupings of ethnic origins that

Table 7: Percentage composition of the population by ethnic origins for province of residence, Canada, 1901 and 1981

Ethnic origin	Total	Nfld.	PEI	NS	NB	Que.	Ont.	Man.	Sask.	Alta.	BC	Yukon	NWT
1901													
British	57.0	..	85.1	78.1	71.7	17.6	79.3	64.4	43.9	47.8	59.6	39.2	0.5
French	30.7	..	13.4	9.8	24.2	80.2	7.3	6.3	2.9	6.2	2.6	6.5	0.2
Other	12.3	..	1.5	12.1	4.1	2.2	13.4	29.3	53.2	46.0	37.8	54.3	99.3
Total	100.0	100.0	100.0	100.0	100.0	100.0	100.0	100.0	100.0	100.0	100.0	100.0	100.0
1981													
British	40.2	92.2	77.0	72.5	53.5	7.7	52.6	36.9	38.3	43.5	51.0	43.6	22.4
French	26.7	2.7	12.2	8.5	36.4	80.2	7.7	7.3	4.9	5.1	3.4	4.7	3.9
Multiple (Br. & Fr.)	6.3	2.6	6.9	7.9	5.5	1.8	7.9	7.1	7.8	9.6	9.1	10.7	4.4
Other European													
German	4.7	0.3	0.7	3.9	0.9	0.5	4.4	10.7	16.9	10.5	6.9	5.6	2.5
Dutch	1.7	0.1	1.1	1.6	0.6	0.1	2.2	3.3	1.8	2.9	2.7	1.7	0.7
Scandinavian	1.2	0.1	0.2	0.3	0.3	0.1	0.5	2.5	4.5	3.5	3.1	3.2	1.3
Polish	1.1	--	0.1	0.3	0.1	0.3	1.4	2.8	1.9	1.7	0.9	0.8	0.5
Russian	0.2	--	--	--	--	--	0.1	0.4	0.7	0.3	0.7	0.2	0.2
Ukrainian	2.2	--	0.1	0.2	0.1	0.2	1.6	9.8	8.0	6.2	2.3	2.8	1.3
Italian	3.1	0.1	0.4	0.2	2.6	5.7	0.9	0.3	1.2	1.2	1.9	0.4	0.5
Portuguese	0.8	--	--	0.1	--	0.4	1.5	0.8	0.1	0.3	0.6	--	0.1
Jewish	1.1	0.1	0.1	0.2	0.1	1.4	1.5	1.5	0.2	0.4	0.5	0.1	0.1
Multiple (Eur. & Other)	1.0	0.1	0.1	0.6	0.2	0.2	1.0	2.3	2.5	2.2	1.5	1.7	0.7
Asiatic	2.5	0.3	0.2	0.4	0.2	0.6	3.1	2.5	1.0	3.2	3.7	1.4	0.7
Other													
Black[1]	0.1	--	--	0.3	--	0.1	0.2	0.1	--	0.1	0.1	--	--
Latin American	0.5	--	--	0.1	--	0.4	0.9	0.4	0.1	0.3	0.2	--	0.1
Native people	1.7	0.6	0.4	0.8	0.7	0.7	0.1	5.9	5.7	2.7	2.4	14.8	55.6
Mult. (Native & Other)	0.3	0.2	0.2	0.2	0.1	0.1	0.3	0.6	0.5	0.5	0.7	2.7	2.4
All other	4.6	0.6	0.7	1.8	0.9	2.6	6.5	4.2	4.8	5.7	5.3	5.3	2.6
Total	100.0	100.0	100.0	100.0	100.0	100.0	100.0	100.0	100.0	100.0	100.0	100.0	100.0

-- Less than 0.05   - Nil or zero   .. Figures not available

[1] Includes African Black, Canadian Black, and Other Black.

SOURCES: Statistics Canada, 1981 Census of Canada, Cat. 92-911 (Ottawa: Minister of Supply and Services, February 1984), Table 1; Dominion Bureau of Statistics, 1961 Census of Canada, Bulletin 7:1-6 (Ottawa: Queen's Printer, 1966), Tables 1, 2, 3.

have occurred over a period of eighty years as a result of differential rates of natural increase and the net effects of both internal and international migration. The net effects of the population dynamics during this period, while not dramatic, have been an increase in the relative concentration of those of French origin in New Brunswick and Quebec, as well as for the population of British origins in both the Atlantic provinces and the three most western provinces. For the remaining combined population of all other origins, its degree of relative concentration declined significantly in the western provinces, and to a lesser extent in several of the Atlantic provinces while increasing in Ontario, Quebec, and in Prince Edward Island. However, with respect to the latter two provinces, the 'other' origins are still under-represented to a considerable degree. Another manifestation of these long-term trends is the increasing ethnic diversity which has characterized all of the provinces' populations, except Quebec, during the most recent intercensal decade, 1971–1981.

Overall, there do not seem to be any startling shifts in the relative concentrations of the major ethnic-origin groups in Canada's major regions. The basic pattern of the geographical ethnic mosaic would seem to have been laid down fairly early in Canada's history by the two founding groups, and their relatively large size would tend to resist the effects of rapid shifts caused by recent migrants responding to the increased opportunities found in Canada's largest metropolitan centres. In the long run, however, the tendency for more rapid industrial and economic development to occur in central Canada and in the far west (and north) can be expected to continue to channel the more recent immigrants, as well as internal migrants of differing origins, into these areas. If this is in fact the case, Canada's ethnic patterns will, in time, shift accordingly.

. . .

NOTES

[1] Data on ethnic populations in this paper are based on the 'ethnic origin' question included in the Canadian Census. The data are not necessarily indicative of the individual's ethnic identity or the strength of his feelings about his identity or identification with an ethnic community. Prior to the 1981 Census of Canada, the census attempted to establish the respondent's ethnic or cultural background, by asking 'to which ethnic or cultural group do you, or your ancestor, on the male side belong on first coming to this continent?' The 1981 census dropped the reference to 'the male side' and left it up to the respondent to choose the appropriate side in cases of ethnic intermarriage. Also, for the first time, the census accepted 'multiple origin' responses and published data for the most frequently occurring combinations.

[2] The problems associated with the collection and interpretation of ethnic-origin data have long been recognized. Unexplained deviations from long-term trends or other apparent anomalies in the data should alert the reader, or user, of ethnic-origin or other census data to possible problems. For example, in Table 3, the rather large increase in the population

of Jewish origins between 1961 and 1971 is largely the result of changes in the 1971 Census editing procedures. Specifically, individuals who reported their religion as Jewish were automatically included in the Jewish ethnic-origin population regardless of the origin reported. Other changes in the census schedules and enumeration procedures may partly account for the larger than expected increase in numbers of English origin and declines in the other British Isles origin groups. More recently, in the 1981 Census of Canada, the decision to permit multiple responses to the ethnic origin question, in addition to dropping the reference to 'the male side' of the respondent's ancestry, has seriously affected the comparability of the 1981 ethnic origin data with respect to earlier censuses. For this reason, and because of the increasing number of immigrants coming from non-European countries, the 1981 census data are presented separately in Table 4, rather than inviting invalid comparisons for some groups by including them in the historical series presented in Table 3. These and other problems are discussed in the 'Introduction' to Volume 1, Part 3, of the *1971 Census of Canada*; and W.O. Boxhill, *A User's Guide to 1981 Census Data on Ethnic Origins*, Statistics Canada, Cat. 99–949 Occasional (Ottawa: Minister of Supply and Services, 1986).

[3] W.E. Kalbach, *The Effect of Immigration on Population*, The Canadian Immigration and Population Study (Department of Manpower and Immigration, Ottawa: Information Canada, 1974), Table 3.2; and, Employment and Immigration Canada, *1983 Immigration Statistics* (Ottawa: Minister of Supply and Services Canada, 1985a), Table 1.

[4] Jacques Henripin, *Trends and Factors of Fertility in Canada*, 1961 Census Monograph (Ottawa: Information Canada, 1972), Table 6.11; Statistics Canada, *1981 Census of Canada*, Cat. 92–906 (Ottawa: Minister of Supply and Services Canada, 1983), Tables 10 and 11.

[5] Statistics Canada, *Vital Statistics, 1971*, Volume 1 (Ottawa: Information Canada, 1974), Tables 5 and 10.

[6] Statistics Canada, *1981 Census of Canada*, Cat. 92–906, Table 10.

[7] See Quebec's Bill 101 for legislation designed to limit access to schooling in the English language for children with non-English mother tongues.

[8] Department of Manpower and Immigration, *The Green Paper on Immigration*, Volumes I–IV, Canadian Immigration and Population Study (Ottawa: Information Canada, 1974).

[9] Canada, House of Commons, Bill C–24, Part I, Section 3, 2nd Session, Thirtieth Parliament, 25–26 Elizabeth II, 1976–77.

[10] Canada, Bill C–24, Part I–pt.7.

[11] Statistics Canada, *1981 Census of Canada*, Cat. 92–913 (Ottawa: Minister of Supply and Services, 1984), Tables 2A and 2B.

PART SEVEN

URBANIZATION

AND

POPULATION

ECOLOGY

GENERAL TRENDS IN URBANIZATION

Historically, rapid increases in population growth have been accompanied by urbanization. These two processes are interrelated. In the early phases of Canada's evolution as a nation, population growth was largely a rural phenomenon, as most people lived on farms; relatively few people resided in large urban areas. However, by the early 1920s the proportion of Canada's population living in urban localities had grown to 48 per cent and the number of cities with more than 100,000 population had increased to six.

After the Depression and war years, Canada witnessed a sharp rise in urban growth. The baby boom, the large wave of new immigrants to Canada, and the prospering economy contributed to an urban boom between 1945 and 1964. The rural population experienced depopulation through the large outflow of migrants towards the metropolitan centres. As a result of these demographic and economic processes, the Canadian population became increasingly concentrated in metropolitan areas, and small towns went into decline.

During this period, the inner city also experienced a decline in population that reflected the so-called 'flight to suburbia', a trend to which the growth of industry on the outer fringes of the city also contributed. Whereas only 54 per cent of Canadians lived in urban centres in 1941, 71 per cent were classified as urban in 1961. In fact, by the early 1960s, nearly 8 million people, out of a total of just over 18 million, lived in 18 urban places with populations of 100,000 or more. Both Montreal and Toronto had, by this time, reached the one million mark in their populations.

The next phase of urban change, from the mid-1960s to the early 1980s, may be characterized as one of deconcentration and decline. Key demographic factors in this development were the baby bust and the lower numbers of international immigrants to Canada. On the economic front, Canada went through a number of recessions accompanied by declines in the economies of central Canada (Ontario and Quebec) in the 1970s. At the same time, however, the resource-based economies of the western provinces (Alberta and British Columbia) were experiencing a boom, and therefore attracted many immigrants from central and eastern Canada. Thus while urban centres in the east were undergoing a slow-down in growth, cities such as Calgary and Edmonton were growing rapidly.

Unexpectedly, this period of urban change saw a more rapid growth of small and medium-sized centres at the expense of the larger metropolitan areas. Other industrialized countries were experiencing a similar phenomenon, which has been labelled 'counterurbanization' or 'deurbanization'. The extent of this phenomenon was relatively minor in Canada in comparison to other countries such as the United States, where it represented a significant shift from the patterns established earlier in history.

During the recession of 1980–82, there was very little growth in urbanization. Fertility had been low for some time, and immigration slowed down in response to the economic downturn. The economies of the western provinces were on the decline and many people moved to the urban areas of central Canada, causing another reversal in the concentration of growth in the urban population. With the economic recovery of 1983 in Ontario, internal migration was largely directed towards large cities like Toronto.

Generally, the post-1981 period has been characterized by a stable slow growth in population. The level of urbanization had reached 76 per cent by 1981 and has remained relatively constant since then. Recently, however, a modest metropolitan revival has been evident at the expense of smaller towns in the urban system of Canada. If there ever was a counterurbanization process in the 1970s, it now appears to have ended, and metropolitan areas are again growing faster than smaller places in the urban hierarchy.

Within the city, downtown growth has accelerated. Many cities have invested in the revitalization of the centre, as increasing numbers of people 'return' from the suburbs to establish permanent residence in the core. This recent process, sometimes referred to as 'gentrification', is part of a larger trend of increased socio-cultural heterogeneity or diversification of the social character of cities. Socio-economic differences in housing are becoming more noticeable in the city; high-rise housing is constructed next to aging neighbourhoods, and upscale housing catering to the upwardly mobile may exist next to downscale residential areas. The gentrification process and the concentration of new-wave immigrants in certain neighbourhoods also contribute to the social and cultural diversity of the contemporary Canadian city. At the same time, the increasing numbers of homeless people and working poor further accentuate the differentiation along socio-economic lines.

In this final section Stone provides an overview of Canadian urbanization in the last 110 years. Placing the Canadian experience in the broader context of world urbanization, he points out that in historical perspective the spread of urban living among the world's peoples is quite recent. Until the beginning of the nineteenth century the concentration of the world population in urban centres reached no more than 5 per cent, whereas in the 160 years from 1800 to 1960 this figure had risen to 25 per cent. Cities of 1,000,000 people or more have existed mainly since the eighteenth century.

According to Stone, in 1666, when the first census of New France was taken there existed no centre of population concentration in excess of 1,000 people. By the first quarter of the nineteenth century, New France had two cities of over 20,000 (Montreal and Quebec), containing in 1825 more than 5 per cent of the colonial population of British North America, which means that during this period Canada was one of the most urbanized regions in the world. The decade after Confederation (1867) represented this nation's 'take-off' towards higher levels of urbanization, and by 1961 Canada was among the top one-fifth of the world's most urbanized countries.

Both demographic and economic factors have played a critical role in the growth of cities in Canada and the concentration of the population in cities. Among the many factors contributing to Canada's urban growth, according to Stone, are international immigration, fertility trends (and natural increase), the concentration of economic activity over geographic areas in the country, the development of transportation and communication routes, the concentration of labour and consumer markets in certain areas of the nation, and the growth of resource industries (e.g. oil) in some parts of the country.

THE CITY

The macro-level changes described in connection with Canadian urbanization must be reflected to some degree in changes at the level of the city. In fact, the contemporary city is undergoing significant change in social, demographic, and economic dimensions.

Ram, Norris, and Skof rely on 1986 census data to provide an overview of change in the inner city between 1981 and 1986. They also incorporate some historical data to show that, for the first time since 1951, inner cities are experiencing an increase in population as compared to their outlying areas. Overall, the growth of population in inner cities between 1981 and 1986 was 5 per cent.

Among their more important conclusions are the following: (1) in general, the inner city has a high concentration of elderly persons and under-representation of children compared with the population of metropolitan areas; (2) inner cities tend to be inhabited mainly by unmarried persons and people who live alone; almost half of all families in the inner city are childless and about 22 per cent are lone-parent families; (3) immigrants comprise a higher proportion of the population in inner cities than in the balance of metropolitan areas; (4) between 1961 and 1986, the concentration of persons with ethnic origins other than British and French has remained consistently higher in inner cities; in 1986 these persons represented 53 per cent of the inner city population; (5) inner cities and their respective outlying areas have become more dissimilar, with the increasing concentration of university-educated population living in the inner city; (6) since the early 1970s the proportion of the labour force engaged in managerial and professional occupations and living in the inner city has increased relative to outlying areas; and (7) there is a wide disparity in median income between inner-city residents (lower) and families in the outlying areas.

Social scientists have used various models to conceptualize the social differentiation in cities. One such model is Homer Hoyt's sector theory (1963) of city structure, which views residential differentiation along socio-economic lines as following a pattern of sectoral strips in the city, with higher-income neighbourhoods aligned along the better transportation routes and/or the most scenic physical areas. Another important model of social area analysis is the concentric zone theory developed by Burgess in the 1920s (1925). This model posits a single centre for the city, which is considered the point of greatest access and greatest competition for space. Population density tends to be higher at the centre and to decrease toward the periphery of the city. According to this theory, persons of high economic status can afford to live at greater distances from the centre and tend to locate farther from the centre than the less economically advantaged. This model predicts an increase in socio-economic differentiation over time along the income dimension as well as in terms of family size, as families tend to prefer suburban residence.

Balakrishnan and Jarvis test this concentric zonal model for Canada using census tract data from the censuses of 1961, 1971, and 1981 for 14 of the largest metropolitan areas of Canada. They find that the concentric gradient pattern not only persists, but may have intensified as far as socio-economic status and family size are concerned. The authors interpret this result as reflecting the strong societal norm of owning a single-family detached dwelling, as well as the development of well-maintained roadways, which make it worthwhile for suburbanites to commute to work in Canadian cities.

Finally, Darroch and Marston examine the relationship between ethnic residential concentration in the city and the continuity of ethnic communities. They argue that ethnic residential concentration is a function of two spatial-demographic variables: urban size (the population size of the city) and the size of the ethnic group. In general, the larger the city, the larger the flow of immigrants to it, and hence the numerical size of ethnic communities in the city. Indeed, urban size and ethnic-community size are viewed as causes of the degree of ethnic residential segregation. Two Canadian examples of this relationship may be found in Toronto and Montreal. Because these metropolitan areas attract many international immigrants, they show great ethnic heterogeneity, and some groups have grown considerably. Relatively large ethnic groups such as Italians are also highly concentrated residentially and have a high degree of ethnic institutional completeness (e.g., churches, clubs, social service associations, etc.). Regarding a high degree of residential concentration as a cause of institutional completeness, Darroch and Marston find that the greater the institutional completeness, the greater the degree of ethnic persistence in urban Canada. Residential concentration intervenes between spatial-demographic factors (such as city size and group numbers) and institutional completeness of ethnic groups.

TECHNICAL NOTES

1. *Urban growth* means the increase in the number of places that are defined as urban. For example, one may compare the number of cities with populations of 100,000 or more in 1961 to the number of such cities in 1981. Urban growth is asymptotic in the sense that it can continue indefinitely. The number of cities that can grow in a given country has no upper limit, but as the numbers of cities increase, the numbers of new cities diminish.

2. *Urbanization* means the change in the percentage of the population that lives in urban areas. The upper limit for urbanization, of course, is 100 per cent.

3. *Urbanism* is a social-psychological phenomenon associated with urban living, characterized by secularism and modern lifestyles, it contrasts with the traditionalism that is the dominant mode of orientation in rural society.

4. A *census metropolitan area* (CMA) is made up of a very large urbanized core together with adjacent urban and rural areas that have a high degree of economic and social integration with that core. A CMA is defined as the main labour market area of an urban area (the urbanized core) of at least 100,000 population, based on the previous census. Once an area becomes a CMA, it continues to be considered a CMA for statistical purposes even if its population later declines.

5. An *urban area* is a continuously built-up area with a population concentration of 1,000 or more and a population density of 400 or more per square kilometre, based on the previous census. To be considered continuous, the built-up area must not have a discontinuity exceeding two kilometres.

   In addition, many other lands used for commercial, industrial, and institutional purposes may be considered 'urban' even if they do not meet the population and density criteria. Examples include commercial and industrial areas, railway yards, airports, parks, golf courses, and cemeteries.

6. The term *rural area* refers to all territory lying outside 'urban areas'.
   (Above adapted from: *Census of Canada 1986*, 'Population and Dwelling Counts; Provinces and Territories', Ottawa, 1987.)

SUGGESTED READING

Anderson, P. William and Yargos Y. Papageorgiou (1992). 'Metropolitan and non-metropolitan population trends in Canada, 1966–1982'. *The Canadian Geographer* 36, 2: 124–44.

Balakrishnan, T.R. (1982). 'Changing patterns of ethnic residential segregation in the metropolitan areas of Canada'. *Canadian Review of Sociology and Anthropology* 19: 92–110.

——— (1986). 'Ethnic residential segregation in the metropolitan areas of Canada. *Canadian Journal of Sociology* 1, 4: 481–98.

Bourne, Larry S. (1991). 'Addressing the Canadian city: contemporary perspectives, trends, and issues'. Pp. 25–44 in Bunting and Filion (1991).

Bunting, Trudi E. (1991). 'Social differentiation in Canadian cities'. Pp. 286–312 in Bunting and Filion (1991).

——— and Pierre Filion, eds (1991). *Canadian Cities in Transition*. Toronto: Oxford University Press.

Burgess, E.W. (1925). 'The Growth of the City'. Pp. 47–62 in R.E. Park, E.W. Burgess and R.D. Mackenzie eds., *The City*. Chicago: University of Chicago Press.

Burke, Mary Anne (1987). 'Urban Canada'. *Canadian Social Trends* 7: 12–18.

Cappon, Daniel (1991). 'Criteria for healthy urban environments'. *Canadian Journal of Public Health* 82 (July/Aug.): 249–58.

Darroch, A. Gordon, and Wilfred G. Marston (1971). 'The social class bases of ethnic residential segregation: The Canadian case'. *American Journal of Sociology* 77, 3: 491–510.

Davis, Kingsley (1955). 'The origin and growth of urbanization in the world'. *American Journal of Sociology* 60 (March): 429–37.

Edmonston, Barry (1983). 'Metropolitan population deconcentration in Canada, 1941–1976'. *Canadian Studies in Population* 10: 49–70.

Hawley, Amos H. (1964). 'World urbanization: Trends and prospects'. Pp. 70–83 in Ronald Freedman, ed., *Population: The Vital Revolution*. Garden City, NJ: Doubleday,

Hoyt, Homer (1963). 'The growth of cities, from 1800 to 1960'. *Land Economics* 39 (May): 167–73.

Keddie, Phillip D., and Alun E. Joseph (1991). 'The turnaround of the turnaround? Rural population change in Canada, 1976 to 1986'. *The Canadian Geographer* 35, 4: 367–79.

Michelson, William H. (1976). *Man and His Urban Environment: A Sociological Approach*. Reading, MA: Addison-Wesley.

Murdie, Robert A. (1971). 'The Social Geography of the City: Theoretical and Empirical Background'. Pp. 279–90 in Larry S. Bourne, ed., *Internal Structure of the City*. New York: Oxford University Press.

Okraku, O. Ishmael (1987). 'Age residential segregation in Canadian cities'. *Canadian Review of Sociology and Anthropology* 24, 3: 431–52.

Pineo, Peter C. (1988). 'Socioeconomic status and the concentric zonal structure of Canadian cities'. *Canadian Review of Sociology and Anthropology* 25, 3: 421–38.

Scientific American (1965). *Cities*. New York: Alfred A. Knopf.

Stafford, James (1980). 'Demographic correlates of urban development'. *Canadian Studies in Population* 7: 67–80.

CHAPTER 25

U R B A N

D E V E L O P M E N T

I N C A N A D A

Leroy O. Stone

. . .

[HISTORICAL OVERVIEW]

When significant European colonization of Canada began in the seventeenth century, town development in Western Europe already had a long history. In 1666, the colony of New France had fewer than 5,000 settlers, while the city of London (England) contained over 400,000 residents (Cudmore and Caldwell, 1938: chap. III). At that time, Montreal, Quebec and Trois-Rivières were tiny villages, each with a population of fewer than 1,000. By 1765, Montreal and Quebec had passed the 5,000 mark but no Canadian centre was as large as 20,000.

By the first quarter of the nineteenth century, Halifax, Montreal and Quebec had become major Canadian centres for trade, trans-shipment of goods and commerce. It is symptomatic of the functions of these centres that the Banks of Montreal and Quebec were founded in 1817 and 1818, respectively, for the purpose of financing trade between England and Canada. By 1818, Halifax was the most important of several shipping centres in the Maritimes (Cudmore and Caldwell, 1938: chap. III). Thus, some significant urban development in Canada may be dated as early as the first quarter of the nineteenth century, if not earlier. It may be recalled that at the turn of the nineteenth century less than 5 per cent of the world's population resided in cities of 20,000 and over, although there were many cities considerably larger than 20,000, and the most highly urbanized country at that time (England and Wales) had already attained a marked degree of urbanization. By 1825, Montreal and Quebec had passed the 20,000 mark, having populations of 32,000 and 22,000, respectively. Trois-Rivières had about 3,000 persons and York, the capital of Upper Canada, 2,000. These four centres comprised 9 per cent of the colonial population of Upper and Lower Canada. In the Maritimes, Saint John had about 11 per cent of New Brunswick's population (74,000) in 1824, and Halifax about 12 per cent of Nova Scotia's (124,000) in 1827 (Cudmore and Caldwell, 1938: chap. III). These data suggest that around 1825 roughly 5 per cent of the colonial population of Upper and Lower Canada and the Maritimes were concentrated in the two centres of 20,000 and over.

In 1851, 7 per cent of the population which subsequently formed the Dominion were concentrated in centres of cities 20,000 and over. Montreal had passed the 50,000 mark, Quebec and Toronto had passed the 30,000 mark, and Halifax and Saint John were among the cities of 20,000 and over (Cudmore and Caldwell, 1938: chap. III). According to Davis (1955: Table 1) the percentage of world population residing in cities of 20,000 and over was still below 5 per cent in 1850. Thus, if the Davis estimate may be accepted as being sufficiently accurate to provide a rough comparison of Canadian and world urbanization, it would appear that at least 20 years before Canada experienced a marked 'take-off' toward high levels of urbanization (between 1871 and 1885) it already had a level of urbanization higher than the world average.

. . .

Within North America, the levels of urbanization shown by Canada and the United States around 1961 seem quite similar. In the 1960 Census of Population, 70 per cent of the population of the conterminous United States plus Alaska and Hawaii were classified as urban (US Census 1961: xiii–xiv), a percentage equal to that shown for Canada in its 1961 census. . . .

In terms of the percentage of population in urban agglomerations of 20,000 and over, the United States was probably ahead of Canada in 1961. Figure 1 shows that in 1960 roughly 57 per cent of the United States population (conterminous US) resided in urban agglomerations of 20,000 and over; the corresponding figure for Canada in 1961 was 52 per cent. However, the gap between Canada and the United States in this respect has been closing since 1921.

About 1961, the percentage of population in urban agglomerations of 100,000 and over was higher for Canada than for the United States (Figure 1), a differential that appeared for the first time (among census years) in 1951. In 1961 roughly one-third of Canada's population resided in such agglomerations as against three-tenths in 1951; in 1960 the United States figure had not yet reached three-

Figure 1: Percentage of population in urban agglomerations of 20,000 and over and of 100,000 and over, Canada and the United States[1], 1851-1961

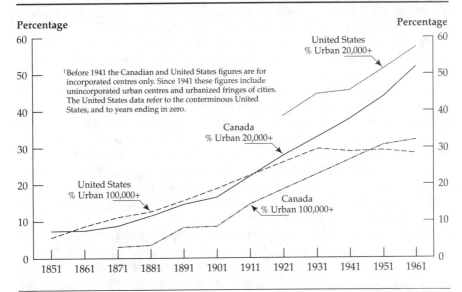

SOURCES: US, 1960 Census of Population, Table 8; Canada, DBS 99–512, 1961 Census, Table 3; DBS 92–535, 1961 Census, Tables 10 and 11; 1951 Census, Vol. I, Tables 12 and 12a; 1890–91 Census, Vol. I, p. 370; 1871 Census, Vol. I, pp. 30, 82, 428; 1851–52 Census, Vol. I, pp. xvii–xix; UN, Population Division, 1966, Tables 2 and 3.

tenths. In comparison, the percentage of the United States population in urban agglomerations of 100,000 and over about 1870 was roughly 11 per cent versus 3 per cent for Canada. Canada's percentage has increased much more rapidly than that of the United States in this century.

Thus, from the earliest phases of the relatively short history of European settlement in Canada, a marked tendency was shown toward the concentration of the colonial population in centres. However, no centre of concentration was over 1,000 in population when the first census of New France was taken in 1666. The colony had two cities of over 20,000 (Montreal and Quebec) by the first quarter of the nineteenth century, and the available data indicate that these centres contained more than five per cent of the colonial population of British North America in 1825, which suggests that Canada may be placed among the world's more highly urbanized regions by 1825. British North America was among the principal regions in regard to the level of urbanization in the decade after Confederation, when it began a 'take-off' toward high levels of urbanization. By 1961 Canada was firmly among the top one-fifth of the world's most highly urbanized countries. Together with the United States, it formed one of the three most highly urbanized of the world regions. Around 1961 the levels of urbanization in Canada and the United States were very similar, at least 70 per cent in both countries.

SOME FACTORS IN CANADIAN URBANIZATION

. . .

In broad generalization, it may be said that Canadian urbanization has partially resulted from and determined the concentration of economic advances at a relatively few specific points in geographical space. This concentration has been brought about partly by forces external to Canada (such as shifts in the commodity structure of demand on the world market, technological changes outside of Canada that affect the comparative advantage of certain types of productive activity in Canada, international migration, and major wars) and partly by internal forces (such as technological changes, shifts in the structure of demand, and decisions by political authorities which influence the structures of the demand and supply of economic goods and services). Important among the factors that have influenced the spatial concentration of economic changes and opportunities are: (a) a sequence of technological developments in the fields of transportation and communication, (b) the intensification of division of labour and of the interdependence of units in production processes, and (c) shifts toward more complex and sophisticated production systems. Particular developments in the geographical concentration of economic changes and opportunities tend, in turn, to produce ramifications that have had a powerful cumulative effect upon the advance of urbanization. These ramifications include the mobility of both people and factors of production, which, in turn, influence (a) regional and rural–urban differentials in the natural increase of population and (b) the attainment of large labour pools and consumer markets in very small geographical areas. The latter is a feature of urban agglomerations that tends to facilitate further advances in the technology of production (and hence further urbanization, up to the upper limits of urbanization). These complexes of factors seem to be evidenced, if only partially so, by the recorded history of Canada.

Canadian urban development probably had its 'take-off' toward high levels of urbanization in the 10–15 years following Confederation in 1867. Upper Canada, Lower Canada and the Maritimes (together) were about 8 to 10 per cent urbanized around 1825 (Cudmore and Caldwell, 1938: chap. III). These regions were about 13 per cent urbanized in 1851, which suggests an average decade increase of about two percentage points in the level of urbanization between 1825 and 1851. The decennial advance in the level of urbanization for these regions increased markedly from 1861–71 to 1871–81. This advance remained near its 1871–81 level in the remaining two decades of the nineteenth century. For Canada as a whole there was a similar upsurge in the decade increase of urbanization in 1871–81 (which is to be expected, since settlement was heavily concentrated in the Maritimes, Quebec and Ontario).

A number of important developments may be associated with the upsurge of Canadian urbanization following Confederation. The 20-year period preceding Confederation had seen the occupation of virtually all of the easily arable land in eastern Canada (Lower, 1946: 182) and the first phase of marked expansion in railways and telegraph networks (Spelt, 1955: 136–7; Cudmore and Caldwell,

1938: 33). In addition, there were some major shifts in the conditions of world trade which were partly responsible for the formation of a Confederation designed to promote, among other things, the development of domestic markets and interregional trade within Canada (Buckley, 1955: 45; Mackintosh, 1939: 15–19). These developments imparted a shock to the pre-1850s complex of economic relations, which was characterized by almost exclusive orientation to primary-product extraction in the economy, by transportation dominated by wooden sailing vessels and water routes, and by considerable isolation of the individual British North American communities (Cudmore and Caldwell, 1938: chap. III; Camu, Weeks, and Sametz, 1964: 44; Mackintosh, 1939: 17–19). The shock provided by the above-mentioned developments in the fields of agricultural activity, of transportation, of world trade, and of political organization (Confederation) produced an expanded scope for the growth of those economic activities which require (or are facilitated by) the agglomeration of population into very small geographical areas.

Later in the nineteenth century there was a sharp expansion of tariffs from 1879 to 1887 (Mackintosh, 1939: 33, 50; Buckley, 1955: 46), and technological changes spurred the development of manufacturing (Bertram, 1963: 171; Spelt, 1955: 138, 171; Buck and Elver, 1964: 5; Corbett, 1957: 122). These post-Confederation developments combined with those occurring in the 1850s and 1860s to generate a surge of industrialization during the last third of the nineteenth century. Important among the ramifications of such developments was a marked step toward the economic integration of Canadian regions (Camu, Weeks, and Sametz, 1964: 48–9), which has been a major influence on the size of the internal market for domestic non-primary production. This whole complex of forces must have generated a great push to the agglomeration of population into urban centres, where the new economic structural changes and opportunities were being concentrated, while the urban centres further facilitated the march of industrialization. Thus, the historical record suggests a whole matrix of major economic and social changes associated with the upsurge of Canadian urbanization following Confederation and with the continued rapid pace of this urbanization in the last third of the nineteenth century.

Beginning around the latter portion of the 1890s the 'urbanizing forces' in Canada sustained a new and powerful augmentation. A tremendous immigration wave (about 1896–1914), extensive western settlement, and the emergence of wheat as a major staple in the Canadian economy formed a three-pronged development which was probably interrelated with the marked upsurge in the decade advance of Canadian urbanization from 1891–1901 to 1901–11. The expansion of wheat production for export became a major force in promoting the integration and interdependence of Canadian regions (with a particularly notable impulse to manufacturing in central Canada), and this expansion had an important multiplier effect upon employment opportunities in the centres where non-primary activities were concentrated—that is, in the urban areas. Thus, the rapid growth of population and the generation of urban employment opportunities (derived ultimately from the expansion of wheat production for export) enhanced the advance of urbanization around the turn of the twentieth century (Mackintosh, 1939: 39, 50; Buckley, 1955: 4, 45).

The First World War brought heavy demands for manufactured products and exerted a marked impulse upon the concentration of economic opportunities in urban areas (Corbett, 1957: 143; Buckley, 1955: 45). The economic transformations of the war period promoted technological changes in agriculture, particularly in western Canada, and these changes mushroomed in the 1920s (Mackintosh, 1939: 87). The expanded use of mechanized farm implements was making heavy inroads into the demand for farm labour. In central Canada, urbanization maintained its record pace of advance from 1901–11 to 1911–21, while the increase of urbanization decelerated markedly in the highly agricultural Prairies.

The Great Depression which began generally in 1929, but was evident in Saskatchewan as early as 1928 (Mackintosh, 1939: chap. 6), was marked by an enormous dampening of the factors promoting urbanization. Immigration and population growth decelerated markedly, the demand for the products of non-primary activities fell off considerably, and the rate of investments [in] technological changes declined greatly. Accompanying this matrix of economic contraction (Hood and Scott, 1957: 15) was a marked downturn in the pace of Canadian urbanization The events of the period surrounding and including the Great Depression comprise an impressive commentary on the integral part played by urbanization in the development of the Canadian economy.

With the advent of the Second World War, Canada entered upon a period of unprecedented industrialization. This war was an important motive force behind some impressive technological changes and mobilization of resources. As stated by Wilson, Gordon, and Judek (1965: 44–5), 'Not only had industrial research begun on a large scale but many entirely new industries had been established (e.g., synthetic rubber, roller bearings, diesel engines, antibiotics, high octane gasoline, aircraft manufacturing, and shipbuilding). Further processing of some manufactured goods hitherto imported likewise gave the Canadian economy a taste of new manufacturing capabilities. . . . In many industries (e.g., steel) basic capacity was permanently enlarged.' And accompanying the transformations of the 1940s was a heavy decline in the agricultural working force (1951 Census, vol. X: 47; Slater, 1960a: 57–8). These changes no doubt were interrelated with a marked upsurge in the level of urbanization, which was further accentuated in the post-war period of unprecedented prosperity.

To the forces let loose by the Second World War must be added in the post-war period the development of new sources of economic opportunity (through an employment-multiplier process) in the rapid growth of the oil, natural gas, pulp and paper, and automobile industries, and the great revolution in transportation and communication facilities which spurted after the turn of the century (Bertram, 1963: 175) and mushroomed after the Second World War (Blumenfeld, 1961). This revolution and the continued economic growth have been key factors in the suburban sprawl and metropolitan growth of the 1950s and 1960s. The recent rapid urbanization has been further enhanced by a post-war immigration wave which has been concentrated upon urban areas (Camu, Weeks, and Sametz, 1964: 72).

. . .

HISTORICAL PATTERN OF RATES OF URBAN POPULATION

The past century has experienced high rates of urban population increase, accompanied by much lower rates of change in rural population. Between 1851 and 1961 the urban population in the area of the three oldest major regions (the Maritimes, Quebec and Ontario) has increased at least 28-fold, while the rural population has increased, at most, twofold (Table 1 . . .). It is notable that the population classified as rural in these three major regions was about 2,000,000 in 1851 and only about 3,500,000 in 1961. Between 1901 and 1961 the urban population in Canada (excluding Newfoundland, Yukon Territory and the Northwest Territories) has increased at least sixfold, while the rural population has increased at most threefold.

. . .

One of the questions which a refined decomposition of the intercensal urban population increase should answer is the following: What has been the relative contribution of international migration to the rate of urban population growth in Canada? A precise answer to this question may not be available due to the large pieces of relevant information which are not contained in the available data. However, the works of Hurd (1943), of Slater (1960b), and of Camu, Weeks, and Sametz (1964: 68–72) indicate that international migration, whose direct impact on population growth is the net external migration, has been a significant contributor to urban population increase in Canada. Figure 2 indicates the strong association between the historical patterns of the intercensal rates of net external migration and of urban population increase.

HISTORICAL PATTERN OF THE ADVANCE OF URBANIZATION

The marked urban–rural differentials in intercensal rates of population increase, indicated [above], imply continued advances in the percentage of population which is urban (Figure 3). Between 1851 and 1961 this percentage (which is being used here as a measure of the level of urbanization) increased at least fivefold (Table 1). Between 1901 and 1961 the degree of urbanization in Canada doubled from 35 per cent to 70 per cent.

The degree of urbanization in Canada has advanced in every decade since 1851, as the foregoing comments on urban–rural differentials in rates of population increase suggest. In eight of the eleven decades from 1851 to 1961 the degree of urbanization in Canada increased by at least five percentage points (Figure 3).

Table 1: Percentage of population urban[1], Canada and provinces, 1851 to 1961

Canada or province	1851	1861	1871	1881	1891	1901
Canada (incl. Newfoundland)	...	...	...	...	...	...
Canada (excl. Newfoundland)	13.1	15.8	18.3	23.3	29.8	34.9
Newfoundland	...	...	...	...	...	...
Maritimes	9.0	9.9	11.9	15.3	18.8	24.5
Prince Edward Island	—	9.3	9.4	10.5	13.1	14.5
Nova Scotia	7.5	7.6	8.3	14.7	19.4	27.7
New Brunswick	14.0	13.1	17.6	17.6	19.9	23.1
Quebec	14.9	16.6	19.9	23.8	28.6	36.1
Ontario	14.0	18.5	20.6	27.1	35.0	40.3
Prairies	...	...	...	...	...	19.3
Manitoba	...	...	—	14.9	23.3	24.9
Saskatchewan	...	...	...	...	...	6.1
Alberta	...	...	...	...	...	16.2
British Columbia	—	—	9.0	18.3	42.6	46.4

	1911	1921	1931	1941	1951	1961
Canada (incl. Newfoundland)	...	...	...	...	62.4	69.7
Canada (excl. Newfoundland)	41.8	47.4	52.5	55.7	62.9	70.2
Newfoundland	...	...	...	...	43.3	50.7
Maritimes	30.9	38.8	39.7	44.1	47.4	49.5
Prince Edward Island	16.0	18.8	19.5	22.1	25.1	32.4
Nova Scotia	36.7	44.8	46.6	52.0	54.5	54.3
New Brunswick	26.7	35.2	35.4	38.7	42.8	46.5
Quebec	44.5	51.8	59.5	61.2	66.8	74.3
Ontario	49.5	58.8	63.1	67.5	72.5	77.3
Prairies	27.9	28.7	31.3	32.4	44.5	57.6
Manitoba	39.3	41.5	45.2	45.7	56.0	63.9
Saskatchewan	16.1	16.8	20.3	21.3	30.4	43.0
Alberta	29.4	30.7	31.8	31.9	47.6	63.3
British Columbia	50.9	50.9	62.3	64.0	68.6	72.6

NOTE: Percentages computed from unrounded figures. Exclusive of the Yukon and Northwest Territories.

[1] From 1851 to 1911 the urban population figures refer to incorporated cities, towns and villages of 1,000 and over only; from 1921 to 1951 the percentages are estimates of the percentages which would have been reported in the respective censuses had the 1961 Census definition and procedures been used; for 1961 the figures are those published according to the 1961 Census definition of 'urban'.

SOURCES: 1921 Census, Vol. I, Table 12; 1931 Census, Vol. I, Tables 1a and 5; 1941 Census, Vol. I, Table 10; 1951 Census, Vol. I, Tables 12, 12a and 13; 1951 Census, Bul. SP-7; 1956 Census, Vol. I, Tables 8 and 9; 1961 Census, DBS 99-511, Table 1—DBS 99-512, Tables 1 and 2—DBS 92-535, Tables 10 and 11—DBS 92-536, Table 12—DBS 92-539—DBS 92-528; DBS, 'Component Parts', 1963; Cudmore and Caldwell (1938), pp. 36-8.

The three decades in which the degree of urbanization has advanced by less than five percentage points were two periods preceding the 'take-off' of industrialization in central Canada (1851–61 and 1861–71) and a period containing much of the Great Depression (1931–41).

Figure 2: Intercensal rates of immigration, net external migration, and urban population increase,[1] Canada,[2] 1851–61 to 1951–61

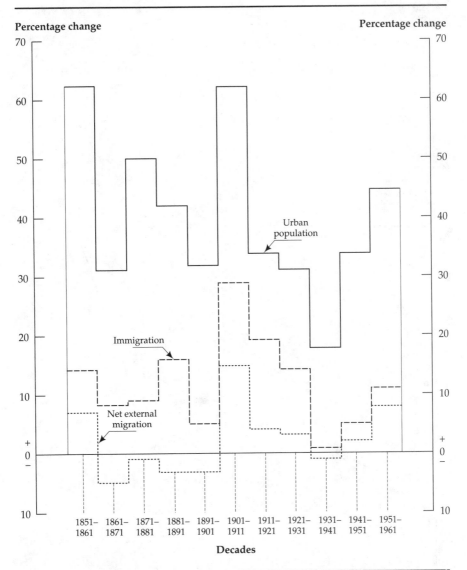

Percentage change

Percentage change

Urban population

Immigration

Net external migration

Decades

1851–
1861

1861–
1871

1871–
1881

1881–
1891

1891–
1901

1901–
1911

1911–
1921

1921–
1931

1931–
1941

1941–
1951

1951–
1961

[1] The rates are formed by dividing the population of Canada at the beginning of the pertinent intercensal period into the respective totals (immigration, net external migration, or urban population increase). 'Immigration' refers to the total number of immigrant arrivals between the censuses in question. 'Net external migration' is the difference between immigration and emigration (defined as the number of persons departing Canada for residence elsewhere). The figures for immigrants and emigrants are estimates having varying degrees of accuracy (see Camu, Weeks, and Sametz, 1964, pp. 56–64 for detailed discussion).

[2] The data for immigrants and for net external migration include Newfoundland (after 1941) and the Yukon and Northwest Territories. These areas are excluded from the urban population data. The implied discrepancy in this chart has a negligible effect on the pattern which the chart is designed to show.

Figure 3: **Percentage of population urban, Canada and major regions, 1851–1961**

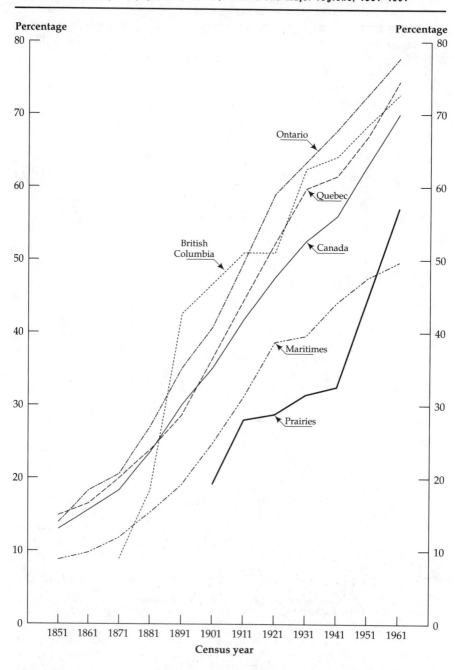

SOURCE: Table 1.

. . .

Considering the decennial percentage point gain in urbanization and the decennial rate of increase in urban population, six historical phases may be identified in the pattern of Canadian urban development from 1851 to 1961. Three of these phases are marked by upturns and three by downturns in the pace of Canadian urban development.

Historical phase	General direction of change in the rate of urban development	Number of decades in which the direction of change is sustained
1851–61 to 1861–71	very slight downturn	1
1861–71 to 1881–91	sharp upturn	2
1881–91 to 1891–1901	slight downturn	1
1891–1901 to 1901–11	moderate upturn	1
1901–11 to 1931–41	moderate downturn	3
1931–41 to 1951–61	very sharp upturn	2

The historical pattern of urban development in Canada is not merely a result of places 'graduating' from rural to urban status and cities enlarging their boundaries through annexation; it is a pattern which is shown by the intercensal growth rates for cities independently of boundary changes. . . .

DIFFERENTIALS REGARDING THE RAPIDITY OF URBANIZATION

. . . Ontario was the first region to be 25 per cent urbanized and it reached this level near 1881. Ontario was joined by British Columbia in being the first to reach the 50 per cent level, attained in 1911. The two-thirds level of urbanization was first shown by Ontario for 1941 and by 1961 Ontario was the only region showing a level higher than three-fourths, although Quebec and British Columbia had levels very close to 75 per cent. Table 2 shows these patterns in greater detail.

. . .

The major regions may also be compared in terms of percentage-point gain in level of urbanization over specific periods. For the entire 1851–1961 period, British Columbia, Ontario and Quebec rank in that order from first to third in regard to percentage-point gain in urbanization. These provinces rank in the identical order from first to third in regard to the amount of advance in level of urbanization from 1851 to 1911, the latter year marking the end of an intercensal decade of unprecedented population growth and western settlement. However, the order changes for the 1911–1961 period when Quebec takes the lead in increase of urbanization, with Ontario and British Columbia following in that order. Since 1941, the Prairies have established a clear lead in increase of urbanization.

Table 2: Census years in which Canada and the major regions reached or surpassed selected levels of urbanization, 1851 to 1961

Canada and major regions	Levels of urbanization[1]				
	25%	**35%**	**50%**	**67%**	**75%**
Canada	1891	1901	1931	1961	[2]
Maritimes	1901	1921	1961	[2]	[2]
Quebec	1891	1901	1921	1951	[2]
Ontario	1881	1891	1911	1941	1961
Prairies	1911	1951	1961	[2]	[2]
British Columbia	1891	1891	1911	1951	[2]

[1] The level of urbanization is measured by the percentage of population classified as urban.

[2] The area in question had not attained the pertinent level of urbanization as of 1961, according to the source data.

SOURCES: 1921 Census, Vol. I, Table 12; 1931 Census, Vol. I, Tables 1a and 5; 1941 Census, Vol. I, Table 10; 1951 Census, Vol. I, Tables 12, 12a and 13; 1951 Census, Bul. SP-7; 1956 Census, Vol. I, Tables 8 and 9; 1961 Census, DBS 99-511, Table 1—DBS 99-512, Tables 1 and 2—DBS 92-535, Tables 10 and 11—DBS 92-536, Table 12—DBS 92-539—DBS 92-528; DBS, 'Component Parts', 1963; Cudmore and Caldwell (1938), pp. 36–8.

Thus it is apparent that there are distinct and systematic differences between the five selected major regions of Canada in regard to the historical pattern of increase in urbanization and in the rapidity of this increase over specified periods and among selected levels of urbanization. The factors responsible for these differences are not discussed in detail but a number of general points may be noted. An explanatory analysis of the regional differentials should be constrained by the facts that (a) the regions differ markedly in regard to the history of considerable settlement, and (b) as the proximity of the upper limit of the level of urbanization is reached it may become more and more difficult to obtain a given increase in urbanization. Having taken these two factors into account, one should then turn to the demographic mechanisms accounting for the regional differentials, and follow this by an attempt to delineate the non-demographic factors underlying (and interacting with) the demographic mechanisms.

SUMMARY

When significant European colonization of Canada began in the seventeenth century, town development in Western Europe and the British Isles already had a long history. However, from its earliest stages colonial settlement in Canada was marked by a tendency for population to be concentrated in very small areas, and the available data suggest that Canada may be placed among the more highly urbanized regions of the world around 1825. (It should be recalled, however, that the levels of world and Canadian urbanization were extremely low around 1825.)

At the time of the 1851 census, less than 15 per cent of the population of British North America resided in urban centres. By 1961, however, Canada was 70 per cent urbanized and was clearly among the most highly urbanized countries in the world. Within North America, the levels of urbanization in Canada and the United States were very similar around 1961.

In the past century Canada has had high rates of urban population increase accompanied by much lower rates of change in rural population. In each of the 11 decennial periods from 1851 to 1961, the percentage increase in Canadian urban population was twice as high as that in rural population. In 10 of the intercensal periods, the Canadian urban population increase exceeded 25 per cent and in five of these periods the rate of increase was higher than 35 per cent.

No marked and sustained upward or downward drift (general trend) is observed in the intercensal rates of urban population increase for Canada; what the data show prominently is a historical pattern of marked fluctuations in these rates. In the curve of intercensal rates of urban population increase, there are very high peaks for 1851–61 and 1901–11, less prominent peaks for 1871–81 and 1951–61, and troughs in 1861–71, 1891–1901 and 1931–41. The historical pattern of the increase is not explained by waves of expansion in the area of urban settlement, and it reflects rates of population growth in urban centres independently of boundary change.

The marked rural–urban differentials in the rate of population increase imply continued advances in the level of Canadian urbanization. In the decades preceding the period of 'take-off' in the industrialization of central Canada (1851–61 and 1861–71) and in the generally depressed 1931–41 decade, the level of Canadian urbanization advanced about two to three percentage points. In all other decades, however, the level of urbanization advanced by at least five percentage points, and the increase reached a peak of seven percentage points in 1901–11, 1941–51 and 1951–61.

Among the five selected major regions of Canada, Ontario, Quebec and British Columbia showed levels of urbanization above 70 per cent in 1961, while in the Maritimes and the Prairies it was less than 60 per cent. Ontario, Quebec and British Columbia have been the most highly urbanized of the five major regions since 1881. Since 1881, the differential between the level of urbanization in this group of regions and that in the Maritimes appears to have widened markedly. The differential between the level of urbanization in the group of Ontario, Quebec and British Columbia and that in the Prairie region widened markedly from 1911 to 1941 but has since narrowed sharply, as the Prairies have led the way in the post-war advance of urbanization. Generally, Ontario has been in the vanguard of Canadian urbanization since Confederation, being among the first to reach the 25 per cent (in 1881), 50 per cent (in 1911) and 75 per cent (in 1961) levels of urbanization. However, for the 1851–1961 period, British Columbia, Ontario and Quebec rank in that order from first to third in regard to the amount of increase in urbanization, while for the 1911–61 period Quebec leads the rank order with Ontario and British Columbia following.

REFERENCES

Bertram, Gordon W. (1963). 'Economic growth in Canadian industry, 1870–1915'. *Canadian Journal of Economics and Political Science* 29 (May): 159–85.

Blümenfeld, H. (1961). 'Transportation in the modern metropolis'. *Queen's Quarterly* 67 (Winter): 640–3.

Buck, W. Keith, and R.B. Elver (1964). *The Canadian Steel Industry*, Mineral Information Bulletin MR 70. Ottawa: Queen's Printer.

Buckley, Kenneth (1955). *Capital Formation in Canada, 1896–1930*. Toronto: University of Toronto Press.

Camu, P., E.P. Weeks and Z.W. Sametz (1964). *Economic Geography of Canada*. Toronto: Macmillan.

Canada. Department of Agriculture. *Census of Canada, 1870–71, Vol. I*. Ottawa: I.B. Taylor, 1873.

—— Department of Agriculture. *Census of Canada, 1890–91, Vol. I*. Ottawa: Queen's Printer, 1893.

—— Dominion Bureau of Statistics. *Sixth Census of Canada, 1921, Vol. I, Population, Number, Sex, and Distribution*. Ottawa: King's Printer, 1924.

—— Dominion Bureau of Statistics. *Seventh Census of Canada, 1931, Vol. I, Summary*. Ottawa: King's Printer, 1936.

—— Dominion Bureau of Statistics. *Eighth Census of Canada, 1941, Vol. I, General Review and Summary Tables*. Ottawa: King's Printer, 1950.

—— Dominion Bureau of Statistics. *Ninth Census of Canada, 1951, Vol. I, Population, General Characteristics*. Ottawa: Queen's Printer, 1953.

—— Dominion Bureau of Statistics. *Ninth Census of Canada, 1951, Vol. X, General Review*. Ottawa: Queen's Printer, 1956.

—— Dominion Bureau of Statistics. *Ninth Census of Canada, 1951, Population, Unincorporated Villages and Hamlets*. Bul. SP-7. Ottawa: Queen's Printer, 1954.

—— Dominion Bureau of Statistics. *Census of Canada, 1956, Vol. I, Population, General Characteristics*. Ottawa: Queen's Printer, 1959.

—— Dominion Bureau of Statistics. *1961 Census of Canada, Population, Unincorporated Villages*. Bul. SP-4, Cat. No. 92–528. Ottawa: Queen's Printer, 1963.

—— Dominion Bureau of Statistics. *1961 Census of Canada, Vol. I, Population, Incorporated Cities, Towns and Villages*. Bul. 1.1–6, Cat. No. 92–535. Ottawa: Queen's Printer, 1962.

—— Dominion Bureau of Statistics. *1961 Census of Canada, Vol. I, Population, Rural and Urban Distribution*. Bul. 1.1–7, Cat. No. 92–536. Ottawa: Queen's Printer, 1963.

—— Dominion Bureau of Statistics. *1961 Census of Canada, Vol. I—Part 1, Population, Historical 1901–1961*. Bul. 1.1–10, Cat. No. 92–539. Ottawa: Queen's Printer, 1963.

—— Dominion Bureau of Statistics. *1961 Census of Canada, General Review, Growth of Population*. Bul. 7.1–1, Cat. No. 99–511. Ottawa: Queen's Printer, 1963.

—— Dominion Bureau of Statistics. *1961 Census of Canada, General Review, Rural and Urban Population*. Bul. 7.1–2, Cat. No. 99–512. Ottawa: Queen's Printer, 1963.

Charles, Enid (1948). *The Changing Size of Family in Canada*. 1941 Census Monograph No. 1. Ottawa: King's Printer.

Childe, V. Gordon (1951). *Man Makes Himself*. New York: New American Library of World Literature, (a Mentor Book).

Clark, S.D. (1961). *Urbanism and the Canadian Society*. Toronto: University of Toronto Press.

Corbett, D.C. (1952). *Urban Growth and Municipal Finance*. Montreal: Canadian Federation of Mayors and Municipalities.

Cudmore, S.A., and H.G. Caldwell (1938). *Rural and Urban Composition of the Canadian Population*. 1931 Census Monograph No. 6. Ottawa: King's Printer.

Davis, Kingsley (1955). 'The origin and growth of urbanization in the world'. *American Journal of Sociology* 60 (March): 429–37.

———— and H.H. Golden (1954). 'Urbanization and the development of pre-industrial areas', *Economic Development and Cultural Change*, 3 (October): 6–26.

Dickinson, Robert E. (1959). 'The growth of the historic city'. Pp. 69–83 in *Readings in Urban Geography* Ed. Harold M. Mayer and Clyde F. Kohn. Chicago: University of Chicago Press.

Fyfe, Stewart (1961). 'Governing urban communities', *Queen's Quarterly* 67 (Winter): 605–17.

Gras, N.S.B. (1922). *An Introduction to Economic History*. New York: Harper and Brothers.

Hauser, Philip M. (1965). 'Introduction' Pp. 1–37 in *The Study of Urbanization* ed. Philip M. Hauser and Leo F. Schnore. New York: John Wiley.

————, and Leo F. Schnore, eds. (1965). *The Study of Urbanization*. New York: John Wiley.

Hawley, Amos H. (1956). *The Changing Shape of Metropolitan America*. Glencoe, Illinois: Free Press.

Hood, William C., and Anthony Scott (1957). *Output, Labour and Capital in the Canadian Economy*. Prepared for the Royal Commission on Canada's Economic Prospects. Ottawa: Queen's Printer.

Hoyt, Homer (1963). 'The growth of cities, from 1800 to 1960'. *Land Economics* 39 (May): 167–73.

Hurd, W. Burton. 'Population trends underlying the potential agricultural development in Canada'. Parts I to III. Prepared for the Committee on Reconstruction. Ottawa (Mimeographed.)

Lampard, Eric (1965). 'Historical aspects of urbanization'. Pp. 519–54 in *The Study of Urbanization*, eds. Philip M. Hauser and Leo F. Schnore. New York: John Wiley.

Lower, Arthur R.M. (1946). *Colony to Nation*. Toronto: Longmans, Green.

Mackintosh, W.A. (1964). *The Economic Background of Dominion-Provincial Relations*. Prepared for the Royal Commission on Dominion-Provincial Relations, 1939. Toronto: McClelland and Stewart. (First published by King's Printer in 1939.)

Mumford, Lewis (1961). *The City in History*. New York: Harcourt, Brace and World.

Slater, David W. (1960a). 'The distribution of urban populations in Canada'. Economics Department, Queen's University, Kingston. (Mimeographed).

———— (1960b). 'The urbanization of people and activities in Canada, including an analysis of components of the growth of urban population'. Department of Economics, Queen's University, Kingston. (Mimeographed).

Spelt, J. (1955). *The Urban Development in South-Central Ontario*. Assen, Netherlands: Van Gorcum.

United Nations. Economic and Social Council (1965). 'World survey of urban and rural population growth'. Preliminary report by the Secretary General to the Population Commission, 13th session. Document E/CN.9/187. New York, 8 March. (Mimeographed).

————. Population Division. 'World Urbanization Trends, 1920–1960'. Paper presented to the Inter-Regional Seminar on Development Policies and Planning in Relation to Urbanization, Pittsburgh, October. (Mimeographed).

United States. Bureau of the Census. *U.S. Census of Population, 1960, Number of Inhabitants, United States Summary*. Final Report PC(1)—1A. Washington: U.S. Government Printing Office.

Wilson, George W., Scott Gordon and Stanislaw Judek (1965). *Canada: an Appraisal of Its Needs and Resources*. Toronto: University of Toronto Press.

CHAPTER 26

THE INNER CITY
IN TRANSITION

Bali Ram, Mary Jane Norris,
and Karl Skof

INTRODUCTION

Canadian cities experienced large-scale suburbanization and inner-city decline during the 1950s and 1960s. However, in recent decades, there has been renewed interest in the inner cities as places of residence. As a result, many cities have made a transition which is reflected in the changing demographic, family, cultural and socio-economic characteristics of the inner-city residents.

This study examines (1) the extent of differences between inner cities and their outlying areas; (2) whether inner cities have become increasingly similar or dissimilar in relation to the remainder of the census metropolitan areas; and (3) whether inner cities have been undergoing revitalization in recent years. By doing so, this study dispels numerous myths about inner cities.

. . .

Canadian censuses provide a variety of data, rich in geographic and socio-economic details. These data have made it possible to undertake this study for 12 census metropolitan areas over the 1951–86 period. A census metropolitan area is the main urban labour-market area of at least 100,000 population. The selected metropolitan areas are Toronto, Montreal, Vancouver, Ottawa–Hull, Edmonton, Calgary, Winnipeg, Quebec, Halifax, Saskatoon, Regina, and Saint John. Census tracts, which are small and socio-economically homogeneous neighbourhoods, formed the basis of defining inner-city boundaries. Data by census tract for the 35-year period were available only for these 12 metropolitan areas. Inner-city boundaries have been held constant for the entire period, while those of the remainder of the metropolitan areas have changed according to annexations.

There is no standard definition of the inner city. The definition used here is based on a previous Statistics Canada study.[1] The delineation of the inner-city area in this earlier study was based on land use and age of development criteria selected in consultation with the planning departments of respective cities. Thus, the inner city refers to the core of the metropolitan area which includes the site of the earliest development of the city, the 'central business district', and the surrounding areas of mixed land uses, with high density residential development. . . .

This study begins with a look at the changing population size and share of the 12 inner cities. Demographic structures and trends between inner cities and their respective outlying areas are then compared. A discussion follows on inner-city/suburb differences in selected trends and patterns of the family.

The analysis then examines how immigrant and ethnic concentrations in inner cities have changed over time. This is followed by a description of the change in socio-economic characteristics. . . . The study concludes with an overall assessment of inner-city/suburb differences, the growing similarities and dissimilarities between the two areas and the extent of renewal of the inner city.

POPULATION OF INNER CITIES

In 1951, there were 15 census metropolitan areas (called metropolitan areas hereafter), with about 40 per cent of Canada's population residing in these areas, and the remaining 60 per cent in non-metropolitan areas. By 1986, the distribution was completely reversed, with 60 per cent of Canadians residing in metropolitan areas. This growing phenomenon is due not only to population growth but also to the effect of areal expansion of metropolitan areas and the addition of new metropolitan areas as other urban centres became larger.

Canada had 25 metropolitan areas in 1986. The 12 areas chosen in this study represent nearly 80 per cent of the total 1986 metropolitan population of some 15 million in Canada. In terms of population, as shown in Table 1, these areas ranged from a low of 121,000 for Saint John to a high of 3,427,000 for Toronto. Their inner-city populations add to almost half a million, representing 4 per cent of their combined total metropolitan population.

Inner-City Share of Total Metropolitan Population

Between 1951 and 1986, the inner cities' share of the total metropolitan area population has declined continuously, from 16 per cent in 1951 to 4 per cent by

Table 1: Population of 12 census metropolitan areas and inner cities, 1986

CMA	Metropolitan area	Inner city
Toronto	3,427,165	128,165
Montreal	2,921,355	93,010
Vancouver	1,380,735	73,960
Ottawa–Hull	819,265	43,590
Edmonton	785,465	18,285
Calgary	671,325	18,840
Winnipeg	625,300	28,325
Quebec	603,265	21,920
Halifax	295,990	10,490
Saskatoon	200,660	4,360
Regina	186,520	8,650
Saint John	121,265	6,845
Total	12,038,310	456,440

SOURCE: 1986 Census of Canada, unpublished data.

1986. This is largely because inner-city boundaries have remained constant while the outlying areas have expanded. In addition, over the 35 years, the population of inner cities has declined by 37 per cent, whereas that of the outlying areas has increased by 200 per cent.

The loss of population in some inner cities has been rather marked, as shown in Table 2. Over the 1951–81 period, the inner-city populations of Montreal, Quebec, Halifax and Regina shrank by more than half. Other centres with significant losses were Ottawa–Hull, Winnipeg, Saskatoon and Saint John. Population reduction in these inner cities during the same 30 years ranged from 42 per cent to 47 per cent. Smaller losses, between 13 per cent and 21 per cent, were experienced by Toronto, Vancouver, Edmonton and Calgary.

Turnaround in Inner-City Population Decline

A turnaround in the long-term decline of inner-city populations occurred during the 1981–86 period. In Toronto, Vancouver, Edmonton and Calgary, it occurred as early as 1976. During 1981–86, all inner cities increased in population, except for Montreal and Saint John which lost population. These recent trends suggest that the historic decline of the inner city has been reversed, and indeed, some observers believe that a 'back-to-the-city' movement has begun.

DEMOGRAPHIC STRUCTURE

In general, Canadian inner cities are characterized by an under-representation of the young and an over-representation of the elderly. In 1986, the population

Table 2: Population of inner cities as a percentage of total metropolitan areas, 1951–1986

CMA	Inner city population					Inner city as % of total metropolitan area				
	1951	1961	1971	1981	1986	1951	1961	1971	1981	1986
	'000					%				
Toronto	143.5	127.1	124.8	114.7	128.2	12.8	7.0	4.7	3.8	3.7
Montreal	219.7	163.0	128.0	93.5	93.0	15.7	7.7	4.7	3.3	3.2
Vancouver	83.9	70.4	72.6	71.6	74.0	15.8	8.9	6.7	5.6	5.4
Ottawa–Hull	80.9	72.1	57.5	43.0	43.6	28.7	16.8	9.5	6.0	5.3
Edmonton	20.4	17.8	20.0	17.8	18.3	11.8	5.3	4.0	2.7	2.3
Calgary	22.0	17.0	17.8	17.3	18.8	15.8	6.1	4.4	2.9	2.8
Winnipeg	45.4	38.2	31.7	26.1	28.3	12.8	8.0	5.9	4.5	4.5
Quebec	50.6	44.3	32.9	21.0	21.9	18.4	12.4	6.8	3.6	3.6
Halifax	24.8	23.1	14.6	10.1	10.5	18.5	12.5	6.6	3.6	3.5
Saskatoon	6.5	5.3	4.4	3.8	4.4	12.2	5.6	3.5	2.5	2.2
Regina	16.8	14.3	11.8	8.3	8.6	23.6	12.7	8.4	5.0	4.6
Saint John	13.2	13.7	12.2	7.1	6.8	16.9	14.3	11.5	6.3	5.6
Total	727.8	606.0	528.3	434.2	456.4	15.8	8.5	5.5	4.0	3.8

SOURCE: 1951–1981 Censuses of Canada, published data for census tracts, and 1986 Census of Canada, unpublished data.

under age 15 formed 9 per cent of the total population of the inner cities, but 20 per cent of the population of outlying areas. Conversely, the population aged 65 and over formed 15 per cent of the population of inner cities, but only 10 per cent of the population of outlying areas.

Population Under Age 15

Consistent with the overall reduction in fertility across Canada, metropolitan areas have recently experienced a marked decline in the proportion of the population in younger age groups. Figure 1 shows that since the peak of the baby boom in the late 1950s, the proportion of the population below age 15 has been in a continuous decline, having fallen from 20 per cent in 1961 to 9 per cent in 1986 for the 12 inner cities under consideration. The corresponding reduction, however, was less pronounced for outlying areas, where between 1961 and 1986 the proportion of the population under age 15 declined from 32 per cent to 20 per cent.

Two factors could have contributed to this trend. First, the fertility rate of inner-city dwellers has probably been declining at a faster pace than the fertility rate of those living in outlying areas. Second, and probably a more important factor, could be selective migration. Probably persons with younger children are more likely to move out of inner-city areas, whereas persons with no children are more likely to move into the city.

Figure 1: Percentage of population by age groups, inner cities and remainder, 1951–1986

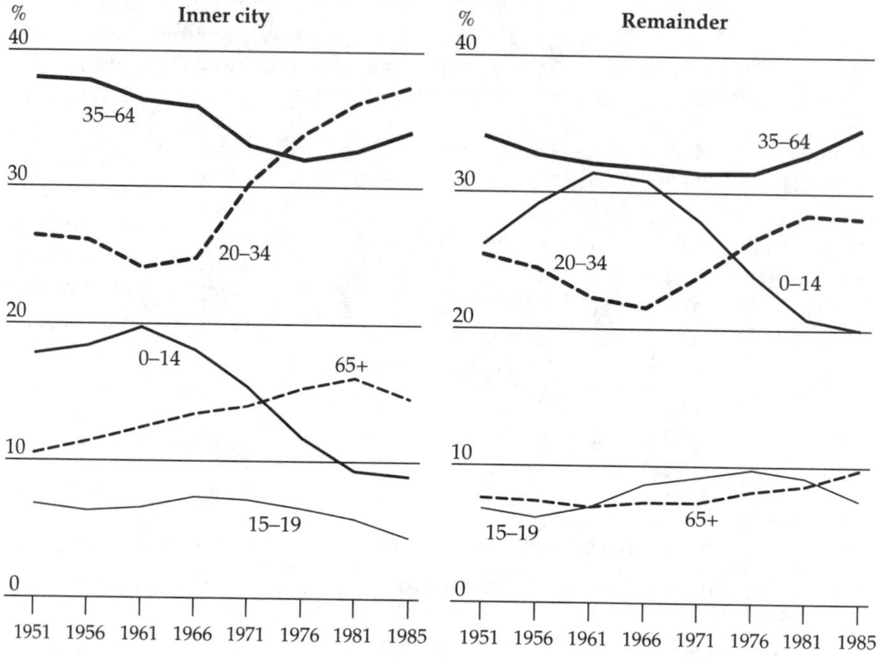

SOURCE: 1951–1981 Censuses of Canada, published data for census tracts, and 1986 Census of Canada, unpublished data.

Working-Age Population

Recently, the population in the age group 20–34 years has become increasingly concentrated in inner cities. Between 1961 and 1986, their proportion increased from 22 per cent to 28 per cent in the outlying areas, but from 24 per cent to 37 per cent in the inner cities. The increase in the concentration of these persons has occurred in all the inner cities except Saskatoon and Regina. Inner-city living may be attractive to these persons for various reasons. Many of them may be single or married with no children or have very young children, and virtually all of them are just beginning their economic life cycle.

Over the years, inner cities have become less attractive to persons with older children. An examination of the concentration of population aged 35–64 in the inner cities over the years verifies this phenomenon. This age group has continually declined as a proportion of the total population within the inner cities, from 38 per cent in 1951 to 34 per cent in 1986.

Over-Representation of the Elderly

While the younger population in the inner cities has declined, the number of people in the older age groups (65 years and over) has been increasing in proportion to the total population. Because of the easy accessibility of goods and services within walking distance and the availability of public transportation, older people tend to prefer living in the inner areas of cities rather than in the suburbs. The period 1976–86 represents a deviation from earlier periods during which the relative concentration of elderly in the inner cities was reduced substantially. In 1976, the proportion of elderly in the inner cities was almost double that in the outlying areas, but was reduced to one and one-half times in 1986. Perhaps there has been a recent tendency for older persons to move out to the suburbs. As well, the increasing concentration of young adults has lowered the share of elderly persons in inner cities. Again, except for Saskatoon and Regina, these patterns hold true for all the inner cities considered. In Saskatoon and Regina, the concentration of the elderly has increased dramatically. Slightly less than a third of the population in these two small urban centres was composed of persons 65 years and over in 1986; the corresponding proportion in 1951 was less than 14 per cent.

As the proportion of the elderly increased in the inner cities, so did the relative concentration of elderly women. In 1956, there were 95 women aged 65 and over for every 100 men in the same age group. By 1986, the ratio had jumped to 166 women for every 100 men. The corresponding change was less evident in the outlying zones of the metropolitan areas than it was in the inner cities, where the overall ratio increased from 118 in 1956 to 151 in 1986.

FAMILY PATTERNS

The traditional popular image of the inner city is sharply distinguished from the suburb in terms of family life. Whereas the suburb is characterized by the 'family type' of neighbourhood, the inner city is viewed as being largely inhabited by unmarried persons who live alone, and by childless families and lone parents. Several measures of family patterns discussed in this section do, in fact, support this view. But the extent of these inner-city/suburban differences varies by metropolitan area, as do some of their trends in family patterns.

Marital Status

One indicator that makes the inner city distinct from its outskirts is the disproportionately high share of its population that is not married (i.e., single, widowed and divorced). This inner-city/suburb difference has been in existence for a long time, but has widened since the 1960s. As shown in Figure 2, the proportion of the inner-city population who are not married increased from 49 per cent in 1961 to 62 per cent in 1986. Similar but less pronounced trends were observed for the

Figure 2: Percentage of population not married, inner cities and remainder, 1951–1986

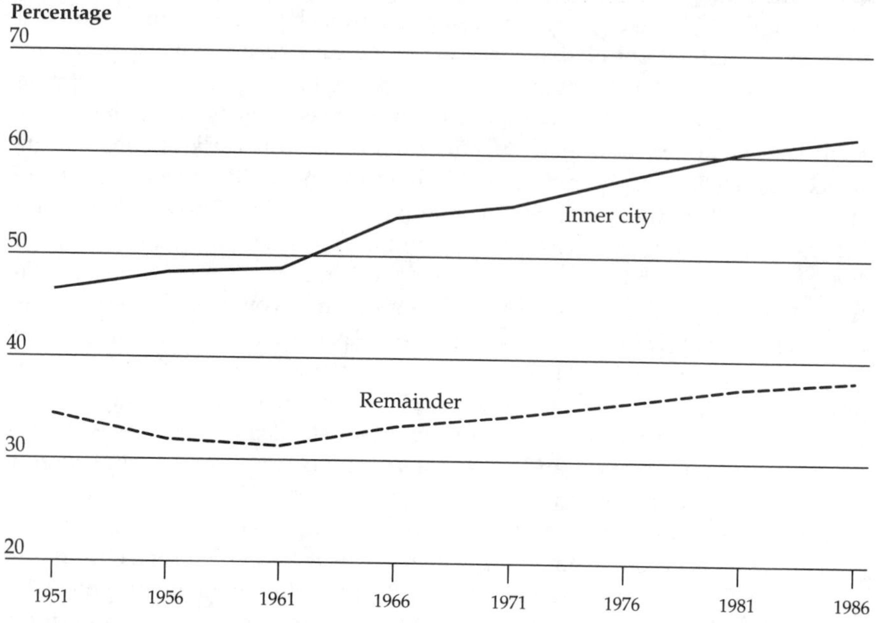

SOURCE: 1951–1981 Censuses of Canada, published data for census tracts, and 1986 Census of Canada, unpublished data.

outlying areas. The more rapid increase in the inner-city areas can be attributed to the increasing concentration of young single persons for whom inner cities tend to serve as 'staging areas' before they marry and move to the suburbs to raise families. It can also be attributed to an increasing proportion of widowed and divorced persons who choose to live in the inner parts of the cities, rather than in the suburbs.

One-Person Households

An interrelated trend which has dramatically influenced various facets of inner-city life is a relatively high concentration of persons living alone. This group is comprised of persons who tend to be not only younger and unmarried, but also may include divorced, widowed or elderly persons whose children have moved out. In 1986, persons living alone constituted more than half (56 per cent) of the households within inner cities, compared with just 22 per cent of households in the outlying areas.

The higher concentration of one-person households in the inner city is not new. In 1951, one-person households accounted for nearly 15 per cent of the inner-city households, compared with just under 5 per cent in the outlying

Table 3: Percentage of total private households with persons living alone, inner cities and remainder, 1951–1986

CMA	Inner city					Remainder				
	1951	1961	1971	1981	1986	1951	1961	1971	1981	1986
	Percentage									
Toronto	9.8	22.5	34.7	51.4	48.9	4.2	7.3	12.2	20.0	19.9
Montreal	14.5	28.0	42.7	56.5	55.9	3.3	7.0	13.1	22.0	23.7
Vancouver	20.4	33.6	47.0	62.4	63.7	8.3	10.9	15.9	23.7	24.2
Ottawa–Hull	10.4	20.9	36.2	54.6	53.4	3.4	5.1	9.9	20.3	20.5
Edmonton	25.6	38.7	49.8	59.9	60.1	6.3	8.0	12.1	19.6	20.9
Calgary	25.4	43.1	51.6	64.0	63.4	8.2	9.3	12.5	18.3	20.8
Winnipeg	17.9	33.4	47.4	58.8	57.2	4.4	7.0	13.6	23.7	23.9
Quebec	9.6	19.5	36.1	53.9	53.9	2.4	4.5	9.8	18.5	20.5
Halifax	8.6	12.0	26.2	45.2	45.4	4.3	5.8	9.3	18.5	18.2
Saskatoon	26.2	40.9	54.6	60.6	60.9	7.6	9.0	15.3	24.3	22.8
Regina	20.4	33.8	50.3	64.5	65.7	5.4	6.3	12.1	20.2	20.2
Saint John	11.9	18.9	26.6	40.7	45.6	5.6	7.4	10.3	17.3	17.9
Total	14.7	27.3	41.4	56.4	55.8	4.7	7.5	12.7	21.0	21.8

SOURCE: 1951–1981 Censuses of Canada, published data for census tracts, and 1986 Census of Canada, unpublished data.

areas. In fact, as shown in Table 3, in the inner cities of Vancouver, Edmonton, Calgary, Saskatoon and Regina more than one-fifth of the households in 1951 were composed of persons living alone, compared with less than 9 per cent in the outlying areas.

These cities have also remained leaders of this phenomenon in later years; by 1981, the proportion of one-person households in their inner cities had increased to three-fifths or more. In Vancouver, Edmonton and Calgary, this trend is largely attributable to a younger single and divorced population, whereas in Saskatoon and Regina it is attributable to an older and widowed population. Other inner cities have also experienced similar increases in varying degrees. In 1986, five of the twelve inner cities under examination had 60 per cent or more of their households composed of persons living alone, while in the remaining seven cities, the proportion was more than 45 per cent. These figures are considerably greater than the national figure of 22 per cent. The higher concentration of persons living alone in the inner cities can be explained mainly by the type of housing, which is primarily suitable for non-family living.

Smaller Families

Changes in family size are related to changes in household composition. On average, families in the inner cities are smaller than those in the outlying areas. In

Figure 3: Index[1] of inner-city families with and without children relative to the total metropolitan areas, 1951–1986

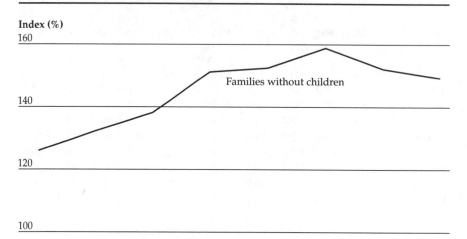

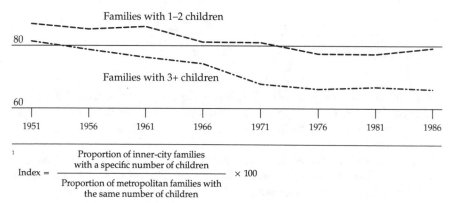

Index (%)

Families without children

Families with 1–2 children

Families with 3+ children

| 1951 | 1956 | 1961 | 1966 | 1971 | 1976 | 1981 | 1986 |

[1]

$$\text{Index} = \frac{\text{Proportion of inner-city families with a specific number of children}}{\text{Proportion of metropolitan families with the same number of children}} \times 100$$

SOURCE: 1951–1981 Censuses of Canada, published data for census tracts, and 1986 Census of Canada, unpublished data.

1986, only 8 per cent of inner-city families, compared with 13 per cent of the families in the remainder of the metropolitan areas, had three or more children. Also, 55 per cent of the families in the outlying areas, but only 42 per cent of the inner-city families had one to two children. Conversely, almost half (49 per cent) of families in the inner cities were without children compared with a third in the outlying areas.

This trend towards smaller families in inner cities is not a new occurrence since the downtown core has traditionally been viewed as a less desirable place for raising large families. With the increasing concentration of smaller families in the inner city, divergence between inner cities and the suburbs in terms of their

Table 4: Lone-parent families as a percentage of all families, inner cities and remainder, 1971-1986

CMA	Inner city				Remainder			
	1971	1976	1981	1986	1971	1976	1981	1986
				Percentage				
Toronto	16.7	17.9	21.0	22.7	8.9	10.0	11.5	12.4
Montreal	19.0	15.7	21.7	23.4	10.9	11.0	13.6	15.7
Vancouver	15.0	13.8	16.3	18.7	10.0	10.3	11.5	12.8
Ottawa–Hull	19.4	17.7	18.8	19.7	9.6	10.6	12.8	13.5
Edmonton	14.4	12.6	12.7	15.7	10.0	10.7	11.6	13.2
Calgary	14.9	17.0	13.6	15.3	9.6	10.2	11.1	12.5
Winnipeg	19.7	18.1	24.3	27.9	10.3	10.9	12.4	13.5
Quebec	22.3	18.9	22.4	26.9	10.8	10.7	12.7	14.6
Halifax	23.5	23.2	25.3	28.8	9.3	10.3	12.6	13.1
Saskatoon	15.2	15.2	16.4	16.9	9.4	10.0	12.3	13.7
Regina	18.7	19.0	20.6	19.8	10.0	9.7	11.8	13.3
Saint John	19.5	21.3	31.3	33.4	11.1	10.7	13.9	15.4
Total	17.9	16.8	20.1	22.1	9.9	10.5	12.3	13.6

SOURCE: 1976 and 1981 Census of Canada, published data for census tracts, and 1971 and 1986 Censuses of Canada, unpublished data.

respective family size has increased over the years, as shown in Figure 3. Since the late 1970s, this trend has somewhat stabilized, probably because there has been an exodus of families at either end of the life cycle and an increased arrival of couples with children into the inner cities.

Lone-Parent Families

Inner cities also tend to have a much higher proportion of lone-parent families than do outlying areas, as shown in Table 4. In 1986, the proportion of families with only one parent was higher in inner cities (22 per cent) than in the remainder of the metropolitan areas (14 per cent). But rates of change over the past decade were similar in the inner cities and their outlying areas. In the inner cities the proportion of families with only one parent increased from 17 per cent in 1976 to 22 per cent in 1986, while in the remainder of the metropolitan areas the increase was from 11 per cent to 14 per cent. During this 10-year period, the various inner cities have differed markedly in their relative concentration of lone-parent families. In 1986, the proportion varied from a low of 15 per cent in Calgary to a high of 33 per cent in Saint John; the corresponding variation in the outlying areas ranged from a low of 12 per cent for Toronto and Calgary to a high of 16 per cent for Montreal.

Table 5: Immigrant population as a percentage of total population, inner cities and remainder, 1961–1986

CMA	Inner city				Remainder			
	1961	1971	1981	1986	1961	1971	1981	1986
				Percentage				
Toronto	40.3	41.0	40.9	39.1	32.7	33.6	37.9	36.3
Montreal	19.5	22.8	27.3	27.1	14.9	14.4	15.8	15.6
Vancouver	48.1	41.4	41.1	37.9	26.8	25.4	29.1	28.4
Ottawa–Hull	13.0	16.0	20.4	19.8	12.0	12.1	13.9	13.7
Edmonton	37.2	26.9	28.3	25.4	22.6	18.0	19.6	18.4
Calgary	41.8	28.8	30.4	32.1	23.6	20.1	21.1	20.7
Winnipeg	33.0	30.4	34.5	34.4	22.9	19.2	18.7	17.5
Quebec	3.3	3.1	4.3	5.8	1.9	2.2	2.2	2.3
Halifax	6.4	8.2	8.9	10.4	7.1	7.2	7.3	7.1
Saskatoon	36.2	30.5	24.3	21.4	16.9	13.3	11.4	9.3
Regina	31.1	24.2	24.5	18.7	15.5	12.1	10.0	9.1
Saint John	7.1	6.2	6.3	6.1	5.4	4.7	5.2	4.7
Total	27.0	28.0	31.3	30.2	21.1	20.6	22.8	22.2

SOURCE: 1961–1981 Censuses of Canada, published data for census tracts, and 1986 Census of Canada, unpublished data.

CULTURAL MILIEU

Ethnicity is one of the most important variables associated with residential segregation in North American cities. Historically, faced with the disadvantages of low incomes, immigrants and ethnic minorities have been channelled into the inner parts of the city. These people have chosen to reside on the edge of the central business district. Most of them have sought low-cost housing that is close to their place of work.

Residential Distribution of Immigrants

In 1961, the foreign-born in Canada (hereafter referred to as immigrants) constituted 27 per cent of the inner-city population but only 21 per cent of the population of the outlying areas. As shown in Table 5, the figure for the inner cities edged slightly upward in the next 25 years to 30 per cent in 1986, but remained relatively stable for the remainder of metropolitan areas. This is considerably higher than the national level of 16 per cent in 1986.

Between 1961 and 1986, the relative proportion of immigrants declined in inner cities, whereas the proportion increased in suburban areas. For example, in Vancouver, a metropolitan area that has traditionally attracted immigrants, the proportion of immigrants in the inner city declined from 48 per cent to 38 per cent, but increased slightly in its outlying parts. During the same period, Toronto, another metropolitan area attractive to immigrants, experienced no change in the concentration of immigrants in its inner city—their proportion ranged between 39 per cent and 41 per cent. In contrast, a slight increase in their already high concentration was observed in the outlying areas. Here, their proportion rose from 33 per cent to 36 per cent. In two other metropolitan areas— Edmonton and Calgary—the immigrant proportion declined both in the inner city and in the outlying areas, although the decline was faster in the inner city. These trends suggest that during 1961–86 there may have been a growing preference for suburban living among the immigrants in these four metropolitan areas.

The growing preference for suburban living tends to be more true of immigrants who have been in Canada for some time, than of recent immigrants. In 1986, 'older' immigrants (those who migrated to Canada before 1978) accounted for almost 80 per cent of the immigrant population in the suburbs, compared with just 65 per cent of immigrants in inner cities. More 'recent' immigrants tend to settle in the inner cities. This tendency was most pronounced in Winnipeg where recent (post-1977) immigrants accounted for over half (53 per cent) of the immigrant population in its inner city compared with just 19 per cent in the rest of the metropolitan area. Neither the inner nor the outer areas of Saskatoon and Regina seem to have attracted as many immigrants.

In the remaining six metropolitan areas (Montreal, Ottawa–Hull, Winnipeg, Quebec, Halifax and Saint John), the residential pattern of immigrants was generally the exact opposite to that described above; overall, the concentration of immigrants grew in the inner cities but not in the balance of the metropolitan areas. In the inner city of Winnipeg, the proportion of immigrants did not change much during 1961–86, having fluctuated between 30 per cent and 34 per cent. But the proportion in the outskirts of the city exhibited a decline during the same period, from 23 per cent to 17 per cent. A similar pattern was observed for Saint John, where the immigrant population in the inner city remained low at 6 per cent to 7 per cent during the 25-year period, while declining elsewhere from 17 per cent to 9 per cent. In the outskirts of Montreal, Ottawa–Hull, Quebec and Halifax, the concentration of immigrants increased only slightly, but in their inner cities, it increased markedly.

The changing patterns of immigrant residential distribution over the 25-year period resulted in a reduction in the number of cities whose inner zones were heavily inhabited by immigrants. In 1961, immigrants constituted more than 30 per cent of the population in seven inner cities: Toronto, Vancouver, Edmonton, Calgary, Winnipeg, Saskatoon and Regina. In 1986, however, there were only four: Toronto, Vancouver, Calgary and Winnipeg.

Ethnic Concentration

Urban analysis of ethnic segregation typically focuses on the changing concentration of ethnic and cultural minorities in the inner city. Because of conceptual changes from one census to another, time-series data on ethnicity are not strictly

Table 6: Index[1] of concentration of ethnic groups other than British or French in the inner cities relative to the total metropolitan areas, 1961–1986

CMA	Inner city			
	1961	1971	1981	1986
Toronto	122	111	102	102
Montreal	103	128	139	138
Vancouver	139	119	110	105
Ottawa–Hull	93	117	121	120
Edmonton	111	98	97	98
Calgary	118	107	103	102
Winnipeg	103	106	116	115
Quebec	154	129	126	203
Halifax	128	117	116	123
Saskatoon	122	113	104	92
Regina	121	119	106	100
Saint John	105	141	109	117
Total	108	110	112	110

[1]

$$\text{Index} = \frac{\text{Proportion of population in ethnic groups other than British or French in the inner city}}{\text{Proportion of population in the ethnic groups other than British or French in the total metropolitan area}} \times 100$$

SOURCE: 1961–1981 Censuses of Canada, published data for census tracts, and 1986 Census of Canada, unpublished data.

comparable; however, they are meaningful when analysed as indices showing their relative representation in the inner city compared with that in the total metropolitan area. As shown in Table 6, the relative concentration of the population from ethnic groups other than British or French has not changed much during 1961–86. Relative to the total metropolitan areas, the representation of these groups remained high in the inner cities. To get a clearer view of the changing residential concentration of persons from ethnic origins other than British or French in the inner city, one must look at the individual cities. In six of the twelve inner cities considered—Toronto, Vancouver, Edmonton, Calgary, Saskatoon and Regina—the relative concentration of these groups has declined markedly. These cities have historically been heavily populated by persons from ethnic groups other than British or French, and perhaps over time they have increasingly moved towards the outlying zones.

Winnipeg is a metropolitan area highly populated by persons from non-British-non-French ethnic origins. Over the years, these groups have become increasingly concentrated in the inner part of this city. In 1986, about three-fourths of the inner-city population of Winnipeg consisted of persons from ethnic groups other than British or French. This proportion is the highest among the 12 cities considered in this study. Winnipeg is unique also because of a high concentration of aboriginal population in its inner parts.

SOCIO-ECONOMIC CHARACTERISTICS

. . .

Education

There are major differences between the inner and the outer parts of metropolitan areas regarding the education level of their residents. In 1986, 16 per cent of Canada's inner-city population and 14 per cent of the suburban population (aged 15 and over) had less than a Grade 9 level of schooling. Certainly, this does not represent a significant difference between the two areas. However, the proportion of the population with Grades 9 to 13 was higher in the outlying areas (38 per cent) than in the inner cities (27 per cent), whereas people with schooling above Grade 13 were more highly concentrated in the inner city than in outlying areas. Compared with only 23 per cent of the residents in the remainder of the metropolitan areas, 36 per cent of the inner-city residents had some university education or a university degree. The percentage of degree holders was also higher in the inner city: 21 per cent of the inner-city population had a university degree, compared with a 12 per cent level among the population in the outlying areas.

In 1971, inner and outer parts of most metropolitan areas were close to each other in terms of the proportion of the population with a university education. Over the next 15 years, this proportion increased in both areas, but much more rapidly in the inner cities, as shown in Table 7. Consequently, the inner and outer areas became increasingly dissimilar in their concentration of the university-educated population. In 1986, there were five metropolitan areas (Toronto, Montreal, Ottawa–Hull, Edmonton and Quebec) where the proportion of the inner-city population having some university education was more than one and a half times larger than that in the suburbs; in 1971, this occurred in only two metropolitan areas—Toronto and Montreal. It appears that inner cities are becoming increasingly attractive to highly educated persons.

Occupation

Inner cities also differ from the outlying areas in the occupational composition of their residents. In 1986, 37 per cent of the labour force residing in the inner cities, compared with only 28 per cent of the labour force residing in the outlying areas, occupied managerial and professional posts. Except for Winnipeg and Saint John, this pattern held true for all metropolitan areas considered, for both males and females. Also, for both sexes combined there was a larger concentration of persons engaged in service occupations in the inner city than in the remainder of the metropolitan area (18 per cent versus 12 per cent). However, in all inner cities,

Table 7: Percentage of population aged 15 and over with some university education or with a university degree, inner cities and remainder, 1971–1986

CMA	Inner city				Remainder			
	1971	1976	1981	1986	1971	1976	1981	1986
	Percentage							
Toronto	24.2	26.6	37.3	42.0	13.2	16.4	20.4	23.3
Montreal	16.7	22.8	30.6	38.7	12.8	16.0	17.1	19.9
Vancouver	15.9	21.1	26.4	29.2	15.1	17.6	22.2	24.4
Ottawa–Hull	18.4	24.9	35.6	41.6	18.2	21.3	24.8	28.2
Edmonton	16.5	19.7	26.1	32.6	14.8	15.8	21.0	21.9
Calgary	15.7	19.5	26.7	30.2	16.6	18.0	24.5	27.3
Winnipeg	11.2	15.5	19.1	21.4	14.2	16.0	19.9	23.3
Quebec	9.6	15.9	21.8	28.0	11.9	14.4	16.2	19.3
Halifax	12.9	15.9	28.9	35.3	16.0	16.3	22.8	26.5
Saskatoon	11.4	25.1	21.3	24.5	18.3	17.2	24.3	26.3
Regina	14.7	14.1	18.5	29.9	15.3	16.3	22.2	25.6
Saint John	9.7	10.5	12.5	19.6	10.0	11.1	15.1	17.6
Total	17.4	22.0	30.1	35.6	13.9	16.6	21.1	22.9

SOURCE: 1971–1981 Censuses of Canada, published data for census tracts, and 1986 Census of Canada, unpublished data.

the proportions of the female labour force in clerical and related occupations were smaller than those in the outlying areas (30 per cent versus 37 per cent).

For the sake of brevity, only three categories—managerial and professional; clerical and related; and services—have been selected to portray the changing occupational composition of the population. Table 8 clearly shows an increasing concentration of the male labour force engaged in managerial and professional occupations in the inner cities (from 24 per cent in 1971 to 37 per cent in 1986), compared with the suburbs (from 22 per cent to 28 per cent). The pattern, though not as pronounced as for males, is also evident for females. This observation, which holds true for all cities covered by this study, provides additional support for the hypothesis that inner cites are becoming, with time, increasingly populated by white-collar workers, often displacing blue-collar workers who may be moving to the suburbs.

This situation is generally reversed for women employed in clerical and related occupations. The relative concentration of the inner-city female labour force in these occupations has declined during 1971–86, since the reduction in the proportion in the clerical and related occupations was more rapid (from 40 per cent to 30 per cent in the inner city than in the outlying areas (from 43 per cent to 37 per cent). This could imply an out-migration of women in clerical and related occupations to outlying areas. But it is more likely a reflection of the recent large entry of suburban middle-class women into the labour force—particularly those with clerical and related skills. These observations suggest again that the inner cities

Table 8: Percentage of labour force engaged in selected occupations by sex, inner cities and remainder, 1971-1986

	Inner city			Remainder		
Occupation	1971	1981	1986	1971	1981	1986
	Percentage					
Male						
Managerial/professional[1]	23.9	33.0	36.9	22.0	26.6	28.1
Clerical and related	12.9	10.9	10.4	11.3	9.4	8.8
Service	19.3	18.4	18.8	10.8	11.0	11.6
Female						
Managerial/professional[1]	26.4	32.4	36.4	21.2	24.7	28.4
Clerical and related	40.2	34.2	29.6	42.9	41.5	37.5
Service	18.2	16.0	16.6	14.0	12.9	13.5

[1] Includes managerial, administrative and related occupations; teaching and related occupations; occupations in medicine and health; occupations in natural sciences, engineering and mathematics; occupations in social sciences and related fields; occupations in religion; and artistic, literary, recreational and related occupations.
SOURCE: 1971, 1981 and 1986 Censuses of Canada, unpublished data.

and the balance of the metropolitan areas have become increasingly dissimilar in terms of the socio-economic status of their respective populations.

Historically, a larger proportion of the labour force engaged in service occupations lived in the inner cities. This is to be expected, given that most service occupations in places such as hotels, restaurants, and so on, are in, or very close to, the inner city. Generally, the situation has persisted over time.

Women's Labour-Force Participation

In general, inner cities are different from their outlying areas in terms of women's labour-force participation. Figure 4 presents the ratio of the labour-force participation rate of women 15 years and over in the inner city and its outlying area relative to the total metropolitan areas during the 1951-86 period. It appears that the gap between the inner city and its outlying areas in terms of the labour-force participation of women has been drastically reduced. In 1951, the women's labour-force participation rate in the inner city was 36 per cent higher than that in the total metropolitan area. Over the next 35 years, the gap was narrowed to just 3 per cent. This increased similarity between the inner cities and the outlying areas was clearly due to a very rapid increase in the labour-force participation of women living in the suburbs. Historically, the suburbs have been characterized by a heavy concentration of child-oriented families, and therefore a large proportion of women who did not participate in the labour force. In recent years, however, an increasing proportion of women living in the suburbs have opted to work outside the home. Another factor motivating these women to enter the labour force has been the faster growth of jobs in the outlying zones of the

---

Figure 4: Index[1] of women's labour-force participation rate in the inner cities and remainder relative to the total metropolitan areas, 1951–1986

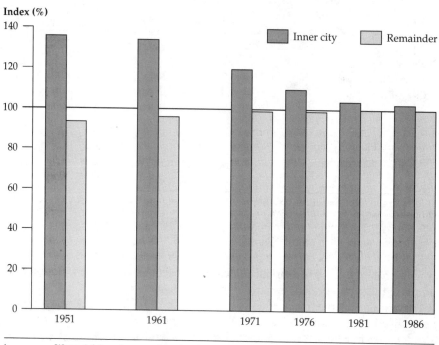

[1]

$$\text{Index} = \frac{\text{Women's labour force participation rate in the inner cities (or remainder)}}{\text{Women's labour force participation rate in the total metropolitan areas}} \times 100$$

SOURCE: 1951–1981 Censuses of Canada, published data for census tracts, and 1986 Census of Canada, unpublished data.

metropolitan areas. Consequently, for women living in the suburbs, finding nearby employment is now easier.

Family Income

Inner cities remain distinct from the outlying areas in terms of income. As shown in Table 9, between 1970 and 1985, the overall median income of census families in inner cities increased, but at a slower rate than for the remainder of the metropolitan areas; the rate of increase was more than twice as high for the outlying areas (28 per cent) as it was for the inner cities (12 per cent). As a result, the income difference between the inner city and the outlying area has widened. In 1970, the median income of inner-city families was 70 per cent of that of families in the outlying areas; by 1985, it had dropped to 62 per cent. This pattern, however, was

Table 9: Median income of census families in constant 1985 dollars, inner cities and remainder, 1970 and 1985

City	1970			1985		
	Inner city	Remainder	$\frac{\text{Inner city}}{\text{Remainder}} \times 100$	Inner city	Remainder	$\frac{\text{Inner city}}{\text{Remainder}} \times 100$
	$	$	%	$	$	%
Toronto	22,689	32,624	70	30,622	41,723	73
Montreal	18,715	27,971	67	24,445	34,646	71
Vancouver	21,620	29,960	72	23,197	38,076	61
Ottawa–Hull	23,977	34,007	71	31,282	43,107	73
Edmonton	23,170	29,997	77	27,367	38,781	71
Calgary	21,258	30,727	69	24,594	41,104	60
Winnipeg	18,552	28,188	66	16,026	36,364	44
Quebec	20,129	27,301	74	21,796	35,284	62
Halifax	18,232	28,393	64	23,747	36,815	65
Saskatoon	21,067	26,541	79	29,536	35,832	82
Regina	19,785	27,606	72	25,422	39,324	65
Saint John	19,825	25,063	79	18,200	31,564	58
Total	21,056	30,003	70	23,639	38,361	62

SOURCE: 1971 and 1986 Censuses of Canada, unpublished data.

reversed in Toronto, Montreal, Ottawa–Hull, Halifax and Saskatoon, where the inner-city family incomes have become closer to those of the remainder of the total metropolitan areas.

A comparison of families by specific income group (in constant 1985 dollars) reflects the same disparity between the inner cities and the outlying areas. Table 10 shows that in 1985, the proportion of inner-city families with incomes less than $20,000 was about twice as high as in outlying areas (39 per cent versus 21 per cent); the pattern was also about the same in 1970 (47 per cent versus 24 per cent), suggesting a similar improvement in family incomes in the inner cities and the suburbs. But the situation was different at the other end of the scale: the proportion of families with incomes of $60,000 or more in outlying areas increased from 8 per cent in 1970 to 19 per cent in 1985, but in the inner city the corresponding increase was from 6 per cent to 15 per cent. It seems that inner cities have attracted an increasing number of high-income families during the 15-year-period. During this period, the most impressive increases in the concentration of families with incomes of $60,000 or more were observed in larger cities: Ottawa–Hull, Calgary, Edmonton, Toronto, Vancouver and Montreal.

. . .

Table 10: Percentage of census families in inner cities and remainder in selected income groups (constant 1985 dollars), 1970 and 1985

| City | % of families in the inner city: | | | | % of families in the remainder: | | | |
| | Less than $20,000 | | $60,000 or more | | Less than $20,000 | | $60,000 or more | |
	1970	1985	1970	1985	1970	1985	1970	1985
				%				
Toronto	43.3	33.0	8.6	22.0	19.9	16.7	10.3	22.7
Montreal	53.5	41.5	7.1	15.8	27.9	25.0	7.6	14.4
Vancouver	45.6	43.1	3.9	9.2	25.0	22.0	8.0	18.1
Ottawa–Hull	39.1	28.3	5.6	19.1	18.8	16.2	12.8	24.5
Edmonton	42.2	31.7	4.7	12.9	23.8	20.9	7.4	18.3
Calgary	47.4	41.0	3.4	10.4	22.2	18.6	8.1	23.5
Winnipeg	54.1	55.8	2.1	3.3	26.0	21.1	6.0	14.4
Quebec	49.7	45.2	5.1	9.8	27.6	22.9	7.3	13.4
Halifax	56.2	42.2	...	7.9	24.4	19.7	6.3	15.8
Saskatoon	47.2	36.7	...	13.4	30.2	23.9	5.0	14.5
Regina	50.8	39.1	...	11.6	28.9	19.5	5.4	18.7
Saint John	50.8	55.0	...	...	33.5	29.4	4.0	9.3
Total	47.3	39.4	5.9	15.2	24.4	20.7	8.5	18.6

... Less than 100 families

SOURCE: 1971 and 1986 Censuses of Canada, unpublished data.

CONCLUSION

By analysing census data from 1951 to 1986, this study has documented the patterns of similarity and dissimilarity between 12 inner cities and their outlying areas, in terms of demographic, family, cultural and socio-economic characteristics. It has also shown that some, though not all, inner cities have been passing through a period of mild transition in recent years, whereby certain long-term historical trends have either slowed down or reversed.

Clearly, there are many sharp contrasts between the inner city and the rest of the metropolitan area. Generally, inner cities are inhabited more by young adults and senior citizens, most of whom are not married, and less by families with school-age children. In contrast to residents in outlying areas, the majority of people in the inner city live alone, reflecting salient differences in life-style. Culturally, inner cities have higher concentrations of immigrants and ethnic groups other than those of British or French origin.

Over the years, some differences have become more pronounced while others have diminished. For example, within the inner city the concentration of young adults aged 20–34 is increasing, whereas the concentration of persons with older children is declining relative to outlying areas. Coincident with these changes is an increase in the proportion of persons with high levels of education, of employees in managerial and professional occupations, and of families with high income in the inner city. At the same time, however, the income gap between the inner city and its outlying areas has widened, such that overall income levels of inner-city dwellers have risen at a slower rate. In addition, some inner-city areas are witnessing a growth in home ownership and a revival in the construction of residential dwellings. Perhaps one of the most telling indicators of revitalization is that, for the first time since 1951, the population of most inner cities grew between 1981 and 1986.

What are the implications of these changes for the future residential development in the inner city? Is the recent revitalization that some inner cities are undergoing just a temporary phenomenon? What lies behind these changes in the inner-city landscape? Perhaps these issues could be examined in the light of factors such as increased costs of transportation, rising house prices in the suburbs, or a 'baby-boom' effect—as more young singles and couples in the early stages of their work careers combine the convenience of downtown living with easier access to jobs and, increasingly, home ownership. Regardless of these factors, however, there are built-in limits to residential renewal, construction and expansion within the inner city itself. The limited space and competition for land use from commercial interests leads to more and more high-rise residential development which is suitable for only certain types of living. One can only speculate on the characteristics of tomorrow's inner city. What has transpired, however, in the changing relationship of the inner city with its outlying area and their growing differences and similarities suggests that the inner city is in transition.

NOTE

[1] *Perspectives Canada III*, Cat. 11–511, pp. 183–240.

CHAPTER 27

IS THE BURGESS CONCENTRIC ZONAL THEORY OF SPATIAL DIFFERENTIATION STILL APPLICABLE TO URBAN CANADA?

T. R. Balakrishnan and George K. Jarvis

In two earlier articles we investigated the applicability of the Burgess theory of concentric zones (Burgess, 1925) to urban Canada in 1961 and 1971 (Balakrishnan and Jarvis, 1976, 1979). Briefly, the Burgess model of concentric zones posits a single centre for the community. The centre is the point of greatest access, the place of greatest competition for space. Land values and population density tend to be higher at central locations and decrease toward the periphery of the city. Persons of higher socio-economic status, who can afford more space (and more often purchase single-family residences) and can pay the costs of greater distance from the centre, tend to be located farther from the centre than the poorer segments of the population. Family units with children are also more likely to choose peripheral neighbourhoods. Households without children are more often located in central parts of the city. There is a body of opinion (Schnore, 1967a; Schnore and Jones, 1969) that says as cities age, the Burgess pattern should become more clear. Also, as cities become larger, centre-periphery differences in socio-economic status and family size should become greater.

We found in our earlier analyses (1976, 1979) that:

1. In general the zonal pattern was evident for family size and to a lesser degree for socio-economic status;
2. The theory was not the only explanatory pattern for Canadian cities; sectors explained even more variation in socio-economic status than did zones; zones explained variation in family size better than sectors;
3. Ethnic status did not show any clear pattern by sectors or zones;
4. The patterns were generally consistent between the two dates.

The purpose of this paper is to provide partial replication of these findings using the 1961, 1971, and 1981 censuses of Canada, by examining variation in socio-economic status and family size by zones in the different metropolitan areas of Canada. The change in the definition of ethnicity in the 1981 census, compounded by the introduction of multiple ethnic origins, has essentially made it impossible to construct a simple and comparable measure of ethnicity status.

The applicability of Burgess zonal theory as a description of North American urban spatial structure was confirmed by many studies using data prior to the mid-sixties (Anderson and Egeland, 1961; Schnore, 1964, 1965, 1967a, 1967b; Haggerty, 1971). As cities grew and population became deconcentrated, the positive relationship between socio-economic status and distance from the centre became more significant. Though deconcentration in Canadian cities may have been more recent than in the United States, the Burgess patterns were substantiated in urban Canada and the US at approximately the same time (Guest, 1969; Murdie, 1969; Schwirian, 1970, 1971; Balakrishnan and Jarvis, 1968, 1976, 1979). Recent writing on urban structure has continued to address the Burgess hypothesis (Choldin and Hanson, 1982). However, urban development in the last two decades has raised serious questions as to the continued relevance of the Burgess formulation. For example, in Canada, based on individual level data rather than tracted data such as ours, Pineo found only modest support for the gradient hypothesis of increasing socio-economic status from the centre of the city (Pineo, 1988).

A number of developments cause one to question the relevance of Burgess concentric zones to urban areas in North America in the 1980s. Dramatic changes have been taking place not only in urban development but in the demographic characteristics of city residents. Many of the functions originally attributed to the central business district have become decentralized. The central city first lost most of its original industrial base, then the population and retail business moved to the suburbs as well (Hawley, 1971).

The zone of transition surrounding the central business district, once defined by Burgess and Park as an area of dilapidated housing and social disorganization, is undergoing revitalization through publicly-funded urban renewal as well as by gentrification (London, Lee and Lipton, 1986; Lee, 1980; Shlay and Rossi, 1981). Real-estate prices, which used to be depressed in this zone, have skyrocketed in many urban areas.

The nature of the modern industrial economy has also changed, with corresponding changes in the occupational composition of the labour force. Blue-collar employment has decreased considerably and white-collar employment has increased. Old, inefficient plants in the middle of cities have often been demolished and moved to the suburbs or to designated industrial parks. Demographic factors, such as declining family size, increased divorce and increased female labour-force participation, have also influenced the residential location choices of people along lines different from those suggested by Burgess. In this paper our purpose is not to look comprehensively at Burgess's concept of zones, but rather to investigate trends in spatial patterns for two factors. These factors, in the past, have been associated with concentric zones. We assess the associations for 1961 through 1981.

DATA AND METHODS

Canada's 14 largest metropolitan areas in the years 1961, 1971 and 1981 were included in the study. Smaller metropolitan areas were excluded because they contained too few census tracts for meaningful statistical analysis. Further, a few census tracts in the selected cities which were very small in population size or for which there were inadequate socio-economic data were also excluded. The total number of tracts covered was 1,331 in 1961, 1,973 in 1971 and 2,628 in 1981.

From the raw data available in the census computer tapes, various measures were calculated for the analysis. A socio-economic status (SES) index was constructed for each census tract by using the values for the tract for three variables: occupation, education and income. It was assumed that a combination of the three variables would measure socio-economic status better than any one of them taken separately. The three variables were operationalized as follows:

Occupation: percentage of employed males in higher-status occupations;
Education: percentage with some high school education;
Income: percentage of families with annual incomes of more than $7,000 in
   1961, $10,000 in 1971 and $20,000 in 1981.

The three variables were first standardized to a mean of 50 and a standard deviation of 10. The individual score for any census tract was given by:

$$y = (x\text{-}\bar{x})/\: \sigma x\: (10) + 50$$

where $\bar{x}$ = the mean score on occupation, education or income for all the census tracts, and σx = the standard deviation of the distribution of x for all the tracts.

The socio-economic status index is then calculated by averaging the standardized scores on occupation, education and income. Family status is measured by the average number of persons per family in each census tract.

Zones were initially constructed by two methods. The first method consisted of grouping the census tracts in concentric zones of one-mile radius from the city centre. One-mile zones resulted in a larger number of zones for the bigger cities than the smaller urban areas. Therefore, four concentric zones were constructed for each city so that each zone had one-fourth of the total census tracts. These quartiles are comparable to the inner four of Burgess's five zones, the fifth being the commuter zone which lies at least partly outside the tracted area. As the simpler and more economical quartile method revealed similar patterns to the more complex one-mile zones, the analysis has concentrated on quartiles.

FINDINGS

Socio-economic Status

The index means in SES for the 14 largest metropolitan areas are presented in Table 1. Over the past three decades the two metropolitan areas in the province of Quebec, Montreal and Quebec City, had mean SES indices lower than the national average of 50.0, as did Windsor, Kitchener–Waterloo, Hamilton and Winnipeg. Ottawa–Hull, Toronto, and the western cities of Edmonton, Calgary, Vancouver and Victoria have SES indices markedly above the national average.

Our interest is not so much in variation among cities, but rather in the variation found within cities. The mean SES indices of census tracts by quartile zones are found in Table 2. With few exceptions (five cities in 1961; four in 1971; and only one in 1981), the lowest SES is found in the census tracts in the centre of the city. Over the three decades, cities increasingly fit the Burgess pattern. The outer zones show a similar though less clear change in pattern. In 1961 the outermost quartile in five cities had the highest SES, a pattern consistent with Burgess. In 1971 the outermost zones in only four cities had the highest SES. However, in 1981, six cities followed this pattern.

Additional analysis of patterns in SES is depicted in Table 3. Of particular interest are three measures relevant to the Burgess model:

1. The *range* is the absolute difference between the mean SES score for the innermost and the outermost quartiles of the census tracts of each city. A wider range is closer to the Burgess pattern.
2. The *percentage increase* represents the relative or percentage increase in SES from the inner to the outer zones. A greater percentage increase more nearly approximates the concentric zone model.
3. The *pattern* is a description of variation from inner to outer zones. 'B' is the expected Burgess pattern, which increases from inner to outer quartiles. '4' increases through three zones, then decreases in the fourth or outer zone. Similarly, '3' represents increase through first and second zones, then decrease from the third zone outward. Various patterns designated 'irr.' are irregular, but usually depart from the gradient pattern only in the case of one zone.

The average range from inner to outer quartiles was 4.5 in 1961, 4.2 in 1971, and 7.4 in 1981. This indicates similar levels in 1961 and 1971 but a strong increase in 1981 in the direction of concentric zones.

Table 1: Mean socio-economic status index of selected metropolitan areas of Canada, 1961, 1971, and 1981

Metropolitan area	1961			1971			1981		
	# of Tracts	Mean	Standard Dev.	# of Tracts	Mean	Standard Dev.	# of Tracts	Mean	Standard Dev.
Montreal	369	48.0	10.5	552	47.1	9.0	629	46.0	9.7
Toronto	301	52.6	10.7	434	52.7	9.4	586	51.8	8.6
Vancouver	117	52.4	8.2	174	52.1	7.0	241	52.6	6.7
Quebec City	71	47.4	8.1	89	47.5	8.2	118	48.0	9.1
Ottawa–Hull	78	54.0	9.4	117	54.3	8.9	173	54.0	9.3
Hamilton	78	47.7	7.0	107	49.5	7.2	142	48.7	8.0
Winnipeg	83	50.7	8.5	102	49.3	7.3	127	48.8	8.6
Edmonton	49	52.6	8.4	80	51.6	6.7	134	53.2	6.5
Calgary	27	52.1	7.1	76	52.8	6.7	115	54.9	6.9
Halifax	29	51.6	8.5	47	51.2	7.6	62	50.8	7.8
Kitchener–Waterloo	29	48.2	6.6	44	49.5	5.1	57	48.0	6.1
London	37	51.6	7.8	57	52.3	7.2	68	50.9	8.2
Windsor	40	47.5	6.8	53	49.8	5.4	53	46.0	6.7
Victoria	23	51.0	5.5	41	51.4	6.3	53	52.7	5.5

Table 2: Mean socio-economic status index by quartile zones for selected metropolitan areas of Canada, 1961, 1971, and 1981

Metropolitan area	1961				1971				1981			
	1st Quartile	2nd Quartile	3rd Quartile	4th Quartile	1st Quartile	2nd Quartile	3rd Quartile	4th Quartile	1st Quartile	2nd Quartile	3rd Quartile	4th Quartile
Montreal	40.9	49.0	50.9	51.6	42.8	46.3	49.9	49.5	41.2	43.8	46.9	51.3
Toronto	46.0	51.5	55.7	56.5	48.0	52.6	55.2	55.0	47.5	50.6	53.1	55.6
Vancouver	52.1	54.0	55.6	49.0	51.3	53.5	54.1	49.4	50.4	53.2	54.3	52.6
Quebec City	46.2	45.9	50.5	46.9	43.9	47.6	54.5	43.6	39.8	47.8	53.5	49.9
Ottawa–Hull	50.1	50.6	57.4	58.4	50.2	52.5	59.8	54.6	46.9	54.7	57.5	56.7
Hamilton	44.7	47.4	48.5	49.6	44.5	49.1	49.7	54.7	42.4	48.9	49.5	54.1
Winnipeg	43.4	50.1	56.7	54.1	43.6	48.0	53.4	52.8	40.0	47.4	52.4	55.3
Edmonton	48.1	51.4	60.7	50.4	50.7	51.6	51.3	53.3	50.1	51.1	54.3	57.5
Calgary	48.4	53.2	54.6	52.1	50.4	52.7	54.0	54.5	50.5	52.5	56.6	60.0
Halifax	51.0	54.5	52.0	47.8	53.2	50.4	49.4	50.6	51.6	50.7	52.3	48.6
Kitchener–Waterloo	46.3	48.8	54.1	44.9	47.0	53.4	51.3	46.6	45.2	50.8	50.3	45.7
London	47.0	50.5	56.3	53.8	48.6	52.4	55.6	52.4	45.1	49.5	55.5	53.0
Windsor	43.7	48.2	47.7	51.7	45.6	49.9	53.7	50.3	39.5	45.2	50.4	49.5
Victoria	48.2	48.0	56.8	52.6	47.3	50.9	57.5	50.4	48.6	51.8	57.4	53.1

Table 3: Patterns in mean ses by quartile zones for Canadian metropolitan areas, 1961, 1971, and 1981

Metropolitan area	1961			1971			1981		
	Range	% increase	Pattern	Range	% increase	Pattern	Range	% increase	Pattern
Montreal	10.7	26	B	6.7	16	4	10.1	25	B
Toronto	10.5	23	B	7.0	15	4	8.1	17	B
Vancouver	-3.1	-6	4	-1.9	-4	4	2.2	4	4
Quebec City	0.7	2	4(Irr.)	-0.3	-1	4	10.1	25	4
Ottawa–Hull	8.3	17	B	4.4	9	4	9.8	21	4
Hamilton	4.9	11	B	10.2	23	B	11.7	28	B
Winnipeg	10.7	25	4	9.2	21	4	15.3	38	B
Edmonton	2.3	5	4	2.6	5	B(Irr.)	7.4	15	B
Calgary	3.7	8	4	4.1	8	B	9.5	19	B
Halifax	-3.2	-6	3	2.6	5	2(Irr.)	-3.0	-6	4
Kitchener–Waterloo	-1.4	-3	4	-0.4	-1	3	0.5	1	3
London	6.8	14	4	3.8	8	4	7.9	18	4
Windsor	8.0	18	B(Irr.)	4.7	10	4	10.0	25	4
Victoria	4.4	9	4	3.1	7	4	4.5	9	4
Means	4.5	10		4.2	9		7.4	17	

The relative increase from inner to outer zones follows a similar pattern. It averaged 10 per cent in 1961, dropped slightly to 9 per cent in 1971, and increased to an average of 17 per cent in 1981. This indicates more marked differentiation of SES levels and that these follow more precisely the Burgess pattern than 1961 and 1971.

The patterns of city zones in 1961 showed four cities with regular and one with an irregular Burgess pattern in SES. Nine cities showed a '4' or '3' pattern. In 1971 only three cities followed a complete Burgess pattern and one of these was irregular. However, in 1981 six cities followed a regular Burgess pattern. Seven followed a '4' pattern. It should be noted that cities with a '4' pattern follow the Burgess direction in two of three intervals between zones. To summarize these patterns in another way, in 1961, 29 of the possible 42 between-zone intervals were in the direction hypothesized by Burgess. In 1971, almost the same number (28) fit the Burgess model. But in 1981, this number had increased to 32 of the possible 42 intervals. Rather than a decrease in the importance of the Burgess hypothesis with regard to SES, there has been a slight increase in its predictive value in the zones of Canadian cities.

Of special interest is the recent change in 1981 toward the Burgess pattern. The two largest cities in Canada, Montreal and Toronto, already show clearly the pattern predicted by the Burgess hypothesis. However, cities which have moved strongly toward this pattern in 1981 are the second rung of cities, smaller in size than Montreal and Toronto, but larger than 500,000 population. In 1961 only two of these cities described a 'B' pattern. In 1971 three did, but one was irregular. In 1981 four of the seven followed the Burgess pattern completely. One can conjecture that these middle-size cities are undergoing the evolutionary processes that Burgess outlined. As the support for this contention is largely limited to one time-period, and the number of cities is small, more observations will be needed to determine whether this is an actual trend or a short-term aberration. In the five smallest metropolitan areas considered here, the Burgess pattern has always been violated, at least in the outermost zone, where the SES indices show a decline. This pattern remained in effect in 1981. One may speculate that as these cities grow in size the Burgess pattern will be more completely extended to these cities as well.

Family Size

The Burgess model indicates that land costs are greater at the centre due to more intense competition among land uses. Family size should increase with distance from the centre as family residential use, especially single-family dwellings, tends to be low-intensity. The centre is peopled by older people, childless couples, single persons and, traditionally, new arrivals in a zone of transition. New arrivals now are more likely to populate the periphery of the city. Later efforts in social area analysis described familism as one of the three original dimensions of urban structure. An important component of this dimension was fertility or number of children. Hence, family size, sensitive as it is to fertility, should vary regularly and in concentric fashion in cities.

Family size, as measured by the mean number of persons in the family, increases uniformly from the first (innermost) to the fourth (outermost) quartile in all the cities. The direct association with distance from the centre is much more pronounced than in the case of socio-economic status. This is not surprising as the residential space requirements of a large family are better met in the suburbs where the single-family dwellings are concentrated. Facilities such as schools, churches, recreation areas, which service large families, tend also to be located farther from the city centre.

There have been some changes between 1961 and 1981 in persons per family in the various cities. In 1961 Quebec cities (Quebec and Montreal), as well as Ottawa-Hull and Halifax had on average a greater number of persons per family, reflecting in part the higher past fertility in these parts of Canada. Both Victoria and Vancouver had a lower than average number of persons per family. Other cities were distributed near the average. By 1981, after all cities had undergone a steep drop in persons per family, the highest levels were found in Toronto, Halifax, and to a lesser extent Hamilton, Windsor, and Ottawa–Hull. Montreal, Vancouver and Quebec City were slightly below average, but the lowest levels were found in Victoria, perhaps related to the large proportion of older persons in that city.

In 1961 the mean number of persons in the innermost quartile of Canadian cities was 3.31, ranging to 3.92 in the most outlying zone (see Table 4). In 1971 the inner zone averaged 3.23 persons per family, and the outer zone averaged 3.85. In 1981 the zones averaged from 2.29 to 3.17. There were slightly fewer persons per family in 1971 than in 1961, but in 1981 the number dropped markedly. In all cases in all years the averages of persons per family in the zones increased with distance from the centre of the city.

Patterns are more uniform for persons per family than on SES. In 1961 the innermost zone had the smallest number of persons per family in 13 of the 14 cities. In 1971 the pattern was similar. By 1981 the pattern had become universal, with all cities reporting their lowest number of persons per family in the innermost zone. In each of the census years examined the outer zones in almost all of the cities (13 of 14 in 1961; 12 of 14 in 1971; 13 of 14 in 1981) had the highest number of persons per family.

The range in persons per family in 1961 varied from 1.08 in Calgary to 0.19 in Victoria (see Table 5). For all cities the mean in 1961 was 0.61. In 1971 cities varied from a range of 1.05 in Edmonton to a range of 0.29 in Kitchener–Waterloo. Overall, the mean of ranges increased slightly to 0.63. By 1981 the range for cities had increased greatly. The smallest range among the zones in that year was 0.66, greater than the mean in 1961 and 1971. Six cities had a range of over 1.00, with Edmonton and Quebec City having the highest at 1.08. The mean of ranges for all cities was 0.90. Moreover, this greater absolute range, or spread of persons per family across zones, occurred with smaller absolute values in persons per family.

With this in mind it is not surprising that the percentage increase across zones increased even more markedly. In 1961 cities averaged an 18 per cent increase in persons per family from the innermost to the outermost zones. This increased to 20 per cent in 1971, but in 1981 was 40 per cent. This indicates much greater

Table 4: Mean persons per family by quartile zones for selected metropolitan areas of Canada, 1961, 1971, and 1981

Metropolitan area	1961				1971				1981			
	1st Quartile	2nd Quartile	3rd Quartile	4th Quartile	1st Quartile	2nd Quartile	3rd Quartile	4th Quartile	1st Quartile	2nd Quartile	3rd Quartile	4th Quartile
Montreal	3.54	3.54	3.61	4.03	3.49	3.40	3.59	3.99	2.29	2.45	2.82	3.16
Toronto	3.24	3.13	3.35	3.73	3.25	3.21	3.54	3.76	2.63	2.72	3.08	3.29
Vancouver	3.09	3.37	3.55	3.66	2.96	3.27	3.54	3.61	2.30	2.67	2.87	3.01
Quebec City	3.83	4.07	4.43	4.64	3.55	3.71	3.98	4.23	2.26	2.67	2.87	3.01
Ottawa–Hull	3.54	3.72	3.97	4.07	3.35	3.61	3.80	4.01	2.30	2.75	2.98	3.27
Hamilton	3.28	3.47	3.50	3.78	3.27	3.54	3.51	3.78	2.45	2.94	2.87	3.24
Winnipeg	3.22	3.35	3.61	3.72	3.14	3.31	3.52	3.82	2.30	2.56	2.82	3.11
Edmonton	3.21	3.68	3.74	4.05	3.06	3.57	3.88	4.10	2.21	2.85	3.23	3.29
Calgary	2.97	3.34	3.74	4.05	3.02	3.47	3.90	4.06	2.13	2.99	3.08	3.20
Halifax	3.50	3.55	3.96	4.32	3.30	3.61	3.93	3.91	2.33	2.79	3.16	3.34
Kitchener–Waterloo	3.37	3.60	3.68	3.79	3.26	3.55	3.66	3.55	2.37	2.79	3.08	3.06
London	3.24	3.46	3.76	3.83	3.21	3.31	3.69	3.73	2.19	2.36	3.02	3.22
Windsor	3.18	3.45	3.84	3.91	3.30	3.54	3.81	3.91	2.36	2.74	3.06	3.22
Victoria	3.13	3.43	3.38	3.32	3.04	3.20	3.44	3.48	1.92	2.32	2.86	2.93
Means	3.31	3.51	3.72	3.92	3.23	3.45	3.70	3.85	2.29	2.69	2.99	3.17

Table 5: Patterns in mean family size by quartiles for Canadian metropolitan areas, 1961, 1971, and 1981

Metropolitan area	1961			1971			1981		
	Range	% increase	Pattern	Range	% increase	Pattern	Range	% increase	Pattern
Montreal	0.49	14	B(Irr.)	0.50	14	B(Irr.)	0.87	38	B
Toronto	0.49	15	B(Irr.)	0.51	16	B(Irr.)	0.66	25	B
Vancouver	0.56	18	B	0.66	22	B	0.71	31	B
Quebec City	0.81	21	B	0.68	19	B	1.08	48	B
Ottawa–Hull	0.53	15	B	0.66	20	B	0.97	42	B
Hamilton	0.50	15	B	0.51	16	B	0.79	32	B(Irr.)
Winnipeg	0.50	15	B	0.68	22	B	0.81	35	B
Edmonton	0.85	26	B	1.05	34	B	1.08	49	B
Calgary	1.08	36	B	1.04	35	B	1.07	50	B
Halifax	0.82	23	B	0.61	18	B	1.01	43	B
Kitchener–Waterloo	0.42	12	B	0.29	9	4	0.69	29	4
London	0.59	18	B	0.52	16	B	1.03	47	B
Windsor	0.74	23	B	0.61	18	B	0.86	36	B
Victoria	0.19	6	3	0.44	15	B	1.01	53	B
Means	0.61	18		0.63	20		0.90	40	B

relative disparity in 1981 from innermost to outermost zones in persons per family.

Examination of overall patterns also indicates some movement toward concentric zone patterns. In 1961 11 cities showed a regular 'B' pattern; two were irregular examples of 'B' pattern; and only one city, Victoria, decreased in number of persons per family from the third zone outward. In 1971 ten cities portrayed a regular 'B' pattern; two showed an irregular 'B' pattern; and two, Halifax and Kitchener–Waterloo, decreased in number of persons per family from the fourth zone outward. As on other indices, the 1981 pattern conforms even more strongly to the Burgess pattern. Twelve cities depicted a 'B' pattern; one was an irregular 'B'; and one decreased in number of persons per family from the fourth zone outward. In 1961, 38 of 42 between-zone intervals were in the direction the Burgess model would have predicted. This was the case for 37 of 42 intervals in 1971 and for 40 of 42 intervals in 1981. This provides further evidence of continued drift toward the Burgess model even for a variable already strongly oriented to the model in 1961.

The range, percentage increase, and pattern in the increase of family size seem to be unaffected by city size. In large, medium-sized, and smaller metropolitan areas there are similar ranges, percentage increase and patterns approaching the Burgess model. Only in Montreal and Toronto, the two largest cities, is there slightly smaller range and percentage increase throughout the three census periods. However, they follow the same trend as other places toward closer conformity to the Burgess pattern.

DISCUSSION

Our analysis shows that changes in urban development in the last several decades, such as urban renewal, gentrification, mass transit systems, as well as other demographic and social changes such as occupational composition and female labour-force participation have not invalidated the association found between SES, family size and concentric zones. Though the original description by Burgess of the character of the zones should be re-examined in modern-day Canadian cities, the gradient pattern itself not only persists but may have intensified as far as socio-economic status and family size are concerned. This is especially evident for medium-sized cities on SES, but the intensification has occurred for all sizes of cities for family size. The relationship with family size remains stronger than that with SES.

We speculate that there are two basic factors which explain the durability of these patterns. First, the norm of owning a single-family, detached dwelling is so embedded in North American culture that those who can afford the time and cost of transportation continue to opt for locations with more of this type of housing, which increase with distance from the centre of cities. This is especially true for those who today have families with children. Smaller families and an increase in marriage dissolutions have not eroded this value. Instead, they have intensified the contrast between two sharply divergent styles of life: the one devoted to singlehood, childlessness, freedom from family commitment and often oriented to cosmopolitan participation in the amenities of the inner zones of refurbished cities; the other devoted to traditional family life, yet attempting to provide a full range of educational opportunities for children, often relying on dual or multiple wage-earners to meet the rising scale of expenses, and living in the suburbs.

Second, though mass transit systems are not widely used in Canada except in Toronto and Montreal, the development of freeways and other roads within cities has been effective enough to enable extensive use of the automobile for the journey to work. In spite of the increase in the area and population size of the metropolitan areas in Canada, for most Canadians the journey to work has not increased proportionately. The majority can still commute comfortably in less than an hour. Therefore, for one with the economic resources, the motivation to move from the centre continues to be strong. Though there may in time be a reversal of this trend due to the process of gentrification, the latter's effect on gradient patterns is not yet strongly noticeable in the concentric zones of the Canadian metropolitan areas described in this study. In any case it is too early to assess its long-term impact at this time.

REFERENCES

Anderson, T.R., and J. Egeland (1961). 'Spatial aspects of social area analysis'. *American Sociological Review* 26: 392-9.

Balakrishnan, T.R., and George K. Jarvis (1968). 'Socioeconomic differentiation in the metropolitan areas of Canada'. Paper presented at the Canadian Association of Sociology and Anthropology, Calgary, Alberta.

—— (1976). 'Socioeconomic differentiation in urban Canada'. *Canadian Review of Sociology and Anthropology* 13, 2: 205-16.

—— (1979). 'Changing patterns of spatial differentiation in urban Canada, 1961-1971'. *Canadian Review of Sociology and Anthropology* 16, 2: 218-27.

Burgess, Ernest W. (1925). 'The growth of the city: an introduction to a research project'. In R.E. Park, E.W. Burgess and R.D. McKenzie, eds, *The City*. Chicago: University of Chicago Press.

Choldin, Harvey M., and Claudine Hanson (1982). 'Status shifts in the city'. *American Sociological Review* 47, 1: 129-41.

Guest, A.M. (1969). 'The applicability of the Burgess zonal hypothesis to urban Canada'. *Demography* 6: 271-7.

Haggerty, Lee J. (1971). 'Another look at the Burgess hypothesis: Time as an important variable'. *American Journal of Sociology* 76, 6: 1084-93.

Hawley, Amos (1971). *Urban Society*. New York: Ronald Press.

Lee, B.A. (1980). 'The disappearance of Skid Row: Some ecological evidence'. *Urban Affairs Quarterly* 16: 81-107.

London, B., B.A. Lee, and S.G. Lipton (1986). 'The determinants of gentrification in the US: A city level analysis'. *Urban Affairs Quarterly* 21: 369-87.

Murdie, R.A. (1969). 'Factorial ecology of metropolitan Toronto: 1951–1961'. Department of Geography, University of Chicago, Research Paper No. 116.

Pineo, Peter C. (1988). 'Socioeconomic status and the concentric zonal structure of Canadian cities'. *Canadian Review of Sociology and Anthropology* 25, 3: 421–38.

Schnore, Leo F. (1964). 'Urban structure and suburban selectivity'. *Demography* 1, 1: 164–76.

——— (1965). *The Urban Scene*. New York: Free Press.

——— (1967a). 'Measuring city-suburban status differentials'. *Urban Affairs Quarterly* 3: 95–108.

——— (1967b). 'On the spatial structure of cities in the two Americas'. In Philip M. Hauser and Leo F. Schnore, eds., *The Study of Urbanization*. New York: Wiley.

Schnore, Leo F., and Joy K.O. Jones (1969). 'The evolution of city-suburban types in the course of a decade'. *Urban Affairs Quarterly* 4: 421–2.

Schwirian, K. (1970). 'Analytical convergence in ecological research: factorial analysis, gradient and sector models'. In J.A. Sweet, ed., *Models of Urban Structure*. Columbus: Ohio State University and Battelle Memorial Institute.

——— (1971). 'The ecological structure of Canadian cities' (unpublished manuscript). Columbus: Ohio State University.

Shlay, Anne B., and Peter Rossi (1981). 'Keeping up the neighbourhood'. *American Sociological Review* 46: 703–19.

CHAPTER 28

PATTERNS OF

URBAN ETHNICITY

Toward a Revised

Ecological Model

A. Gordon Darroch and Wilfred G. Marston

INTRODUCTION

In this paper we formulate a conceptual linkage between three apparently disparate orientations in recent urban analysis. These are (1) the ethnic assimilation–
pluralism debate, especially in light of the apparent renaissance of ethnic identity
and subcommunities and the persistence of ethnic stratification in urban areas;
(2) the surprising persistence of ethnic residential segregation and concentration;
and (3) the renewed interest in the theoretical importance of demographic parameters as factors in the social organization of urban life in general and ethnic subcultures in particular. We base our discussions on a wide, though selective,
literature drawn from urban research in the United States and Canada. We refor-
mulate the links between the basic demographic parameters (both the absolute
and the relative size of urban populations and subgroups) and ethnic residential
patterns on the one hand and the persistence, or indeed, 'emergence' of ethnic
communities and forms of ethnic stratification on the other. Specifically, we draw

on several recent contributions to the analysis of urban ethnicity to formulate a model in which specific patterns of *interaction* between urban size and the relative size and the residential patterns of the ethnic groups are key conditions giving rise to processes that sustain urban ethnic pluralism and stratification. . . .

ETHNIC RESIDENTIAL PATTERNS

. . .

The analysis of residential patterns has been a prominent, though very largely a separate, field of study in urban ethnic and racial relations. It has been pursued as an extension of the theoretical and methodological lead of the Chicago school (Park, 1950; Hawley, 1950; Lieberson, 1963; Duncan and Lieberson, 1959). However, studies of assimilation or pluralism in the wider cultural and structural sense have often given only passing consideration to residential patterns, for example, by treating the persistence of residential segregation as an *indicator* of pluralism (or of 'failed assimilation'), or as a contingent condition mirroring more fundamental social processes (see, for example, Gordon, 1964; Metzger, 1971; note especially the criticism of Gordon's influential work by Kantrowitz, 1973 in this respect). This peripheral position of residential patterns in the larger analysis of ethnicity is evident in the fact that most textbooks on Race and Ethnic Relations give only passing, if any, attention to ethnic residential segregation.

Of course, urban ecologists share part of the blame for this less-than-central position of residential patterns in the study of ethnicity. For the most part, the description of trends and patterns of residential segregation has been taken as a sufficient research focus, it being acknowledged that this does, however, leave open the question of the actual processes that produce the segregation, not to mention the question of its social consequences (cf. Darroch and Marston, 1971; Farley, 1977). To be sure, most studies begin by referring to such classic statements as Park's (1926), to the effect that spatial relations are so frequently correlated with social relations that the spatial may be taken as an index of social patterns; or to Hawley's (1944: 674) view that 'Redistribution of a minority group in the same territorial pattern as that of the majority group results in a dissipation of subordinate status and an assimilation of the subjugated group into the social structure'. But, by and large, these analytical statements are employed to justify the measurement of segregation trends and patterns rather than to serve as a starting point for further theoretical or empirical analysis. Thus, these studies have provided a wealth of descriptive information on segregation trends and patterns, but they frequently stop short of exploring the ways in which these trends and patterns influence inter- and intra-ethnic relations or ethnic stratification and conflict.

Despite this apparent conceptual hesitation, recent literature has revealed a resurgence of interest in the importance of spatial parameters for social organization, an interest pursued at several levels of analysis, ranging from interpersonal relations to institutional functions (cf. Hall, 1966; Ebbesen et al., 1976). More directly significant for urban sociology is the fact that a growing number of studies document the wider social impact of spatial patterns of urban ethnic life, though they do not attempt to place them in a more complex interpretive framework. For example, Lieberson's (1963) well-known study found that the ability to speak English, American citizenship, and occupational improvement were positively linked to reductions in residential segregation for white ethnic groups in ten US cities. Roof (1972) demonstrated that for southern US cities, at least, segregation directly affects educational inequality, which in turn affects occupational inequality and income inequality. Steger (1973) has indicated how residential segregation clearly stifles income opportunities for Blacks. He estimates that the total cost of income opportunity deprivation resulting from residential segregation exceeds ten billion dollars annually in the United States. Drawing on such studies Marston and Van Valey (1979) have argued that the residential segregation of ethnic and racial groups is alone probably sufficient to prevent any significant structural assimilation. . . . Other studies have indicated that physical distance and social isolation encourage the institutionalization of inequalities in such key realms as education and social services (McEntire, 1960; Williams, 1964).

As part of a growing body of research, such studies seem fully to justify Hawley's early insistence on the role of residential patterns as a condition that critically limits inter-ethnic relations and, hence, limits individual opportunity and equality in the institutions of the wider, competitive society. However, a few studies have begun to hint that implications of ethnic residential patterns go beyond the question of limitations on assimilation and equality of access to society-wide institutions. These studies investigate the role of residential patterns in the emergence and maintenance of viable ethnic subcultures. In this sense, they explore the implications of spatial patterns for sustaining cultural pluralism, rather than in the restricting of assimilation.

Empirical studies of the relation of urban ethnic segregation to ethnic subcultural life are particularly scarce. For a North American city as a whole, in fact, there is only one study of which we are aware. It warrants some comment. Following a provocative analysis by Breton (1964) of the effect of ethnic 'institutional completeness'[1] on ethnic identity, Driedger and Church (1974) and Driedger (1978) present strong empirical evidence that residential segregation is a condition of the maintenance of institutional completeness, in which services required by members of an ethnic group are provided by the ethnic community itself, given its spatial boundedness.

Driedger and Church discovered that the French in Winnipeg were strongly tied to their community, staunch supporters of their own institutions, and also highly segregated residentially. Moreover, as the extent of their residential segregation increased over time, the French maintained ethnic isolation in the original areas of institutional concentration and, as well, kept their residential mobility within the original settlement area.

The Scandinavians, on the other hand, never developed an isolated pattern of residence and traditionally maintained few ethnically based religious, educational and other institutions. The Jews, while moving out of their original areas of concentration into the suburbs, re-established their religious and cultural institutions in their new residential location. In other words, their upward social mobility gave rise to inter-neighborhood geographic mobility, but residential segregation and institutional completeness were re-established in the new suburban neighbourhood(s).

In a later study of Winnipeg, Driedger (1978) concluded that 'the urban French community by means of residential segregation, with limited out mobility, has maintained a French culture within a fairly complete ethnic institutional framework' (193). In contrast to this experience, he observed that the Ukrainians are beginning to move out of their original neighbourhoods and the strength of their institutional completeness is weakening. Moreover, the Poles, who were never a heavily concentrated population, had correspondingly never developed a high level of institutional completeness in Winnipeg.

The comparative inter-ethnic analysis undertaken by Driedger and his colleagues is unique, but several other recent works have taken a similarly fresh look at the relation of spatial boundaries to ethnic community life. Suttles's (1968) ethnographic study of the social significance of territory and neighbourhood in slum areas . . . has led to an impressive reconsideration of the significance of spatial patterns in the 'social construction of communities' (1972). Further, several authors have begun to review studies of urban ethnicity in a new light, arguing that common structural conditions form an essential foundation for the maintenance of white ethnic identities and communities in urban areas (Yancey et al., 1976) and are also the foundation of a distinctive Black urban 'ethnicity' (Taylor, 1979). The most significant feature of the latter studies is the insistence on the structural basis of ethnicity, which is itself understood to be a cultural formation. The approach challenges the assimilationist implications of most prior theory and research.

In the following analysis we attempt to formulate a model which draws together the implications of an analysis of residential patterns as they limit inter-ethnic relations and, simultaneously, as a key structural condition giving rise to the formation and maintenance of urban ethnic subcultures. The development of such a model, however, requires some consideration of the basic spatial conditions of urban areas and ethnic communities as well as of the problems of their measurement. We discuss the measurement problem briefly and only in so far as it is essential to a specification of the issues at hand.

Residential Patterns: Segregation vs. Concentration

It is our contention that failure to solve the problem of measurement has been one of the central limitations in the analysis of residential patterns as a structural condition of urban life. The most common measures of residential patterns— measures of residential 'segregation'—simply fail to capture aspects of the spatial patterns which may be *most* important in influencing ethnic relations and community formation.

Traditionally, residential segregation has been taken to mean the difference in the distribution of two ethnic groups, or of other groups, throughout an urban area. A high level of residential segregation implies that most members of a given

Figure 1

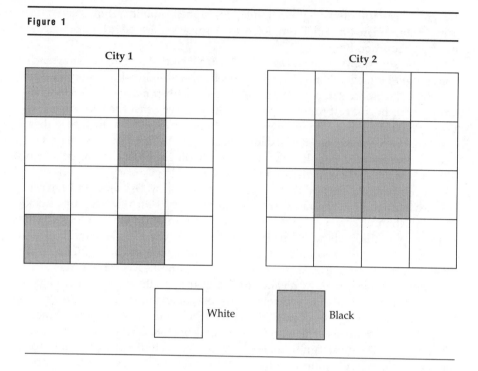

ethnic group live in neighbourhoods inhabited predominantly by members of that group only. By contrast, a low level of residential segregation implies that most members of a given ethnic group live in neighbourhoods that contain a high percentage of members from another or other ethnic groups.

Most studies of residential segregation employ an 'index of dissimilarity' as a measure of the degree of residential separation between two groups; for example, between ethnic minorities and a majority group, between ethnic minorities or between two occupational or other status groups (see Duncan and Duncan, 1955 or Taeuber and Taeuber, 1965 for a discussion of the strengths and weaknesses of this measure). The index is a summary measure of the degree of residential separation between two groups over an entire urban area. It does not however reflect either the pattern of separation or the location tendencies of either group. Take, for example, [two] hypothetical cases, examples in which the shaded areas represent an entirely Black population of a city, the blank areas an entirely white population. (See Figure 1).

In both cases the segregation index between Blacks and whites is at its maximum, since there are no subareas containing both Blacks and whites. Clearly, though, city 1 represents a 'scattered' pattern and city 2 represents a 'concentrated' pattern. The differences are of considerable sociological interest. For example, *ceteris paribus*, the probability of physical contact and, hence, of sustained social contact between Blacks and whites is greater in the first case. Moreover, a concentrated pattern, especially for relatively large ethnic groups, makes possible the establishment of institutions, services and stores that cater primarily to that group. Of course, this is exactly the kind of 'institutional completeness' which may be essential for sustaining the boundaries of ethnic or racial communities.

Now the question of adequate measurement, and especially the question of the limits of an index of segregation, has not gone unnoticed. There is a quite lively and continuing discussion about alternative measures and their limitations and advantages (Cortese et al., 1976; Winship, 1977; Farley, 1977). There are also some valuable analyses comparing the implications of different measures (Erbe, 1975; Rosenberg and Lake, 1976). In general there is sufficient evidence to suggest that one proceed with caution when relying upon the usual measure of segregation, 'the index of dissimilarity', as the sole measure of residential distributions, especially when the intention is to assess the impact of spatial patterning on ethnicity in urban areas.

Our discussion of measurement only touches the several issues raised in the methodological literature, but we wish to draw attention to the likelihood that one feature of residential patterning missed by conventional measures may be of particular significance in the context of the revival of interest in urban ethnic pluralism. We shall argue in the following section that the aspect of residential patterning most critical to an understanding of the structural basis of urban ethnic pluralism is the extent to which an ethnic group is *concentrated* in sufficient numbers, say, to 'dominate' the life of a neighbourhood.

DEMOGRAPHIC PARAMETERS OF URBAN ETHNICITY

In much of contemporary sociology, the stature of demographic parameters parallels that of spatial parameters. Variables such as sheer size, relative size of sub-populations, and population composition have been treated peripherally, in that they are typically considered as 'useful background information'. It hasn't always been that way. In the nineteenth century and early in this century, demographic parameters were central to several notable accounts of the nature of social life (Durkheim, 1955; Simmel, 1950; Park, 1926; Wirth, 1938). In recent decades such parameters have been largely dismissed as too obvious, too simplistic, or perhaps even as non-sociological, at least in the predominant interpretations of urban life (Gans, 1962).[2]

Again, however, there appears to be a resurgence of sociological interest in the potential explanatory power of demographic parameters, as there has been in ethnic pluralism itself. This interest is seen in studies of small groups (Steiner, 1972; Tucker and Friedman, 1972; Shaw, 1976), of formal organizations (Blau, 1970; Mayhew et al., 1972); of communities (Fischer, 1975, 1976; Kasarda, 1974) and of societies (Kasarda, 1974; Nolan, 1979). The theoretical formulations of Fischer (1975, 1976) and Blau (1970, 1977) are of particular relevance to our proposed model.

Fischer has offered an imaginative reconsideration of the role that demographic factors play in a 'subcultural theory of urbanism'. His analysis provides a framework for a specification of the ways in which demographic variables affect processes of pluralism and forms of ethnic conflict. Fischer's arguments provide the basis for our development of a more complete model of urban ethnic pluralism.

The main purpose of Fischer's revisionist theory is to account for the unique character of large urban areas, specifically in terms of their capacity to generate forms of unconventional behaviour—deviance, innovation, political dissidence, and so forth. While unconventional behaviour represents the central focus of his overall argument, its relevance to urban ethnicity is both direct and compelling. In fact, it is precisely the maintenance of ethnic subcultures that Fischer finds most persuasive as an exemplification of his theory.

Fischer's central argument is deceptively simple. Most generally, he contends 'that urbanism independently affects social life . . . ' (1976: 35). Fischer uses the term 'urbanism' rather idiosyncratically to refer to urban size and density. More commonly the term 'urbanization' would be used, but Fischer makes a very specific analytic argument that size and density have independent effects on other aspects of urban life. Specifically, his subcultural theory of urbanism contends that the foremost social consequence of increasing urban size is the promotion of diverse subcultures. Thus people in large urban areas live in meaningful social worlds and 'These worlds are inhabited by persons who share relatively distinctive traits (like ethnicity and occupation), who tend to interact especially with one another, and who manifest a relatively distinct set of beliefs and behaviors' (1976: 36; it should be noted that Fischer uses the terms *subculture* and *social world* interchangeably).

Fischer (1976: 37) argues that there are two basic ways in which large urban size produces the urban mosaic of 'little social worlds':

> 1) Large communities attract migrants from wider areas than do small towns, migrants who bring with them a great variety of cultural backgrounds, and thus contribute to the formation of a diverse set of social worlds. 2) Large size produces . . . structural differentiation—occupational specialization, the rise of specialized institutions, and of special interest groups. To each of these structural units are usually attached subcultures . . . . In these ways, urbanism generates a variety of social worlds.

The impact of urban population concentration goes beyond the creation of distinct social worlds or subcultures. Fischer argues that large urban areas also tend systematically to 'intensify' these social worlds through two powerful processes. The first process is based on the attainment of *critical mass*, that is, 'a population size large enough to permit what would otherwise be only a small group of individuals to become a vital, active subculture' (1976: 37). The relevance of critical mass to urban ethnicity is made abundantly clear in the following passages:

> Sufficient numbers allow them to support institutions—clubs, newspapers, and specialized stores, for example, that serve the group; allow them to have a visible and affirmed identity, to act together in their own behalf, and to interact extensively with each other (Fischer, 1976: 37).

The second process of subcultural intensification results from contacts between subcultures which are enhanced by the other demographic condition of urbanism, *density*.

> People in different social worlds often do touch . . . But in doing so, they sometimes rub against one another to recoil, with sparks flying upward. Whether the encounter is between blacks and Irish, hardhats and hippies, or town and gown, people from one subculture often find people in another subculture threatening, offensive, or both. A common reaction is to embrace one's own social world all the more firmly, thus contributing to its further intensification (Fischer, 1976: 38).

Fischer's interpretation is intentionally abstract, or analytic, as he calls it. Hence, he is specifying *tendencies* in urban processes due alone to demographic conditions, rather than focusing on the peculiarities of any given, historical case. Specifically, following Fischer, we argue that the larger the ethnic groups, the greater the expected ethnic subcultural intensity, with a corresponding high rate of *intra*-ethnic social contact and involvement in ethnic social networks. By the same token, the greater the number and size of ethnic groups, the more likely competition and conflict will emerge amongst them.

Though his analysis presents a model of the bases of urban pluralism, Fischer acknowledges that the impact of urbanism is by no means unidirectional. He is fully aware of the forces inherent in increased size, diversity, and, at least by implication, density, that encourage increased inter-ethnic contact and perhaps even assimilation. A major way in which ethnic identity and intensity may be undermined in large urban areas is through the growth of *alternative* bases of association such as subcultures founded on occupation, life-style or special interests. The tension between such countervailing forces is a central feature of Fischer's analysis, and sets it apart from conventional assimilationist views:

> These subcultures attract individuals' allegiance and modify the values of ethnic groups. Yet, at the same time, the urban effect of larger numbers within ethnic groups and the subcultural opposition among them should have the same vitalizing effects for ethnic groups that they do for other subcultures. We should expect, therefore, to observe both processes — weakening and strengthening — and see them working against each other (1976: 128).

Fischer then considers the conditions which tend to tip the balance in a tug of war between the forces of ethnic subcultural intensification and the forces of dissolution. He suggests that the demographic parameters of a city are the key. In the case of small ethnic groups in a large urban area, 'defections and dilutions will predominate', whereas, in the case of large ethnic groups in a large or small city, 'cohesion and cultural integrity should both be maintained, perhaps even deepened' (1976: 128).

The significance of demographic parameters is further supported by two observations recently put forward by Peter Blau. The first statement (1970) amounts to a specification of Fischer's theory and the second (1977) lends substantial reinforcement to it. In considering the implications of the size of formal organizations, Blau noted that as organizations increase in size (number of employees) they routinely become more structurally differentiated—vertically, horizontally, and territorially. However, and more significantly, the increase in structural differentiation does not 'keep pace' (increases at a declining rate) with the increase in overall organizational size; thus the number of employees per unit of the organization also increases with organizational size.

While to our knowledge there is as yet no empirical support for it, we believe it is useful to apply this same principle to the relationship between increasing urban size and ethnic diversity. Blau's perspective, like Fischer's, is analytic, focusing on social structural tendencies resulting from essentially demographic conditions. Thus, it is entirely plausible that as urban areas increase in size (number of residents) the number of identifiable ethnic groups also increases, but, in general, at a rate which is lower than the rate of population growth. Consequently, larger urban areas not only have more ethnic groups, but the population of each ethnic group also tends to be larger than in smaller urban areas. The application of Blau's argument to urban areas clarifies Fischer's argument that urban size itself creates diversity and in turn tends to produce the 'critical mass' of given ethnic (or other) groups within the urban area.

Blau's other work (1977) adds support to Fischer's theory. Specifically, he addresses the question of which groups have higher rates of intergroup associations than others and why they do. At an entirely structural level of analysis, he argues,

> the arithmetic properties of groups imply the theorem that in the relation between any two groups, the rate of intergroup associations of the smaller group exceeds that of the larger. This first theorem applies to three forms of associations and all their specific manifestations: 1) the proportion intermarried (or having another exclusive association as mutual best friends) in the smaller group exceeds that in the larger; 2) the mean number of intergroup associates in the smaller group exceeds that in the larger; 3) the mean amount of time spent in intergroup association is greater for the smaller than for the larger group (1977: 35).

Blau means by intergroup relations, of course, ties *between* groups. Conversely, then, the argument parallels Fischer's view that a small ethnic group is more likely to experience weakened ties *among* the members of the ethnic group than is a large ethnic group. We take these specifications of the demographic conditions of urban ethnicity as a point of departure for proposing a model of the ecological bases of urban ethnic pluralism which integrates both spatial and demographic considerations.

A MODEL OF URBAN ETHNIC PLURALISM: ECOLOGICAL CONDITIONS

A review of the issues regarding spatial and demographic aspects of urban ethnicity strongly suggests that both sets of parameters have similar, if not identical, effects on ethnic pluralism. For example, we argued that ethnic residential patterns, especially residential concentration, directly contribute to the development and maintenance of ethnic subcultures characterized by institutional com-

Figure 2

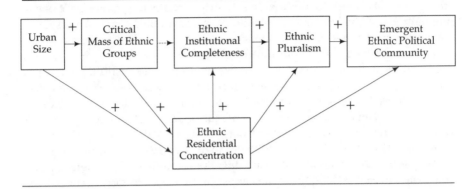

pleteness. In Fischer's theory, it is increasing size and diversity which give rise to a 'critical mass' of individuals of a given ethnicity and directly contributes to the 'intensification' of ethnic subcultures. By 'intensification' Fischer refers to the strength of subcultural beliefs, values, norms and customs (1975: 1325).

For the most part, these apparently parallel processes generating urban ethnicity have been dealt with separately. On the one hand, studies of ethnic residential segregation have rarely considered the impact of urban size, diversity or critical mass, especially as they may interact with segregation in affecting the nature of urban ethnic communities.[3] On the other hand, Fischer does not explicitly consider the possibility that the impact of urbanism on ethnic patterns may be significantly mediated by residential patterning.

Our proposed model of the basic processes involved takes urban size itself and the 'critical mass' of ethnic groups as related in the manner which Fischer and Blau suggest. We argue further that the separate and joint effects of size and mass on the intensity of ethnic pluralism or, in the case of any given group, on the strength of ethnic identity and density of ethnic networks, are significantly mediated by ethnic residential patterning. Specifically, we have taken residential concentrations of ethnic populations to be the primary intervening variable in a process in which the demographic parameters affect ethnic pluralism, that is, affect both the number of ethnic subcultures and their 'intensity', to use Fischer's term again. Since we have already argued that both the 'critical mass' of an ethnic population and residential concentrations have their major impact on ethnic subcultures, by way of sustaining the institutional completeness of the ethnic community, the latter too should be entered into the model as a separate intervening and mediating factor.

In schematic form, the model may be presented as [in Figure 2]:

If we ignore for the moment the residential concentration variable and read straight across the model, it follows Fischer's essential argument. That is, as urban areas increase in population so too do the number of ethnic groups (structural differentiation). Following Blau, we suggest that the rate at which the number of ethnic groups increases does not in general keep pace with the rate of growth of the urban population. Thus, as urban areas grow the number of residents within each ethnic group also tends to increase. In turn this increases the possibility of one or more ethnic groups attaining a population size we have called a 'critical mass'. It is a feature of both Fischer's and our model that the lower limit of this critical mass remains unspecified, though presumably not unspecifiable.

In turn, a precondition of a full complement of ethnic institutions is some critical mass of ethnic group members who can avail themselves of these services and functions. Institutional completeness, therefore, greatly facilitates the development and maintenance of intense ethnic subcultures, in that it encourages the context within which social interactions, both secondary and primary, are confined to the ethnic group itself. Finally, to the extent that an ethnic group has developed a subculture within which identification and social interaction are primarily internal to the group, it is significantly easier to mobilize a political constituency, for example, that views issues and problems along ethnic lines. In a later discussion we trace some of the possible implications of ethnic mobilization for ethnic stratification.

The importance of critical mass in this process can also be illustrated in Suttles's (1968) study of the Addams area in Chicago. Of the four ethnic groups inhabiting the area only the Puerto Ricans were noticeably threatened by an erosion of their subculture (blacks, Italians, and Mexican-Americans being the other three groups). Suttles argues that this erosion is due to the lack of supporting institutions, particularly an ethnic church, which in turn he attributes to the relatively small number of Puerto Ricans; in the terms of the model, it is due to an insufficient critical mass.

It is possible, however, to specify certain conditions within which urban size and critical mass would contribute significantly less to institutional completeness and in turn to ethnic pluralism than is suggested in the above discussion. Consider a situation in which a particular ethnic group residing in a large urban area has the critical mass necessary to develop and maintain institutional completeness and an intense sub-cultural life. However, for various reasons, the ethnic group is residentially dispersed throughout the urban area so that in any given neighbourhood its members do not make up a majority of the population. This situation would arise from either of the following two processes: (1) ethnic group members selected housing primarily on the basis of socio-economic factors, with ethnicity playing no role at all, or (2) ethnic group members tended to select housing on the basis of their ethnic affiliation, but these housing areas were 'scattered' throughout the urban area. In the latter case ethnic group members might be 'concentrated' in a number of small pockets, but each pocket would tend to be too small to facilitate the maintenance of ethnic institutions and dense social networks confined to the ethnic neighbourhood.

Thus the model we present indicates that the residential concentration of ethnic populations seems most likely to be a key structural variable which, in effect, intensifies or heightens the relations between the initial demographic preconditions of ethnic pluralism and the several aspects of the ethnic communities 'institutional completeness' engendered by such concentration. We ﬞntional assumptions about the inevitability of ethnic assimilation as a ﬞustrialization and urbanization. We suggest that it is precisely the of urban size, ethnic group size and residential and institutional ﬞ affects the balance of processes leading toward individual assimila- ﬞnatively, toward the maintenance of distinct ethnic communities and ﬞic identities. This balance has to be understood in terms of several ﬞ ms or levels of assimilation and ethnic relations. . . .

NOTES

jointly authored; sections of it draw directly from unpublished manuscripts ﬞMarston

completeness at its extreme would mean that ethnic group members 'would ﬞ make use of native institutions for the satisfaction of any of their needs, such ﬞ, work, food and clothing, medical care, or social assistance' (Breton, 1964:

exception to the relegation of demographic parameters to the 'background' ﬞcro-theories of racial/ethnic relations which incorporate such factors as the of minority populations as a central independent variable in accounting for ﬞination and socio-economic inequalities. Influenced by the theoretical formu- ﬞlliams (1947) and Allport (1954), a number of researchers have found that the ﬞlative size of a minority, (1) the greater the degree of discrimination against y (Blalock, 1956, 1967) and (2) the greater the majority-minority disparities in occupational status (Blalock, 1967; Brown and Fuguitt, 1972; Turner, 1951; Neidert, 1977). In a similar vein, Karning (1979) found that city size is signi- ﬞfavorably associated with over twenty measures of Black economic, political, development.

ﬞiptive studies of racial residential segregation which have controlled for ﬞnd the relative size of the Black population demonstrate that segregation is ﬞrger urban areas and where Blacks make up a higher percentage of the total . . . These conclusions are qualified to the extent that the only measure of ﬞatterning was a measure of segregation (dissimilarity index), which does for the relative size of the minority populations or reflect other aspects of ﬞrns, as noted above.

ﬞowledge, the only study that directly addresses the interaction of demo- ﬞspatial parameters with respect to ethnicity is Balakrishnan's (1976) analysis ﬞsidential segregation in urban Canada. He considered the impact of urban ﬞdiversity, and ethnic group size on the level of ethnic residential segregation ﬞen metropolitan areas in Canada. He found segregation to be positively ﬞith total population size and with the percentage of the total population ﬞnon-British and, to a lesser extent, with the size of the ethnic group itself. measure of ethnic diversity, *per se*, was not significantly associated with levels. Although this study invites further analysis, it also employs the con- ﬞeasure of residential segregation and, hence, may not capture important ﬞsidential patterning.

Figure 3: A simple interaction model of ethnic pluralism

Residential pattern

Ethnic size	Scattered	Concentrated
Small	1	2
Large	3	4

themselves, including their institutional base, the intensity of their relations and identities and eventually the possibilities of their social and political mobiliza- tion. The model indicates, by a dashed arrow, that we rather suspect that Fischer's proposed direct effect of the critical mass of a subgroup on the intensification of subgroup life may indeed be entirely or primarily mediated by the role of residen- tial concentrations. His original model perhaps subsumes such intermediary conditions under the general notions of intensification, but we have given a detailed justification for the specification.

The model may be viewed in another light. We may consider the size of ethnic subgroups as a variable, rather than as a question of some minimum threshold, as conveyed by the concept of 'critical mass'. In this case, the implications for ethnic pluralism are surprisingly informative, even in the most simple situations created by the interaction of just two of the variables, ethnic group size and ethnic residential patterns. The simple cross-tabulation of the two is shown [in Figure 3], where the difference between large and small populations refers to populations above and below the threshold defined as a 'critical mass', and the distinction between a scattered and concentrated pattern is consistent with the distinction drawn earlier.

The social implications of Case 1 are straightforward. A relatively small ethnic group, residentially distributed in a scattered pattern, has both demographic and spatial conditions working against it with regard to resisting pressures toward assimilation. In this situation there would be limited chances of developing and maintaining ethnically bounded services and functions because of the lack of (1) critical mass and (2) a territorially concentrated population. Moreover it is likely that the rate of inter-ethnic contact at both the secondary and primary levels would be relatively high in this situation. Ethnic identities may still be sustained, but in the absence of ethnic neighbourhoods and the subcultural life they nurture.

Case 2 represents a situation where demographic and spatial parameters affect ethnicity in opposing ways. On the one hand, the relatively small size operates to encourage assimilation and discourage subcultural intensity. On the other hand, the concentrated residential pattern provides the setting for maintaining multiple ethnic institutions which counter assimilation pressures. A basic question about such concentration is whether or not there are sufficient numbers of the ethnic group to 'dominate' the neighbourhood in its institutional makeup, that is, to have it become socially recognized as a neighbourhood with a particular ethnic character. For example, a study of the city of Flint, Michigan (Marston and Zinn, 1979), revealed that both Arab and Hispanic populations tended to be concentrated in a few areas, but never sufficiently to make up the majority, or even to give the areas a predominantly Arab or Hispanic character.

Case 3 is perhaps the most interesting in the sense that it might be possible to compare the impact of differing residential patterns for one ethnic group in a single urban area. We might expect in the case of a relatively large ethnic population which tends to be scattered throughout an urban area that at least one of the neighbourhoods would contain a fairly large concentration of that group. This would typically be the original settlement area in the inner city and the one which many ethnic group members left to take up residence in a more scattered pattern throughout the rest of the urban area. In other words, this case compares the effects upon ethnicity of social life in a neighbourhood composed almost entirely of persons of the same ethnic origin with social life in an ethnically heterogeneous neighbourhood. There has been some research with respect to the sense of alienation among Blacks in America which makes such a comparison, but with conflicting results to date. In some cases, Blacks tend to be less alienated and have less of a sense of powerlessness in a virtually all-Black ghetto than in racially mixed areas (Wilson, 1971), and in others just the reverse pattern was found (Bullough, 1967; Kapsis, 1979). To our knowledge, no attempt has been made to assess the extent to which the location of ethnic enclaves within an urban area results in assimilation and/or pluralist tendencies. The present model of the interaction of ethnic group size and residential patterning provides a framework for research and a clear set of hypotheses.

Case 4 represents the classic situation of the development and maintenance of urban ethnic pluralism, or from a somewhat different perspective, it represents the ideal situation for 'emergent' ethnicity. Here we have both demographic and spatial parameters favouring the development of ethnic pluralism. It represents the situation in which the necessary *critical* mass is *residentially concentrated* so that a given ethnic group simply has the opportunity to exercise a dominant influence upon the way of life in a residential area. Yancey et al. (1976: 392) have made the same point in suggesting that the 'ecological' structure of cities is a catalyst in the social definition and maintenance of urban ethnicity. The strength of ethnic networks and the frequency of ethnic interaction, they argue, are enhanced by common occupational positions, residential concentration and stability and a dependence on common institutions. These are not the only conditions under which ethnic identity and interaction may be maintained, in our view, but they are conditions that enhance the sense of ethnic community boundary and salience in everyday life.

The model we have discussed also specifies that the size of urban areas is a prior condition affecting the form of the interaction between the size of an ethnic population and its residential concentration, and their consequences for ethnic

pluralism. In this we follow Fischer (1976). Clearly it specify various forms of this complex association; consequences one could expect in cases of relativel which tend to be residentially scattered in large met son to similar ethnic groups in smaller cities and to these small ethnic groups were quite highly concer this tend to minimize the differences in their effect u and small urban environments? These complex inte *ceteris paribus*, as we have done throughout, woul Fischer's convincing argument that urbanization en ing forces. To reiterate the argument noted earlier, sheer variety of alternative social worlds and ways of community attachments as a result of increasing the variety of other groups and identities. At the same tir mass' and institutional completeness of ethnic grou them, tend to strengthen ethnic attachments (1976 cities both processes are weakened.

We do not attempt a full specification of the varie three variables, urban size, ethnic subgroup size ar ing, but draw attention to the advantages of the fo rates both demographic and spatial parameters. V that ethnic residential concentration is the key va effects, since it is under conditions of concentrated ethnic institutional density, that the boundaries of a community are most likely to offset counteractin And this is likely the case in urban areas of varying processes may be quite variable.

The model presented above draws together the a and spatial factors in an explanation of urban el referred to recent works, the import of which might ist to the extent that they take very seriously the racial communities are actively formed by their n structural conditions. . . .

CONCLUSION

We have tried to formulate a model that specifies the demographic and spatial parameters for urban eth that there are clear advantages in including both k analysis. While both demographic and spatial featu some independent influence on ethnic groups, we the interaction between them provides a more pow to assess the basic structural conditions underlyi short, the model emphasizes the significance of rather than the more common notion of segregati

REFERENCES

Allport, Gordon (1954). *The Nature of Prejudice*. Reading, MA.: Addison-Wesley.

Balakrishnan, T.R. (1976). 'Ethnic residential segregation in the metropolitan areas of Canada'. *Canadian Journal of Sociology* 1: 481–98.

Blalock, Hubert M., Jr. (1956). 'Economic discrimination and Negro increase'. *American Sociological Review* 21: 584–8.

—— (1967). *Toward A Theory of Minority Group Relations*. New York: Wiley.

Blau, Peter (1970). 'A formal theory of differentiation in organizations'. *American Sociological Review* 35: 201–18.

—— (1977). 'A macrosociological theory of social structure'. *American Journal of Sociology* 83: 26–52.

Breton, Raymond (1964). 'Institutional completeness of ethnic communities and the personal relations of immigrants'. *American Journal of Sociology* 70: 193–205.

Brown, David L. and Glenn V. Fuguitt (1972). 'Percent nonwhite and racial disparity in nonmetropolitan cities in the south'. *Social Science Quarterly* 53: 573–82.

Bullough, Bonnie (1967). 'Alienation in the ghetto'. *American Journal of Sociology* 72: 469–78.

Cortese, C.F., R.F. Falk and J.K. Cohen (1976). 'Further considerations on the methodological analysis of segregation indices'. *American Sociological Review* 41: 889–93.

Darroch, A. Gordon and Wilfred G. Marston (1971). 'The social class basis of ethnic residential segregation: The Canadian case'. *American Journal of Sociology* 77: 491–510.

Driedger, Leo (1977). 'Toward a perspective on Canadian pluralism: Ethnic identity in Winnipeg'. *Canadian Journal of Sociology* 2: 77–95.

—— (1978). 'Ethnic boundaries: A comparison of two urban neighborhoods'. *Sociology and Social Research* 62: 193–211.

—— and Glenn Church (1974). 'Residential segregation and institutional completeness. A comparison of ethnic minorities'. *Canadian Review of Sociology and Anthropology* 11: 390–52.

Duncan, Otis, Dudley and Beverley Duncan (1955). 'A methodological analysis of segregation indices'. *American Sociological Review* 20: 210–17.

Duncan, Otis, Dudley and Stanley Lieberson (1959). 'Ethnic segregation and assimilation'. *American Journal of Sociology* 64: 364–74.

Durkheim, Emile (1955). *The Division of Labour in Society*. New York: Free Press.

Ebbesen, Ebbe B., Glenn L. Kjos, and Vladimer J. Konleni (1976). 'Spatial ecology: Its effects on the choice of friends and enemies'. *Journal of Experimental Social Psychology* 12: 505–18.

Erbe, Brigitte Mack (1975). 'Race and socioeconomic segregation'. *American Sociological Review* 40: 801–12.

Farley, Renolds (1977). 'Residential segregation in urbanized areas of the United States in 1970: An analysis of social class and racial differences'. *Demography* 14: 497–518.

Fischer, Claude S. (1975). 'Toward a subcultural theory of urbanism'. *American Journal of Sociology* 80: 1319–41.

—— (1976). *The Urban Experience*. New York: Harcourt, Brace.

Frisbie, W. and Lisa Neidert (1977). 'Inequality and the relative size of minority populations: A comparative analysis'. *American Journal of Sociology* 82: 1007–30.

Gans, Herbert (1962). *The Urban Villagers*. New York: Macmillan.

Gordon, Milton (1964). *Assimilation in American Life*. New York: Oxford.

Hall, Edward T. (1966). *The Hidden Dimension*. Garden City, New York: Doubleday.

Hawley, Amos (1944). 'Dispersion vs. segregation: Apropos of a solution of race problems'. Papers of The Michigan Academy of Arts and Letters 30: 667–74.

—— (1950). Human Ecology. New York: Ronald Press.

Kantrowitz, Nathan (1973). Ethnic and Racial Segregation in the New York Metropolis. New York: Praeger.

Kapsis, Robert E. (1979). 'Powerlessness in racially changing neighborhoods'. Urban Affairs Quarterly 14: 424–42.

Karning, Albert K. (1979). 'Black economic, political and cultural development: Does city size make a difference'. Social Forces 57: 1194–2009.

Kasarda, John (1974). 'The structural implications of social system size'. American Sociological Review 39: 19–28.

Lieberson, Stanley (1963). Ethnic Patterns in American Cities. New York: Free Press.

—— (1972). 'Stratification in ethnic groups'. Pp. 199–211 in A.H. Richmond, ed., Readings in Race and Ethnic Relations. London: Pergamon.

Marston, Wilfred G. and Thomas L. Van Valey (1979). 'The role of residential segregation in the assimilation process'. Annals of the American Academy of Political and Social Science 441: 13–25.

Marston, Wilfred G. and Maxine Baca Zinn (1979). 'Impact of urbanization on ethnic subcultures and assimilation'. Unpublished report.

Mayhew, R.H., R.L. Levinger, J.M. McPherson and T.F. James (1972). 'System size and structural differentiation in formal organizations'. American Sociological Review 37: 629–33.

McEntire, Davis (1960). Residence and Race. Berkeley: University of California.

Metzger, Paul L. (1971). 'American sociology and Black assimilation: Conflicting perspectives'. American Journal of Sociology 76: 627–47.

Nolan, Patrick (1979). 'Size and administrative intensity of nations'. American Sociological Review 44: 110–25.

Park, Robert E. (1926). 'The urban community as a spatial pattern and a moral order'. In Ernest W. Burgess, ed., The Urban Community. Chicago: University of Chicago Press.

—— (1950). Race and Culture. Glencoe, Illinois: Free Press.

Roof, W. Clark (1972). 'Residential segregation of Blacks and racial inequality in southern cities: Toward a causal model'. Social Problems 19: 393–407.

Rosenberg, Terry J. and Robert W. Lake (1976). 'Toward a revised model of residential segregation and succession: Puerto Ricans in New York, 1960–1970'. American Journal of Sociology 81: 1142–50.

Shaw, Marvin E. (1976). Group Dynamic: The Psychology of Small Group Behavior. New York: McGraw-Hill.

Simmel, Georg (1950). The Sociology of Georg Simmel. Trans. and ed. by Kurt Wolff. New York: Free Press of Glencoe.

Steger, Wilbur A. (1973). 'Economic and social costs of residential segregation'. Pp. 83–113 in Marion Clawson, ed., Modernizing Urban Land Policy. Baltimore: Johns Hopkins.

Steiner, Ivan D. (1972). Group Process and Productivity. New York: Academic Press.

Suttles, Gerald (1968). The Social Order of the Slum. Chicago: University of Chicago.

—— (1969). 'Anatomy of a Chicago slum'. Pp. 42–57 in G.T. Marx and N. Goodman, ed., Sociology: Classic and Popular Approaches. New York: Random House.

—— (1972). The Social Construction of Communities. Chicago: University of Chicago.

Taeuber, Karl E. and Alam F. Taeuber (1965). Negroes In Cities. Chicago: Aldine.

Taylor, Ronald (1979). 'Black ethnicity and the persistence of ethnogenesis'. American Journal of Sociology 84: 1401–23.

Tucker, James and S. Thomas Friedman (1972). 'Population density and group size'. *American Journal of Sociology* 77: 742–49.

Turner, Ralph (1951). 'The relative position of Negro males in the labor force of large American cities'. *American Sociological Review* 16: 524–29.

Williams, Robin (1947). *The Reduction of Intergroup Tensions: A Survey of Research on Problems of Ethnic, Racial and Religious Group Relations*. New York: S & R Council.

——— (1964). *Strangers Next Door*. Englewood Cliffs: N.J.: Prentice Hall.

Wilson, Robert A. (1971). 'Anomie in the ghetto: A study of neighborhood type, race and anomie'. *American Journal of Sociology* 77: 67–88.

Winship, Christopher (1977). 'A revaluation of indexes of segregation'. *Social Forces* 55: 1058–1066.

Wirth, Louis (1938). 'Urbanism as a way of life'. *American Journal of Sociology* 34: 1–24.

Yancey, William L., Eugene P. Ericksen and Richard N. Juliani (1976). 'Emergent ethnicity: a review and reformulation'. *American Sociological Review* 41: 391–403.

Pistol $20